EVERYMAN'S LIBRARY

EVERYMAN,
I WILL GO WITH THEE,
AND BE THY GUIDE,
IN THY MOST NEED
TO GO BY THY SIDE

WILLIAM SHAKESPEARE

Comedies

with an Introduction by Tony Tanner
General Editor – Sylvan Barnet

VOLUME 2

EVERYMAN'S LIBRARY

226

This book is one of 250 volumes in Everyman's Library
which have been distributed to 4500 state schools
throughout the United Kingdom.
The project has been supported by a grant of £4 million
from the Millennium Commission.

First included in Everyman's Library, 1906

ISBN 1-85715-226-3

A CIP catalogue record for this book is available from the
British Library

Published by Everyman Publishers plc,
Gloucester Mansions, 140A Shaftesbury Avenue,
London WC2H 8HD

Distributed by Random House (UK) Ltd.,
20 Vauxhall Bridge Road, London SW1V 2SA

COMEDIES

CONTENTS

Introduction

The Merchant of Venice xi
The Merry Wives of Windsor xl
Much Ado About Nothing liv
As You Like It lxxiv
Twelfth Night ciii
All's Well That Ends Well cxxvii
Measure for Measure cliv

Select Bibliography clxxxiii

Chronology cxc

THE MERCHANT OF VENICE 1

THE MERRY WIVES OF WINDSOR 105

MUCH ADO ABOUT NOTHING 217

AS YOU LIKE IT 319

TWELFTH NIGHT 425

ALL'S WELL THAT ENDS WELL 531

MEASURE FOR MEASURE.. 651

INTRODUCTION

THE MERCHANT OF VENICE (1596)

Which is the merchant here? And which the Jew?

(IV, i, 173)

... see how yond justice rails upon yond simple thief. Hark, in thine ear: change places, and, handy-dandy, which is the justice, which is the thief?

(*King Lear* IV, vi, 153-6)

When Portia, disguised as Balthasar, 'a young and learned doctor', enters the Court of Justice in Venice, her first business-like question is 'Which is the merchant here? And which the Jew?' It is an astonishing question. We know that Shylock would have been dressed in a 'gaberdine', because, we are told, Antonio habitually spits on it. This was a long garment of hard cloth customarily worn by Jews who, since 1412, had been obliged to wear a distinctive robe extending down to the feet. Shylock would have been literally a 'marked' man (in a previous century he would have had to wear a yellow hat). Antonio, a rich merchant who invariably comes 'so smug upon the mart' (where 'smug' means sleek and well-groomed, as well as our sense of complacently self-satisfied), is more likely to have been dressed in some of the 'silk' in which he trades (look at the sumptuously dressed Venetian merchants in Carpaccio's paintings to get some idea). It would have been unmissably obvious which was the merchant and which was the Jew. So, is that opening question just disingenuousness on Portia–Balthasar's part – or what?

The first Act is composed of three scenes set in the three (relatively) discrete places, or areas, each of which has its distinct voices, values, and concerns. Together, they make up the world of the play. I will call these – Rialto Venice; Belmont (Portia's house, some indeterminate distance from Venice, probably best thought of as being like one of those lovely Renaissance palaces still to be seen in the Veneto); and Ghetto

Venice (Shylock's realm). The word 'ghetto' never appears in
the play, and, as John Gross has pointed out, Shakespeare
makes no mention of it. But the name Ghetto Nuovo (meaning
New Foundry) was the name of the island in Venice on which
the Jews were effectively sequestered (and from which the
generic use of 'ghetto' derives); and clearly Shylock lives in a
very different Venice from the Venice enjoyed by the confident
Christian merchants. Hence my metaphoric use of the name
for what, in Shakespeare, is simply designated as a 'public
place'. The opening lines of the three scenes are, in sequence:

In sooth I know not why I am so sad.
It wearies me, you say it wearies you ...

By my troth, Nerissa, my little body is aweary of this great world.

Three thousand ducats – well.

Sadness and weariness on the Rialto and in Belmont; money
matters in the Ghetto. Is there any inter-connection? Can
anything be done?

Antonio speaks first, which is quite appropriate since *he* is
the 'Merchant' of the title – not, as some think, Shylock. Had
Shakespeare wanted Shylock signalled in his title, he could
well have called his play *The Jew of Venice*, in appropriate
emulation of Marlowe's *The Jew of Malta* (1589), which was
playing in London in 1596 when Shakespeare (almost certainly) started his own play, and which he (most certainly)
knew and, indeed, deliberately echoed at certain key points (of
which, more by and by). But Shylock is a very different figure
from Barabas, who degenerates into a grotesque Machiavellian monster. In fact, Shylock only appears in five of the
twenty scenes of the play; though he is overwhelmingly the
figure who leaves the deepest mark – 'incision' perhaps (see
later) – on the memory. He shuffles off, broken, beaten, and
ill – sadder and wearier than anyone else in Venice or
Belmont – at the end of Act IV, never to return. But, while
the triumph and victory belong unequivocally to Portia, it is
the Jew's play.

However, Antonio is our merchant, and very Hamlet-ish he
is, too. He sounds an opening note of inexplicable melancholy:

INTRODUCTION

> But how I caught it, found it, or came by it,
> What stuff 'tis made of, whereof it is born,
> I am to learn ...
>
> (I, i, 3-5)

We might later have a guess at at least some of the 'stuff' it is made of, but for now Salerio and Solanio (another of those effectively indistinguishable Rosencrantz-and-Guildenstern couples Shakespeare delights in – it offers another 'which-is-which?' puzzle in a lighter key) try to commiserate with him and cheer him up. And in their two speeches, Shakespeare – breathtakingly – manages to convey a whole sense of mercantile Renaissance Venice. Of course, they say, you are understandably worried – 'your mind is tossing on the ocean' – about your 'argosies' (a very recent English word for large merchant ships, coming from the Venetian Adriatic port of Ragusa – and also used in Marlowe's play). Salerio, packing all the pride and confident arrogance of imperial, incomparable Venice into his lines, imagines those ship as 'rich burghers on the flood', or 'pageants [magnificent floats in festival and carnival parades] of the sea', which

> Do overpeer the petty traffickers
> That cursy [curtsy] to them, do them reverence,
> As they fly by them with their woven wings.
>
> (I, i, 12-14)

Other seafaring traders are 'petty traffickers': Venetian merchants, attracting and exacting worldwide admiration and deference, are something quite superbly else. Solanio chimes in, evoking a merchant's necessary anxieties about winds, maps, ports, piers, and everything that, he says, 'might make me fear/Misfortune to my ventures' – 'ventures' is a word to watch. Salerio develops the theme, imagining how everything he saw on land would somehow remind him of shipwrecks.

> Should I go to church
> And see the holy edifice of stone
> And not bethink me straight of dangerous rocks,
> Which touching but my gentle vessel's side
> Would scatter all her spices on the stream,
> Enrobe the roaring waters with my silks –

And in a word, but even now worth this,
And now worth nothing?

(I, i, 29–36)

'But now a king, now thus,' says Salisbury when he watches
King John die, pondering the awesome mortality of kings
(*King John* V, vii, 60). In this Venice there is much the same
feeling about the loss of one of their argosies, monarchs (or
burghers – it was a republic) of the sea as they were. And what
a sense of riches is compacted into the lines imagining spices
scattered on the stream, and waves robed in silk – an image of
spilt magnificence if ever there was one.

It is important to note Salerio's reference to 'church ... the
holy edifice of stone'. In one of those contrasts dear to artists,
the stillness and fixity of the holy edifice of stone is to be seen
behind the flying ships on the tossing oceans and flowing
streams – the eternal values of the church conjoined with, and
in some way legitimizing, the worldly wealth-gathering of the
sea-venturing, transient merchants; the spiritual ideals sustain-
ing the material practices. For Venice was a holy city (the
Crusades left from there), as well as the centre of a glorious
worldly empire. It was an object of awe and fascination to the
Elizabethans. Indeed, as Philip Brockbank suggested, Venice
was for Renaissance writers what Tyre was for the prophet
Isaiah – 'the crowning city, whose merchants are princes,
whose traffickers are the honourable of the earth' (Isaiah
23:8). But Tyre was also a 'harlot' who made 'sweet melody',
and Isaiah prophesies that it 'shall commit fornication with all
the kingdoms of the world' (Venice was also famed, or
notorious, for its alleged sensualities – in Elizabethan London
there was a brothel simply named 'Venice'). But, also this
about Tyre:

And her merchandise and her hire shall be holiness to the Lord: it
shall not be treasured nor laid up; for her merchandise shall be for
them that dwell before the Lord, to eat sufficiently, and for durable
clothing.

(Isaiah 23:18)

Traditionally, religion is ascetic and preaches a rejection of
worldly goods. But here we see religion and the 'use of riches'

creatively reconciled – and by spending, not hoarding. As Tyre, so Venice. But there is, in Isaiah, an apocalyptic warning – that God will turn the whole city 'upside down' and 'scatter' the inhabitants:

And it shall be, as with the people, so with the priest ... as with the buyer, so with the seller; as with the lender, so with the borrower; as with the taker of usury, so with the giver of usury to him.
The land shall be utterly emptied, and utterly spoiled: for the Lord hath spoken this word.

(24:2, 3)

Ruskin would say that this was effectively what *did* happen to Venice. But that is another story. The point for us here is that the Venetian setting of his play allowed Shakespeare to pursue his exploratory interest in (I quote Brockbank):

the relationship between the values of empire and those of the aspiring affections, human and divine; those of the City of Man and those of the City of God ... between the values we are encouraged to cultivate in a mercantile, moneyed and martial society, and those which are looked for in Christian community and fellowship; between those who believe in the gospel teachings of poverty, humility and passivity, and those who (as the creative hypocrisy requires) pretend to.

Returning to the play, Solanio says that if Antonio is not sad on account of his 'merchandise', then he must be in love. Antonio turns away the suggestion with a 'Fie, fie!' As it happens, I think this is close to the mark, but we will come to that. Here Solanio gives up on trying to find a reason for Antonio's gloom –

> Then let us say you are sad
> Because you are not merry; and 'twere as easy
> For you to laugh and leap, and say you are merry.

(I, i, 47–9)

And he leaves with Salerio, who says to Antonio – 'I would have stayed till I had made you merry.' 'Merry' is a lovely word from old English, suggesting pleasing, amusing, agreeable, full of lively enjoyment. 'To be merry best becomes you,' says Don Pedro to the vivacious Beatrice, 'for out o' question, you were born in a merry hour' (*Much Ado* II, i, 327–9) – and we feel he has chosen just the right word. The princely merchants of Venice favour the word, for, in their aristocratic way, they believe in 'merriment'. It is an unequivocally positive word; it has no dark side, and carries no shadow. Yet in this play, Shakespeare makes it become ominous. When Shylock suggests to Antonio that he pledges a pound of his flesh as surety for the three thousand ducat loan, he refers to it as a 'merry bond', signed in a spirit of 'merry sport' (I, iii, 170, 142). The word has lost its innocence and is becoming sinister. The last time we hear it is from Shylock's daughter Jessica in Belmont – 'I am never merry when I hear sweet music' (V, i, 69). After her private duet with Lorenzo, nobody speaks to Jessica in Belmont and these are, indeed, her last words in the play. It is hard to feel that she will be happily asssimilated into the Belmont world. Something has happened to 'merry-ness', and although Belmont is, distinctly, an abode of 'sweet music', a note of un-merry sadness lingers in the air.

When Bassanio enters with Gratiano, he says to the departing Salerio and Solanio, as if reproachfully, 'You grow exceeding strange; must it be so?' (I, i, 67). It is a word which recurs in a variety of contexts, and it reminds us that there is 'strangeness' in Venice, centring on Shylock, whose 'strange apparent cruelty' (IV, i, 21) is some sort of reflection of, response to, the fact that he is treated like 'a stranger cur' (I, iii, 115) in Venice. And he is, by law, an alien in the city – the stranger within. Gratiano then has a go at Antonio – 'You look not well, Signior Antonio' ('I am not well' says Shylock, as he leaves the play – IV, i, 395: now the merchant, now the Jew. Sickness circulates in Venice, along with all the other 'trafficking').

> You have too much respect upon the world;
> They lose it that do buy it with much care.
> Believe me, you are marvelously changed.
>
> (I, i, 74–6)

His scripture is a little awry here: what people lose who gain the whole world is the *soul*, not the world. A *mondain* Venetian's slip, perhaps. But we are more likely to be alerted by the phrase 'marvelously changed'. As we have seen, Shakespearian comedy is full of marvellous changes, and we may be considering what transformations, marvellous or otherwise, occur in this play. In the event, the 'changes' turn out to be far from unambiguous 'conversions'. Somewhere behind all these conversions is the absolutely basic phenomenon whereby material is converted into 'merchandise' which is then converted into money – which, as Marx said, can then convert, or 'transform' just about anything into just about anything else. It is perhaps worth remembering that Marx praised Shakespeare, in particular, for showing that money had the power of a god, while it behaved like a whore. Shakespeare, he said, demonstrates that money 'is the visible divinity – the transformation of all human and natural properties into their contraries, the universal confounding and distorting of things: impossibilities are soldered together by it'.

Jessica willingly converts to Christianity, hoping for salvation, at least from her father's house, but it hardly seems to bring, or promise, any notable felicity or grace. Shylock is forced to convert – which, however construed by the Christians (he would thereby be 'saved'), is registered as a final humiliation and the stripping away of the last shred of his identity. When Portia gives herself to Bassanio, she says:

> Myself, and what is mine, to you and yours
> Is now converted.
>
> (III, ii, 166–7)

and this is to be felt as a willing conversion, a positive transformation – just as she will, like a number of other heroines, 'change' herself into a man to effect some genuine salvation. Sad Antonio, it has to be said, is not much changed at all at the end – though his life has been saved, and his ships have come sailing in. Venice itself, as represented, is hardly changed; not, that is, renewed or redeemed – though it is a good deal more at ease with itself for having got rid of Shylock – if that is what it *has* done. One hardly feels that the realm has been purged, and that the malcontent threatening the joy of the festive conclusion has been happily exorcized. The play

COMEDIES

does not really end quite so 'well' as that. It is not a
'metamorphic' celebration.

It is Bassanio's plea for financial help from Antonio that
concludes the first scene, and the way in which he does so is
crucial to an appreciation of what follows. He admits that he
has 'disabled mine estate' by showing 'a more swelling port'
than he could afford. 'Swelling port' is 'impressively lavish
lifestyle', but I think we will remember the 'portly sail' of the
Venetian argosies just referred to, 'swollen' by the winds (cf.
the 'big-bellied sails' in *A Midsummer Night's Dream*). The
Venetian princely way of life is both pregnant and distended –
fecund and excessive. However inadvertently, Bassanio is
recognizing a key word by using it. He is worried about his
'great debts':

> Wherein my time, something too prodigal,
> Hath left me gaged.

(I, i, 129–30)

Shylock calls Antonio a 'prodigal Christian', and it was always
a fine point to decide to what extent 'prodigality' was com-
patible with Christianity (think of the parables of the Prodigal
Son, and the Unjust Steward), and to what extent it contra-
vened Christian doctrine. It is one of those words which looks
two ways, pointing in one direction to the magnanimous
bounty of an Antony, and in the other to the ruinous
squandering of a Timon. Clearly, the munificent prodigality
of Antonio is in every way preferable to the obsessive meanness
and parsimony of Shylock. But there is a crucial speech on this
subject, tucked away, as was sometimes Shakespeare's wont,
where you might least expect it. Salerio and Gratiano are
whiling away the time in front of Shylock's house, waiting to
help Lorenzo in the abduction of Jessica. Salerio is saying that
lovers are much more eager to consummate the marriage than
they are to remain faithful ('keep obliged faith') subsequently.
'That ever holds' says Gratiano:

> All things that are
> Are with more spirit chasèd than enjoyed.
> How like a younger or a prodigal
> The scarfèd bark puts from her native bay,

Hugged and embracèd by the strumpet wind!
How like the prodigal doth she return,
With over-weathered ribs and ragged sails,
Lean, rent, and beggared by the strumpet wind!
(II, vi, 12–19)

An apt enough extended metaphor in a mercantile society, and the Venetians must have seen many a ship sail out 'scarfed' (decorated with flags and streamers) and limp back 'rent'. It may be added that Gratiano is something of a cynical young blade. But the speech stands as a vivid reminder of one possible fate of 'prodigality', *and* of marriage. Ultimately of Venice too, perhaps.

Bassanio, whatever else he is (scholar, courtier) is a 'prodigal', and he wants to clear his 'debts'. Antonio immediately says that 'my purse, my person' (a nice near pun, given the close inter-involvement of money and body in this play) 'lie all unlocked to your occasions' (I, i, 139). This open liberality might be remembered when we later hear the frantically retentive and self-protective Shy*lock* (a name not found outside this play) repeatedly warning Jessica to 'look to my house ... lock up my doors ... shut doors after you' (II, v, 16, 29, 52). The difference is clear enough, and need not be laboured. Antonio also positively invites Bassanio to 'make waste of all I have' (I, i, 157) – insouciantly negligent aristocrats like to practise what Yeats called 'the wasteful virtues'. The contrast with 'thrifty' Shylock, again, does not need underlining.

But Bassanio has another possible solution to his money problems; one which depends on 'adventuring' and 'hazard'.

In Belmont is a lady richly left;
And she is fair and, fairer than that word,
Of wondrous virtues ...
Nor is the wide world ignorant of her worth,
For the four winds blow in from every coast
Renownèd suitors, and her sunny locks
Hang on her temples like a golden fleece,
Which makes her seat of Belmont Colchos' strond,
And many Jasons come in quest of her.
O my Antonio, had I but the means
To hold a rival place with one of them,

I have a mind presages me such thrift
That I should questionless be fortunate!

(I, i, 161–3, 167–76)

Antonio, all his wealth at sea, at the moment has neither
'money, nor commodity'; but he will use his 'credit' to get 'the
means'. He will borrow the *money* from Shylock to finance
Bassanio's quest of a second *golden* fleece. So it is that the
seemingly discrete worlds of the Ghetto, the Rialto, and
Belmont are, from the beginning, inter-involved.

Rich – fair – virtuous; 'worth' indeed, and well figured by
mythologizing Portia's 'sunny locks' into a 'golden fleece'.
Perhaps unsurprisingly, we are back into Ovid. Helle, the
daughter of Athamas and Nephele, tried to escape from her
stepmother Ino on a golden-fleeced ram. Unfortunately, she
fell off into the sea then named after her – the Hellespont. Her
brother, however, did escape, and sacrificed the ram in
gratitude. The ram became the constellation Aries, and Jason
was sent on a mission to recover the fleece. This probably tells
you more than you want to know, or be reminded of. The
more relevant point is that Jason won the golden fleece with
the help of the dark magic of Medea, whom he married. So he
returned with two prizes from 'Colchos' strond' (Colchis, on
the Black Sea, was Medea's homeland). We will encounter
another echo of Medea; but the further point to remember
here is that Jason was the least heroic of heroes, and that he
deserted Medea just as he had previously deserted Hypsipyle.
Jonathan Bate says that Jason was 'an archetype of male
deceit and infidelity', and, albeit in very different circumstances, we do see Bassanio being 'unfaithful' to Portia almost
immediately after their marriage. Portia wants to see Bassanio
as a 'Hercules', the *most* heroic of heroes; but the question must
remain to what extent he is, in fact, a Jason in Hercules'
clothing (since we're talking about sheep and fleeces). And
one more point. Jason won the fleece *and* a wife. For Bassanio
the fleece *is* the wife. Fittingly, when he opens the right casket,
he finds a 'golden mesh' – a painting of Portia's 'sunny locks'.
This, it has to be said, was the 'gold' he came for. To keep the
analogy alive in our minds, after Bassanio has won Portia,
Gratiano exults 'We are the Jasons, we have won the Fleece'

(III, ii, 241); and Salerio, keeping the mercantile line of thought going, replies – 'I would you had won the fleece that he Antonio hath lost!' (III, ii, 242). 'Fleece' equals 'fleets'? Perhaps. Certainly there is some connection (not necessarily an identification) between Portia, her hair, her gold, Rialto wealth, and – somewhere – Ghetto ducats. Bassanio could not be/play Jason–Hercules winning the Portia–fleece, without the help of Shylock mediated through Antonio.

Venice, as we have seen it and will see it, is overwhelmingly a man's world of public life; it is conservative, dominated by law, bound together by contracts, underpinned by money – and closed. Belmont is run by women living the private life; it is liberal, animated by love, harmonized by music and poetry ('fancy'), sustained by gold – and open. However cynical one wants to be, it will not do to see Belmont as 'only Venice come into a windfall' (Ruth Nevo). It is better to see it as in a line of civilized, gracious retreats, stretching from Horace's Sabine farm, through Sidney's Penshurst, Jane Austen's Mansfield Park, up to Yeats's Coole Park. As Brockbank said, such places ideally offered 'the prospect of a protected life reconciling plenitude, exuberance, simplicity and order'. It was Sidney who said that 'our world is brazen, the poets only deliver a golden', and you might see Belmont as a kind of 'golden' world which has been 'delivered' from the 'brazen' world of trade and money. (The art-gold which builds the statues at the end of *Romeo and Juliet* is not the same as the money-gold with which Romeo buys his poison.) Yes, somewhere back along the line, it is grounded in ducats; but you must think of the churches, palaces, art works and monuments of the Renaissance, made possible by varying forms of patronage, and appreciate that the 'courtiers, merchants and bankers of the Renaissance found ways of transmuting worldly goods into spiritual treasure' (Brockbank). Belmont is a privileged retreat from Venice; but, as Portia will show, it can also fruitfully engage with it.

In scene two we are in Belmont, and Portia is weary. Partly, surely, because she must be bored stiff with the suitors who have come hopefully buzzing round the honey-pot – the silent Englishman, the mean Scotsman, the vain Frenchman, the drunken German, and so on, as she and Nerissa amuse themselves discussing their different intolerabilities. But, more importantly, because she is under the heavy restraint of a paternal interdiction (familiar enough in comedy, though this one comes from beyond the grave). She has been deprived of *choice* – and she wants a mate.

> The brain may devise laws for the blood, but a hot temper leaps o'er a cold decree; such a hare is madness the youth to skip o'er the meshes of good counsel the cripple. But this reasoning is not in the fashion to choose me a husband. O me, the word 'choose'! I may neither choose who I would nor refuse who I dislike, so is the will of a living daughter curbed by the will of a dead father. Is it not hard, Nerissa, that I cannot choose one, nor refuse none?
>
> (I, ii, 17–26)

Then we learn from Nerissa about the lottery of the caskets, which she thinks was the 'good inspiration' of a 'virtuous' and 'holy' man. We shall see. But we note that, in this, Belmont (in the form of Portia) is as much under the rule of (male) law as Venice. There are 'laws for the blood' in both places, and they may by no means be 'leaped' or 'skipped' over. In other comedies we have seen inflexible, intractable, unmitigatable law magically, mysteriously melt away or be annulled. Not in this play. Here the law is followed, or pushed, to the limit – and beyond. Indeed, you might say that Belmont has to come to Venice to help discover this 'beyond' of the law.

And now, in scene three, we are in Shylock's Venice; and we hear for the first time what will become an unmistakable voice – addressing, as it were, the bottom line in Venice: 'three thousand ducats – well'. Shylock speaks in – unforgettable – prose, and this marks something of a crucial departure for Shakespeare. Hitherto, he had effectively reserved prose for exclusively comic (usually 'low') characters. With Shylock, this all changes (with Falstaff too, who emerges shortly after Shylock – though arguably he is, at inception, still something of a comic character). For Shylock is not a comic character. He has a power, a pain, a passion, a dignity – and, yes, a savagery, and a suffering – which, whatever they are, are not comic. And here I would like, if possible, to discredit and disqualify two damagingly irrelevant attitudes to the play. The first is the one which accuses it of anti-Semitism. This really is, with the best will in the world, completely beside the point. There *were* Jews in Renaissance European cities; they *were* often the main money-lenders; no doubt some of them *were* extortionate. Christians who borrowed from them no doubt *did* develop strong antagonistic, resentful feelings towards them (as people invariably do towards those to whom they are in any way 'indebted' – 'Why do you hate me so much; what have I done for you recently?' is, here, a pertinent Jewish joke). And, equally assumable, some Jews came to harbour very understandable feelings of anger and revenge against the people who, at once, used and reviled them. So much is history: so much – I risk – is fact. And Shakespeare knew his facts. Interested in every aspect of human behaviour, for him an archaically vengeful Jew was as plausible a figure as an evil monarch, a betraying friend, a cowardly soldier, an ungrateful daughter.

A more insidious view is that which maintains that Shylock is intended to be 'a purely repellent or comic figure' because 'conventionality' would have it so. These are the words of E. E. Stoll, from a regrettably influential essay written in 1911. Like it or not, he said, that is how Jews were regarded by the Elizabethans, and Shakespeare, 'more than any other poet, reflected the settled prejudices and passions of his race'. 'How can we,' he concluded, 'for a moment sympathize with Shylock unless at the same time we indignantly turn, not only against Gratiano, but against Portia, the Duke, and all Venice as well?' The baneful insensitivity and crass unintelligence of these remarks merit no response, and I would not have resurrected them were it not for the fact that, in our understandably squeamish post-Holocaust time, reasons (justifications, *excuses*) for even performing the play sometimes run along those lines. As I have said before, if something hurts or worries us, you may be very sure that it hurt and worried Shakespeare, and the idea of happily laughing the broken Shylock off stage is simply unthinkable. Now. And then. And some of that 'indignant turning' on Venice, which Stoll found so inconceivable, may well not be out of place. We have here, certainly a 'comedy' as conventionally constituted – group solidarity reconfirmed, a threat disarmed and extruded; but there is something sour, sad, even sick in the air – at the end as at the beginning. As we regard the contented figures at Belmont, we may well agree with Ruth Nevo that 'we do not feel that they are wiser than they were. Only that they have what they wanted.' In pursuit of his vengeance, Shylock becomes a monstrous figure, as does anyone who takes resentment, hatred, and revenge, to extremes. But the play is not a melodrama or morality play, and that is certainly not all there is to him.

On his first appearance, Shylock establishes his 'Jewishness' by, among other things, revealing his adherence to Jewish dietary rules – 'I will not eat with you, drink with you, nor pray with you' (I, iii, 345). (But why, then, does he later agree to go to supper with the 'prodigal Christian', which in any case he would not have been allowed to do, since the Jews were locked up in their island at night? On this, and all matters concerning Jews in contemporary Venice, and London, see John Gross's comprehensive *Shylock*. I suppose Shakespeare wants to get him out of the way so Jessica can rob him and flee.) When Antonio appears, Shylock reveals a darker side of his nature in an 'aside' (as we have often seen, potential villains tend to reveal themselves and their intentions in soliloquies or asides – to us).

> I hate him for he is a Christian;
> But more, for that in low simplicity
> He lends out money gratis, and brings down
> The rate of usance here with us in Venice.
> ...
> He hates our sacred nation, and he rails,
> Even there where merchants most do congregate,
> On me, my bargains, and my well-won thrift,
> Which he calls interest. Cursèd be my tribe
> If I forgive him.
>
> (I, iii, 39-42, 45-9)

Shylock gives three good reasons for his hating of Antonio – insofar as one can have good reasons for hatred: personal, professional, tribal. This is interesting in view of his response during the trial scene, when he is asked why he would not prefer to have ducats rather than Antonio's flesh:

INTRODUCTION

> So can I give no reason, nor I will not,
> More than a lodged hate and a certain loathing
> I bear Antonio ...
>
> (IV, i, 59–61)

In his two comedies which follow shortly, Shakespeare includes two, relatively minor, characters who cannot find, or offer, any explanation for the irrational hatreds they feel (Oliver in *As You Like It*, and Don John in *Much Ado*). Shylock is a much larger and more complex figure; and, like Iago – Shakespeare's greatest study of 'motiveless malignity' – he can find motives (more plausible than Iago's), but ultimately reveals that he is acting under the compulsion of a drive which defeats and outruns explanation. The phenomenon was clearly starting to engage Shakespeare's serious attention.

His crucial opening exchange with Antonio really defines the central concern of the play. He has already mentioned 'usance' ('a more clenly name for usury' in contemporary terms), 'thrift' (which means both prosperity and frugality – 'thrift, Horatio, thrift') and 'interest'. And 'usury', of course, is the heart of the matter. Any edition of the play will tell you that the law against lending money at interest was lifted in 1571, and a rate of ten percent was made legal. Queen Elizabeth depended on money borrowed at interest, so did most agriculture, industry, and foreign trade by the end of the sixteenth century (according to R. H. Tawney). So, indeed, did Shakespeare's own Globe Theatre. Plenty of Christians lent money at interest (including Shakespeare's own father); and Bacon, writing 'Of Usury' in 1625, said 'to speak of the abolishing of usury is idle'. Antonio, scattering his interest-free loans around Venice, is certainly an 'idealized' picture of the merchant, just as Shylock sharpening his knife to claim his debt, is a 'demonized' one. This is John Gross's point, and it could be seen as a version of what psychoanalysts call 'splitting', as a way of dealing with confused feelings: Melanie Klein's good mother – figure of our hopes and desires, that would be Antonio; and bad mother – object of our fears and aggressions, Shylock. But Aristotle and Christianity had spoken against usury, and there was undoubtedly a good deal of residual unease and ambivalence about it. Ruthless usurers were thus especially hated and abused, and since Jews were identified as quintessential usurious money-lenders (and, of course, had killed Christ), they were available for instant and constant execration. This must certainly be viewed as a collective hypocrisy – one of those 'projections' by which society tries to deal with a bad conscience (not that Shakespeare would have seen many Jews in London; it is estimated that there were fewer than two hundred at the time). Shakespeare was not addressing a contemporary problem;* rather, he was exploring some of the ambivalences and hypocrisies, the value clashes and requisite doublenesses, which inhere in, and attend upon, all commerce.

The play is full of commercial and financial terms: 'moneys', 'usances', 'bargains', 'credit', 'excess' and 'advantage' (both used of usury and profit), 'trust', 'bond' (which occurs vastly more often than in any other play: curiously 'contract' is *not* used – Shakespeare wants us to focus on 'bond'), 'commodity' (you may recall the 'smooth-faced gentleman, tickling commodity ... this commodity, this bawd, this broker, this all-changing word' from *King John*), and 'thrift'. Launcelot Gobbo is 'an unthrifty knave', while Jessica flees from her father's house with 'an unthrift love'. This last serves as a reminder that both here and elsewhere in Shakespeare the language of finance and usury could be used as a paradoxical image of love (happiness accrues and passion grows by a form of *natural* interest). You will hear it in Belmont as well as on the Rialto. When Portia gives herself to Bassanio, she, as it were, breaks the bank:

> I would be trebled twenty times myself,
> A thousand times more fair, ten thousand times more rich,
> That only to stand high in your account,
> I might in virtues, beauties, livings, friends,
> Exceed account.

> (III, ii, 153–7)

---

*Though there had been an outbreak of anti-Semitism in 1594, after the execution of Roderigo Lopez, a Portuguese Jew accused by Essex of trying to poison Queen Elizabeth.

Rich place, Belmont; generous lover, Portia!

The absolutely central exchange occurs when Antonio and Shylock discuss 'interest', or 'borrowing upon advantage'. 'I do never use it' declares Antonio (what is the relationship between 'use' and 'usury'? Another consideration.) Shylock replies, seemingly rather inconsequentially: 'When Jacob grazed his uncle Laban's sheep . . .' Antonio brings him to the point. 'And what of him? Did he take interest?' Shylock seems to prevaricate: 'No, not take interest – not as you would say/ Directly int'rest', and then recounts the story from Genesis. This tells how Jacob tricked – but is that the right word? – his exploitative uncle, Laban: they agreed that, for his hire, Jacob should be entitled to any lambs in the flocks he was tending, that were born 'streaked and pied'. Following the primitive belief that what a mother sees during conception has an effect on the offspring, Jacob stripped some 'wands' (twigs or branches), so that some were light while others were dark, and 'stuck them up before the fulsome ewes' as the rams were impregnating them. In the subsequent event, a large number of 'parti-colored lambs' were born, which of course went to Jacob. Nice work; but was it also sharp practice? Or was it both, and so much the better? Or, does it matter? Not as far as Shylock is concerned:

> This was a way to thrive, and he was blest;
> And thrift is blessing if men steal it not.
>
> (I, iii, 86–7)

'Ewes' may be a pun on 'use'; and for Shylock, it is as legitimate to use ewes in the field as it is to use usury on the 'mart'. Not so for Antonio:

> This was a venture, sir, that Jacob served for,
> A thing not in his power to bring to pass,
> But swayed and fashioned by the hand of heaven.
> Was this inserted to make interest good?
> Or is your gold and silver ewes and rams?

And Shylock:

> I cannot tell; I make it breed as fast.
>
> (I, iii, 88–93)

Antonio's last line effectively poses *the* question of the play.

It was a line often quoted (or more often, slightly misquoted) by Ezra Pound in his increasingly unbalanced vituperations against usury and Jews. The root feeling behind it is that it is somehow *unnatural* for inorganic matter (gold, silver, money) to reproduce itself in a way at least analogous to the natural reproductions in the organic realm. 'They say it is against nature for *Money* to beget *Money*,' says Bacon, quoting Aristotle, and Pope catches some of the disgust the notion could arouse, in a simple couplet:

> While with the silent growth of ten per cent
> In dirt and darkness hundreds stink content.

This enables Antonio to reject Shylock's self-justifying analogy: Jacob's story does *not* 'make interest good', because he was having, or making, a 'venture', and the result was, inevitably, 'swayed and fashioned' by – heaven? nature? some power not his own. This, revealingly, was how Christian commentators of the time justified Jacob's slightly devious behaviour (as Frank Kermode pointed out) – he was making a *venture*. Antonio's ships are 'ventures', and Bassanio is on a venture when he 'adventures forth' to Belmont. It seems that the element of 'risk' (= to run into danger) and 'hazard', purifies or justifies the act. As 'hazard' was originally an Arabian word for a gaming die, this would seem to enable gambling to pass moral muster as well. Perhaps it does. Whatever, there is seemingly *no* risk, as well as no nature, in usury. Shylock's answer, that he makes his money 'breed as fast', is thought to tell totally against him; and Antonio's subsequent remark, 'for when did friendship take /A breed for barren metal of his friend?' (I, iii, 130–31), is taken to orient our sympathies, and values, correctly. But this won't quite do.

Because, like it or not, money most certainly *does* 'breed'. It may not literally copulate, but there is no way round the metaphor. Sigurd Burckhardt is the only commentator I have read who has seen this clearly, and he wrote: 'metal ["converted" into money] is not barren, it does breed, is pregnant with consequences, and capable of transformation into life and art'. For a start, it gets Bassanio to Belmont, and the obtaining of Portia and the Golden Fleece (or Portia *as a* golden fleece). And – as if to signal his awareness of the proximity, even similitude, of the two types of 'breeding', with the lightest of touches – when Gratiano announces he is to marry Nerissa at the same time as Bassanio marries Portia, Shakespeare has him add, 'we'll play with them the first boy for a thousand ducats' (III, ii, 214). You 'play' for babies, and you 'play' for ducats. Which also means that when Shylock runs through the streets crying 'O my ducats! O my daughter!' (echoing Marlowe's Barabas who cries out 'oh, my girl, my gold', but when his daughter *restores* his wealth to him), we should not be quite so quick to mock him as the little Venetian urchins. He may not use his money to such life-enhancing and generous ends as some of the more princely Venetians; but he *has* been doubly bereaved (which literally means – robbed, *reaved*, on all sides).

Having mentioned that robbery, I will just make one point about the Jessica and Lorenzo sub-plot. However sorry we may feel for Jessica, living in a 'hell' of a house with her father, the behaviour of the two lovers is only to be deprecated. Burckhardt is absolutely right again: 'their love is lawless, financed by theft and engineered by a gross breach of trust'. Jessica 'gilds' herself with ducats, and throws a casket of her father's wealth down to Lorenzo ('Here, catch this casket; it is worth the pains', II, vi, 33 – another echo-with-a-difference of Marlowe's play, in which Abigail throws down her father's wealth from a window, to her *father*). This is an anticipatory parody, travesty rather, of Portia, the Golden (not 'gilded') Fleece, waiting to see if Bassanio will pass the test of *her* father's caskets (containing wisdom, rather than simple ducats). He 'hazards' all; this couple risk nothing. They squander eighty ducats in a night – folly, not bounty. Jessica exchanges the ring her mother gave her father as a love-pledge, for – a monkey! They really do make a monkey out of marriage – I will come to their famous love duet in due course. Theirs is the reverse, or inverse, of a true love match. It must be intended to contrast with the marriage made by Bassanio and Portia. Admittedly, this marriage also involves wealth – as it does paternal caskets; but, and the difference is vital, wealth *not gained or used in the same way*.

Those caskets.* Shakespeare took nearly everything that he wanted for his plot (including settings, characters, even the ring business in Act V) from a tale in *Il Pecorone* (*The Dunce*), a collection of stories assembled by Giovanni Fiorentino, published in Italy in 1558 – everything except the trial of the caskets. In the Italian story, to win the lady, the hero has to demonstrate to her certain powers of sexual performance and endurance. Clearly, this was not quite the thing for a Shakespearian heroine. So Shakespeare took the trial-by-caskets from a tale in the thirteenth-century *Gesta Romanorum*, which had been translated into English. Here, a young woman has to choose between three vessels – gold, silver, lead – to discover whether she is worthy to be the wife of the Emperor's son. All we need note about it is one significant change that Shakespeare made in the inscriptions on the vessels/caskets. Those on the gold and silver ones are effectively the same in each case – roughly, 'Who chooseth me shall gain/get what he desires/deserves'. But in the medieval tale, the lead casket bears the inscription '*Thei that chese me, shulle fynde in me that God hath disposid*'. Now, since the young woman is a good Christian, she could hardly have been told more clearly that this was the one to go for. It is, we may say, no test at all. Shakespeare changes the inscription to 'Who chooseth me must give and hazard all he hath' (II, vii, 9). This is a very different matter. Instead of being promised a placid and predictable demonstration of

---

*My editor does not like footnotes, but I would briefly like to draw attention to an interesting paper on 'The Theme of the Three Caskets' by Freud (Collected Papers IV), not mentioned by commentators on this play whom I have read. He points out how often the theme of having to choose between three women recurs through myth and folk tale (Paris with the three goddesses, the Prince with Cinderella and her two sisters – not to mention Lear and his three daughters); and how, invariably, the 'right' choice is the seemingly least likely one – Cinderella, Cordelia, the lead casket (caskets, of course, represent women). Freud wonders whether, in some refracted way, they figure 'the three forms taken on by the figure of the mother as life proceeds: the mother herself, the beloved who is chosen after her pattern, and finally the Mother Earth who receives him again'. No direct relevance, I think, to the play. But interesting.

piety rewarded, we are in that dangerous world of risk and hazard which, at various levels, constitutes the mercantile world of the play. And to the prevailing lexicon of 'get' and 'gain', has been added the even more important word – 'give'. One of the concerns of the play is the conjoining of *giving* and *gaining* in the most appropriate way, so that they may 'frutify' together (if I may borrow Launcelot Gobbo's inspired malapropism). 'I come by note, *to give and to receive*,' Bassanio announces to Portia (III, ii, 140 – my italics). Which is no less than honesty.

While she is anxiously waiting as Bassanio inspects the caskets, Portia says:

> Now he goes,
> With no less presence, but with much more love,
> Than young Alcides [Hercules], when he did redeem
> The virgin tribute paid by howling Troy
> To the sea monster. I stand for sacrifice;
> The rest aloof are the Dardanian wives,
> With blearèd visages come forth to view
> The issue of th' exploit. Go, Hercules!

(III, ii, 53–60)

The 'virgin tribute' was Hesione, and her rescue by Hercules is described in Book XI of Ovid's *Metamorphoses* (where it is preceded by stories concerning Orpheus, who turned everything to music, and Midas, who turned everything to gold – they are both referred to in the play, and are hovering mythic presences behind it). Portia's arresting claim – 'I stand for sacrifice' – resonates through the play; to be darkly echoed by Shylock in court – 'I stand for judgment ... I stand here for law' (IV, i, 103, 142). When she says 'stand for', does she mean 'represent' or 'embody'; or does she imply that she is in danger of being 'sacrificed' to the law of her father unless rescued by right-choosing Hercules–Bassanio? Or is it just that women are always, in effect, 'sacrificed' to men in marriage, hence the 'bleared visages' of those 'Dardanian wives'? Something of all of these, perhaps. In the event, it is Portia herself who effectively rescues or – her word – 'redeems', not Troy, but Venice. Bassanio (courtier, scholar, and fortune-seeker) is, as we have seen, if not more, then as much Jason as Hercules. The point is, I think, that he has to be *both* as cunning as the one *and* as bold as the other. The 'both-ness' is important.

This is how Bassanio thinks his way to the choice of the correct casket:

> So may the outward shows be least themselves;
> The world is still deceived with ornament.
> In law, what plea so tainted and corrupt,
> But being seasoned with a gracious voice,
> Obscures the show of evil?

(III, ii, 73-7)

One of his examples of the deceptiveness of 'outward shows' is:

> How many cowards whose hearts are all as false
> As stairs of sand, wear yet upon their chins
> The beards of Hercules and frowning Mars,
> Who inward searched, have livers white as milk!

(III, ii, 83-6)

A Hercules concealing the false heart and milk-white liver for which, as it happens, Jason was renowned – who can Bassanio have in mind? He even says that 'snaky golden locks' on a woman often turn out to be wigs taken from corpses – so perhaps we would even do well to blink at Portia, while Bassanio praises the 'golden mesh' of her hair, though of course she proves true and real enough. I am sure Shakespeare wants us to notice how analogies can sometimes circle round on the characters who offer them. Bassanio, moralizing hard, returns to his theme of 'ornament':

> Thus ornament is but the guilèd shore
> To a most dangerous sea, the beauteous scarf
> Veiling an Indian beauty; in a word,
> The seeming truth which cunning times put on
> To entrap the wisest.

(III, ii, 97-101)

This, *mutatis mutandis*, is a theme in Shakespeare from first to last – 'all that glisters is not gold', and so on (II, vii, 65). Bassanio is on very sure ground in rejecting the gold and silver and opting for lead, *in the context of the test*. But – ornament: from *ornare* – to equip, to adorn. Now, if ever there was an equipped and adorned city, it was Venice. It is aware of dangerous seas and treacherous shores, of course; but it is also a city of beauteous scarves, and silks and spices – and what are they but 'ornaments' for the body and for food? Bassanio is an inhabitant and creation of an ornamented world, and is himself, as we say, an 'ornament' to it. So why does he win by going through a show of rejecting it? He wins, because he realizes that he has to subscribe to the unadorned modesty of lead, *even while* going for the ravishing glory of gold. *That* was the sort of complex intelligence Portia's father had in mind for his daughter. Is it hypocrisy? Then we must follow Brock-bank and call it 'creative hypocrisy'. It recognizes the compromising, and willing-to-compromise, doubleness of values on which a worldly society (a society in the world) necessarily rests, and by which it is sustained. The leaden virtues, and the golden pleasures. Bothness.

Such is the reconciling potency of Belmont; and Portia seals the happy marriage with a ring. But, meanwhile, Shylock is waiting back in Venice for his pound of flesh, and he *must* be satisfied. Must – because he has the law on his side, and Venice lives by law; its wealth and reputation depend on honouring contracts and bonds – as Shylock is the first to point out. 'If you deny my bond, let the danger light/Upon your charter and your city's freedom!' Portia, as lawyer Balthasar, agrees: 'There is no power in Venice/Can alter a decree established' (IV, i, 38–9, 217–18). 'I stay here on my bond' (IV, i, 241) – if Shylock says the word 'bond' once, he says it a dozen times (it occurs over thirty times in this play – never more than six times in other plays). We are in a world of law where 'bonds' are absolutely binding. Portia's beautiful speech exhorting to 'mercy' is justly famous; but, as Burckhardt remarked, it is impotent and useless in this 'court of justice', a realm which is under the rule of the unalterable letter of the law. Her sweet and humane lyricism founders against harsh legal literalism. The tedious, tolling reiteration of the word 'bond' has an effect which musicians know as 'devaluation through repetition'. The word becomes emptier and emptier of meaning, though still having its deadening effect. It is as if they are all in the grip of a mindless mechanism, which brings them to a helpless, dumb impasse, with Shylock's dagger quite legally poised to strike. Shylock, it is said, is adhering to the old Hebraic notion of the law – an eye for an eye. He has not been influenced by the Christian saying of St Paul: 'The letter killeth but the spirit giveth life.' For Shylock, the spirit *is* the letter; and Antonio can only be saved *by* the letter. It is as though Portia will have to find resources in literalism which the law didn't know it had.

And so, the famous moment of reversal.

> Tarry a little; there is something else.
> This bond doth give thee here no jot of blood;
> The words *expressly* are 'a pound of flesh.'
> Take then thy bond ...
> Shed thou no blood, nor cut thou less nor more
> But just a pound of flesh.
>
> (IV, i, 304–7, 324–5 – my italics)

(Compare Cordelia's 'I love your Majesty/According to my bond, no more nor less', *King Lear* I, i, 94–5; scrupulous exactness in honouring a bond turns out to be the most reliable way of recognizing it, in both cases.) Ex-press: to press out. Portia squeezes new life and salvation out of the dead and deadly law – and not by extenuation or circumvention or equivocation. 'How every fool can play upon the word!' says Lorenzo, in response to Launcelot's quibbles. But you can't 'play' your way out of the Venetian law courts. Any solution must be found within the precincts of stern, rigorous law. 'The Jew shall have all justice ... He shall have merely justice and his bond' (IV, i, 320, 338). And, to Shylock: 'Thou shalt have justice more than thou desir'st' (315). Portia makes literalism yield a life-saving further reach. Truly, the beyond of law.

Life-saving for Antonio – and for Venice itself, we may say. But not, of course, for Shylock. He simply crumples; broken by his own bond, destroyed by the law he 'craved'. But prior to this, his speeches have an undeniable power, and a strangely compelling sincerity. Necessarily un-aristocratic, and closer to the streets (and the Ghetto life back there somewhere), his

speech in general has a force, and at times a passionate directness, which makes the more 'ornamented' speech of some of
the more genteel Christians sound positively effete. Though
his defeat is both necessary and gratifying – the cruel hunter
caught with his own device – there is something terrible in the
spectacle of his breaking. 'I pray you give me leave to go from
hence. I am not well' (IV, i, 394–5). And Gratiano's cruel,
jeering ridicule, with which he taunts and lacerates Shylock
through the successive blows of his defeat, does Christianity,
does humanity, no credit. I think we can 'indignantly turn' on
him – for a start. Like the malcontent or kill-joy in any
comedy, Shylock has to be extruded by the regrouping,
revitalized community, and he is duly chastised, humiliated,
stripped, and despatched – presumably back to the Ghetto.
He is never seen again; but it is possible to feel him as a dark,
suffering absence throughout the final Act in Belmont. And in
fact, he does make one last, indirect 'appearance'. When
Portia brings the news that Shylock has been forced to leave
all his wealth to Jessica and Lorenzo, the response is – 'Fair
ladies, you drop manna in the way/Of starved people' (V, i,
294–5). 'Manna' was, of course, what fell from heaven and fed
the children of Israel in the wilderness. This is the only time
Shakespeare uses the word; and, just for a second, its deploy-
ment here – at the height of the joy in Christian Belmont –
reminds us of the long archaic biblical past stretching back
behind Shylock, who also, just for a second, briefly figures, no
matter how unwillingly, as a version of the Old Testament
God, providing miraculous sustenance for *his* 'children' (a
point made by John Gross).

But why did not Shakespeare end his play with the climactic
defeat of Shylock – why a whole extra Act with that ring
business? Had he done so, it would have left Venice unequivocally triumphant, which perhaps he didn't quite want. This is
the last aspect of the play I wish to address, and I must do so
somewhat circuitously. Perhaps Shylock's most memorable
claim is:

I am a Jew. Hath not a Jew eyes? Hath not a Jew hands, organs,
dimensions, senses, affections, passions? – fed with the same food, hurt
with the same weapons, subject to the same diseases, healed by the

same means, warmed and cooled by the same winter and summer as
a Christian is? If you prick us, do we not bleed?

$$(\text{III, i, } 55\text{-}61)$$

That last question, seemingly rhetorical (of course you do),
but eventually crucial (Shylock seems to have overlooked the
fact that if he pricks Antonio, *he* will bleed too), is prepared
for, in an admittedly small way, by the first suitor to attempt
the challenge of the caskets. The Prince of Morocco starts by
defending the 'shadowed livery' of his 'complexion', as against
'the fairest creature northward born':

> And let us make incision for your love
> To prove whose blood is reddest, his or mine.

$$(\text{II, i, } 6\text{-}7)$$

So, a black and a Jew claiming an equality with white
Venetian gentles/gentiles (another word exposed to examination in the course of the play), which I have not the slightest
doubt Shakespeare fully accorded them (the princely Morocco, in fact, comes off rather better than the silvery French
aristocrat who follows him). And Morocco's hypothetical
'incision' anticipates the literal incision which Shylock seeks to
make in Antonio. When Bassanio realizes that Portia is going
to ask to see her ring, which he has given away, he says in an
aside:

> Why, I were best to cut my left hand off
> And swear I lost the ring defending it.

$$(\text{V, i, } 177\text{-}8)$$

So, there may be 'incisions' made 'for love', from hate, and out
of guilt. Portia describes the wedding ring as:

> A thing stuck on with oaths upon your finger,
> And so riveted with faith unto your flesh.

$$(\text{V, i, } 168\text{-}9)$$

Riveting on is, I suppose, the opposite of Shylock's intended
cutting out; but, taken together, there is a recurrent linking of
law (oaths, bonds, rings) – and flesh. The play could be said to
hinge on *two* contracts or bonds, in which, or by which, the

law envisions, permits, requires, ordains, the exposing of a part of the body of one party to the legitimate penetration (incision) by the other party to the bond. If that party is Shylock, the penetration/incision would be done out of hate – and would prove mortal; if that other party is Bassanio it should be done out of love – and give new life. Shylock swears by his 'bond'; Portia works through her 'ring'.

It should be noted that, in the last Act, when Bassanio is caught out with having given Portia's ring away to Balthasar, he stands before Portia as guilty and helpless as Antonio stood before Shylock. And, like Shylock, she insists on the letter of the pledge, and will hear no excuses and is not interested in mercy. Like Shylock too, she promises her own form of 'fleshly' punishment (absence from Bassanio's bed, and promiscuous infidelity with others). As with the word 'bond' in the court scene, so with the word 'ring' in this last scene. It occurs twenty-one times, and at times is repeated so often that it risks suffering the semantic depletion which seemed to numb 'bond' into emptiness. *Both* the word 'bond' and the word 'ring' – and all they represent in terms of binding and bonding – are endangered in this play. But the law stands – and continues to stand. Bonds must be honoured or society collapses; there is nothing Bassanio can do. Then, just as Portia-as-Balthasar found a way through the Venetian impasse, so Portia-as-Portia has the life-giving power to enable Bassanio to *renew* his bond – she gives him, mysteriously and to him inexplicably, the same ring, for a second time. (She has mysterious, inexplicable good news for Antonio, too, about the sudden safe arrival of his ships.) A touch of woman's magic. For Portia is one of what Brockbank called Shakespeare's 'creative manipulators' (of whom Prospero is the last). Like Vincentio (in *Measure for Measure*), she uses 'craft against vice'. She can be a skilful man in Venice (a veritable Jacob), and a tricky, resourceful, ultimately loving and healing woman in Belmont (a good Medea with something of the art of Orpheus – both figures invoked in the scene). She can gracefully operate in, and move between, both worlds. Because she is, as it were, a man–woman, as good a lawyer as she is a wife (more 'both-ness'), she figures a way in which law and love, law and blood, need not be mutually exclusive and opposed forces. She shows how they, too, can 'frutify' together.

The person who both persuades Bassanio to give away his ring, and intercedes for him with Portia ('I dare be bound again') is Antonio. He is solitary and sad at the beginning, and is left alone at the end. He expresses his love for Bassanio in an extravagant, at times tearful way. It is a love which seems to be reciprocated. In the court scene, Bassanio protests to Antonio that:

> life itself, my wife, and all the world
> Are not with me esteemed above thy life.
> I would lose all, ay sacrifice them all
> Here to this devil, to deliver you.

Portia (she certainly does 'stand for sacrifice'!), permits herself an understandably dry comment:

> Your wife would give you little thanks for that
> If she were by to hear you make the offer.

(IV, i, 283–8)

Perhaps this is why she decides to put Bassanio to the test with the ring. I have already had occasion to recognize the honourable tradition of strong male friendship, operative at the time. I also know that 'homosexuality', as such, was not invented until the late nineteenth century. I am also totally disinclined to seek out imagined sexualities which are nothing to the point. But Antonio is so moistly, mooningly in love with Bassanio (and so conspicuously uninvolved with, and un-attracted to, any woman), that I think that his nameless sadness, and seemingly foredoomed solitariness, may fairly be attributed to a homosexual passion, which must now be frus-trated since Bassanio is set on marriage. (Antonio's message to Bassanio's wife is 'bid her be judge/Whether Bassanio had not once a love', which implies 'lover' as much as 'friend'; revealingly, Antonio's one remaining desire is that Bassanio should witness the fatal sacrifice he is to make for him.) Even then, we might say that that is neither here nor there. Except for one fact. Buggery and usury were *very* closely associated or connected in the contemporary mind as unnatural acts.

INTRODUCTION

Shylock is undoubtedly a usurer, who becomes unwell; but if Antonio is, not to put too fine a point on it, a bugger, who is also unwell ...

Perhaps some will find the suggestion offensively irrelevant; and perhaps it is. But the atmosphere in Venice–Belmont is not unalloyedly pure. The famous love duet between Lorenzo and Jessica which starts Act V, inaugurating the happy post-Shylock era – 'In such a night ... ' – is hardly an auspicious one, invoking as it does a faithless woman (Cressid), one who committed suicide (Thisbe), an abandoned woman (Dido), and a sorceress (Medea whose spells involved physical mutilation), before moving on to a contemporary female thief – Jessica herself. I hardly think that she and Lorenzo will bear any mythological 'ornamenting'. And that theft has become part of the texture of the Belmont world. It is a place of beautiful music and poetry – and love; but with perhaps just a residual something-not-quite-right lingering from the transactions and 'usages' of Ghetto–Rialto Venice. (The very last word of the play is a punningly obscene use of 'ring' by Gratiano, the most scabrous and cynical voice in Venice – again, a slightly off-key note.) There is moonlight and candle-light for the nocturnal conclusion of the play, but it doesn't 'glimmer' as beautifully as it did at the end of *A Midsummer Night's Dream*. Portia says:

> This night methinks is but the daylight sick;
> It looks a little paler. 'Tis a day
> Such as the day is when the sun is hid.

(V, i, 124–6)

A little of the circulating sickness has reached Belmont. The play *is* a comedy; but Shakespeare has here touched on deeper and more potentially complex and troubling matters than he had hitherto explored, and the result is a comedy with a difference. And, of course, it is primarily Shylock who *makes* that difference.

Now, let's go back to the beginning. 'Which is the merchant here? And which the Jew?' It turns out to be a good question.

*

COMEDIES

THE MERRY WIVES OF WINDSOR (1597)

What tempest, I trow, threw this whale, with so many tuns of oil in
his belly, ashore at Windsor?

(II, i, 62-4)

The whale is Falstaff; the speaker is merry wife Mrs Ford; and
the question is a good one. What *is* Falstaff doing in Windsor?
Ephesus, Padua, Verona, Navarre, Athens, Messina, Arden,
Illyria, Rousillon – Shakespeare habitually set his romantic
comedies in exotic-sounding placeless places, as often as not in
somewhat timeless times as well. But in this play we are in a
completely recognizable contemporary Windsor. This comedy, like T. S. Eliot's history, is 'now and England'. There are
identifiable inns, chapels, rivers and parks. The characters sup
on good Elizabethan fare – hot venison pasty, possets, Banbury cheese, stewed prunes. They climb stiles, and keep dogs.
The women 'wash, wring, brew, bake, scour, dress meat and
drink, make the beds' (I, iv, 94-5) – though I suppose that
they have been doing that for time out of mind. Still, it all
contributes to the feeling that we are amid the familiar
domestic routines of a small Elizabethan country town. Since
we last encountered Falstaff – not to mention Bardolph, Pistol,
Nym, Shallow, Mistress Quickly – in the reign of Henry IV,
i.e. some two centuries earlier (though, if we had been
Elizabethan playgoers, it would have been an extremely
recent encounter), it is necessarily something of a surprise
(though hardly an unwelcome one for us, whatever it might be
for the good wives of the town) to see the debauched old rogue
trying to wing it and make out in Elizabethan Windsor. The
question is – is it the *same* Falstaff?

When Falstaff says: 'If it should come to the ear of the court
how I have been transformed, and how my transformation
hath been washed and cudgeled, they would melt me out of
my fat drop by drop, and liquor fishermen's boots with me'
(IV, v, 93-8), it suggests that he is the same man we saw
bantering with the 'wild Prince' (also referred to in this play).
On the other hand, he does not seem to know Mistress
Quickly, who is herself recognizably the same, yet manifestly
different. One school of thought holds that this Falstaff is 'a

new character with an old name'. Another, exemplified by
Ruth Nevo, confidently asserts that 'the character of Falstaff
has not changed – the craft, the shrewdness, the brass, the zest
are all there'. Against that, set H. B. Charlton: 'His wits have
lost all their nimbleness.' It has to be said that Charlton's
reading is strange to the point of derangement. He sees the
play as a 'cynical revenge which Shakespeare took on the
hitherto unsuspecting gaiety of his own creative exuberance'.
He maintains it was a sense of 'bitter disillusionment' that
allowed Shakespeare 'to call the contemptible caricature of
The Merry Wives of Windsor by the name of Sir John Falstaff'.
He speaks of 'malicious laceration', and 'a crime worse than
parricide'. You rub your eyes in disbelief.

This is the sort of disagreement which can get literary
criticism a bad name. Have these critics read the same play?
An attempt to adjudicate between such contradictory views is
hardly called for. The point, surely, is that Shakespeare has
taken a recently created and very successful character,
retained a number of his most distinguishing characteristics
(verbal inventiveness, resilience, and so on), but placed him in
an entirely different setting and situation. On his own turf, in
the easy-going inns of London, Falstaff is more or less the boss;
in the respectable bourgeois world of a quiet country town, he
is a fish out of water – or better, a beached whale, as the good
lady has it. So that in some ways he is bound to look rather
different. It has been suggested that one reason for the
reappearance of Falstaff in an unlikely setting was the request
of the Queen. This tradition, or legend, was started in the
eighteenth century by Dennis and Rowe. 'She was so well
pleas'd with that admirable Character of *Falstaff* in the two
Parts of *Henry IV*, that she commanded him to continue it for
one Play more, and to shew him in Love. This is said to be the
Occasion of his Writing *The Merry Wives of Windsor*.' The
Arden editor, H. J. Oliver, pertinently comments that it is
unlikely that the Queen would have asked to see Falstaff 'in
love' if she had seen him with Doll Tearsheet in *2 Henry IV* – a
consideration which adds to the evidence that the play was
written in 1597, immediately after the first part of *Henry IV*. Dr
Johnson was sceptical about the legend, and in his comment

offers a powerful account of what makes Falstaff Falstaff. 'Shakespeare knew what the Queen, if the story be true, seems not to have known, that by any real passion of tenderness, the selfish craft, the careless jollity, and the lazy luxury, must have suffered so much abatement, that little of his former cast would have remained. Falstaff could not love, but by ceasing to be Falstaff. He could only counterfeit love, and his professions could be prompted, not by the hope of pleasure, but of money.' Dr Johnson is, of course, absolutely right. Falstaff in Windsor does need money – but I will come back to him.

There *is* a love plot in the play, involving the sweet English maid, Anne Page, and the young gentleman, Fenton, who 'dances', 'has eyes of youth', 'writes verses', 'speaks holiday', and 'smells April and May' (III, ii, 63–5). A perfectly matched couple. Together, they conspire to circumvent her obstructive parents. There is no more basic plot to comedy than this, but as a whole the play is not a romantic comedy. Nor is it a satire, as, say, in the manner of Jonson. No one is savaged, no one is relentlessly ridiculed, no one is deflated beyond restoration. Falstaff has his discomforts, but as he dusts himself down at the end, he is effectively unscathed – and off to supper with everyone. Jealous Ford has to be made to look *and* feel ridiculous, if only for the easing of his good wife. But, on the whole, no grievances are laceratingly felt, no grudges are unforgivingly borne (with perhaps one tiny exception). People are mocked, but the mocking is merry: there is quarrelling, but it is dissolved in laughter and hospitality. Inviting everyone in for dinner near the beginning, Page says 'Come, gentlemen, I hope we shall drink down all unkindness' (I, i, 189–90). At the end, his wife repeats the invitation – 'let us every one go home,/And laugh this sport o'er by a country fire' (V, v, 243–4). This is the prevailing benign atmosphere of the play.

If anything, it is almost a kind of farce, centring on the blundering mishaps of Falstaff, and the foiled misprisions of Ford. It has been called a 'citizen comedy', and compared to, among others, Dekker's *Shoemaker's Holiday* (1599). Bullough points out that a number of realistic comedies of town life (i.e. not the court or the palace or the manor) were written in the last few years of the sixteenth century. It *is* extremely funny, sometimes in a slapstick, or Box-and-Cox sort of way, and gives unfailing pleasure (though not to poor Professor Charlton); but it remains something of an anomaly among Shakespeare's comedies. Written almost entirely in prose, it seems strange that it follows the iridescent magic of *A Midsummer Night's Dream*; and with its elements of knock-about farce, it feels odd that it precedes the sophisticated courtly brilliance of *Much Ado About Nothing*. And why Windsor between Athens and Messina; why so unmistakably contemporary England? It is a play which unarguably shows signs of hurried composition. There are lots of loose ends; situations are set up but not resolved; incomplete episodes are left unintegrated into the play (whatever happened to the German horse-thieves?); several unemployed characters seem to have no real role, though we are happy enough to see them enter and speak their bits, however inconsequential they may seem. (Who would be without Slender, in whom, said F. S. Boas, 'not only do we see intellect flickering with its last feeble glimmer, but the will attenuated almost to vanishing point. Palpitating on the brink of nonentity, he clings for support to the majestic figure of Shallow.' With just a few strokes, Shakespeare has created an unforgettable figure. And, as H. J. Oliver says, Slender's proposal to Anne – III, iv – is perhaps the funniest proposal in English literature, matching anything in Jane Austen.)

A possible answer to all these questions about a play which somehow does not seem to 'fit' in the line of Shakespeare's development, was first suggested by J. L. Hotson, who said that the play could have been written specifically, and hastily, for the Garter festivities in April/May 1597. William Green developed this idea in his *Shakespeare's Merry Wives of Windsor*, and I shall simply summarize briefly some of his work. In Act V, scene v, there is a reference to 'our radiant Queen'; and Mistress Quickly as Queen of the Fairies sends the boys dressed as fairies to 'Windsor Castle' with orders to 'strew good luck ... on every sacred room'. She tells them to scour 'the several chairs of Order', mentions the 'loyal blazon', refers to 'the Garter's compass', and instructs them to write *Honi soit qui mal y pense* in flowers (this, of course, is the motto of the

Order of the Garter). Earlier in the play, Mistress Quickly notes that the town is filling with courtiers, while Dr Caius says he is hurrying to court for a 'grand affair'. Clearly, an installation of Knights-Elect to the Order of the Garter is about to take place in Windsor. And in the real Windsor too. William Green: 'Now the Windsor setting makes sense, for if Shakespeare chose to allude to a Garter installation, what more appropriate place to locate the play than in Windsor, home of the Order of the Garter since the fourteenth century? Moreover, what need to state that the preparation of castle and chapel is for this ceremonial? The Elizabethans knew that the only Garter rite celebrated in Windsor was an installation – this by decree of Elizabeth in 1567. And the Elizabethans – at least those in courtly circles during the late 1590s – further knew what Garter installation Shakespeare was referring to – that of May, 1597.' One of the individuals to be named to the Order on this occasion was George Carey, the second Lord Hunsdon. Hunsdon was patron of Shakespeare's company at this time. He was also a favourite cousin of Queen Elizabeth, and the not unreasonable speculation is that the Queen's request for another Falstaff play was conveyed through Hunsdon. Tradition further has it that he had to write it in fourteen days, perhaps to be ready for presentation at the April 1597 St George's Day festivities. This last bit cannot be verified, of course; but, on this occasion, the whole line of conjecture makes a lot of sense in that it explains much that is otherwise inexplicable about this anomalous play.

The main incidents are all to be found in earlier European and English stories and farces. The themes of the presumptuous suitor punished; and the jealous husband fooled; and, indeed, the forbidding parents foiled, are all old and familiar. Shakespeare, of course, infuses new life into them, and weaves them together brilliantly, even if there are some bits left hanging out. The play opens with some comical talk of coats of arms, old family lines, prerogatives and titles – suitable enough for a Garter entertainment, quickly moving on to talk of 'pretty virginity' and family inheritances, and soon settling into its central bourgeois concerns – marriage, money, and class. A speech by Fenton (a Gentleman, and thus out of his class with the Pages and Fords) brings these matters together. He is explaining to Anne Page why her father disapproves of him:

> He doth object I am too great of birth,
> And that my state being galled with my expense,
> I seek to heal it only by his wealth.
> Besides these, other bars he lays before me:
> My riots past, my wild societies;
> And tells me 'tis a thing impossible
> I should love thee but as a property.
>
> (III, iv, 4-10)

Here is a defining bourgeois wariness – suspicion of the upper classes as dissolute and wasteful; belief that they are after middle-class daughters to get at their money. The defining word is 'property'. Anne, refreshingly, replies by saying 'May be he tells you true'. Good for her! Though with a very small part, Anne is one of those independent young women who very definitely refuse to behave like property when men – or parents – try to treat them as such. (Anne's reaction to the proposal that she marry Caius shows commendable spirit and that gay inventiveness which is the hallmark of the Shake-spearian comic heroine: 'I had rather be set quick i' th' earth,/ And bowled to death with turnips', III, iv, 86-7.) But the possession of property is what the bourgeois live by, and live for, and by this reckoning wives and daughters *are* a form of property. Being robbed, being cuckolded, and being duped are all forms of that great bourgeois dread – theft. And there is a great deal of stealing and cheating going on, or being attempted, in this play, both by the visitors and among the locals. Marilyn French pointed out that 'everyone in the play cozens, is cozened, or both' (except Page's son, William – too young for it). Certainly, the words 'cozen', 'cozened', 'cozen-age' are heard more frequently in this play than in any other. 'I would all the world might be cozened, for I have been cozened and beaten too' (IV, v, 92-3) is a late cry from Falstaff. Shakespeare has found his integrating master-theme.

Once settled in his room at the Garter Inn, where he doubtless feels most at home, Falstaff is soon talking about 'filching' and theft with his ruffianly followers. As he later admits to Pistol (whom he nicely addresses as 'thou unconfinable baseness' – given his size, a perfect self-description) – 'I, I, I myself sometimes, leaving the fear of God on the left hand and hiding mine honor in my necessity, am fain to shuffle, to hedge, and to lurch' (II, ii, 23–6) – three words for cheating and pilfering. He soon makes clear his intentions concerning two local wives, candidly revealing his venal, commercial motives.

I am about thrift. Briefly, I do mean to make love to Ford's wife. I spy entertainment in her: she discourses, she carves, she gives the leer of invitation ... the report goes she has all the rule of her husband's purse ... I have writ me here a letter to her; and here another to Page's wife, who even now gave me good eyes too ... She bears the purse too. She is a region in Guiana, all gold and bounty. I will be cheater to them both, and they shall be exchequers to me. They shall be my East and West Indies, and I will trade to them both.

(I, iii, 42–71)

He has lost none of his expansive opulence of language, his gift for the fecund phrase ('the leer of invitation' is marvellous). The images of trading, banking, and exotic foreign lands to be explored and exploited for their riches have, of course, a contemporary aptness. By one of those tricks whereby language has it both ways, 'cheater' denominates both an escheator, an official who looked after lapsed estates which were forfeit to the crown; and someone who defrauds. Momentarily, looking after becomes indistinguishable from taking away – and indeed, you can't always tell guardianship from theft, or protection from subtraction. Falstaff aims to be every way a 'cheater'. For this, and for the shameless fatuity of his vain assumption that the two respectable wives are consumed with lust for his grotesque body, he must and will be punished.

The details of the plots or schemes whereby – out of fear of the madly jealous Ford – Falstaff is inveigled, first, into a laundry basket full of filthy clothes which is then emptied in a muddy ditch near the Thames, and secondly, into wearing the gown of the fat woman of Brainford, to be cudgelled from the house by an irate Ford ('Out of my door, you witch, you rag, you baggage, you polecat, you runnion!', IV, ii, 180–82, this is Punch and Judy stuff) – these details require no comment. They are part of the unambiguous, depthless fun of the play. His third punishment, however, merits a little consideration. Mrs Page draws on a folk figure called Herne the Hunter, said to roam at midnight in Windsor Forest with 'great ragg'd horns' upon his head, blasting trees and taking cattle. The plan is to persuade Falstaff to dress up in some horns and, disguised as Herne the Hunter, keep an assignation with the two wives in the forest at midnight. He will then be exposed and lightly tormented – pinches and little taper burns – by children dressed as fairies. Amazingly enough, fresh from a dousing and a beating, Falstaff agrees to keep the tryst in the recommended horn disguise. This is sometimes seen as showing his limitless gullibility, or the degrading unquenchability of his lust and desperation. But such responses quite miss the tone. If anything, you have to admire the old boy for returning *yet again* to a manifestly and disastrously lost cause.

But something more than that. This is his soliloquy as he stands in his preposterous disguise next to the oak tree at midnight, waiting for his women:

The Windsor bell hath struck twelve; the minute draws on. Now, that hot-blooded gods assist me! Remember, Jove, thou wast a bull for thy Europa; love set on thy horns. O powerful love, that in some respects makes a beast a man; in some other, a man a beast. You were also, Jupiter, a swan for the love of Leda. O omnipotent love, how near the god drew to the complexion of a goose! A fault done first in the form of a beast. O Jove, a beastly fault! And then another fault in the semblance of a fowl; think on't, Jove; a foul fault! When gods have hot backs, what shall poor men do? For me, I am here a Windsor stag; and the fattest, I think, i' th' forest. Send me a cool rut-time, Jove, or who can blame me to piss my tallow? Who comes here? My doe?

(V, v, 1–16)

This is the only time that this play reaches back to the great pagan world of Ovid. The speech has a depth of perspective, a richness of reference, a wealth of suggestion, not found elsewhere in the play. Of course, the figure of fat old Falstaff in his horns invoking the Greek gods is comic – mock-epic. But, as he stands there, opening up the myths of divine promiscuity, he becomes a reminder of more awesome things and figures. At a simple level, horned Falstaff evokes both a satyr waiting to couple with his nymphs, and a cuckold, the generically emasculated male. But he is also effectively a reincarnation of the figure of Actaeon, habitually represented as having a stag's head, a human body, and wearing hunter's clothes. Actaeon is the huntsman who accidentally caught sight of the goddess Diana naked while bathing. As punishment for this profane act, Diana turns him into a stag, in which form he is hunted down and torn to pieces by his own dogs.* Shakespeare (along with other Renaissance writers) uses the myth as a figure of self-destructive sexual desire. As in *Twelfth Night*:

> O when mine eyes did see Olivia first
> Methought she purged the air of pestilence;
> That instant was I turned into a hart,
> And my desires, like fell and cruel hounds,
> E'er since pursue me.

(I, i, 18–22)

Pistol, telling Ford that Falstaff is in pursuit of his wife, describes him as 'Like Sir Actaeon he, with Ringwood at thy heels' (II, i, 117). (Because of his horns, Actaeon was an Elizabethan name for a cuckold, and Ford thinks, quite wrongly, that he will expose his trusting friend Page as being 'a secure and willful Actaeon', III, ii, 39. After this play, the name never appears again in Shakespeare.) Actaeon was punished for his sexual transgression or presumption, and so it will be with this contemporary version of Actaeon, preying in Windsor Forest. But instead of real dogs – pretend fairies.

Actaeon is very brutally torn to pieces by his own dogs:

---

*Thirty-five of them: Shakespeare delighted in dogs' names, and he must have relished in this list – Blackfoot, Tracker, Glance, Glutton, Ranger, Rover, Stalker, Storm, Hunter, Woodman, Dingle, Snatch, Catch, Shepherd, Spot, Gnasher, Tigress, Courser, Lightfoot, Strong, Sooty, Branch, Woolf, Cyprian, Spartan, Tempest, Clinch, Blackie, Shag, Furie, Whitetooth, Barker, Blackhair, Killer, Climber.

Good. But it's not Tray, Blanche and Sweetheart.

> Now they are all around him, tearing deep
> Their master's flesh, the stag that is no stag.

By contrast, Falstaff is pinched by children dressed as fairies. As the sound of real hunting approaches, he can discard his horns in a way unavailable to luckless Actaeon. Thus the stage direction: *And a noise of hunting is made within, and all the Fairies run away. Falstaff pulls off his buck's head and rises.* Falstaff, we may note, always rises, rises again, after every fall. He always has done. This (characteristic) draining of the actual violence from Ovid's story may be seen in different ways – as a 'demetaphorization' of Ovid's terrible image; as a domestication of the wilder pagan story; as a comic reminder, as Falstaff pulls his stage-prop buck's head off, that we no longer live in a mythic age – this is theatre within theatre. François Laroque adds a slightly more sombre note:

In this final scene, Falstaff plays the role of a 'scape-deer', abandoned to the mercies of the fairies and elves by whom he is cornered. Beneath the farce, there clearly lie primitive myths associated with the notions of sacrifice, courage and metamorphosis. The dynamic of the images is intended to reveal the 'accursed side of festivity' in which what Jeanne Roberts calls 'the "innocent" revenge of its night-wandering spirits' in truth masks a scene of ritual sacrifice or sacred lynching.

Perhaps, though that sounds a shade heavy to me. Bearing in mind the fairies, we might do better to think of the only other visibly metamorphosed comic figure – Bottom among his elves. He had his moment of visionary glory; and the figure of Falstaff as a Windsor stag, invoking as precedent the polymorphous amorous exploits of Jove, has a certain overreaching splendour which momentarily eclipses both past and imminent humiliations.

Despite those humiliations, Falstaff remains throughout a figure of real comic stature; not just because of the size of his body, but through his relationship *to* that body.

Sayest thou so, old Jack? Go thy ways; I'll make more of thy old body than I have done. Will they yet look after thee? Wilt thou, after the expense of so much money, be now a gainer? Good body, I thank thee.

(II, ii, 138–42)

The accounts he gives of his misadventures – 'you may know by my size that I have a kind of alacrity in sinking', 'Think of that, a man of my kidney – think of that – that am as subject to heat as butter; a man of continual dissolution and thaw' (see the speeches in III, v, 1–18 and 94–121) – are not the words of a broken man. He can be funnier about his own body than anybody else. With his rich elaborations, he transforms what was pure knock-about farce into something of grander proportions and resonances – mock epic perhaps, but the epic note is there. Even when he discovers that the fairies were only children, his rhetoric lends a kind of dignity to the delusion:

And these are not fairies? I was three or four times in the thought they were not fairies; and yet the guiltiness of my mind, the sudden surprise of my powers, drove the grossness of the foppery into a received belief, in despite of all the teeth of rhyme and reason, that they were fairies.

(V, v, 124–9)

This is to make simple, scared error into a complex moral and psychological experience. Perhaps it always is – again these are not the words of a terminally humiliated man. He says, soberly enough, 'I do begin to perceive that I am made an ass' (V, v, 122) – an ass, rather than the bull and swan he was hoping to emulate. It is a clear enough piece of self-recognition. Thus it is that, after the assembled group submit him to a sustained bout of insults – 'hodge-pudding', 'bag of flax', 'old, cold, withered, and of intolerable entrails', 'slander-ous as Satan', 'given to fornications, and to taverns, and sack and wine and metheglins' and so on – he seems notably unbruised by the onslaught. His reply is hardly a flinching one: 'Well, I am your theme. You have the start of me; I am dejected ... Use me as you will' (V, v, 165–8). 'Well, I am your theme' ... hardly a cry from the cross. They will 'use' him by inviting him to supper. And he has the next-to-last laugh, when it is disclosed that Anne and Fenton have foiled the Pages and are now married. 'When night dogs run, all sorts of deer are chased' (V, v, 240) comments Falstaff with the wisdom of experience. He knows he is not the only ass in the forest. The man is intact.

1

INTRODUCTION

The other figure who needs punishing, or humiliating back into his senses, is the jealous husband, Ford. He is subject to what Evans calls 'fery fantastical humors and jealousies' (III, iii, 168), and Evans warns him 'you must ... not follow the imaginations of your own heart' (IV, ii, 153). All of Windsor knows that he is off his head in this matter, and his wife clearly has some grim times with him. He has one monologue, after posing as Mr Brooke to persuade Falstaff to seduce his wife, only to gather that, as Falstaff thinks, the matter is already well in hand, which reveals him to be pathological. This is at II, ii, 286–312, the key part running from 'See the hell of having a false woman! My bed shall be abused, my coffers ransacked, my reputation gnawn at' – the bourgeois triple nightmare – to the deranged cry 'God be praised for my jealousy'. The Arden editor, along with others, thinks that in Ford, jealousy 'is depicted "in the round"', and that Ford's suffering is 'acute'. The alternative view sees Ford, with his obsessive, repetitive, knee-jerk suspicions, as a 'humour' figure (such figures, in whom, to simplify, a single characteristic or temperamental trait completely predominates, were becoming popular in drama towards the end of the sixteenth century). If his jealousy is 'in the round', then he is anticipating Othello and we suffer with him and sympathize. If he is a 'humour' figure, he could easily appear in a Ben Jonson satire and we should laugh at him and condemn. I suppose you take your pick. It is very hard for Shakespeare not to humanize what he touches, and he does not offer the skeletally thinned-down humour-figures of a Ben Jonson. On the other hand, given the manifest virtue and probity of his wife, and the attitude of his fellow citizens – 'the lunatic is at it again' – I think he is more of an amplified humour than an inchoate Othello. Still, jealousy is a phenomenon which can always generate tragedy, and in this comedy, it has to be very thoroughly defused. Shakespeare has just the verb for it; they have to '*scrape* the figures out of [his] brains' (IV, ii, 212 – my italics). By the end, we are to take it that they have succeeded.

There are other characters who are something between humours and humans, types and individuals – Mistress Quickly, Welsh parson–schoolmaster Evans, the French doctor Caius, the jovial benign Host, Pistol, Bardolph, Nym, Slender, Shallow. Whatever they contribute to the movement of the main plots – and here and there they do – as a group they contribute hugely to the rippling laughter of the play as a whole. This is mainly a matter of language. When Henry James returned to America after a long absence, he was taken aback by the variety of accents, the weird immigrant manglings of English, he heard in the cafés on New York's East Side – 'torture-rooms of the living idiom' he called them. The world of Shakespeare's Windsor is more a funhouse than a torture-room, but English certainly gets put through the wringer. When Mistress Quickly accuses Caius of the 'abusing of God's patience and the King's English' (I, iv, 5-6), she hits the mood of the play; as does Page when he says of Nym 'Here's a fellow frights English out of his wits' (II, i, 135-6). When Evans hears Bardolph say 'the gentleman had drunk himself out of his five sentences', he pedantically comments 'It is his "five senses." Fie, what the ignorance is!' (I, i, 169-71). He is hardly one to talk. More than the pinching and burning in the final scene, what causes Falstaff most pain is the way Evans speaks to him. 'Have I lived to stand at the taunt of one that makes fritters of English?' (V, v, 146-7). We hardly need to know that 'fritters' were bits of fried batter: it is the perfect word. Mistress Quickly contributes her inspired malapropisms – a 'fartuous ... civil modest wife' (II, ii, 97-8); or, trying to cheer up the half-drowned Falstaff and reassure him of Mrs Page's honest intentions, 'She does so take on with her men; they mistook their erection.' 'So did I mine' replies Falstaff somewhat grimly – what else could he possibly say? (III, v, 39-41). The admirable Host, tricking Evans and Caius out of their intended duel, says 'Disarm them, and let them question. Let them keep their limbs whole and hack our English' (III, i, 72-3). That is the mood of the play. The only wounding is of the English language (it is possible that Caius storms off angrily at the end after he discovers he has 'married' a boy – 'Be-gar, I'll raise all Windsor', V, v, 211 – but I think it is quite wrong to see him as a Malvolio figure). The Host proves a perfect reconciler between the doctor and the priest. 'Shall I lose my doctor? No; he gives me the potions and the motions.

Shall I lose my parson, my priest, my Sir Hugh? No; he gives me the proverbs and the no-verbs. Give me thy hand, terrestrial; so. Give me thy hand, celestial; so. Boys of art, I have deceived you both; I have directed you to wrong places. Your hearts are mighty, your skins are whole, and let burnt sack be the issue. Come, lay their swords to pawn. Follow me, lad of peace ... ' (III, i, 97–105). It is as amiable a little speech as you will find in Shakespeare. In general we can say that Shakespeare has not had so much fun with the English language – whether indulging its over-spilling plenitude with Falstaff (and triplets are everywhere – 'accoutrement, complement, and ceremony', 'a knot, a ging, a pack', 'speak, breathe, discuss', etc.), or letting it run wildly off the leash with Mistress Quickly, Evans, Caius, and others – since *Love's Labor's Lost*. Take the play as a whole and Evans is right – 'It is admirable pleasures and fery honest knaveries' (IV, iv, 80–81).

But we must not forget the 'merry wives' of the title. Mrs Page and Mrs Ford are distinctly *not* 'humours' or types, and they admirably demonstrate that 'Wives may be merry, and yet honest too' (IV, ii, 100) And they, after all, are the ones who initiate the plots – this is where the real, inventive power is in Windsor. Together, they are the master-minder. They have the comic initiative – not the men. So adroit in London, in Windsor Falstaff is nowhere (he is even humiliated in female clothes – the only time a *man* cross-dresses in Shakespeare). Ruth Nevo sees this as part of a central development in the role of Shakespeare's comic heroines. 'The transmission to the women of a masculine comic energy, of racy wit and high spirits, of irony and improvisation, of the uninhibited zest for mockery which were the prerogatives of maverick and adventurous males, was a gradual process' – Beatrice, Rosalind, Viola to follow. Nevo suggests that the transfer of comic energies to the women required the emasculation of Falstaff. This may well be true, and in an important sense this play belongs to the women. But Falstaff has that one moment of commanding presence as he stands there like a stag (at bay, as it turns out) and proclaims – 'When gods have hot backs, what shall poor men do?'

It is another good question.

COMEDIES

MUCH ADO ABOUT NOTHING (1598)

> There is some strange misprision in the princes.
>
> (IV, i, 184)

> Of this matter
> Is little Cupid's crafty arrow made,
> That only wounds by hearsay.
>
> (III, i, 21–3)

This is a comedy built around, generated by, 'misprision' (to be heard again in *Twelfth Night* and *All's Well*) and 'hearsay' (Shakespeare's only use of the word). It is also perhaps Shakespeare's most perfectly constructed play, every part in its place, and working so smoothly and easily as to make the whole work seem like a piece of effortless, seamless spontaneity. You can't see the joins, or hear the engine – from this point of view, it is a Rolls-Royce of a play. Swinburne was justified in his claim that 'for absolute power of composition, for faultless balance and blameless rectitude of design, there is unquestionably no creation of his hand that will bear comparison with *Much Ado About Nothing*'. He built on previous work (understandably enough – he was writing at an astonishing rate; averaging two plays a year throughout this decade). He had experimented with contrasting heroines in *The Taming of the Shrew*: one, docile and submissive; the other, sharp-tongued and wilful. They were wooed by equally contrasting suitors: one, conventionally romantic; the other, resolutely unsentimental. Bianca and Kate will blossom into Hero and Beatrice, while Lucentio and Petruchio will mutate into Claudio and Benedick. Wooing could be this, wooing could be that – worth exploring further for comic, dramatic possibilities. And the combative relationship between Kate and Petruchio proved capable of a rich turn in the debonair duelling and sparring between Berowne and Rosaline in *Love's Labor's Lost* – good basis here for the 'merry war' between Beatrice and Benedick. That play had shown that there was a lot of potential for amusing badinage and banter in concentrating on a courtly circle – particularly if the characters are engaged in wooing games. 'Cupid' is invoked some ten times in both *Love's Labor's Lost* and *Much Ado About Nothing* (much more often than elsewhere), and they could be well called Shakespeare's Cupid plays. 'Wit' and 'woo' are words which – again – occur far more often in these two plays than in any others (except for 'woo' in *The Taming of the Shrew*); and, if I may be allowed to press a noun into service as a verb, we might say that 'to wit' and 'to woo', 'witting' and 'wooing', go together, flow together, as interrelated activities and drives. As the anonymous contemporary commentator said, they are both 'borne in the sea that brought forth Venus'.

But, while *Love's Labor's Lost* was an incomparable entertainment, it was hardly a play; for the simple reason that, when all was said and done, it lacked a plot. Couldn't really do that again. And a good way to make sure of a plot, as Shakespeare was learning, was to have a plotter *in* the play. So he invented, or imported (the figure of the saturnine, melancholic, Machiavellian malcontent was becoming a familiar one on the Elizabethan stage), Don John. When Hero's maid, Ursula, announces near the end – 'Don John is the author of all' (V, ii, 97), she speaks more truly than she knows; for without his malign, contriving mischief, there would not be a play. And Shakespeare, the other 'author', had a plot to draw on – a story he knew in at least three versions (by Ariosto, Bandello, Belleforest). There are variations and differing elaborations in each version, but the basic plot involves a jealous lover engaged to be married to a pure heroine; a wicked intriguer who contrives a 'demonstration' (for the lover) of the heroine's sexual impurity by persuading a maid to impersonate her and let one of his accomplices in through her bedroom window; the shared belief in the heroine's guilt, and her public condemnation followed by her apparent death; her concealment and the subsequent exposure of the villainy against her; her re-emergence and return, leading to the appropriate happy conclusion. Shakespeare took, as usual, many details from these sources, including names and the setting in Messina, though of course making his own distinctive modifications and changes. The theme of the supposed death of the heroine prompted him to redeploy the way he had *and Juliet*; to give the figure of the Friar a different kind of wisdom and authority; and to begin to explore the regenerative possibilities in the feigned death motif (which would come to full fruition in the last plays). Since the romance story in his sources was entirely devoid of any comedy, he invented Dogberry and Verges and the Watch as a – literally – indispensable plebeian adjunct to the rather closed and rarefied world of the court. They amplify the sense of a varied and interrelated society in Messina. With all these elements to hand, all Shakespeare had to do was to interweave them, and then fill in the words. Which, of course, is when it all starts to become quite unique.

A word about the title. It can certainly mean just what it seems to mean – to 'make great ado about small matters' is another contemporary formulation. In addition, a Victorian editor (Richard Grant White) maintained that, in Elizabethan pronunciation 'nothing' and 'noting' sounded much the same, and that the plot of the play depends on 'noting' – watching, judging, noting, often incorrectly. This is certainly central to the play, and there is an odd bit of banter between Balthasar and Don Pedro, just before Balthasar sings his famous song 'Sigh no more, ladies'.

> *Balthasar*. Note this before my notes:
>   There's not a note of mine that's worth the noting.
> *Don Pedro*. Why, these are very crotchets that he speaks!
>   Note notes, forsooth, and nothing!

> (II, iii, 54–7)

(The song itself is full of dire warnings to the ladies: 'Men were deceivers ever ... To one thing constant never ... The fraud of men was ever so ... ' – apt enough, in view of what is to transpire.) I am actually a little dubious about 'nothing' and 'noting' having been homophonic, though this has become part of the standard reading of the play.

But there were other associations around 'nothing' for the Elizabethans, which, indeed, a Victorian critic would have gone out of his way not to 'note'. To my knowledge, Roger Sales was the first person to spell these out. A 'thing' was common slang for the phallus, so 'no thing' could be used –

mockingly, even insultingly – of the female genitalia.
Remember Hamlet and Ophelia:

> *Hamlet.* Do you think I meant country matters?
> *Ophelia.* I think nothing, my lord.
> *Hamlet.* That's a fair thought to lie between maids' legs.
> *Ophelia.* What is, my lord?
> *Hamlet.* Nothing.

(Hamlet III, ii 119–24)

And thus Benedick and Beatrice, as they finally reveal their
attraction for each other:

> *Benedick.* I do love nothing in the world so well as you. Is not that
> strange?
> *Beatrice.* As strange as the thing I know not.

(IV, i, 266–8)

Sales suggests that 'the title probably offered both a sexual
statement and, more importantly, the promise of more sexual
jokes to come. Benedick and Beatrice fulfil such expectations,
even during the play's potentially sombre moments.' It is
perhaps worth remembering that the main males in the play
are just back from a victory in some unspecified war which is
now over. The Elizabethans used to say that armies in
peacetime were like chimneys in summer (and the phallic
aspect of a chimney is appropriate). It is now *après la guerre*,
and it will take something, it will take 'nothing' – it will take
women – to get these unemployed soldier–chimneys smoking
again. As Claudio says:

> But now I am returned and that war-thoughts
> Have left their places vacant, in their rooms
> Come thronging soft and delicate desires ...

(I, i, 291–3)

Just so.

The court of Messina is a new kind of world in Shakespeare's comedies. It is as though he has decided to shed most
of the usual romantic trappings – of landscapes, disguisings,
dialogues. There is no Belmont adjacent to this Messina. The
play is mostly in prose, with few opportunites for self-inflaming
lyricism. It has been called (by David Stevenson) 'the most

realistic of Shakespeare's love comedies'; and, while Rossiter did not diagnose a lack of feeling in the play, he felt he detected a certain '*hard*' quality – 'a bright hardness runs through the play'. Bright it is: it glitters and sparkles and flashes. These people are so quick and inventive; yet so nonchalant and casual, withal. There is so much happy, self-delighting intelligence and mental alertness in the air – what Rossiter called 'impetuous exuberance' and 'competitive vitality'. Wit abounds; and it is not the cerebral wit of a Voltaire, but something altogether more expansive, unexpected, joyous. Coleridge compared it to 'the flourishing of a man's stick while he is walking, in the full flow of animal spirits, a sort of exuberance of hilarity which ... resembles a conductor, to distribute a portion of gladness to the surrounding air' (quoted by A. R. Humphreys in his Arden edition).

Though this atmosphere is a function of the whole group, with Dogberry and Verges making a distinctive, illiterate contribution, the leading generators are, of course, Beatrice and Benedick (for a while, the play became known as *Benedick and Beatrice*). Beatrice in particular, though she is said to be 'too curst' and 'shrewd of tongue', is a far cry from the earlier 'shrew', and is Shakespeare's most complex and attractive heroine to date. 'I was born to speak all mirth and no matter' she says gaily, though of course there is matter in her mirth. On Don Pedro's appreciative reply, 'out o' question you were born in a merry hour', she is quick with another turn of the conversation:

No, sure, my lord, my mother cried; but then there was a star danced, and under that was I born. Cousins, God give you joy!

(II, i, 326–32)

Out of question, she has a dancing mind, and it gives *us* joy. One is happy to believe the ensuing description of her by her uncle, Leonato:

There's little of the melancholy element in her, my lord. She is never sad but when she sleeps, and not ever sad then; for I have heard my daughter say she hath often dreamt of unhappiness and waked herself with laughing.

(II, i, 338–42)

'You will never run mad, niece,' he says elsewhere (I, i, 89), and – out of question – hers is a mind of the most felicitous sanity.

But to Benedick she is Lady Disdain, Lady Tongue, a chatterer, a parrot-teacher, 'infernal Ate [goddess of discord] in good apparel' (II, i, 253-4) – 'she speaks poniards, and every word stabs' (II, i, 245-6). She 'turns ... every man the wrong side out' (III, i, 68), and she can take a simple word and so play with it and torment it that Benedick, invariably beaten, has to concede, somewhat complainingly: 'Thou hast frighted the word out of his right sense, so forcible is thy wit' (V, ii, 55-6). To Beatrice, Benedick is a stuffed man, a braggart, caught like a disease, the Prince's jester, a dull fool, and so on. They are both resolutely unsentimental, positively misogamous in their resistance to the idea, ideal, of marriage. How much of his misogyny, and how much of her shrewishness is the expression of genuine feeling, and how much is – playfully or defensively – assumed, can hardly be ascertained; probably even by themselves. (At one point, Beatrice speaks of 'taming my wild heart to thy loving hand', III, i, 112. If this, far more self-controlled, 'shrew' is to be 'tamed', she will tame *herself*.) Even before they are tricked into love and partly (only partly) let their defences down, they are clearly obsessed with each other. From the first moment, they cannot let each other alone. 'I wonder that you will still be talking, Signior Benedick; nobody marks you' says Beatrice, clearly revealing that she has been 'marking' him for all of the approximately thirty seconds he has been in the room in the first scene. 'What, my dear Lady Disdain! Are you yet living?' counters Benedick, and they are off – for the rest of the play. What they engage in is 'flouting' – another word which occurs more often here than in any other play. The word comes from *fluiten*, an old Dutch verb meaning to whistle, play the flute, and hiss – thence to the Elizabethan sense of 'to treat mockingly, with derision'. Given the sort of hissing, whistling music this pair make together, it is a very suitable word for them.

And it is clear that they have a history. Beatrice's first backward reference may be somewhat cryptic. 'He set up his bills here in Messina and challenged Cupid at the flight; and my uncle's fool, reading the challenge, subscribed for Cupid and challenged him at the burbolt' (I, i, 37-40). But later, when laughingly accused of having lost the heart of Benedick with her scolding mockery, her answer is quite unambiguous. 'Indeed, my lord, he lent it me awhile, and I gave him use for it, a double heart for his single one. Marry, once before he won it of me with false dice; therefore your Grace my well say I have lost it' (II, i, 275-9). She once thought he loved her, and returned his love with interest ('use'): but he was playing – and playing with false dice. Having been once bitten, perhaps it is not surprising – attack being the best form of defence – that she is so self-protectively aggressive towards him. For his part, there seems to be some fear of women underlying his virile scorn for 'love'. 'Prove that ever I lose more blood with love than I will get again with drinking, pick out mine eyes with a ballad maker's pen and hang me up at the door of a brothel house for the sign of blind Cupid' (I, i, 241-5). Without wishing to get psychoanalytical, this does sound like castration anxiety. There is no significant metamorphosis in this comedy, but there is a joke about it. When Benedick is wondering whether he will ever be so foolish as to fall in love like Claudio, he muses: 'May I be so converted and see with these eyes? I cannot tell; I think not. I will not be sworn but love may transform me to an oyster' (II, iii, 22-4). In the event, this is just what happens. After he has succumbed to love and rejoins his friends, Benedick glumly announces 'Gallants, I am not as I have been' (III, ii, 15). His friends proceed to tease and rag him, and like any good oyster, he most uncharacteristically says not a word. He has, as we say, clammed up. Even at the end, his capitulation bears all the marks of apprehensive reluctance – 'I cannot woo in festival terms ... I love thee against my will ... Thou and I are too wise to woo peaceably' (V, ii, 41, 67, 72). And the 'merry war' is hardly over by the end, which smacks more of truce than victory. Their last words to each other are:

Benedick. Come, I will have thee; but, by this light, I take thee for pity.
Beatrice. I would not deny you; but, by this good day, I yield upon great persuasion, and partly to save your life, for I was told you were in a consumption.

Benedick. Peace! I will stop your mouth. [*Kisses her*.]

(V, iv, 92–7)

Long before this, we can see that they were made for each other.

Benedick's penultimate words are 'Prince, thou art sad; get thee a wife, get thee a wife! There is no staff more reverend than one tipped with horn' (V, iv, 122–4). It is fitting that almost his last word should be 'horn'. The play is full of jokes about cuckoldry, which are also jokes about sexual appetite, since the 'horn' symbolized both; so that, for a man to be 'horn-mad' means he could be wild with jealousy, or sexually insatiable – or both. There is, throughout, a great deal of bawdy word-play, by the women as well as the men. This takes place exclusively at court, and is perhaps a function of idleness and luxury. The unluxuried, uneducated figures certainly have cleaner, if less nimble, tongues; perhaps they do not have much time to think about such things. (Incidentally, George Bernard Shaw was very huffy about Benedick, asserting that he 'is not a wit but a blackguard', thus showing that, like many promiscuous men, Shaw was also a prig.)

Beatrice sees the relations between the sexes in terms of dance. She says to her cousin: 'hear me, Hero: wooing, wedding, and repenting is as a Scotch jig, a measure, and a cinquepace. The first suit is hot and hasty like a Scotch jig (and full as fantastical); the wedding, mannerly modest, as a measure, full of state and ancientry; and then comes Repentance and with his bad legs falls into the cinquepace faster and faster, till he sink into his grave' (II, i, 71–9). The play indeed has wooing, wedding, and repentance – danced at different paces and with different steps. Immediately after this speech, the 'revelers' enter, masked, and there is an actual dance. In a way, it is a version of the play in little. Couples pair off, and engage in deceitful words behind false faces. It occasions the one explicit Ovidian reference in an exchange between Don Pedro and Hero:

Don Pedro. My visor is Philemon's roof; within the house is Jove.
Hero. Why then, your visor should be thatched.

(II, i, 95–7)

lxi

The humble peasants Baucis and Philemon hospitably entertained the disguised Jove in their simple thatched cottage – the moral playfully drawn here is that you can never be sure what may be inside a misleadingly simple container. 'Seeming' and 'being' will, not for the first time in Shakespeare, turn out to be a serious theme of the play. Another couple have a related exchange. Ursula identifies her masked partner, correctly, as Antonio.

Antonio. To tell you true, I counterfeit him.
Ursula. ... You are he, you are he!
Antonio. At a word I am not.
Ursula. Come, come, do you think I do not know you by your
    excellent wit? Can virtue hide itself? Go to, mum, you are he.
    Graces will appear, and there's an end.

(II, i, 115–23)

Serious matters, lightly touched upon. Can a person 'counterfeit' himself, herself? Does virtue sometimes hide itself; may graces be sometimes *un*apparent? Matters to be more seriously explored. This leads easily to a third exchange, between the masked Beatrice and Benedick. Beatrice quotes something said by 'Signior Benedick':

    Benedick. What's he?
    Beatrice. I am sure you know him well enough.
    Benedick. Not I, believe me.

(II, i, 131–3)

Do they know each other behind their masks? Indeed, do they know each other, or even themselves, *without* their masks? *Are* they ever, truly and fully, *un*masked? Benedick may very well be speaking simple truth when he protests that he does not know him(self) 'well enough'. Is the truth in the mask, or behind it? Describing this encounter, Benedick says: 'she misused me past the endurance of a block! ... my very visor [mask] began to assume life and scold with her' (II, i, 237–40). Is the *real* life in the 'assumed' life of the mask? Perhaps. Perhaps not. This masked ball is only a game of seeming and deceit; but deceiving words, false names, and misleading dress will produce the play-acted defamation of Hero – with the most unseeming, unseemly, results. But, in general, life in this

Messina is much like a varying dance in which you can never be *absolutely* sure when or whether the masks are finally off. It is not unusual for a comedy to end with weddings and then a dance. But, here again, they do things in Messina a bit differently. 'Let's have a dance *ere* we are married, that we may lighten our own hearts and our wives' heels' (V, iv, 117–19 – my italics). It is the concluding desire of the play, and Benedick gets his way. Meanwhile, above Messina, the dancing stars look down.

You may be sure that a dancing society takes care about how it is dressed, so it is hardly surprising that the word 'fashion' occurs far more often in this play than elsewhere (fifteen times). It comes from *facere*, and it has the straight-forward, honest meaning of 'to make, to shape', as in what a craftsman does. But it soon acquired a potentially somewhat more sinister usage to indicate a more manipulative activity – to *re*-shape or *mis*-shape. As when Brutus says of a possible recruit to his conspiracy – 'Send him but hither, and I'll fashion him' (*Julius Caesar* II, i, 220). The Friar in this play uses it in this sense, but positively – 'doubt not but success/Will fashion the event in better shape' (IV, i, 233–4). And planning the – benign – deception of Benedick and Beatrice to bring them 'into a mountain of affection th' one with th' other', Don Pedro says 'I would fain have it a match, and I doubt not but to fashion it' (II, i, 362–3). The malign plotter, Borachio, promises – 'I will so fashion the matter that Hero shall be absent' (II, ii, 48–9). Given the right, and the wrong, motive, anyone can 'fashion' any appearance they choose. Craftsman-ship gone wild.

As a noun, 'fashion' soon came to refer to custom or mode, including in matters of manners and clothing, which is, I suppose, its dominant meaning today. 'He wears his faith but as the fashion of his hat; it ever changes with the next block [mould for the latest shape of hat]' (I, i, 71–3) – is one of Beatrice's earliest tart, pejorative comments on Benedick. Beatrice herself perhaps goes to the other extreme:

> No, not to be so odd, and from all fashions,
> As Beatrice is, cannot be commendable.

(III, i, 72–3)

That is Hero's opinion, who, we infer, does not deviate from fashion one inch either way. A good girl. But even when Benedick sees Beatrice as goddess of discord, Ate, he adds – 'in good apparel' (II, i, 253). They must all have been beautifully dressed. But the most interesting use of the word comes when Borachio is recounting to Conrade the villainy he has just perpetrated on Don John's behalf. Instead of simply describing what he did (pretend to enter Hero's bedroom with the somewhat unwitting aid of Margaret), Borachio – to Conrade's understandable bemusement – embarks on a disquisition on fashion. The exchange is seldom commented on, but I think it is a key to an appreciation of the play.

Borachio. Thou knowest that the fashion of a doublet, or a hat, or a cloak, is nothing to a man.
Conrade. Yes, it is apparel.
Borachio. I mean the fashion.
Conrade. Yes, the fashion is the fashion.
Borachio. Tush! I may as well say the fool's the fool. But seest thou not what a deformed thief this fashion is?

(At this point, the listening Watch pick up on what they take to be a thief named 'Deformed'. Mr Deformed takes on a life of his own, and by the end has acquired a lock *and key* in his ear. But the admirable Watch are not all wrong; there are quite a lot of 'Deformed's about.)

Borachio. Seest thou not, I say, what a deformed thief this fashion is? How giddily 'a turns about all the hotbloods between fourteen and five-and-thirty? ...
Conrade. All this I see; and I see that the fashion wears out more apparel than the man. But art not thou thyself giddy with the fashion too, that thou hast shifted out of thy tale into telling me of the fashion?
Borachio. Not so neither. But know that I have tonight wooed Margaret, the Lady Hero's gentlewoman, by the name of Hero.

(III, iii, 117-47)

At the end of the play, Benedick sums up – 'for man is a giddy thing, and this is my conclusion' (V, iv, 107-8). If you dance too fast, or for too long, you are likely to become 'giddy' (coming from a word meaning 'possessed by a god'!); something of this seems to be happening in Messina. The point forcefully made here is that this is a society governed, for good and bad, by fashion. This is underlined by the very next scene, in which Hero and Margaret discuss dresses, ruffs, sleeves, skirts, pearls, silver lace, cloth of gold, and so on, in connection with Hero's wedding dress – 'your gown's a most rare fashion, i' faith' (III, iv, 14–15). A concern for fashion is good in that it makes people care about beautiful appearances and elegant manners – 'style', in short. But it can be bad or dangerous in that the 'apparel' may be more regarded than what may, or may not, lie beneath it; as the rogue himself says, with the usual insight of the wicked, fashion, apparel – doublets, hats, cloaks – 'is nothing to a man' i.e. reveals nothing of the real person. Messina tends to live by fashion (perhaps this gives the slightly hard and glittering feel which Rossiter sensed), and this makes it vulnerable to 'fashioned' appearances – both benign and malign. 'De-formation' either way. (This is why Borachio precedes his description of deception with a discussion of fashion – he knows very well that they are intimately related; if not, indeed, at bottom, the same phenomenon.) Which brings us to 'misprision' and 'hearsay'.

To begin to understand why this play proceeds so purringly, one must appreciate how elegantly Shakespeare has plotted the plottings 'authored' by his characters. Both the malign plot to deceive Claudio into poisonous jealousy, and the benign plot to trick Benedick and Beatrice into 'a mountain of affection th' one with th' other' (II, i, 362), depend upon staged hoaxes, and eavesdropping by the deluded, concealed victims. Taken in by, and relying upon, varied forms of 'hearsay', they fall into the 'trap' of 'misprision' (literally, mistaking), and 'misprizing' (estimating value wrongly); leading to misunderstandings, misinterpretations, misapprehensions – things going amiss. It is a world in which appearances cannot be trusted – men are not what they seem; words are not what they say. When the Watch ask Dogberry what they should do to recalcitrant drunks, he says 'you may say they are not the men you took them for' (III, iii, 49). In Messina, you may say that again. The two 'plotters' follow hard on each other's heels. Don Pedro exits, promising to 'practice on Benedick', and claiming 'we are the only love-gods' (II, i, 382), to be replaced by Borachio, explaining to Don John how he will 'practice' on Claudio. He will, says Borachio, 'hear me call Margaret Hero, hear Margaret term me Claudio' ('hearsay' indeed), and:

I will so fashion the matter that Hero shall be absent; and there shall appear such seeming truth of Hero's disloyalty that jealousy shall be called assurance and all the preparation overthrown.

(II, ii, 48-52)

Here we have, in embryonic form, what will be the whole plot of *Othello*; and, to the extent that Don Pedro plays a 'love-god', we may say that Borachio takes the role of an Iago–devil, manipulating appearances for diabolical ends. And problems concerning '*seeming* truth' pervade Shakespeare from first to last.

But if, in some ways, the plots run in parallel, in other ways they are antithetical, as Bullough pointed out. Hero and Claudio, following romantic conventions almost mindlessly, are effortlessly brought together with the help of experienced mediators. They are then jarringly separated by 'hearsay' and false report. It is exactly the other way round with Beatrice and Benedick. Resisting all conventions of courtship, they seem entirely at their ease in unwedded singleness. It would seem an almost impossible task to bring them into union – though, here again, deft mediators and a judicious use of 'hearsay' and false report accomplish what Don Pedro specifically likens to 'one of Hercules' labors' (II, i, 360 – shades of the Ur-Tamer, Petruchio!). The two plots become inter-involved, thus providing dramatic momentum (coming to a peak, perhaps, with Beatrice's arresting, and testing, order to her new-found lover – 'kill Claudio', IV, i, 287). One can profitably take the point made by Carol Neely:

Together the two plots maintain an equilibrium between male control and female initiative, between male reform and female submission, which is characteristic of the romantic comedies. In this play, wit clarifies the vulnerability of romantic idealization while romance alters the static, self-defensive gestures of wit.

lxvi

The very different wooings, and eventual matings, of these two interlocking couples, enable Shakespeare to probe and explore myriad aspects of possible relations between the sexes – in the real world – more brilliantly and searchingly than in any previous play.

The play effectively starts with a 'hearing', Claudio announcing his love for Hero ('If my passion change not shortly,' he adds, ominously as it turns out) – followed by an '*over*hearing'. 'The Prince and Count Claudio, walking in a thick-pleached alley in mine orchard, were thus much overheard by a man of mine' (I, ii, 7–10). The 'man' gets it wrong, of course, as will all the other differing overhearers to follow (with widely varying results) – overhearing is invariably *mis*hearing. The man thinks that the Prince is avowing his love for Hero, whereas, in fact, he is promising to woo her on Claudio's behalf. The error is quick to circulate, as errors are; and, during the masked dance, Don John, pretending that he thinks he is talking to Benedick, is happy to stab Claudio with the information that Don Pedro is 'enamored on Hero'. The main point here is that Claudio *instantly* takes this as ascertained truth. ''Tis certain so. The Prince woos for himself' (II, i, 172). People are not to be trusted. 'Let every eye negotiate for itself/And trust no agent' (II, i, 176–7). This is just a preliminary version of the main plot. Don John promises to demonstrate Hero's infidelity on the eve of the wedding. Don't trust me, intimates Don John, trust what you will see. 'If you dare not trust that you see, confess not that you know. If you will follow me, I will show you enough' (III, ii, 115–17). If you will 'follow' him (and his slanders and faked 'evidence'), he certainly will show you enough. It doesn't take much – just a few clothes, and a misleading dialogue. Iago, who also leads while pretending only to 'show', can do it with a single handkerchief. What Claudio is too culpably gullible to realize is that, while he thinks his eye is 'negotiating' for itself, he is in fact 'trusting' another 'agent' – but this time, not one who helps to make his marriage, but one who seeks to work his ruin. We, the audience, do not see the 'scene' put on for Claudio's benefit – a shrewd decision on Shakespeare's part since it keeps us, too, in a world of 'hearsay' and report – but we gather that Claudio was, again, instantly convinced of Hero's infamy by what he saw and heard. And even Don Pedro, who accompanied him, was taken in – later insisting that Hero was 'charged with nothing/But what was true, and very full of proof' (V, i, 104–5). This is what Othello will call 'ocular proof' and to 'trust' and 'follow' it can have disastrous, tragic results. This is part of Shakespeare's growing concern about what sort of evidence can be relied on; indeed, what 'evidence' really was. In the realm of human feeling and action, can you ever, finally, *prove* anything?

The benign deception of Benedick and Beatrice is a different sort of affair, although we notice that the credulousness of the 'overhearers' is once more immediate. Plato recognizes different forms of deceit – the manifestly wicked kind; the legitimate deceits of warfare (ambushes); and the good, or useful, or 'medicinal' lie, which you might tell a friend for his own good (when he is about to do himself some harm). We should place 'the false sweet bait' and 'honest slanders' (III, i, 33, 84) with which Benedick and Beatrice are baited, hooked and landed (hunting and angling images dominate these scenes), in this last category of Plato's. If there can be such a thing as 'the lie beneficent' (and Plato's authority is hardly negligible), then this is what the 'plotters' use on Benedick and Beatrice. And, of course, there is another possible twist. Without knowing or intending it, they may *actually* be telling the (hidden) truth about Beatrice's and Benedick's feeling – in which case, their inventions serve the honourable role of revelations.

The apparent paradox of 'honest slanders' may serve as a reminder that the word 'slander' (and 'slanderous', 'slandered') occurs far more often in this play than elsewhere. And while we may say that Beatrice and Benedick are 'slandered' into love, Hero is, officially at least, 'slandered to death by villains', 'Done to death by slanderous tongues' (V, i, 88; V, iii, 3). Shakespeare had an acute sense of (and revulsion for) the gratuitous, irreparable damage than can be done by malicious slander (what Spenser, with a comparable loathing, allegorized as the Blatant Beast). There is an enormous delight in word-play throughout, but there is a concurrent suspicion of the wayward power of tongues, and of the man who is, as it were, all tongue. 'But manhood is melted into cursies, valor into compliment, and men are only turned into tongue, and trim ones too' (IV, i, 317-19). The tongue set free may 'transshape' virtues into vices, evil into good, and anything into anything. The word 'transshape' only appears in this play (V, i, 169), like 'hearsay', and it is clearly all part of Shakespeare's particular interest here in 'misprision' (that Shakespeare himself 'transshapes' life into art, is only another aspect of this endlessly complex matter). When Constable Dogberry brings Conrade and Borachio before the Prince, for once, in his muddled way, he puts his wobbling lexical finger on the central matter – his rambling redundancies are spot on.

Marry, sir, they have committed false report; moreover, they have spoken untruths; secondarily, they are slanders; sixth and lastly, they have belied a lady; thirdly, they have verified unjust things; and to conclude, they are lying knaves.

(V, i, 214-18)

I don't see how Solomon himself could have said it much better than that! And it is because so many people in this Messina are given to 'committing false report' (of very varying degrees of seriousness), that when Beatrice comes forward, after 'overhearing' accounts of Benedick's love for her, and says – to herself and us – 'and I believe it *better than reportingly*' (III, i, 115-16 – my italics), we thrill to feel that she has stepped beyond the tangled world of hearsay and misprision, into the more serious, more risky world of 'trust' (it doesn't matter if we think she is – the more, or less – deceived). Shakespeare uses the word 'report' hundreds of times, but the curious adverb 'reportingly' just this once. It is, perhaps, that people in this Messina tend to live *too* reportingly (which is why 'slander' thrives), and Shakespeare is intimating that there must be a better way than that.

The drama of *The Merchant of Venice* gathers to a head and finally breaks in Act IV in the courtroom. Something very similar happens in the fourth Act of *Much Ado* though this time the scene is a chapel. In both cases, a key civic ritual is interrupted, disrupted, turned askew – first a trial; now a wedding. And in both scenes, there is an identical moment

lxix

which turns out to be the turning point of the play. I will come to this. The outburst which profanes and violates the holy orderliness of the chapel ceremony is precipitated by 'mis-*prision*' leading to 'mis*prizing*' – the two errors being often, of course, closely inter-involved. That second word is, in fact, only used of Beatrice in this play:

> Disdain and Scorn ride sparkling in her eyes,
> Misprizing what they look on.
>
> (III, i, 51–2)

But Beatrice's disvaluing, or devaluing, remarks are a form of non-lethal mockery; at bottom, a sometimes astringent merriment. A 'sparkling'. But there is nothing merry or sparkling about Claudio's public 'misprizing' of Hero in church. He has already promised to 'shame her ... in the congregation' if Don John 'proves' her infidelity, which leads to these comments:

> *Don Pedro.* O day untowardly turned!
> *Claudio.* O mischief strangely thwarting!
>
> (III, ii, 127–8)

Don John is the embodiment of the will to 'thwart'. It is one of his favoured words, and, seemingly, 'thwarting' is the only activity which gives him a perverse sort of pleasure. (As a word, it draws together crooked, crossed, transverse; to twist, oppose, frustrate – the quintessential drive to block and spoil.) Don John thus 'turns' the play away from its planned felicitous route to marriage and happiness – he derails the comedy. It will take another 'turn' to regain that route, set things to rights, and repair the damage.

And shame Hero 'in the congregation', Claudio duly does – with words of extraordinary virulence and loathing:

> There, Leonato, take her back again.
> Give not this rotten orange to your friend.
> She's but the sign and semblance of her honor.
> . . .
>
> Would you not swear,
> All you that see her, that she were a maid,
> By these exterior shows? But she is none.

> She knows the heat of a luxurious bed;
> Her blush is guiltiness, not modesty.
>
> (IV, i, 30-32, 37-41)

And to Hero directly:

> Out on thee, seeming! I will write against it.
> . . .
> But you are more intemperate in your blood
> Than Venus, or those pamp'red animals
> That rage in savage sensuality.
>
> (IV, i, 55, 58-60)

'Seeming' is, indeed, one of Shakespeare's great themes, and *he* wrote against or about it continually. The irony here, of course, is precisely that Claudio has been taken in by signs, semblances, and seeming. But, hearing Claudio's amazingly immoderate, intemperate language, one feels that something else is going on as well. Benedick's comment, 'This looks not like a nuptial' (IV, i, 67), must rank as the understatement of the play.

But what *does* it look like? Let's start with that orange, since, oddly, it is the only orange in Shakespeare (there is an 'orange-tawny beard' in *A Midsummer Night's Dream*, and an 'orange-wife' in *Coriolanus*). To refer to a woman as a 'rotten orange' is to allude disgustedly to her private parts, suggesting not only promiscuity but venereal disease (the relatively recent rampant spread of syphilis was a major worry in Shakespeare's London). Shakespeare has prepared for this startlingly unpleasant image, by having Beatrice, earlier, describe Claudio as 'civil as an orange, and something of that jealous complexion' (II, i, 291-2). The pun is on civil/Seville (Seville oranges, as far as I can find out, were the only oranges known in Shakespeare's London - presumably for jam-making). Hero, it need hardly be said, is nothing of a 'rotten orange' - no woman less so. The oranges are in Claudio's head - the very colour and contents of his sexually unbalanced (immature? prurient? lubricious? frightened?), distinctly male, imagination. I make that stress because, in his nauseated, nauseous outburst against female sexuality, Claudio is only the first of a number of men in Shakespeare who indulge in similar inflamed and disgusted tirades - they include Angelo, Troilus, Hamlet, Othello,

Posthumus, Leontes. Whether these speeches reveal something about Shakespeare's own ambivalent feelings and fears concerning female sexuality may be left to the individual to decide, since it is a manifestly imponderable question. I would only point out that, in every case, the fears and suspicions are groundless, the accusations utterly wild, the revulsion totally unjustified by anything that is discoverably the case – *all* misprision and misprizing. (I have left out Lear's famous denunciation since, considering the antics of Goneril and Regan, it might be felt that he has a point.) For what it is worth, I think Shakespeare is saying, showing, something about the nature of male sexual imaginings.

None of this is of any help to Hero who, confronted with such incomprehensible and insane accusations, can only respond by swooning. Her shame, defamation, and rejection reach apparent completeness when her own father cries out – 'Let her die' (IV, i, 153). At which point, the Friar steps forward – 'Hear me a little'. He then advances the defining wisdom of the play: 'There is some strange misprision in the princes' (IV, i, 184), a consideration which seems to occur to no one else except Beatrice (followed, quickly enough, by Benedick). When all seems lost, irremediable, unredeemable, the Friar stops all the hopelessness with – 'Pause awhile' (IV, i, 199). This echoes Portia's 'Tarry a little', and has exactly the same effect and function. Here the play begins to 'turn' again; turn back, this time, to the right track, though it will involve quite a detour. I have written elsewhere of the importance of the 'pause' (during which things may be 'scanned'), and 'the pauser, reason', in the tragedies. 'Tarry a little' and 'Pause awhile' are adumbrations of this crucial moment (Hamlet tarries and pauses, arguably for too long; Macbeth doesn't want to tarry and pause at all). The 'pause' is what arrests an apparently headlong and unstoppable rush of the dramatic action to disaster. The interposed gap of reflection opens up the possibility of another way. In the two comedies under discussion, it allows the action to be pulled back from veering off into tragedy. And here, the Friar is crucial.

This Friar has a more important, more creative, role than the well-wishing, would-be helper of Romeo and Juliet. The latter suggested the 'feigned death' of Juliet stratagem as simply a trick, a tactic, for gaining time. This Friar sees the same device as having far greater potential:

> And publish it that she is dead indeed;
> . . .
> Marry, this well carried shall on her behalf
> Change slander to remorse; that is some good.
> But not for that dream I on this strange course,
> But on this travail look for greater birth.
>
> (IV, i, 203, 209–12)

Greater birth – he has in mind a process involving remorse, repentance, and regeneration. This theme of (apparent) death, followed by (greater) rebirth, will be most fully worked out in the last plays. Success, says the Friar, 'Will fashion the event in better shape' (IV, i, 234) – this is the most positive use of 'fashion' in the play, suggesting an almost god-like activity or magic. Thus, his last advice to Hero sounds the note – a note of 'strangeness' – which will dominate the rest of the play; and which will be heard again hereafter.

> For to strange sores strangely they strain the cure.
> Come, lady, die to live. This wedding day
> Perhaps is but prolonged. Have patience and endure.
>
> (IV, i, 251–3)

With the indispensable help of the Watch – 'What your wisdoms could not discover, these shallow fools have brought to light', as Borachio says (V, i, 231–3), a very Shakespearian note – the plot to defame Hero is revealed, and it remains for Claudio to perform rites of mourning and repentance. Hence the scene at Hero's monument, before the final reconciliation scene when Claudio agrees to marry, as he thinks, 'another Hero'; who, of course, turns out to be the same Hero, to the bewilderment of the onlookers. 'She died, my lord, but whiles her slander lived' (V, iv, 66), explains her father. And the Friar, who has become, in effect, the director of the play, issues a last promise and instruction:

> All this amazement can I qualify,
> When, after that the holy rites are ended,

I'll tell you largely of fair Hero's death.
Meantime let wonder seem familiar,
And to the chapel let us presently.

(V, iv, 67–71)

One can see the intention. This is a very important development in Shakespeare's comedies and the slightly mysterious, benignly inventive and ministering Friar is something of an embryonic Prospero. But, arguably, the figures of Claudio and Hero (and Don John) are insufficiently developed for this part of the play to generate the sort of 'wonder' which will so richly and rarely suffuse the last plays. For a lot of people, the play *is*, primarily, *Beatrice and Benedick*.

I have noted that Shakespeare sometimes marks the distinctive light in which his comedies conclude – the 'glooming' morning at the end of *Romeo and Juliet*; followed by the wonderful 'glimmering' which illuminates the finale of *A Midsummer Night's Dream*; then, the more equivocal 'daylight sick' in which *The Merchant of Venice* is concluded. Here the light, as you might expect, is, finally, good enough.

Good morrow, masters; put your torches out.
The wolves have preyed, and look, the gentle day,
Before the wheels of Phoebus, round about
Dapples the drowsy east with spots of gray.
Thanks to you all, and leave us. Fare you well.

(V, iii, 24–8)

The wolves *have* preyed; but in Messina, clearly, the sun also rises.

*

AS YOU LIKE IT (1599)

happy is your Grace
That can translate the stubbornness of fortune
Into so quiet and so sweet a style.

(II, i, 18–20)

Your If is the only peacemaker. Much virtue in If.

(V, iv, 102–3)

My way is to conjure you.

(Epilogue, 10–11)

INTRODUCTION

This is, unambiguously, the happiest of Shakespeare's comedies. Happiest, in this sense – there is certainly evil (or a kind of folk-tale figuring of evil) in the first Act: a cruel elder brother dispossessing a younger brother; a tyrannical younger brother usurping the rightful dukedom of an elder brother; the unjust banishment of the manifestly good characters. But by the end, not a trace of that initial, initiating evil remains. And there are no ritual expulsions, exclusions, expurgations; no defeats, no punishments, no disappointments even; no one is hunted down, hunted out. The evil characters are simply, perhaps miraculously, 'converted' (key word). Old Adam, who foresees a time

> When service should in my old limbs lie lame
> And unregarded age in corners thrown.
>
> (II, iii, 41-2)

– graphic lines, which perfectly describe the old servant, Freers, at the end of *The Cherry Orchard*, when he is left, lying down, abandoned and forgotten in the empty house – is spared that indignity, and simply fades out of the play when he has served his loyal turn. (In Shakespeare's source, Adam is made 'Captain of the Kings Gard ... that Fortune might everie way seeme frolicke', and I will return to Fortune's frolics.) Importantly, Adam is not there at the close to remind us of the distinctly uncomic seventh age of man, which, in Jaques' mordant words, is:

> second childishness and mere oblivion,
> Sans teeth, sans eyes, sans taste, sans everything.
>
> (II, vii, 165-6)

The play ends with a completely clean sheet, as it were. To be sure, the sour and melancholy Jaques refuses to join in the final harmonizing dance of multiple weddings (four – more than in any other Shakespearian comedy), and blissful reconciliations and restorations. But, as he leaves, he is no scapegoat, no spoil-sport kill-joy to be chased from the feast. Nobody wants him to go. 'Stay, Jaques, stay,' implores the Duke. You do not hear people saying 'Stay, Shylock, stay', or 'Stay, Malvolio, stay'. By voluntarily absenting himself from the concluding celebrations, he, wittingly or not, indicates or demonstrates that there are people, things, which remain inconvertible, unaccommodatable, inassimilable to the great comic resolutions on offer. He, and he alone, cannot, or will not, be 'converted'. 'Will you, won't you, will you, won't you, won't you join the dance?' says the whiting to the snail, in the Mock Turtle's song (*Alice in Wonderland*). Well, Jaques *won't*. 'I am for other than for dancing measures,' he says in a tone of disdainful refusal, as the concluding celebrations commence (V, iv, 193). Jaques is He Who Will Not Be Included. He consciously and deliberately withdraws from what Rosalind nicely calls 'the full stream of the world' (III, ii, 410). The stream which the others, we may take it, will happily rejoin. But I will come back to Jaques.

After the opening outburst of evil in Act I, during which the holy bonds of family are brutally broken as brother turns unnaturally on brother, and the good are banished from manor and court, effectively all the rest of the play takes place in the Forest of Arden, where the banished take refuge. The woods of the Ardennes, somewhere between Bordeaux and Lyons, were well established as a pastoral region; and the Forest of Arden (not, of course, on any map) was the setting for the pastoral romance on which Shakespeare based his play (Thomas Lodge's *Rosalynde* – of which more later). 'Pastoral' literally means pertaining to shepherds (from *pascere* – to graze), and pastoral poetry habitually describes the loves and sorrows of (very poetical and musical) shepherds and shepherdesses, living a rustic, idle and innocent life in some imagined Golden Age or ideali zed Arcadia (the founding, generative texts are the Idylls of Theocritus and the Eclogues of Virgil). It is, of course, a distinctly urban (or courtly) and sophisticated genre, convention-driven and highly artificial – and most successful when it never pretends to be anything else. Pastoral romances tend to show heroes and heroines from the outside ('real') world (often the court), becoming, out of whatever exigency, temporary sojourners of this Arcadian 'world elsewhere', and then returning to their own world, usually in better shape. At the time Shakespeare wrote this play, there was something of a vogue for pastoral and woodland (Robin Hood) plays, and Shakespeare's contribution is an unparalleled exploration of the genre of pastoral. He leads his characters into the curiously suspended, time-out-of-time, pastoral moment or interlude, and then sets about exposing, testing, mocking, celebrating, elaborating pastoral's conventions, assumptions, and pretensions – in the process, not only laying bare its manifest limitations, but also revealing new possibilities in its artifice – its obvious artificiality.

Shakespeare gives the clearest possible indication of the world we are heading for in the first scene when Charles the wrestler gives Oliver news of the whereabouts of the banished Duke Senior.

They say he is already in the Forest of Arden, and a many merry men with him; and there they live like the old Robin Hood of England. They say many young gentlemen flock to him every day, and fleet the time carelessly as they did in the golden world.

(I, i, 111–15)

That 'golden world' is the Golden Age, the first age of man, in the first book of Ovid's *Metamorphoses*.

> The world untroubled lived in leisured ease.
> Earth willingly, untouched, unwounded yet
> By hoe or plough, gave all her bounteous store;
> Men were content with nature's food unforced,
> And gathered strawberries on the mountainside
> And cherries and the clutching bramble's fruit,
> And acorns fallen from Jove's spreading tree.
> Springtime it was, always, for ever spring ...

(I, 101–8)

A vegetarian diet; and permanent spring. But in the Forest of Arden, the Duke and his men are terrific eaters of meat and keen killers of deer; and the winters, by all accounts, are dreadful. (According to the classical myth, retold by Ovid, seasonal variations entered the world after the fall of Saturn, and the declension of mankind into the Silver Age. There *is* a slight feeling of permanent springtime in Shakespeare's Arden, but Duke Senior and his merry men inhabit the fallen world and experience 'The seasons' difference', as the icy fang/And churlish chiding of the winter's wind', II, i, 6–7.) There is also, in Shakespeare's play, a fallen acorn, but it turns out to be the hero, Orlando.

Celia. I found him under a tree, like a dropped acorn.
Rosalind. It may well be called Jove's tree when it drops forth fruit.

(III, ii, 233-5)

Shakespeare is having his fun. But somewhat more serious matters are being engaged as well. Shakespeare is not simply offering some wry, undermining comments on the myth of a Golden Age which never was, and never could have been. It is that in part of course, but his aim is not simply demolition. He knew, if only from his own early life, what country life was actually like, and he here allows some rural realities to enter and impinge on – if you like, contest, and even contaminate (but *not* destroy) – the unactual, pastoral Arden. In addition to bad weather and bloody hunting, there are some distinctly unpastoral, even unpleasant, characters in this Arden. Corin reminds us of the realities of the helpless bondage of villeinage:

> But I am shepherd to another man
> And do not shear the fleeces that I graze.
> My master is of churlish disposition
> And little recks to find the way to heaven
> By doing deeds of hospitality.
> Besides, his cote, his flocks, and bounds of feed
> Are now on sale, and at our sheepcote now,
> By reason of his absence, there is nothing
> That you will feed on ...

(II, iv, 78-86)

There *is* 'hospitality' in this forest (it is the crucial, originary, cultural value); but, fleetingly, there is the chill shadow of its absence as well. Audrey, William, even Sir Oliver Mar-text (all Shakespeare's additions to his source), come from a different world from that of Silvius and Phebe, with whom they nevertheless rub shoulders, as it were. Or, rather, they seem to come from the 'real' world (say, round Stratford), while the others emerge, fully-formed, from pastoral convention – and very unreal, and sometimes silly, they seem. I might add that, in addition to the direct references to the Golden Age, there are also glancing allusions to the Garden of Eden, and the 'fall' that ended *that* idyll. The first character to be addressed in the play is 'Adam', while Duke Senior refers to 'the penalty of Adam' (II, i, 5) – seasonal variation followed that 'fall' as well. Shakespeare also introduces a snake into his Arden/Eden which was not there in his source. And there is some interesting play to do with the matter of 'ribs', as there is in Genesis, to which I will return. Not for the first time, Shakespeare is conflating pagan (or classical) and Hebraic–Christian myths, and bringing his own questioning eye to bear on them.

Certainly, the play starts with expulsion – not from, but *to* a radically reconstituted and re-imagined Eden/Arden. The expellers – the cruel Oliver who plans to burn his younger brother, Orlando, in his lodging, and the tyrant Frederick who, having usurped his elder brother's kingdom, now suddenly banishes that brother's daughter, Rosalind – seem more like figures from Ovid's fourth, last age of man – the Age of Iron, a time of terminal degeneration.

> In that hard age
> Of baser vein all evil straight broke out,
> And honour fled and truth and loyalty,
> Replaced by fraud, deceit and treachery
> And violence and wicked greed for gain.
> . . .
> Friend was not safe from friend, nor father safe
> From son-in-law, *and kindness rare between*
> *Brother and brother* . . .
>
> (I, 128–32, 48–50 – my italics)

That's the Age they come from; that's where they belong. There is also a distinct hint at the sort of unmotivated malignity we have seen occupying Shakespeare's interest a number of times already: 'I hope I shall see an end of him; for my soul, yet I know not why, hates nothing more than he,' Oliver confesses right at the start (I, i, 157–9). The sudden eruptiveness of evil is manifested in Frederick – 'his malice 'gainst the lady/Will suddenly break forth' (I, ii, 272–3) warns Le Beau, and it promptly does in the next scene. Villains, right enough. Yet they bear some of the lineaments of the menacing figures in folk tale (from which, indeed, the story ultimately derives), or the threatening ogre/giant types in fairy tales. They are even imaginable in pantomime. The evils which are sketched out or, as it were, succinctly anthologized in them, seem real enough. But they, somehow, are not, quite. After the initial flurry of compacted nastiness, we *know* things are going to be all right. As Celia and Rosalind set out for the forest at the end of Act I, Celia says:

> Now go in we content
> To liberty, and not to banishment.
>
> (I, iii, 135–6)

By an affirmative inversion, 'banishment' is turned into 'liberty'. It is the first in a series of vital 'conversions' which runs through the play.

Once Shakespeare has got his good characters out of harm's way and safely into the Forest of Arden, what does he do with them to generate a play? It is a pertinent question since the play has almost no plot (in this, and in some of its atmosphere and effects it has some resemblance to *Love's Labor's Lost*) – no plotters, no schemers, no intrigue; nothing and no one to circumvent, outmanoeuvre, or supplant (though, of course, a couple to flee from at the start). There are none of the usual obstacles to provoke a devised and pursued line of action. There is, mainly, just love, and talk of love. Very pastoral. Except, this being Shakespeare, it is pastoral with a difference. In this connection, it is instructive to note where Shakespeare deviates from his source – what he deletes, changes, and adds. In addition to the realistic 'country copulatives' I have mentioned, he adds the sophisticated, melancholic, cynical Jaques who brings a crucial tartness and bitterness to the 'sweet especial scene' of this green and pleasant pastoral interlude. And, perhaps even more importantly, he adds Touchstone, the first of his professional court jesters, or 'allowed fools'. He has, of course, brought on fools, buffoons, and 'clowns' (from an old word for clod) before. But they were, more or less, sublimely unaware of their folly, daftness, or general incompetence. To be sure, there are distinct glimpses of a self-aware shrewdness and ironic questioningness in Launce (*The Two Gentlemen of Verona*) and Launcelot Gobbo (*The Merchant of Venice*), but Touchstone is something else again; a major innovation who inaugurates a line which will run through Feste, Lavatch, Lear's Fool, and Trinculo. Touchstone problematizes every aspect of court and country he meanderingly encounters.

What Shakespeare dropped from Thomas Lodge's *Rosalynde* is also illuminating. He kept the plot line, along with incidents and names, *almost* intact. But he cuts out almost all the violence. In Lodge, the younger brother Rosader suffers from his elder brother Saladyne's malevolent plan – 'though he be a Gentleman by nature, yet forme him anew, and make him a peasant by nourture' – just as Orlando is deliberately brought-*down*, rather than being properly brought-up, by Oliver. 'He lets me feed with his hinds, bars me the place of a brother, and, as much as in him lies, mines my gentility with my education' (I, i, 18-20). Shakespeare is greatly interested in the respective influences of nature and nurture in our lives, and the relation between innate 'gentility' and the refining furtherances of 'education'. Indeed, the opening scene is a debate concerning 'breeding', 'gentility', 'education', 'blood', 'gentlemanlike qualities', 'the courtesy of nations', 'nature', and 'fortune'. But, to stay with the matter of violence. Rosader is driven 'halfe mad' by his treatment, and when he finally rebels he erupts into such murderous anger that he kills many people and devastates and empties his elder brother's house. Orlando, driven beyond endurance by Oliver – 'You have trained me like a peasant, obscuring and hiding from me all gentlemanlike qualities' (I, i, 66-7) – merely 'seizes' Oliver, after Oliver has added insolence to injury by striking him. Orlando is a good wrestler, and he once draws his sword when he is desperate to get food for the starving Adam. But he is distinctly not a violent man.

Now I think Shakespeare is engaging in some sort of a deep joke here which I am not sure I fully understand. Shakespeare keeps a lot of Lodge's names – notably, Adam, Rosalind, Aliena, and Ganymede – but he changes Rosader to Orlando. The most famous Orlando was of course Ariosto's *Orlando Furioso* (1532), which was translated, and indeed performed (in a play by Greene), in 1591. In Ariosto, Orlando is a man of mighty angers, and when he *finds* poems on trees concerning his beloved Angelica and her love for another, he gets very *furioso* indeed, tearing up forests and destroying towns as he raves across the continents. Very different from our English Orlando, who is, if anything, given to great mildness – not to mention the fact that he puts the poems on the trees himself. Perhaps Shakespeare said to himself – let's see what we can do with an Orlando *Un*furioso.

That he effectively wanted to drain all the violence from his source is made very clear by a change to the ending. In Lodge, the wicked, usurping King of France brings an army to the Forest of Arden in an attempt to slaughter his banished brother and his men. Battle is duly joined, and the bad figures are defeated or slain. Shakespeare has it otherwise. The bad Duke Frederick (nothing so specific as 'France' for the strange placeless geography of this play):

> Addressed a mighty power, which were on foot
> In his own conduct, purposely to take
> His brother here and put him to the sword;
> And to the skirts of this wild wood he came,
> Where, meeting with an old religious man,
> After some question with him, was converted
> Both from his enterprise and from the world ...
>
> (V, iv, 156–62)

Similarly, Oliver, Orlando's 'unnatural' elder brother, undergoes a change – metamorphosis again – as his motiveless malignity drops from him once he enters the forest:

> *Celia.* Was't you that did so oft contrive to kill him?
> *Oliver.* 'Twas I. But 'tis not I. I do not shame
>   To tell you what I was, since my conversion
>   So sweetly tastes, being the thing I am.
>
> (IV, iii, 135–8)

'Twas I. But 'tis not I. How many characters in Shakespeare's comedies have occasion to say that, in one form or another! Shakespeare wants his Forest of Arden to be a place of slightly magical 'conversions', as well as unchanging country copulatives. Conversion at all levels. Duke Senior's opening speech in

INTRODUCTION

Arden celebrates life in the woods as being 'more sweet' than the 'painted pomp' of the 'envious court' and 'public haunt'. 'Sweet are the uses of adversity,' he claims, which enables them to:

> Finds tongues in trees, books in the running brooks,
> Sermons in stones, and good in everything.
>
> (II, i, 12, 16–17)

This provokes Amiens to exclaim:

> happy is your Grace
> That can translate the stubbornness of fortune
> Into so quiet and so sweet a style.
>
> (II, i, 18–20)

This is a good description of what Shakespeare himself does – translate the stubbornness of fortune into so sweet a style. We begin to notice the recurrence of the word 'sweet'. Oliver tells of Orlando pacing through the forest 'Chewing the food of sweet and bitter fancy' (IV, iii, 103), and we can appreciate how necessary is the sourness of Jaques, not to mention the saltiness of Touchstone, to prevent this pastoral from becoming *too* 'sweet'. But sweet it is, and is meant to be. Shakespeare does away with the decisive effects of violence to explore and draw attention to the possibilities of 'conversion' and 'translation'. Con-vert – to turn completely: trans-late – to carry across, into another place, another language. Life *is* 'stubborn'; it does not easily or readily turn and carry in the ways we would like it to. The sweet magic of this play is really Shakespeare's demonstration of the converting, translating powers of the imagination. Not as fortune has it, but as *we* like it.

There is one other change to the source – a small addition – which invariably goes unnoticed. There is of course the wrestling tournament in Lodge, at which Rosader/Orlando is successful, and catches Rosalind's eye and heart. Characteristically, the wrestling is a degree more lethal in Lodge, but I am more interested in something which Lodge does not mention and Shakespeare does. In Lodge, details of the wrestling include references to broken necks, limbs, sinews,

and chests – but not ribs. Shakespeare mentions *only* broken
ribs. To explain what I think is going on, I must bring together
a few quotations, noting the words 'sport' and 'fall'. When we
first see Rosalind and Celia they are trying to 'devise sports',
and Rosalind says – 'Let me see, what think you of falling in
love?' (I, ii, 24). When Le Beau brings them news of the
wrestling immediately after this conversation, he starts by
declaring 'Fair princess, you have lost much good sport' (I, ii,
95). He describes how Charles, the Duke's wrestler, has
despatched three brothers, breaking their 'ribs'. Touchstone is
quick off the mark:

But what is the sport, monsieur, that the ladies have lost?
Le Beau. Why, this that I speak of.
Touchstone. Thus men may grow wiser every day. It is the first time
that ever I heard breaking of ribs was sport for ladies.

To which Rosalind adds:

But is there any else longs to see this broken music in his sides? Is there
yet another dotes upon rib-breaking?

(I, ii, 125–34)

Shortly after Orlando has tried 'one fall' with Charles, 'throwing' him, and, in another sense 'throwing' Rosalind as well,
Celia admonishes Rosalind:

Celia. Come, come, wrestle with thy affections.
Rosalind. O, they take the part of a better wrestler than myself!
Celia. O, a good wish upon you! You will try in time, in despite of
a   fall.

(I, iii, 21–5)

('Try' is sometimes amended to 'cry', meaning you will cry
when your time comes, in the throes of labour. But 'try' is in
the Folio and as the Duke has just said to Orlando 'You shall
try but one fall', it makes perfectly good sense as it is – you will
risk a (sexual) bout in due course.) The concluding quotation
I need is, of course, from Genesis:

And the Lord God caused a deep sleep to fall upon Adam, and he
slept: and he took one of his ribs, and closed up the flesh instead
thereof;

INTRODUCTION

And the rib which the Lord God had taken from man, made he a woman, and brought her unto the man.
And Adam said, This is now bone of my bones, and flesh of my flesh: she shall be called Woman, because she was taken out of Man.

$$(2:\ 21-3)$$

Arden is not Eden – what with the inclement weather, the blood sports, and feudal servitude; but the emphasis on ribs, the punning play on 'fall', not to mention Adam, and the added snake, make it clear that Shakespeare intends us to hear refracted echoes of the first book of the Bible. To what end, it may be asked? Eve tempted Adam, and Adam fell – we all fell. To what extent was it a 'fortunate fall'? Redemption is not on Shakespeare's mind here; he is more concerned with love, love between the two sexes so mysteriously engineered in Eden and thus, unavoidably, sexual love. He is taking a laughing look back to that mythical time when the whole man–woman business began. Physical lovemaking can be indistinguishable from wrestling – the combative and the erotic seem to merge into each other, and wrestling with emotions is only one metaphorical step away ('I'll wrestle with you in my strength of love,' says Antony to Caesar, *Antony and Cleopatra* III, ii, 62, while Orlando, for his part, is 'overthrown', not by Charles, but by Rosalind). Sexual congress usually involves a literal fall – down to the horizontal – but it also re-enacts the primal fall when Adam succumbed to the seduction of Eve. Rosalind is not Eve, though she certainly has more knowingness, quicker wits, arguably more guile and certainly more attractiveness, than anyone else in the Forest of Arden. She is Eve-ish at least in her irresistibility; and she has certainly eaten well of the Tree of Knowledge – to beneficent, and what used to be called life-enhancing, effect. So perhaps yes, a *fortunate* fall.

Rosalind certainly wants a literal, legalized, fall with Orlando; but, or perhaps and, with her lightness of touch she does turn love and loving into a kind of 'sport'. We tend to restrict 'sport' to those activities invariably covered in the last section of the newspaper, but the word was much more capacious for Shakespeare and he uses it from first play to last. It can cover any kind of amusement, pastime, frolic, diversion, distraction. Those last two words come from verbs meaning, literally, turn away, and drag away. 'Sport' comes from disport – literally, carry away. Once again, we seem to have a positive turning, carrying activity. In Nathaniel Hawthorne's tale, 'Endicott and the Red Cross', he describes a young woman in Puritan Salem who has been forced to wear the letter A on her gown. 'And even her own children knew what that initial signified. Sporting with her infamy, the lost and desperate creature had embroidered the fatal token in scarlet cloth, with golden thread, and the nicest art of needlework; so that the capital A might have been thought to mean Admirable, or any thing rather than Adultress.' She is clearly a forerunner of Hester Prynne in *The Scarlet Letter* – though in that novel, for his own reasons Hawthorne never uses the word 'adultress', and the A is even more possibly polysemous, suggesting Art, America, Almost Anything you care to read off it. But it is that fine phrase 'sporting with her infamy' that I want. Here is a playing which transforms stigma into adornment, punishment into play, guilt into grace. This is sport as art – something, indeed, to outwit the stubbornness of fortune, and hard, unbending Puritans, alike. Rosalind lives in a happier land and a more hospitable climate – no stigma for her to cope with, no infamy to transform (unless you include the initial banishment, which the two girls instantly change into 'liberty'). But she does turn love into a sport of the highest kind. We start with the rather primitive sport of wrestling (which perhaps also suggests the primitiveness of carnal embraces); but by the end, the sport of love is 'converted' into an art – and Rosalind is the artist. Indeed, such a fine artist that some critics have been prompted to call this play, *her* play, Mozartian.

In their opening scene, Celia deflects Rosalind's suggestion of sporting with love.

Rosalind. What shall be our sport then?
Celia. Let us sit and mock the good housewife Fortune from her wheel, that her gifts may henceforth be bestowed equally.

(I, ii, 29–32)

And they begin to banter about how Fortune's 'benefits' are often 'mightily misplaced'. But when Celia points out that honesty and beauty rarely go together, Rosalind insists on a distinction:

Nay, now thou goest from Fortune's office to Nature's. Fortune reigns in gifts of the world, not in the lineaments of Nature.

(I, ii, 39-41)

Nature is what you are born with; Fortune is what you get thereafter. It is of course an unstable opposition or differentiation, and the matter can be argued in different ways – Orlando is a gentleman by Nature, but he had the good Fortune to be born of a noble father, as well as the bad Fortune to have such a rotten elder brother, while the workings of Nature make Rosalind fall Fortunately in love with him, and so on. It is rather like contemporary debates about Nature/Culture (or Nurture). If you inquire deeply enough, the distinction starts to disappear or become meaningless – particularly down among the genes. Emerson has it sufficiently succinctly – 'Nature, that made the carpenter, made the house.' But we still know what we mean when we say that a man is born a male = nature, while the culture he is born into will decree how he will manifest his masculinity. These distinctions are meaningful, if, finally, provably ungrounded. They are useful in discussions considering *why* we are *what* we are. Similarly, the Elizabethans loved debates concerning the relative powers, and spheres of influence, of Nature and Fortune, more or less apotheosized as the case may be. Celia, in this particular bantering bout, makes the important point that 'Nature hath given us wit to flout at Fortune' (I, ii, 44). 'Mind is life's self-criticism,' said George Bernard Shaw; and the simple, though very important point, is that – like Pascal's thinking reed which can protest even as the boulder crushes it – we *can* 'take issue' with whatever particular sea of troubles rolls our way, and, not indeed 'end them', but 'flout' them. Listen to Rosalind.

References to, and invocations of, Fortune are seeded throughout Lodge's *Rosalynde* – indeed, I gave up counting after the word had already occurred twenty times. Among many rather sobering pronouncements, there is this doleful contention: 'when Fortune hath done her worst, then Love comes in to begin a new tragedie'. From one point of view and in another genre, the mighty misplacements of Fortune's 'benefits' might well be the prelude to tragedy. But – as far as Shakespeare is concerned in this play – not here, not now. There is also this in Lodge, from 'Alinda's [= Shakespeare's Celia] Comfort to Perplexed Rosalynde': 'If then Fortune aimest at the fairest, be patient Rosalynde: for first by thine exile thou goest to thy father: nature is higher prised than wealth, & the love of ones parents ought to bee more precious than all dignities.' Shakespeare refers to 'the natural bond of sisters' (I, ii, 266), and there is a deep feeling throughout his plays that it is more 'natural' to honour familial bonds than it is to break them; more 'natural' to be Cordelia than to be Goneril and Regan, though they all came, by the way of 'nature', from the same womb. Thus the initial actions of Oliver and Frederick, prizing wealth higher than love of family, have made the court (which should be 'cultivated') an 'unnatural' realm. True court-esy has fled to the forest, and, by a pastoral inversion–conversion which Shakespeare enjoys, genuine culture can only be found in the realm of nature.

In this play, all true civility, hospitality (courtly, and rustic), refinement, and respect for the bondings of love and family, is to be found in Arden. This is nicely brought out when Orlando, desperate to find food for the starving Adam, approaches Duke Senior and his men with drawn sword. There follows this central exchange:

> *Duke.* Art thou thus boldened, man, by thy distress,
>   Or else a rude despiser of good manners,
>   That in civility thou seem'st so empty?
> *Orlando.* You touched my vein at first. The thorny point
>   Of bare distress hath ta'en from me the show
>   Of smooth civility; yet am I inland bred
>   And know some nurture.
> ...
> *Duke.* What would you have? Your gentleness shall force
>   More than your force move us to gentleness.
>
> (II, vii, 91-7, 101-3)

'Show of smooth civility' makes it sound as if civility is only a veneer which can be (hypocritically) assumed – as it undoubtedly can (and is still preferable to coarse candour). It is all part of the big question – how deep does 'civility' go, reach, come from? Being 'inland bred' is, precisely, not being 'out-landish' – doubtless unfair to many of the inhabitants of our 'outlands', but meaning well brought up. But that, as we have seen, is just what Orlando has not been – it is his prime complaint – and he has been allowed all too little of the 'nurture' he should have enjoyed. To the extent that he is a 'gentleman', it is by 'nature'. And 'gentle' is the word. He replies to the Duke:

> Speak you so gently? Pardon me, I pray you.
> I thought that all things had been savage here
> ...
> Let gentleness my strong enforcement be;
> In the which hope I blush, and hide my sword.
> (II, vii, 106-7, 118-19)

We are told that only human beings can blush – it is one of our distinguishing traits – and then, only those sufficiently prin-cipled to be capable of shame are, presumably, liable to the revealing suffusion. In this play, all shameless savagery is to be found in the court. Only the forest is 'gentle' (though, we are reminded, not always and in all parts) – and has a gentling influence. As soon as Oliver and Frederick reach it, they are 'converted'.

Jaques is, perhaps, hardly to be described as 'gentle'. He has been seen as Shakespeare's mockery of the growing cult of the Melancholic Man, the Malcontent; or a wearied, debauched and now disillusioned *fin se siècle* figure (his famous speech on 'all the world's a stage' is, among other things, a self-conscious allusion to the Globe Theatre – where the play was performed – having just opened in 1599, when the play was almost certainly written). Commentators differ as to the effect his bitter presence has on the Arcadian atmosphere of Arden. The editor of the Arden edition thinks that Jaques has no specific sense of personal injury; that 'in Arden, his cynicism looks ridiculous'; and that he is 'a satirist in a milieu proof against satire'. A. D. Nuttall, by contrast, maintains that 'because he is radically wretched he is a walking affront to the felicity of Arden', and that, while he does not endanger the pastoral idyll, he is a threat to Duke Senior and 'marks the mendacity of the situation'. The case Nuttall makes is an interesting one. He compares Jaques to Caliban, maintaining that 'Caliban is that of which Jaques is the social sophistication'. As outsiders, they are both opposed, in their different ways, to the preferred harmony of society. Nuttall bases his case on the fact that they are both characterized as being less than human by their respective masters (Duke Senior says of Jaques 'I think he be transformed into a beast,/For I can nowhere find him like a man', II, vii, 1–2; while Prospero calls Caliban 'a thing most brutish', 'not honored with a human shape', *The Tempest* I, ii, 357; I, ii, 283–4). Awareness of the possibility of downward or degenerative metamorphosis is in Shakespeare from the start, though it might be thought that the Duke is joking while Prospero manifestly is not. But it turns out to be a rather pointed joke since, as Nuttall shows, shortly afterwards the Duke rounds on Jaques with a kind of lashing, disgusted anger, otherwise unheard in Arden, but certainly heard when Prospero castigates Caliban.

> For thou thyself hast been a libertine,
> As sensual as the brutish sting itself;
> And all th' embossèd sores and headed evils
> That thou with license of free foot hast caught,
> Wouldst thou disgorge into the general world.
>
> (II, vii, 65–9)

Jaques is notably unmoved by the attack, and, losing no cool, defends himself suavely and effortlessly. And perhaps that's it – the Duke is angry because Jaques will not join in his Robin Hood game, thus effectively giving it the lie. He remains out of the reach of the Duke's power and influence – as of course he does at the end. Both Caliban and Jaques are recalcitrant to their governors; and while Caliban is, supposedly, finally domesticated, Jaques enacts a possibly deeper unassimilability – *un*convertibility. Nuttall suggests that 'it is not a waste of the imagination to consider Jaques as a Caliban who has been civilized' – or, we might add, over-civilized; there are reminders in the play of how, as 'we ripe' we also 'rot', and Jaques may be a case of an over-ripeness giving way to a premature rottenness. Or perhaps he was never truly civilized at all. Or perhaps he is something else again – a cold voice from the outlands commenting acidly on inland cultural presumptions. Whatever, he is a provoking figure; and he certainly provokes the otherwise always equable Duke.

We first hear of him weeping over a dying stag, wounded by the Duke's hunters. Noting that the stag is ignored by a 'careless herd/Full of the pasture', Jaques, so a lord reports, broke out into what amounted to a condemnation of the world's heartlessness.

'Sweep on, you fat and greasy citizens,
'Tis just the fashion; wherefore do you look
Upon that poor and broken bankrupt there?'
Thus most invectively he pierceth through
The body of the country, city, court,
Yea, and of this our life, swearing that we
Are mere usurpers, tyrants, and what's worse,
To fright the animals and to kill them up
In their assigned and native dwelling place.

(II, i, 55–63)

There is no plausible case to be made out for Jaques as a potential Animal Rights sympathizer. He enjoys wrong-footing people, making them uneasy in their assumed positions and aims, so it pleases him to take the negative line – most inventively – and see the usurped Duke as himself a kind of usurper of the forest animals. The Duke seems unmoved, and purports to enjoy Jaques in his 'sullen fits', but he cannot exactly relish having his forest lifestyle cast in that light. There is a touch of self-deception in his rather self-contratulatory Sherwood Forestry, and it is better that it should be audibly pointed out. For his part, Jaques prefers to 'avoid' the Duke as being 'too disputable' (II, v, 30). He doesn't care for the company of 'Signior Love', Orlando, either – 'let's meet as little as we can', and Orlando has as little liking for 'Monsieur Melancholy' – 'I do desire we may be better strangers' (III, ii, 255–6). He doesn't get on much better with Ganymede–Rosalind, to whom he boasts of his unique, *sui generis*, 'melancholy of mine own' and his 'humorous sadness' (IV, i, 15–19). Rosalind declares that she prefers merriness to sadness, and he quickly leaves. He certainly sees himself as a serious satirist, 'anatomizing' folly, trying to 'cleanse the foul body of th' infected world' (II, vii, 60); but perhaps he might best be regarded as, more generally, a requisite principle of dissonance. Early on, when the Duke is told that Jaques has been caught in an uncharacteristically 'merry' mood 'hearing of a song' (there are, incidentally, more songs in this play than in any other – the forest is full of music, as is Prospero's Isle), the Duke exclaims:

> If he, compact of jars, grow musical,
> We shall have shortly discord in the spheres.
>
> (II, vii, 5–6)

If *Jaques* starts becoming harmonious, the very music of the spheres will go out of tune, because he lives by disagreement and by being contrary, and he can only be what the other isn't. He is 'compact of jars' – *composed* of discord, not just occasionally discordant: we have lost much of the force of the old word 'jar', but for Shakespeare it carried a powerful harshness (civil wars were civil jars). Jaques lives by and for 'jars': he *is* the jarring sound which makes you appreciate what true harmony is, and as such he is, in this play, indispensable. It would be an immeasurably weaker, more flaccid affair without him. It is oddly fitting that he is given what is effectively the final 'bequeathing' speech, which lays out all their futures. He delivers it with strange dignity and authority, before taking his 'jars' away from a scene of what must be by now, for him, altogether too much harmony.

The person in the forest whom Jaques finds most congenial, or enjoyable, or even estimable, is, of course, Touchstone, whom he extols in his first actual speech. 'A fool, a fool! I met a fool i' th' forest,/A motley fool!' (II, vii, 12–13). As Jaques describes him, Touchstone 'hath been a courtier', and his somewhat scrambled brain is 'crammed' with all sorts of unusual observations 'the which he vents/In mangled forms'. A mangling man is bound to appeal to a jarring man. And Jaques concludes his eulogy – 'O that I were a fool!/I am ambitious for a motley coat.' He has met his welcome contrary – and equal (II, vii, 40–43). Touchstone is (as I have mentioned) a new kind of fool in Shakespeare, and the decision to bring him into the pastoral was as inspired as the introduction of Jaques. He is called, variously, 'Nature's natural' (I, ii, 47) and 'clownish fool' (I, iii, 128), yet, silly as he sometimes seems, he is really, as we say, nobody's fool. He has his wits about him, but uses them in unusual, unpredictable ways. Those critics – there are some – who think he simply spouts nonsense, are themselves the more deceived – fooled, we might say. Duke Senior is closer to the mark when he says – 'He uses his folly like a stalking horse, and under the presentation of that he shoots his wit' (V, iv, 106–7).

That he is going to be an antithetical presence in the Arden pastoral, he makes clear with his first words in the forest. 'Ay, now am I in Arden, the more fool I. When I was at home, I was in a better place, but travelers must be content' (II, iv, 15–17). (Perhaps pertinently, Jaques also sees himself as 'a traveler', IV, i, 20 – these two are rootless, they drift anywhere.) Touchstone has a mocking, or undermining, or teasing – or simply rude – word for everyone, Duke or peasant, court lady or goat-girl. And only he can reduce aloof Jaques to helpless laughter. He is sophisticated enough to cite Ovid – the last time the Roman poet appears by name in Shakespeare. In his wooing of Audrey, which serves as a tolerably rank burlesque of the courtly and poetic courtship which elsewhere prevails in Arden, Touchstone strikes an ironic pose:

I am here with thee and thy goats, as the most capricious poet, honest Ovid, was among the Goths.

(III, iii, 6–8)

The joke is multiple. Goths were pronounced 'Goats' in Elizabethan England; Latin goats were '*capers*', and not-so-honest Ovid was exiled among the Gothic Getae for writing some distinctly *caper*icious poetry (*Ars Amatoria*); while Touchstone is intending some strictly goatish business with goat-girl Audrey. Not the usual pastoral tone. Jaques (listening and speaking aside) responds with a by now familiar allusion to Ovid's *Metamorphoses*:

O knowledge ill-inhabited, worse than Jove in a thatched house!

(III, iii, 9–10)

In *Much Ado* the story was invoked in connection with misleading appearances: here Jaques refers to finding things in incongruous places – for the impoverished Baucis and Philemon were surprisingly courteous and generous to the disguised Jove. In a pastoral play where harshness and rejection reign at court and love and hospitality have removed to the forest, the allusion is especially apt (as Lodge says in his pastoral – 'crownes have crosses when mirth is in cottages').

Touchstone's attitude to love is unequivocally carnal, sexual, without romantic sentiment or rhetoric. Introducing himself to Duke Senior at the end he says: 'I press in here, sir, amongst the rest of the country copulatives, to swear and to forswear, according as marriage binds and blood breaks' (V, iv, 56-8). 'Copulatives' was the Latinate term for couples about to get married (those who would couple); but of course it cannot but bring to mind the fact that an important part of love between young men and women involves copulation. Copulate is what the animals do, as Touchstone reminds the honest shepherd, Corin – 'That is another simple sin in you: to bring the ewes and the rams together and to offer to get your living by the copulation of cattle' (III, ii, 78-80). It is what humans do, too, but the high, idealizing romantic love of conventional pastoral does not care to look that way (though Rosalind glances at it a couple of times). Touchstone *only* looks that way, lining himself up with the animals. 'As the ox hath his bow, sir, the horse his curb, and the falcon her bells, so a man hath his desires; and as pigeons bill, so wedlock would be nibbling' (III, iii, 76-9). Shakespeare never ever suggests that love can be reduced to sexual gratification, and Touchstone's view of the matter is hardly endorsed in a play dominated by Rosalind. But a full love importantly includes it, and to ignore or occlude the fact is to risk vaporizing away into the simpering silliness of a Silvius. Silvius is true to the pastoral convention which produced him; but Shakespeare, of course, is true to life. So he sends Touchstone to press in, not just among the country copulatives, but among the courtly and Arcadian romantic lovers as well. He also reminds them – and us – that 'We that are true lovers run into strange capers; but as all is mortal in nature, so is all nature in love mortal in folly'

(II, iv, 51-4). In Barber's words, Touchstone 'forestalls potential audience cynicism' – we will hardly find a more deflationary, unromantic voice than his. It is because of Touchstone wandering around the forest – with Jaques on the loose as well – that we have pastoral with a difference; which includes a much more comprehensive consideration of what might be held in that 'captious and inteemable sieve' of a word (I steal from *All's Well That Ends Well*) – love. (He is once called a 'whetstone', and he *is* a sort of 'touchstone' – he does serve to sharpen things up, and, indirectly, test their real qualities. There are also some sparks.)

One of the most important encounters he has is with Corin. Like their betters, they discuss manners, breeding, art and nature, with the good Corin – he has an honest rustic dignity which is proof against mockery and not reducible to pastoral convention – giving at least as good as he gets. Arguably better. 'Those that are good manners at the court are as ridiculous in the country as the behavior of the country is most mockable at the court' (III, ii, 45-8). True. And there is truth, too, in what seems like Touchstone's equivocating answer to Corin's question – 'how like you this shepherd's life?'

Truly, shepherd, in respect of itself, it is a good life; but in respect that it is a shepherd's life, it is naught. In respect that it is solitary, I like it very well; but in respect that it is private, it is a very vile life. Now in respect it is in the fields, it pleaseth me well; but in respect it is not in the court, it is tedious. As it is a spare life, look you, it fits my humor well; but as there is no more plenty in it, it goes much against my stomach.

(III, ii, 13-21)

I have seen this described as a piece of double-talking nonsense to bamboozle the simple Corin, but of course it is nothing of the kind. You can look at the same thing in different ways, from different perspectives. One description need not cancel out another. Indeed, if it is an equally plausible description, it supplements the first and we are the richer. Of course you can look at the same life with courtly eyes, and with country eyes. That is what Shakespeare himself is doing, with the implicit exhortation – be flexible, be plural, be inclusive. Monocularity is impoverishing.

Touchstone's proposed rough-and-ready country marriage with Audrey (a rural reality, called a hedge-wedding), serves as a contrast, perhaps a travesty, in advance, of the mock marriage played out by Rosalind–Ganymede and Orlando just two scenes later. (Not so mock either. Harold Brooks pointed out that an espousal, called in legal terms *sponsalia per verba de praesenti*, takes place if the couple declare that they take each other as husband and wife right now, at this very moment. Marriage by this means was, apparently, still valid in the sixteenth century. This gives an extra piquancy to the scene. No wonder Rosalind is so particularly high-spirited and playful afterwards. It's not every day that a girl gets married, even if the husband doesn't realize it has happened!) Touchstone, regretting that his Ovidian wit cannot be appreciated by the simple Audrey ('I am not a slut, though I thank the gods I am foul', III, iii, 36), says to her 'Truly, I would the gods had made thee poetical', and the following exchange is vital to the whole play:

Audrey. I do not know what poetical is. Is it honest in deed and word? Is it a true thing?
Touchstone. No, truly; for the truest poetry is the most feigning, and lovers are given to poetry, and what they swear in poetry may be said as lovers they do feign.

(III, iii, 16–21)

Is it a true thing? No one better to ask than, indirectly, Shakespeare, whose whole play may be seen as an extended pondering and answering of this deepest of questions. Touchstone's response is both cynical-sounding and arrestingly to the point. The question as to whether poets were liars was a commonly debated one, and Touchstone's succinct formulation – 'the truest poetry is the most feigning' – goes to the heart of the matter. It depends on hearing 'fain' behind, or within 'feign' – etymologically unrelated but exact homophones (a moment later Jaques says 'I would fain see this meeting', III, iii, 44, as they prepare for the wedding). 'Feign' comes from *fingere* – to form, conceive, contrive, subsequently to pretend. 'Fain' – gladly, willingly – comes from an old word for joy, and indicates desire. We can fashion a pretend-form of what it is

we want. Poetry – art – thus becomes a glad contrivance
through which we project and dramatize our desires. Seen this
way, the truest poetry *is* the most feigning–faining – the
highest artifice satisfying our deepest needs. Life re-presented
just as we would like it.

Curiously enough, Jaques interrupts the hedge-wedding –
perhaps not liking to see a court man (even a court fool) go
rustic; perhaps because he is turning ascetic and religious, and
is disgusted by such country 'copulatives' (at the end, he leaves
to seek out the company of a 'convertite').

And will you, being a man of your breeding, be married under a bush
like a beggar? Get you to church, and have a good priest that can tell
you what marriage is.

(III, iii, 80–83)

Touchstone and Audrey duly join all the other couples in
honourable wedlock at the end, though Jaques himself foresees
that Touchstone will 'break' his 'bond' within two months – a
courtier/animal (Ovid/goat) to the end. But Touchstone
makes one more crucial contribution to the play. Just before
the end, concerning the matter of lying and quarrelling, he
gives a brilliant account of 'the degrees of the lie'. His two long
speeches here (V, iv, 69–82, 90–103) are often seen as a
mockery, a parody, of the minutely discriminated niceties of
court etiquette. Possibly (although avoiding the brutality of
duelling through adroit formulaic politeness is not a trivial
matter); but they make a point on which the – peaceful –
conclusion of the play depends. Again, as so often in the play,
there is a concern with manners – and the taming of incipient
violence. At issue is how you may avoid coming to blows over
an accusation of lying. 'O sir, we quarrel in print, by the book,
as you have books for good manners. I will name you the
degrees.' And so he does – Retort Courteous, Quip Modest,
Reply Churlish, Reproof Valiant, Countercheck Quarrelsome, Lie with Circumstance, Lie Direct.

All these you may avoid but the Lie Direct, and you may avoid that
too, with an If. I knew when seven justices could not take up [settle] a
quarrel, but when the parties were met themselves, one of them
thought but of an If: as, 'If you said so, then I said so'; and they shook

hands and swore brothers. Your If is the only peacemaker. Much
virtue in If.

(V, iv, 96-103)

Almost immediately, the figure of Hymen enters to soft music,
and the play resolves itself in the doubly manifest artifice of a
Masque.

If – such a small, but such a potent conjunction (from the
old Norse *ef*, but ultimately, and fittingly – when did humans
start thinking alternatively? – 'of unknown origin'). It opens
up a whole new space of conditionality and supposition – the
world of might be, could be, should be; the boundless realm of
may-be. This tiny little sound significantly reveals that the
human mind, while it is eager to establish actualities, also
wants to entertain possibilities. Theatre drama itself depends
on a massive 'If', being conditional on what Coleridge called
'the willing suspension of disbelief' (cf. Dr Johnson – in
connection with Shakespeare's plays – 'delusion, *once delusion be
admitted*, knows no certain limit' – my italics). The title of one
of Pirandello's most famous plays is *Cosi e, se vi pare!* –
translated as *It Is So! (If You Think So)*. In this case, the satire
is against malign gossips, who insist that what they speculat-
ively like to imagine about a family is the actual truth
concerning that family. This is the dark downside of the
willingness to believe in one's own ill-founded fabrications and
projections. But in art, consciously deployed, it can bring great
benefits. Hans Vaihinger wrote a work entitled *The Philosophy
of 'As if'*, and what it had to say about the rich role that
possible, plausible, provisional fictions may play in our life and
thinking had an influence on Wallace Stevens – a poet of 'If' if
ever there was one ('The final belief is to believe in a fiction,
which you know to be a fiction, there being nothing else'). I
will stray no further afield into the theory of fictions. But in his
theatre, Shakespeare can give Pirandello's title a happy turn,
and say – *if* you are willing to believe, make-believe, in
Rosalind and the others, as *they* believe, make-believe in
Hymen and the Masque orchestrating the peaceful, harmonious conclusion, if you can just think so; then, for a time
anyway, it is so. Much virtue in If.

Much virtue in Rosalind, too – 'the mannish Rosalind' as

Henry James interestingly called her; Lodge's 'amorous Girle–boye'. Like 'If', she is, in this play, 'your only peacemaker': she arranges, directs, and stages the gathering harmonizations and couplings with which the action concludes. (For the *dénouement* she plans, she has an 'if' – five of them – for all the unsatisfied lovers as she promises them, variously, contentment: 'I will content you if what pleases you contents you, and you shall be married tomorrow' and so on, V, ii, 108–119. If you follow my commands, it will all be as you would like it.) She is also the leading actor–actress in her own play. We have seen, once before, a boy actor playing a girl playing a boy who describes playing a girl (Julia in *The Two Gentlemen of Verona*); here, we have a further refinement, since here the heroine plays a boy who then proceeds to play at being – herself! One may well feel that this disorienting recesssional device can hardly be taken further. When Rosalind–Ganymede – teasing, provocative – says to Orlando (who is, we may note, a rather simple, straightforward lad, with none of the sparkling wit of a Berowne or a Benedict):

Come, woo me, woo me; for now I am in a holiday humor and like enough to consent. What would you say to me now, an I were your very very Rosalind?

(IV, i, 64–7)

she is at play in the wide world of the conditional ('an' = 'if'), and having tremendous fun. It is a game with an agreeable sexual piquancy and ambiguity, for both of them perhaps. At the same time, she *is* his 'very very Rosalind'; here the 'most feigning' ('I would cure you, if you would but call me Rosalind', III, ii, 416; let's pretend) is also the simple truth. Just so, when she entices Orlando into the mock marriage, it is, did he but know it, also a real one. Touchstone's definition of the 'truest poetry' is perceptibly justified.

Once she assumes men's clothes, it is as if boundless performing energies are released in her. She becomes positively Protean, a virtuoso of transformations. Seemingly, she can do anything, play anyone, every kind of woman and man (except a physically tough one: she faints at the sight of Orlando's blood, though she tries to pretend it is a 'counterfeit' swoon. But, for once, this is *not* 'feigning'; there are limits even to her creative simulations. Involuntarily, she is very very true to her woman's tenderness.) Being no longer confined to a woman's restricted role, Rosalind is free to enter more deeply into masculine proclivities and potencies than any of the other Shakespearian heroines who assume male disguise. Like Portia, she becomes the master–mistress of the whole situation. She is the central consciousness in the forest, where she takes control. Ultimately, she runs things. Her disguise affords her detachment, even while her engaged feelings ensure her involvement; so that she can comment ironically, wisely, angrily (to Phebe), wryly, sadly, happily on all the lovers, including herself. She can look at love from every angle, so that her vision and comprehension is much wider and more inclusive than the partial attitudes displayed by goatish Touchstone and soppy Silvius. Yeats once said of John Donne that he could be as metaphysical as he pleased because he could be as physical as he pleased. Adapting this, we may say that Rosalind can be as romantic as she pleases because she can be as realistic as she pleases – and knows to be necessary. Orlando, a conventional hero–romantic lover all the way down, maintains that he will love 'for ever and a day'.

Rosalind. Say 'a day,' without the 'ever.' No, no, Orlando. Men are
    April when they woo, December when they wed. Maids are May
    when they are maids, but the sky changes when they are wives.
                                                     (IV, i, 139–42)

By her own account, Rosalind is 'many fathom deep' in love; but her enlarged forest consciousness knows that love, too, has its seasons.

What Rosalind will not tolerate is affectation, humourless pretensions, and self-deception. Hence her rebuke to the coquettish Phebe:

But mistress, know yourself. Down on your knees,
        And thank heaven, fasting, for a good man's love.
                                                     (III, v, 57–8)

Know thyself. Bullough pointed out that it is really with this play that self-knowledge starts to become an important theme for Shakespeare, and he added that this state is easier to achieve in the green world than in the court – Rosalind's forest, Lear's heath, Prospero's island. It is as if the green world was a place of unavoidable honesties, irrefutable exposures. Touchstone, wonderfully cryptic, at one point says to Rosalind: 'You have said; but whether wisely or no, let the forest judge' (III, ii, 121-2). As who should say – the forest will always find you out. The difficulties of achieving self-knowledge (and the resistances to, and avoidances of it) are central to the great tragedies. Lear, tragically in the event, 'hath ever but slenderly known himself' (I, i, 295-6). While Macbeth, who knows himself only too well, moves tragedy into a new key when he realizes 'To know my deed, 'twere best not know myself' (II, ii, 72). But, in this play, self-knowledge is arrived at through, and in, comedy. And it is the 'amorous Girle–boye' Rosalind, by common consent the most delightful of all Shakespeare's heroines, who is the principal enabler, just as it is she who arranges the concluding multiple marriages. Though, to do this, she has to have recourse to a little 'conjuring'.

At the end, Ganymede reverts to being very Rosalind who, having made 'all this matter even' (V, iv, 18), then, in the Epilogue, reverts to being a, by this time very hermaphroditic, boy actor. This final step back into the *he*ness of the actor from the *she*ness of the character ensures that gender distinctions remain provocatively problematical to the end – as David Carroll nicely says about this final appearance of the amorous girl–boy character/boy–girl actor – 'we had forgotten she was not a woman'. In that Epilogue, he/she says 'My way is to conjure you'. *Con-jurare* is to band together with an oath, thence to conspire, to plot, to exorcize: also (OED) 'to constrain to appear by invocation ... effect, bring out, by juggling ... produce magical effects by natural means, perform marvels, cause to appear to the fancy'. Thus, a 'conjurer' can be one who (seriously) conjures up spirits, and one who (admittedly) uses legerdemain to 'produce magical effects'. Clever tricks or solemn summonings. Conjuring can be a kind of feigning, and vice-versa. You could hardly find better words for what Shakespeare does in the theatre, and how he does it.

And it all depends on a kind, on many kinds, of 'magic'. A 'Magus' was a member of an ancient Persian priestly caste (the *magi* were the wise men from the East who came to worship the child Jesus); anglicized as 'mage' it can mean a wise man or a magician. Perhaps, also, a Shakespeare. Certainly, a Rosalind. Promising Orlando a happy resolution to his longings, she tells him:

> Believe then, if you please, that I can do strange things. I have, since I was three year old, conversed with a magician, most profound in his art and yet not damnable ... it is not impossible to me, if it appear not inconvenient to you, to set her [Rosalind] before your eyes tomorrow, human as she is, and without any danger.

(V, ii, 58–68)

Of course it is 'not impossible' since she *is* Rosalind; and anything less than 'inconvenient' to Orlando than seeing Rosalind, it is hard to imagine. By his own account, he is by now close to bursting. So why the mystification; why this circuitous route to happiness? Why the ensuing artifice; the staging of Hymen? Shakespeare wants us to see the magic, and also see it for what it is. It is a conjuring trick; it is also a serious invocation working to wondrous effect. Note that it is good magic, white magic – 'not damnable'. This is the first time that Shakespeare brings benign magic into his drama (Richard III was execrated as a 'black magician' – fair enough). And of course, that drama will culminate in the awesome magic of Prospero. And what more fitting words for Shakespeare himself than 'a magician, most profound in his art and yet not damnable'. Rosalind is acting as his deputy.

Hymen is the spirit of concord:

> Then is there mirth in heaven
> When earthly things made even
>   Atone together
> . . .
> Peace ho! I bar confusion:
> 'Tis I must make conclusion
>   Of these most strange events.

(V, iv, 108–10, 125–7)

So should the best comedies end; with bad things 'atoned' for, and people at one with each other. In this play, Shakespeare shows – to perfection – how to bring it off. A final point. The last song of the play is to Hymen.

> Wedding is great Juno's crown,
>   O blessed bond of board and bed!
> 'Tis Hymen peoples every town;
>   High wedlock then be honorèd.
> Honor, high honor, and renown
> To Hymen, god of every town!

(V, iv, 141-6)

The last song in Lodge's *Rosalynde* is a true eclogue, about a shepherd and his lass who finally marry 'And fore God Pan did plight their troth'. Pan was an essentially rural god; Shakespeare, realist and now Londoner, wants the final stress of his play to look back to the town. Though only after the testing, healing forest has judged. And the magic has worked.

*

TWELFTH NIGHT (1601)

> *Viola.* I am not that I play. Are you the lady of the house?
> *Olivia.* If I do not usurp myself, I am.

(I, v, 182-4)

> *Olivia.* I prithee tell me what thou think'st of me.
> *Viola.* That you do think you are not what you are.
> *Olivia.* If I think so, I think the same of you.
> *Viola.* Then think you right. I am not what I am.
> *Olivia.* I would you were as I would have you be.
> *Viola.* Would it be better, madam, than I am?

(III, i, 140-45)

Julia dressed as a page-boy in order to follow and serve her faithless lover, Proteus (*The Two Gentlemen of Verona*); Portia dressed as a man to enter the male world of the law and rescue her husband's friend; Rosalind adopted 'a swashing and a martial outside' to reduce the dangers to two helpless women fleeing into the forest from the court (*As You Like It*). But Viola, in what is sometimes called the last of Shakespeare's 'happy comedies', gives no clear reason for assuming male disguise. After being rescued from the shipwreck, she finds herself without role and direction in a strange land. 'And what should I do in Illyria?' (I, ii, 3) she rhetorically asks the good captain who has saved her. She asks who governs in Illyria and learns about Orsino and his love for the lady Olivia. After being told that Olivia has 'abjured the sight/And company of men', Viola responds:

> O that I served that lady,
> And might not be delivered to the world,
> Till I had made mine own occasion mellow,
> What my estate is.

(I, ii, 41-4)

The Captain points out apparently insuperable difficulties, and Viola switches to the Duke.

> I prithee (and I'll pay thee bounteously)
> Conceal me what I am, and be my aid
> For such disguise as haply will become
> The form of my intent. I'll serve this duke.
> Thou shalt present me as an eunuch to him;
> It may be worth thy pains.

(I, ii, 52-7)

The Arden editors comment that this indicates 'neither a deep-laid scheme nor an irresponsible caprice' and add in a footnote: '"Till I had made mine own occasion mellow" will pass in the theatre. There is, and can be, no sound reason given for her taking service with either Olivia or Orsino: this is simply required by the plot, from which Shakespeare has dropped the original motivation of the heroine's disguise (to serve the man she secretly loves).' Certainly, Shakespeare can set his plot in motion in any way he wants, and he is under no obligation to provide motivated reasons for opening actions. But, since the theme of a woman dressing up as a page or servant to gain proximity to a man is a very familiar one from a number of sixteenth-century plays and narratives (mainly Italian), and since her motive is *always* the fact that she *already* loves that man, Shakespeare's decision to drop that traditional reason, indeed to obscure if not erase motive altogether, is perhaps worth a little more consideration than a parenthesis in a footnote.

Considering her speech to the Captain, Barber admires 'the aristocratic, free and easy way she [Viola] settles what she will do'; and later, 'Viola's spritely language conveys the fun she is having in playing a man's part, with a hidden womanly perspective about it. One cannot quite say that she is playing in a masquerade, because disguising *just* for the fun of it is a different thing. But the same sort of festive pleasure in transvestism is expressed.' Twelfth Night concluded the twelve days of Christmas festivities which traditionally was a period of 'misrule', when the world could, temporarily, be turned upside down, or inside out (like Feste's glove), and clothes, genders and identities swapped around. (See François Laroque on this.) So 'festive pleasure in transvestism' seems to point in the right direction. But I am intrigued that Viola should resolve to go as a 'eunuch'. Some editions will tell you that Shakespeare dropped this idea, or simply forgot all about it. But I wonder if he did. For instance, when the letter from 'THE FORTUNATE UNHAPPY' reminds Malvolio that 'Some are born great, some achieve greatness, and some have greatness thrust upon 'em' (II, v, 144-5), it is engaging in a barely submerged parody of the biblical verse:

For there are some eunuchs, which were so born from their mother's womb: and there are some eunuchs, which were made eunuchs of men: and there be eunuchs, which have made themselves eunuchs for the kingdom of heaven's sake. He that is able to receive it, let him receive it.

(Matthew 19:12)

Something is going on in this play about what it is to be, and to fail to be, properly gendered; what it is for nature to draw to her 'bias', or swerve from it. I think Viola's resolve to enter Illyria as a eunuch will stand a little more pondering. Ruth Nevo can see that it matters, and she interprets it in her own way. Noting Viola's 'ambivalence' about whom to serve, she writes:

But she does not fly to the Countess Olivia for succour, woman to woman, despite her sympathy for a fellow-mourner. Instead she chooses to be *adventurously epicene* in the Duke's entourage. Viola escapes her feminine state but at the cost of a (symbolic) castration: it is as a eunuch (to account for her voice) that she will 'sing,/And speak to him in many sorts of music' (I, ii, 57).

(my italics). William Carroll also raises the question – 'But why a eunuch?' – and his answer is instructive:

Shakespeare's initial choice of the eunuch role may have been for pragmatic reasons. 'Cesario' would not be sexually identified and as a neutral figure could more easily become a confidant of Olivia. But somewhere along the way, Shakespeare changed his mind and dropped the idea, perhaps because Viola is already a eunuch as far as Viola goes; and a *man* playing a eunuch affords comic possibilities, but a woman playing a eunuch – nothing. As the play continues, we see that Cesario must in fact be essentially bisexual, not neuter, as Viola is both firm and flexible, both deliberate and careless, both committed and disengaged.

Suppose we think of this play as centring on a figure who sets out to be 'adventurously epicene' and discovers that s/he is, has to be, 'bisexual, not neuter' – the would-be eunuch who became the inadvertent hermaphrodite. How or why might a great romantic comedy emerge from such a proposition, it might be asked? That is what I will try to explore.

'Epicene' comes from *epi-* (close up) *koinos* (common). Epicene nouns, in Greek and Latin, are words which have only one form for both the masculine and feminine case – for example, *poeta* is morphologically feminine and grammatically masculine, and refers to a poet of either sex. We can say, then, that it elides marks of sexual difference, and brings two into one. This is what Viola, for her own reasons, sets out to do. 'Hermaphrodite' is, of course, Hermes plus Aphrodite, and refers to a being who has all the sexual characteristics (and equipment) of both sexes, and thus transforms one into two. Such a natural anomaly would be something of a monster. Yet it is just such a being that Viola finds herself, impossibly, turning into. As she recognizes, when she refers to herself as 'poor monster':

> What will become of this? As I am man,
> My state is desperate for my master's love.

> As I am woman (now alas the day!),
> What thriftless sighs shall poor Olivia breathe?
>
> (II, ii, 36-9)

At the start, we saw Viola wavering between the Countess and the Duke – this way or that way? At the end she tells her brother what has happened since their separation:

> All the occurrence of my fortune since
> Hath been between this lady and this lord.
>
> (V, i, 257-8)

– which we might also hear as saying, I have spent my time being something between a lady and a lord. When Viola–Cesario first makes her way to Olivia's house, Olivia asks Malvolio 'Of what personage and years is he?' Malvolio has a rather elaborate answer:

Not yet old enough for a man nor young enough for a boy; as a squash is before 'tis a peascod, or a codling when 'tis almost an apple. 'Tis with him in standing water, between boy and man.

> (I, v, 155-8)

This reminds me of the image Antony uses for Octavia:

> the swan's-down feather
> That stands upon the swell at the full of tide,
> And neither way inclines.
>
> (*Antony and Cleopatra* III, ii, 48-50)

Twelfth Night is one of the most watery of Shakespeare's plays, so Malvolio's image is particularly appropriate. We may feel that young Viola, fresh from the sea, is sexually still labile, not yet fully differentiated; that, for the moment, she 'neither way inclines' (I need hardly point out, by now, how having a boy actor play the girl would add to this effect). But Malvolio's description also points, however unawarely, to another figure who is of central importance in this play – Narcissus. Once again, we are back with Ovid. Here is how he describes Narcissus:

> Narcissus now had reached his sixteenth year
> And seemed both man and boy; and many a youth
> And many a girl desired him ...

Drinking from a pool, he sees:

> A form, a face, and loved with leaping heart
> A hope unreal and thought the shape was real.
> Spellbound he saw himself . . .

He falls in love with his own 'fleeting image' and Ovid comments:

> You see a phantom of a mirrored shape;
> Nothing itself . . .

In Ovid's account, he simply pines away on the bank, and after his death is turned into a white and yellow flower. But there also grew up a version of the myth which had Narcissus drowning trying to kiss and embrace his own reflection. It is this version which Shakespeare draws on in both of his major poems:

> Narcissus so himself himself forsook,
> And died to kiss his shadow in the brooke.
>
> (*Venus and Adonis*)

> That, had Narcissus seen her as she stood,
> Self-love had never drowned him in the flood.
>
> (*The Rape of Lucrece*)

'O, you are sick of self-love, Malvolio' – these are the first words Olivia speaks to her steward (I, v, 90), and we learn from Maria that he likes 'practicing behavior to his own shadow' (II, v, 16). He is, indeed, a very obvious study in narcissism in a comically exaggerated form (even his grotesque cross-garters are the Narcissus colour – yellow, as pointed out by Jonathan Bate). But there is subtler and more serious narcissism in the leading figures in Illyria – Olivia and Orsino, both in danger of drowning in various forms of self-love. The indeterminate, could-seemingly-go-either-way, Viola–Cesario will change all that. Prior to her arrival, we feel that a curious stasis, or even stagnation, prevailed in Illyria – the sterile, repetitious, self-directed, self-obsessed emotions of the Duke and Countess going, growing, nowhere. Viola proves to be the crucial catalyst for change, emergence, growth. She herself, despite her 'standing-water' status and appearance, is decidedly *not* a Narcissus. She is more reminiscent of the other key figure in the myth – Echo. Echo was a nymph who used to distract Juno's attention by her talking, while Jove had his way with other nymphs. As a punishment, Juno reduced her powers of speech to the ability to repeat the last words of any voice she hears. Echo falls in love with Narcissus, who rejects her in disgust. Echo takes her shame to the woods, 'yet still her love endures and grows on grief'. She wastes away and is finally just a discarnate voice, left to echo the wailing of the water dryads, mourning the death of Narcissus. There is something of all this in two of Viola's key speeches, when she is, as it were, talking indirectly about her own love, since her disguise has reduced her to something of an echo (repeating Orsino's overtures to Olivia, and Olivia's rejections to Orsino). Unlike Echo, she can release herself, anonymously, in lyric flights of poetry. What would she do if *she* loved Olivia?

> Make me a willow cabin at your gate
> And call upon my soul within the house;
> Write loyal cantons of contemnèd love
> And sing them loud even in the dead of night;
> Hallo your name to the reverberate hills
> And make the babbling gossip of the air
> Cry out 'Olivia!'

(I, v, 269-75)

As Jonathan Bate says, 'babbling gossip of the air' is effectively an explicit reference to Echo; but the beauty of the poetry is all her own. No wonder Olivia reacts with 'You might do much'. After all her proud, house-bound, self-bound, posturing mourning for her brother, this is, perhaps, her first encounter with a genuinely felt and powerfully expressed emotion of love, and, her narcissism cracked open, she finds it irresistible.

Similarly, there is something of the faithful though fading Echo in her account of the hopeless love suffered by her imaginary sister, indirectly, of course, describing her own. 'And what's her history?' asks the Duke, confident that no woman's love could match his own.

> A blank, my lord. She never told her love,
> But let concealment, like a worm i' th' bud,

Feed on her damask cheek. She pined in thought;
And, with a green and yellow melancholy,
She sat like Patience on a monument,
Smiling at grief. Was not this love indeed?

(II, iv, 111–16)

Her answer has some general force. The history of women is all too often 'a blank'; theirs tend to be the unwritten lives – 'hidden from history', as they say. And Viola also feels she is blanked out, having made herself invisible as a woman in front of the man she now loves. But from the deep feeling in her words, we surely agree that this is 'love indeed'. Characteristically, the Duke's only response is to ask if the sister died or not. He cannot hear the cadences of true feeling, preferring his own music-fed moods of languorous sentimentality and affected infatuation. Viola remains something of a hapless Echo to Orsino to the end. His emergence from narcissism is extremely peremptory, if indeed it happens. At the end, learning that Cesario is a woman, he agrees to take her, on account of her expressed devotion to him.

Give me thy hand,
And let me see thee in thy woman's weeds.

(V, i, 272–3)

It is notable that we never see Viola back in her 'woman's weeds' – as we do the triumphant Rosalind, and Portia and Julia. It is possible that Orsino actually prefers her as Cesario – the adoring, beautiful boy servant. For the audience, at least, she remains the ambiguous Viola–Cesario composite figure she has become. It is also notable that after this moment when she is accepted by the Duke, she never says another word throughout the remaining one hundred and thirty-five lines of the play – as if faithful Echo has finally, fully, faded away. (Rosalind, of course, had the last word – lots of them – in a masterly, confident epilogue.) Jonathan Bate's suggestion about Viola–Echo is a good one. 'Echo functions in Ovid as an alternative to self-love: had Narcissus responded to her love, neither of them would have been destroyed. Viola's function is to enable characters to respond, to see that love requires echoing instead of narcissism.' Though I suppose since Echo can only give you back your own words – just as mirrors and ponds give you back your own image – she might well contribute to your narcissism. It is only while Viola is Cesario that she finds that enlargement of voice which Shakespeare's heroines characteristically enjoy once they have assumed male disguise. With the mention of 'woman's weeds' to be re-assumed, Viola is, seemingly, silenced. As Jonathan Bate says, you can either read this, happily, as indicating that she has done her work in Illyria (released the lord and lady from their narcissism), and now has her husband–reward; or, rather more darkly, as intimating, as wife, her history will return to being 'a blank'.

I have not mentioned Sebastian, but he of course is Viola's other half; Shakespeare here, once again, having recourse to the 'divisible indivisibility' of identical twins, though this time of opposite sexes. This multiplies and deepens the thematic possibilities of identity and gender confusion when one twin decides to go same-sex. This move in turn allows Viola an experience, a perception, not vouchsafed to the other cross-dressing heroines – the possible dangers of this device.

> Disguise, I see thou art a wickedness
> Wherein the pregnant enemy does much.
>
> (II, ii, 27–8)

With identical twins, Shakespeare can put on stage the apparently bewildering phenomenon whereby one is two, and two are one. It is a visible rendering of the more ineffable two-into-one mystery of marriage. In one case literally, in the other metaphorically, therein is number slain (*The Phoenix and the Turtle*).

> How have you made division of yourself?
> An apple cleft in two is not more twin
> Than these two creatures. Which is Sebastian?
>
> (V, i, 222–4)

says Sebastian's loyal lover, Antonio (and that, incidentally, is the last we hear from him. Like that other spokesman for homosexual devotion, also named Antonio – in *The Merchant of Venice* – he is just vaguely left out of things at the end as others pair up, or leave.) The Duke's response to the seemingly impossible phenomenon is famous:

> One face, one voice, one habit, and two persons –
> A natural perspective that is and is not.
>
> (V, i, 216-17)

Just before Sebastian enters, poor Andrew comes rushing in with his broken head, claiming that seemingly cowardly Cesario has turned out to be 'the very devil incardinate' (V, i, 182-3). He surely means 'incarnate' but 'incardinate' is happier than he knows, since it would mean 'without number' (a point made by William Carroll), which fits someone who is apparently both one and two, and, as a 'eunuch', nought – hence, no 'cardinal' number will serve. With reference to 'incarnate', commentators sometimes make the point that Twelfth Night marked the Eve of Epiphany, which saw the announcement of another yet more mysterious incarnation. This might seem a little far-fetched, were it not for Sebastian's strange response when Viola accuses him of being the spirit of her dead brother.

> A spirit I am indeed,
> But am in that dimension grossly clad
> Which from the womb I did participate.
>
> (V, i, 236-8)

It is a strange way of saying, I am still a body; but the somewhat hieratic turn of phrase does indeed invoke a reminder of God putting on flesh – which is, I suppose, the ultimate two-in-one miracle. Certainly, the last scene of the play, while not in any way explicitly religious, should gradually be bathed in a sense of expanding wonder.

This wonder is connected with the sea – as it will increasingly be in Shakespeare's last plays. The sea is the unstable element of mutability and transformation; people crossing the sea often undergo strange sea-changes. On land, it can surge into people's metaphors. The play starts with Orsino asking for 'excess' of music, so that 'surfeiting,/The appetite may sicken and so die'. Shakespeare is to refer to 'the never-surfeited sea' (*The Tempest* III, iii, 55), and it is not surprising

that Orsino's melancholy insatiability turns his thoughts
seawards.

> O spirit of love, how quick and fresh art thou,
> That, notwithstanding thy capacity,
> Receiveth as the sea. Nought enters there,
> Of what validity and pitch soe'er,
> But falls into abatement and low price
> Even in a minute.
>
> (I, i, 9-14)

He is both right, and very wrong. The sea drowns, but it can
also save and renew. As the very next scene reveals, Viola
'entered' the sea, was wrecked, but has been 'saved'; and, so
far from falling into 'abatement and low price', will bring
some much-needed quickness and freshness to stagnating
Illyria. She thinks her brother drowned, though the Captain
last saw him holding 'acquaintance with the waves', riding
them 'like Arion on the dolphin's back' (I, ii, 15). The
dolphin, famously, shows his back above the element he lives
in (see *Antony and Cleopatra* V, ii, 89-90). Feste, making a
contemporary joke of it, says to Viola–Cesario 'Who you are
and what you would are out of my welkin; I might say
"element," but the word is overworn' (III, i, 58-60). But he is
right; fresh-from-the-sea Viola effectively comes from another
element (as does her brother, Sebastian, who, we will learn,
was 'redeemed' from 'the rude sea's enraged and foamy
mouth', V, i, 78. The sister 'saved', the brother 'redeemed' –
the words are, surely, not idly chosen.) ('I am not of your
element' says Malvolio to, really, everyone, III, iv, 130, and
that's true, too – he is in a bleak, unpeopled, self-incarcerating
element of his own making – imaged by the darkened room in
which he is imprisoned to cure his 'madness'.) Sea-going
touches everyone's speech: 'she is the list of my voyage' (III, i,
77-8); 'you are now sailed into the North of my lady's opinion'
(III, ii, 26-7); 'board her, woo her, assail her' (I, iii, 56); 'Will
you hoist sail, sir? ... No ... I am to hull here a little longer' (I,
v, 201-3). There are also Olivia's copious tears, which we hear
about before we see her – 'she will veilèd walk,/And water
once a day her chamber round/With eye-offending brine'

(I, i, 29–31), 'brine' serving to bring the sea into the house. Sebastian also weeps for a lost sibling – 'She is drowned already, sir, with salt water, though I seem to drown her remembrance again with more' (II, i, 30–32). Even land-locked Sir Toby is like a 'drowned' man when he is 'in the third degree of drink' (I, v, 134–5). The play is, as it were, awash with liquidity. Viola, we recall, started out as 'standing water'. And it is her words on learning of the possible salvation of her brother which, above all, determine the atmosphere at the end of the play.

> O, if it prove,
> Tempests are kind, and salt waves fresh in love!
>
> (III, iv, 395–6)

That is probably the most defining sentence in Shakespearian comedy: salt becomes fresh; wreckage generates love; the world turns kind. Briney blessings. (See Introduction to *Comedies* Volume 1.)

Something of this prevailing liquidity reflects a certain incipient uncertainty and instability in the identities and emotions of some of the characters. The Duke is, by all accounts including his own, very labile. Feste, with the clown's licence, tells him as much to his face. He minces his words, ironically, with what sounds like elaborate nonsense; but the truth is all there.

Now the melancholy god protect thee, and the tailor make thy doublet of changeable taffeta, for thy mind is a very opal. I would have men of such constancy put to sea, that their business might be everything, and their intent everywhere; for that's it that always makes a good voyage of nothing.

> (II, iv, 73–8)

Shot-silk and the opal both change colour endlessly according to light and movement – the Duke is, to all intents and purposes, permanently tossing about on the waves, or, as Shakespeare will later, breathtakingly, put it, 'lackeying the varying tide' (*Antony and Cleopatra* I, iv, 46). Feste has his man. Up to a point, the Duke concedes as much. He generalizes to Cesario:

> Our fancies are more giddy and unfirm,
> More longing, wavering, sooner lost and worn,
> Than women's are.
>
> (II, iv, 33-5)

Of himself he claims:

> For such as I am all true lovers are,
> Unstaid and skittish in all motions else
> Save in the constant image of the creature
> That is beloved.
>
> (II, iv, 17-20)

To define true constancy turns out to be one of the concerns of the play. Claiming that his passion is greater than any woman could feel – because their hearts 'lack retention' – he again, revealingly and inappropriately, invokes the sea:

> But mine is all as hungry as the sea
> And can digest as much. Make no compare
> Between that love a woman can bear me
> And that I owe Olivia.
>
> (II, iv, 101-4)

The sea is his image for unsatisfiability; it is also the world's image for inconstancy. As is now familiar from Shakespeare's comedies, it is the woman who will show 'retention'.

Ironically, Orsino exhorts Cesario to an immovable constancy – on his behalf:

> Be not denied access, stand at her doors,
> And tell them there thy fixèd foot shall grow
> Till thou have audience.
>
> (I, iv, 16-18)

Viola obeys him – pretty literally, according to Malvolio:

he says he'll stand at your door like a sheriff's post, and be the supporter to a bench, but he'll speak with you.

> (I, v, 146-8)

To be as fixed as a post and as stiff as a bench-leg is, certainly, one kind of constancy, and we may say of Viola that she holds her ground (except when it comes to dùelling). But, clearly, there is constancy and constancy. There is this little exchange

in the last Act before things have started to sort themselves
out.

> *Duke.* Still so cruel?
> *Olivia.* Still so constant, lord.
> *Duke.* What, to perverseness?

> (V, i, 110-12)

There is such a thing as bad constancy – as, for instance, in the
extreme case of Malvolio. Now *there's* someone who really is as
stiff as a post. He manifests just that inflexibility and intracta-
bility, that refusal to change, which always shows itself as a
negative feature in Shakespeare's comedies. But then, opal-
headed fickleness and shot-silk variability are not exactly, in
and of themselves, positive virtues. Here again, we see Shakespeare interested in trying to identify the best combination of
openness to change and aptness for commitment, adaptation
and 'retention', yielding and holding fast, flexibility and
stability. Orsino and Olivia, initially at least, certainly don't
have it; they are both constant to their chosen 'perverseness'.
It is Viola who best shows it – the nimblest of shape-shifters,
not to say gender-crossers, who yet remains absolutely steadfast and loyal.

In this connection, another piece of advice, or rather
another order, which Orsino gives his nuncio, Cesario, points
to larger issues – 'Be clamorous and leap all civil bounds' (I, iv,
21). In the immediately preceding scene, we have just heard
Maria advise Sir Toby 'Ay, but you must confine yourself
within the modest limits of order' (I, iii, 8-9), and we have
seen Sir Andrew literally dancing and leaping his way out at
the end of the scene, at Sir Toby's incitement: 'Let me see thee
caper. Ha, higher; ha, ha, excellent!' (I, iii, 137-8). As often
happens in Shakespearian comedy, the characters messing
around below stairs offer, unintentionally of course, a crude
and literal parody of things going on metaphorically at the
higher, courtly level. Viola has already made a great leap
across the gender gap; she thereby certainly does *not* keep
'within the modest limits of order' as far as the prescribed
behaviour for women was concerned; and, speaking as a
humble, abject messenger to a great lady, her sometimes tart

and independent (though always courteous) remarks to Olivia could sometimes be said to 'leap all civil bounds', at least to the eye of convention.

In this connection, it is worth considering something said by Sebastian in *his* first scene on the sea-coast. Whither are you 'bound', asks the life-saving and already devoted Antonio? Sebastian has no plans, directions, or aims. 'My determinate voyage is mere extravagancy' (II, i, 11–12). 'Extravagancy' means 'wandering', but there is more in the word than that. As, much later, the American writer Thoreau realized: 'I fear chiefly lest my expression may not be *extra-vagant* enough – may not wander far enough beyond the narrow limits of my daily experience, so as to be adequate to the truth of which I have been convinced. *Extra vagance!* it depends on how you are yarded. The migrating buffalo, which seeks new pastures in another latitude, is not extravagant like the cow which kicks over the pail, leaps the cow-yard fence, and runs after her calf, in milking time. I desire to speak somewhere *without* bounds . . .' (*Walden* – Conclusion). Characters in Illyria strike one as being very 'yarded' indeed – house-bound in innutrient, self-devouring emotional states. The place is certainly in need of some extra-vagance. And Viola starts the play by, if I may so put it without offence, leaping over 'the cow-yard fence'. With the advent of the shipwrecked twins, 'extravagancy' has entered the country. Pails are duly kicked over, 'civil bounds' will be broken and transgressed. In her very first audience with Olivia, Viola–Cesario soon departs from the 'poetical' encomium which she has prepared. Instinctively, she starts speaking frankly to Olivia, then realizes 'But this is from my commission' (I, v, 187). When, perhaps on a woman's impulse, Viola asks to see her face, Olivia gently chides 'You are now out of your text' (I, v, 231–2), but complies anyway. Viola's refreshing sincerity is irresistible in the elegant but self-stultifying airlessness of Illyria. Viola must depart from her commission to bring about some requisite reinvigoration. She is certainly 'out of her text' in Illyria – indeed, she is out of her sex. She must, indeed, 'leap all civil bounds' – and textual ones. She will break free from conventional prescriptions. 'Yarding' fences need to be jumped in Illyria: Sir Toby's and

Sir Andrew's drunken caperings are amusing, but no good for the purpose. Viola will find the way. Sebastian has the way made for him.

When Olivia first sees Sebastian and, of course, thinks he is Cesario, she begs him into her house with endearing familiarity. Though quite uncomprehending, Sebastian – it is a point in his favour – accepts the invitation. We may say that he trustingly embraces his good fortune.

> What relish is in this? How runs the stream?
> Or I am mad, or else this is a dream.
> Let fancy still my sense in Lethe steep;
> If it be thus to dream, still let me sleep!
>
> (IV, i, 60-63)

'Relish' is nice: this, whatever it is, tastes good to Sebastian, and he is man enough to trust his senses. The 'stream' quickly turns into a 'flood' as Olivia showers gifts on him and hastens to hustle him to the altar. Given the prevailing watery imagery, we can justifiably say that Sebastian goes with the flow.

> And though 'tis wonder that enwraps me thus,
> Yet 'tis not madness.
> . . .
> For though my soul disputes well with my sense
> That this may be some error, but no madness,
> Yet doth this accident and flood of fortune
> So far exceed all instance, all discourse,
> That I am ready to distrust mine eyes
> And wrangle with my reason that persuades me
> To any other trust but that I am mad,
> Or else the lady's mad. Yet, if 'twere so,
> She could not sway her house, command her followers,
> Take and give back affairs and their dispatch
> With such a smooth, discreet, and stable bearing
> As I perceive she does. There's something in't
> That is deceivable. But here the lady comes.
>
> (IV, iii, 3-4, 9-21)

So she does; and with neither the chance nor the inclination to resist, he is off to church to be married.

There are observations to be made concerning this episode

which have relevance for the whole play. In the comparable incident in a work which Shakespeare certainly drew on for some plot details (*Riche his Farewell to Militarie Profession*, 1581), the lady, Julina, persuades the mistaken man, Silvio, not to church but to bed. He, knowing perfectly well that he is the sexual beneficiary of a case of mistaken identity, ungallantly skips town next morning, leaving the lady (a widow) embarrassingly pregnant. This apparently minor change in the direction of decorum makes one realize anew how very little actual sexual reference there is in a play which, when you think about it, offers virtually unlimited opportunity for almost every kind of heterosexual and homosexual allusion or innuendo (for instance, in most of the source narratives using the girl-dressed-as-page theme, the infatuated great lady invariably falls on him–her physically). Call it taste, call it what you like, but Shakespeare leaves the overt sex out – or, rather, he leaves it to take care of itself. The only bawdy, and it is very explicit, occurs in Olivia's putative letter to Malvolio – 'These be her very C's, her U's, and her T's, and thus makes she her great P's' (II, v, 87–9). Like our not dissimilar word, 'cut' was familiar slang for the female genitals, and P's speaks for itself. This manifest obscenity is there for a purpose. It is a measure of poor Sir Andrew's simplicity that he doesn't understand ('Her C's, her U's, and her T's? Why that?' You may be sure the audience laughed at that!); just as it is a measure of Malvolio's blind self-infatuation that he does not notice. He is too busy 'crushing' the more enigmatic 'M.O.A.I.' to form his own name. (Incidentally, O.A.I. occur in both Olivia and Viola which are, of course, effectively anagrams of each other; in which connection I like Leonard Barkan's comment that it is as if there is 'a kind of enigma of coalescing identity that hangs over the apparent frivolities of the play'.) No one is more interested in the whole man–woman business, and any ancillary swerving affective intensities, than Shakespeare, and he perfectly well appreciated the comedy (as well as the pathos) latent in misdirected sexual desires. But he eschewed the naming and showing of parts. Besides, he has a lot invested in the sanctity of marriage. (See the priest's speech starting 'A contract of eternal bond of love', V, i, 156–61.)

Sebastian mistaken by Olivia is a replay of Antipholus of Syracuse mistaken by Adriana, and anyone who has a memory of *The Comedy of Errors* will recognize how much *Twelfth Night* reworks situations and themes from that earlier, Plautine play. Like Antipholus, Sebastian doesn't know whether he is awake or dreaming, sane or mad, and, like him, he goes along with his unforeseen and inexplicable good fortune. Here a word might be said about 'madness' (and 'witchcraft', mentioned in both plays). The word 'mad' occurs more often in this play than in any other of Shakespeare's (twenty times). Just about everybody in Illyria is called 'mad' by one character or another, on one occasion or another. 'Are all the people mad?' cries an exasperated and non-comprehending Sebastian at one point (IV, i, 27), and this is the tone of the times. But most (not all) of the supposed 'madness' is simply the confusion caused by the 'extravagant' and unco-ordinated arrival in Illyria of identical twins unaware of each other's presence (it had the same effect in Ephesus in the earlier play, where the word 'mad' occurs seventeen times – second highest rate). True, Olivia says of her uncle Toby, 'He speaks nothing but madman' (I, v, 105–6), but that refers to his drunken burblings: Malvolio is conspiratorially locked up to 'cure' his stage-managed madness; but as he, rightly, claims – 'I am as well in my wits as any man in Illyria' (IV, ii, 109–10). How well that is, individual spectators may decide; but this play is decidedly not a study in lunacy and mental derangement. What Shakespeare is interested in here is the dramatic possibilities latent in the obvious comedy of mistaken identity. Profounder themes are touched on. Can we trust what we see, what we hear? Do we know who we are? Come to that, as we watch Viola–Cesario moving between lord and lady, do we know *what* we are? Questions of identity and self-knowledge are often rather tortuously engaged, as in the quotation set at the start of this introduction. When Feste engages with Sebastian, thinking of course that he is Cesario, he is brusquely rebuffed. Feste defends himself with heavy irony: 'No, I do not know you ... nor your name is not Master Cesario; nor this is not my nose neither. Nothing that is so is so' (IV, i, 5–9). This is still comedy; but take a turn into seriousness, and you could soon arrive at Macbeth's incipient mental malfunctioning in which 'nothing is/But what is not' (I, iii, 141-2). Frank Kermode calls *Twelfth Night* 'a comedy of identity, set on the borders of wonder and madness'. As he invariably does, he has caught the mood of the play. But we might remember Sebastian's judgement – 'though 'tis wonder that enwraps me thus/Yet 'tis not madness'. As I said, this is still comedy, and wonder prevails. Real madness must wait for the tragedies (and not wait long; *Hamlet* was, almost certainly, Shakespeare's next play – 'to define true madness,/What is't but to be nothing else but mad?', Polonius tautologously raises the big question, II, ii, 93-4).

Prior to the arrival of Viola and Sebastian, life in Illyria seems to adhere to a very fixed, repetitive text – Orsino swoons, Olivia weeps, Sir Toby drinks. Nothing changes. So it goes. The twins bring with them, though they cannot know it, the germ of a new life – the galvanizing disease of love. Not for the first time in Shakespeare's comedies, this is exactly the image used. Thus Olivia's reaction after her first encounter with Viola–Cesario:

> How now?
> Even so quickly may one catch the plague?
> Methinks I feel this youth's perfections
> With an invisible and subtle stealth
> To creep in at mine eyes. Well, let it be.
>
> (I, v, 295-9)

Among other things, this gives a premonitory edge to the first words spoken by Sir Toby, two scenes previously:

What a plague means my niece to take the death of her brother thus? I am sure care's an enemy to life.

(I, iii, 1-3 – my italics)

So it is: though to be completely care-less or care-free will not do either. Care, as we say, must be responsibly taken. Narcissists, too easily caring only for their own images, do not manage this. Which is why, paradoxically, the Illyrians need the disease of love – to get them out of their mirrors and into true

COMEDIES

relationships. This is the force behind Sebastian's reassuring
words to Olivia who, after all, has impulsively married herself
to a completely strange male.

> So comes it, lady, you have been mistook.
> But nature to her bias drew in that.
> You would have been contracted to a maid ...
>
> (V, i, 259-61)

This is a central Shakespearian belief: left to itself, nature goes
this way rather than that way. It is *biased* – towards dutiful
daughters, faithful wives, heterosexual marriages. But, of
course, humans do not leave nature to itself; they buck the
bias, and bring into play every kind of perverse swerving –
which is why we have Shakespearian drama; because you
cannot have five Acts of Desdemona and Cordelia rehearsing
the predictable texts of their fidelity. Well, you could; but it
wouldn't be drama. Surprised by love, Olivia makes another
striking comment:

> Fate, show thy force; ourselves we do not owe [=own].
> What is decreed must be – and be this so!
>
> (I, v, 311-12)

Ourselves we do not know; ourselves we do not own – these
could be said to be two of Shakespeare's central concerns as his
comedies deepen towards tragedy. It is difficult enough to
know yourself – myriad-minded Hamlet doesn't know what *a*
self might be; Othello? Lear? they fight self-knowledge until
almost the end. Macbeth knows himself all right; but what
about 'owning' yourself – knowing what you are going to do,
and why you are going to do it; being completely *responsible* for
your deeds? Even Macbeth falls down there, as probably we
all do. Self-possession is a crucially difficult matter. It is
perhaps no wonder that Olivia, thus early, relinquishes matters to the 'force' of 'Fate'; just as, two scenes later, Viola
hands things over to Time:

> O Time, thou must untangle this, not I;
> It is too hard a knot for me t' untie.
>
> (II, ii, 40-41)

This spirit of resignation to the solving or resolving forces of larger powers is more familiar from the tragedies. 'Well, let it be' says 'plague'-struck Olivia when Viola–Cesario leaves after their first conversation: 'Let be' says Hamlet, as he is about to submit to the final, poisoned, duel. What can you do? 'The readiness is all' – certainly; what both plays discover is that some people are readier than others. Comedy does not usually put down such deep feelers; and, indeed, Shakespeare is about to abandon the genre – even in this play, he is stretching it towards something else.

So what then, finally, of Shakespeare's Illyria? It is not Verona, or Messina, or Arden – not Windsor either, though one can imagine Sir Toby drinking with Falstaff at the Garter Inn. In Ovid, it is where shipwrecked Cadmus lands, not knowing that his daughter, Io, has been both saved and transformed. Bullough suggests that this vague place on a little-known coast allowed Shakespeare to mix Mediterranean romance plausibly with Northern realism (not that many Elizabethans would have known or cared, Illyria was on the coast of Yugoslavia – at this time of writing, unhappily more renowned for atrocity than romance). There is no alternative realm in this play – no forest, no Belmont; but there is a running contrast between the elegant, rather melancholy-mannered court of Orsino, where people speak verse (there is much rather Italianate talk of manners and courtesy); and the much more easy-going, belching, swigging, knock-about household of Olivia, where prose predominates (except when infatuation drives Olivia into poetry). The atmosphere at court seems dominated by music and melancholy, while over at Olivia's house there seems to be a permanent nocturnal drinking party. Maria is, certainly, 'as witty a piece of Eve's flesh as any in Illyria' (I, v, 27-8), and the joke she plays on Malvolio is perhaps the funniest thing in Shakespeare, no matter how often seen or read (at least, that is my experience). But there is a feeling that the revels have been going on for too long. There is no more revealing moment than when, having had 'sport royal' with Malvolio and fooled him 'black and blue', Sir Toby suddenly says to Maria 'I would we were well rid of this knavery' (IV, ii, 69-70). To use a chilling line of

Emily Dickinson's, 'the jest has crawled too far'. Laroque is perhaps too grim when he detects 'the boredom of a world grown old' and says that, here, 'festivity seems doomed to sterile, boring repetition. The veteran champions of festivity have become the pensioners of pleasure. The Puritans may be odious and malicious, but the old merrymakers are plain ridiculous.' This is, arguably, too censorious a view. But you see his point. There is something pathetic about poor, exploited, Sir Andrew ('for many do call me fool', II, v, 82), and I have a good deal of sympathy with Dr Johnson's view that it is unfair to mock his 'natural fatuity'. Sir Toby, seen rather generously by Barber as 'gentlemanly liberty incarnate', is agreeable inasmuch as he is festively anti-Malvolio and pro-cakes and ale; but his unscrupulous abuse of Sir Andrew's mindlessly trusting gullibility is unattractive, and he reveals a brutally unpleasant side in his final exchange with him. They have both been wounded by Sebastian, and Sir Andrew, rather sweetly, says – 'I'll help you, Sir Toby, because we'll be dressed together'. Sir Toby's very unsweet response is:

Will you help – an ass-head and a coxcomb and a knave, a thin-faced knave, a gull?

(V, i, 205-7)

These are his last words to Sir Andrew, who is not heard from again. Not nice.

Assorted Illyrians, then, repeating fixed routines until they are disrupted into new life by the arrival of Viola and Sebastian from the sea. But Feste the clown seems to come from somewhere else again. Barber says 'the fool has been over the garden wall into some such world as the Vienna of *Measure for Measure*', and that feels right. He is not as bitter or cynical as Touchstone. He sings, he fools, he begs; he talks nonsense for tips. But you feel that he has seen a wider, darker world than the predominantly sunny Illyria. 'Anything that's mended is but patched; virtue that transgresses is but patched with sin, and sin that amends is but patched with virtue' (I, v, 45-8). You don't acquire that kind of shrewd, worldly knowingness by tippling with Sir Toby. When Olivia starts by saying 'Take the fool away' (I, v, 37), he nimbly turns the tables on her, saying 'Misprision in the highest degree. Lady, *cucullus non facit monachum*. That's as much to say as, I wear not motley in my brain' (I, v, 54-6). There is no taking away of this fool; he will be there to the very end, when, quite decisively, he has the last words. 'Misprision' is a good defining word for what is going on around him, for people are constantly mis-taking themselves or others. The cowl does not make the monk is his Latin tag; and he is anything but a fool in his brain. The male outfit does not make the man, either, as Viola will both learn and demonstrate. Just what people *do* wear in their brains is, of course, a matter of continuously increasing interest for Shakespeare. There is another glance at Viola–Cesario when Feste is persuaded to put on a gown and beard to play the curate, Sir Topas, and further madden Malvolio. 'Well, I'll put it on, and I will dissemble myself in't, and I would I were the first that ever dissembled in such a gown' (IV, ii, 4-6). Orsino, more correctly than he knows, says approvingly to his new page, Cesario – 'all is semblative a woman's part' (I, iv, 34). Viola later admits to Olivia that she is 'out of my part' (I, v, 177). What *is*, or should be, her 'part' – is she most herself when she is 'sembling', or when she is 'dissembling'? People are often not what they seem, and seldom just what they wear. Among other things, Feste serves to open up doors onto problems of identity.

He opens up words, too; or rather, he shows that they are infinitely malleable, and can be made to do anything. Anyone who can say, as he does to Malvolio concerning the dark room in which he is imprisoned – 'it hath bay windows transparent as barricadoes, and the clerestories toward the south north are as lustrous as ebony' (IV, ii, 37-9) – clearly has language completely at his disposal. He calls himself Olivia's 'corrupter of words' (III, i, 37), and inasmuch as he can seduce words into doing anything, break them up this way and that, it is an apt enough self-designation. It is Feste who provides one of the key images of the play when he remarks to Viola: 'To see this age! A sentence is but a chev'ril glove to a good wit. How quickly the wrong side may be turned outward! (III, i, 11-13). Quite a lot of things get turned inside out, or are reversed, in this play; just as there is 'midsummer madness' (III, iv, 58) in the depths of winter. Wandering between court and house, fooling and singing for a living but profoundly unattached, Feste can truly say – in this most liquid of plays – 'I am for all waters' (IV, ii, 65).

There is bad blood between him and Malvolio from the beginning, as you would expect between the humourless and vain would-be social climber and the professional anarch. Malvolio starts by sneering at Feste – 'Unless you laugh and minister occasion to him, he is gagged' (I, v, 86–7). Malvolio sounds an uncomfortably discordant tone in Illyria, rather as Shylock does in Venice. There are, indeed, similarities between these two figures (I have seen it suggested that, in his depiction of the sober but unpleasantly grasping Jew, Shakespeare was actually aiming at the figure of the contemporary Puritan businessman). Whether or not Malvolio is a Puritan is hardly relevant. As Barber says of him, he is more of a businessman who 'would like to be a rising man, and to rise he *uses* sobriety and morality'. It is curious that Shakespeare allows the releasing of 'THE MADLY USED MALVOLIO' to occupy the last part of the play, while Viola stands silently by. Malvolio, of course, fills the traditional role of the kill-joy spoil-sport who is scapegoated out of the final happy ensemble. Though it has to be said that, compared with the flood of marriages which concludes *As You Like It*, this is a rather reduced and muted ending – with half the characters absent and the main hero and heroine completely silent. Feste gets his dig in to the infuriated Malvolio – 'And thus the whirligig of time brings in his revenges' (V, i, 378–9). Whether we think he has been 'most notoriously abused', or whether, with Fabian, we think his punishment – for his 'stubborn and uncourteous parts' – 'may rather pluck on laughter than revenge' (V, i, 368), will depend on individual weightings. He is certainly not the broken man that Shylock is, as he storms out crying 'I'll be revenged on the whole pack of you!' Indeed, we may take Barber's neat point: 'One could moralize the spectacle by observing that, in the long run, in the 1640s, Malvolio *was* revenged on the whole pack of them' (he is referring to the closure of the theatres by the Puritans).

For all the spreading wonderment in the last Act, we have a sense that this is comedy on the turn. There is that shockingly violent outburst from Orsino, when he thinks his Cesario has secretly married Olivia:

> But this your minion, whom I know you love,
> And whom, by heaven I swear, I tender dearly,
> Him will I tear out of that cruel eye
> Where he sits crownèd in his master's spite.
> Come, boy, with me. My thoughts are ripe in mischief.
> I'll sacrifice the lamb that I do love
> To spite a raven's heart within a dove.

(V, i, 125-31)

There is an ugly side to the man, for all the elegance of his court, and the refinement of his manners. A comparably ugly side is revealed to jolly Sir Toby, when he turns so unpleasantly on Sir Andrew. There is the strange silencing of Viola, as well as the unappeased fury of Malvolio. There is even that surgeon, who, when he is needed, it turns out has been drunk since eight in the morning – which sounds something more than festive. The Duke speaks of 'golden time' at the end (V, i, 384), but the glow is fading. Feste, clearly aware of life's rougher weather, ends the play with his song about the wind and the rain, with its reiterated reminder that 'the rain it raineth every day'. As a matter of fact, he leaves one verse out.

> He that has and a little tiny wit,
>   With heigh-ho, the wind and the rain,
> Must make content with his fortunes fit,
>   Though the rain it raineth every day.

But he, or someone very like him, will sing it to the truly mad King Lear, during conditions which are unimaginable in Illyria (*King Lear* III, ii, 74-7).

*

ALL'S WELL THAT ENDS WELL (1603)

Clown. O madam, yonder's my lord your son with a patch of velvet on's face; whether there be a scar under't or no, the velvet knows, but 'tis a goodly patch of velvet. His left cheek is a cheek of two pile and a half, but his right cheek is worn bare.

Lafew. A scar nobly got, or a noble scar, is a good liv'ry of honor; so
belike is that.
Clown. But it is your carbonadoed face.

(IV, v, 95–102)

The hero is home from the wars – or is he the villain? Half his
face is covered in velvet, but what is it concealing – a noble scar,
sign of honour; or the marks made by incisions made to drain
syphilitic ulcers, a wound of shame? Only the velvet knows. In
this, Bertram's face is rather like the play itself. Part of it is plain
and simple – a bare cheek; but part of it is covered in a thick pile
of velvet language, and it is not always clear what, exactly, is
going on. As if only the language knows. There is certainly not
much that is comic about the play; Barber excluded it from his
work, *Shakespeare's Festive Comedy*, on the well-justified grounds
that there is nothing festive in it. There is a clown; but he is 'a
shrewd knave and an unhappy' (IV, v, 64) – 'shrewd' here
meaning 'bitter', an apt word for the mood of much of the play.
The Clown suggests that Parolles contributes to 'the world's
pleasure and the increase of laughter' (II, iv, 37), and Parolles
himself is tricked 'for the love of laughter', said twice (III, vi, 34
and 41). But the words are curiously hollow: while there may
be the occasional rictus, sign of incipient mirth, here true
laughter dies on the lips. The play as a whole better fits Mark
Twain's definition of a German joke – 'no laughing matter'. It
is fairly obviously from the same hand which (almost certainly)
had recently written *Troilus and Cressida* and *Hamlet*, and
Shakespeare is opening up strange territories for his own
purposes. The play leaves us with residual uncertainties –
undecidabilities; as if we never are to learn *exactly* what has been
going on under the velvet. But one thing is certain and clear.
Shakespeare has taken something very simple and transformed
it into something very complicated.

The simple story on which he based his play is in Boccaccio's
Decameron (Day III, story ix), effectively translated by William
Painter in *The Palace of Pleasure* (published in 1566 and 1575) –
a work which Shakespeare certainly knew. This tale brings
together two themes familiar from folk or fairy tales – these are
usually called 'the sick king' (whose apparently incurable
ailing affects the whole kingdom); and 'the impossible tasks'

(usually set for a woman before she can gain her beloved). The tale also avails itself of the 'bed trick' (or 'substitute coupling') which was curiously popular in Shakespeare's time (apparently, over twenty contemporary plays make use of it). It is a short, direct, unambiguous tale – all situation, complication, and resolution. It is enacted by what Muriel Bradbrook called 'shrewd unsentimental vigorous Italians', without a whiff of psychological probing. Here is Painter's summary of the little 'Novel'.

Giletta a Phisition's doughter of Narbon, healed the French King of a Fistula, for reward whereof she demaunded Beltramo Counte of Rossiglione to husband. The Counte being married against his will, for despite fled to Florence, and loved another. Giletta his wife, by pollicie founds means to lye with her husbande, in place of his lover, and was begotten with childe of two sonnes: which knowen to her husband, he received her againe, and afterwards he lived in great honour and felicitie.

There it is. A sick king, a reluctant courtier, a clever wife; one, two, three – six pages, and the tale is told. The figures are types; there is no characterization or individuation, never mind complex psychological motivation. Shakespeare changes all that, completely transforming the romance atmosphere and environment, bringing the whole story out of the remote distance of folk tale into all sorts of troubling proximities, and introducing all manner of proliferations, circumlocutions and complications. Indeed, what he did with his simple source is a wonder.

Let us just consider some of the additions and changes he made in substantive matters of character and plot. He gives Bertram a mother, the Countess of Rousillon, a maternal figure of the utmost sweetness and compassionate concern ('the most beautiful old woman's part ever written', according to George Bernard Shaw). He gives her a companion in her palace, Lafew, 'an old lord'. Together, these two wise and good patricians stand for, and embody, the moral standards and high good manners of an older, and nobler, order, which was generous, seemly and fair – almost, one feels, an *ancien régime* of feudal honour, graciousness and courtesy, which is giving way to a cruder, coarser, less principled generation (it is sometimes remarked that all the virtuous characters at court in this play turn out to be elderly). The play starts in an autumnal register, with two noble fathers lately dead, and a king seemingly sickening unto death – and it can hardly be said to move towards a springtime of regeneration.

The best, we feel, is past. The sick king remembers the words of one of his now-dead friends:

> 'Let me not live,' quoth he,
> 'After my flame lacks oil, to be the snuff
> Of younger spirits, whose apprehensive senses
> All but new things disdain; whose judgments are
> Mere fathers of their garments; whose constancies
> Expire before their fashions.'

> (I, ii, 58–63)

We have heard much of garments and fashions in the comedies, and of the besetting problems of changeableness and constancy. For this play, Shakespeare brings on a character who is, effectively, composed *entirely* of garments and inconstancies, with speech to match. I will come back to this extraordinary creation – Parolles; suffice it here to say that in his cavalier rejection of court values (of *all* values), he is not to be mistaken for a Falstaff or a Shylock. In their extremely corporeal presence, these two men embody and inhabit a world outside of, if adjacent to, the official citadels of the constituted authorities. Perhaps they *have* to be vanquished, marginalized, or extruded; but they have an undeniable, potentially damaging and threatening, reality. None of this applies to Parolles – he is something new in Shakespeare. There is a story by Edgar Allan Poe called 'The Man Who Was Used Up', concerning a flashy, fashionable socialite. The narrator goes to visit him at his private address, during the daytime. On being admitted to his room, all he can see is a little heap of clothes on the floor. The heap begins to assemble itself, with the aid of all sorts of artificial devices, into the recognizable fashionable figure who haunts the evening salons. But the narrator has seen what there really is to the man. There is something of this about Parolles; though it should be stressed that even when he seems most washed-up, he is never, ever, 'used up'. There is nothing to him – but he is inextinguishable.

If Bertram is representative of the 'younger spirits' poised to take over, then we may well sympathize with the sick king's wish to be 'quickly ... dissolved from my hive' (I, ii, 66). This Bertram is not going to bring any honey home (syphilis is more likely). It is notable that Shakespeare makes Bertram plunge himself far deeper into ignominy and disgrace than does his original, compounding his dishonesty and treachery in the perversely protracted fifth Act. Shakespeare certainly seems to want to make Bertram blacker than black, with *no* extenuations. (The proposition, sometimes advanced, that the simple young lad is seduced and led astray by the demon, Parolles, won't do. Even if accepted, it would only make Bertram even more stupid and corruptible than he already appears. But Bertram is his own man. It just happens that it is a particularly rotten sort of man to be.) Whether, by the same token, Shakespeare wants to make Helena appear whiter than white, is a more complex and interesting question, here deferred. We may, however, note that Shakespeare increases the social distance between Bertram and Helena – in the original, Helena is independently wealthy and much closer to being Bertram's equal. Whether this goes any way towards helping to explain her adoration or his revulsion, must be left to individual response (for me it doesn't, but I can see that for some it might).

It will come as no surprise to anyone even slightly familiar with Shakespeare's treatment of his sources to learn that he markedly compressed the more leisurely time-scheme of the original. But it is worth drawing attention to one particular result of this contraction. In the original, Giletta (the Helena figure), having arranged the 'bed trick' with her husband, repeats it 'manye other times so secretly, as it was never knowen'. She not only conceives, but is delivered of, 'two goodly sonnes' which 'were very like unto their father'. When she produces the two sons at the final revelatory feast, Beltramo (Bertram) accepts the children as his – 'they were so like hym' – and 'abjected his obstinate rigour'. In Shakespeare's play, the contrived illicit/licit bedding is a one-night-only affair; and when Helena *finally* confronts Bertram with 'evidence' of his paternity of her child in the final scene, she is – pregnant. Without pushing the matter too pointlessly far, there is surely a signal difference between confronting a man with two bouncing baby boys who are his spitting image, and standing, visibly pregnant, in front of him and asserting that you are carrying his child. Paternity is notoriously difficult to establish incontrovertibly, and this seemingly slight plot change is characteristic of the widespread introduction of uncertainty – or the draining or diffusing away of certainty – which marks this play. All you can feel at the end is that it is, indeed, a conclusion 'pregnant' with possibilities. We cannot possibly see which way things will turn out – what, if you like, is waiting to be born.

I have mentioned that Shakespeare added a clown – given, deliberately as one supposes, the rather unpleasant name of Lavatch. His is a sneering, bawdy, nihilistic voice; and as a figure he is closer to Thersites than to Touchstone and Feste. We are a long way from Arden and Illyria. The other figures to be added by Shakespeare are some French captains and Florentine soldiers. This is more interesting than it perhaps sounds, and pursuing the matter a little further may provide us with an oblique approach to the strangeness of this play. In Boccaccio's little story, the unwilling Beltramo, having been virtually forced into marrying Giletta, pretends to be return- ing home but immediately takes flight into Italy. This is what we are told. 'And when he was on horseback hee went not thither but took his journey into Tuscane, where under- standing that the Florentines and Senois were at warres, he determined to take the Florentines parte, and was willingly received and honourablie entertained, and was made captaine of a certain nomber of men, continuing in their service a long time.' And that is all we hear about the wars, and Beltramo's soldiering. See how Shakespeare elaborates and complicates it.

> *King.* The Florentines and Senoys are by th' ears,
> Have fought with equal fortune, and continue
> A braving war.
> *First Lord.*　　　So 'tis reported, sir.
> *King.* Nay, 'tis most credible. We here receive it
> A certainty, vouched from our cousin Austria,

> With caution, that the Florentine will move us
> For speedy aid; wherein our dearest friend
> Prejudicates the business, and would seem
> To have us make denial.
> *First Lord.*   His love and wisdom,
> Approved so to your Majesty, may plead
> For amplest credence.
> *King.*   He hath armed our answer,
> And Florence is denied before he comes;
> Yet, for our gentlemen that mean to see
> The Tuscan service, freely have they leave
> To stand on either part.
>
> (I, ii, 1–14)

The Florentines were fighting the Sienese (Senoys) in Boccaccio, but what is Austria doing here, which was, anyway, in no sense France's 'dearest friend'? Be that as it may – Austria '*prejudicates* the business', a word Shakespeare uses nowhere else (this is not mere pedantry on my part – he forces a number of rather awkward and unusual words into service in *All's Well That Ends Well* which he does not use elsewhere; this is part of the thick velvet side of the play). But 'judicating' all round seems rather precarious and insecure in this play: though Austria apparently deserves 'amplest *credence*' (another rather formal 'silver' word, used only in this play and in *Troilus and Cressida*), and though the King vows he will deny Florence help – he then says he will let his men take whichever side they like. So much for the 'amplest credence' of 'our dearest friend'. A quite unnecessary scene; unless Shakespeare wants to show that, despite the high-sounding, sonorous language, loyalties and friendship are fading all round.

There is a comparably supererogatory-seeming scene somewhat later, in the Duke's palace in Florence.

> *Duke.* So that from point to point now have you heard
> The fundamental reasons of this war,
> Whose great decision hath much blood let forth,
> And more thirsts after.
> *First Lord.*   Holy seems the quarrel
> Upon your Grace's part; black and fearful
> On the opposer.
> *Duke.* Therefore we marvel much our cousin France

Would in so just a business shut his bosom
Against our borrowing prayers.
Second Lord.   Good my lord,
The reasons of our state I cannot yield,
But like a common and an outward man
That the great figure of a council frames
By *self-unable* motion; therefore dare not
Say what I think of it, since I have found
Myself in my incertain grounds to fail
As often as I guessed.

(III, i, 1–16 – my italics)

The quarrel between the holy and the black might certainly be said to be engaged by the confrontation of Helena and Bertram, but we are given no insight into the apparently elemental issues at stake in the war. In this, we are somewhat in the position of the Second Lord. It's easy enough to get the hang of what he says – I can't really tell you anything about our reasons of state because I am always outside the council chamber. I just have to make guesses and here I'm as wrong as often as I'm right. But he 'frames' his guesses by '*self-unable* motion'. Not only is this another word (or compound-word) that Shakespeare never uses elsewhere; my guess is that this is its only appearance in the whole of English literature. Obviously it refers to some kind, or degree, of incompetence or disability or just inability. But it is an unusual mouthful for a second lord. However we can readily respond to his feeling that he is in 'incertain grounds'. In this play, so are we.

In the event, Bertram and the other young French blades decide to fight for Florence; but not, we understand, from any feelings of siding with an honourable (or even holy) cause. Boredom seems to be one motive (they 'surfeit on their ease', III, i, 18); while Bertram has his own determinants.

This very day,
Great Mars, I put myself into thy file!
Make me but like my thoughts and I shall prove
A lover of thy drum, hater of love.

(III, iii, 8–11)

The word 'drum' does not appear in the translation of Boccaccio's tale; it occurs more often in this play than in any other by Shakespeare. Such a foregrounding of the 'drum' might seem to suggest that Shakespeare wants to invoke the martial and heroic values – perhaps to set up a tension between the masculine claims and appeal of Mars against the feminine enticements and allure of Venus. This could make for a perfectly good drama (there is something of it in *Antony and Cleopatra*), but it is not the case in this curiously skewed play. The next voiced concern about the drum comes from Parolles, as the Florentine army re-enters the city, presumably return-ing from battle. 'Lose our drum! Well' (III, v, 87). It is his only line in the scene. Now, it was well known that for a regiment to lose its drum (which bore the regimental colours) was some form of ultimate military disgrace. But here, it appears that *only* Parolles cares about the loss. The general attitude of the soldiers is expressed by that Second Lord, speaking, as it were, without velvet. 'A pox on't, let it go, 'tis but a drum' (III, vi, 46). As though only he feels the dishonour, Parolles grandiloquently vows to recover the lost drum. But if empty, say-anything-noisy, Parolles is the only voice speaking up for traditional notions of honour, then one has to feel that the old values are in a parlous state. In the event, his vainglorious boast that he will go and reclaim the drum is used by the other drum-indifferent officers to trick Parolles and catch him out in all his hypocrisies, mendacities, treacheries, betrayals, cowardices, and whatever else of abject baseness a man is capable of. Parolles is caught out all right; but whatever military dignity and honour may have been associated with the drum is entirely sullied and degraded by its being the central point in this farcical exposure of the least brave and heroic of men. But truly, no one here gives a damn about 'the drum' and whatever traditions of valour and honour it may symbolize.

Parolles, the manifestly pseudo courtier and soldier, a 'counterfeit module' (IV, iii, 104), a creature of 'scarves' (military sashes) and 'bannerets' is, variously and then com-prehensively, seen through, 'smoked' (III, vi, 106), and 'found' out (III, vi, 95; V, ii, 46). This, it should be noted, is exactly what happens to the one man willing to believe in him and accept him as a companion, if not a guide – Bertram.

Where Parolles is literally blindfolded and bamboozled and frightened into revealing the extent of his utter cowardice, Bertram is more subtly and elaborately hoodwinked before his final, devastating, unmasking. Not for the first time in Shakespeare, the sub-plot parodies the main one, with worrying, undermining consequences. It becomes something of a question to what extent Parolles and Bertram (for all his true blue blood) might not be two of a kind. But where Bertram, for the most part, seems to alternate between sullen aphasia and a crude or cloddish manner of speaking (Helena is 'my clog' – II, v, 55), Parolles, as his name suggests, has any number of words at his disposal. And as we listen to his facile, improvising, opportunistic, unprincipled loquaciousness, we realize that this is a new voice in Shakespeare.

Nadia Fusini has suggested that Parolles is related to the *picaro* (= rogue, scoundrel) figure who was emerging in Spanish fiction (and probably in European cities) in the second half of the sixteenth century (the first 'picaresque' novel is usually taken to be the anonymous *Lazarillo de Tormes*, 1554). The *picaro* is a deracinated, lower-class figure (an orphan, a discharged servant, some piece of social flotsam), with no family, belonging nowhere, owning nothing, who moves on, takes whatever is going, and lives by his wits. He has no aims, ambitions, or goals – or rather, he has one: survival. In the form of Parolles – I think Nadia Fusini is right – he has found his way onto the Shakespearian stage. Wise old Lafew sees him for what he is from the start – not deserving the title of 'man'. 'Yet art thou good for nothing but taking up, and that thou'rt scarce worth' (II, iii, 208–9). For Lafew, Parolles is totally transparent: 'thy casement I need not open, for I look through thee. Give me thy hand' (II, iii, 215–16). (I would just note that this sort of quite unanticipated shift of tone – you're obviously a total fraud; shake hands – occurs quite often. Having promised to deny Florence any help, the King immediately says his men can fight for whom they like; similarly, in the last scene, when Bertram offers an incredibly contorted and implausible explanation of his conduct, the King says 'Well excused' and then goes on to describe the excuse as totally inadequate – V, iii, 55–72. That somewhat unnerving,

unpredictable discontinuity of response is another characteristic of this strange play.)

But Parolles really reveals himself in the episode of his
supposed attempt heroically to recapture the lost drum. He
quickly realizes he has made a boast he cannot possibly carry
out, and he turns on – his own tongue. 'I find my tongue is too
foolhardy ... Tongue, I must put you into a butter-woman's
mouth, and buy myself another of Bajazet's mule if you prattle
me into these perils' (IV, i, 29-30, 42-4). Iago calculates every
cutting, killing word – Parolles will simply say anything if he
thinks it might please or impress on a particular occasion. We
have the expression – his tongue ran away with him; Parolles is
a cautionary example of the vagabond tongue which will
stray, roam, run, rush anywhere – because his utterance is not
rooted in, or motivated by, anything except an instinct to
smooth, mollify, and get by. It duly 'prattles him into perils'.
And when he thinks he has been captured by foreign enemies
(it is apt that he is completely taken in by figures gabbling
actual nonsensical gibberish – in a play in which quite a lot of
the speech moves towards the edges of comprehensibility),
Parolles reveals, as it were, his true colours: 'Let me live, sir, in
a dungon, i' th' stocks, or anywhere, so I may live' (IV, iii,
256-8). It is the eternal cry of the *picaro*. It is not surprising
that he adds, in an aside: 'I'll no more drumming. A plague of
all drums!' (IV, iii, 312-13).

But he attains his zenith, or nadir – hard to say which –
when, after his stream of betrayal and calumny of everything
and everyone, his fellow officers 'unmuffle' him, and he stands
exposed in what you might think was the last degree of
ignominy. His reaction? 'Who cannot be crushed with a plot?'
(IV, iii, 340). There is no other line quite like this in the whole
of Shakespeare. To be sure, Falstaff dusts himself off fairly
breezily after he realizes he has been made 'an ass' in *Merry
Wives*. But his attitude is more resigned – you win some, you
lose some, and as you get older you lose more. But Parolles is
another creature entirely. It is not that he is beyond shame.
He has clearly never known what shame is – or guilt, or
morality, or principle, or loyalty, or anything else by which
society has tried to bind, and bond, and dignify itself. He is

not, certainly not, *evil*. He is nothing at all. But there he breathingly is, demanding to live. His soliloquy, after his fellow officers leave him alone with his disgrace, is uttered, one feels, with a certain placidity and peace of mind, and is in some way definitive:

> Yet am I thankful. If my heart were great
> 'Twould burst at this. Captain I'll be no more,
> But I will eat and drink and sleep as soft
> As captain shall. Simply the thing I am
> Shall make me live. Who knows himself a braggart,
> Let him fear this; for it will come to pass
> That every braggart shall be found an ass.
> Rust, sword; cool, blushes; and Parolles live
> Safest in shame! Being fooled, by fool'ry thrive!
> There's place and means for every man alive.
> I'll after them.

> (IV, iii, 345-55)

If my heart were great – but it isn't, and that's that. 'Simply the thing I am shall make me live' – it is a far cry from Richard's 'I am myself alone'. It is the difference between heroic, overreaching Renaissance individualism, and an impoverished cluster of the most basic appetites. With Parolles, we could join the mean streets of the twentieth-century city. But he won't die, and you won't shake him off – 'I'll after them.' This is the point of his final exchange with Lafew (who can't resist teasing him – 'How does your drum?'). Parolles is a suppliant: 'It lies in you, my lord, to bring me in some grace, for you did bring me out' (V, ii, 49-50). (Bertram will also, shortly, need someone to bring him in some grace.) Lafew at first responds chidingly: 'Out upon thee, knave! Dost thou put upon me at once both the office of God and the devil? One brings thee in grace and the other brings thee out.' (Again, a larger theme is glanced at – do, can, humans take on the office of God, and the devil?) But he concludes compassionately: 'Sirrah, inquire further after me. I had talk of you last night; though you are a fool and a knave you shall eat. Go to, follow' (V, ii, 51-7). This is part of the final muted mood of this curious 'comedy'; not, certainly, festive – but nobody, not even the fools and knaves, will starve.

INTRODUCTION

The most succinct comment on Parolles comes from a lord who overhears some of his shameless self-communings (if nothing else, Parolles knows himself clearly and unself-deludingly enough) – 'Is it possible he should know what he is, and be that he is?' (IV, i, 45–6). That is the wonder of the man. Not that he is a rogue (nothing new there); but that he seems oblivious to notions of roguery (no wallowing in villainy here, no determined embrace of evil) – he just doesn't care. It is a little frightening – ethical discourse would be meaningless to him; he is completely unreachable on such matters. Yet there he stands like the rest of us – a hungry human being. But meanwhile, during the Florentine military scenes, Bertram is acquitting himself even more dishonourably. The timing is nice – his fellow captains have set the trap for Parolles and promise Bertram some 'sport': 'When his disguise and he is parted, tell me what a sprat you shall find him' (III, vi, 107–8). (It will, of course, be only a matter of time before Bertram's 'disguise and he is parted' as well.) But Bertram first wants to pursue some other sport, with a local lass (Diana).

> *Second Lord.* But you say she's honest.
> *Bertram.* That's all the fault.
>
> (III, vi, 115–16)

Fault indeed, when a lass should be tiresomely 'honest': but whatever happened to the chivalric code, the courtier's code, the gentleman's code, all the codes? And the other captains see Bertram, what he is, as clearly as they see through Parolles.

> *Second Lord.* He hath perverted a young gentlewoman here in Florence, of a most chaste renown, and this night *he fleshes his will in the spoil of her honor*; he hath given her his monumental ring, and thinks himself made in the unchaste composition.
> *First Lord.* Now, God delay our rebellion! As we are ourselves, what things are we!
>
> (IV, iii, 15–21 – my italics)

The italicized words express a powerful, vehement disgust. This man is a disgrace – he is sunk in spoilt honour. And there is a curious half-echo of the recent comment on Parolles – 'Is it possible he should know what he is, and be that he is?': 'As we are ourselves, what things are we!' There is a scent here of a sort of weary incredulousness at just how awful humans can be, which lingers in the louring air of the play.

Bertram thinks he is buying Diana's body by giving her his 'monumental ring'. There is such a ring in the original tale; it is one of the wife's 'impossible' tasks to get it off her husband's finger. Shakespeare adds a second ring, which, among other things, allows for further complications and attenuations in the last scene (and, not incidentally, allows Bertram to double his ignominy). Rings (female) and drums (male) should symbolize some kind of honour, and Shakespeare brings both into the foreground of his play; not just to point up the always possible struggle between the ring and the drum (and all they stand for), but also to show them both sullied, devalued, degraded. The drum is simply a farcical factor in Parolles' disgrace. The 'monumental ring' should fare better: in Bertram's own words to Diana when, following instructions, she requests it:

> It is an honor 'longing to our house,
> Bequeathèd down from many ancestors,
> Which were the greatest obloquy i' th' world
> In me to lose.

To which Diana has an unanswerable reply:

> Mine honor's such a ring;
> My chastity's the jewel of our house,
> Bequeathèd down from many ancestors,
> Which were the greatest obloquy i' th' world
> In me to lose.

(IV, ii, 42–9)

So Bertram makes the 'unchaste composition' (bargain, arrangement): 'Here, take my ring./My house, mine honor, yea, my life be thine' (IV, ii, 51–2). As Helena predicted he would:

> a ring the County wears,
> That downward hath succeeded in his house

From son to son some four or five descents
Since the first father wore it. This ring he holds
In most rich choice; yet, in his idle fire,
To buy his will it would not seem too dear,
Howe'er repented after.

(III, vii, 22-8)

There is something rather awesomely biblical about 'the first father': cumulatively, it feels as if there were some ancient, even primal, virtue, as well as dynastic honour and paternal potency, mystically lodged in the ring. The more profane and sacrilegious, then, Bertram's easy surrendering it as part of a dirty deal – 'to buy his will' (lust). So much for the regimental drum; so much for the family ring. 'Obloquy' indeed ('obloquy' – to be everywhere spoken against: there is, indeed, nothing to be said *for* Bertram by the time Shakespeare has finished with him).

Helena also has something handed down to her by her father which she, by contrast, respects, preserves, and puts to beneficial use.

You know my father left me some prescriptions
Of rare and proved effects, such as his reading
And manifest experience had collected
For general sovereignty.

(I, iii, 223-6)

'General sovereignty' is a rather vague phrase which could mean 'universal supremacy' as well as, more specifically, master medicines which cure all. From the first scene, this now dead father is credited with having had strange, mysterious, almost miraculous powers; his 'skill was almost as great as his honesty; had it stretched so far, would have made nature immortal, and death should have play for lack of work' (I, i, 20-23). These mysterious powers – they become increasingly important in Shakespeare – seem to be in some sort religious, or more than mundane, though with no suggestions of any orthodox theology. Ruskin once said that Shakespeare's religion is 'occult behind his magnificent equity', and we will hardly find a better formulation. There are certainly sugges-

tions of 'occult' (concealed, hidden, secret) powers in this, as
in later plays; and, in the material form of his almost magical
prescriptions, Helena has inherited something of her father's
power which, we come to feel, is spiritual as well.

Trying to persuade the sceptical sick King to let her try to
cure him, she says that her father gave her one very special
'receipt' which 'He bade me store up as a triple eye,/Safer than
mine own two' (II, i, 110–11). Wilson Knight, who was much
drawn to such things, happily asserted that this was the
' "triple eye" of occult doctrine and practice – located on the
forehead, and used in spirit-healing as a source of powerful
rays'. Something of that, perhaps: but, as Philip Brockbank
pointed out, the 'triple' or third eye was most traditionally an
attribute of the goddess Prudentia; it was also a bawdy way
(common in Jacobean drama) of referring to virginity. This is
more to the point. Impoverished and orphaned Helena will
have to be nothing if not prudent if she is to make her way in
this increasingly ruthless society; and her virginity – traditionally associated with magic power – is indeed her most valuable
'receipt' which she will have to deploy with the utmost care
(and, in the event, deviousness).

The King, having experienced many failed attempts to
ameliorate his condition, is no longer 'credulous of cure',
adding that the 'most learnèd doctors ... have concluded':

> That laboring art can never ransom nature
> From her inaidable estate.

> (II, i, 120–21)

That one sentence covers a major part of the thrust of
Shakespeare's dramatic explorations – particularly the later
ones. To what extent *is* nature 'inaidable' (another strong,
angular word used solely this once by Shakespeare); and how
might 'laboring art' (medicine–drama) in some way 'ransom'
it? In the event, the King submits to Helena, and proves to be
'aidable' through her, paternally-derived, 'laboring art'. He is
cured, and the reactions to this apparent miracle are notable
(Bertram, typically, has no significant reaction at all and stays
sullen-dumb). For Lafew, it justifies the faith of an older
world:

They say miracles are past, and we have our philosophical persons, to make modern and familiar, things supernatural and causeless. Hence it is that we make trifles of terrors, ensconcing ourselves into seeming knowledge, when we should submit ourselves to an unknown fear.

(II, iii, 1–6)

When Ruskin compared his contemporary, faithless, complacent Victorians, with the pious Venetians of the Middle Ages, he saw a vast difference between 'the calculating, smiling, self-governed man, and the believing, weeping, wondering, struggling, Heaven-governed man'. Lafew feels something of this about the difference between his generation and Bertram's, and it is a deep concern of the play to what extent life, lives, might be said to be, in some way, 'Heaven-governed'. Lafew also reads from what must be a broadsheet ballad (such as would have been quickly produced to welcome the recovery of the King): 'A showing of a heavenly effect in an earthly actor' (II, iii, 24). One feels that it is somehow characteristic of Shakespeare to have ascribed what is, in effect, the most succinct description possible of the central action of the play, to an anonymous pamphlet. For we, as audience, are invited to watch seemingly 'heavenly effects' brought about by, or through 'earthly actors' (agents – but play-actors as well) – provoking us, perhaps, into peripheral ponderings about the larger relations between heaven and earth. But it is important always to bear in mind – in view of frequent attempts to sanctify and spiritualize her – that Helena is, unambiguously, an *earthly* actor.

But perhaps the most enthusiastic response to the miraculous cure comes from – Parolles. 'Why, 'tis the rarest argument of wonder that hath shot out in our latter times' (II, iii, 7–8). 'Shot out' is rather odd; one hardly knows whether he is thinking of comets or guns. But 'arguments of wonder' feature increasingly in Shakespeare's later comedies, and Parolles' comment is entirely fitting. But then he piles on the words, trying to match Lafew's more gravely measured expressions of awe. The 'very hand of heaven,' says Lafew; Parolles seeks to go one better – 'great power, great transcendence' (II, iii, 32–6). We must pause on that last word. Not only is it yet another word which Shakespeare uses only in this play; the OED gives it as the first example of its use in English! Wilson Knight wrote that 'what is remarkable in this play is the more near-distance, immediate and detailed, treatment of transcendence'. Now, clearly there are intimations of transcendence hovering intermittently around Helena. But Parolles is a man who devalues everything he embraces, sullies everything he speaks. It was Parolles, remember, who seemed to make the strongest plea on behalf of the honour of the regimental drum. So when he speaks up so positively for the recognition of 'transcendence' (I like to think of him as the first man in England to do so!), we are bound to wonder just how much weight and authentic content the word carries – or is meant to carry.

Nevertheless, Helena has attracted something more than admiration from the commentators. For Coleridge, she was 'Shakespeare's loveliest character'; Bullough finds her 'entirely good' (though not witty after the first scene); Wilson Knight, never one to modify his raptures, found her 'almost beyond the human ... almost a divine or poetic principle' – certainly a 'miracle worker', and 'a channel, or medium, of the divine, or cosmic powers'. She is, he says, 'the supreme development of Shakespeare's conception of feminine love'. Most find her 'a ministering angel' (healing the King); though some have regarded her use of the bed trick as rather odiously manipulative. Clearly she is the central character (though Charles I apparently found Parolles the chief attraction!), and the whole play revolves and evolves around her. And she is various. Angelic she may be; but she certainly wants to go to bed with Bertram. As the anonymous ballad unambiguously reminds us, she is an '*earthly* actor'. And the first Act reveals that she certainly commands a number of different styles and voices – at least three – and we will start there.

Her first words are something of a quibble – 'I do affect a sorrow indeed, but I have it too' (I, i, 57) – suggesting that she is aware that the emotions you show are not always in synchrony with the emotions you feel. Her first soliloquy starts, rather strikingly, with the admission that paternal veneration has been somewhat dislodged – 'I think not on my father':

> I have forgot him; my imagination
> Carries no favor in't but Bertram's.
>
> (I, i, 85-9)

But, she realizes, doting on him is like loving a 'star' (there are lots of stars in this play), 'he is so above me', she is 'not in his sphere' (I, i, 92-5). Since he has left for Paris, all she can do, she rather extravagantly says, is 'my idolatrous fancy/Must sanctify his relics', as if to turn desire into hagiolatry. Then Bertram's friend Parolles enters, and Helena reacts:

> I love him for his sake,
> And yet I know him a notorious liar,
> Think him a great way fool, solely a coward...
>
> (I, i, 105-7)

– another example of the discontinuous – not to say contradictory – response I have already mentioned as being strangely characteristic of this play. Her tone then changes radically as she and Parolles engage in some extended, and fairly earthy, banter about 'virginity' – how to keep it; when best to lose it. At this point, seemingly irrelevant matters – yet they are to be central concerns of the play. Here, Helena speaks a tolerably tough sort of prose. 'Bless our poor virginity from underminers and blowers-up! Is there no military policy how virgins might blow up men?' (I, i, 126-8). 'Pollicie' was what Giletta employed to regain her husband, and it would be only a slight exaggeration to say that Helena rather satisfactorily 'blows up' Bertram by the end of the play. Parolles' response comes in the form of one of dozens of paradoxes and seeming oxymorons which bestrew the play. 'Virginity by being once lost may be ten times found; by being ever kept it is ever lost' (I, i, 136-8). More oxymorons follow when Helena imagines Bertram at court:

> His humble ambition, proud humility;
> His jarring, concord, and his discord, dulcet;
> His faith, his sweet disaster; with a world
> Of pretty, fond, *adoptious* christendoms
> That blinking Cupid gossips. Now shall he –
> I know not what he shall.
>
> (I, i, 178-83 – my italics)

She can't keep it up; and small wonder, since it is not at all clear what on earth she is talking about (I have italicized another word which only occurs in this play). Not for the last time, one has a sense of an over-ornate language taking over from the speakers and covering parts of the play in a thick, semi-incomprehensible, velvet.

When Parolles leaves, Helena, with an utterly different voice, shifts into rhymed couplets for a soliloquy full of that incantatory, apodictic confidence which is often generated by couplets in Shakespeare (it is with just such incantatory couplets that Helena will, effectively, mesmerize the initially sceptical King into trying her 'remedy' for him).

> Our remedies oft in ourselves do lie,
> Which we ascribe to heaven; the fated sky
> Gives us free scope; only doth backward pull
> Our slow designs when we ourselves are dull.
> What power is it which mounts my love so high,
> That makes me see, and cannot feed mine eye?
> The mightiest space in fortune nature brings
> To join like likes, and kiss like native things.
>
> (I, i, 223–30)

Helena here sees and speaks with what we might indeed call almost occult clarity. We *do* have some 'free scope', though living under a 'fated sky' – Helena is recognizing the reality and force of free will in a world of everywhere more powerful influences. Whatever power it is that makes her yearn for Bertram – call it what you like; spiritual, carnal – its strength cannot be denied, even if it unacceptably transgresses an all but sacrosanct class barrier. And, yes – nature can join what fortune seems to have placed far apart (the debate about their respective powers is joined again). Helena is clearing her ground for action – already thinking about going to Paris to cure the King:

> my project may deceive me,
> But my intents are fixed, and will not leave me.
>
> (I, i, 235–6)

It is the first scene, and Helena has already started to plot.

There follows an interview with Bertram's mother, the

Countess, and Helena reverts to blank verse for a mode of speaking marked by ellipsis, ambiguity and cicumlocution. Before the interview, there is an exchange – preparatory as one comes to feel – between the Countess and the Clown, in which the Countess asks the Clown why he wants to get married. 'My poor body, madam, requires it' and 'I have other holy reasons, such as they are' (I, iii, 28, 32). It is generally thought that, this Clown being as he is, 'holy' is probably a bawdy pun, perhaps 'reasons' (raisings), too. It is tolerably clear that Helena's body 'requires' Bertram; the question will be – how unobscenely 'holy' are her other reasons? The Steward then tells the Countess that he has heard Helena soliloquizing about her love for Bertram. The reaction of the Countess – to herself – is one of profound understanding:

> Even so it was with me, when I was young;
> If ever we are nature's, these are ours; this thorn
> Doth to our rose of youth rightly belong;
> Our blood to us, this to our blood is born.
> It is the show and seal of nature's truth.
>
> (I, iii, 130–34)

I find it almost touching that the Arden editor thinks that 'these' (line two above) refers to 'situations'. They are, surely, importunate sexual desires, so thorningly and prickingly born in us. As Shakespeare here recognizes, with his own matchless directness, they come with our blood. Certainly we are 'nature's'; the question, here and always, is what we do about that ineluctable fact.

Confronted by the Countess, in a kindly enough manner, with the discovered fact of loving her son, Helena prevaricates and prevaricates, until the Countess is provoked to say – 'Go not about' (I, iii, 190). It is an injunction or imperative which could be issued to many other figures in this play, in which the dominant (though not exclusive) mode is, indeed, to 'go about' and about – to the point of provoking an irritated impatience in other characters and audience alike. It is a play in which, for the most part, directness is drowned, or relentlessly abjured; (in the interests of tolerance, we might, perhaps, remember John Donne's lines to the effect that 'he who truth would seek, about must and about must go'). Admitting the fact in her own baroque, or indeed Mannerist, way, Helena says:

> I know I love in vain, strive against hope;
> Yet, in this *captious and inteemable* sieve,
> I still pour in the waters of my love,
> And lack not to lose still. Thus, Indian-like,
> Religious in mine error, I adore
> The sun that looks upon his worshipper
> But knows of him no more.
>
> (I, iii, 203-9 – my italics)

'Love' as a 'sieve' which will take as much as you pour into it, but which doesn't pour anything back, is a recognizable image for the relationship between the selfless/selfish love of Helena/ Bertram. But, 'captious and inteemable' (italicized because, again, unique to this play)? This is amazingly wrought utterance. (We might compare, from the previous scene, the King's phrase 'On the catastrophe and heel of pastime', I, ii, 57: it recognizably means simply 'towards the end of his pleasure or recreation', but what an extraordinarily rich, redundant way of saying it! Such formulations, both dazzling and perverse, are the hallmark of this play.) Helena ends her confessional speech in riddles. She is one who can only:

> But lend and give where she is sure to lose;
> That seeks not to find that her search implies,
> But, riddle-like, lives sweetly where she dies.
>
> (I, iii, 217-19)

In fact, the whole play tends towards riddle.

When Helena claims her reward for successfully curing the King, and moves to choose a man for her husband, she says:

> Now, Dian, from thy altar do I fly,
> And to imperial Love, that god most high,
> Do my sighs stream.
>
> (II, iii, 75-7)

The real 'Diana' in the play is the chaste Florentine girl so-

named, whom Bertram seeks to debauch, and who helps
Helena in her plot to gain access to Bertram's bed. Helena
(whose namesake's sexual attractiveness was the 'cause ... the
Grecians sacked Troy', as the Clown reminds us – I, iii, 72) has
to enter the arena of sexual love – *use* her virginity – to achieve
her ends, physical or spiritual as they may be. Bertram, of
course, rejects 'a poor physician's daughter' with deep 'disdain', thus exciting the King's anger:

> 'Tis only title thou disdain'st in her, the which
> I can build up. Strange is it that our bloods,
> Of color, weight, and heat, poured all together,
> Would quite confound distinction, yet stands off
> In differences so mighty.
> . . .
>   Good alone
> Is good, without a name; vileness is so:
> The property by what it is should go,
> Not by the title. She is young, wise, fair;
> In these to nature she's immediate heir;
> And these breed honor.
>
>   (II, iii, 118-22, 129-34)

There is much undeniable wisdom here, and we should
recognize that, though it comes from a king, it represents a
potential threat to all distinctions, differences, titles, names –
with only 'nature' left to 'breed honor'. Though, of course, at
the beginning and at the end of the day we *are* nature's.
Certainly, Helena is good; and, make no mistake, Bertram is
'vile'. Nature certainly humbles class hierarchy here. The
matter has been in question from the beginning. Helena
profits from both culture and nature; from what 'her *education*
promises' and the 'disposition she *inherits*' – 'she *derives* her
honesty and *achieves* her goodness' (I, i, 42-7 – my italics).
Bertram, by starkly emphasized contrast, inherits his father's
'shape' and 'title' (name), but none of his 'manners'; and his
ineducable wilfulness takes him from bad to worse. It is all
part of that ongoing debate in Shakespeare concerning the
relationship between, precisely, what we 'derive' and what we
'achieve'. In rejecting Helena, Bertram sufficiently reveals
himself in all his amoral obtuseness:

> Proud, scornful boy, unworthy this good gift,
> That dost in vile misprision shackle up
> My love and her desert...

> (II, iii, 152-4)

says the furious King (to be soon after echoed by the Countess condemning her son's 'misprizing of a maid too virtuous'). We have encountered 'misprision' among princes before. Shakespeare was very attuned to all the arrogance and 'prejudicating' blindness that can come with name and title.

When Helena receives Bertram's 'dreadful' letter ('Till I have no wife, I have nothing in France', III, ii, 76), with its apparently impossible conditions, her first reaction seems to be to blame herself and retreat:

> I will be gone;
> My being here it is that holds thee hence.
> Shall I stay here to do't? No, no, although
> The air of paradise did fan the house
> And angels officed all. I will be gone.

> (III, ii, 127-31)

When Helena speaks such, indeed, 'angelic' poetry, one can understand Wilson Knight's enthusiasm. She suddenly seems to come from somwhere else. In the next scene, the aura of holiness around Helena increases as the Countess reads the letter from her in which she announces:

> I am Saint Jaques' pilgrim, thither gone.
> Ambitious love hath so in me offended
> That barefoot plod I the cold ground upon,
> With sainted vow my faults to have amended.

> (III, iv, 4-7)

– as if her love was a sin to be expiated. To the Countess, this makes her son appear, by contrast, even worse.

> What angel shall
> Bless this unworthy husband? He cannot thrive,
> Unless her prayers, whom heaven delights to hear
> And loves to grant, reprieve him from the wrath
> Of greatest justice.

> (III, iv, 25-9)

Helena certainly seems a good deal closer to God than Bertram, and in most readings of the play she does indeed become the 'angel' who forgives, blesses, and thus redeems her *very* 'unworthy husband'. And perhaps that is right – it is certainly an interpretation the play permits. But there is a point worth noting. In Boccaccio, Giletta, on receiving the rejection letter from her husband, immediately sets about planning to perform the impossible conditions. Her announcement that she is departing on a perpetual pilgrimage is simply a concealing ruse – she heads straight for Florence and Beltramo. Most readers of Shakespeare's play think that Helena's penitential religious feelings are sincere, and her intention to be a pilgrim, genuine. Perhaps they are. But why then did Shakespeare have her say she is 'Saint Jaques' pilgrim' (not mentioned in the source)? To any Elizabethan audience this would mean that she was going to the shrine of Saint James at Compostella. Now, as Dr Johnson remarked, drily as one feels, Florence is 'somewhat out of the road from Rousillon to Compostella'. So it is; but Florence is where Helena turns up in the next scene. By accident; by chance; is she just going a *very* long way round? Inconceivable, surely. The Arden editor thinks that 'Saint Jaques' is simply Shakespeare's mistake; but I doubt that, too. It looks more like false bait to me. And in Florence she soon has her plot arranged, along with some semi-specious-sounding justifications and rationalizations for it.

> Why then tonight
> Let us assay our plot, which, if it speed,
> Is wicked meaning in a lawful deed,
> And lawful meaning in a lawful act,
> Where both not sin, and yet a sinful fact.
> But let's about it.

(III, vii, 43–8)

Since they are, in fact, arranging for a wife to go to bed with her husband, it is lawful enough. As for the deception – well, 'craft against vice', as the Duke will say in *Measure for Measure*. Nevertheless, Helena has to find her way to the deed through paradox and ambiguity. But, in the world of this play, that is too often what you need.

The last scene, in which everything is finally, *finally*, made clear, is marked by prolix protractions, elaborate mendacities, futile denials, and maddening evasions. There is also a lot about 'haggish age', forgetting, oblivion, and 'th' inaudible and noiseless foot of Time' (V, iii, 41). In one extraordinary contorted and mannered speech, (fantastically different from his usual semi-literate thuggish mode, V, iii, 44-55), Bertram attempts to convince the court that he has always actually, really, loved Lafew's daughter, Maudlin – the unlikeliest of unlikely stories. When pressed about the second ring (which Helena put on Bertram's hand during the dark night of their consummation), Diana prevaricates – no, she didn't buy it; no, she didn't find it; no, she wasn't given it; no, she wasn't lent it. At which point, the exasperated King sends her off to prison – and one can sympathize; the obfuscations seem almost to be getting out of hand. (Of course, Diana simply never *had* the ring – but, when once we practise to deceive . . .) Helena finally appears, clearing everything up, and in a dozen, businesslike lines, claims Bertram as 'doubly won' (V, iii, 314), and effects needed clarifications and reconciliations. Even more brusquely, in a couple of peremptory lines Bertram asks pardon and promises love (by this time he seems pretty crushed). There is no sense of great happiness; certainly no feeling of either ecstatic personal reunion, or welcome social regeneration. More a feeling of somewhat weary relief that the rather wretched business has finally been tidied up and is at last all over. 'All's well that ends well' says Helena, optimistically, twice (V, iv, 35; V, i, 25); but the King's concluding comment sounds more appropriate – 'All yet *seems* well . . . ' (V, iii, 333 – my italics).

This is not intended to be reductive about Helena and her role as saviour (of Bertram, as well as the King); it is possible to see her as an instrument of the Divine, or more than human, Will, without failing to discern that she is a woman who very much wants her man. The final completion of the marriage can be seen as the climax to a mysterious, providential design, as well as clever Helena's personal triumph. Like other heroines before her, she is resourceful enough to take over the play, thus appearing as some sort of superior power in control; but, for all that, she is an earthly actor. Perhaps it is best to see the advantage she takes of her 'free scope' implementing, complementing, working in conjunction with the 'fated sky'. She may say, modestly and piously, to the King:

> But most it is presumption in us when
> The help of heaven we count the act of men...
>
> (II, i, 153-4)

but this is her incantatory couplet mode, when she takes on the role of a sort of priestess. Elsewhere, she stakes everything on the acts of women – starting with herself; 'the help of heaven' may operate in its own way, but it is hardly to be passively counted on. That her acts involve deception (including a feigned death – another one!) is more a comment on the world in which she has to act and find her way, than on her personal morality. It remains something of a puzzle why she should want the despicable Bertram so much; Shakespeare has clearly gone out of his way to make sure he has *no* redeeming feature (though I suppose we are to assume he has patrician good looks). Some think that Shakespeare does this to make Helena's love, mercy and forgiveness seem almost divinely beneficent, and that may well be right; for love and forgiveness *are* miracles – earthly miracles. But there remains a sense of residual mystery to the play – as I suggested, it is as if half of it were concealed by the strange velvet of its language, like Bertram's handsome but probably pox-scarred face. The play opens with a riddle – 'In delivering my son from me I bury a second husband' (I, i, 1-2), thus the Countess bids farewell to her son, playing on 'delivering' as 'giving birth' and 'letting go'; and it goes on riddling to the end – thus Diana:

> Dead though she be, she feels her young one kick.
> So there's my riddle: one that's dead is quick.
> And now behold the meaning.
> *Enter Helena*
>
> (V, iii, 302-4)

Helena is the answer to the riddle; but she is herself a riddle. And the riddles are deep. Burials yielding deliveries; the dead strangely transformed to the quick – though the great tragedies are still to come, we are already well on the way to the last plays.

*

COMEDIES

MEASURE FOR MEASURE (1604)

> Which is the wiser here, Justice or Iniquity?
>
> (II, i, 172)

> What's this? What's this? Is this her fault or mine?
> The tempter or the tempted, who sins most?
>
> (II, ii, 162-3)

This is a worryingly claustrophobic play. It opens in some unspecified room, perhaps in the Duke's palace, only to show the Duke making rather furtive arrangements to leave ('I'll privily away', I, i, 67); we are next in a street, peopled mainly by characters who bring the fetid reek of the brothel with them; thence to a Friar's cell in a monastery, and thence to the coolness of a nunnery. The important scenes in Act II take place in a courtroom and then a smaller ante-room, where the atmosphere grows more intense and stifling. For all of Act III and most of Act IV we are in a prison, with one excursion to a moated grange. Act V does, at last, bring all the characters into a 'public space near the city gate'; but although this is, as it should be, a site for clarifications, uncoverings, revelations, solvings – people and events finally appearing in their true light, as it were – the longing for fresh, refreshing air and expansive breathing space, which grows throughout the play, is hardly satisfied.

There is nothing romantic about this Vienna, in which the play is set – no nearby Belmont, no reachable Forest of Arden. No 'green world' at all, really; only a 'moated grange' and a reference to Angelo's garden. One would hardly look for release and revivification in a garden belonging to Angelo. Interestingly, it is a 'garden circummured with brick' (IV, i, 28). Shakespeare invents the word 'circummured' for this play, and never uses it again. It means – obviously enough – walled around, or walled in. Not surprisingly, it is the perfect word for the world of this play, for these are 'circummured' people. Literally, of course – if not in the courtroom or the brothel, then in the secular prison or the holier confinement of monastery or nunnery. (There are no domestic spaces or scenes in what Mary Lascelles rightly called 'this strangely *un-familied* world'.) But a lot of the main characters are walled up mentally and emotionally – say 'humanly' – as well. In this respect, the three main characters are oddly similar. The Duke likes to avoid his people and 'assemblies', and prefers to withdraw – 'I have ever loved the life removed' (I, iii, 8). Angelo, in the Duke's own terms, is 'precise ... scarce confesses/That his blood flows, or that his appetite/Is more to bread than stone' (I, iii, 50–53); he is 'a man of stricture and firm abstinence' who has blunted his 'natural edge/With profits of the mind, study and fast' (I, iii, 12 and I, iv, 60–61); he is the very type of the repressed, self-immuring Puritan – except, as we might say, when his blood is up. We first see Isabella in a nunnery 'wishing a more strict restraint/Upon the sisterhood' – this, in the famously strict order of Saint Clare (I, iv, 4–5). She, too, seems dedicated to a cloistral sequestering, and a chaste coldness – except when *her* blood is up, when she displays, in Walter Pater's words, 'a dangerous and tigerlike changefulness of feeling'. In their very different ways, all three find that they cannot live 'the life removed'. The Duke's apparent abdication is the prelude to his disguised descent into the lives of his people; thrust into high office and rendered effectively omnipotent, the apparently bloodless Angelo finds himself swamped with lust and driven to (attempted) murder; Isabella is drawn out of the nunnery, never to return – unavoidably involved in the plots and snares of the distinctly 'fallen' world of Vienna. But these emergings from the various retreats of withdrawal and withholding – both actual and temperamental 'murings' – are hardly liberations into a new-found freedom. For Vienna, like Hamlet's Denmark, is itself a prison.

As portrayed here, there are two worlds in this Vienna – the realm of the palace, the monastery, the lawcourt, the nunnery; but something has gone wrong with authority and things go variously, and sometimes dreadfully, amiss, until they are rather desperately righted at the end: then the brothel world, with its atmosphere of compulsive yet joyless lust, listless lawlessness, disease, degeneration and decay, where things, unchecked, go from bad to worse (or just from bad to bad). Lucio, something of a Mercutio, something of a Parolles, and something all himself, buzzes between the two worlds – and all realms come together in the prison, which becomes, through its occupants, at once brothel, lawcourt, nunnery – and, did but the others know it, the palace is there as well. Normality – if we may so designate reciprocal love and reproductive sexuality – is represented solely by Claudio and Juliet, the only genuine 'couple' in the play. Their sexual intercourse is described as 'our most mutual entertainment' (I, ii, 157), and the act was, both agree, 'mutually committed' (II, iii, 27). These are the only times the word appears in the play: apart from this couple, there is no 'mutuality' in this world – and he is in prison under sentence of death, while she is allowed barely sixty words, hardly there at all. There just doesn't seem to be any ordinary, straightforward love around. This hapless couple apart, we are confronted with, on the one hand, a merciless and tyrannous legalism, a ferocious and rancid chastity, and whatever it is the Duke thinks he's up to; on the other, 'mere anarchy' and '*concupiscible* intemperate lust' (V, i, 98). This is the only time Shakespeare uses the italicized word (or any of its derivatives); it comes ultimately from *cupere*, to desire, which can be innocent enough; but the word, just by its sound, irresistibly suggests extreme lubricity and uncontrolled sexual desire. Admittedly, these are Isabella's words about Angelo, but one feels that Shakespeare came to share some of her nausea at the idea of unbridled sexuality. And the fact that Angelo succumbs to a more terrifying and deranging lust than is manifested by any of the brothel regulars, tells us something about Puritans, certainly, but more generally enforces the recognition that the realms of authority and anarchy are not so firmly and stably separate and discrete as society, perhaps, likes to imagine. Of course, sex is always *potentially* a great leveller. What the law – any law – can do about sex, is one of the problems explored by the play. And it has got to do something – unless you regard Isabella's hysterical chastity, and Mistress Overdone's punks and stewed prunes, as viable options.

Interestingly and perhaps understandably – the prospect of

a few drinks at Mistress Overdone's is surely more appealing than the idea of arguing forensics with Angelo – some major critics have shown themselves disinclined to be censorious about scenes involving the denizens of the brothel world. Dr Johnson found them 'very natural and pleasing', which could make you wonder how he spent his evenings in London, if we didn't know better. Walter Pater is even more enthusiastic. 'It brings before us a group of persons, attractive, full of desire, vessels of the genial, seed-bearing powers of nature, a gaudy existence flowering out over the old court and city of Vienna, a spectacle of the fullness and pride of life which to some may seem to touch the verge of wantonness.' *Touch the verge*! One applauds the tolerance, but perhaps has to deprecate the idealizing – some of the figures are amiable enough, and they certainly provide the only *comedy* in the play; but they are meant, surely, to be seen as emissaries from a pretty foul and degraded world. These critics, and many others, are in part responding to the telling poetry Lucio uses to plead the case of Claudio and Juliet to ice-maiden Isabella:

> Your brother and his lover have embraced;
> As those that feed grow full, as blossoming time
> That from the seedness the bare fallow brings
> To teeming foison, even so her plenteous womb
> Expresseth his full tilth and husbandry.
>
> (I, iv, 40–44)

Put like *that* (no coarse brothel squalor in these lines – we are out in the fields we never see, and I doubt Lucio's competence in husbandry) it seems like the most natural thing in the world. Which of course it is – one more example of the ongoing miracle of nature's bounty. And the death sentence passed on Claudio *is* an absurdity as well as an atrocity. Pompey lives by being a bawd:

Escalus. Is it a lawful trade?

Pompey. If the law would allow it, sir.

Escalus. But the law will not allow it, Pompey; nor it shall not be allowed in Vienna.

Pompey. Does your worship mean to geld and splay all the youth of the city?

COMEDIES

Escalus. No, Pompey.
Pompey. Truly, sir, in my poor opinion, they will to't, then.

(II, i, 226-33)

Of course they will. We scarcely need a play by Shakespeare to remind us that you – they – cannot stamp out legally unsanctioned sexual behaviour, nor decree it away. Pompey makes a sharper point. It *would* be legal if the legitimating authorities legalized it – the law is, at bottom, as tautologous as that. It certainly cannot invoke the authority of nature, since nature not only allows unrestricted sexuality, it seems positively to demand it. The law can either invoke the will of God; or point to the requirements of civic order and decency; or simply rule by fiat, fear, and force. These are complex and perennial matters: how and to what extent a society controls the sexuality of its members is perhaps its most abiding problem and concern (even today, different societies have different ideas about what to do about the world's oldest profession – legalize it? tolerate it? wink at it? ghetto-ize it? try to eradicate it? But whatever they decide, you may be sure people 'will to't'.)

As he does so often, Shakespeare, in this play, has taken familiar tales and themes and synthesized them in a completely original way, giving them a twist in the process. There are three such discernible in this play, usually referred to (following Arden editor J. W. Lever) as the story of the Corrupt Magistrate (also called 'The Monstrous Ransom' by Mary Lascelles); the legend of the Disguised Ruler; and the tale of the Substituted Bedmate. The first story turns on the abuse of authority and power and must be as old as Authority itself. A generic version would have a woman pleading to a local authority for the life of her husband, under sentence of death for murder. The authority promises to release the husband if the wife will sleep with him. She does; but he executes the husband anyway. The wife appeals to the great ruler of the land, and the corrupt authority is ordered to marry the wronged wife (to make her respectable) and is then executed. An eye for an eye – very satisfying. In his *Hecatommithi* (1565), Cinthio, offering a more romantic version, made certain changes to the plot, which were adopted by Shake-

INTRODUCTION

speare. The husband and wife become brother and sister; the brother's original crime was not murder but seduction of a virgin; the brother is not executed after all; and the sister pleads for and obtains mercy for the corrupt magistrate who is now her husband. Much happier all round. According to Lever, 'The end of the story was explicitly designed to show the courtesy, magnanimity, and justice of the Emperor Maximian.' This has particular contemporary relevance for Shakespeare's play, written as it was the year after James I came to the throne (1603) – of which, more later. A more recent source for Shakespeare was George Whetstone's two-part play, *Promos and Cassandra* (1578). These two leading figures, greatly altered, mutate into Angelo and Isabella. Their two great interviews occur at about the same stages in both plays, and for two Acts, Shakespeare follows Whetstone's structure and scene sequence quite closely. He also takes over some minor characters, characteristically altered and in-dividualized – though he added Elbow and Froth, Abhorson and the crucial Barnardine, Lucio and Mariana, and effec-tively reinvents the great ruler, since, as Bullough pointed out, 'in no other version of the tale is the overlord given the same prominent part'. Of course, Shakespeare's masterstroke, which changes everything, is to make the heroine a novitiate nun, and to have her *refuse* to sacrifice her chastity to save the life of her brother.

The stories of monarchs moving among their people in disguise are likewise numerous and ancient. The Roman Emperor Alexander Severus was famous for it: here is Sir Thomas Elyot writing about Severus in *The Image of Governance* (1541) – a title with obvious relevance for Shakespeare's play.

[he] used many tymes to disguise hym selfe in dyvers straunge facions. ... and woulde one day haunte one parte of the citee, an other day an other parte ... to see the state of the people, with the industrie or negligence of theym that were officers.

The figure of the Disguised Ruler had become popular on the contemporary stage: in Shakespeare's play he becomes the crucial mediating, moderating and *manipulating* figure. The

Substituted Bedmate – the bed trick – was an even more familiar and popular motif which Shakespeare has, of course, used before, not least in the immediately preceding *All's Well That Ends Well*. But by bringing in Mariana, who is sort of Angelo's fiancée, to be the substitute; and by having Isabella, who is almost a nun, agree to the trick, Shakespeare opens up all sorts of legal, moral and spiritual issues. As, of course, does the whole play.

One general point should be made about the genre of this strange play. Just at this time, the emergent genre of 'Mongrell tragicomedy' (as Sidney called it), was being 'theorized' by one Guarini in his *Compendio della Poesia Tragicomica* (1601). I quote Lever's summary of Guarini's defence of the 'mongrel'. 'The form was defined as a close blend or fusion of seeming disparates; taking from tragedy "its great characters, but not its great action; a likely story, but not a true one ... delight, not sadness; danger, not death"; and from comedy "laughter that was not dissolute, modest attractions, a well-tied knot, a happy reversal, and, above all, the comic order of things."' Shakespeare's play hardly meets all these requirements, even though it does end with the marriages, pardons and reconciliations, and apparent harmonizations of 'the comic order of things' – even Lucio, who looks set to act as the usual requisite scapegoat excluded from the final ensemble, is forgiven. So all *seems* well. But what laughter there is is resolutely 'dissolute'; the arranged marriages have not been sought and pursued by the couples involved – there is no genuine *love* (as opposed to lust) in this play – but are imposed by the Duke (we get no sense of Claudio and Juliet as a happy couple); the knots don't come across as very 'well-tied' (Isabella doesn't even get to answer the Duke's unprecedentedly peremptory proposal of marriage); there is certainly danger rather than death, but not much of a sense of delight or happiness comes off the resolving reversals. The questions raised by the play remain unanswered – are perhaps unanswerable. A. P. Rossiter's redefinition of Tragicomedy comes nearer the mark. 'Tragicomedy is an art of inversion, deflation and paradox. Its subject is tragicomic man; and my repetition is not tautology, because genuine tragicomedy is marked by telling generalizations about the

INTRODUCTION

subject, *man*, of a seriousness which is unexpected in comedy and may seem incongruous with it.' He takes up a term first used by F. S. Boas in 1896, when he described *Troilus and Cressida*, *All's Well That Ends Well*, *Measure for Measure* and *Hamlet* as 'Problem Plays'. Rossiter says that in these 'problem plays', 'we are *made to feel the pain* – of the distressing, disintegrating possibilities of human meanness (ignobility and treachery, craft and selfishness)'. Such plays, he suggests, are marked by '*shiftingness*. All the firm points of view or *points d'appui* fail one', and human experience 'seems only describable in terms of *paradox*'.

The play opens with a ruler announcing his imminent 'absence'. It is all rather stealthy – he wants to slip away silently and secretly; unnoticed and unaccompanied. He gives absolutely no reason or explanation for this un-ducal move. It is not how rulers were expected to behave – it is as if he is abdicating from the responsibilities of his regal role, which for Elizabethans would serve as a dire presage of civil disorder to come in his 'absence', an opening to be taken up again in *King Lear* which can be seen as another experiment in civil disorder ensuant on the self-removal of the keystone of the state. The Duke will return in a very public way with full pomp and ceremony – we hear him ordering trumpets at the city gates. The experiment – or whatever it was – is over, and he will appear as a true Duke again.

His opening speech is also strange. The first line has a fine, royal ring to it:

Of government the properties to unfold...

(I, i, 3)

– and we feel we are in for another eloquent speech like the one given by Ulysses on 'degree' (*Troilus and Cressida*), this time on the 'properties of government', an always urgent concern for the Elizabethans. But no – that won't be necessary, he says to Escalus, *you* know all about that already. He seems to promise one thing, then fails to deliver, or goes off in another direction. This is how he is going to behave, apparently. Near the end, an increasingly bewildered Escalus complains: 'Every letter he hath writ hath *disvouched* other'

(IV, iv, 1). It is an ungainly negative – rather as if one should say dis-confirm, dis-call, un-speak – and Shakespeare has invented it for this play. Again we can see the rightness of the word – this is to be a disvouching Duke; it is one of the seemingly ungainly ways in which he works. But to return to that opening line: the coming play *will* 'unfold' the properties of government – the properties; and the difficulties, the obligations, the temptations, the abuses, the failures – all the *un*-properties too. 'Unfold' is a crucial word in the play, and has become very important for Shakespeare. Near the end, when Isabella thinks her appeal to the Duke has been incredulously denied, she cries out:

> Then, O you blessèd ministers above,
> Keep me in patience, and with ripened time
> Unfold the evil which is here wrapped up
> In countenance.

(V, i, 115–18)

She is anticipating Cordelia in *King Lear*; and, indeed, how wrapped-up evil does, finally, get 'unfolded', may be said to be the main concern of Shakespeare's tragedies. It is certainly the theme of the second half of this play – and a tricky and messy business it turns out to be. Not for the first time, Shakespeare has given us a clear pointer into his play in the first line.

The Duke's next speech is to Angelo, and the word recurs:

> Angelo
> There is a kind of character in thy life,
> That to th' observer doth thy history
> Fully unfold.

(I, i, 26–9)

'Character' is to be another crucial word in the play. It was coming to have something of our meaning – the qualities that make up a person, say. But the stronger meaning was of a distinctive mark, an inscription, a graphic symbol (hence handwriting), an engraving (coming, indeed, from the Greek word for the instrument used for marking, scratching). You can read Angelo from the outside – the marks reveal the man. Dramatic irony of course – it will take a great deal to 'fully unfold' Angelo. Some writing *is* reliably legible. In the very next scene Claudio tells Lucio:

> The stealth of our most mutual entertainment
> With character too gross is writ on Juliet.
>
> (I, ii, 157–8)

She is manifestly pregnant, which is a true indication of our sexual coupling. When the disguised Duke wants to persuade the uncertain Provost to follow his plan, he shows him 'the hand and seal of the Duke', adding 'You know the character' (IV, ii, 195–6). The Provost hesitates no longer. However, when the returning Duke greets Angelo thus:

> O, your desert speaks loud, and I should wrong it
> To lock it in the wards of covert bosom,
> When it deserves, with characters of brass,
> A forted residence 'gainst the tooth of time
> And razure of oblivion …
>
> (V, i, 9–13)

he is engaging in deliberate, penetrative irony. Isabella is of course right to denounce the misleading appearance of Angelo:

> even so may Angelo,
> In all his dressings, caracts [characters, distinctive badges], titles, forms,
> Be an arch-villain.
>
> (V, i, 55–7)

As in other plays, but here with unusually excoriating power, Shakespeare is engaging that central problem of 'seeming' – what signs, which 'characters', can you trust? The Duke's last line before disappearing is:

> Hence shall we see,
> If power change purpose, what our *seemers* be.
>
> (I, iii, 53–4 – my italics)

It is the only time Shakespeare used that particular cognate of the word.

To return to the Duke's first speech to Angelo. He continues with an important exhortation.

Thyself and thy belongings
Are not thine own so proper as to waste
Thyself upon thy virtues, they on thee.
Heaven doth with us as we with torches do,
Not light them for themselves; for if our virtues
Did not go forth of us, 'twere all alike
As if we had them not.

(I, i, 29–35)

He is drawing on the Bible, of course:

No man, when he hath lighted a candle, covereth it with a vessel, or putteth it under a bed; but setteth it on a candlestick, that they which enter in may see the light...

(Luke 8:16)

and the episode with the woman who has an 'issue' of blood:

And Jesus said, Somebody hath touched me: for I perceive that *virtue is gone out of me*.

(Luke 8:46 – my italics)

The injunction is, effectively, for Angelo to give up all that isolated study and fasting and put his private virtues to public use. But the words could be self-admonitory – 'it's about time *I* emerged from "the life removed" and did something' (as he is, rather rumly, about to) and they could be addressed proleptically to the nunnery-seeking Isabella, who elevates her own chastity over her brother's life. 'I cannot praise a fugitive and cloistered virtue, unexercised and unbreathed, that never sallies out and sees her adversary' – Milton's words could almost have Isabella in mind (I think Jocelyn Powell first noted this). In Isabella's case, we might add the line from Langland – 'Chastity without charity is chained in hell.' As I suggested, there are odd psychic similarities in the three main players. In their different ways, they do step out from 'the life removed'; and we see what, variously, goes forth from them.

Two scenes later the Duke is in a monastery ... explaining to Friar Thomas why he is disappearing, and handing over his 'absolute power' to Angelo. Presumably because of his preference for 'the life removed', he has allowed the 'strict statutes and most biting laws' of the city to slip, so that now:

INTRODUCTION

> Liberty plucks Justice by the nose;
> The baby beats the nurse, and quite athwart
> Goes all decorum...

(I, iii, 29-31)

– the world upside down. Whatever else this means, it indicates that he has been responsible for some sort of dereliction of duty and neglect of good 'government'. The play shows what he tries to do about it. Here is his plan. Instal Angelo in his, the Duke's, office:

> And to behold his sway,
> I will, as 'twere a brother of your order,
> Visit both prince and people. Therefore, I prithee,
> Supply me with the habit and instruct me
> How I may formally in person bear
> Like a true friar.

(I, iii, 43-8)

At a stroke, Shakespeare opens another dimension to his play. As Duke, Vincentio represents the acme of temporal power; then, 'in disguising the Duke as Friar Shakespeare intends to raise questions of spiritual responsibility inherent in the course of temporal power' (Powell). The King was, of course, head of the Church in England, so this image of the composite, dual nature of authority – the Duke–Friar – would, again, have carried a contemporary relevance. But this dual figure also allows Shakespeare to address Renaissance theories of the law and government (the appropriate administering of Vienna), *and* to draw on the teaching of the Church and the sayings of the Bible (matters concerning repentance, forgiveness, charity, mercy) – crimes, and sins; the control of man as body; the salvation of man as soul. And what is it for a mere, mortal *man* to have 'authority' over *other* men? Shakespeare has hardly gone as deep as this before now.

When the cat's away ... and when the *Duke's* away (or living the 'life removed'), the rats seem to take over the city.

> Our natures do pursue,
> Like rats that ravin down their proper bane,
> A thirsty evil, and when we drink, we die.

(I, ii, 131-3)

Thus Claudio, on his way to prison, sentenced to death, under Angelo's new dispensation, for fornication. It is a powerful image. Whether the 'thirsty evil' is 'too much liberty' or simply lechery, the transposition of the epithet makes it seem as if the evil is drinking the rats. 'Bane' is poison, and is presumably the arsenic put down to kill rats – it induces thirst and when the rats drink to slake that thirst, they die. The greedy attempt to satisfy our insatiable appetites inevitably proves mortal. And the appetite in this play is sexual – lust is everywhere on the loose. Immediately after the Duke's initial departure, the brothel people – customers and providers – are on the scene. Whenever these people are present they bring with them a certain air of rank vitality, which certainly seems preferable to the stunning hypocrisy of Angelo. But it should not be romanticized. Sex is degraded into crude lechery ('groping for trouts in a peculiar river', I, ii, 92; 'filling a bottle with a tundish funnel', III, ii, 173), and is everywhere associated with disease, disfigurement, treatment for syphilis – rotting, stinking. We can all respond to the foul, bawdy talk since we all have a component of animal sexuality, while fewer of us are pathological puritans. But the vitality is verminous, and points to beastliness and the disorder of a completely non-moral world. Sex can, of course, lead to 'blossoming' and 'teeming foison', as invoked in Lucio's entirely out of character and – in this play – dissonant bit of pastoralizing to Isabella (even he won't talk dirty to 'a thing enskied and sainted', I, iv, 34); but hardened vice is something else – a thirsty evil – and the harvest is death. It is with a characteristically deft touch that Shakespeare has Pompey invited to become an executioner's assistant in prison. Abhorson, the resident professional executioner, finds the idea insulting to his trade: 'A bawd, sir? Fie upon him! He will discredit our mystery.' But the Provost's reply is definitive: 'Go to, sir; you weigh equally; a feather will turn the scale' (IV, ii, 28–31). There's nothing to choose between them – in their different ways they both dispense death.

The first two scenes of Act II show the result of the Duke's 'absence' (in a sense, he has absented himself from office for years). The subtle balancings, adjustments, temperings, reparations and restitutions of the law as it should be administered, have collapsed into the stark alternatives of chaos and tyranny. In the first scene, the under-deputy Escalus, who clearly shares what we are to believe was the Duke's habitually lax tolerance, tries to make some sense out of constable Elbow's malapropisms (he is bringing in the denizens of a 'naughty house' whom he refers to as 'notorious benefactors', II, i, 50), and Pompey Bum's weirdly inconsequential ramblings (Angelo won't hear him out – 'This will last out a night in Russia/When nights are longest there', II, i, 133-4 – and leaves Escalus to pass sentence). It becomes a parody of what should be the properly conducted arguments for the prosecution and defence in a decent court of law. Ethics are dissolved – logic and relevance nowhere to be found. It is comical enough; but if this is 'law' in Vienna, then the law is indeed an ass, or as Angelo would say, 'a scarecrow' (II, i, 1). Escalus simply gets lost – 'Which is wiser here, Justice or Iniquity?' (II, i, 172), and ends muddle-headedly ordering Pompey to go on just as he is – 'Thou art to continue now, thou varlet; thou art to continue' (II, i, 191). Tolerance is invariably preferable to harshness; but you really can't run a city this way. *Not* good 'government'.

Then, in the next scene, we see Angelo, newly invested with 'absolute power', in action when Isabella comes to intercede for her brother. 'Absolute' is a word which attaches itself to Angelo; and he certainly merits the criticism addressed by Volumnia to Coriolanus – another fanatic – 'You are too absolute' (*Coriolanus* II, ii, 39). 'Precise' is another word which sticks to him; this is appropriate since Puritans (and this was a time of Puritan reform agitation in England) *were* self-confessedly and boastingly 'precise' – meaning strict in observance. But it is curiously appropriate that 'precise' comes from *prae-caedere* meaning to cut short, abridge, since this is just what Angelo wants to do to lusty young men, if not to sexuality itself. (In an excellent essay, Paul Hammond makes the neat point that 'precise' Angelo 'needs to be tackled by imprecise means, by approximate, devious, and even lying methods' – as we shall see.) The 'removing' Duke instructs Angelo as he leaves:

> In our remove be thou at full ourself;
> Mortality and mercy in Vienna
> Live in thy tongue and heart.
>
> (I, i, 43-5)

He has, he says, 'lent him [Angelo] our terror, dressed him with our love' (I, i, 19). Angelo, we quickly see, has gone for terror and mortality, and dropped the mercy and love. This scene (Act II, scene ii) is the first of two interviews with Isabella, and I might just say here that these two scenes are like nothing else in the whole of Shakespeare for white-hot, scorching psychological power, and intensity mounting to exploding point. Before looking at these incandescent exchanges, I want to insert a quotation from Henry James: 'Great were the obscurity and ambiguity in which some impulses lived and moved – the rich gloom of their combinations, contradictions, inconsistencies, surprises.' ('The Papers') – different era; same phenomenon. As we are about to see dramatically enacted.

Isabella and Angelo are both absolutists – in this, they are two of a kind. Isabella almost gives up before she has started, as one intransigent idealist conceding to another:

> O just but severe law!
> I had a brother, then. Heaven keep your honor.
>
> (II, ii, 41-2)

Indeed, whatever else we might think of the *louche* Lucio, we must recognize that it is only his prompting of Isabella ('You are too cold') that finally saves Claudio's life. As the legalistic Angelo coldly reiterates:

> Your brother is a forfeit of the law,
> And you but waste your words.
>
> (II, ii, 71-2)

Isabella's temper begins to rise, and with it her eloquence:

> Why, all the souls that were were forfeit once;
> And He that might the vantage best have took
> Found out the remedy. How would you be,

INTRODUCTION

> If He, which is the top of judgment, should
> But judge you as you are?
>
> (II, ii, 73-7)

'Remedy' is a key word in the play (occurring more often than in any other); ranging from Pompey's 'remedy' as described by Elbow – 'Nay, if there be no remedy for it, but that you will needs buy and sell men and women like beasts' (III, ii, 1-3), to God's remedy, through Christ, for the sins of men. But we are neither beasts nor gods, and some other 'remedy' for our ills and confusions must be found. Angelo's implacable 'no remedy' (II, ii, 48) means a reign of terror – the Duke will have to find a better way.

The first interview is a terrible collision between insistent Christianity and intractable law; and since we are not in the nunnery but rather in the realm of the social law where Angelo owns the discourse, as we used to say, Angelo is bound to win. But Isabella's passionate rhetoric continues to gain in heat and power, until Angelo seems to flinch a little – 'Why do you put these sayings on me?'; and Isabella thrusts home:

> Because authority, though it err like others,
> Hath yet a kind of medicine in itself,
> That skins the vice o' th' top; go to your bosom,
> Knock there, and ask your heart what it doth know
> That's like my brother's fault; if it confess
> A natural guiltiness such as is his,
> Let it not sound a thought upon your tongue
> Against my brother's life.
>
> (II, ii; 134-41)

Angelo turns aside to murmur: 'She speaks, and 'tis/Such sense, that my sense breeds with it' (II, ii, 141-2). She's got him! But not quite in the way she intended. When Isabella has left, Angelo *does* knock on his bosom to ask what's there – and to his horror, he finds foulness.

> What's this? What's this? Is this her fault or mine?
> The tempter or the tempted, who sins most?
> Ha, not she. Nor doth she tempt; but it is I
> That, lying by the violet in the sun,
> Do as the carrion does, not as the flow'r,

> Corrupt with virtuous season. Can it be
> That modesty may more betray our sense
> Than woman's lightness? Having waste ground enough,
> Shall we desire to raze the sanctuary,
> And pitch our evils there? O fie, fie, fie!
> What dost thou, or what art thou, Angelo?
> Dost thou desire her foully for those things
> That make her good?

(II, ii, 162–74)

There is no more electrifying speech in Shakespeare. And note the aptness, as well as the power, of his images. The same sun which brings the flowers to bloom (as in Lucio's blossoming fields), makes dead flesh even more putrid. And 'evils' was a word for privies – thus, why should I want to devastate the temple-pure Isabella by using her as a place of excrement? The sewer-like, stinking lust of old Vienna – it is the world, after all, of Pompey *Bum*, an unusual, but surely deliberately designated, surname – has erupted in Angelo himself.

Isabella's sound 'sense' has started his 'sense' (sensuality) 'breeding', and we shortly hear the results in a long soliloquy, uttered in the feverish anticipation of Isabella's imminent second visit. His religion is in tatters and is now no help to him:

> When I would pray and think, I think and pray
> To several subjects: heaven hath my empty words,
> Whilst my invention, hearing not my tongue,
> Anchors on Isabel: heaven in my mouth,
> As if I did but only chew his name,
> And in my heart the strong and swelling evil
> Of my conception.

(II, iv, 1–7)

This, of course, is like Claudius trying to pray in *Hamlet*: 'My words fly up, my thoughts remain below:/ Words without thoughts never to heaven go' (III, iii, 97–8), and there is something anticipatory of Macbeth's 'swelling act' (I, ii, 128) as well. The other 'swelling' in the play is Juliet's pregnancy. As so often in Shakespeare, it becomes a dramatic question of increasing urgency whether the 'swelling evil' will outgrow and obliterate the good signs of new life. Angelo's tormented state is one which increasingly attracts Shakespeare's scrutiny (compare Macbeth's 'pestered' senses). Here it makes Angelo realize the utter falseness of his position of authority:

> O place, O form,
> How often dost thou with thy case [outside], thy habit [dress],
> Wrench awe from fools, and tie the wiser souls
> To thy false seeming! Blood, thou art blood.
>
> (II, iv, 12-15)

It is a King Lear-like moment of sudden devastating realization ('a dog's obeyed in office', IV, vi, 161); and this almost torrential uprushing of blood in its undeniable, unstaunchable reality, will also afflict Othello. We are already in Shakespeare's tragic world.

The second interview with Isabella is even more powerful than the first – a sustained crescendo to a heart-stopping climax. Angelo, deploying his legal skills to serve his lust, uses specious arguments and a deformed (not to say depraved) logic to manoeuvre Isabella into an impossible position. When he advances the apparently hypothetical case that she might save her brother if she would 'lay down the treasures of your body' (II, iv, 96), she responds with a revealing passion:

> Th' impression of keen whips I'd wear as rubies,
> And strip myself to death as to a bed
> That longing have been sick for, ere I'd yield
> My body up to shame.
>
> (II, iv, 101-4)

It is hard not to hear the distorted (masochistic?) sexuality which goes into these overheated words in favour of cold chastity. Better her brother die than she lose that priceless treasure. This enables Angelo to pin her on the contradiction in her stance and arguments. 'Were not you, then, as cruel as the sentence/That you have slandered so?' (II, iv, 109-10). There would be no point here in tracing all the twists and turns in this desperate, gripping disputation. Isabella believes – or purports to believe – that Angelo is engaging in somewhat perverse casuistry; as it were, trying to fend off the real import in, or behind, his words as long as possible. Angelo begins to lose patience: 'Nay, but hear me./Your sense pursues not mine;

either you are ignorant,/Or seem so, crafty; and that's not good' (II, iv, 73-5). So – 'I'll speak more gross'. No more sophistry, no more forensics – 'Plainly conceive, I love you ... My words express my purpose' (II, iv, 141, 148). Isabella can no longer deflect or evade his intention, and cries out in outrage – 'Seeming, seeming!/I will proclaim thee, Angelo' (II, iv, 150-51). But 'absolute' Angelo now gives himself over absolutely to lust and corrupt abuse of authority:

> Who will believe thee, Isabel?
> My unsoiled name, th' austereness of my life,
> My vouch against you, and my place i' th' state,
> Will so your accusation overweigh,
> That you shall stifle in your own report,
> And smell of calumny. I have begun,
> And now I give my sensual race the rein.
> Fit thy consent to my sharp appetite,
> Lay by all nicety and prolixious blushes,
> That banish what they sue for; redeem thy brother
> By yielding up thy body to my will ...

(II, iv, 154-64)

or I will have him *tortured* to death. Angelo makes his exit with the chillingly triumphant line – 'Say what you can, my false o'erweighs your true' (II, iv, 170). It is a terrifying speech, laying bare the awesome potential for evil there is in 'absolute power'. As for Isabella – what can she do? 'To whom should I complain? Did I tell this,/Who would believe me?' (II, iv, 171-2). But, whatever happens, she is absolutely firm about one resolve – 'More than our brother is our chastity' (II, iv, 185). Thus ends this extraordinary Act – in a state of total impasse, a sort of throbbing paralysis, with incredibly urgent matters of life and death hanging in the air. Isabella has, after all, only twenty-four hours.

This is only the end of Act II: no play could continue at this level of intensity for long. It carries over to the next scene, in the prison, in which the Duke disguised as a friar seeks to reconcile Claudio to dying – 'Be absolute for death' and so on (III, i, 5-41). It is a long speech and a curious one for a friar,containing not a trace or hint of Christian hope, redemption, the soul, the after-life, immortality, whatever. It is, in fact, much more in the tradition of the ancient Stoics, the overall drift being that, when it comes to life, you are better off without it. This is certainly a tenable position; but, for a man of God, an odd one to advance. It denies man any dignity and honour, and human existence any point or value. It could have been spoken by Hamlet, and is in keeping with the bleak mood which often prevails in these 'problem plays', but it is hard to see what the Duke–Friar is up to. However, that turns out to be true of a lot of what he does. This is followed by the mountingly intense scene between Isabella and her brother which comes to a head when Claudio learns that there *is*, in fact, a 'remedy' (III, i, 61 – i.e. Isabella's going to bed with Angelo) and after an initial brave attempt to respond to her appeal to his nobility and sense of honour, he understandably breaks down – 'Ay, but to die, and go we know not where' (III, i, 118-32). It is an incredibly powerful speech (justly famous), and you can feel the dread of death whipping through it like an icy wind. It is a fear which must surely touch all mortals at one time or another, whatever they believe. 'Sweet sister, let me live' (III, i, 133) – anyone can understand the appeal. Her answer reveals the hysterical nature of her abhorrence of unchastity.

> Die, perish! Might but my bending down
> Reprieve thee from thy fate, it should proceed.
> I'll pray a thousand prayers for thy death,
> No word to save thee.

(III, i, 144-7)

Here is a flaring up of that 'vindictive anger' Pater noted in the young novitiate. The impasse is now complete: Claudio, surely, dies tomorrow.

Then the Duke–Friar steps forward and says 'Vouchsafe a word, young sister, but one word' (III, i, 152) – and the play suddenly changes. For one thing, it shifts into prose. Up till now, all the main characters have spoken in verse; the low life, as usual, alone speaking prose (and even Lucio speaks verse to Isabella). From now on, nearly all the exchanges are conducted in prose until the last Act, which returns to verse, but verse of a rather flat, formal kind – more geared to making pronouncements than discoveries. Claudio's fear-of-death speech is the last of the searing, intensely dramatic, image-packed verse which brings the second Act of the play to its almost unbearably intense pitch. After the Duke–Friar moves into prose, everything seems to get quieter and slow down: the mode changes, the mood changes, the atmosphere changes, the pace changes – instead of dramatic confrontations and agonistic struggles, we have a more narrative mode of intrigue and arrangement. It is quite a shock. As Brockbank says, 'we pass from Shakespeare's poetry at its most urgent and explora-tory to the easy lies and evasions of the Duke's "crafty" talk'. We also move from 'consummate psychological insight' (Wilson Knight) to something much more like Romance, and as we approach this strange second part of the play, we would do well to bear in mind Brockbank's reminder that Shakespeare is 'the romantic playwright, using Romance tricks to recover order from human disarray'. And so, in his way, is the Duke.

One result of this shift is that everything now centres on the disguised Duke, and Isabella – the Isabella we have seen in verbal combat with Angelo – disappears. Unlike most of Shakespeare's other comic heroines, she fades away into obedient submission and docile compliance. 'Fasten your ear on my advisings ... be directed ... be ruled' is the Duke's line to her; and advised, directed and ruled she duly is. She becomes almost dumbly passive, and remains silent for the last eighty-five lines of the play. Marcia Poulsen describes her as 'speechless, a baffled actress who has run out of lines', and sees her as a 'victim of bad playwriting' – the Duke's, that is; but also perhaps Shakespeare's. She diagnoses an 'unusual sense of female powerlessness' in this play, and thinks the play as a whole 'explores the incompatibility of patriarchal and comic structures'. This may be a rather too contemporary way of looking at it; but it is true that while Isabella starts with something of the independence and spirit of a Beatrice, a Rosalind (without, of course, the humour), all the life and vitality drain out of her. Shakespeare invented another woman, Mariana, who is just as bidden and obedient as Isabella. When, at the Duke–Friar's urging, the two women join hands as 'vaporous night approaches' in the sad, suggestive moated grange (impossible to forget Tennyson's poem), he 'seems almost to merge them together into a single being' (Jocelyn Powell). Strong female identity seems to be waning in the dusk – generic 'Woman' is as wax in the Duke's hands. Certainly, it becomes entirely the Duke's play, the Duke's world.

Many critics have noticed a gradual loss of autonomy and spontaneity in the characters, as the Duke moves them around (Lucio and Barnardine excepted – I'll come to them). William Empson said the Duke manipulates his subjects 'as puppets for the fun of seeing them twitch'. Manipulate them he certainly does, but is it just 'for fun'? Was Hazlitt correct in saying that the Duke is 'more absorbed in his own plots and gravity than anxious for the welfare of the state'? How we answer these questions and charges will determine how we view and value the second part of the play; for many people have become understandably impatient at the excruciating attenuations and prolongations involved in the Duke's complicated and often inept plottings and stagings. Why so devious when the power and authority is his to reclaim at any second he chooses? That, it must be said, would hardly be the 'remedy' he seeks for the people and condition of Vienna. Nobody and nothing would be changed – Claudio's execution could be stayed, and Angelo's hypocrisy exposed, but the previous civic disarray would not be radically healed. You *could* see the Duke engaged in an uncertain experiment to see how – or even if – justice and mercy can be combined in a moderate, mediating, measured way – *not* by the 'measure for measure' of the Old Law. When the Duke – as Duke – urges the fittingness of the execution of Angelo to Isabella, he says:

> The very mercy of the law cries out
> Most audible, even from his proper tongue,
> 'An Angelo for Claudio, death for death!'
> Haste still pays haste, and leisure answers leisure;
> Like doth quit like, and Measure still for Measure.
>
> (V, i, 410–14)

He is, of course, alluding to a saying in Matthew, but, as with so many of the arguments he uses, he is twisting it somewhat, so what he misleadingly calls 'the *mercy* of the law' turns out to be old-style vengeance – an eye for an eye. One can only surmise that, as with the seemingly perverse and cruel, prolonged pretence that Claudio is really dead, he is testing Isabella; educating her out of *her* absolutism – her first instinct certainly was for violent revenge on Angelo ('I will to him and pluck out his eyes', IV, iii, 121) – into *true* mercy and forgiveness, bringing her to the point when she will actually plead for Angelo's life, albeit in stiltedly legalistic terms. Perhaps, as Lever suggests, he is re-educating her 'cloistered virtue' into a virtue which can serve as an active force in the real world. Similarly, the seemingly perverse way he prolongs his apparent faith in Angelo, and the consequent public humiliation of Isabella (and Mariana) can be appreciated if, as Jocelyn Powell suggests, we see him as showing Isabella what she would have been up against if he really *had* been absent. Of *course* trusted Angelo would have got away with it, with no redress for the women. This in turn shows all of us just how fragile and vulnerable justice is.

Perhaps it does seem like 'a mad fantastical trick of him to steal from the state' (III, ii, 94) as Lucio says, but he should be seen as engaged in a difficult and circuitous quest – to see for himself the condition he has allowed his state to fall into, and to try what shifts and stratagems might put things to rights. When he says

> My business in this state
> Made me a looker-on here in Vienna,
> Where I have seen corruption boil and bubble
> Till it o'errun the stew...

(V, i, 317-20)

he is speaking as the Friar, but also as the Duke. The idea of absconding from his manifest role, but still surveying his realm, has some sort of a precedent in the notion of a *deus absconditus*, an idea which goes back to the Old Testament ('Verily thou *art* a god that hidest thyself, O God of Israel, the Saviour', Isaiah 45:15). But we should certainly not be tempted to regard the Duke as an incarnate figure of God. Some nourishment for this idea is provided by the lines of Angelo, when the Duke is revealed in Act V:

> O my dread lord,
> I should be guiltier than my guiltiness,
> To think I can be undiscernible,
> When I perceive your Grace, like pow'r divine,
> Hath looked upon my passes.
>
> (V, i, 369-73)

From this, some critics (notably Wilson Knight) have gone on to treat the whole play as an orthodox Christian allegory based on the gospel teaching. This is very wide of the mark. The Duke – like the English kings – rules by divine right; but he is, himself, a 'deputy elected by the Lord' – just as he appoints Angelo to be *his* 'Deputy'. When Angelo comes before the Duke to be judged, it is an image of the position the Duke himself (like everyone else) will be in before the truly divine God. On earth, he is only '*like* pow'r divine'. That he seeks to act as a sort of secular providence, sometimes coercively, sometimes fumblingly, is a better description. Centrally, he is a seventeenth-century ruler, trying to work out the best way to rule – getting the balance of justice and mercy right.

But he is also, as is often noted, a sort of playwright and theatre director, and not always a very good one – certainly, he does not have Prospero's serene power. He makes mistakes, stratagems don't work as he intends, some things (and people) he just cannot control, and he loses his temper in a rather unducal way. That is part of the point of the somehow admirable brute obstinacy and total intransigence of Barnardine (no 'seemer', he), whose execution is part of one of the Duke's more desperate plots. The following scene is illustrative of the limits to the Duke's power. The Duke tells Barnardine he is to die:

Barnardine. I swear I will not die today for any man's persuasion.
Duke. But hear you –
Barnardine. Not a word. If you have anything to say to me, come to my ward, for thence will not I today. *Exit.*

(IV, iii, 60-64)

'Not a word' is a marvel of insolence, and the Duke is left spluttering with impotent rage. There is a similar point in the Duke's inability to shake Lucio off, or make him shut up.

COMEDIES

Lucio's talk is scabrous and obscene, and he often appears in an unamiable light; but some of the few comic moments occur (or so I find) when the disguised Duke, hearing himself traduced and mocked ('the old fantastical Duke of dark corners', IV, iii, 160), simply can't get rid of him – 'Nay, friar, I am a kind of burr; I shall stick' (IV, iv, 181) and again when the Duke, increasingly irritated, simply can't get Lucio to stay silent in the last, big juridical scene. Unlike Isabella, these two will *not* be directed or advised. An allegorical reading of the play has nothing to say regarding the Duke's helplessness with burrs that insist on sticking.

In the strange couplets, gnomic rather than theophanic, in which the Duke soliloquizes at the end of Act III, he tells us something of his strategies and intentions, concluding:

> Craft against vice I must apply:
> With Angelo tonight shall lie
> His old betrothèd but despisèd;
> So disguise shall, by th' disguisèd,
> Pay with falsehood false exacting,
> And perform an old contracting.

(III, ii, 280–85)

This is the sort of questionable ethical casuistry we heard in *All's Well That Ends Well*; I will out-disguise disguise, beat falsehood with more falsehood – exactly, use 'craft against vice'. It has been called 'redemptive deceit' and 'creative deception', and it certainly requires some such paradoxical gloss. 'Craft' might be taken to include stagecraft, and the Duke certainly uses quite a few tricks of the trade, not always successfully or convincingly. (Brockbank made the nice point that he seems to invent the moated grange, Mariana, and Angelo's previous engagement – which exactly mirrors that between Claudio and Juliet, down to the blocked dowry which prevents both marriages – as a sort of desperate remedy, 'finding a theatrical solution to an otherwise insoluble human problem'.) Everything seems to come right in the end – just about, more or less – but without any of the feeling of joyful regeneration and renewal, a world transformed, that a truly successful comedy should arouse.

clxxviii

INTRODUCTION

If the Duke is, in truth, not a very good playwright, the unanswerable question is to what extent his failings are Shakespeare's failings as well. Some critics think that the dramaturgical ineptness is Shakespeare's, and no one can deny that after the thrilling drama of Act II, the play seems to slacken and lose force. But, arguably, no play could continue at that level of intensity, and perhaps we should see the Duke – with an awakened concern for 'good government' – as trying, with rather hastily devised tricks and ruses (time is short), to steer things into calmer, quieter waters, patching up a solution to the impasse which has so quickly developed. Perhaps Shakespeare is, in fact, exposing the often rather crude and necessarily mendacious ways in which any playwright somehow stitches things together for a tolerably harmonious conclusion. Perhaps he is also showing how easily and rapidly evil can burst out and take over – in a man, in a city (the first two Acts); and how difficult and awkward it is to achieve some sort of restitution and bring about a balanced, precarious, justice (the last three Acts).

One thing is certainly true and is often remarked on – while attempting to minister to all his subjects in both worldly and spiritual matters, the Duke does not learn anything about himself. Indeed, he is in danger of becoming something of a cipher – the *type* of good governor. It is possible that this might be related to the recent accession of James I. It has long been suggested that the Duke was intentionally modelled on the King, who was also the patron of Shakespeare and his company. If he was meant to be so viewed, then the Duke could hardly have been given the sort of turbulent and developing inwardness we associate with Shakespeare's main characters – that would have been *lesè majesté*. James I's *Basilicon Doron* had been published in 1603, and was, we may say, required reading. Shakespeare certainly knew it, and, as has been noted by scholars, many of the concerns and exhortations articulated in that book could equally well have come from the Duke. I give two examples:

even in your most vertuous actions, make ever moderation to be the chief ruler. For although holinesse be the first and most requisite qualitie of a Christian, yet ... moderate all your outwarde actions

clxxix

flowing there-fra. The like say I nowe of Justice ... For lawes are ordained as rules of vertuous and sociall living, and not to be snares to trap your good subjectes: and therefore the lawe must be interpreted according to the meaning, and not to the literall sense ... And as I said of Justice, so I say of Clemencie ... *Nam in medio stat virtus*.

And (this for Angelo, say):

he cannot be thought worthie to rule and command others, that cannot rule and dantone his own proper affections and unreasonable appetites ... be precise in effect, but sociall in shew ...

It is perhaps relevant that James issued a proclamation 'for the reformation of great abuses in Measures' (again, 1603). The King also insisted that certain laws that had fallen into disuse or abeyance should be tightened up. He showed irritation if his proclamations were not obeyed (the Duke and Barnardine), was apparently over-sensitive in his reactions to calumny (the Duke and Lucio), and wanted to visit the Exchange in secret to observe the behaviour of his subjects, though it proved impossible to maintain the secrecy. In short, many similarities between the Duke and James I are discernible and there is extensive work on this topic; I have listed helpful items in the bibliography. However, I think it would be wrong to see the figure of the Duke as simply a flattering idealized version of James I. The Duke is far from faultless and infallible; and one of the forceful demonstrations of the play is that you cannot simply translate abstract precepts concerning conduct and justice (such as are to be found in *Basilicon Doron*) into the actual human flesh-and-blood realm of mixed motives, contradictory passions, and endless ambiguities of word and deed. If James I *did* see himself in Duke Vincentio, he should have found it a cautionary experience.

How do you legislate for a carnal world; how can justice keep up with human wickedness; what kind of 'government' – in the individual, in the state – is both possible and desirable? These are some of the urgent questions the play dramatically explores. Pater catches well the prevailing ethical concerns of the play:

Here the very intricacy and subtlety of the moral world itself, the difficulty of seizing the true relations of so complex a material, the

INTRODUCTION

difficulty of just judgment, of judgment that shall not be unjust, are the lessons conveyed ... we notice the tendency to dwell on mixed motives, the contending issues of action, the presence of virtues and vices alike in unexpected places, on 'the hard choice of two evils', on the 'imprisoning' of men's 'real intents'.

This Vienna is a very long way from the Forest of Arden – but very close to Elsinore and Venice.

King's College, Cambridge   Tony Tanner

TONY TANNER was Professor of English and American Literature in Cambridge University, and Fellow of King's College. His publications include *The Reign of Wonder, City of Words, Adultery and the Novel* and *Venice Desired*, as well as studies of Jane Austen, Henry James, Saul Bellow and Thomas Pynchon. He died in 1998.

SELECT BIBLIOGRAPHY

BIOGRAPHY
The standard biography is now Samuel Schoenbaum, *William Shake-speare: A Documentary Life*, Oxford University Press, Oxford, 1975. A shortened version of this excellent volume was published in 1977. For those interested in Shakespearian mythology, Schoenbaum has also produced *Shakespeare's Lives*, Clarendon Press, Oxford, 1970, a witty dissection of the myriad theories concerning the playwright's identity and the authorship of the plays. Rather in the same vein is Anthony Burgess, *Shakespeare*, Penguin, London, 1972, a lively introduction to the presumed facts of the poet's life, enhanced by novelistic licence.

BIBLIOGRAPHY
Among the vast quantity of Shakespeare criticism it is probably only useful to list texts which are both outstanding and easily available. This I do below. For further information the serious student may consult the bibliographies of works listed. There are also three major journals which record the flow of critical work: the *Shakespeare Quarterly*; and the *Shakespeare Survey* and *Shakespeare Studies* which are published annually.

CRITICISM
The two indispensable Shakespearian critics are Johnson and Coleridge. Their dispersed comments are collected in *Samuel Johnson on Shakespeare*, ed., H. R. Woodhuysen, Penguin, London, 1989, and S. T. Coleridge, *Shakespearian Criticism*, two vols., Everyman's Library, London, 1960.

THE COMEDIES: GENERAL

BARBER, C. L., *Shakespeare's Festive Comedy*, 1959.
BARKAN, L., *The Gods Made Flesh*, 1986.
BATE, J., *Shakespeare and Ovid*, 1993.
BERRY, R., *Shakespeare's Comedies*, 1972.
BRADBROOK, M. C., *The Growth and Structure of Elizabethan Comedy*, 1955.
BROWN, J. R., (ed.), *The Early Shakespeare* (Stratford-upon-Avon Studies), 1961.
—*Shakespearian Comedy* (Stratford-upon-Avon Studies), 1972.
CALDERWOOD, J. C., *Shakespeare's Metadrama*, 1971.
CARROLL, W. C., *The Metamorphoses of Shakespearean Comedy*, 1985.
CHAMPION, L., *The Evolution of Shakespeare's Comedies*, 1973.

COMEDIES

CHARLTON, H. B., *Shakespearian Comedy*, 1938.
EDWARDS, P., *Shakespeare and the Confines of Art*, 1968.
EVANS, B., *Shakespeare's Comedies*, 1960.
FRYE, N., *A Natural Perspective*, 1965.
HERRICK, M. T., *Comic Theory in the Sixteenth Century*, 1950.
HUSTON, J. D., *Shakespeare's Comedies of Play*, 1981.
KAHN, C., *Man's Estate: Masculine Identity in Shakespeare*, 1981.
LAROQUE, F., *Shakespeare's Festive World*, 1991.
LEGGATT, A., *Shakespeare's Comedy of Love*, 1974.
LEVIN, H., *Playboys and Killjoys*, 1987.
MCFARLAND, T., *Shakespeare's Pastoral Comedy*, 1972.
MUIR, K., (ed.), *Shakespeare: The Comedies*, 1968.
NEVO, R., *Comic Transformations in Shakespeare*, 1980.
PARROTT, T. M., *Shakespearian Comedy*, 1949.
PETTET, E. C., *Shakespeare and the Romance Tradition*, 1949.
PHIALAS, P. G., *Shakespeare's Romantic Comedies*, 1966.
SALINGAR, L., *Shakespeare and the Traditions of Comedy*, 1976.
SCRAGG, L., *Shakespeare's Mouldy Tales*, 1992.
SORELIUS, G., *Shakespeare's Early Comedies*, 1993.
WELSFORD, E., *The Fool*, 1935.
WILSON, J. D., *Shakespeare's Happy Comedies*, 1962.
YOUNG, D., *The Heart's Forest: A Study of Shakespeare's Pastoral Plays*, 1972.

Many of the above books contain chapters on the individual plays collected in this volume. What follows may be regarded as suggested supplementary reading.

THE MERCHANT OF VENICE
BAMBER, L., *Comic Women, Tragic Men*, 1982.
BARNET, S., 'Prodigality and Time in *The Merchant of Venice*', PMLA 87, 1972.
BROCKBANK, P., 'Parables for the City', in *On Shakespeare*, 1989.
BROWN, J. R., ed., the Arden edition, Routledge, 1988.
—'The Realization of Shylock: A Theatrical Criticism', in *Early Shakespeare*, 1961.
BURCKHARDT, S., *Shakespearean Meanings*, 1968.
CARDOZO, J., *The Contemporary Jew in the Elizabethan Drama*, 1925.
COGHILL, N., 'The Governing Idea', Shakespeare Quarterly 1, 1948.
GEARY, K., 'The Nature of Portia's Victory', Shakespeare Survey 37, 1984.
GROSS, J., *Shylock*, 1992.
NOVY, M., *Love's Argument*, 1984.

SELECT BIBLIOGRAPHY

PALMER, J., *Comic Characters of Shakespeare*, 1946.

RABKIN, N., *Shakespeare and the Problem of Meaning*, 1980.

THE MERRY WIVES OF WINDSOR

BRYANT, J., 'Falstaff and the Renewal of Wonder', PMLA 89, 1974.

CROFTS, J., *Shakespeare and the Post Horses*, 1937.

ERICKSON, P., 'The Order of the Garter, the cult of Elizabeth, and the class-gender tension in *The Merry Wives of Windsor*', in *Shakespeare Reproduced: The Text in History and Ideology*, 1987.

FRENCH, M., *Shakespeare's Division of Experience*, 1982.

FRYE, N., 'Characterisation in Shakespearean Comedy', Shakespeare Quarterly 4, 1953.

GREEN, W., *Shakespeare's Merry Wives of Windsor*, 1962.

HINLEY, J., 'Comic Scapegoats and the Falstaff of *The Merry Wives of Windsor*', Shakespeare Studies 15, 1982.

PARROTT, M., *Shakespearean Comedy*, 1949.

ROBERTS, J., *Shakespeare's English Comedy:* The Merry Wives of Windsor *in Context*, 1979.

MUCH ADO ABOUT NOTHING

BERGER, H., 'Against the Sink-a-Pace: Sexual and Family Politics in *Much Ado About Nothing*', Shakespeare Quarterly 33, 1982.

CRANE, M., *Shakespeare's Prose*, 1951.

EVERETT, B., '*Much Ado About Nothing*', Critical Quarterly 3, 1961.

HUNTER, G., 'Lyly and Shakespeare', in *John Lyly*, 1962.

MUESCHKE, P. and MUESCHKE, M., 'Illusion and Metamorphosis in *Much Ado About Nothing*', Shakespeare Quarterly 18, 1967.

MULRYNE, J., *Shakespeare: Much Ado About Nothing*, 1965.

NEELY, C., *Broken Nuptials in Shakespeare's Plays*, 1985.

PROUTY, C., *The Sources of* Much Ado About Nothing, 1950.

ROSSITER, A., '*Much Ado About Nothing*', in *Angel with Horns*, 1961.

SALES, R., *Shakespeare's* Much Ado About Nothing (Penguin Critical Study), 1987.

STAUFFER, D., *Shakespeare's World of Images*, 1949.

STEVENSON, D., *The Love-Game Comedy*, 1946.

WESTLUND, J., *Shakespeare's Reparative Comedies*, 1984.

AS YOU LIKE IT

BARNET, S., 'Strange Events: Improbability in *As You Like It*', Shakespeare Studies 4, 1969.

BARTON, A., Shakespeare's Sense of an Ending', in *Shakespearean Comedy*, Stratford-upon-Avon Studies 14, 1972.

COMEDIES

FREY, C., 'As You Like It as a Comedy of Reconciliation', in Comedy: New Perspectives, 1978.

GARDNER, H., 'As You Like It', in More Talking of Shakespeare, 1959.

GOLDSMITH, R., Wise Fools in Shakespeare, 1955.

HALIO, J., 'No Clock in the Forest: Time in As You Like It', Studies in English Literature: 1500–1900, 2, 1962.

HAYLES, N., 'Sexual Disguise in As You Like It and Twelfth Night', Shakespeare Survey 32, 1979.

ISER, W., 'The Dramatization of Double Meaning in As You Like It', Theatre Journal 35, 1983.

JENKINS, H., 'As You Like It', Shakespeare Survey 8, 1955.

KIMBROUGH, R., 'Androgyny Seen Through Shakespeare's Disguise', Shakespeare Quarterly 33, 1982.

KUHN, M., 'Much Virtue in If', Shakespeare Quarterly 28, 1977.

MONTROSE, L., 'The Place of a Brother in As You Like It', Shakespeare Quarterly 32, 1981.

NUTTALL, A., 'Two Unassimilable Men', in Shakespearean Comedy, Stratford-upon-Avon Studies 14, 1972.

PIERCE, R., 'The moral language of Rosalynde and As You Like It', Studies in Philology LXVIII, 1971.

SHAW, J., 'Fortune and Nature in As You Like It', Shakespeare Quarterly 6, 1955.

TAYLOR, M., 'As You Like It: the penalty of Adam', Critical Quarterly XV, 1973.

YOUNG, D., The Heart's Forest: A Study of Shakespeare's Pastoral Plays, 1972.

TWELFTH NIGHT

BARNET, S., 'Charles Lamb and the Tragic Malvolio', Philological Quarterly 33, 1954.

EDWARDS, P., Shakespeare and the Confines of Art, 1968.

EVANS, G., 'Shakespeare's Fools', in Shakespearean Comedy, Stratford-upon-Avon Studies 14, 1972.

EVERETT, B., 'Or What You Will', Essays in Criticism 35, 1985.

HOLLANDER, J., 'Twelfth Night and the Morality of Indulgence', Sewanee Review 67, 1959.

JENKINS, H., 'Shakespeare's Twelfth Night', Rice Institute Pamphlet 45, 1959.

KERMODE, F., 'The Mature Comedies' in The Early Shakespeare, Stratford-upon-Avon Studies 3, 1961.

LEECH, C., Twelfth Night and Shakespearean Comedy, 1959.

LEWALSKI, B., 'Thematic Patterns in Twelfth Night', Shakespeare Studies 1, 1965.

SELECT BIBLIOGRAPHY

LOTHIAN, J. M. and CRAIK, T.W., eds., the Arden edition, Routledge, 1989.

PETTER, E., *Shakespeare and the Romance Tradition*, 1949.

PRESTON, D., 'The Minor Characters in *Twelfth Night*', Shakespeare Quarterly 21, 1970.

SALINGAR, L., 'The Design of *Twelfth Night*, Shakespeare Quarterly 9, 1958.

SUMMERS, J., 'The Masks of *Twelfth Night*', University of Kansas City Review 22, 1955.

ALL'S WELL THAT ENDS WELL

ARTHOS, J., *The Art of Shakespeare*, 1964.

BRADBROOK, M., 'Virtue is the True Nobility', Review of English Studies 1, 1950.

BROOKE, N., *'All's Well That Ends Well'*, Shakespeare Survey 30, 1977.

CAMPBELL, O., *Shakespeare's Satire*, 1943.

COLE, H., *The 'All's Well' Story from Boccaccio to Shakespeare*, 1981.

ELLIS-FERMOR, U., 'Some functions of verbal music in drama', Shakespeare Jahrbuch XC, 1954.

FRYE, N., *The Myth of Deliverance*, 1982.

HALIO, J., *'All's Well That Ends Well'*, Shakespeare Quarterly 15, 1964.

HUNTER, G., ed., the Arden edition, Routledge, 1989.

HUNTER, R., *Shakespeare and the Comedy of Forgiveness*, 1965.

KIRSCH, A., *Shakespeare and the Experience of Love*, 1981.

KRAPP, G., 'Parolles', in *Shakespearian Studies*, 1916.

LAWRENCE, W., *Shakespeare's Problem Comedies*, 1931.

LEECH, C., 'The theme of ambition in *All's Well*', ELH 21, 1954.

PRICE, J., *The Unforunate Comedy*, 1968.

ROSSITER, A., *'All's Well That Ends Well'*, in *Angel With Horns*, 1961.

SMALLWOOD, R., 'The Design of *All's Well That Ends Well*', Shakespeare Survey 25, 1972.

WESTLUND, J., *Shakespeare's Reparative Comedies*, 1984.

WHEELER, R., *Shakespeare's Development in the Problem Plays*, 1981.

WILSON, H., 'Dramatic Emphasis in *All's Well*', Huntington Library Quarterly XIII, 1949-50.

MEASURE FOR MEASURE

BENNETT, J., Measure for Measure *as Royal Entertainment*, 1966.

BRADBROOK, M., 'Authority, Truth and Justice in *Measure for Measure*', Review of English Studies 17, 1941.

BROCKBANK, P., 'The Theatre of God's Judgments', in *On Shakespeare*, 1989.

COMEDIES

DURHAM, W., 'What art thou, Angelo?', University of California Publications in English, VIII (2), 1951.

FOAKES, R., *Shakespeare: The Dark Comedies to the Last Plays*, 1971.

GLESS, D., *Measure for Measure: The Law and the Convent*, 1979.

HAMMOND, P., 'The Argument of *Measure for Measure*', English Literary Renaissance 16, 1986.

HAWKINS, H., *Measure for Measure*, 1987.

HUNTER, R., *Shakespeare and the Comedy of Forgiveness*, 1965.

JAMIESON, M., 'The Problem plays 1920–1970: A Retrospect', Shakespeare Survey 25, 1972.

KNIGHTS, L. C., 'The Ambiguity of *Measure for Measure*, Scrutiny 10, 1942.

LEVER, J., ed., the Arden edition, Routledge, 1989.

LASCELLES, M., *Shakespeare's* Measure for Measure, 1953.

MAXWELL, J., '*Measure for Measure*: The Play and the Themes', Proceedings of the British Academy 60, 1974.

MILES, R., *The Problem of* Measure for Measure, 1976.

PATER, W., *Appreciations*, 1889.

POULSON, M., 'The Constriction of Female Power in *Measure for Measure*', Shakespeare Quarterly 35, 1984.

POWELL, J., 'Theatrical *trompe l'oeil* in *Measure for Measure*', Shakespearean Comedy, Stratford-upon-Avon Studies 14, 1972.

ROSSITER, A., '*Measure for Measure*', in *Angel with Horns*, 1961.

SCHANZER, E., *The Problem Plays of Shakespeare*, 1963.

SHELL, M., *The End of Kinship: Measure for Measure, Incest, and the Ideal of Universal Siblinghood*, 1988.

STEVENSON, D., 'The Role of James I in Shakespeare's *Measure for Measure*', ELH 26, 1959.

SOUTHALL, R., '*Measure for Measure* and the Protestant Ethic', Essays in Criticism XI, 1961.

THOMAS, V., *The Moral Universe of Shakespeare's Problem Plays*, 1987.

TILLYARD, E., *Shakespeare's Problem Plays*, 1950.

WILSON KNIGHT, G., '*Measure for Measure* and the Gospels', in *The Wheel of Fire*, 1949.

CHRONOLOGY

DATE	AUTHOR'S LIFE	LITERARY CONTEXT
1564	Born in Stratford, Warwickshire, the eldest surviving son of John Shakespeare, glover and occasional dealer in wool, and Mary Arden, daughter of a prosperous farmer.	Birth of Christopher Marlowe.
1565	John Shakespeare elected Alderman of Stratford.	Clinthio: *Hecatommithi*.
1566	Birth of Shakespeare's brother Gilbert.	Edwards: *Damon and Pythias*. Gascoigne: *Supposes*.
1567		Udall: *Roister Doister*. Golding: *The Stories of Venus and Adonis and of Hermaphroditus and Salamcis*.
1568	His father is elected bailiff.	Gascoigne: *Jocasta*. Wilmot: *Tancred and Gismunda*. Second Edition of Vasari's *Lives of the Artists*.
1569	Probably starts attending the petty school attached to the King's New School in Stratford. Birth of his sister Joan.	
1570	His father involved in money-lending.	
1571	John Shakespeare is elected Chief Alderman and deputy to the new bailiff.	
1572		Whitgift's *Answer* to the 'Admonition' receives Cartwright's *Reply*, beginning the first literary debate between Anglicans and Puritans.
1573		Tasso: *Aminta*.
1574	Probably enters the Upper School (where studies include rhetoric, logic, the Latin poets, and a little Greek). Birth of his brother Richard.	

Death of Michelangelo. Birth of Galileo.

Rebellion against Spain in the Netherlands. Birth of the actor Edward Alleyn.
Birth of the actor Richard Burbage.

Mary Stuart flees to England from Scotland.

Northern Rebellion.

Excommunication of Elizabeth. *Baïf's* Academy founded in Paris to promote poetry, music and dance.
Ridolfi Plot. Puritan 'Admonition' to Parliament.

Dutch rebels conquer Holland and Zeeland. Massacre of St Bartholomew's Day in Paris.

Accession of Henry III and new outbreak of civil war in France. First Catholic missionaries arrive in England from Douai. Earl of Leicester's Men obtain licence to perform within the City of London.

COMEDIES

DATE	AUTHOR'S LIFE	LITERARY CONTEXT
1575		*Gammer Gurton's Needle* is printed.
1576		Castiglione's *The Book of the Courtier* banned by the Spanish Inquisition. George Gascoigne: *The Steel Glass*.
1577		John Northbrooke's attack in *Treatise wherein Dicing, Dancing, Vain Plays etc are reproved*.
1578	Shakespeare family fortunes are in decline, and John is having to sell off property to pay off his increasing debts.	Sidney writes *The Lady of May* and begins the 'Old' *Arcadia*. George Whetstone: *Promos and Cassandra*. John Lyly: *Euphues, the Anatomy of Wit*. Pierre de Ronsard, leader of the Pléiade, publishes his *Sonnets pour Hélène*. He is said to have exercised a considerable influence on the English sonnet-writers of the sixteenth century.
1579		Spenser: *The Shepherd's Calendar*. North: translation of Plutarch. Gossen: *The School of Abuse, and Pleasant Invective against Poets, Pipers, Players etc*.
1580	Birth of Shakespeare's brother Edmund.	Sidney: *Apologie for Poetrie*. Lodge: *Defense of Plays*.
1581		John Newton's translation of Seneca's *Ten Tragedies*. Barnaby Rich: *Apolonius and Silla*.
1582	Shakespeare marries Anne Hathaway, a local farmer's daughter, 7 or 8 years his senior, who is already pregnant with their first child.	Tasso: *Gerusalemme Liberata*. Watson: *Hekatompathia* (First sonnet sequence published in England). Whetstone: *Heptameron of Civil Discourses*. Sidney begins *Astrophel and Stella* and the 'New' *Arcadia*. Lope de Vega writing for the Corrals in Madrid.

CHRONOLOGY

HISTORICAL EVENTS

Kenilworth Revels.

Restricted by the City of London's order that no plays be performed within
the City boundaries, James Burbage of The Earl of Leicester's Men builds
The Theatre only just outside the boundaries in Shoreditch. The Blackfriars
Theatre is built. End of civil war in France. Observatory of Uraniborg built
for the Danish astronomer, Tycho Brahe. Death of Titian.
Drake's circumnavigation of the world. The Curtain Theatre built. Birth of
Rubens.

First visit to England of the duc d'Alencon as a suitor to Elizabeth,
provoking much opposition to a French match. The Corral de la Cruz built
in Madrid.

Spanish conquest of Portugal. Jesuit mission arrives in England from Rome
led by Edmund Campion and Parsons.
Stricter enforcement of treason laws and increased penalties on recusants.
Campion captured and executed. Northern provinces of the Netherlands
renounce their allegiance to Phillip II, and invite the duc d'Alencon to be
their sovereign.
Sir Walter Ralegh established in the Queen's favour. The Corral del Principe
built in Madrid.

DATE	AUTHOR'S LIFE	LITERARY CONTEXT
1583	Birth of their daughter Susanna.	
1583-4	The players' companies of the Earls of Essex, Oxford and Leicester perform in Stratford.	Giordarno Bruno visits England.
1584		Bruno publishes *La cena de le Ceneri* and *Spaccio della bestia trionfante*. Reginald Scott: *The Discovery of Witchcraft*.
1585	Birth of Shakespeare's twins Hamnet and Judith. The following years until 1592 are the 'Lost Years' for which no documentary records of his life survive, only legends such as the one of deer-stealing and flight from prosecution, and conjectures such as ones that he became a schoolmaster, travelled in Europe, or went to London to be an actor as early as the mid 1580s.	Death of Pierre de Ronsard. Bruno: *De gli eroici furori*, dedicated to Sidney.
1586		Timothy Bright: *A Treatise of Melancholy*.
1586-7	Five players' companies visit Stratford, including the Queen's, Essex's, Leicester's and Stafford's.	
1587		Holinshed: *Chronicles of England, Scotland and Ireland*. Marlowe: First part of *Tamburlaine the Great* acted. New edition of *The Mirror for Magistrates*.
1588		Marlowe: Second part of *Tamburlaine*. Thomas Kyd: *The Spanish Tragedy*. Lope de Vega, serving with the Armada, writes some of *The Beauty of Angelica*.

CHRONOLOGY

HISTORICAL EVENTS

First meeting of the Durham House Set led by Ralegh, Northumberland and Harriot, to promote mathematics, astronomy and navigation. Archbishop Whitgift leads more extreme anti-Puritan policy. Throckmorton plot, involving the Spanish ambassador.

Death of d'Alencon. Assassination of William of Orange. The Teatro Olimpico, Vicenza, built by Palladio.

England sends military aid to the Dutch rebels under the command of Leicester. Ralegh organizes the colonization of Virginia.

Babington plot. Death of Sir Philip Sidney. Rise of the Earl of Essex. Colonization of Munster.

Execution of Mary Stuart. Drake's raid on Cadiz.

Defeat of the Armada. Death of the Earl of Leicester. The first of the Puritan Marprelate Tracts published.

COMEDIES

DATE	AUTHOR'S LIFE	LITERARY CONTEXT
1589	The earliest likely date at which Shakespeare began composition of his first play (1 *Henry VI*) when he would have been working as an actor at The Theatre, with Burbage's company.	Marlowe: *The Jew of Malta*. Thomas Nashe: *The Anatomy of Absurdity*. Richard Hakluyt: *Principal Navigations, Voyages and Discoveries of the English nation*.
1590	2 *Henry VI*, 3 *Henry VI*.	Spenser: first 3 books of *The Faerie Queen*. Publication of Sidney's 'New' *Arcadia*. Nashe: *An Almond for a Parrot*, one of the Marprelate Tracts. Greene: *Menaphon*. Guarina: *The Faithful Shepherd*.
1590–92	Performances of *Henry VI*, parts 2 and 3, *Titus* and *The Shrew* by the Earl of Pembroke's Men.	
1591	*Richard III* and *The Comedy of Errors* written.	Spenser's *Complaints* which includes his translation of fifteen of Joachim du Bellay's sonnets – du Bellay was a member of the Pléiade and responsible for its manifesto. Sir John Harington's translation of *Orlando Furioso*. Publication of Sidney's *Astrophel and Stella*.
1592	First recorded reference to Shakespeare as an actor and playwright in Greene's attack in *The Groatsworth of Wit* describing him as 'an upstart crow'.	Samuel Daniel: *Delia*. Marlowe's *Edward II* and *Doctor Faustus* performed. *Arden of Feversham* printed. Nashe: *Strange News*.
1592–4	*Titus Andronicus* written.	
1593	Publication of *Venus and Adonis*, dedicated to the Earl of Southampton. The *Sonnets* probably begun.	Marlowe: *Massacre of Paris*. *The Phoenix Nest*, miscellany of poems including ones by Ralegh, Lodge and Breton. Barnabe Barnes: *Parthenophil and Parthenope*. George Peele: *The Honour of the Garter*. Lodge: *Phillis*. Nashe: *Christ's Tears over Jerusalem*
1593–4	*The Taming of the Shrew*; *The Two Gentlemen of Verona*.	

CHRONOLOGY

HISTORICAL EVENTS

Failure of the Portugal expedition. Henry III of France assassinated.
English military aid sent to Henry of Navarre. Marlowe's tutor, Francis
Ket, burned at the stake for atheism.

English government discovers and suppresses the Puritan printing press.

Earl of Essex given command of the English army in France. The last fight
of the *Revenge* under Spanish attack.

Capture of Madre de Dios. Split in the main players' company.
Shakespeare and Burbage's group remain at The Theatre, Alleyn's move to
the Rose on Bankside. Plague in London: the theatres closed.

Marlowe arrested on blasphemy charges and murdered two weeks later.
Kyd arrested for libel. Henry of Navarre converts to Catholicism in order
to unite France.

DATE	AUTHOR'S LIFE	LITERARY CONTEXT
1593–6		John Donne writing his early poems, the Satires and Elegies.
1594	*The Rape of Lucrece* dedicated to his patron Southampton. *The Comedy of Errors* and *Titus Andronicus* performed at the Rose. Shakespeare established as one of the shareholders in his company, The Chamberlain's Men, which performs before the Queen during the Christmas festivities.	Daniel: *Cleopatra*. Spenser: *Amoretti* and *Epithalamion*. Drayton: *Idea's Mirror*. Nashe: *The Terrors of the Night*, *The Unfortunate Traveller*. Greene: *Friar Bacon and Friar Bungay*.
1594–5	*Love's Labor's Lost* and *Romeo and Juliet* written.	
1595	*Richard II*.	Daniel: *The First Four Books of the Civil Wars between the two houses of Lancaster and York*. Sidney: *Defence of Poesy* published. Ralegh: *The Discovery of the Empire of Guiana*.
1595–6	*A Midsummer Night's Dream*.	
1596	Death of his son, Hamnet. *The Merchant of Venice*. Shakespeare living in Bishopsgate ward. His father, John, is granted a coat of arms. *King John* written.	Lodge: *Wits Miserie*. First complete edition of Spenser's *Faerie Queen*.
1597	*Henry IV* Part 1. First performance of *The Merry Wives of Windsor*. Shakespeare's company now under the patronage of the new Lord Chamberlain, Hunsdon. In Stratford, Shakespeare buys New Place, the second largest house in the town, with its own orchards and vines.	John Donne writes 'The Storme' and 'The Calme'. Francis Bacon: first edition of *Essays*. Jonson and Nashe imprisoned for writing *The Isle of Dogs*.
1597–8	*Henry IV* Part 2.	
1598	*Much Ado About Nothing*. Shakespeare one of the 'principal comedians' with Richard Burbage, Heminge and Cordell in Jonson's *Every Man in his Humour*. For the second year, Shakespeare is listed as having failed to pay tax levied on all householders.	Publication of Sidney's *Works* and of Marlowe's *Hero and Leander* (together with Chapman's continuation). *Seven Books of the Iliads* (first of Chapman's Homeric translations). Meres: *Palladia Tamia*. New edition of Lodge's *Rosalynde*.

HISTORICAL EVENTS

Henry of Navarre accepted as King in Paris. Rebellion in Ireland. The London theatres re-open. The Swan Theatre is built. Ralegh accused of blasphemy.

France declares war on Spain. Failure of the Indies voyage and death of Hawkins. Ralegh's expedition to Guiana.

England joins France in the war against Spain. Death of Drake. Raid on Cadiz led by Essex. In long-standing power struggle with Essex, Robert Cecil is appointed Secretary of State.

Islands Voyage led by Essex and Ralegh. The government suppresses the *Isle of Dogs* at the Swan and closes the theatres. Despite the continued hostility of the City of London, they soon re-open. James Burbage builds the second Blackfriars Theatre. Death of James Burbage.

Peace between France and Spain. Death of Philip II. Tyrone defeats the English at Armagh. Essex appointed Lord Deputy of Ireland.

COMEDIES

DATE	AUTHOR'S LIFE	LITERARY CONTEXT
1598 *cont.*		Lope de Vega: *La Arcadia*. James VI of Scotland: *The True Law of Free Monarchies*.
1599	*As You Like It, Henry V, Julius Caesar*. Shakespeare one of the shareholders in the Globe Theatre. He moves lodgings to Bankside. Publication of *The Passionate Pilgrim*, a miscellany of 20 poems, at least 5 by Shakespeare.	Jonson: *Every Man out of his Humour*. Dekker: *The Shoemaker's Holiday*. Sir John Hayward: *The First Part of the Life and Reign of King Henry IV*. Greene's translation of *Orlando Furioso*.
1600		'England's Helicon'.
1601	*Twelfth Night. Hamlet* (performed with Burbage as the Prince and Shakespeare as the Ghost). *The Phoenix and the Turtle*. The Lord Chamberlain's Men paid by one of Essex's followers to perform *Richard II* on the day before the rebellion. Death of John Shakespeare.	
1601–2	*Troilus and Cressida*.	
1602	Shakespeare buys more property in Stratford.	
1603–4	*All's Well That Ends Well*.	
1603	Shakespeare's company now under the patronage of King James. Shakespeare is one of the principal tragedians in Jonson's *Sejanus*.	Montaigne's *Essays* translated into English. Thomas Heywood: *A Woman Killed with Kindness*.
1604	Shakespeare known to be lodging in Silver Street with a Huguenot family called Mountjoy. *Othello*; first performance of *Measure for Measure*.	Chapman: *Bussy d'Ambois*. Marston: *The Malcontent*.
1604–5	Ten of his plays performed at court by the King's Men.	
1605	First performance of *King Lear* at the Globe, with Burbage as the King, and Robert Armin as the Fool. Shakespeare makes further investments in Stratford,	Cervantes: *Don Quixote* (part one). Bacon: *The Proficience and Advancement of Learning*. Jonson and Inigo Jones: *The Masque of Blackness*.

CHRONOLOGY

The Burbage brothers, Richard and Cuthbert, pull down The Theatre and, with its timbers, build the Globe on Bankside. Essex's campaign fails in Ireland, and after returning without permission to court he is arrested. The government suppresses satirical writings, and burns pamphlets by Nashe and Harvey.

Essex released but still in disgrace. The Fortune Theatre built by Alleyn and Henslowe. Bruno executed for heresy by the Inquisition in Rome. Essex's Rebellion. Essex and Southampton arrested, and the former executed. Spanish invasion of Ireland. Monopolies debates in Parliament.

Spanish troops defeated in Ireland.

Death of Elizabeth, and accession of James I. Ralegh imprisoned in the Tower. Plague in London. Sir Thomas Bodley re-founds the library of Oxford University.

Peace with Spain. Hampton Court Conference.

Gunpowder Plot.

COMEDIES

DATE	AUTHOR'S LIFE	LITERARY CONTEXT
1605 *cont.*	buying a half interest in a lease of tithes.	Jonson and co-authors imprisoned for libellous references to the court in *Eastward Ho*.
1605–6		Jonson: *Volpone*.
1606	First performance of *Macbeth*.	John Ford's masque *Honour Triumphant*.
1607	*Antony and Cleopatra*. Susanna marries John Hall, a physician. Death of Shakespeare's brother Edmund, an actor.	Tourneur's *The Revenger's Tragedy* printed. Barnes: *The Devil's Charter*.
1607–8	*Timon of Athens, Coriolanus, Pericles*.	
1608	Shakespeare one of the shareholders in the Blackfriars Theatre. Death of his mother.	Lope de Vega: *Peribanez*. Beaumont and Fletcher: *Philaster*. Jonson and Jones: *The Masque of Beauty*. Donne writes *La Corona*. Twelve books of Homer's *Iliad* (Chapman's translation).
1609	Publication, probably unauthorized, of the quarto edition of the *Sonnets* and *A Lover's Complaint*.	Jonson and Jones: *The Masque of Queens*. Donne's 'The Expiration' printed; 'Liturgie' and 'On the Annunciation' written. Bacon: *De Sapientia Veterum*. Lope de Vega: *New Art of Writing Plays for the Theatre*.
1609–10	*Cymbeline*.	
1610		Donne: *Pseudo-Martyr* printed and *The First Anniversarie* written. Jonson: *The Alchemist*. Beaumont and Fletcher: *The Maid's Tragedy*.
1610–11	*The Winter's Tale*.	
1611	*The Tempest* performed in the Banqueting House, Whitehall. Simon Forman records seeing performances of *Macbeth, The Winter's Tale* and *Cymbeline*.	Beaumont and Fletcher: *A King and No King, The Knight of the Burning Pestle*. Tourneur: *The Atheist's Tragedy*. Jonson and Jones: *Masque of Oberon*. Authorized Version of the Bible. Sir John Davies: *The Scourge of Folly*.

CHRONOLOGY

HISTORICAL EVENTS

Monteverdi: *Orfeo*.
Bacon appointed Solicitor General.

Galileo's experiments with the telescope confirm the Copernican theory.
Kepler draws up 'Laws of Planetary Motion'. Twelve-year Truce between
Spain and Netherlands.

Galileo: *The Starry Messenger*. Assassination of Henry IV of France.
Parliament submits the Petition of Grievances.

The Inquisition of Rome begins investigating Galileo.

COMEDIES

DATE	AUTHOR'S LIFE	LITERARY CONTEXT
1611 *cont.*		Donne writes the *The Second Anniversarie* and a 'A Valediction: forbidding mourning'.
1612	Shakespeare appears as a witness in a Court of Requests case involving a dispute over a dowry owed by his former landlord, Mountjoy, to his son-in-law, Belott. Death of his brother Gilbert.	Webster: *The White Devil* printed. Tourneur: *The Nobleman*. Lope de Vega: *Fuente Ovejuna*.
1613	At a performance of his last play, *Henry VIII*, the Globe Theatre catches fire and is destroyed. As part of the court celebrations for the marriage of Princess Elizabeth, The King's Men perform 14 plays, including *Much Ado*, *Othello*, *The Winter's Tale* and *The Tempest*. Death of his brother Richard.	Sir Thomas Overbury: *The Wife*. Donne: 'Good Friday' and 'Epithalamion' on Princess Elizabeth's marriage. Cervantes: *Novelas ejemplares* – a collection of short stories.
1614	In Stratford, Shakespeare protects his property interests during a controversy over a threat to enclose the common fields.	Jonson: *Bartholomew Fair*. Webster: *The Duchess of Malfi*. Ralegh: *The History of the World*.
1615	The Warwick Assizes issue an order to prevent enclosures, which ends the dispute in Stratford.	Cervantes publishes 8 plays and *Don Quixote* (part two).
1616	Marriage of his daughter Judith to Thomas Quincy, a vintner, who a month later is tried for fornication with another woman whom he had made pregnant. Death of Shakespeare (23 April).	Jonson: *The Devil is an Ass*. Jonson publishes his *Works*.
1623	The players Heminge and Condell publish the plays of the First Folio.	

CHRONOLOGY

Death of Henry, Prince of Wales.

Marriage of Princess Elizabeth to Frederick, Elector Palatine. Bacon appointed Attorney-General.

The second Globe and the Hope Theatre built.

Inquiry into the murder of Sir Thomas Overbury in the Tower implicates the wife of the King's favourite, Somerset.

Ralegh released from the Tower to lead an expedition to Guiana; on his return he is executed.

WILLIAM SHAKESPEARE

THE
MERCHANT
OF VENICE

Edited by Kenneth Myrick

[*Dramatis Personae*

THE DUKE OF VENICE
THE PRINCE OF MOROCCO ⎫
THE PRINCE OF ARAGON ⎭ suitors to Portia
ANTONIO, a merchant of Venice
BASSANIO, his friend, suitor to Portia
GRATIANO ⎫
SALERIO ⎬ friends to Antonio and Bassanio
SOLANIO ⎭
LORENZO, in love with Jessica
SHYLOCK, a Jew
TUBAL, a Jew, his friend
LAUNCELOT GOBBO, a clown, servant to Shylock
OLD GOBBO, father to Launcelot
LEONARDO, servant to Bassanio
BALTHASAR ⎫
STEPHANO ⎭ servants to Portia
PORTIA, an heiress
NERISSA, her waiting woman
JESSICA, daughter to Shylock
Magnificoes of Venice, Officers of the Court of Justice,
   Jailer, Servants, and other Attendants

Scene: Venice and Belmont]

THE MERCHANT
OF VENICE

[ACT I

Scene I. *Venice. A street.*]

Enter Antonio, Salerio, and Solanio.

ANTONIO In sooth I know not why I am so sad.
    It wearies me, you say it wearies you;
    But how I caught it, found it, or came by it,
    What stuff 'tis made of, whereof it is born,
    I am to learn;   5
    And such a want-wit sadness makes of me
    That I have much ado to know myself.

SALERIO Your mind is tossing on the ocean,
    There where your argosies with portly sail—
    Like signiors and rich burghers on the flood,   10
    Or as it were the pageants of the sea—
    Do overpeer the petty traffickers
    That cursy to them, do them reverence,
    As they fly by them with their woven wings.

SOLANIO Believe me, sir, had I such venture forth,   15
    The better part of my affections would

Text references are printed in **bold** type; the annotation follows in roman type.
I.i.1. **sad** sober, depressed 5 **am to learn** need to learn, cannot guess (the incomplete line indicates a short pause) 6 **want-wit** dull fellow 6 **sadness** depression 8 **ocean** (pronounced "ó-ce-an") 9 **argosies** great merchant ships 9 **portly** stately 11 **pageants** floats, splendidly decorated wagons in the shape of castles, dragons, etc. 13 **cursy** curtsy, bow 15 **venture** unpredictable enterprise

3

Be with my hopes abroad. I should be still
Plucking the grass to know where sits the wind,
Peering in maps for ports and piers and roads;
20   And every object that might make me fear
Misfortune to my ventures, out of doubt
Would make me sad.

SALERIO   My wind cooling my broth
Would blow me to an ague when I thought
What harm a wind too great might do at sea.
25   I should not see the sandy hourglass run
But I should think of shallows and of flats,
And see my wealthy *Andrew* docked in sand,
Vailing her high top lower than her ribs
To kiss her burial. Should I go to church
30   And see the holy edifice of stone
And not bethink me straight of dangerous rocks,
Which touching but my gentle vessel's side
Would scatter all her spices on the stream,
Enrobe the roaring waters with my silks—
35   And in a word, but even now worth this,
And now worth nothing? Shall I have the thought
To think on this, and shall I lack the thought
That such a thing bechanced would make me sad?
But tell not me! I know Antonio
40   Is sad to think upon his merchandise.

ANTONIO Believe me, no. I thank my fortune for it,
My ventures are not in one bottom trusted,
Nor to one place; nor is my whole estate
Upon the fortune of this present year.
45   Therefore my merchandise makes me not sad.

SOLANIO Why then you are in love.

ANTONIO   Fie, fie!

SOLANIO Not in love neither? Then let us say you are sad

17 **still** always   19 **roads** harbors   23 **ague** trembling fit   27 **Andrew** the name
of a ship   28 **Vailing** lowering, in recognition of a superior   32 **gentle** noble and
gentle; hence, splendid and frail   35, 36 **this, nothing** (spoken with an emphatic
gesture)   38 **bechanced** should it happen   42 **bottom** ship

4

Because you are not merry; and 'twere as easy
For you to laugh and leap, and say you are merry
Because you are not sad. Now by two-headed Janus,   50
Nature hath framed strange fellows in her time:
Some that will evermore peep through their eyes
And laugh like parrots at a bagpiper,
And other of such vinegar aspect
That they'll not show their teeth in way of smile   55
Though Nestor swear the jest be laughable.

Enter Bassanio, Lorenzo, and Gratiano.

Here comes Bassanio, your most noble kinsman,
Gratiano, and Lorenzo. Fare ye well;
We leave you now with better company.

SALERIO I would have stayed till I had made you merry,   60
If worthier friends had not prevented me.

ANTONIO Your worth is very dear in my regard.
I take it your own business calls on you,
And you embrace th' occasion to depart.

SALERIO Good morrow, my good lords.   65

BASSANIO Good signiors both, when shall we laugh? Say,
when?
You grow exceeding strange; must it be so?

SALERIO We'll make our leisures to attend on yours.
Exeunt Salerio and Solanio.

LORENZO My Lord Bassanio, since you have found
Antonio,
We two will leave you; but at dinner time   70
I pray you have in mind where we must meet.

BASSANIO I will not fail you.

GRATIANO You look not well, Signior Antonio.

50 **two-headed Janus** Roman god of entrances and hence of all beginnings;
depicted with two faces, one cheerful, one sad, symbolizing the uncertainty of the
future (Solanio suggests that Antonio is as strange a figure as Janus)   51 **strange**
marvelously queer   56 **Nestor** the oldest and most venerable Greek leader in the
Trojan War; a type of gravity and wisdom   61 **prevented** forestalled   67 **strange**
distant

You have too much respect upon the world;
75   They lose it that do buy it with much care.
Believe me, you are marvelously changed.

ANTONIO I hold the world but as the world, Gratiano—
A stage, where every man must play a part,
And mine a sad one.

GRATIANO   Let me play the fool!
80   With mirth and laughter let old wrinkles come,
And let my liver rather heat with wine
Than my heart cool with mortifying groans.
Why should a man whose blood is warm within
Sit like his grandsire, cut in alabaster?
85   Sleep when he wakes? And creep into the jaundice
By being peevish? I tell thee what, Antonio—
I love thee, and 'tis my love that speaks—
There are a sort of men whose visages
Do cream and mantle like a standing pond,
90   And do a willful stillness entertain
With purpose to be dressed in an opinion
Of wisdom, gravity, profound conceit,
As who should say, "I am Sir Oracle,
And when I ope my lips, let no dog bark!"
95   O my Antonio, I do know of these
That therefore only are reputed wise
For saying nothing; when I am very sure
If they should speak, would almost dam those ears,
Which hearing them would call their brothers fools.
100   I'll tell thee more of this another time.

74 **respect upon** regard for   81 **liver** one of the supposed seats of the passions
82 **mortifying groans** groans supposed to deaden vitality (by drawing blood from
the heart)   85 **jaundice** disease thought to be caused by peevishness   89 **cream
and mantle** become impassive like thick cream on a bowl of milk, or a mantle of
scum on a pond   90 **entertain** assume   91 **opinion** reputation (as in line 102)
92 **profound conceit** power of forming profound conceptions   93 **I am Sir
Oracle** i.e., I am as wise as a Greek oracle (inspired by the gods)   98 **dam** (often
emended to "damn," and probably a pun: If these silent and reputedly wise men
ever did speak, the abundance of their foolish words would not only dam up the
ears of the listeners, but also make the listeners call the formerly silent men fools,
and thus bring on the listeners the penalty of damnation which is pronounced on
all who apply this term to a brother-man. See Matthew 5:22)

But fish not with this melancholy bait
For this fool gudgeon, this opinion.
Come, good Lorenzo. Fare ye well awhile;
I'll end my exhortation after dinner.

LORENZO Well, we will leave you then till dinner time.   105
I must be one of these same dumb wise men,
For Gratiano never lets me speak.

GRATIANO Well, keep me company but two years moe,
Thou shalt not know the sound of thine own tongue.

ANTONIO Fare you well; I'll grow a talker for this gear.   110

GRATIANO Thanks i' faith; for silence is only commendable
In a neat's tongue dried and a maid not vendible.
                    Exeunt [Gratiano and Lorenzo].

ANTONIO Is that anything now?

BASSANIO Gratiano speaks an infinite deal of nothing,
more than any man in all Venice. His reasons are as   115
two grains of wheat hid in two bushels of chaff: you
shall seek all day ere you find them, and when you
have them they are not worth the search.

ANTONIO Well, tell me now, what lady is the same
To whom you swore a secret pilgrimage   120
That you today promised to tell me of?

BASSANIO 'Tis not unknown to you, Antonio,
How much I have disabled mine estate,
By something showing a more swelling port
Than my faint means would grant continuance.   125
Nor do I now make moan to be abridged

101-2 **But ... gudgeon** don't cultivate melancholy to gain a reputation for silent
wisdom, for the judgment of the multitude is stupid ("gudgeon" = proverbially
foolish fish)   108 **moe** more ("moe" is the old positive form of which "more" was
the comparative)   110 **gear** stuff (a mild jest, showing that Gratiano has cheered
Antonio for a moment)   112 **neat's tongue** beef tongue   112 **vendible** salable,
i.e., marriageable   124 **something** somewhat   124 **swelling port** impressive style
of living   125 **grant continuance** allow me to continue   126 **abridged** cut down

From such a noble rate; but my chief care
Is to come fairly off from the great debts
Wherein my time, something too prodigal,
130   Hath left me gaged. To you, Antonio,
I owe the most in money and in love,
And from your love I have a warranty
To unburden all my plots and purposes
How to get clear of all the debts I owe.

135   ANTONIO I pray you, good Bassanio, let me know it,
And if it stand as you yourself still do,
Within the eye of honor, be assured
My purse, my person, my extremest means
Lie all unlocked to your occasions.

140   BASSANIO In my schooldays, when I had lost one shaft
I shot his fellow of the selfsame flight
The selfsame way, with more advisèd watch,
To find the other forth; and by adventuring both
I oft found both. I urge this childhood proof
145   Because what follows is pure innocence.
I owe you much, and like a willful youth
That which I owe is lost; but if you please
To shoot another arrow that self way
Which you did shoot the first, I do not doubt,
150   As I will watch the aim, or to find both,
Or bring your latter hazard back again
And thankfully rest debtor for the first.

ANTONIO You know me well, and herein spend but time
To wind about my love with circumstance;
155   And out of doubt you do me now more wrong
In making question of my uttermost

127 rate scale   129 my time, something too prodigal the lavish way I spent my
time   130 gaged pledged   136 still always   139 occasions needs   140 shaft
arrow   141 fellow duplicate   141 selfsame flight identical in size and in the
feathers   142 advisèd considered   144 proof experience   145 pure innocence
childlike sincerity   146 like a willful youth i.e., like one who neglected sound
advice and learned by making mistakes   150 or either   151 hazard thing risked
154 To wind ... circumstance to approach my love circuitously with elaborate
talk

8

Than if you had made waste of all I have.
Then do but say to me what I should do
That in your knowledge may by me be done,
And I am prest unto it. Therefore speak.   160

BASSANIO In Belmont is a lady richly left;
And she is fair and, fairer than that word,
Of wondrous virtues. Sometimes from her eyes
I did receive fair speechless messages.
Her name is Portia, nothing undervalued   165
To Cato's daughter, Brutus' Portia;
Nor is the wide world ignorant of her worth,
For the four winds blow in from every coast
Renownèd suitors, and her sunny locks
Hang on her temples like a golden fleece,   170
Which makes her seat of Belmont Colchos' strond,
And many Jasons come in quest of her.
O my Antonio, had I but the means
To hold a rival place with one of them,
I have a mind presages me such thrift   175
That I should questionless be fortunate!

ANTONIO Thou know'st that all my fortunes are at sea;
Neither have I money, nor commodity
To raise a present sum. Therefore go forth;
Try what my credit can in Venice do.   180
That shall be racked even to the uttermost
To furnish thee to Belmont, to fair Portia.
Go presently inquire, and so will I,
Where money is; and I no question make
To have it of my trust or for my sake.   *Exeunt.*   185

---

160 **prest unto it** ready to aid you in it (from Latin *praesto*, at hand, ready)
161 **richly left** left rich   163 **virtues** powers and gifts (a more inclusive word than
today)   165-66 **nothing undervalued/To** of no less value than   166 **Brutus'
Portia** famed for her intellectual gifts, her resolution, and her wifely devotion (see
Julius Caesar, II.i. 233-308)   171 **seat** estate   171 **Colchos' strond** the shore east
of the Black Sea where Jason won the Golden Fleece   175 **a mind presages me**
a presentiment that foretells me   175 **thrift** thriving, success   178 **commodity**
merchandise   181 **racked** stretched to the point of torture (as on the rack)
183 **presently** instantly   185 **of my trust or for my sake** on my credit or on the
basis of friendship

[Scene II. *Belmont. Portia's house.*]

Enter Portia with her waiting woman, Nerissa.

PORTIA By my troth, Nerissa, my little body is aweary
of this great world.

NERISSA You would be, sweet madam, if your miseries
were in the same abundance as your good fortunes
5   are; and yet for aught I see, they are as sick that surfeit with too much as they that starve with nothing.
It is no mean happiness, therefore, to be seated in
the mean; superfluity comes sooner by white hairs,
but competency lives longer.

10   PORTIA Good sentences, and well pronounced.

NERISSA They would be better if well followed.

PORTIA If to do were as easy to know what were good
to do, chapels had been churches, and poor men's
cottages princes' palaces. It is a good divine that fol-
15   lows his own instructions; I can easier teach twenty
what were good to be done, than to be one of the
twenty to follow mine own teaching. The brain may
devise laws for the blood, but a hot temper leaps
o'er a cold decree; such a hare is madness the youth
20   to skip o'er the meshes of good counsel the cripple.
But this reasoning is not in the fashion to choose me
a husband. O me, the word "choose"! I may neither
choose who I would nor refuse who I dislike, so is
the will of a living daughter curbed by the will of

I ii.1 **troth** faith   5–6 **surfeit** are overfed, glutted   7, 8 **mean** (1) slight (2) golden
mean   8 **comes sooner by** acquires sooner   9 **competency** a modest but
comfortable fortune   10 **sentences** sententious maxims   13 **had been** would
have been   18 **blood** passion   18 **hot temper** ardent temperament   19 **cold
decree** decision made in cold judgment   20 **meshes** nets for catching small
creatures   21 **in the fashion** of the sort   24 **will ... will** wish ... last will and
testament

a dead father. Is it not hard, Nerissa, that I cannot   25
choose one, nor refuse none?

NERISSA Your father was ever virtuous, and holy men
at their death have good inspirations. Therefore the
lott'ry that he hath devised in these three chests of
gold, silver, and lead, whereof who chooses his mean-   30
ing chooses you, will no doubt never be chosen by
any rightly but one who you shall rightly love. But
what warmth is there in your affection towards any of
these princely suitors that are already come?

PORTIA I pray thee overname them; and as thou namest   35
them I will describe them, and according to my description level at my affection.

NERISSA First, there is the Neapolitan prince.

PORTIA Ay, that's a colt indeed, for he doth nothing but
talk of his horse, and he makes it a great appropri-   40
ation to his own good parts that he can shoe him
himself. I am much afeard my lady his mother
played false with a smith.

NERISSA Then is there the County Palatine.

PORTIA He doth nothing but frown—as who should say,   45
"And you will not have me, choose!" He hears
merry tales and smiles not; I fear he will prove the
weeping philosopher when he grows old, being so
full of unmannerly sadness in his youth. I had
rather be married to a death's-head with a bone in   50
his mouth than to either of these. God defend me
from these two!

NERISSA How say you by the French lord, Monsieur Le
Bon ?

PORTIA God made him, and therefore let him pass for a   55
man. In truth, I know it is a sin to be a mocker, but

---

26 refuse none refuse any   40-41 appropriation ... parts personal accomplish-
ment added to his talents   44 County Count   46 And if   47-48 the weeping
philosopher i.e., another Heraclitus   49 unmannerly sadness unbecoming
seriousness

he! Why, he hath a horse better than the Neapolitan's,
a better bad habit of frowning than the Count Palatine; he is every man in no man. If a throstle sing,
60 he falls straight a-cap'ring; he will fence with his own
shadow. If I should marry him, I should marry
twenty husbands. If he would despise me, I would
forgive him; for if he love me to madness, I shall
never requite him.

65 NERISSA What say you then to Falconbridge, the young
baron of England?

PORTIA You know I say nothing to him, for he under-
stands not me, nor I him. He hath neither Latin,
French, nor Italian; and you will come into the court
70 and swear that I have a poor pennyworth in the English. He is a proper man's picture, but alas, who can
converse with a dumbshow? How oddly he is suited!
I think he bought his doublet in Italy, his round
hose in France, his bonnet in Germany, and his be-
75 havior everywhere.

NERISSA What think you of the Scottish lord, his neighbor?

PORTIA That he hath a neighborly charity in him, for he
borrowed a box of the ear of the Englishman and
80 swore he would pay him again when he was able. I
think the Frenchman became his surety and sealed
under for another.

NERISSA How like you the young German, the Duke of
Saxony's nephew?

85 PORTIA Very vilely in the morning when he is sober, and
most vilely in the afternoon when he is drunk. When
he is best he is a little worse than a man, and when he

59 **throstle** song thrush   61 **should ... should** were to ... would be obliged to
71 **proper** handsome   73 **doublet** upper garment, corresponding to the modern
coat   73-74 **round hose** lower garment, combining the functions of breeches and
stockings   76-81 **Scottish lord ... Frenchman** (an allusion to the French promises
of aid to the Scots against the English, promises that were often broken)   83 **German**
(Germans were proverbially heavy drinkers)

is worst he is little better than a beast. And the worst
fall that ever fell, I hope I shall make shift to go
without him.   90

NERISSA If he should offer to choose, and choose the
right casket, you should refuse to perform your
father's will if you should refuse to accept him.

PORTIA Therefore, for fear of the worst, I pray thee set
a deep glass of Rhenish wine on the contrary casket,   95
for if the devil be within and that temptation without,
I know he will choose it. I will do anything, Nerissa,
ere I will be married to a sponge.

NERISSA You need not fear, lady, the having any of these
lords. They have acquainted me with their determi-   100
nations; which is indeed to return to their home, and
to trouble you with no more suit, unless you may be
won by some other sort than your father's imposition, depending on the caskets.

PORTIA If I live to be as old as Sibylla, I will die as   105
chaste as Diana unless I be obtained by the manner
of my father's will. I am glad this parcel of wooers
are so reasonable, for there is not one among them but
I dote on his very absence; and I pray God grant them
a fair departure.   110

NERISSA Do you not remember, lady, in your father's
time, a Venetian, a scholar and a soldier, that came
hither in company of the Marquis of Montferrat?

PORTIA Yes, yes, it was Bassanio!—as I think, so was he
called.   115

NERISSA True, madam. He, of all the men that ever my
foolish eyes looked upon, was the best deserving a
fair lady.

87-88 best ... beast (a pun, "beast" being pronounced almost like "best." Such
quibbles were not necessarily comic, but were considered clever and interesting)
89 make shift find a way   103 sort manner   103-4 imposition command
105 Sibylla the Cumean Sibyl (Apollo promised her as many years of life as were
the grains of sand she was holding in her hand)

PORTIA I remember him well, and I remember him
120   worthy of thy praise.

Enter a Servingman.

How now? What news?

SERVINGMAN The four strangers seek for you, madam,
to take their leave; and there is a forerunner come
from a fifth, the Prince of Morocco, who brings word
125   the Prince his master will be here tonight.

PORTIA If I could bid the fifth welcome with so good
heart as I can bid the other four farewell, I should
be glad of his approach. If he have the condition of a
saint and the complexion of a devil, I had rather he
130   should shrive me than wive me. Come, Nerissa. Sirrah, go before. Whiles we shut the gate upon one
wooer, another knocks at the door.   *Exeunt.*

[Scene III. *Venice. A public place.*]

Enter Bassanio with Shylock the Jew.

SHYLOCK Three thousand ducats—well.

BASSANIO Ay, sir, for three months.

SHYLOCK For three months—well.

BASSANIO For the which, as I told you, Antonio shall be
5   bound.

SHYLOCK Antonio shall become bound—well.

---

122 **four strangers** (apparently Shakespeare originally described four suitors,
then added two more, and forgot to change "four" to "six")   130-31 **Sirrah** (a regu-
lar form of address to a social inferior. Portia speaks to the servant) I.iii.5 **bound**
under legal obligation as cosigner of the bond

BASSANIO May you stead me? Will you pleasure me? Shall I know your answer?

SHYLOCK Three thousand ducats for three months, and Antonio bound.   10

BASSANIO Your answer to that.

SHYLOCK Antonio is a good man.

BASSANIO Have you heard any imputation to the contrary?

SHYLOCK Ho no, no, no, no! My meaning in saying he is   15
a good man, is to have you understand me that he is
sufficient. Yet his means are in supposition: he hath
an argosy bound to Tripolis, another to the Indies;
I understand, moreover, upon the Rialto, he hath a
third at Mexico, a fourth for England—and other   20
ventures he hath, squand'red abroad. But ships are
but boards, sailors but men; there be land rats and
water rats, water thieves and land thieves—I mean
pirates—and then there is the peril of waters, winds,
and rocks. The man is, notwithstanding, sufficient.   25
Three thousand ducats—I think I may take his bond.

BASSANIO Be assured you may.

SHYLOCK I will be assured I may. And that I may be assured, I will bethink me. May I speak with Antonio?

BASSANIO If it please you to dine with us.   30

SHYLOCK Yes, to smell pork, to eat of the habitation
which your prophet the Nazarite conjured the devil
into! I will buy with you, sell with you, talk with you,
walk with you, and so following; but I will not eat
with you, drink with you, nor pray with you. What   35
news on the Rialto? Who is he comes here?

---

7 **May** can   7 **stead** be of service to   12 **good man** good business risk (Bassanio takes the word as referring to moral character)   17 **sufficient** adequate, responsible 17 **in supposition** doubtful   19 **Rialto** famous bridge in Venice, the center of commercial activity   24 **pirates** (pronounced "pi-rats," with quibble on "rats") 32 **the Nazarite** Christ (the allusion is to the episode in Mark 5:1-13, Luke 8:26-33)

Enter Antonio.

BASSANIO This is Signior Antonio.

SHYLOCK [*Aside*] How like a fawning publican he
          looks.
          I hate him for he is a Christian;
40   But more, for that in low simplicity
          He lends out money gratis, and brings down
          The rate of usance here with us in Venice.
          If I can catch him once upon the hip,
          I will feed fat the ancient grudge I bear him.
45   He hates our sacred nation, and he rails,
          Even there where merchants most do congregate,
          On me, my bargains, and my well-won thrift,
          Which he calls interest. Cursèd be my tribe
          If I forgive him.

BASSANIO   Shylock, do you hear?

50   SHYLOCK I am debating of my present store,
          And by the near guess of my memory
          I cannot instantly raise up the gross
          Of full three thousand ducats. What of that?
          Tubal, a wealthy Hebrew of my tribe,
55   Will furnish me. But soft, how many months
          Do you desire? [*To Antonio*] Rest you fair, good
          signior!
          Your worship was the last man in our mouths.

ANTONIO Shylock, albeit I neither lend nor borrow
          By taking nor by giving of excess,
60   Yet to supply the ripe wants of my friend,
          I'll break a custom. [*To Bassanio*] Is he yet
          possessed
          How much ye would?

---

38 **publican** (sometimes glossed as a Roman tax-gatherer, as in Matthew 11:17
and 31:30 f., and sometimes as an Elizabethan innkeeper. Perhaps Shylock uses it
as an inexact but bitter term of reproach) 39 **for** because 42 **usance** interest
43 **upon the hip** at a disadvantage (a term in wrestling) 47 **thrift** prosperity
50 **present store** stock of ready money 52 **gross** whole amount 55 **soft** hold,
stay 61 **possessed** apprised 62 **would** desire

SHYLOCK   Ay, ay, three thousand ducats.

ANTONIO And for three months.

SHYLOCK I had forgot—three months, you told me so.
Well then, your bond. And let me see—but hear you: 65
Methoughts you said you neither lend nor borrow
Upon advantage.

ANTONIO   I do never use it.

SHYLOCK When Jacob grazed his uncle Laban's sheep—
This Jacob from our holy Abram was,
As his wise mother wrought in his behalf,   70
The third possessor; ay, he was the third—

ANTONIO And what of him? Did he take interest?

SHYLOCK No, not take interest—not as you would say
Directly int'rest. Mark what Jacob did:
When Laban and himself were compremised   75
That all the eanlings which were streaked and pied
Should fall as Jacob's hire, the ewes being rank
In end of autumn turnèd to the rams;
And when the work of generation was
Between these woolly breeders in the act,   80
The skillful shepherd pilled me certain wands,
And in the doing of the deed of kind
He stuck them up before the fulsome ewes,
Who then conceiving, did in eaning time
Fall parti-colored lambs, and those were Jacob's.   85
This was a way to thrive, and he was blest;
And thrift is blessing if men steal it not.

ANTONIO This was a venture, sir, that Jacob served for,
A thing not in his power to bring to pass,
But swayed and fashioned by the hand of heaven.   90
Was this inserted to make interest good?
Or is your gold and silver ewes and rams?

66 **Methoughts** it seemed to me   67 **advantage** interest   68 **Jacob** (see Genesis
30:25-43; 31:1-13)   75 **were compremised** had reached an agreement   81 **pilled**
stripped   81 **me** (the ethical dative)   82 **kind** nature   84 **eaning** lambing   88 **venture** unpredictable enterprise

SHYLOCK I cannot tell; I make it breed as fast.
But note me, signior—

ANTONIO   Mark you this, Bassanio,
95   The devil can cite Scripture for his purpose.
An evil soul producing holy witness
Is like a villain with a smiling cheek,
A goodly apple rotten at the heart.
O what a goodly outside falsehood hath!

SHYLOCK Three thousand ducats—'tis a good round
100   sum.
Three months from twelve—then let me see, the
rate—

ANTONIO Well, Shylock, shall we be beholding to you?

SHYLOCK Signior Antonio, many a time and oft
In the Rialto you have rated me
105   About my moneys and my usances.
Still have I borne it with a patient shrug,
For suff'rance is the badge of all our tribe.
You call me misbeliever, cutthroat dog,
And spet upon my Jewish gaberdine,
110   And all for use of that which is mine own.
Well then, it now appears you need my help.
Go to, then. You come to me and you say,
"Shylock, we would have moneys"—you say so,
You that did void your rheum upon my beard
115   And foot me as you spurn a stranger cur
Over your threshold! Moneys is your suit.
What should I say to you? Should I not say,
"Hath a dog money? Is it possible
A cur can lend three thousand ducats?" Or
120   Shall I bend low, and in a bondman's key,
With bated breath, and whisp'ring humbleness,
Say this:

98 goodly fine-appearing   102 beholding beholden, obligated   104 rated berated,
reviled   106 Still always   107 suff'rance long-suffering   109 gaberdine the
distinctive gown or mantle of the Jews   112 Go to, then (an exclamation suggesting annoyance)   114 rheum spittle

"Fair sir, you spet on me on Wednesday last,
You spurned me such a day, another time
You called me dog; and for these courtesies   125
I'll lend you thus much moneys"?

ANTONIO   I am as like to call thee so again,
To spet on thee again, to spurn thee too.
If thou wilt lend this money, lend it not
As to thy friends—for when did friendship take   130
A breed for barren metal of his friend?—
But lend it rather to thine enemy,
Who if he break, thou mayst with better face
Exact the penalty.

SHYLOCK   Why look you, how you storm!
I would be friends with you, and have your love,   135
Forget the shames that you have stained me with,
Supply your present wants, and take no doit
Of usance for my moneys; and you'll not hear me.
This is kind I offer.

BASSANIO   This were kindness.

SHYLOCK   This kindness will I show: 140
Go with me to a notary; seal me there
Your single bond, and, in a merry sport,
If you repay me not on such a day,
In such a place, such sum or sums as are
Expressed in the condition, let the forfeit   145
Be nominated for an equal pound
Of your fair flesh, to be cut off and taken
In what part of your body pleaseth me.

ANTONIO   Content, in faith. I'll seal to such a bond,
And say there is much kindness in the Jew.   150

BASSANIO   You shall not seal to such a bond for me!
I'll rather dwell in my necessity.

131 breed for barren metal interest (Aristotelian doctrine held that money,
unlike living things, cannot reproduce)   133 break become insolvent   137 doit
tiny Dutch coin, valued at one-eighth of an English penny   139 kind kind and
natural (in contrast to usurious dealings)   142 single without further security
150 kindness natural friendliness

ANTONIO Why fear not, man; I will not forfeit it.
Within these two months—that's a month before
155 This bond expires—I do expect return
Of thrice three times the value of this bond.

SHYLOCK O father Abram, what these Christians are,
Whose own hard dealings teaches them suspect
The thoughts of others! Pray you tell me this:
160 If he should break his day, what should I gain
By the exaction of the forfeiture?
A pound of man's flesh taken from a man
Is not so estimable, profitable neither,
As flesh of muttons, beefs, or goats. I say
165 To buy his favor I extend this friendship.
If he will take it, so; if not, adieu.
And for my love I pray you wrong me not.

ANTONIO Yes, Shylock, I will seal unto this bond.

SHYLOCK Then meet me forthwith at the notary's;
170 Give him direction for this merry bond,
And I will go and purse the ducats straight,
See to my house, left in the fearful guard
Of an unthrifty knave, and presently
I'll be with you.   *Exit.*

ANTONIO   Hie thee, gentle Jew.
175 The Hebrew will turn Christian; he grows kind.

BASSANIO I like not fair terms and a villain's mind.

ANTONIO Come on. In this there can be no dismay;
My ships come home a month before the day.
                                                    Exeunt.

---

160 **break his day** break his promise to pay on the due date   166 **adieu**
(probably the word has the original meaning, "I commend you to God")   167 **And...
wrong me not** i.e., and for the friendship I have shown you, please don't mis-
judge me in the future   172 **fearful** hazardous   173 **unthrifty knave** careless
youngster   173 **presently** instantly   174 **gentle Jew** courteous Jew (with a pun
on "gentile")

[ACT II

Scene I. *Belmont. Portia's house.*]

[Flourish of cornets.] Enter [the Prince of] Morocco, a tawny Moor all in white, and three or four Followers accordingly, with Portia, Nerissa, and their Train.

MOROCCO   Mislike me not for my complexion,
The shadowed livery of the burnished sun,
To whom I am a neighbor and near bred.
Bring me the fairest creature northward born,
Where Phoebus' fire scarce thaws the icicles,   5
And let us make incision for your love
To prove whose blood is reddest, his or mine.
I tell thee, lady, this aspect of mine
Hath feared the valiant. By my love I swear,
The best-regarded virgins of our clime   10
Have loved it too. I would not change this hue,
Except to steal your thoughts, my gentle queen.

PORTIA   In terms of choice I am not solely led
By nice direction of a maiden's eyes.
Besides, the lott'ry of my destiny   15

II.i.2 **shadowed** dark   2 **livery** uniform for a king's or nobleman's retainers
5 **Phoebus'** the sun-god's   6 **make incision** cut our flesh   8 **aspect** (pronounced "a-spèct")   9 **feared the valiant** caused the valiant to fear   13 **In terms of choice** with respect to my choice   14 **nice** fastidious

21

Bars me the right of voluntary choosing.
But if my father had not scanted me,
And hedged me by his wit to yield myself
His wife who wins me by that means I told you,
20   Yourself, renownèd Prince, then stood as fair
As any comer I have looked on yet
For my affection.

MOROCCO   Even for that I thank you.
Therefore I pray you lead me to the caskets
To try my fortune. By this scimitar,
25   That slew the Sophy, and a Persian prince
That won three fields of Sultan Solyman,
I would o'erstare the sternest eyes that look,
Outbrave the heart most daring on the earth,
Pluck the young sucking cubs from the she-bear,
30   Yea, mock the lion when 'a roars for prey,
To win thee, lady. But alas the while,
If Hercules and Lichas play at dice
Which is the better man, the greater throw
May turn by fortune from the weaker hand.
35   So is Alcides beaten by his page,
And so may I, blind Fortune leading me,
Miss that which one unworthier may attain,
And die with grieving.

PORTIA   You must take your chance,
And either not attempt to choose at all,
40   Or swear before you choose, if you choose wrong
Never to speak to lady afterward
In way of marriage. Therefore be advised.

MOROCCO Nor will not. Come, bring me unto my
        chance.

PORTIA First, forward to the temple; after dinner
Your hazard shall be made.

---

17 **scanted** limited   18 **hedged me by his wit** fenced me in by his clever intellect
25 **Sophy** Shah of Persia   27 **o'erstare** outstare 30 **'a** he   32 **Lichas** Hercules'
page   35 **Alcides** Hercules   42 **be advised** consider well   43 **Nor will not** nor
will I (ever woo another for my wife)

MOROCCO   Good fortune then,   45
To make me blest or cursèd'st among men!
                    [*Flourish of cornets.*] *Exeunt.*

[Scene II. *Venice. A street.*]

Enter [Launcelot Gobbo,] the Clown, alone.

LAUNCELOT Certainly my conscience will serve me to
run from this Jew my master. The fiend is at
mine elbow and tempts me, saying to me, "Gobbo,
Launcelot Gobbo, good Launcelot," or "good
Gobbo," or "good Launcelot Gobbo—use your   5
legs, take the start, run away." My conscience says,
"No. Take heed, honest Launcelot; take heed,
honest Gobbo," or as aforesaid, "honest Launcelot
Gobbo, do not run; scorn running with thy heels."
Well, the most courageous fiend bids me pack.   10
"Fia!" says the fiend; "away!" says the fiend. "For
the heavens, rouse up a brave mind," says the
fiend, "and run." Well, my conscience hanging about
the neck of my heart says very wisely to me, "My
honest friend Launcelot, being an honest man's   15
son"—or rather an honest woman's son, for indeed
my father did something smack, something grow
to, he had a kind of taste—Well, my conscience
says, "Launcelot, budge not." "Budge," says the
fiend. "Budge not," says my conscience. "Con-   20
science," say I, "you counsel well." "Fiend," say I,
"you counsel well." To be ruled by my conscience,

II.ii.9 **scorn running with thy heels** (1) scorn to run away with your feet
(2) scorn utterly to run   11 **Fia!** (from Italian *via*, away)   11-12 **For the heavens**
by heaven, or for heaven's sake (in either case a grotesque thing for the fiend to
say)   17-18 **did something smack ... had a kind of taste** (both phrases
indicate a tendency to vice)

23

I should stay with the Jew my master who (God
bless the mark!) is a kind of devil; and to run away
25   from the Jew, I should be ruled by the fiend who,
saving your reverence, is the devil himself. Certainly
the Jew is the very devil incarnation; and in my
conscience, my conscience is but a kind of hard conscience to offer to counsel me to stay with the Jew.
30   The fiend gives the more friendly counsel. I will run,
fiend; my heels are at your commandment, I will
run.

Enter Old Gobbo with a basket.

GOBBO Master young man, you, I pray you, which is
the way to Master Jew's?

35   LAUNCELOT [*Aside*] O heavens, this is my true-begotten
father who, being more than sand-blind, high-
gravel-blind, knows me not. I will try confusions
with him.

GOBBO Master young gentleman, I pray you which is
40   the way to Master Jew's?

LAUNCELOT Turn up on your right hand at the next
turning, but at the next turning of all, on your left;
marry, at the very next turning turn of no hand,
but turn down indirectly to the Jew's house.

45   GOBBO Be God's sonties, 'twill be a hard way to hit!
Can you tell me whether one Launcelot that dwells
with him, dwell with him or no?

LAUNCELOT Talk you of young Master Launcelot?
[*Aside*] Mark me now! Now will I raise the
50   waters.—Talk you of young Master Launcelot?

23-24 **God bless the mark!** (used, like "saving your reverence" in line 26, to
avert a bad omen)   27 **incarnation** (blunder for "incarnate")   36 **sand-blind**
dull of sight   36-37 **high-gravel-blind** (Launcelot's comic superlative for "sand-
blind")   43 **marry** (a mild interjection, originally an oath, by the Virgin Mary)
45 **Be God's sonties** by God's little saints   49-50 **raise the waters** rouse a storm
of emotion (a nautical metaphor?)

GOBBO No master, sir, but a poor man's son. His
father, though I say't, is an honest exceeding poor
man and, God be thanked, well to live.

LAUNCELOT Well, let his father be what 'a will, we talk
of young Master Launcelot.   55

GOBBO Your worship's friend, and Launcelot, sir.

LAUNCELOT But I pray you, ergo old man, ergo I beseech you, talk you of young Master Launcelot?

GOBBO Of Launcelot, an't please your mastership.

LAUNCELOT Ergo, Master Launcelot. Talk not of Master   60
Launcelot, father, for the young gentleman, according to Fates and Destinies and such odd sayings, the
Sisters Three and such branches of learning, is indeed deceased, or as you would say in plain terms,
gone to heaven.   65

GOBBO Marry, God forbid! The boy was the very staff
of my age, my very prop.

LAUNCELOT [Aside] Do I look like a cudgel or a hovel-
post, a staff, or a prop? Do you know me, father?

GOBBO Alack the day, I know you not, young gentle-   70
man, but I pray you tell me, is my boy—God rest
his soul—alive or dead?

LAUNCELOT Do you not know me, father?

GOBBO Alack, sir, I am sand-blind! I know you not.

LAUNCELOT Nay, indeed if you had your eyes you might   75
fail of the knowing me. It is a wise father that knows
his own child. Well, old man, I will tell you news of
your son. [Kneels, with his back to his father.] Give
me your blessing. Truth will come to light; murder

51 No master (as a servant, Launcelot has no claim to the title of master)
52-53 exceeding ... to live poverty-stricken and well-to-do   56 Your worship's
friend (he politely insists on his son's humble status)   57 ergo therefore   59 an't
if it   68-69 Do I ... a prop? (spoken directly to the audience)   69, 73 father (a
term of courtesy often used by the young to the old, without implying blood
relationship)

80   cannot be hid long—a man's son may, but in the
            end truth will out.

       GOBBO Pray you, sir, stand up. I am sure you are not
            Launcelot, my boy.

       LAUNCELOT Pray you let's have no more fooling about
85   it, but give me your blessing. I am Launcelot—your
            boy that was, your son that is, your child that
            shall be.

       GOBBO I cannot think you are my son.

       LAUNCELOT I know not what I shall think of that; but
90   I am Launcelot, the Jew's man, and I am sure
            Margery your wife is my mother.

       GOBBO Her name is Margery indeed! I'll be sworn, if
            thou be Launcelot thou art mine own flesh and
            blood. Lord worshipped might he be, what a beard
95   hast thou got! Thou hast got more hair on thy chin
            than Dobbin my fill-horse has on his tail.

       LAUNCELOT [Rises] It should seem then that Dobbin's
            tail grows backward. I am sure he had more hair of
            his tail than I have of my face when I last saw him.

100   GOBBO Lord, how art thou changed! How dost thou
            and thy master agree? I have brought him a present.
            How 'gree you now?

       LAUNCELOT Well, well; but for mine own part, as I have
            set up my rest to run away, so I will not rest till I
105   have run some ground. My master's a very Jew. Give
            him a present? Give him a halter! I am famished
            in his service; you may tell every finger I have with
            my ribs. Father, I am glad you are come. Give me
            your present to one Master Bassanio, who indeed
110   gives rare new liveries. If I serve not him I will run

---

94 **beard** (the sand-blind father places his hand on his son's head, and mistakes
Launcelot's fashionable long hair for a huge beard) 96 **fill-horse** cart horse
104 **set up my rest** wagered all (with word play on "rest" and "run")
106 **halter** hangman's noose 107 **tell** count

as far as God has any ground. O rare fortune, here comes the man. To him, father, for I am a Jew if I serve the Jew any longer.

Enter Bassanio, with [Leonardo and] a Follower or two.

BASSANIO You may do so, but let it be so hasted that supper be ready at the farthest by five of the clock. 115 See these letters delivered, put the liveries to making, and desire Gratiano to come anon to my lodging.
[*Exit one of his men.*]

LAUNCELOT To him, father!

GOBBO God bless your worship!

BASSANIO Gramercy. Wouldst thou aught with me?   120

GOBBO Here's my son, sir, a poor boy—

LAUNCELOT Not a poor boy, sir, but the rich Jew's man, that would, sir, as my father shall specify—

GOBBO He hath a great infection, sir, as one would say, to serve—   125

LAUNCELOT Indeed, the short and the long is, I serve the Jew, and have a desire, as my father shall specify—

GOBBO His master and he, saving your worship's reverence, are scarce cater-cousins.   130

LAUNCELOT To be brief, the very truth is that the Jew, having done me wrong, doth cause me, as my father, being I hope an old man, shall frutify unto you—

GOBBO I have here a dish of doves that I would bestow upon your worship, and my suit is—   135

---

117 **anon** straightway   120 **Gramercy** many thanks (French *grand merci*)
124 **infection** (Gobbo's mistake for "affection," i.e., liking)   130 **cater-cousins**
great friends   133 **frutify** (for "fructify," a blunder for a word like "signify")

LAUNCELOT In very brief, the suit is impertinent to myself, as your worship shall know by this honest old
man, and though I say it, though old man, yet poor
man, my father.

140 BASSANIO One speak for both. What would you?

LAUNCELOT Serve you, sir.

GOBBO That is the very defect of the matter, sir.

BASSANIO I know thee well; thou hast obtained thy suit.
Shylock thy master spoke with me this day,
145 And hath preferred thee, if it be preferment
To leave a rich Jew's service to become
The follower of so poor a gentleman.

LAUNCELOT The old proverb is very well parted between thy master Shylock and you, sir. You have
150 the grace of God, sir, and he hath enough.

BASSANIO Thou speak'st it well. Go, father, with thy
son;
Take leave of thy old master and inquire
My lodging out. [To a Servant] Give him a livery
More guarded than his fellows'. See it done.

155 LAUNCELOT Father, in. I cannot get a service; no! I have
ne'er a tongue in my head! Well! [Studies his palm.]
If any man in Italy have a fairer table which doth
offer to swear upon a book—I shall have good fortune! Go to, here's a simple line of life. Here's a
160 small trifle of wives. Alas, fifteen wives is nothing;
eleven widows and nine maids is a simple coming-in
for one man. And then to scape drowning thrice,
and to be in peril of my life with the edge of a feather-
bed! Here are simple scapes. Well, if Fortune be a
165 woman, she's a good wench for this gear. Father,

---

136 **impertinent** (for "pertinent")   142 **defect** (for "effect")   145 **preferred**
recommended for a higher position   148 **proverb** (such as, "He that hath
the grace of God hath enough")   154 **guarded** ornamented   157 **table** palm
164 **scapes** escapes   165 **gear** business, i.e., the good fortune that he pretends to
read in his palm

come. I'll take my leave of the Jew in the twinkling.
Exit Clown [Launcelot, with Old Gobbo].

BASSANIO I pray thee, good Leonardo, think on this:
These things being bought and orderly bestowed,
Return in haste, for I do feast tonight
My best-esteemed acquaintance. Hie thee, go.   170

LEONARDO My best endeavors shall be done herein.

Enter Gratiano.

GRATIANO Where's your master?

LEONARDO   Yonder, sir, he walks.
                                       Exit Leonardo.

GRATIANO Signior Bassanio!

BASSANIO Gratiano!

GRATIANO I have suit to you.

BASSANIO   You have obtained it!   175

GRATIANO You must not deny me. I must go with you
  to Belmont.

BASSANIO Why then you must. But hear thee, Gratiano:
Thou art too wild, too rude, and bold of voice—
Parts that become thee happily enough
And in such eyes as ours appear not faults;   180
But where thou art not known—why, there they
  show
Something too liberal. Pray thee take pain
To allay with some cold drops of modesty
Thy skipping spirit, lest through thy wild behavior
I be misconst'red in the place I go to,   185
And lose my hopes.

GRATIANO   Signior Bassanio, hear me:
If I do not put on a sober habit,
Talk with respect, and swear but now and then,

182 **liberal** free (a kind word to describe Gratiano!) 185 **misconst'red** miscon-
strued 187 **habit** (1) bearing (2) garment

Wear prayer books in my pocket, look demurely—
190   Nay more, while grace is saying hood mine eyes
Thus with my hat, and sigh and say Amen,
Use all the observance of civility
Like one well studied in a sad ostent
To please his grandam, never trust me more.

195   BASSANIO Well, we shall see your bearing.

GRATIANO Nay, but I bar tonight. You shall not gauge
        me
By what we do tonight.

BASSANIO   No, that were pity.
I would entreat you rather to put on
Your boldest suit of mirth, for we have friends
200   That purpose merriment. But fare you well;
I have some business.

GRATIANO And I must to Lorenzo and the rest,
But we will visit you at supper time.   *Exeunt.*

[Scene III. *Venice. Shylock's house.*]

Enter Jessica and [Launcelot] the Clown.

JESSICA I am sorry thou wilt leave my father so;
Our house is hell, and thou a merry devil
Didst rob it of some taste of tediousness.
But fare thee well; there is a ducat for thee.
5   And, Launcelot, soon at supper shalt thou see
Lorenzo, who is thy new master's guest.
Give him this letter; do it secretly.
And so farewell. I would not have my father
See me in talk with thee.

192 **civility** civilized behavior   193 **sad ostent** sober and earnest appearance

30

LAUNCELOT Adieu! Tears exhibit my tongue. Most   10
    beautiful pagan, most sweet Jew, if a Christian do
    not play the knave and get thee, I am much de-
    ceived. But adieu! These foolish drops do some-
    thing drown my manly spirit. Adieu!

JESSICA Farewell, good Launcelot.   [*Exit Launcelot.*]   15
    Alack, what heinous sin is it in me
    To be ashamed to be my father's child!
    But though I am a daughter to his blood,
    I am not to his manners. O Lorenzo,
    If thou keep promise, I shall end this strife,   20
    Become a Christian and thy loving wife!   *Exit.*

[Scene IV. *Venice. A street.*]

Enter Gratiano, Lorenzo, Salerio, and Solanio.

LORENZO Nay, we will slink away in supper time,
    Disguise us at my lodging, and return
    All in an hour.

GRATIANO We have not made good preparation.

SALERIO We have not spoke us yet of torchbearers.   5

SOLANIO 'Tis vile, unless it may be quaintly ordered,
    And better in my mind not undertook.

LORENZO 'Tis now but four of clock. We have two
    hours
    To furnish us.

II.iii.10 **Adieu** (perhaps not merely "good-bye," but "I commend you to God")
10 **exhibit** (for "inhibit")   11-13 **if a … deceived** (perhaps Launcelot is giving a
hint of what happens in II.v, but perhaps "do" should be emended to "did," and
"get" should be understood in the sense of "beget") II.iv.5 **spoke us yet of torchbearers** talked about getting torchbearers (who were regularly used in this sort of
street festivity)   6 **quaintly ordered** artfully arranged

Enter Launcelot [with a letter].

Friend Launcelot, what's the news?

10   LAUNCELOT And it shall please you to break up this,
       it shall seem to signify.

     LORENZO I know the hand. In faith, 'tis a fair hand,
       And whiter than the paper it writ on
       Is the fair hand that writ.

     GRATIANO   Love-news, in faith!

15   LAUNCELOT By your leave, sir.

     LORENZO Whither goest thou?

     LAUNCELOT Marry, sir, to bid my old master the Jew
       to sup tonight with my new master the Christian.

     LORENZO Hold here, take this. [*Gives money.*] Tell
       gentle Jessica
20   I will not fail her. Speak it privately.
                              Exit Clown [Launcelot].
       Go, gentlemen;
       Will you prepare you for this masque tonight?
       I am provided of a torchbearer.

     SALERIO Ay marry, I'll be gone about it straight.

     SOLANIO And so will I.

25   LORENZO   Meet me and Gratiano
       At Gratiano's lodging some hour hence.

     SALERIO 'Tis good we do so.   *Exit [with Solanio].*

     GRATIANO Was not that letter from fair Jessica?

     LORENZO I must needs tell thee all. She hath directed
30   How I shall take her from her father's house,
       What gold and jewels she is furnished with,
       What page's suit she hath in readiness.
       If e'er the Jew her father come to heaven,

---

10 **break up** open   13 **it** i.e., the hand   17 **bid** ask   19, 34 **gentle** charming and
possessed of all attributes of a lady (with a pun on "gentile," as elsewhere)

32

It will be for his gentle daughter's sake;
And never dare misfortune cross her foot,   35
Unless she do it under this excuse,
That she is issue to a faithless Jew.
Come, go with me; peruse this as thou goest.
Fair Jessica shall be my torchbearer.

Exit [*with Gratiano*].

[Scene V. *Venice. Before Shylock's house.*]

Enter [*Shylock the*] *Jew and* [*Launcelot,*] *his man
that was the Clown.*

SHYLOCK Well, thou shalt see, thy eyes shall be thy
    judge,
The difference of old Shylock and Bassanio.—
What, Jessica!—Thou shalt not gormandize
As thou hast done with me.—What, Jessica!—
And sleep, and snore, and rend apparel out.—   5
Why, Jessica, I say!

LAUNCELOT   Why, Jessica!

SHYLOCK Who bids thee call? I do not bid thee call.

LAUNCELOT Your worship was wont to tell me I could
    do nothing without bidding.

Enter Jessica.

JESSICA Call you? What is your will?   10

SHYLOCK I am bid forth to supper, Jessica.
There are my keys. But wherefore should I go?
I am not bid for love—they flatter me.
But yet I'll go in hate, to feed upon
The prodigal Christian. Jessica my girl,   15

35 **cross her foot** cross her path   37 **faithless** lacking the Christian faith   39 **torchbearer** i.e., disguised as a page   II.v.3 **What** (exclamation ·of impatience like
"Why" in line 6)

> Look to my house. I am right loath to go.
> There is some ill a-brewing towards my rest,
> For I did dream of moneybags tonight.

LAUNCELOT I beseech you, sir, go. My young master
20   doth expect your reproach.

SHYLOCK So do I his.

LAUNCELOT And they have conspired together. I will
not say you shall see a masque, but if you do, then
it was not for nothing that my nose fell a-bleeding
25   on Black Monday last at six o'clock i' th' morning,
falling out that year on Ash Wednesday was four
year in th' afternoon.

SHYLOCK What, are there masques? Hear you me,
      Jessica:
> Lock up my doors; and when you hear the drum
30 > And the vile squealing of the wry-necked fife,
> Clamber not you up to the casements then,
> Nor thrust your head into the public street
> To gaze on Christian fools with varnished faces;
> But stop my house's ears—I mean my casements;
35 > Let not the sound of shallow fopp'ry enter
> My sober house. By Jacob's staff I swear
> I have no mind of feasting forth tonight;
> But I will go. Go you before me, sirrah.
> Say I will come.

LAUNCELOT   I will go before, sir.
40   Mistress, look out at window for all this:
        There will come a Christian by
        Will be worth a Jewess' eye.   [Exit.]

---

18 **tonight** last night (the premonition is serious for Shylock, comic for the audience)
20 **reproach** (Launcelot's word for "approach")   25 **Black Monday** Easter Monday
26-27 **falling ... afternoon** (apparently Launcelot means "four years ago on Ash
Wednesday," but he may be intentionally talking nonsense)   30 **wry-necked fife**
fife-player with neck twisted to one side (the mouthpiece of the Elizabethan fife
was set at an angle, and these words are therefore sometimes taken to mean the
instrument; but Shylock would be less scornful of the instrument than of the gay
fool with his neck at a crazy angle)   33 **varnished faces** painted masks (Shylock
no doubt puns on "varnished" in the sense of "insincere")

SHYLOCK What says that fool of Hagar's offspring, ha?

JESSICA His words were "Farewell, mistress"—nothing
    else.

SHYLOCK The patch is kind enough, but a huge feeder,   45
    Snail-slow in profit, and he sleeps by day
    More than the wildcat. Drones hive not with me;
    Therefore I part with him, and part with him
    To one that I would have him help to waste
    His borrowed purse. Well, Jessica, go in;   50
    Perhaps I will return immediately.
    Do as I bid you, shut doors after you.
    Fast bind, fast find,
    A proverb never stale in thrifty mind.   *Exit.*

JESSICA Farewell; and if my fortune be not crost,   55
    I have a father, you a daughter, lost.   *Exit.*

[Scene VI. *Venice. Before Shylock's house.*]

Enter the Masquers, Gratiano and Salerio.

GRATIANO This is the penthouse under which Lorenzo
    Desired us to make stand.

SALERIO   His hour is almost past.

GRATIANO And it is marvel he outdwells his hour,
    For lovers ever run before the clock.

SALERIO O ten times faster Venus' pigeons fly   5
    To seal love's bonds new-made, than they are wont
    To keep obligèd faith unforfeited!

---

43 **Hagar's offspring** Ishmael, son of Abraham by the servant Hagar (mother and
son were cast out by Abraham after Isaac's birth)   45 **patch** fool   46 **in profit** in
any profitable activity   II.vi.1 **penthouse** shelter formed by a projecting roof
5 **Venus' pigeons** (they drew her chariot)   7 **obligèd faith** faith pledged (in
marriage)

35

GRATIANO That ever holds. Who riseth from a feast
    With that keen appetite that he sits down?
10 Where is the horse that doth untread again
    His tedious measures with the unbated fire
    That he did pace them first? All things that are
    Are with more spirit chasèd than enjoyed.
    How like a younger or a prodigal
15 The scarfèd bark puts from her native bay,
    Hugged and embracèd by the strumpet wind!
    How like the prodigal doth she return,
    With over-weathered ribs and ragged sails,
    Lean, rent, and beggared by the strumpet wind!

Enter Lorenzo.

20 SALERIO Here comes Lorenzo: more of this hereafter.

LORENZO Sweet friends, your patience for my long
        abode.
    Not I but my affairs have made you wait.
    When you shall please to play the thieves for wives,
    I'll watch as long for you then. Approach;
25 Here dwells my father Jew. Ho, who's within?

[Enter] Jessica above [in boy's clothes].

JESSICA Who are you? Tell me for more certainty,
    Albeit I'll swear that I do know your tongue.

LORENZO Lorenzo, and thy love.

JESSICA Lorenzo certain, and my love indeed,
30 For who love I so much? And now who knows
    But you, Lorenzo, whether I am yours?

LORENZO Heaven and thy thoughts are witness that
        thou art.

JESSICA Here, catch this casket; it is worth the pains.
    I am glad 'tis night, you do not look on me,

---

11 **measures** paces 14 **younger** younger son 15 **scarfèd** decorated with scarfs
(i.e., flags and streamers) 18 **over-weathered** long exposed to stormy weather
21 **abode** delay 34 **'tis night, you** (an ellipsis, "and" being understood)

For I am much ashamed of my exchange.   35
But love is blind, and lovers cannot see
The pretty follies that themselves commit;
For if they could, Cupid himself would blush
To see me thus transformèd to a boy.

LORENZO Descend, for you must be my torchbearer.   40

JESSICA What, must I hold a candle to my shames?
They in themselves, good sooth, are too too light.
Why, 'tis an office of discovery, love,
And I should be obscured.

LORENZO   So are you, sweet,
Even in the lovely garnish of a boy.   45
But come at once;
For the close night doth play the runaway,
And we are stayed for at Bassanio's feast.

JESSICA I will make fast the doors and gild myself
With some moe ducats, and be with you straight.   50
                                    [*Exit above.*]

GRATIANO Now by my hood, a gentle and no Jew!

LORENZO Beshrow me but I love her heartily!
For she is wise, if I can judge of her,
And fair she is, if that mine eyes be true,
And true she is, as she hath proved herself;   55
And therefore, like herself, wise, fair, and true,
Shall she be placèd in my constant soul.

                Enter Jessica [below].

What, art thou come? On, gentlemen, away!
Our masquing mates by this time for us stay.
                        Exit [with Jessica and Salerio].

                Enter Antonio.

ANTONIO Who's there?   60

35 exchange i.e., of clothes   42 light immodest (with a pun)   43 office of
discovery task in which my disguise will be revealed   45 garnish pleasing attire
47 close secret   50 moe more   51 gentle refined lady (with the usual pun on
"gentile")   52 Beshrow (a light word for "curse")

GRATIANO Signior Antonio?

ANTONIO Fie, fie, Gratiano, where are all the rest?
'Tis nine o'clock, our friends all stay for you.
No masque tonight. The wind is come about;
65   Bassanio presently will go aboard.
I have sent twenty out to seek for you.

GRATIANO I am glad on't. I desire no more delight
Than to be under sail and gone tonight.

Exeunt.

[Scene VII. *Belmont. Portia's house.*]

[*Flourish of cornets.*] *Enter Portia with Morocco
and both their Trains.*

PORTIA Go, draw aside the curtains and discover
The several caskets to this noble Prince.
Now make your choice.

MOROCCO This first, of gold, who this inscription bears,
"Who chooseth me shall gain what many men
5   desire."
The second, silver, which this promise carries,
"Who chooseth me shall get as much as he deserves."
This third, dull lead, with warning all as blunt,
"Who chooseth me must give and hazard all he
hath."
10   How shall I know if I do choose the right?

PORTIA The one of them contains my picture, Prince.
If you choose that, then I am yours withal.

MOROCCO Some god direct my judgment! Let me see—

---

65 **presently** at this present moment   II.vii.1 **discover** reveal   8 **as blunt** as
blunt as the lead is dull (with quibbles on "blunt" in the senses of "abrupt in
speech and manner" and of "not sharp," and on "dull" in the senses of "not
sharp" and "not shining")

I will survey th' inscriptions back again.
What says this leaden casket?   15
"Who chooseth me must give and hazard all he hath."
Must give—for what? For lead! Hazard for lead?
This casket threatens; men that hazard all
Do it in hope of fair advantages.
A golden mind stoops not to shows of dross;   20
I'll then nor give nor hazard aught for lead.
What says the silver with her virgin hue?
"Who chooseth me shall get as much as he deserves."
As much as he deserves? Pause there, Morocco,
And weigh thy value with an even hand: 25
If thou be'st rated by thy estimation,
Thou dost deserve enough, and yet enough
May not extend so far as to the lady;
And yet to be afeard of my deserving
Were but a weak disabling of myself.   30
As much as I deserve? Why that's the lady!
I do in birth deserve her, and in fortunes,
In graces, and in qualities of breeding;
But more than these, in love I do deserve.
What if I strayed no farther, but chose here?   35
Let's see once more this saying graved in gold:
"Who chooseth me shall gain what many men
    desire."
Why that's the lady! All the world desires her;
From the four corners of the earth they come
To kiss this shrine, this mortal breathing saint.   40
The Hyrcanian deserts and the vasty wilds
Of wide Arabia are as throughfares now
For princes to come view fair Portia.
The watery kingdom, whose ambitious head
Spets in the face of heaven, is no bar   45
To stop the foreign spirits, but they come
As o'er a brook to see fair Portia.
One of these three contains her heavenly picture.
Is't like that lead contains her? 'Twere damnation

26 estimation reputation   30 disabling undervaluing   41 Hyrcanian deserts
Persian deserts (famous for savage beasts)

39

50   To think so base a thought; it were too gross
      To rib her cerecloth in the obscure grave.
      Or shall I think in silver she's immured,
      Being ten times undervalued to tried gold?
      O sinful thought! Never so rich a gem
55   Was set in worse than gold. They have in England
      A coin that bears the figure of an angel
      Stampèd in gold—but that's insculped upon;
      But here an angel in a golden bed
      Lies all within. Deliver me the key.
60   Here do I choose, and thrive I as I may!

PORTIA There, take it, Prince; and if my form lie there,
      Then I am yours.   [*He opens the golden casket.*]

MOROCCO   O hell! What have we here?
      A carrion Death, within whose empty eye
      There is a written scroll! I'll read the writing.
65   "All that glisters is not gold;
          Often have you heard that told.
          Many a man his life hath sold
          But my outside to behold;
          Gilded tombs do worms infold.
70   Had you been as wise as bold,
          Young in limbs, in judgment old,
          Your answer had not been inscrolled.
          Fare you well, your suit is cold."
      Cold indeed, and labor lost.
75   Then farewell heat, and welcome frost!
      Portia, adieu. I have too grieved a heart
      To take a tedious leave. Thus losers part.
                        Exit [*with his Train. Flourish of cornets*].

PORTIA A gentle riddance. Draw the curtains, go.
      Let all of his complexion choose me so.   *Exeunt.*

---

50 **it were too gross** lead would be too coarse (bodies of wealthy persons were
often encased in lead)   51 **cerecloth** waxed embalming cloth   51 **obscure** (accent
on first syllable)   57 **insculped** sculptured   58 **angel** i.e., Portia's picture   63 **Death**
death's head   65 **All … gold** (proverbial)   72 **inscrolled** written on the scroll
78 **gentle** well-bred   79 **complexion** temperament (not merely coloring)

[Scene VIII. *Venice. A street.*]

Enter Salerio and Solanio.

SALERIO Why, man, I saw Bassanio under sail;
　With him is Gratiano gone along,
　And in their ship I am sure Lorenzo is not.

SOLANIO The villain Jew with outcries raised the Duke,
　Who went with him to search Bassanio's ship.　　　　5

SALERIO He came too late, the ship was under sail.
　But there the Duke was given to understand
　That in a gondola were seen together
　Lorenzo and his amorous Jessica.
　Besides, Antonio certified the Duke　　　　　　　10
　They were not with Bassanio in his ship.

SOLANIO I never heard a passion so confused,
　So strange, outrageous, and so variable
　As the dog Jew did utter in the streets:
　"My daughter! O my ducats! O my daughter!　　　15
　Fled with a Christian! O my Christian ducats!
　Justice! The law! My ducats and my daughter!
　A sealèd bag, two sealèd bags of ducats,
　Of double ducats, stol'n from me by my daughter!
　And jewels—two stones, two rich and precious
　　stones,　　　　　　　　　　　　　　　　　20
　Stol'n by my daughter! Justice! Find the girl!
　She hath the stones upon her, and the ducats!"

SALERIO Why, all the boys in Venice follow him,
　Crying his stones, his daughter, and his ducats.

SOLANIO Let good Antonio look he keep his day,　　25
　Or he shall pay for this.

II.viii.4 villain low-bred fellow (not scoundrel; a vaguer term than today)
12 passion emotional outburst 25 keep his day pay on the exact day appointed

41

SALERIO   Marry, well rememb'red.
I reasoned with a Frenchman yesterday,
Who told me, in the narrow seas that part
The French and English there miscarrièd
30   A vessel of our country richly fraught.
I thought upon Antonio when he told me,
And wished in silence that it were not his.

SOLANIO You were best to tell Antonio what you hear.
Yet do not suddenly, for it may grieve him.

35   SALERIO A kinder gentleman treads not the earth.
I saw Bassanio and Antonio part.
Bassanio told him he would make some speed
Of his return; he answered, "Do not so.
Slubber not business for my sake, Bassanio,
40   But stay the very riping of the time;
And for the Jew's bond which he hath of me,
Let it not enter in your mind of love.
Be merry, and employ your chiefest thoughts
To courtship and such fair ostents of love
45   As shall conveniently become you there."
And even there, his eye being big with tears,
Turning his face, he put his hand behind him,
And with affection wondrous sensible
He wrung Bassanio's hand; and so they parted.

50   SOLANIO I think he only loves the world for him.
I pray thee let us go and find him out,
And quicken his embracèd heaviness
With some delight or other.

SALERIO   Do we so.   *Exeunt*.

27 **reasoned** talked 28 **narrow seas** English Channel 30 **fraught** freighted
39 **Slubber** hurry over in a slovenly way 42 **mind of love** loving thoughts (probably about both Antonio and Portia) 44 **ostents** shows, expressions 48 **affection wondrous sensible** wonderfully strong emotion 52 **quicken his embracèd heaviness** lighten the gloom which he has embraced

[Scene IX. *Belmont. Portia's house.*]

Enter Nerissa and a Servitor.

NERISSA Quick, quick I pray thee, draw the curtain
    straight.
    The Prince of Aragon hath ta'en his oath,
    And comes to his election presently.
    [*Flourish of cornets.*] *Enter Aragon, his Train, and
    Portia.*

PORTIA Behold, there stand the caskets, noble Prince.
    If you choose that wherein I am contained,   5
    Straight shall our nuptial rites be solemnized;
    But if you fail, without more speech, my lord,
    You must be gone from hence immediately.

ARAGON I am enjoined by oath to observe three things:
    First, never to unfold to any one   10
    Which casket 'twas I chose; next, if I fail
    Of the right casket, never in my life
    To woo a maid in way of marriage;
    Lastly, if I do fail in fortune of my choice,
    Immediately to leave you and be gone.   15

PORTIA To these injunctions everyone doth swear
    That comes to hazard for my worthless self.

ARAGON And so have I addressed me. Fortune now
    To my heart's hope! Gold, silver, and base lead.
    "Who chooseth me must give and hazard all he hath."   20
    You shall look fairer ere I give or hazard.
    What says the golden chest? Ha, let me see!
    "Who chooseth me shall gain what many men desire."

II.ix.1 **straight** at once   3 **election** choice   3 **presently** at this present moment,
instantly   18 **so** on these terms   18 **have I addressed me** I have addressed
myself (to this affair)

43

What many men desire—that "many" may be meant
25   By the fool multitude that choose by show,
Not learning more than the fond eye doth teach,
Which pries not to th' interior, but like the martlet
Builds in the weather on the outward wall,
Even in the force and road of casualty.
30   I will not choose what many men desire,
Because I will not jump with common spirits
And rank me with the barbarous multitudes.
Why then, to thee, thou silver treasure house!
Tell me once more what title thou dost bear.
35   "Who chooseth me shall get as much as he deserves."
And well said too, for who shall go about
To cozen fortune, and be honorable
Without the stamp of merit? Let none presume
To wear an undeservèd dignity.
40   O that estates, degrees, and offices
Were not derived corruptly, and that clear honor
Were purchased by the merit of the wearer!
How many then should cover that stand bare!
How many be commanded that command;
45   How much low peasantry would then be gleanèd
From the true seed of honor! And how much honor
Picked from the chaff and ruin of the times
To be new varnished. Well, but to my choice.
"Who chooseth me shall get as much as he deserves."
50   I will assume desert. Give me a key for this,
And instantly unlock my fortunes here.

[*He opens the silver casket.*]

PORTIA Too long a pause for that which you find there.

---

25 **By** with regard to   26 **fond** foolish   27 **martlet** martin, a bird   29 **in ...
casualty** exposed to the tyrannic force of mischance and lying in the open road
31 **jump with** accord with   37 **cozen** cheat   40 **degrees** ranks   40 **offices**
official positions   43 **cover** wear hats, in sign of authority   45 **gleanèd** picked
out, as in gleaning grain (cf. line 47, "Picked from the chaff")   46 **seed of honor**
descendants of ancient nobility   48 **To be new varnished** to have the luster of
their family restored   52 **Too ... there** (probably an aside)

ARAGON What's here? The portrait of a blinking idiot
Presenting me a schedule! I will read it.
How much unlike art thou to Portia!   55
How much unlike my hopes and my deservings!
"Who chooseth me shall have as much as he
   deserves."
Did I deserve no more than a fool's head?
Is that my prize? Are my deserts no better?

PORTIA To offend and judge are distinct offices,   60
And of opposèd natures.

ARAGON   What is here?
"The fire seven times tried this;
Seven times tried that judgment is
That did never choose amiss.
Some there be that shadows kiss;   65
Such have but a shadow's bliss.
There be fools alive iwis,
Silvered o'er, and so was this.
Take what wife you will to bed,
I will ever be your head.   70
So be gone; you are sped."
Still more fool I shall appear
By the time I linger here.
With one fool's head I came to woo,
But I go away with two.   75
Sweet, adieu. I'll keep my oath,
Patiently to bear my wroath.   [*Exit with his Train.*]

PORTIA Thus hath the candle singed the moth.
O these deliberate fools! When they do choose,
They have the wisdom by their wit to lose.   80

NERISSA The ancient saying is no heresy:
Hanging and wiving goes by destiny.

PORTIA Come draw the curtain, Nerissa.

54 **schedule** scroll   60–61 **To offend ... natures** the offender is not to judge
himself   62 **fire** (pronounced fī-er)   62 **this** i.e., the silver of the casket   67 **iwis**
certainly   68 **Silvered o'er** i.e., with the gray hair usually associated with wisdom
70 **I** "the blinking idiot" of line 53   71 **you are sped** you have achieved your
fortune   77 **wroath** heavy lot (?)   80 **wit** cleverness

Enter Messenger.

MESSENGER Where is my lady?

PORTIA   Here. What would my lord?

85   MESSENGER Madam, there is alighted at your gate
        A young Venetian, one that comes before
        To signify th' approaching of his lord,
        From whom he bringeth sensible regreets,
        To wit, besides commends and courteous breath,
90   Gifts of rich value. Yet I have not seen
        So likely an ambassador of love.
        A day in April never came so sweet
        To show how costly summer was at hand,
        As this forespurrer comes before his lord.

95   PORTIA No more, I pray thee. I am half afeard
        Thou wilt say anon he is some kin to thee,
        Thou spend'st such high-day wit in praising him.
        Come, come, Nerissa, for I long to see
        Quick Cupid's post that comes so mannerly.

100   NERISSA Bassanio, Lord Love, if thy will it be!

                                                Exeunt.

---

84 **What would my lord?** (a gay, jesting retort to the messenger's "my lady")
88 **sensible regreets** a quibble: greetings (1) expressing strong feeling, and
(2) conveying tangible gifts   90 **Yet I have not seen** not yet have I seen   91 **likely**
promising   93 **costly** rich, plenteous   94 **forespurrer** advance messenger (one
who spurs his horse ahead of his party)   97 **high-day wit** imagination befitting a
festive occasion   99 **post** messenger   100 **Lord Love** god of love

[ACT III

Scene I. *Venice. A street.*]

[Enter] Solanio and Salerio.

SOLANIO Now what news on the Rialto?

SALERIO Why, yet it lives there unchecked that Antonio
hath a ship of rich lading wracked on the narrow
seas—the Goodwins I think they call the place—
a very dangerous flat, and fatal, where the carcasses   5
of many a tall ship lie buried as they say, if my gossip Report be an honest woman of her word.

SOLANIO I would she were as lying a gossip in that, as
ever knapped ginger or made her neighbors believe
she wept for the death of a third husband. But it is   10
true, without any slips of prolixity or crossing the
plain highway of talk, that the good Antonio, the
honest Antonio—O that I had a title good enough to
keep his name company!—

SALERIO Come, the full stop.   15

SOLANIO Ha, what sayest thou? Why the end is, he hath
lost a ship.

SALERIO I would it might prove the end of his losses.

III.i.2 **it lives there unchecked** it is reported without dispute   3-4 **narrow seas**
English Channel   4 **Goodwins** Goodwin Sands, a shoal   6-7 **gossip** talkative
comrade   9 **knapped** snapped, bit   11 **slips of prolixity** long-winded lies
11-12 **crossing ... talk** going counter to honest speech   15 **Come, the full stop**
come to the end of your sentence

47

SOLANIO Let me say Amen betimes, lest the devil cross
my prayer, for here he comes in the likeness of a Jew.

Enter Shylock.

How now, Shylock? What news among the merchants?

SHYLOCK You knew, none so well, none so well as you,
of my daughter's flight.

SALERIO That's certain. I for my part knew the tailor
that made the wings she flew withal.

SOLANIO And Shylock for his own part knew the bird
was fledge, and then it is the complexion of them
all to leave the dam.

SHYLOCK She is damned for it.

SALERIO That's certain, if the devil may be her judge.

SHYLOCK My own flesh and blood to rebel!

SOLANIO Out upon it, old carrion! Rebels it at these
years?

SHYLOCK I say my daughter is my flesh and my blood.

SALERIO There is more difference between thy flesh and
hers than between jet and ivory, more between your
bloods than there is between red wine and Rhenish.
But tell us, do you hear whether Antonio have had
any loss at sea or no?

SHYLOCK There I have another bad match! A bankrout, a prodigal, who dare scarce show his head on
the Rialto, a beggar that was used to come so smug
upon the mart! Let him look to his bond. He was
wont to call me usurer. Let him look to his bond. He
was wont to lend money for a Christian cursy. Let
him look to his bond.

---

19 **betimes** promptly   28 **fledge** feathered, able to fly   28 **complexion** natural
disposition   33 **Rebels it** (a contemptuous pun on "flesh and blood" in the sense
of fleshly desire)   41-42 **bankrout** bankrupt   43 **smug** well-groomed   46 **cursy**
courtesy

SALERIO Why, I am sure if he forfeit thou wilt not take
his flesh. What's that good for?

SHYLOCK To bait fish withal. If it will feed nothing else,   50
it will feed my revenge. He hath disgraced me, and
hind'red me half a million, laughed at my losses,
mocked at my gains, scorned my nation, thwarted
my bargains, cooled my friends, heated mine enemies—and what's his reason? I am a Jew. Hath not   55
a Jew eyes? Hath not a Jew hands, organs, dimensions, senses, affections, passions?—fed with the
same food, hurt with the same weapons, subject to
the same diseases, healed by the same means, warmed
and cooled by the same winter and summer as a   60
Christian is? If you prick us, do we not bleed? If you
tickle us, do we not laugh? If you poison us, do we
not die? And if you wrong us, shall we not revenge?
If we are like you in the rest, we will resemble you in
that. If a Jew wrong a Christian, what is his humil-   65
ity? Revenge! If a Christian wrong a Jew, what
should his sufferance be by Christian example? Why
revenge! The villainy you teach me I will execute, and
it shall go hard but I will better the instruction.

Enter a Man from Antonio.

[MAN] Gentlemen, my master Antonio is at his house,   70
and desires to speak with you both.

SALERIO We have been up and down to seek him.

Enter Tubal.

SOLANIO Here comes another of the tribe. A third cannot be matched, unless the devil himself turn Jew.
Exeunt Gentlemen [Solanio, Salerio, and Man].

SHYLOCK How now, Tubal! What news from Genoa?   75
Hast thou found my daughter?

56-57 **dimensions** limbs, features, etc.   57 **affections** feelings   65-66 **what is
his humility?** what does his Christian humility amount to?

TUBAL I often came where I did hear of her, but cannot
find her.

SHYLOCK Why there, there, there, there! A diamond
80 gone cost me two thousand ducats in Frankford! The
curse never fell upon our nation till now; I never felt
it till now. Two thousand ducats in that, and other
precious, precious jewels. I would my daughter were
dead at my foot, and the jewels in her ear! Would she
85 were hearsed at my foot, and the ducats in her coffin!
No news of them? Why, so! And I know not what's
spent in the search. Why thou loss upon loss—the
thief gone with so much, and so much to find the
thief!—and no satisfaction, no revenge, nor no ill
90 luck stirring but what lights o' my shoulders, no sighs
but o' my breathing, no tears but o' my shedding.

TUBAL Yes, other men have ill luck too. Antonio, as I
heard in Genoa—

SHYLOCK What, what, what? Ill luck, ill luck?

95 TUBAL Hath an argosy cast away coming from Tripolis.

SHYLOCK I thank God, I thank God! Is it true, is it true?

TUBAL I spoke with some of the sailors that escaped the
wrack.

SHYLOCK I thank thee, good Tubal. Good news, good
100 news! Ha, ha! Heard in Genoa?

TUBAL Your daughter spent in Genoa, as I heard, one
night fourscore ducats.

SHYLOCK Thou stick'st a dagger in me. I shall never see
my gold again. Fourscore ducats at a sitting, fourscore
105 ducats!

TUBAL There came divers of Antonio's creditors in my
company to Venice that swear he cannot choose but
break.

108 **break** go bankrupt

SHYLOCK I am very glad of it. I'll plague him; I'll torture
him. I am glad of it.   110

TUBAL One of them showed me a ring that he had of
your daughter for a monkey.

SHYLOCK Out upon her! Thou torturest me, Tubal. It
was my turquoise; I had it of Leah when I was a
bachelor. I would not have given it for a wilderness   115
of monkeys.

TUBAL But Antonio is certainly undone.

SHYLOCK Nay, that's true, that's very true. Go, Tubal,
fee me an officer; bespeak him a fortnight before.
I will have the heart of him if he forfeit, for were he   120
out of Venice I can make what merchandise I will.
Go, Tubal, and meet me at our synagogue; go, good
Tubal; at our synagogue, Tubal.   *Exeunt.*

[Scene II. *Belmont. Portia's house.*]

*Enter Bassanio, Portia, Gratiano, [Nerissa,] and
all their Trains.*

PORTIA I pray you tarry; pause a day or two
Before you hazard, for in choosing wrong
I lose your company. Therefore forbear awhile.
There's something tells me (but it is not love)
I would not lose you; and you know yourself   5
Hate counsels not in such a quality.
But lest you should not understand me well—
And yet a maiden hath no tongue but thought—
I would detain you here some month or two
Before you venture for me. I could teach you   10

114 Leah Shylock's wife   119 officer (to arrest Antonio)   119 bespeak engage
121 merchandise wealth   III.ii.6 in such a quality in such a manner of speech
as I am using to you

How to choose right, but then I am forsworn.
So will I never be. So may you miss me.
But if you do, you'll make me wish a sin—
That I had been forsworn. Beshrow your eyes!
15 They have o'erlooked me and divided me;
One half of me is yours, the other half yours—
Mine own I would say; but if mine then yours,
And so all yours! O these naughty times
Puts bars between the owners and their rights!
20 And so, though yours, not yours. Prove it so,
Let fortune go to hell for it, not I.
I speak too long, but 'tis to peize the time,
To eche it and to draw it out in length,
To stay you from election.

BASSANIO   Let me choose,
25 For as I am, I live upon the rack.

PORTIA Upon the rack, Bassanio? Then confess
What treason there is mingled with your love.

BASSANIO None but that ugly treason of mistrust,
Which makes me fear th' enjoying of my love.
30 There may as well be amity and life
'Tween snow and fire, as treason and my love.

PORTIA Ay, but I fear you speak upon the rack,
Where men enforcèd do speak anything.

BASSANIO Promise me life, and I'll confess the truth.

PORTIA Well then, confess and live.

35 BASSANIO   Confess and love
Had been the very sum of my confession!
O happy torment, when my torturer
Doth teach me answers for deliverance.

14 **Beshrow** curse (but a playful word)   15 **o'erlooked** bewitched   18 **naughty**
wicked   20 **Prove it so** if it should prove so   22 **peize** weigh down, hence retard
23 **eche** eke out, i.e., lengthen   25 **rack** instrument of torture, on which the body
was pulled with great force, often breaking the joints; used to force confessions,
especially in trials for treason   27 **What treason ... love** (spoken playfully)
33 **enforcèd** compelled (by torture)   38 **answers for deliverance** answers to
free me from torture

But let me to my fortune and the caskets.

PORTIA Away then! I am locked in one of them;   40
If you do love me, you will find me out.
Nerissa and the rest, stand all aloof.
Let music sound while he doth make his choice;
Then if he lose he makes a swanlike end,
Fading in music. That the comparison   45
May stand more proper, my eye shall be the stream
And wat'ry deathbed for him. He may win;
And what is music then? Then music is
Even as the flourish when true subjects bow
To a new-crownèd monarch. Such it is   50
As are those dulcet sounds in break of day,
That creep into the dreaming bridegroom's ear
And summon him to marriage. Now he goes,
With no less presence, but with much more love,
Than young Alcides, when he did redeem   55
The virgin tribute paid by howling Troy
To the sea monster. I stand for sacrifice;
The rest aloof are the Dardanian wives,
With blearèd visages come forth to view
The issue of th' exploit. Go, Hercules!   60
Live thou, I live. With much, much more dismay
I view the fight than thou that mak'st the fray.

A song the whilst Bassanio comments on the
caskets to himself.

Tell me where is fancy bred,
Or in the heart, or in the head?
How begot, how nourishèd?   65
    Reply, reply.
It is engend'red in the eyes,

---

44 swanlike end an end like the swan's (who was supposed never to sing until it sang
enchantingly at its death)   49 flourish fanfare of trumpets   54 presence noble
bearing   55 Alcides Hercules   56 virgin tribute Hesione, Priam's sister, who
was offered as a divine sacrifice to be devoured by a sea monster; Hercules slew the
monster and saved her   61 Live thou if thou live   61 dismay alarm and terror
62 fray combat   63 fancy love based only on the senses, especially the sight

With gazing fed, and fancy dies
In the cradle where it lies.
70   Let us all ring fancy's knell.
I'll begin it—Ding, dong, bell.
ALL   Ding, dong, bell.

BASSANIO So may the outward shows be least
themselves;
The world is still deceived with ornament.
75   In law, what plea so tainted and corrupt,
But being seasoned with a gracious voice,
Obscures the show of evil? In religion,
What damnèd error but some sober brow
Will bless it, and approve it with a text,
80   Hiding the grossness with fair ornament?
There is no vice so simple but assumes
Some mark of virtue on his outward parts.
How many cowards whose hearts are all as false
As stairs of sand, wear yet upon their chins
85   The beards of Hercules and frowning Mars,
Who inward searched, have livers white as milk!
And these assume but valor's excrement
To render them redoubted. Look on beauty,
And you shall see 'tis purchased by the weight,
90   Which therein works a miracle in nature,
Making them lightest that wear most of it:
So are those crispèd snaky golden locks,
Which maketh such wanton gambols with the wind
Upon supposèd fairness, often known
95   To be the dowry of a second head,
The skull that bred them in the sepulcher.
Thus ornament is but the guilèd shore
To a most dangerous sea, the beauteous scarf

73 So thus   73 least themselves least like what they really are   74 still continually   79 approve it with a text prove it by a biblical text   86 livers white as milk (a pale liver supposedly caused cowardice)   87 excrement excrescence, outer appearance   88 redoubted dreaded   91 lightest (a pun on "light" in the sense of unchaste)   92 crispèd curled   93 wanton playful   95 dowry gift of property, i.e., hair from a dead person's head   97 guilèd full of guile, treacherous

Veiling an Indian beauty; in a word,
The seeming truth which cunning times put on   100
To entrap the wisest. Therefore then, thou gaudy
   gold,
Hard food for Midas, I will none of thee;
Nor none of thee, thou pale and common drudge
'Tween man and man. But thou, thou meager lead
Which rather threaten'st than dost promise aught,   105
Thy paleness moves me more than eloquence;
And here choose I. Joy be the consequence!

PORTIA [*Aside*] How all the other passions fleet to air,
As doubtful thoughts, and rash-embraced despair,
And shudd'ring fear, and green-eyed jealousy.   110
O love, be moderate, allay thy ecstasy,
In measure rain thy joy, scant this excess!
I feel too much thy blessing. Make it less
For fear I surfeit.

BASSANIO [*Opening the leaden casket*] What find I here?
Fair Portia's counterfeit! What demigod   115
Hath come so near creation? Move these eyes?
Or whether, riding on the balls of mine,
Seem they in motion? Here are severed lips
Parted with sugar breath; so sweet a bar
Should sunder such sweet friends. Here in her hairs   120
The painter plays the spider, and hath woven
A golden mesh t' entrap the hearts of men
Faster than gnats in cobwebs. But her eyes—
How could he see to do them? Having made one,
Methinks it should have power to steal both his   125
And leave itself unfurnished. Yet look how far

99 **Indian** East Indian, hence dusky   103 **pale and common drudge** pale hack
worker, i.e., silver   104 **meager** poverty-stricken, of slight value   112 **scant** lessen
114 **surfeit** grow sick with too much, i.e., too much joy   115 **counterfeit** image
115 **demigod** i.e., half-divine painter   117 **the balls of mine** my eyeballs   119 **so
sweet a bar** i.e., Portia's breath   120 **sweet friends** i.e., her lips   123 **Faster**
tighter   126 **unfurnished** not provided with its mate (since the picture of the first
eye has taken away both of the painter's eyes)

The substance of my praise doth wrong this shadow
In underprizing it, so far this shadow
Doth limp behind the substance. Here's the scroll,
130   The continent and summary of my fortune.

"You that choose not by the view
Chance as fair, and choose as true.
Since this fortune falls to you,
Be content and seek no new.
135   If you be well pleased with this
And hold your fortune for your bliss,
Turn you where your lady is,
And claim her with a loving kiss."

A gentle scroll. Fair lady, by your leave.

[Kisses her.]

140   I come by note, to give and to receive.
Like one of two contending in a prize,
That thinks he hath done well in people's eyes,
Hearing applause and universal shout,
Giddy in spirit, still gazing in a doubt
145   Whether those peals of praise be his or no—
So, thrice-fair lady, stand I even so,
As doubtful whether what I see be true,
Until confirmed, signed, ratified by you.

PORTIA You see me, Lord Bassanio, where I stand,
150   Such as I am. Though for myself alone
I would not be ambitious in my wish
To wish myself much better, yet for you
I would be trebled twenty times myself,
A thousand times more fair, ten thousand times more
     rich,
155   That only to stand high in your account,
I might in virtues, beauties, livings, friends,

127, 129 **The substance** Portia herself   127, 128 **this shadow** her picture
130 **The continent and summary** that which contains and sums up   132 **Chance
as fair** haye as fair fortune   139 **gentle** courteous, well-bred   140 **by note**
according to instructions (in lines 137-38)   141 **prize** contest for a prize, as in a
tournament   145 **his** intended for him   155 **account** esteem, regard   156 **livings**
possessions

Exceed account. But the full sum of me
Is sum of something—which, to term in gross,
Is an unlessoned girl, unschooled, unpracticed;
Happy in this, she is not yet so old   160
But she may learn; happier than this,
She is not bred so dull but she can learn;
Happiest of all, is that her gentle spirit
Commits itself to yours to be directed,
As from her lord, her governor, her king.   165
Myself, and what is mine, to you and yours
Is now converted. But now I was the lord
Of this fair mansion, master of my servants,
Queen o'er myself; and even now, but now,
This house, these servants, and this same myself   170
Are yours, my lord's. I give them with this ring,
Which when you part from, lose, or give away,
Let it presage the ruin of your love
And be my vantage to exclaim on you.

BASSANIO Madam, you have bereft me of all words.   175
Only my blood speaks to you in my veins,
And there is such confusion in my powers
As, after some oration fairly spoke
By a belovèd prince, there doth appear
Among the buzzing pleasèd multitude;   180
Where every something being blent together
Turns to a wild of nothing, save of joy
Expressed and not expressed. But when this ring
Parts from this finger, then parts life from hence!
O then be bold to say Bassanio's dead!   185

NERISSA My lord and lady, it is now our time,
That have stood by and seen our wishes prosper,
To cry "good joy." Good joy, my lord and lady!

---

157 **account** computation   158 **term in gross** describe in broad terms   167 **converted** changed, i.e., made yours   167 **But now** only now   173 **presage** foretell   174 **vantage to exclaim on** opportunity to cry out against (lines 173-74 spoken playfully)   179 **prince** (a feminine as well as a masculine noun; hence suitably applied to Portia)

GRATIANO My Lord Bassanio, and my gentle lady,
190   I wish you all the joy that you can wish—
    For I am sure you can wish none from me;
    And when your honors mean to solemnize
    The bargain of your faith, I do beseech you
    Even at that time I may be married too.

195 BASSANIO With all my heart, so thou canst get a wife.

GRATIANO I thank your lordship, you have got me one.
    My eyes, my lord, can look as swift as yours:
    You saw the mistress, I beheld the maid.
    You loved, I loved; for intermission
200   No more pertains to me, my lord, than you.
    Your fortune stood upon the caskets there,
    And so did mine too, as the matter falls;
    For wooing here until I sweat again,
    And swearing till my very roof was dry
205   With oaths of love, at last—if promise last—
    I got a promise of this fair one here
    To have her love, provided that your fortune
    Achieved her mistress.

PORTIA   Is this true, Nerissa?

NERISSA Madam, it is, so you stand pleased withal.

210 BASSANIO And do you, Gratiano, mean good faith?

GRATIANO Yes, faith, my lord.

BASSANIO Our feast shall be much honored in your
    marriage.

GRATIANO We'll play with them the first boy for a
    thousand ducats.

215 NERISSA What, and stake down?

GRATIANO No, we shall ne'er win at that sport, and stake
    down.

191 **from** away from   195 **so** provided   199 **intermission** paušing   203 **again**
i.e., again and again   204 **roof** roof of the mouth   205 **if promise last** if her
promise holds   215 **stake down** a betting term (with an off-color pun)

But who comes here? Lorenzo and his infidel!
What, and my old Venetian friend Salerio!

*Enter Lorenzo, Jessica, and Salerio, a Messenger
from Venice.*

BASSANIO Lorenzo and Salerio, welcome hither,   220
If that the youth of my new int'rest here
Have power to bid you welcome. By your leave,
I bid my very friends and countrymen,
Sweet Portia, welcome.

PORTIA   So do I, my lord.
They are entirely welcome.   225

LORENZO I thank your honor. For my part, my lord,
My purpose was not to have seen you here,
But meeting with Salerio by the way,
He did entreat me past all saying nay
To come with him along.

SALERIO   I did, my lord,   230
And I have reason for it. Signior Antonio
Commends him to you.   [*Gives Bassanio a letter.*]

BASSANIO   Ere I ope his letter,
I pray you tell me how my good friend doth.

SALERIO Not sick, my lord, unless it be in mind,
Nor well, unless in mind. His letter there   235
Will show you his estate.   *Open the letter.*

GRATIANO Nerissa, cheer yond stranger; bid her
    welcome.
Your hand, Salerio. What's the news from Venice?
How doth that royal merchant, good Antonio?
I know he will be glad of our success;   240
We are the Jasons, we have won the Fleece.

218 **infidel** one who lacks the true faith (Gratiano applies the term playfully to
Jessica; cf. II.vi.51)   221 **int'rest** claim   232 **Commends him to you** sends you
his best wishes   236 **estate** state, condition   239 **royal merchant** merchant
prince

SALERIO I would you had won the fleece that he hath
    lost!

PORTIA There are some shrowd contents in yond same
    paper
    That steals the color from Bassanio's cheek:
245   Some dear friend dead, else nothing in the world
    Could turn so much the constitution
    Of any constant man. What, worse and worse?
    With leave, Bassanio—I am half yourself,
    And I must freely have the half of anything
    That this same paper brings you.

250 BASSANIO   O sweet Portia,
    Here are a few of the unpleasant'st words
    That ever blotted paper! Gentle lady,
    When I did first impart my love to you,
    I freely told you all the wealth I had
255   Ran in my veins—I was a gentleman.
    And then I told you true; and yet, dear lady,
    Rating myself at nothing, you shall see
    How much I was a braggart. When I told you
    My state was nothing, I should then have told you
260   That I was worse than nothing; for indeed
    I have engaged myself to a dear friend,
    Engaged my friend to his mere enemy
    To feed my means. Here is a letter, lady,
    The paper as the body of my friend,
265   And every word in it a gaping wound
    Issuing lifeblood. But is it true, Salerio?
    Hath all his ventures failed? What, not one hit?
    From Tripolis, from Mexico and England,
    From Lisbon, Barbary, and India,
270   And not one vessel scape the dreadful touch
    Of merchant-marring rocks?

SALERIO   Not one, my lord.
    Besides, it should appear that if he had

---

242 **fleece** (pun on "fleets")   243 **shrowd** evil, grievous; literally "cursed"
259 **state** estate, fortune   261 **engaged** pledged   262 **mere** absolute   273 **present** ready

The present money to discharge the Jew,
He would not take it. Never did I know
A creature that did bear the shape of man   275
So keen and greedy to confound a man.
He plies the Duke at morning and at night,
And doth impeach the freedom of the state
If they deny him justice. Twenty merchants,
The Duke himself, and the magnificoes   280
Of greatest port have all persuaded with him,
But none can drive him from the envious plea
Of forfeiture, of justice, and his bond.

JESSICA When I was with him, I have heard him swear
To Tubal and to Chus, his countrymen,   285
That he would rather have Antonio's flesh
Than twenty times the value of the sum
That he did owe him; and I know, my lord,
If law, authority, and power deny not,
It will go hard with poor Antonio.   290

PORTIA Is it your dear friend that is thus in trouble?

BASSANIO The dearest friend to me, the kindest man,
The best-conditioned and unwearied spirit
In doing courtesies, and one in whom
The ancient Roman honor more appears   295
Than any that draws breath in Italy.

PORTIA What sum owes he the Jew?

BASSANIO For me, three thousand ducats.

PORTIA   What, no more?
Pay him six thousand, and deface the bond.
Double six thousand and then treble that,   300
Before a friend of this description
Shall lose a hair through Bassanio's fault.
First go with me to church and call me wife,
And then away to Venice to your friend!

273 discharge pay 276 confound ruin, destroy 278 impeach ... state charge
that Venice is no free state 280–81 magnificoes/Of greatest port nobles of
highest dignity 282 envious malignant 293 The best-conditioned of the best
disposition 299 deface destroy

305   For never shall you lie by Portia's side
With an unquiet soul. You shall have gold
To pay the petty debt twenty times over;
When it is paid, bring your true friend along.
My maid Nerissa and myself meantime
310   Will live as maids and widows. Come away!
For you shall hence upon your wedding day.
Bid your friends welcome, show a merry cheer;
Since you are dear bought, I will love you dear.
But let me hear the letter of your friend.

315   [BASSANIO (*Reads*)] "Sweet Bassanio, my ships have
all miscarried, my creditors grow cruel, my estate is
very low, my bond to the Jew is forfeit. And since in
paying it, it is impossible I should live, all debts are
cleared between you and I if I might but see you at
320   my death. Notwithstanding, use your pleasure. If
your love do not persuade you to come, let not my
letter."

PORTIA O love, dispatch all business and be gone!

BASSANIO Since I have your good leave to go away,
325   I will make haste; but till I come again
No bed shall e'er be guilty of my stay,
Nor rest be interposer 'twixt us twain.   *Exeunt.*

[Scene III. *Venice. A street.*]

*Enter [Shylock] the Jew and Solanio and Antonio
and the Jailer.*

SHYLOCK Jailer, look to him. Tell not me of mercy.
This is the fool that lent out money gratis.
Jailer, look to him.

ANTONIO   Hear me yet, good Shylock.

311 **shall hence** must go hence

SHYLOCK I'll have my bond! Speak not against my bond!
  I have sworn an oath that I will have my bond.   5
  Thou call'dst me dog before thou hadst a cause,
  But since I am a dog, beware my fangs.
  The Duke shall grant me justice. I do wonder,
  Thou naughty jailer, that thou art so fond
  To come abroad with him at his request.   10

ANTONIO I pray thee hear me speak.

SHYLOCK I'll have my bond. I will not hear thee speak.
  I'll have my bond, and therefore speak no more.
  I'll not be made a soft and dull-eyed fool,
  To shake the head, relent, and sigh, and yield   15
  To Christian intercessors. Follow not.
  I'll have no speaking; I will have my bond.

Exit Jew.

SOLANIO It is the most impenetrable cur
  That ever kept with men.

ANTONIO   Let him alone;
  I'll follow him no more with bootless prayers.   20
  He seeks my life. His reason well I know:
  I oft delivered from his forfeitures
  Many that have at times made moan to me.
  Therefore he hates me.

SOLANIO   I am sure the Duke
  Will never grant this forfeiture to hold.   25

ANTONIO The Duke cannot deny the course of law;
  For the commodity that strangers have
  With us in Venice, if it be denied,
  Will much impeach the justice of the state,
  Since that the trade and profit of the city   30
  Consisteth of all nations. Therefore go.
  These griefs and losses have so bated me
  That I shall hardly spare a pound of flesh

III.iii.9 **naughty** wicked 9 **fond** foolish 19 **kept** dwelt 20 **bootless** unavailing
22 **forfeitures** penalties that he could have legally exacted 27 **commodity** commercial advantage 27 **strangers** foreigners 32 **griefs** pains 32 **bated** reduced

Tomorrow to my bloody creditor.
35   Well, jailer, on. Pray God Bassanio come
To see me pay his debt, and then I care not! *Exeunt.*

[Scene IV. *Belmont. Portia's house.*]

Enter Portia, Nerissa, Lorenzo, Jessica, and
[Balthasar,] a Man of Portia's.

LORENZO Madam, although I speak it in your presence,
You have a noble and a true conceit
Of godlike amity, which appears most strongly
In bearing thus the absence of your lord.
5   But if you knew to whom you show this honor,
How true a gentleman you send relief,
How dear a lover of my lord your husband,
I know you would be prouder of the work
Than customary bounty can enforce you.

10   PORTIA I never did repent for doing good,
Nor shall not now; for in companions
That do converse and waste the time together,
Whose souls do bear an egal yoke of love,
There must be needs a like proportion
15   Of lineaments, of manners, and of spirit;
Which makes me think that this Antonio,
Being the bosom lover of my lord,
Must needs be like my lord. If it be so,
How little is the cost I have bestowed
20   In purchasing the semblance of my soul
From out the state of hellish cruelty!
This comes too near the praising of myself;

III.iv.2 **conceit** idea, conception 3 **amity** friendship 7 **lover** friend 8–9 **prouder** ... **you** prouder of this action than even your habitual kindness can make you 12 **converse and waste** associate and spend 13 **egal** equal 20 **purchasing** gaining 20 **semblance** likeness (Portia refers to the old idea that a genuine friend or lover is a second self. Antonio is like Bassanio, and therefore like Portia)

Therefore no more of it. Hear other things:
Lorenzo, I commit into your hands
The husbandry and manage of my house,   25
Until my lord's return. For mine own part,
I have toward heaven breathed a secret vow
To live in prayer and contemplation,
Only attended by Nerissa here,
Until her husband and my lord's return.   30
There is a monast'ry two miles off,
And there we will abide. I do desire you
Not to deny this imposition,
The which my love and some necessity
Now lays upon you.

LORENZO   Madam, with all my heart;   35
  I shall obey you in all fair commands.

PORTIA My people do already know my mind,
  And will acknowledge you and Jessica
  In place of Lord Bassanio and myself.
  So fare you well till we shall meet again.   40

LORENZO Fair thoughts and happy hours attend on you!

JESSICA I wish your ladyship all heart's content.

PORTIA I thank you for your wish, and am well pleased
  To wish it back on you. Fare you well, Jessica.
               Exeunt [Jessica and Lorenzo].
Now, Balthasar,   45
As I have ever found thee honest-true,
So let me find thee still. Take this same letter,
And use thou all th' endeavor of a man
In speed to Padua. See thou render this
Into my cousin's hands, Doctor Bellario;   50
And look what notes and garments he doth give
  thee
Bring them, I pray thee, with imagined speed
Unto the tranect, to the common ferry

25 husbandry care 33 imposition task that I impose 51 look what whatever
52 imagined speed speed of imagination 53 tranect ferry

Which trades to Venice. Waste no time in words
55   But get thee gone. I shall be there before thee.

BALTHASAR Madam, I go with all convenient speed.

[Exit.]

PORTIA Come on, Nerissa; I have work in hand
That you yet know not of. We'll see our husbands
Before they think of us.

NERISSA   Shall they see us?

60   PORTIA They shall, Nerissa, but in such a habit
That they shall think we are accomplishèd
With that we lack. I'll hold thee any wager,
When we are both accoutered like young men,
I'll prove the prettier fellow of the two,
65   And wear my dagger with the braver grace,
And speak between the change of man and boy
With a reed voice, and turn two mincing steps
Into a manly stride, and speak of frays
Like a fine bragging youth; and tell quaint lies,
70   How honorable ladies sought my love,
Which I denying, they fell sick and died—
I could not do withal! Then I'll repent,
And wish, for all that, that I had not killed them.
And twenty of these puny lies I'll tell,
75   That men shall swear I have discontinued school
Above a twelvemonth. I have within my mind
A thousand raw tricks of these bragging Jacks,
Which I will practice.

NERISSA   Why, shall we turn to men?

PORTIA Fie, what a question's that,
80   If thou wert near a lewd interpreter!

---

56 **convenient speed** speed suited (to this emergency)   60 **habit** garment,
i.e., men's clothes   61 **accomplishèd** provided   64 **prettier** more dashing
65 **braver grace** finer masculine grace   67 **reed** high or squeaky, like the sound
of a reed pipe   69 **quaint** clever and elaborate   72 **I could not do withal** I could
not help it   73 **for all that** in spite of that   77 **Jacks** fellows   78 **turn to** turn
into (with an off-color pun; cf. I.iii.78)   80 **lewd** bad

66

But come, I'll tell thee all my whole device
When I am in my coach, which stays for us
At the park gate; and therefore haste away,
For we must measure twenty miles today.   *Exeunt*.

[Scene V. *Belmont. A garden*.]

Enter [Launcelot the] Clown and Jessica.

LAUNCELOT Yes truly; for look you, the sins of the father
are to be laid upon the children. Therefore, I promise you I fear you. I was always plain with you, and
so now I speak my agitation of the matter. Therefore be o' good cheer, for truly I think you are   5
damned. There is but one hope in it that can do you
any good, and that is but a kind of bastard hope
neither.

JESSICA And what hope is that, I pray thee?

LAUNCELOT Marry, you may partly hope that your fa-   10
ther got you not—that you are not the Jew's daughter.

JESSICA That were a kind of bastard hope indeed! So
the sins of my mother should be visited upon me.

LAUNCELOT Truly then, I fear you are damned both by
father and mother. Thus when I shun Scylla your   15
father, I fall into Charybdis your mother. Well, you
are gone both ways.

JESSICA I shall be saved by my husband. He hath
made me a Christian.

LAUNCELOT Truly, the more to blame he! We were   20

III.v.1-2 **sins ... children** (see Exodus 20:5)   3 **fear you** fear for you   4 **agitation** (blunder for "cogitation")   12 **So** thus   18 **saved by my husband** (see
1 Corinthians 7:14)

Christians enow before, e'en as many as could well
live one by another. This making of Christians will
raise the price of hogs; if we grow all to be pork-
eaters, we shall not shortly have a rasher on the
25   coals for money.

Enter Lorenzo.

JESSICA I'll tell my husband, Launcelot, what you say.
Here he comes.

LORENZO I shall grow jealous of you shortly, Launcelot, if you thus get my wife into corners.

30   JESSICA Nay, you need not fear us, Lorenzo. Launcelot
and I are out. He tells me flatly there's no mercy
for me in heaven because I am a Jew's daughter; and
he says you are no good member of the commonwealth, for in converting Jews to Christians you raise
35   the price of pork.

LORENZO [*To Launcelot*] I shall answer that better to
the commonwealth than you can the getting up of
the Negro's belly. The Moor is with child by you,
Launcelot!

40   LAUNCELOT It is much that the Moor should be more
than reason; but if she be less than an honest woman, she is indeed more than I took her for.

LORENZO How every fool can play upon the word! I
think the best grace of wit will shortly turn into
45   silence, and discourse grow commendable in none
only but parrots. Go in, sirrah; bid them prepare for
dinner.

LAUNCELOT That is done, sir. They have all stomachs.

21 **enow** enough   21 **before** before you turned Christian   22 **one by another**
one off another   24 **rasher** slice of bacon   28 **jealous** jealous   31 **out** at odds
38 **Moor** (pronounced "more"; hence Launcelot quibbles on "much," "more,"
and "Moor")   41 **honest** chaste   44 **grace** virtue

LORENZO Goodly Lord, what a wit-snapper are you!
Then bid them prepare dinner.   50

LAUNCELOT That is done too, sir. Only "cover" is the
word.

LORENZO Will you cover then, sir?

LAUNCELOT Not so, sir, neither! I know my duty.

LORENZO Yet more quarreling with occasion! Wilt   55
thou show the whole wealth of thy wit in an instant?
I pray thee understand a plain man in his plain
meaning: go to thy fellows, bid them cover the table,
serve in the meat, and we will come in to dinner.

LAUNCELOT For the table, sir, it shall be served in; for   60
the meat, sir, it shall be covered; for your coming
in to dinner, sir, why let it be as humors and conceits shall govern.   *Exit Clown [Launcelot].*

LORENZO O dear discretion, how his words are suited!
The fool hath planted in his memory   65
An army of good words; and I do know
A many fools that stand in better place,
Garnished like him, that for a tricksy word
Defy the matter. How cheer'st thou, Jessica?
And now, good sweet, say thy opinion—   70
How dost thou like the Lord Bassanio's wife?

JESSICA Past all expressing. It is very meet
The Lord Bassanio live an upright life,
For having such a blessing in his lady,
He finds the joys of heaven here on earth;   75
And if on earth he do not merit it,

---

51 **cover** cover the table (Launcelot proceeds to quibble on "cover" in the sense of
"wear a hat") 55 **quarreling with occasion** caviling at every opportunity
60 **table** (1) the piece of furniture (2) the meal 61 **covered** i.e., to be kept
hot 62–63 **humors and conceits** fancies and notions 64 **dear discretion**
precious common sense 64 **suited** fitted together (?) dressed up (?) 67 **A many**
(an old idiom for a large number) 68 **Garnished** decked out 69 **the matter**
good sense 69 **How cheer'st thou** how is it with thee (the implication is that he
kisses her)

In reason he should never come to heaven.
Why, if two gods should play some heavenly match
And on the wager lay two earthly women,
80   And Portia one, there must be something else
Pawned with the other, for the poor rude world
Hath not her fellow.

LORENZO   Even such a husband
Hast thou of me as she is for a wife.

JESSICA Nay, but ask my opinion too of that!

85   LORENZO I will anon. First let us go to dinner.

JESSICA Nay, let me praise you while I have a stomach.

LORENZO No, pray thee, let it serve for table-talk;
Then howsome'er thou speak'st, 'mong other things
I shall digest it.

JESSICA   Well, I'll set you forth.
                                        Exit [*with Lorenzo*].

---

79 **lay** stake   80 **something else** i.e., to make the wager fair   86 **stomach** (a pun
on "desire" [to praise you] and an "appetite" for dinner)   88 **howsome'er** however
89 **I'll set you forth** I'll give a fine account of you

[ACT IV

Scene I. *Venice. A court of justice.*]

Enter the Duke, the Magnificoes, Antonio,
Bassanio, [Salerio,] and Gratiano [with others].

DUKE What, is Antonio here?

ANTONIO Ready, so please your Grace.

DUKE I am sorry for thee. Thou art come to answer
A stony adversary, an inhuman wretch,
Uncapable of pity, void and empty   5
From any dram of mercy.

ANTONIO   I have heard
Your Grace hath ta'en great pains to qualify
His rigorous course; but since he stands obdurate,
And that no lawful means can carry me
Out of his envy's reach, I do oppose   10
My patience to his fury, and am armed
To suffer with a quietness of spirit
The very tyranny and rage of his.

DUKE Go one, and call the Jew into the court.

SALERIO He is ready at the door; he comes, my lord.   15

IV.i.1 **What** why (interjection)   6 **dram** mite, drop (literally an eighth of an
ounce)   7 **qualify** moderate   10 **his envy's reach** the reach of his malignant hate
13 **tyranny and rage** savagery and passion

71

Enter Shylock.

DUKE Make room, and let him stand before our face.
Shylock, the world thinks, and I think so too,
That thou but leadest this fashion of thy malice
To the last hour of act; and then 'tis thought
20 Thou'lt show thy mercy and remorse more strange
Than is thy strange apparent cruelty;
And where thou now exacts the penalty,
Which is a pound of this poor merchant's flesh,
Thou wilt not only loose the forfeiture,
25 But touched with human gentleness and love,
Forgive a moiety of the principal,
Glancing an eye of pity on his losses,
That have of late so huddled on his back—
Enow to press a royal merchant down
30 And pluck commiseration of his state
From brassy bosoms and rough hearts of flint,
From stubborn Turks and Tartars never trained
To offices of tender courtesy.
We all expect a gentle answer, Jew.

SHYLOCK I have possessed your Grace of what I
35   purpose,
And by our holy Sabbath have I sworn
To have the due and forfeit of my bond.
If you deny it, let the danger light
Upon your charter and your city's freedom!
40 You'll ask me why I rather choose to have
A weight of carrion flesh than to receive
Three thousand ducats. I'll not answer that,
But say it is my humor. Is it answered?
What if my house be troubled with a rat,
45 And I be pleased to give ten thousand ducats

16 our (the royal "we," appropriate in giving an order, but in the next line the
Duke uses "I," the informal singular, suited for a personal appeal to Shylock's
feelings) 20 remorse compassion 20 strange wonderful 21 strange astonishing 24 loose release 26 moiety portion 29 Enow enough 29 royal
merchant merchant prince 34 expect await 34 gentle befitting a gentleman
35 possessed informed 38-39 danger ... freedom (cf. III.iii. 27-31)

To have it baned? What, are you answered yet?
Some men there are love not a gaping pig,
Some that are mad if they behold a cat,
And others, when the bagpipe sings i' th' nose,
Cannot contain their urine; for affection,   50
Master of passion, sways it to the mood
Of what it likes or loathes. Now for your answer:
As there is no firm reason to be rend'red
Why he cannot abide a gaping pig,
Why he a harmless necessary cat,   55
Why he a woollen bagpipe, but of force
Must yield to such inevitable shame
As to offend, himself being offended;
So can I give no reason, nor I will not,
More than a lodged hate and a certain loathing   60
I bear Antonio, that I follow thus
A losing suit against him. Are you answered?

BASSANIO This is no answer, thou unfeeling man,
    To excuse the current of thy cruelty!

SHYLOCK I am not bound to please thee with my
    answers.   65

BASSANIO Do all men kill the things they do not love?

SHYLOCK Hates any man the thing he would not kill?

BASSANIO Every offense is not a hate at first.

SHYLOCK What, wouldst thou have a serpent sting thee
    twice?

ANTONIO I pray you think you question with the Jew.   70
    You may as well go stand upon the beach

46 baned poisoned   47 gaping pig young roast pig, often served with fruit in its
open mouth (Shylock invokes the old theory of natural antipathy to explain his
hatred of Antonio, thus concealing the real cause; cf. I.iii. 39-42)   50 affection
natural sympathy or antipathy   51 passion powerful emotion   54-56 he ... he ...
he (pronounced with heavy emphasis; this man ... that man ... another)   56 of
force of necessity, against his will   57 shame (as in line 50, above)   60 lodged
fixed   60 certain assured, steadfast   65 bound bound by law   70 think you
question remember you argue

And bid the main flood bate his usual height;
You may as well use question with the wolf,
Why he hath made the ewe bleat for the lamb;
75   You may as well forbid the mountain pines
To wag their high tops and to make no noise
When they are fretten with the gusts of heaven;
You may as well do anything most hard
As seek to soften that—than which what's harder?—
80   His Jewish heart. Therefore I do beseech you
Make no moe offers, use no farther means,
But with all brief and plain conveniency
Let me have judgment, and the Jew his will.

BASSANIO For thy three thousand ducats here is six.

85   SHYLOCK If every ducat in six thousand ducats
Were in six parts, and every part a ducat,
I would not draw them. I would have my bond.

DUKE How shalt thou hope for mercy, rend'ring none?

SHYLOCK What judgment shall I dread, doing no wrong?
90   You have among you many a purchased slave,
Which like your asses and your dogs and mules
You use in abject and in slavish parts,
Because you bought them. Shall I say to you,
"Let them be free! Marry them to your heirs!
95   Why sweat they under burdens? Let their beds
Be made as soft as yours, and let their palates
Be seasoned with such viands"? You will answer,
"The slaves are ours." So do I answer you:
The pound of flesh which I demand of him
100   Is dearly bought, is mine, and I will have it.
If you deny me, fie upon your law!
There is no force in the decrees of Venice.
I stand for judgment. Answer; shall I have it?

DUKE Upon my power I may dismiss this court
105   Unless Bellario, a learned doctor

72 **main flood bate his** ocean at high tide reduce its   77 **fretten** fretted   82 **brief and plain** **conveniency** suitable brevity and directness   87 **draw** take   92 **parts** duties

Whom I have sent for to determine this,
Come here today.

SALERIO   My lord, here stays without
A messenger with letters from the doctor,
New come from Padua.

DUKE Bring us the letters. Call the messenger.   110

BASSANIO Good cheer, Antonio! What, man, courage
     yet!
The Jew shall have my flesh, blood, bones, and all,
Ere thou shalt lose for me one drop of blood.

ANTONIO I am a tainted wether of the flock,
Meetest for death. The weakest kind of fruit   115
Drops earliest to the ground, and so let me.
You cannot better be employed, Bassanio,
Than to live still, and write mine epitaph.

     Enter Nerissa [dressed like a Lawyer's Clerk].

DUKE Came you from Padua, from Bellario?

NERISSA From both, my lord. Bellario greets your
     Grace.   [*Presents a letter.*]   120

BASSANIO Why dost thou whet thy knife so earnestly?

SHYLOCK To cut the forfeiture from that bankrout there.

GRATIANO Not on thy sole, but on thy soul, harsh Jew,
Thou mak'st thy knife keen; but no metal can—
No, not the hangman's ax—bear half the keenness   125
Of thy sharp envy. Can no prayers pierce thee?

SHYLOCK No, none that thou hast wit enough to make.

GRATIANO O be thou damned, inexecrable dog,
And for thy life let justice be accused!
Thou almost mak'st me waver in my faith,   130

---

114 **tainted wether** infected ram   115 **Meetest** fittest   125 **hangman's** executioner's   125 **bear** have   126 **envy** malignant hate   128 **inexecrable** most
execrable, detestable   129 **And ... accused** (a much debated line. Probably, "Let
justice be accused because you have been allowed to live so long")

To hold opinion with Pythagoras
That souls of animals infuse themselves
Into the trunks of men. Thy currish spirit
Governed a wolf who, hanged for human slaughter,
135   Even from the gallows did his fell soul fleet,
And whilst thou layest in thy unhallowed dam,
Infused itself in thee; for thy desires
Are wolvish, bloody, starved, and ravenous.

SHYLOCK Till thou canst rail the seal from off my bond,
140   Thou but offend'st thy lungs to speak so loud.
Repair thy wit, good youth, or it will fall
To cureless ruin. I stand here for law.

DUKE This letter from Bellario doth commend
A young and learned doctor to our court.
Where is he?

145 NERISSA   He attendeth here hard by
To know your answer whether you'll admit him.

DUKE With all my heart. Some three or four of you
Go give him courteous conduct to this place.
Meantime the court shall hear Bellario's letter.

150 [CLERK (*Reads*)] "Your Grace shall understand that at
the receipt of your letter I am very sick; but in the
instant that your messenger came, in loving visita-
tion was with me a young doctor of Rome. His name
is Balthasar. I acquainted him with the cause in
155   controversy between the Jew and Antonio the
merchant. We turned o'er many books together.
He is furnished with my opinion which, bettered
with his own learning, the greatness whereof I cannot enough commend, comes with him at my impor-
160   tunity to fill up your Grace's request in my stead.

131 **Pythagoras** Greek philosopher of the 6th century B.C. who taught the doctrine
of the transmigration of souls ⌐134 **hanged for human slaughter** (wolves, dogs,
and other animals were sometimes hanged for killing or attacking people; hence the
phrase "hangdog look") 135 **fell** fierce 136 **dam** mother of an animal, here a
she-wolf 141-42 **fall/To cureless ruin** i.e., like a house too long out of repair
160 **fill up** satisfy

I beseech you let his lack of years be no impediment
to let him lack a reverend estimation, for I never
knew so young a body with so old a head. I leave
him to your gracious acceptance, whose trial shall
better publish his commendation."   165

Enter Portia for Balthasar,
[dressed like a Doctor of Laws].

DUKE You hear the learn'd Bellario, what he writes;
    And here, I take it, is the doctor come.
    Give me your hand. Come you from old Bellario?

PORTIA I did, my lord.

DUKE   You are welcome; take your place.
    Are you acquainted with the difference   170
    That holds this present question in the court?

PORTIA I am informèd throughly of the cause.
    Which is the merchant here? And which the Jew?

DUKE Antonio and old Shylock, both stand forth.

PORTIA Is your name Shylock?

SHYLOCK   Shylock is my name.   175

PORTIA Of a strange nature is the suit you follow,
    Yet in such rule that the Venetian law
    Cannot impugn you as you do proceed.
    [*To Antonio*] You stand within his danger, do you
        not?

ANTONIO Ay, so he says.

PORTIA   Do you confess the bond?   180

ANTONIO I do.

PORTIA   Then must the Jew be merciful.

---

162 **to let** to cause   164 **trial** conduct when brought to the test   170 **difference**
dispute   171 **question** case under judicial examination   172 **throughly** thoroughly   172 **cause** case   176 **strange** astonishing   177 **in such rule that** within the
rule so that   179 **danger** power to harm

SHYLOCK On what compulsion must I? Tell me that.

PORTIA The quality of mercy is not strained;
It droppeth as the gentle rain from heaven
185　Upon the place beneath. It is twice blest;
It blesseth him that gives and him that takes.
'Tis mightiest in the mightiest; it becomes
The thronèd monarch better than his crown.
His scepter shows the force of temporal power,
190　The attribute to awe and majesty,
Wherein doth sit the dread and fear of kings;
But mercy is above this scept'red sway;
It is enthronèd in the hearts of kings,
It is an attribute to God himself,
195　And earthly power doth then show likest God's
When mercy seasons justice. Therefore, Jew,
Though justice be thy plea, consider this:
That, in the course of justice, none of us
Should see salvation. We do pray for mercy,
200　And that same prayer doth teach us all to render
The deeds of mercy. I have spoke thus much
To mitigate the justice of thy plea;
Which if thou follow, this strict court of Venice
Must needs give sentence 'gainst the merchant there.

205　SHYLOCK My deeds upon my head! I crave the law,
The penalty and forfeit of my bond.

PORTIA Is he not able to discharge the money?

BASSANIO Yes, here I tender it for him in the court,
Yea, twice the sum. If that will not suffice,
210　I will be bound to pay it ten times o'er
On forfeit of my hands, my head, my heart.

---

183 **strained** constrained, compelled 198-99 **That ... salvation** (referring to
the doctrine that God can justly condemn every man, since none is free of sin)
209 **twice** (in lines 226 and 233 "thrice" the money has been offered, and editors
therefore commonly emend "twice" to "thrice," on the assumption that here the
compositor misread the manuscript. But in line 84 the offered amount is indeed
double—six thousand ducats for three thousand—and therefore emendation to
"thrice" still leaves an inconsistency, unless the point is that as Bassanio's fears for
Antonio grow, he raises the offer)

If this will not suffice, it must appear
That malice bears down truth. And I beseech you,
Wrest once the law to your authority.
To do a great right, do a little wrong,   215
And curb this cruel devil of his will.

PORTIA It must not be. There is no power in Venice
Can alter a decree establishèd.
'Twill be recorded for a precedent,
And many an error by the same example   220
Will rush into the state. It cannot be.

SHYLOCK A Daniel come to judgment! Yea, a Daniel!
O wise young judge, how I do honor thee!

PORTIA I pray you let me look upon the bond.

SHYLOCK Here 'tis, most reverend Doctor, here it is.   225

PORTIA Shylock, there's thrice thy money off'red thee.

SHYLOCK An oath, an oath! I have an oath in heaven;
Shall I lay perjury upon my soul?
No, not for Venice!

PORTIA   Why, this bond is forfeit;
And lawfully by this the Jew may claim   230
A pound of flesh, to be by him cut off
Nearest the merchant's heart. Be merciful.
Take thrice thy money; bid me tear the bond.

SHYLOCK When it is paid, according to the tenure.
It doth appear you are a worthy judge;   235
You know the law, your exposition
Hath been most sound. I charge you by the law,
Whereof you are a well-deserving pillar,
Proceed to judgment. By my soul I swear
There is no power in the tongue of man   240
To alter me. I stay here on my bond.

214 **Wrest ... authority** for once twist the law a little and subject it to your
authority   222 **A Daniel come to judgment** the young biblical hero who
secured justice for Susannah (See Apocrypha, Susannah: 42-64)   234 **tenure**
conditions   241 **stay** take my stand

ANTONIO Most heartily I do beseech the court
　　To give the judgment.

PORTIA　　　　　　　Why then, thus it is:
　　You must prepare your bosom for his knife—

245 SHYLOCK O noble judge! O excellent young man!

PORTIA For the intent and purpose of the law
　　Hath full relation to the penalty,
　　Which here appeareth due upon the bond.

SHYLOCK 'Tis very true. O wise and upright judge!
250 How much more elder art thou than thy looks!

PORTIA Therefore lay bare your bosom.

SHYLOCK　　　　　　　　　Ay, his breast—
　　So says the bond, doth it not, noble judge?
　　"Nearest his heart"; those are the very words.

PORTIA It is so. Are there balance here to weigh
　　The flesh?

255 SHYLOCK   I have them ready.

PORTIA Have by some surgeon, Shylock, on your
　　charge,
　　To stop his wounds, lest he do bleed to death.

SHYLOCK Is it so nominated in the bond?

PORTIA It is not so expressed, but what of that?
260 'Twere good you do so much for charity.

SHYLOCK I cannot find it; 'tis not in the bond.

PORTIA You, merchant, have you anything to say?

ANTONIO But little. I am armed and well prepared.
　　Give me your hand, Bassanio; fare you well.
265 Grieve not that I am fall'n to this for you,
　　For herein Fortune shows herself more kind
　　Than is her custom: it is still her use

247 **Hath full relation to** is related inseparably to   254 **balance** (plural) scales
256 **on your charge** at your expense   267 **still her use** ever her custom

To let the wretched man outlive his wealth,
To view with hollow eye and wrinkled brow
An age of poverty; from which ling'ring penance   270
Of such misery doth she cut me off.
Commend me to your honorable wife.
Tell her the process of Antonio's end,
Say how I loved you, speak me fair in death;
And when the tale is told, bid her be judge   275
Whether Bassanio had not once a love.
Repent but you that you shall lose your friend,
And he repents not that he pays your debt;
For if the Jew do cut but deep enough,
I'll pay it instantly with all my heart.   280

BASSANIO Antonio, I am married to a wife
Which is as dear to me as life itself;
But life itself, my wife, and all the world
Are not with me esteemed above thy life.
I would lose all, ay sacrifice them all   285
Here to this devil, to deliver you.

PORTIA Your wife would give you little thanks for that
If she were by to hear you make the offer.

GRATIANO I have a wife who I protest I love.
I would she were in heaven, so she could   290
Entreat some power to change this currish Jew.

NERISSA 'Tis well you offer it behind her back;
The wish would make else an unquiet house.

SHYLOCK These be the Christian husbands! I have a
    daughter;
Would any of the stock of Barabbas   295
Had been her husband, rather than a Christian!
We trifle time. I pray thee pursue sentence.

273 process whole story   276 love friend (with a quibble on "love," in the sense of "lover")   277 Repent but you if you but feel sorrow   278 And he repents not then he regrets not   280 with all my heart (a quibble on "heart" in the senses of soul and of the physical organ)   295 Barabbas (1) the thief freed by Pilate when the people demanded that Christ be crucified (2) the name of the villainous hero in Marlowe's *The Jew of Malta*

PORTIA A pound of that same merchant's flesh is thine.
The court awards it, and the law doth give it—

300 SHYLOCK Most rightful judge!

PORTIA And you must cut this flesh from off his breast.
The law allows it, and the court awards it.

SHYLOCK Most learned judge! A sentence! Come, prepare!

PORTIA Tarry a little; there is something else.
305   This bond doth give thee here no jot of blood;
The words expressly are "a pound of flesh."
Take then thy bond, take thou thy pound of flesh;
But in the cutting it, if thou dost shed
One drop of Christian blood, thy lands and goods
310   Are by the laws of Venice confiscate
Unto the state of Venice.

GRATIANO O upright judge! Mark, Jew. O learned
judge!

SHYLOCK Is that the law?

PORTIA   Thyself shalt see the act;
For, as thou urgest justice, be assured
315   Thou shalt have justice more than thou desir'st.

GRATIANO O learned judge! Mark, Jew. A learned
judge!

SHYLOCK I take this offer then. Pay the bond thrice
And let the Christian go.

BASSANIO   Here is the money.

PORTIA Soft!
320   The Jew shall have all justice. Soft, no haste;
He shall have nothing but the penalty.

GRATIANO O Jew! An upright judge, a learnèd judge!

PORTIA Therefore prepare thee to cut off the flesh.
Shed thou no blood, nor cut thou less nor more
325   But just a pound of flesh. If thou tak'st more

Or less than a just pound, be it but so much
As makes it light or heavy in the substance
Or the division of the twentieth part
Of one poor scruple—nay, if the scale do turn
But in the estimation of a hair—   330
Thou diest, and all thy goods are confiscate.

GRATIANO A second Daniel! A Daniel, Jew!
Now, infidel, I have you on the hip!

PORTIA Why doth the Jew pause? Take thy forfeiture.

SHYLOCK Give me my principal, and let me go.   335

BASSANIO I have it ready for thee; here it is.

PORTIA He hath refused it in the open court.
He shall have merely justice and his bond.

GRATIANO A Daniel still say I, a second Daniel!
I thank thee, Jew, for teaching me that word.   340

SHYLOCK Shall I not have barely my principal?

PORTIA Thou shalt have nothing but the forfeiture,
To be so taken at thy peril, Jew.

SHYLOCK Why, then the devil give him good of it!
I'll stay no longer question.

PORTIA   Tarry, Jew!   345
The law hath yet another hold on you.
It is enacted in the laws of Venice,
If it be proved against an alien
That by direct or indirect attempts
He seek the life of any citizen,   350
The party 'gainst the which he doth contrive
Shall seize one half his goods; the other half
Comes to the privy coffer of the state;
And the offender's life lies in the mercy

---

326 just exact 327 substance amount 328 division portion 328-29 twentieth ... scruple i.e., one grain 330 estimation value 345 stay no longer
question remain for no more talk 352 seize take possession of 353 privy
coffer equivalent to the British Privy Purse, money provided for the monarch's
own use

355   Of the Duke only, 'gainst all other voice.
        In which predicament I say thou stand'st,
        For it appears by manifest proceeding
        That indirectly, and directly too,
        Thou hast contrived against the very life
360   Of the defendant, and thou hast incurred
        The danger formerly by me rehearsed.
        Down therefore, and beg mercy of the Duke.

GRATIANO Beg that thou mayst have leave to hang
              thyself!
        And yet, thy wealth being forfeit to the state,
365   Thou hast not left the value of a cord;
        Therefore thou must be hanged at the state's charge.

DUKE That thou shalt see the difference of our spirit,
        I pardon thee thy life before thou ask it.
        For half thy wealth, it is Antonio's;
370   The other half comes to the general state,
        Which humbleness may drive unto a fine.

PORTIA Ay, for the state, not for Antonio.

SHYLOCK Nay, take my life and all! Pardon not that!
        You take my house, when you do take the prop
375   That doth sustain my house. You take my life
        When you do take the means whereby I live.

PORTIA What mercy can you render him, Antonio?

GRATIANO A halter gratis! Nothing else, for God's sake!

ANTONIO So please my lord the Duke and all the court
380   To quit the fine for one half of his goods,
        I am content; so he will let me have
        The other half in use, to render it
        Upon his death unto the gentleman
        That lately stole his daughter.
385   Two things provided more: that for this favor
        He presently become a Christian;

356 **predicament** situation   361 **rehearsed** cited   369 **For** as for   371 **may drive unto a fine** may persuade me to reduce to a fine   380 **quit** remit   381 **so provided**   382 **in use** in trust, to use in his business   386 **presently** instantly

84

The other, that he do record a gift
Here in the court of all he dies possessed
Unto his son Lorenzo and his daughter.

DUKE He shall do this, or else I do recant   390
The pardon that I late pronouncèd here.

PORTIA Art thou contented, Jew? What dost thou say?

SHYLOCK I am content.

PORTIA   Clerk, draw a deed of gift.

SHYLOCK I pray you give me leave to go from hence.
I am not well. Send the deed after me,   395
And I will sign it.

DUKE   Get thee gone, but do it.

GRATIANO In christ'ning shalt thou have two godfathers.
Had I been judge, thou shouldst have had ten
    more—
To bring thee to the gallows, not to the font.
                                    Exit [Shylock].

DUKE Sir, I entreat you home with me to dinner.   400

PORTIA I humbly do desire your Grace of pardon.
I must away this night toward Padua,
And it is meet I presently set forth.

DUKE I am sorry that your leisure serves you not.
Antonio, gratify this gentleman,   405
For in my mind you are much bound to him.
                            Exit Duke and his Train.

BASSANIO Most worthy gentleman, I and my friend
Have by your wisdom been this day acquitted
Of grievous penalties, in lieu whereof,
Three thousand ducats due unto the Jew   410
We freely cope your courteous pains withal.

---

390 recant retract   398 ten more i.e., to make a jury of twelve   404 serves you
not is not sufficient for you   405 gratify show your gratitude to   409 in lieu
whereof in return for   411 We freely cope of our own free will we requite

ANTONIO And stand indebted, over and above,
In love and service to you evermore.

415 PORTIA He is well paid that is well satisfied,
And I, delivering you, am satisfied,
And therein do account myself well paid;
My mind was never yet more mercenary.
I pray you know me when we meet again.
I wish you well, and so I take my leave.

420 BASSANIO Dear sir, of force I must attempt you further.
Take some remembrance of us as a tribute,
Not as fee. Grant me two things, I pray you—
Not to deny me, and to pardon me.

PORTIA You press me far, and therefore I will yield.
425 Give me your gloves; I'll wear them for your sake.
                    [*Bassanio takes off his gloves.*]
And for your love I'll take this ring from you.
Do not draw back your hand; I'll take no more,
And you in love shall not deny me this.

BASSANIO This ring, good sir, alas, it is a trifle!
430 I will not shame myself to give you this.

PORTIA I will have nothing else but only this,
And now methinks I have a mind to it.

BASSANIO There's more depends on this than on the
value.
The dearest ring in Venice will I give you,
435 And find it out by proclamation.
Only for this, I pray you pardon me.

PORTIA I see, sir, you are liberal in offers.
You taught me first to beg, and now methinks
You teach me how a beggar should be answered.

440 BASSANIO Good sir, this ring was given me by my wife,
And when she put it on she made me vow
That I should neither sell nor give nor lose it.

428 in love in your good will to me   433 the value the ring's value   436 Only
... pardon me only as for this ring, I beg you to excuse me

PORTIA That 'scuse serves many men to save their gifts.
　And if your wife be not a madwoman,
　And know how well I have deserved this ring,   445
　She would not hold out enemy forever
　For giving it to me. Well, peace be with you!
　　　　　　　　　　　　　　Exeunt [Portia and Nerissa].

ANTONIO My Lord Bassanio, let him have the ring.
　Let his deservings, and my love withal,
　Be valued 'gainst your wife's commandement.   450

BASSANIO Go, Gratiano, run and overtake him;
　Give him the ring, and bring him if thou canst
　Unto Antonio's house. Away, make haste!
　　　　　　　　　　　　　　Exit Gratiano.
　Come, you and I will thither presently,
　And in the morning early will we both   455
　Fly toward Belmont. Come, Antonio.   *Exeunt.*

[Scene II. *Venice. A street.*]

Enter [Portia and] Nerissa, [disguised as before].

PORTIA Inquire the Jew's house out, give him this deed,
　And let him sign it. We'll away tonight
　And be a day before our husbands home.
　This deed will be well welcome to Lorenzo.

Enter Gratiano.

GRATIANO Fair sir, you are well o'erta'en.   5
　My Lord Bassanio upon more advice
　Hath sent you here this ring, and doth entreat
　Your company at dinner.

PORTIA　　　　　　　That cannot be.

450 commandement (four syllables) IV.ii.1 this deed the deed of gift for Lorenzo and Jessica 6 upon more advice on further consideration

His ring I do accept most thankfully,
10 And so I pray you tell him. Furthermore,
I pray you show my youth old Shylock's house.

GRATIANO That will I do.

NERISSA   Sir, I would speak with you.
[*Aside to Portia*] I'll see if I can get my husband's
    ring,
Which I did make him swear to keep forever.

PORTIA [*Aside to Nerissa*] Thou mayst, I warrant. We
15   shall have old swearing
That they did give the rings away to men;
But we'll outface them, and outswear them too.
Away, make haste! Thou know'st where I will tarry.

NERISSA Come, good sir, will you show me to this
    house?   [*Exeunt.*]

15 **old swearing** a lot of hard swearing

[ACT V

Scene I. *Belmont. A garden before Portia's house.*]

Enter Lorenzo and Jessica.

LORENZO The moon shines bright. In such a night as
    this,
  When the sweet wind did gently kiss the trees
  And they did make no noise, in such a night
  Troilus methinks mounted the Troyan walls,
  And sighed his soul toward the Grecian tents   5
  Where Cressid lay that night.

JESSICA   In such a night
  Did Thisbe fearfully o'ertrip the dew,
  And saw the lion's shadow ere himself,
  And ran dismayed away.

LORENZO   In such a night
  Stood Dido with a willow in her hand   10
  Upon the wild sea banks, and waft her love
  To come again to Carthage.

V.i.1–23 (the lovers' playful contest in verse-making belongs to a type of poetic dialogue as old as Virgil's *Eclogues*)   4 **Troilus** hero of Chaucer's *Troilus and Cressida* and of Shakespeare's play of the same title; a type of the faithful lover   6 **Cressid** Cressida, a type of the faithless woman   7 **Thisbe** heroine of the tragic tale of *Pyramus and Thisbe* in Ovid's *Metamorphoses*   10 **Dido** Queen of Carthage whom Aeneas loved but abandoned at the call of duty   10 **willow** proverbially associated with forsaken love   11 **waft** waved (with the willow branch)

JESSICA   In such a night
   Medea gathered the enchanted herbs
   That did renew old Aeson.

LORENZO   In such a night
15   Did Jessica steal from the wealthy Jew,
   And with an unthrift love did run from Venice
   As far as Belmont.

JESSICA   In such a night
   Did young Lorenzo swear he loved her well,
   Stealing her soul with many vows of faith,
   And ne'er a true one.

20   LORENZO   In such a night
   Did pretty Jessica, like a little shrow,
   Slander her love, and he forgave it her.

JESSICA I would out-night you, did nobody come;
   But hark, I hear the footing of a man.

Enter [Stephano,] a Messenger.

25   LORENZO Who comes so fast in silence of the night?

MESSENGER A friend.

LORENZO A friend? What friend? Your name I pray
   you, friend.

MESSENGER Stephano is my name, and I bring word
   My mistress will before the break of day
30   Be here at Belmont. She doth stray about
   By holy crosses where she kneels and prays
   For happy wedlock hours.

LORENZO   Who comes with her?

MESSENGER None but a holy hermit and her maid.
   I pray you, is my master yet returned?

---

13 **Medea** princess and sorceress who helped Jason to obtain the Golden Fleece, and later was deserted by him 14 **Aeson** father of Jason, restored to youth by Medea 15 **steal** (a pun) steal money, steal away 16 **unthrift love** (a pun) a love which disregards wealth, and a lover without wealth 21 **shrow** shrew 31 **holy crosses** (a common sight in Renaissance Italy; used to mark shrines on hilltops, beside roads, etc.)

LORENZO He is not, nor we have not heard from him.   35
    But go we in, I pray thee, Jessica,
    And ceremoniously let us prepare
    Some welcome for the mistress of the house.

Enter [Launcelot, the] Clown.

LAUNCELOT Sola, sola! Wo ha! Ho sola, sola!

LORENZO Who calls?   40

LAUNCELOT Sola! Did you see Master Lorenzo and
    Mistress Lorenzo? sola, sola!

LORENZO Leave holloaing, man! Here.

LAUNCELOT Sola! Where? Where?

LORENZO Here!   45

LAUNCELOT Tell him there's a post come from my
    master, with his horn full of good news. My master
    will be here ere morning.   *[Exit.]*

LORENZO Sweet soul, let's in, and there expect their
    coming.
    And yet no matter; why should we go in?   50
    My friend Stephano, signify, I pray you,
    Within the house, your mistress is at hand,
    And bring your music forth into the air.
                      [Exit Stephano.]
    How sweet the moonlight sleeps upon this bank!
    Here will we sit and let the sounds of music   55
    Creep in our ears; soft stillness and the night
    Become the touches of sweet harmony.
    Sit, Jessica. Look how the floor of heaven
    Is thick inlaid with patens of bright gold.
    There's not the smallest orb which thou behold'st   60
    But in his motion like an angel sings,

39 **Sola** (Launcelot imitates a courier's horn)   47 **horn full of good news**
(Launcelot puns on the cornucopia, "the horn of plenty")   49 **expect** await
57 **Become** befit   57, 67 **touches** notes produced by touching, the strings or
stops of a musical instrument   59 **patens** tiles

Still quiring to the young-eyed cherubins;
Such harmony is in immortal souls,
But whilst this muddy vesture of decay
65   Doth grossly close it in, we cannot hear it.

[*Enter Musicians.*]

Come ho, and wake Diana with a hymn!
With sweetest touches pierce your mistress' ear
And draw her home with music.   *Play music.*

JESSICA I am never merry when I hear sweet music.

70   LORENZO The reason is, your spirits are attentive.
For do but note a wild and wanton herd
Or race of youthful and unhandled colts
Fetching mad bounds, bellowing and neighing loud,
Which is the hot condition of their blood:
75   If they but hear perchance a trumpet sound,
Or any air of music touch their ears,
You shall perceive them make a mutual stand,
Their savage eyes turned to a modest gaze
By the sweet power of music. Therefore the poet
Did feign that Orpheus drew trees, stones, and
80   floods;
Since naught so stockish, hard, and full of rage
But music for the time doth change his nature.
The man that hath no music in himself,
Nor is not moved with concord of sweet sounds,
85   Is fit for treasons, stratagems, and spoils;
The motions of his spirit are dull as night,
And his affections dark as Erebus.
Let no such man be trusted. Mark the music.

---

62 **quiring** making music (a reference to the music of the spheres. It was thought that the harmonious movement of the spheres, in Ptolemaic astronomy, produced a heavenly music inaudible to human ears)   64 **muddy vesture of decay** earthy garment subject to decay, i.e., the body   66 **Diana** goddess of the moon and of chastity   71 **wanton** frolicsome, untrained   74 **hot condition** impetuous nature 77 **make a mutual stand** stand still by common consent   80 **Orpheus** famous legendary Greek poet and musician   81 **stockish** blockish, dull   81 **rage** passion 85 **spoils** plundering   86 **motions** inward promptings   87 **affections** emotions 87 **Erebus** the dark underworld of the Greeks

Enter Portia and Nerissa.

PORTIA That light we see is burning in my hall;
    How far that little candle throws his beams!   90
    So shines a good deed in a naughty world.

NERISSA When the moon shone we did not see the
    candle.

PORTIA So doth the greater glory dim the less.
    A substitute shines brightly as a king
    Until a king be by, and then his state   95
    Empties itself, as doth an inland brook
    Into the main of waters. Music, hark!

NERISSA It is your music, madam, of the house.

PORTIA Nothing is good, I see, without respect;
    Methinks it sounds much sweeter than by day.   100

NERISSA Silence bestows that virtue on it, madam.

PORTIA The crow doth sing as sweetly as the lark
    When neither is attended; and I think
    The nightingale, if she should sing by day
    When every goose is cackling, would be thought   105
    No better a musician than the wren.
    How many things by season, seasoned are
    To their right praise and true perfection!
    Peace! [*Music ceases.*] How the moon sleeps with
      Endymion,
    And would not be awaked.

LORENZO   That is the voice,   110
    Or I am much deceived, of Portia.

---

91 **naughty** evil   94 **substitute** deputy   95-96 **his state/Empties itself** i.e., his own glory merges into the king's   97 **main of waters** ocean   99 **without respect** without reference to circumstances   103 **attended** heeded   107-8 **by season ... perfection** by the right occasion are made ready to receive their fitting praise and attain their full perfection   109 **Peace! How the** (the quarto reads "Peace, how the"; editors often emend to "Peace, ho! The")   109 **Endymion** a handsome shepherd, beloved of Diana   109-10 **Peace ... awaked** addressed to the musicians

PORTIA He knows me as the blind man knows the
  cuckoo,
    By the bad voice.

LORENZO   Dear lady, welcome home.

PORTIA We have been praying for our husbands' welfare,
115   Which speed we hope the better for our words.
    Are they returned?

LORENZO   Madam, they are not yet,
    But there is come a messenger before
    To signify their coming.

PORTIA   Go in, Nerissa.
    Give order to my servants that they take
120   No note at all of our being absent hence—
    Nor you, Lorenzo—Jessica, nor you.

                              [*A tucket sounds.*]

LORENZO Your husband is at hand; I hear his trumpet.
    We are no telltales, madam; fear you not.

PORTIA This night methinks is but the daylight sick;
125   It looks a little paler. 'Tis a day
    Such as the day is when the sun is hid.

    Enter Bassanio, Antonio, Gratiano, and their Followers.

BASSANIO We should hold day with the Antipodes,
    If you would walk in absence of the sun.

PORTIA Let me give light, but let me not be light,
130   For a light wife doth make a heavy husband,
    And never be Bassanio so for me.
    But God sort all! You are welcome home, my lord.

BASSANIO I thank you, madam. Give welcome to my
    friend.

---

121 s.d. **tucket** trumpet call (Bassanio, like every nobleman, had his individual
tucket)   127 **Antipodes** dwellers on the opposite side of the earth   129, 130 **light,
heavy** (Portia quibbles on "light" in the senses of radiance, unchaste, and of little
weight, and on "heavy" in the senses of weighty and despondent, weighed down
with trouble)   132 **God sort all** let God ordain all according to his wisdom

This is the man, this is Antonio,
To whom I am so infinitely bound.   135

PORTIA You should in all sense be much bound to him,
For, as I hear, he was much bound for you.

ANTONIO No more than I am well acquitted of.

PORTIA Sir, you are very welcome to our house.
It must appear in other ways than words;   140
Therefore I scant this breathing courtesy.

GRATIANO [*To Nerissa*] By yonder moon I swear you do
me wrong!
In faith, I gave it to the judge's clerk.
Would he were gelt that had it, for my part,
Since you do take it, love, so much at heart.   145

PORTIA A quarrel, ho, already! What's the matter?

GRATIANO About a hoop of gold, a paltry ring
That she did give me, whose posy was
For all the world like cutler's poetry
Upon a knife, "Love me, and leave me not."   150

NERISSA What talk you of the posy or the value?
You swore to me when I did give it you
That you would wear it till your hour of death,
And that it should lie with you in your grave.
Though not for me, yet for your vehement oaths,   155
You should have been respective and have kept it.
Gave it a judge's clerk! No, God's my judge,
The clerk will ne'er wear hair on's face that had it!

GRATIANO He will, and if he live to be a man.

NERISSA Ay, if a woman live to be a man.   160

GRATIANO Now by this hand, I gave it to a youth,
A kind of boy, a little scrubbèd boy

136 in all sense (1) in all reason (2) in all senses 138 acquitted of freed from
141 breathing courtesy courtesy that is only breath, i.e., words 144 gelt castrated
144 for my part so far as I care 148 posy (a contraction of "poesy," i.e., "poetry")
motto (inscribed on a ring) 151 What why 155 Though not for me if not for
my sake 156 respective regardful, heedful 162 scrubbèd stunted

No higher than thyself, the judge's clerk,
A prating boy that begged it as a fee.
165   I could not for my heart deny it him.

PORTIA   You were to blame—I must be plain with you—
To part so slightly with your wife's first gift,
A thing stuck on with oaths upon your finger,
And so riveted with faith unto your flesh.
170   I gave my love a ring, and made him swear
Never to part with it; and here he stands.
I dare be sworn for him he would not leave it
Nor pluck it from his finger, for the wealth
That the world masters. Now in faith, Gratiano,
175   You give your wife too unkind a cause of grief.
And, 'twere to me, I should be mad at it.

BASSANIO [*Aside*] Why, I were best to cut my left hand off
And swear I lost the ring defending it.

GRATIANO   My Lord Bassanio gave his ring away
180   Unto the judge that begged it, and indeed
Deserved it too; and then the boy, his clerk
That took some pains in writing, he begged mine;
And neither man nor master would take aught
But the two rings.

PORTIA   What ring gave you, my lord?
185   Not that, I hope, which you received of me.

BASSANIO   If I could add a lie unto a fault,
I would deny it; but you see my finger
Hath not the ring upon it—it is gone.

PORTIA   Even so void is your false heart of truth.
190   By heaven, I will ne'er come in your bed
Until I see the ring!

NERISSA   Nor I in yours
Till I again see mine!

---

172 **leave it** let it go   174 **masters** possesses   175 **unkind** unnaturally cruel
176 **mad** in a frenzy   186 **fault** faulty act

BASSANIO   Sweet Portia,
  If you did know to whom I gave the ring,
  If you did know for whom I gave the ring,
  And would conceive for what I gave the ring,   195
  And how unwillingly I left the ring
  When naught would be accepted but the ring,
  You would abate the strength of your displeasure.

PORTIA If you had known the virtue of the ring,
  Or half her worthiness that gave the ring,   200
  Or your own honor to contain the ring,
  You would not then have parted with the ring.
  What man is there so much unreasonable,
  If you had pleased to have defended it
  With any terms of zeal, wanted the modesty   205
  To urge the thing held as a ceremony?
  Nerissa teaches me what to believe;
  I'll die for't but some woman had the ring!

BASSANIO No, by my honor, madam! By my soul
  No woman had it, but a civil doctor,   210
  Which did refuse three thousand ducats of me
  And begged the ring, the which I did deny him,
  And suffered him to go displeased away,
  Even he that had held up the very life
  Of my dear friend. What should I say, sweet lady?   215
  I was enforced to send it after him.
  I was beset with shame and courtesy.
  My honor would not let ingratitude
  So much besmear it. Pardon me, good lady!
  For by these blessèd candles of the night,   220
  Had you been there, I think you would have begged
  The ring of me to give the worthy doctor.

PORTIA Let not that doctor e'er come near my house.

---

195 **conceive for what** form a conception of why 201 **honor to contain**
honorable duty to retain 205 **terms of zeal** ardent language 205-6 **wanted . . .
ceremony** would have been so lacking in modesty as to urge a claim on the thing
you were keeping as a hallowed symbol 210 **civil doctor** doctor of civil law
217 **beset with shame and courtesy** assailed by feelings of shame and the
obligations of courtesy

Since he hath got the jewel that I loved,
225   And that which you did swear to keep for me,
I will become as liberal as you;
I'll not deny him anything I have,
No, not my body nor my husband's bed.
Know him I shall, I am well sure of it.
230   Lie not a night from home. Watch me like Argus.
If you do not, if I be left alone—
Now by mine honor which is yet mine own,
I'll have that doctor for mine bedfellow.

NERISSA   And I his clerk. Therefore be well advised
235   How you do leave me to mine own protection.

GRATIANO   Well, do you so. Let not me take him then!
For if I do, I'll mar the young clerk's pen.

ANTONIO   I am th' unhappy subject of these quarrels.

PORTIA   Sir, grieve not you; you are welcome not with-
      standing.

240   BASSANIO   Portia, forgive me this enforcèd wrong,
And in the hearing of these many friends
I swear to thee, even by thine own fair eyes,
Wherein I see myself—

PORTIA   Mark you but that!
In both my eyes he doubly sees himself,
245   In each eye one. Swear by your double self,
And there's an oath of credit.

BASSANIO   Nay, but hear me.
Pardon this fault, and by my soul I swear
I never more will break an oath with thee.

ANTONIO   I once did lend my body for his wealth,
250   Which but for him that had your husband's ring

226 **liberal** (1) licentious (2) generous   230 **Argus** a monstrous giant of Greek
myth, with a hundred eyes; a type of never-failing watchfulness   234 **be well
advised** be very careful   236 **take** get hold of   237 **pen** (double entendre)
240 **this enforcèd wrong** this wrong I was forced to commit   245 **double self** a
quibble (1) twofold image (2) double-dealing character   246 **oath of credit** oath
to be believed (spoken in irony)   249 **wealth** welfare

Had quite miscarried. I dare be bound again,
My soul upon the forfeit, that your lord
Will never more break faith advisedly.

PORTIA   Then you shall be his surety. Give him this,
And bid him keep it better than the other.   255

ANTONIO   Here, Lord Bassanio. Swear to keep this ring.

BASSANIO   By heaven, it is the same I gave the doctor!

PORTIA   I had it of him. Pardon me, Bassanio,
For by this ring the doctor lay with me.

NERISSA   And pardon me, my gentle Gratiano,   260
For that same scrubbèd boy, the doctor's clerk,
In lieu of this, last night did lie with me.

GRATIANO   Why, this is like the mending of highways
In summer, where the ways are fair enough.
What, are we cuckolds ere we have deserved it?   265

PORTIA   Speak not so grossly. You are all amazed.
Here is a letter; read it at your leisure.
It comes from Padua from Bellario.
There you shall find that Portia was the doctor,
Nerissa there her clerk. Lorenzo here   270
Shall witness I set forth as soon as you,
And even but now returned. I have not yet
Entered my house. Antonio, you are welcome,
And I have better news in store for you
Than you expect. Unseal this letter soon;   275
There you shall find three of your argosies
Are richly come to harbor suddenly.
You shall not know by what strange accident
I chancèd on this letter.

ANTONIO   I am dumb!

BASSANIO   Were you the doctor, and I knew you not?   280

253 advisedly deliberately   262 In lieu of in return for   265 cuckolds husbands
of faithless wives   266 amazed utterly bewildered; literally, entangled in a maze
or labyrinth   278 strange astonishing

GRATIANO Were you the clerk that is to make me
  cuckold?

NERISSA Ay, but the clerk that never means to do it,
  Unless he live until he be a man.

BASSANIO Sweet Doctor, you shall be my bedfellow.
285 When I am absent, then lie with my wife.

ANTONIO Sweet lady, you have given me life and living!
  For here I read for certain that my ships
  Are safely come to road.

PORTIA   How now, Lorenzo?
  My clerk hath some good comforts too for you.

290 NERISSA Ay, and I'll give them him without a fee.
  There do I give to you and Jessica
  From the rich Jew, a special deed of gift,
  After his death, of all he dies possessed of.

LORENZO Fair ladies, you drop manna in the way
  Of starvèd people.

295 PORTIA   It is almost morning,
  And yet I am sure you are not satisfied
  Of these events at full. Let us go in,
  And charge us there upon inter'gatories,
  And we will answer all things faithfully.

300 GRATIANO Let it be so. The first inter'gatory
  That my Nerissa shall be sworn on is,
  Whether till the next night she had rather stay,
  Or go to bed now, being two hours to day.
  But were the day come, I should wish it dark
305 Till I were couching with the doctor's clerk.
  Well, while I live I'll fear no other thing
  So sore, as keeping safe Nerissa's ring. *Exeunt.*

FINIS

288 **road** anchorage 295 **starvèd people** (Lorenzo, though of good social position, was, like Bassanio, far from rich) 296–97 **not satisfied … full** not fully satisfied how these events came to pass 298 **charge us there upon** load us with questions 298 **inter'gatories** interrogatories, i.e., questions formally drawn up to be put to a defendant or witness and answered under oath 301 **sworn on** sworn to under oath

Textual Note

The exact date of the play's composition is uncertain, but the play was in existence in 1598, when Francis Meres mentioned it in *Palladis Tamia*, and it may have been written as early as 1596, if the reference to the ship *Andrew* in I.i.27 is indebted —as has been conjectured—to news of the capture of the Spanish ship *St. Andrew* in the Cádiz expedition. In 1598 and in 1600 the play was entered in the Stationers' Register. It was first published in a quarto (Q1) in 1600. The interesting part of the title page runs thus: "The most excellent/ Historie of the Merchant/ of Venice./ With the extreame crueltie of Shylocke the Iewe/ towards the sayd Merchant, in cutting a iust pound/ of his flesh: and the obtayning of Portia/ by the choyse of three/ chests./ As it hath beene diuers times acted by the Lord/ Chamberlaine his Seruants./ Written by William Shakespeare." The absence of some necessary stage directions (e.g., entrances of some characters who later speak) suggests that the copy for this quarto could not have been a promptbook. Conversely, there are some bits of evidence that suggest the copy was very close to Shakespeare's manuscript; for example, such a stage direction as "Enter Portia for Balthazar" seems to reflect an author's conception of his action. But plays that are commonly thought to be printed from Shakespeare's manuscript usually have some confusions in them, the result of a somewhat illegible manuscript, and *The Merchant* lacks such confusions. Probably, then, the printer's copy for the first quarto was a scribe's careful and clean copy of the manuscript—but, of course, it is unwise to be dogmatic about such matters.

In 1619 a second quarto (Q2) appeared, falsely dated 1600. Q2 was based on Q1, and though it corrects some palpable errors in Q1, Q2 has no independent authority. In 1623 the play was again reprinted, in the First Folio, again from Q1. And again, of course, there are some slight departures from Q1, ranging from misprints to the addition of some interesting stage directions that doubtless reflect playhouse practice. The most notable are directions calling for the flourishing of cornets.

Q1, then, the only authoritative text, and the source of all others, serves as the basis for the present edition, but some changes have been made. Solanio, Salarino, and Salerio have, as in most modern editions, been reduced to Solanio and Salerio. (Possibly Shakespeare began with three such characters in mind, but as he worked he apparently found he could make do with two, and Salarino disappeared. The name Salarino—which in Q1 occurs in stage directions at I.i; II.iv, vi, viii; III.i—in this edition is replaced by Salerio. Salarino is a diminutive of Salerio, and it is possible that Shakespeare did not intend them to be distinct. In any case, the name Salerio must stay, because it appears in the dialogue as well as in the stage directions.) Spelling and punctuation have been modernized, and speech prefixes have been regularized (e.g., we give "Shylock," though Q1 varies between "Shylock," "Shy.," and "Iew"). Act divisions, first introduced in the Folio, are given, and for ease of reference, the scene divisions established by the Globe edition are given. These additions, like necessary stage directions that are not found in Q1, are enclosed in square brackets. A superfluous stage direction ("*Enter Tubal,*" at III.i.74) has been deleted, the positions of a few stage directions are slightly altered, and obvious typographical errors have been corrected. Other departures from Q1 are listed below, the adopted reading given first, in bold type, the rejected reading in roman type. If the adopted reading comes from Q2 or F, that fact is indicated.

I.i.27 **docked** docks   113 **Is** It is
I.ii.59 **throstle** Trassell
II.i.s.d. **Morocco** Morochus   35 **page** rage
II.ii.99 **last** [Q2] lost
II.vii.69 **tombs** timber
II.viii.39 **Slubber** [Q2, F] slumber
III.i.100 **Heard** heere
III.ii.67 **eyes** [F] eye   81 **vice** voyce
III.iii.s.d. **Solanio** Salerio
III.iv.49 **Padua** Mantua   50 **cousin's** [Q2, F] cosin   81 **my** [Q2, F] my my
III.v.21 **e'en** [Q2, F] in   27 **comes.** come?   77 **merit it** meane it, it
84 **a wife** [F] wife
IV.i.30 **his state** [Q2, F] this states   31 **flint** [Q2] flints   51 **Master**

TEXTUAL NOTE

Maisters   74 **bleat** [F] bleake   75 **mountain** [F] mountaine of   100 **is mine** as
mine   229 **No, not** [Q2] Not not   396 **Gratiano** [Q2, F] Shy [lock]
V.i.41-42 **Master Lorenzo and Mistress Lorenzo?** M. Lorenzo, & M.
Lorenzo   49 **Sweet soul** [concludes Launcelot's speech]   51 **Stephano** [Q2]
Stephen   87 **Erebus** [F] Terebus 152 **it you** [Q2, F] you

WILLIAM SHAKESPEARE

THE MERRY WIVES OF WINDSOR

Edited by William Green

[*Dramatis Personae*

SIR JOHN FALSTAFF
FENTON, a young gentleman
SHALLOW, a country justice
SLENDER, nephew to Shallow
FORD }
PAGE } two citizens of Windsor
WILLIAM PAGE, a boy, son to Page
SIR HUGH EVANS, a Welsh parson
DOCTOR CAIUS, a French physician
HOST OF THE GARTER INN
BARDOLPH ⎫
PISTOL ⎬ followers of Falstaff
NYM ⎭
ROBIN, page to Falstaff
SIMPLE, servant to Slender
RUGBY, servant to Doctor Caius
MISTRESS FORD
MISTRESS PAGE
ANNE PAGE, her daughter
MISTRESS QUICKLY, servant to Doctor Caius
Servants to Page, Ford, etc.

Scene: Windsor and the neighborhood]

THE MERRY WIVES
OF WINDSOR

ACT I

Scene I. [*Before Page's house.*]

Enter Justice Shallow, Slender, [and] Sir Hugh Evans.

SHALLOW Sir Hugh, persuade me not; I will make a Star-chamber matter of it. If he were twenty Sir John Falstaff's, he shall not abuse Robert Shallow, Esquire.

SLENDER In the county of Gloucester, Justice of Peace, and Coram.   5

SHALLOW Ay, cousin Slender, and Custalorum.

SLENDER Ay, and Ratolorum too; and a gentleman born, Master Parson, who writes himself Armigero, in any bill, warrant, quittance, or obligation   10 —Armigero.

Text references are printed in **bold** type; the annotation follows in roman type.
I.i.1 **Sir** title used before the first name of ordinary priests   2 **Star-chamber** court having jurisdiction over cases of riot, forgery, and other specific offenses   6 **Coram** i.e., Quorum (term for justices with specific legal qualifications)   7 **Custalorum** i.e., Custos Rotulorum (a chief justice)   8 **Ratolorum** Slender's garbling of rotulorum   9-10 **Armigero** esquire

SHALLOW Ay, that I do, and have done any time these
three hundred years.

SLENDER All his successors gone before him hath
15   done't; and all his ancestors that come after him
may. They may give the dozen white luces in
their coat.

SHALLOW It is an old coat.

EVANS The dozen white louses do become an old coat
20   well. It agrees well, passant; it is a familiar beast
to man, and signifies love.

SHALLOW The luce is the fresh fish. The salt fish is an
old coat.

SLENDER I may quarter, coz?

25   SHALLOW You may, by marrying.

EVANS It is marring indeed, if he quarter it.

SHALLOW Not a whit.

EVANS Yes, py'r lady. If he has a quarter of your
coat, there is but three skirts for yourself, in my
30   simple conjectures. But that is all one. If Sir John
Falstaff have committed disparagements unto you,
I am of the Church, and will be glad to do my be-
nevolence to make atonements and compromises
between you.

35   SHALLOW The Council shall hear it. It is a riot.

---

16 give display 16 luces pikes (fish) 17 coat coat of arms 20 passant
walking (heraldic) 22-23 The luce ... old coat (obscure line probably containing an involved play on the words "salt" and "saltant" [heraldic term for
describing a leaping position for small animals or vermin], "luce" and "louse,"
"old coat" [as a garment], "coat of arms," and cod [the fish—sometimes pronounced as a homonym of "coat"]. Also, there may be a reference to the coat-of-
arms of the Fishmongers Company which is a composite of the arms of the older
Saltfishmongers and those of the Freshfishmongers) 24 quarter add arms to
one's family coat 24 coz kinsman 28 py'r lady by our Lady (the use of "p" for
"b" here is the first of Evans' Welsh pronunciations) 35 Council King's Council
sitting as the Court of Star-chamber

EVANS It is not meet the Council hear a riot. There is no fear of Got in a riot. The Council, look you, shall desire to hear the fear of Got, and not to hear a riot. Take your vizaments in that.

SHALLOW Ha! O' my life, if I were young again, the 40 sword should end it.

EVANS It is petter that friends is the sword, and end it. And there is also another device in my prain, which peradventure prings goot discretions with it. There is Anne Page, which is daughter to Master George 45 Page, which is pretty virginity.

SLENDER Mistress Anne Page? She has brown hair, and speaks small like a woman?

EVANS It is that fery person for all the 'orld, as just as you will desire. And seven hundred pounds of 50 moneys, and gold and silver, is her grandsire, upon his death's-bed—Got deliver to a joyful resurrections—give, when she is able to overtake seventeen years old. It were a goot motion if we leave our pribbles and prabbles, and desire a marriage be- 55 tween Master Abraham and Mistress Anne Page.

SHALLOW Did her grandsire leave her seven hundred pound?

EVANS Ay, and her father is make her a pretty penny.

SHALLOW I know the young gentlewoman. She has 60 good gifts.

EVANS Seven hundred pounds and possibilities is goot gifts.

SHALLOW Well, let us see honest Master Page. Is Falstaff there? 65

EVANS Shall I tell you a lie? I do despise a liar as I do despise one that is false, or as I despise one that is

39 vizaments i.e., advisements   48 small gentle   55 pribbles and prabbles petty bickerings   62 possibilities prospects of inheritance

not true. The knight Sir John is there; and, I beseech
you, be ruled by your well-willers. I will peat the
70   door for Master Page. [*Knocks.*] What, ho! Got
pless your house here.

PAGE [*Within*] Who's there?

EVANS Here is Got's plessing, and your friend, and
Justice Shallow; and here young Master Slender,
75   that peradventures shall tell you another tale, if
matters grow to your likings.

[*Enter*] *Master Page.*

PAGE I am glad to see your worship well. I thank you
for my venison, Master Shallow.

SHALLOW Master Page, I am glad to see you. Much
80   good do it your good heart! I wished your venison
better—it was ill killed. How doth good Mistress
Page?—and I thank you always with my heart, la,
with my heart.

PAGE Sir, I thank you.

85   SHALLOW Sir, I thank you; by yea and no, I do.

PAGE I am glad to see you, good Master Slender.

SLENDER How does your fallow greyhound, sir? I
heard say he was outrun on Cotsall.

PAGE It could not be judged, sir.

90   SLENDER You'll not confess, you'll not confess.

SHALLOW That he will not. 'Tis your fault, 'tis your
fault. 'Tis a good dog.

PAGE A cur, sir.

SHALLOW Sir, he's a good dog, and a fair dog. Can

---

81 **ill killed** (1) improperly killed (?) (2) possibly a reference to Falstaff's doing the
killing (see I.i. 109-10)   87 **fallow** brownish yellow   88 **Cotsall** the Cotswold
hills in Gloucestershire (locale of the Cotswold Games and center for coursing)
91 **fault** misfortune

there be more aid? He is good and fair. Is Sir John   95
Falstaff here?

PAGE Sir, he is within. And I would I could do a good
office between you.

EVANS It is spoke as a Christians ought to speak.

SHALLOW He hath wronged me, Master Page.   100

PAGE Sir, he doth in some sort confess it.

SHALLOW If it be confessed, it is not redressed. Is not
that so, Master Page? He hath wronged me; indeed,
he hath. At a word, he hath, believe me. Robert
Shallow, Esquire, saith he is wronged.   105

PAGE Here comes Sir John.

[Enter Sir John] Falstaff, Bardolph, Nym, [and] Pistol.

FALSTAFF Now, Master Shallow, you'll complain of me
to the King?

SHALLOW Knight, you have beaten my men, killed my
deer, and broke open my lodge.   110

FALSTAFF But not kissed your keeper's daughter?

SHALLOW Tut, a pin! This shall be answered.

FALSTAFF I will answer it straight. I have done all this.
That is now answered.

SHALLOW The Council shall know this.   115

FALSTAFF 'Twere better for you if it were known in
counsel. You'll be laughed at.

EVANS Pauca verba; Sir John, goot worts.

FALSTAFF Good worts? Good cabbage!—Slender, I
broke your head. What matter have you against   120
me?

112 pin trifle 116-17 in counsel privately 118 pauca verba few words
(Latin) 119 worts (1) words (2) cabbage-like plant 120 matter dispute (but in
the next line it has the senses of "brain matter" and "cause")

SLENDER Marry, sir, I have matter in my head against you, and against your cony-catching rascals, Bardolph, Nym, and Pistol. They carried me to the tavern and made me drunk, and afterwards picked my pocket.

125

BARDOLPH [*Drawing his sword*] You Banbury cheese!

SLENDER Ay, it is no matter.

PISTOL [*Also draws*] How now, Mephostophilus!

130 SLENDER Ay, it is no matter.

NYM [*Drawing*] Slice, I say! *Pauca, pauca*. Slice! That's my humor.

SLENDER Where's Simple, my man? Can you tell, cousin?

135 EVANS Peace, I pray you. Now let us understand. There is three umpires in this matter, as I understand; that is, Master Page, *fidelicet*, Master Page, and there is myself, *fidelicet*, myself; and the three party is, lastly and finally, mine Host of the Garter.

140 PAGE We three to hear it and end it between them.

EVANS Fery goot. I will make a prief of it in my notebook, and we will afterwards 'ork upon the cause with as great discreetly as we can.

FALSTAFF Pistol!

145 PISTOL He hears with ears.

EVANS The tevil and his tam! What phrase is this, "He hears with ear"? Why, it is affectations.

FALSTAFF Pistol, did you pick Master Slender's purse?

SLENDER Ay, by these gloves, did he—or I would I
150   might never come in mine own great chamber again

123 cony-catching cheating   127 **Banbury cheese** (noted for its thinness, a reference to Slender's build)   129 **Mephostophilus** i.e., devil (from Marlowe's *Dr. Faustus*)   132 **humor** temperament   137 **fidelicet** i.e., *videlicet*, namely   139 **Garter** Garter Inn

else—of seven groat's in mill-sixpences, and two
Edward shovel-boards, that cost me two shilling
and two pence apiece of Yed Miller, by these
gloves.

FALSTAFF Is this true, Pistol?   155

EVANS No, it is false, if it is a pickpurse.

PISTOL Ha, thou mountain-foreigner! Sir John and
   master mine,
I combat challenge of this latten bilbo.
Word of denial in thy *labras* here!
Word of denial! Froth and scum, thou liest!   160

SLENDER By these gloves, then 'twas he.

NYM Be advised, sir, and pass good humors. I will say
   "marry trap" with you, if you run the nuthook's
   humor on me. That is the very note of it.

SLENDER By this hat, then he in the red face had it; for   165
   though I cannot remember what I did when you
   made me drunk, yet I am not altogether an ass.

FALSTAFF What say you, Scarlet and John?

BARDOLPH Why, sir, for my part, I say the gentleman
   had drunk himself out of his five sentences.   170

EVANS It is his "five senses." Fie, what the ignorance is!

BARDOLPH And being fap, sir, was, as they say, cashiered; and so conclusions passed the careers.

SLENDER Ay, you spake in Latin then too. But 'tis no

---

151 **groats** coins worth fourpence   151 **mill-sixpences** i.e., milled coins
152 **Edward shovel-boards** shillings from the reign of Edward VI used in the
game of shovelboard (rare coins by the 1590s)   153 **Yed** i.e., Ed, Edward
157 **mountain-foreigner** i.e., Welshman   158 **latten bilbo** brass sword
159 **labras** lips   163 **marry trap** (a term of insult)   163-64 **run the nuthook's
humor** i.e., think to involve me with the law (*nuthook* = constable)   168 **Scarlet
and John** Robin Hood's companions (alluding to Bardolph's red face)   172 **fap**
drunk   172-73 **cashiered** robbed   173 **conclusions passed the careers** (an
obscure line possibly meaning "and that brought the matter to a speedy end" or
"he got what he deserved" —from "pass a careire," a term in horsemanship)

175 matter. I'll ne'er be drunk whilst I live again, but in
honest, civil, godly company, for this trick. If I be
drunk, I'll be drunk with those that have the fear of
God, and not with drunken knaves.

EVANS So Got 'udge me, that is a virtuous mind.

180 FALSTAFF You hear all these matters denied, gentlemen;
you hear it.

[Enter] Anne Page [with wine], Mistress Ford [and]
Mistress Page [following].

PAGE Nay, daughter, carry the wine in; we'll drink
within.   *[Exit Anne Page.]*

SLENDER O heavens! This is Mistress Anne Page.

185 PAGE How now, Mistress Ford!

FALSTAFF Mistress Ford, by my troth, you are very well
met. By your leave, good mistress.   *[Kisses her.]*

PAGE Wife, bid these gentlemen welcome. Come, we
have a hot venison pasty to dinner. Come, gentle-
190 men, I hope we shall drink down all unkindness.
[Exeunt all except Shallow, Slender, and Evans.]

SLENDER I had rather than forty shillings I had my
Book of Songs and Sonnets here.

[Enter] Simple.
How now, Simple, where have you been? I must
wait on myself, must I? You have not the Book of
195 Riddles about you, have you?

SIMPLE Book of Riddles? Why, did you not lend it to
Alice Shortcake upon Allhallowmas last, a fortnight afore Michaelmas?

SHALLOW Come, coz; come, coz; we stay for you. A
200 word with you, coz. Marry, this, coz: there is as

192 **Book of Songs and Sonnets** an anthology published by Tottel in 1557,
commonly called Tottel's *Miscellany* 197 **Allhallowmas** All Saint's Day,
November 1 198 **Michaelmas** St. Michael's Day, September 29 200 **Marry**
(mild oath from "By Mary")

'twere a tender, a kind of tender, made afar off by Sir Hugh here. Do you understand me?

SLENDER Ay, sir, you shall find me reasonable. If it be so, I shall do that that is reason.

SHALLOW Nay, but understand me.   205

SLENDER So I do, sir.

EVANS Give ear to his motions. Master Slender, I will description the matter to you, if you be capacity of it.

SLENDER Nay, I will do as my cousin Shallow says. I   210
pray you pardon me. He's a Justice of Peace in his country, simple though I stand here.

EVANS But that is not the question. The question is concerning your marriage.

SHALLOW Ay, there's the point, sir.   215

EVANS Marry, is it, the very point of it—to Mistress Anne Page.

SLENDER Why, if it be so, I will marry her upon any reasonable demands.

EVANS But can you affection the 'oman? Let us com-   220
mand to know that of your mouth, or of your lips; for divers philosophers hold that the lips is parcel of the mouth. Therefore, precisely, can you carry your goot will to the maid?

SHALLOW Cousin Abraham Slender, can you love her?   225

SLENDER I hope, sir, I will do as it shall become one that would do reason.

EVANS Nay, Got's lords and his ladies! You must speak possable, if you can carry her your desires towards her.   230

201 tender offer 201 afar off indirectly 207 motions proposals 212 simple
though as sure as 222 divers various 222 parcel part 229 possable
positively

SHALLOW That you must. Will you, upon good dowry, marry her?

SLENDER I will do a greater thing than that, upon your request, cousin, in any reason.

235 SHALLOW Nay, conceive me, conceive me, sweet coz. What I do is to pleasure you, coz. Can you love the maid?

SLENDER I will marry her, sir, at your request; but if there be no great love in the beginning, yet heaven
240 may decrease it upon better acquaintance when we are married and have more occasion to know one another. I hope upon familiarity will grow more contempt. But if you say, "Marry her," I will marry her; that I am freely dissolved, and dissolutely.

245 EVANS It is a fery discretion answer, save the faul' is in the 'ort "dissolutely." The 'ort is, according to our meaning, "resolutely." His meaning is goot.

SHALLOW Ay, I think my cousin meant well.

SLENDER Ay, or else I would I might be hanged, la.

[Enter Anne Page.]

250 SHALLOW Here comes fair Mistress Anne.—Would I were young for your sake, Mistress Anne.

ANNE The dinner is on the table. My father desires your worships' company.

SHALLOW I will wait on him, fair Mistress Anne.

255 EVANS Od's plessed will! I will not be absence at the grace.   *[Exeunt Shallow and Evans.]*

ANNE Will't please your worship to come in, sir?

SLENDER No, I thank you, forsooth, heartily; I am very well.

260 ANNE The dinner attends you, sir.

SLENDER I am not a-hungry, I thank you, forsooth.

235 **conceive me** understand me   245 **faul'** fault   255 **Od's** God's

[*To Simple*] Go, sirrah, for all you are my man, go wait upon my cousin Shallow. [*Exit Simple.*] A justice of peace sometimes may be beholding to his friend for a man. I keep but three men and a boy   265
yet, till my mother be dead. But what though? Yet I live like a poor gentleman born.

ANNE I may not go in without your worship; they will not sit till you come.

SLENDER I' faith, I'll eat nothing. I thank you as much   270
as though I did.

ANNE I pray you, sir, walk in.

SLENDER I had rather walk here, I thank you. I bruised my shin th' other day with playing at sword and dagger with a master of fence—three veneys for   275
a dish of stewed prunes—and, by my troth, I cannot abide the smell of hot meat since. Why do your dogs bark so? Be there bears i' th' town?

ANNE I think there are, sir; I heard them talked of.

SLENDER I love the sport well, but I shall as soon   280
quarrel at it as any man in England. You are afraid if you see the bear loose, are you not?

ANNE Ay, indeed, sir.

SLENDER That's meat and drink to me now. I have seen Sackerson loose twenty times, and have taken him   285
by the chain; but, I warrant you, the women have so cried and shrieked at it, that it passed. But woman, indeed, cannot abide 'em; they are very ill-favored rough things.

[*Enter Page.*]

PAGE Come, gentle Master Slender, come. We stay for   290
you.

SLENDER I'll eat nothing; I thank you, sir.

262 **sirrah** (term of address used to inferiors)   275 **veneys** bouts   280 **the sport** i.e., bearbaiting   285 **Sackerson** (a famous bear)

PAGE By cock and pie, you shall not choose, sir!
Come, come.

295 SLENDER Nay, pray you, lead the way.

PAGE Come on, sir.

SLENDER Mistress Anne, yourself shall go first.

ANNE Not I, sir; pray you keep on.

SLENDER Truly, I will not go first; truly, la! I will not
300 do you that wrong.

ANNE I pray you, sir.

SLENDER I'll rather be unmannerly than troublesome.
You do yourself wrong, indeed, la!   *Exeunt.*

Scene II. [*Before Page's house.*]

Enter Evans and Simple.

EVANS Go your ways, and ask of Doctor Caius' house,
which is the way; and there dwells one Mistress
Quickly, which is in the manner of his nurse, or
his dry nurse, or his cook, or his laundry, his
5 washer, and his wringer.

SIMPLE Well, sir.

EVANS Nay, it is petter yet. Give her this letter, for it
is a 'oman that altogether's acquaintance with Mistress Anne Page; and the letter is to desire and re-
10 quire her to solicit your master's desires to Mistress
Anne Page. I pray you be gone. I will make an end
of my dinner; there's pippins and seese to come.
                                                    Exeunt.

---

293 **cock and pie** (an oath)   I.ii.4 **dry nurse** i.e., housekeeper   12 **pippins and
seese** apples and cheese

Scene III. [*Falstaff's room in the Garter Inn.*]

Enter Falstaff, Host, Bardolph, Nym, Pistol,
[and Robin, the] Page.

FALSTAFF Mine Host of the Garter!

HOST What says my bully rook? Speak scholarly and
wisely.

FALSTAFF Truly, mine Host, I must turn away some of
my followers.   5

HOST Discard, bully Hercules, cashier. Let them wag;
trot, trot.

FALSTAFF I sit at ten pounds a week.

HOST Thou'rt an emperor—Caesar, Keisar, and Pheazar. I will entertain Bardolph: he shall draw,   10
he shall tap. Said I well, bully Hector?

FALSTAFF Do so, good mine Host.

HOST I have spoke; let him follow. [*To Bardolph*] Let
me see thee froth and lime. I am at a word; fol-
low.   [*Exit.*]   15

FALSTAFF Bardolph, follow him. A tapster is a good
trade. An old cloak makes a new jerkin; a withered
servingman, a fresh tapster. Go, adieu.

BARDOLPH It is a life that I have desired. I will thrive.

I.iii.2 **bully rook** (friendly term of address used by the Host) 6 **wag** depart
8 **I sit at** my expenses run 9 **Keisar** Kaiser 9-10 **Pheazar** vizier 10 **entertain** employ 10 **draw** draw liquor 11 **tap** serve as tapster 14 **froth and lime**
i.e., cheat the customers by putting a big head of foam on the beer or by
adulterating wine with lime 14 **I am at a word** i.e., I speak briefly

20   PISTOL   O base Hungarian wight! Wilt thou the spigot
        wield?   [*Exit Bardolph.*]

     NYM   He was gotten in drink. Is not the humor con-
        ceited?

     FALSTAFF   I am glad I am so acquit of this tinderbox.
25   His thefts were too open. His filching was like an
        unskillful singer: he kept not time.

     NYM   The good humor is to steal at a minute's rest.

     PISTOL   "Convey," the wise it call. "Steal?" Foh, a fico
        for the phrase!

30   FALSTAFF   Well, sirs, I am almost out at heels.

     PISTOL   Why then, let kibes ensue.

     FALSTAFF   There is no remedy. I must cony-catch, I
        must shift.

     PISTOL   Young ravens must have food.

35   FALSTAFF   Which of you know Ford of this town?

     PISTOL   I ken the wight. He is of substance good.

     FALSTAFF   My honest lads, I will tell you what I am
        about.

     PISTOL   Two yards, and more.

40   FALSTAFF   No quips now, Pistol. Indeed, I am in the
        waist two yards about. But I am now about no
        waste; I am about thrift. Briefly, I do mean to make
        love to Ford's wife. I spy entertainment in her: she
        discourses, she carves, she gives the leer of invi-
45   tation. I can construe the action of her familiar
        style; and the hardest voice of her behavior, to be
        Englished rightly, is, "I am Sir John Falstaff's."

---

20 base Hungarian wight i.e., beggarly fellow   **22 gotten** begotten   **22-23 conceited** ingenious   **24 acquit** rid   **27 minute's rest** i.e., in the shortest possible
interval   **28 fico** fig   **30 out at heels** penniless   **31 kibes** chilblains   **33 shift**
devise some stratagem   **36 ken** know   **44 carves** shows courtesy

PISTOL He hath studied her well, and translated her
will, out of honesty into English.

NYM The anchor is deep. Will that humor pass?   50

FALSTAFF Now, the report goes she has all the rule of
her husband's purse. He hath a legion of angels.

PISTOL As many devils entertain. And "To her, boy,"
say I.

NYM The humor rises; it is good. Humor me the   55
angels.

FALSTAFF I have writ me here a letter to her; and here
another to Page's wife, who even now gave me
good eyes too, examined my parts with most judicious oeillades. Sometimes the beam of her view   60
gilded my foot, sometimes my portly belly.

PISTOL [*Aside*] Then did the sun on dunghill shine.

NYM [*Aside*] I thank thee for that humor.

FALSTAFF O, she did so course o'er my exteriors with
such a greedy intention that the appetite of her eye   65
did seem to scorch me up like a burning-glass.
Here's another letter to her. She bears the purse too.
She is a region in Guiana, all gold and bounty. I
will be cheater to them both, and they shall be
exchequers to me. They shall be my East and West   70
Indies, and I will trade to them both. [*To Pistol*]
Go, bear thou this letter to Mistress Page; [*To
Nym*] and thou this to Mistress Ford. We will
thrive, lads, we will thrive.

PISTOL Shall I Sir Pandarus of Troy become,   75
And by my side wear steel? Then Lucifer take all!

49 honesty chastity   49 English (probably with a pun on *ingle* = paramour)
50 The anchor is deep (an obscure line possibly meaning [1] it is a deeply
thought-out scheme or [2] That wine keg [i.e., Falstaff] is a deep thinker [from
"anker," a wine keg])   52 angels gold coins worth about ten shillings   60 oeillades
amorous glances   69 cheater (1) escheator, official who looked after the king's
escheats (2) one who defrauds   75 Sir Pandarus (the go-between in Chaucer's
Troilus and Criseyde, from whose name the word "pander" comes)

NYM I will run no base humor. Here, take the humor-
letter. I will keep the havior of reputation.

FALSTAFF [*To Robin*] Hold, sirrah, bear you these
letters tightly.
80   Sail like my pinnance to those golden shores.
Rogues, hence, avaunt! Vanish like hailstones, go!
Trudge, plod away o'th' hoof; seek shelter, pack!
Falstaff will learn the humor of the age:
French thrift, you rogues-myself and skirted
page.   [*Exeunt Falstaff and Robin.*]

PISTOL Let vultures gripe thy guts! For gourd and
85   fullam holds,
And high and low beguiles the rich and poor.
Tester I'll have in pouch when thou shalt lack,
Base Phrygian Turk!

NYM I have operations which be humors of revenge.

90   PISTOL Wilt thou revenge?

NYM By welkin and her star!

PISTOL With wit or steel?

NYM With both the humors, I.
I will discuss the humor of this love to Page.

95   PISTOL And I to Ford shall eke unfold
How Falstaff, varlet vile,
His dove will prove, his gold will hold,
And his soft couch defile.

NYM My humor shall not cool. I will incense Page to
100   deal with poison. I will possess him with yellowness, for the revolt of mind is dangerous. That is
my true humor.

---

79 **tightly** well   82 **pack** be off   84 **French thrift** (an allusion to the French
custom then current to use one page instead of many serving men)   85 **gourd and
fullam** kinds of false dice   86 **high and low** numbers on the dice
87 **Tester** sixpence   88 **Base Phrygian Turk** (term of insult)   91 **welkin** sky
94 **discuss** declare   100-1 **yellowness** i.e., jealousy

PISTOL Thou art the Mars of malcontents. I second
   thee; troop on.   *Exeunt*.

Scene IV. [*A room in Dr. Caius' house.*]

Enter Mistress Quickly [and] Simple.

QUICKLY [*Calling*] What, John Rugby! ([*Enter*] *John
   Rugby*.) I pray thee, go to the casement and see if
   you can see my master, Master Doctor Caius, coming. If he do, i' faith, and find anybody in the house,
   here will be an old abusing of God's patience and   5
   the King's English.

RUGBY I'll go watch.

QUICKLY Go, and we'll have a posset for't soon at
   night, in faith, at the latter end of a sea-coal fire.
   [*Exit Rugby*.] An honest, willing, kind fellow, as   10
   ever servant shall come in house withal; and, I
   warrant you, no telltale, nor no breedbate. His
   worst fault is that he is given to prayer: he is something peevish that way, but nobody but has his
   fault. But let that pass.—Peter Simple you say your   15
   name is?

SIMPLE Ay, for fault of a better.

QUICKLY And Master Slender's your master?

SIMPLE Ay, forsooth.

QUICKLY Does he not wear a great round beard like a   20
   glover's paring knife?

I.iv.5 old great, plenty of   8 posset hot milk curdled with ale or wine   9 sea-
coal coal brought by sea   11 withal with   12 breedbate mischiefmaker
14 peevish silly

SIMPLE No, forsooth. He hath but a little whey face, with a little yellow beard—a Cain-colored beard.

QUICKLY A softly-sprighted man, is he not?

25 SIMPLE Ay, forsooth. But he is as tall a man of his hands as any is between this and his head. He hath fought with a warrener.

QUICKLY How say you? O, I should remember him. Does he not hold up his head, as it were, and strut
30 in his gait?

SIMPLE Yes, indeed does he.

QUICKLY Well, heaven send Anne Page no worse fortune. Tell Master Parson Evans I will do what I can for your master. Anne is a good girl, and I
35 wish—

[Enter Rugby.]

RUGBY Out, alas! Here comes my master!

QUICKLY We shall all be shent. Run in here, good young man; go into this closet. He will not stay long. *[Shuts Simple in the chamber.]* What, John
40 Rugby! John, what, John, I say! Go, John, go in-quire for my master. I doubt he be not well, that he comes not home. *[Exit Rugby.]*

[Sings.] "And down, down, adown-a," &c.

[Enter] Doctor Caius.

CAIUS Vat is you sing? I do not like dese toys. Pray
45 you go and vetch me in my closset *un boitier vert*—a box, a green-a box. Do intend vat I speak? A green-a box.

QUICKLY Ay, forsooth, I'll fetch it you. *[Aside]* I am

22 whey i.e., pale (the Folio gives "wee," perhaps a dialectal pronunciation)
23 **Cain-colored** i.e., reddish-yellow (traditional color of Cain's beard in tapestries)
24 **softly-sprighted** gentle-spirited   25-26 **tall a man of his hands** i.e., valiant
27 **warrener** gamekeeper   37 **shent** scolded   38 **closet** private room   41 **doubt**
fear   44 **toys** foolish nonsense   46 **intend** hear (Fr. *entendre*)

124

glad he went not in himself. If he had found the
young man, he would have been horn-mad.   [*Exit.*]   50

CAIUS Fe, fe, fe, fe! *Ma foi, il fait fort chaud. Je m'en
vais à la Cour—la grande affaire.*

QUICKLY [*Returning with the box*] Is it this, sir?

CAIUS *Oui; mette le au mon pocket: dépêche,* quickly.
Vere is dat knave Rugby?   55

QUICKLY What, John Rugby! John!

[*Enter Rugby.*]

RUGBY Here, sir.

CAIUS You are John Rugby, and you are Jack Rugby.
Come, take-a your rapier and come after my heel
to de court.   60

RUGBY 'Tis ready, sir, here in the porch.

CAIUS By my trot, I tarry too long. Od's me! *Qu'ai
j'oublié?* Dere is some simples in my closset dat
I vill not for de varld I shall leave behind.
[*Crosses to the chamber.*]

QUICKLY [*Aside*] Ay me, he'll find the young man   65
there, and be mad.

CAIUS O *diable, diable!* Vat is in my closset? Villainy!
Larron! [*Pulls Simple out.*] Rugby, my rapier!

QUICKLY Good master, be content.

CAIUS Verefore shall I be content-a?   70

QUICKLY The young man is an honest man.

CAIUS Vat shall de honest man do in my closset? Dere
is no honest man dat shall come in my closset.

50 **horn-mad** enraged   51-52 **Ma foi ... grande affaire** faith, it is very hot. I
am going to the Court—the grand affair.   54 **Oui ... dépêche** yes; put it in my
pocket; be quick   62 **trot** i.e., troth   62-63 **Qu'ai j'oublié** what have I forgotten
63 **simples** medicinal herbs   68 **Larron** thief

QUICKLY I beseech you, be not so phlegmatic. Hear
75 the truth of it. He came of an errand to me from
Parson Hugh.

CAIUS Vell?

SIMPLE Ay, forsooth, to desire her to—

QUICKLY Peace, I pray you.

80 CAIUS Peace-a your tongue.—Speak-a your tale.

SIMPLE To desire this honest gentlewoman, your maid,
to speak a good word to Mistress Anne Page for
my master in the way of marriage.

QUICKLY This is all, indeed, la! But I'll ne'er put my
85 finger in the fire, and need not.

CAIUS Sir Hugh send-a you?—Rugby, *baille* me some
paper. Tarry you a little-a while.   [*Writes.*]

QUICKLY [*Aside to Simple*] I am glad he is so quiet. If
he had been throughly moved, you should have
90 heard him so loud, and so melancholy. But notwithstanding, man, I'll do you your master what good
I can; and the very yea and the no is, the French
doctor, my master—I may call him my master, look
you, for I keep his house; and I wash, wring, brew,
95 bake, scour, dress meat and drink, make the beds,
and do all myself—

SIMPLE [*Aside to Quickly*] 'Tis a great charge to
come under one body's hand.

QUICKLY [*Aside to Simple*] Are you avised o' that? You
100 shall find it a great charge. And to be up early and
down late; but notwithstanding—to tell you in your
ear, I would have no words of it—my master himself is in love with Mistress Anne Page. But notwithstanding that, I know Anne's mind. That's
105 neither here nor there.

---

74 phlegmatic (Quickly's error for "choleric") 86 baille fetch 97 charge burden

CAIUS You jack'nape, give-a dis letter to Sir Hugh.
By gar, it is a shallenge. I vill cut his troat in de
Park; and I vill teach a scurvy jackanape priest to
meddle or make. You may be gone; it is not good
you tarry here. [*Exit Simple.*] By gar, I vill cut all   110
his two stones; by gar, he shall not have a stone to
trow at his dog.

QUICKLY Alas, he speaks but for his friend.

CAIUS It is no matter-a ver dat. Do not you tell-a me
dat I shall have Anne Page for myself? By gar, I   115
vill kill de Jack priest; and I have appointed mine
Host of de Jarteer to measure our weapon. By gar,
I vill myself have Anne Page.

QUICKLY Sir, the maid loves you, and all shall be well.
We must give folks leave to prate. What the good-   120
year!

CAIUS Rugby, come to the court vit me. [*To Quickly*]
By gar, if I have not Anne Page, I shall turn your
head out of my door. Follow my heels, Rugby.
                              [*Exeunt Caius and Rugby.*]

QUICKLY [*Calling after Caius*] You shall have An—   125
fool's-head of your own. No, I know Anne's mind
for that. Never a woman in Windsor knows more
of Anne's mind than I do, nor can do more than I
do with her, I thank heaven.

FENTON [*Offstage*] Who's within there, ho?   130

QUICKLY Who's there, I trow? Come near the house,
I pray you.

                    [*Enter*] Fenton.

FENTON How now, good woman. How dost thou?

---

106 jack'nape coxcomb   111 stones testicles   116 Jack (term of contempt)
117 measure our weapon i.e., umpire the duel   120-21 good-year (a meaningless expletive)   125 An (1) Anne (2) an   131 trow wonder   131 Come near i.e.,
enter

QUICKLY The better that it pleases your good worship
135   to ask.

FENTON What news? How does pretty Mistress Anne?

QUICKLY In truth, sir, and she is pretty, and honest,
and gentle—and one that is your friend. I can tell
you that by the way, I praise heaven for it.

140 FENTON Shall I do any good, think'st thou? Shall I not
lose my suit?

QUICKLY Troth, sir, all is in His hands above. But notwithstanding, Master Fenton, I'll be sworn on a
book she loves you. Have not your worship a wart
145   above your eye?

FENTON Yes, marry, have I. What of that?

QUICKLY Well, thereby hangs a tale. Good faith, it is
such another Nan; but, I detest, an honest maid as
ever broke bread. We had an hour's talk of that wart.
150   I shall never laugh but in that maid's company.
But, indeed, she is given too much to allicholy
and musing. But for you—well, go to.

FENTON Well, I shall see her today. Hold, there's
money for thee; let me have thy voice in my behalf.
155   If thou seest her before me, commend me—

QUICKLY Will I? I' faith, that we will. And I will tell
your worship more of the wart the next time we
have confidence, and of other wooers.

FENTON Well, farewell, I am in great haste now.

160 QUICKLY Farewell to your worship. [*Exit Fenton.*]
Truly, an honest gentleman. But Anne loves him not,
for I know Anne's mind as well as another does.
Out upon't, what have I forgot?   *Exit.*

---

137 **honest** chaste   148 **such another Nan** i.e., charming female   148 **detest**
(Quickly's error for "protest")   151 **allicholy** melancholy

Scene I. [*Before Page's house.*]

Enter Mistress Page [*with a letter*].

MRS. PAGE What, have 'scaped love letters in the holiday time of my beauty, and am I now a subject
for them? Let me see.   [*Reads.*]

"Ask me no reason why I love you, for though Love
use Reason for his precisian, he admits him not for   5
his counselor. You are not young, no more am I.
Go to then, there's sympathy. You are merry, so
am I. Ha, ha, then there's more sympathy. You
love sack, and so do I. Would you desire better
sympathy? Let it suffice thee, Mistress Page—at   10
the least, if the love of soldier can suffice—that I
love thee. I will not say, pity me—'tis not a soldier-
like phrase; but I say, love me. By me,
       Thine own true knight,
       By day or night,   15
       Or any kind of light,
       With all his might
       For thee to fight,
          John Falstaff."

What a Herod of Jewry is this! O wicked, wicked   20
world. One that is well-nigh worn to pieces with
age to show himself a young gallant! What an un-

II.i.1-2 **in the holiday time** i.e., in my youth 5 **precisian** inflexible spiritual
advisor 9 **sack** Spanish white wine 20 **Herod of Jewry** (portrayed as a ranting
villain in the miracle plays)

129

weighed behavior hath this Flemish drunkard
picked—with the devil's name!—out of my con-
25   versation that he dares in this manner assay me?
Why, he hath not been thrice in my company.
What should I say to him? I was then frugal of my
mirth—Heaven forgive me! Why, I'll exhibit a
bill in the parliament for the putting down of men.
30   How shall I be revenged on him? For revenged I
will be, as sure as his guts are made of puddings.

[Enter] Mistress Ford.

MRS. FORD Mistress Page! Trust me, I was going to
your house.

MRS. PAGE And, trust me, I was coming to you. You
35   look very ill.

MRS. FORD Nay, I'll ne'er believe that. I have to show
to the contrary.

MRS. PAGE Faith, but you do, in my mind.

MRS. FORD Well, I do then; yet I say I could show you
40   to the contrary. O Mistress Page, give me some
counsel.

MRS. PAGE What's the matter, woman?

MRS. FORD O woman, if it were not for one trifling
respect, I could come to such honor.

45   MRS. PAGE Hang the trifle, woman; take the honor.
What is it? Dispense with trifles. What is it?

MRS. FORD If I would but go to hell for an eternal
moment or so, I could be knighted.

MRS. PAGE What? Thou liest. Sir Alice Ford? These
50   knights will hack; and so thou shouldst not alter
the article of thy gentry.

22-23 **unweighed** inconsiderate   23 **Flemish drunkard** (the Flemish were
notorious for heavy drinking)   24-25 **conversation** behavior   28 **exhibit** submit
29 **putting down** suppressing   31 **puddings** sausages   50 **hack** (meaning not
clear in this context; a double entendre on giving indiscriminate blows with a
sword is possible)   51 **article of thy gentry** character of your rank

MRS. FORD We burn daylight. [*Giving her a letter*]
Here, read, read! Perceive how I might be knighted.
I shall think the worse of fat men as long as I have
an eye to make difference of men's liking. And   55
yet he would not swear; praised women's modesty;
and gave such orderly and well-behaved reproof to
all uncomeliness that I would have sworn his disposition would have gone to the truth of his words.
But they do no more adhere and keep place to-   60
gether than the Hundredth Psalm to the tune of
"Greensleeves." What tempest, I trow, threw this
whale, with so many tuns of oil in his belly, ashore
at Windsor? How shall I be revenged on him? I
think the best way were to entertain him with hope   65
till the wicked fire of lust have melted him in his
own grease. Did you ever hear the like?

MRS. PAGE [*Comparing the two letters*] Letter for letter, but that the name of Page and Ford differs.—
To thy great comfort in this mystery of ill opin-   70
ions, here's the twin brother of thy letter. But let
thine inherit first, for I protest mine never shall. I
warrant he hath a thousand of these letters, writ
with blank space for different names—sure, more—
and these are of the second edition. He will print   75
them, out of doubt; for he cares not what he puts
into the press, when he would put us two. I had
rather be a giantess and lie under Mount Pelion.
Well, I will find you twenty lascivious turtles ere
one chaste man. [*Gives both letters to Mrs. Ford.*]   80

MRS. FORD Why, this is the very same: the very hand,
the very words. What doth he think of us?

---

52 **burn daylight** waste time   55 **make difference of** discriminate between
55 **liking** looks   58 **uncomeliness** improper behavior   58-59 **his disposition
... words** i.e., appearances are deceiving   62 **Greensleeves** popular love ballad
70-71 **ill opinions** i.e., sullied reputations   78 **Mount Pelion** (mountain in
Thessaly noted in mythology for the attempt of the giants to reach heaven by
piling Mount Ossa on Pelion)   79 **turtles** turtledoves (noted for their fidelity to
their mates)

MRS. PAGE Nay, I know not. It makes me almost ready
to wrangle with mine own honesty. I'll entertain
85   myself like one that I am not acquainted withal; for
sure, unless he know some strain in me that I know not
myself, he would never have boarded me in
this fury.

MRS. FORD "Boarding" call you it? I'll be sure to keep
90   him above deck.

MRS. PAGE So will I. If he come under my hatches,
I'll never to sea again. Let's be revenged on him.
Let's appoint him a meeting, give him a show of
comfort in his suit, and lead him on with a fine-
95   baited delay till he hath pawned his horses to mine
Host of the Garter.

MRS. FORD Nay, I will consent to act any villainy
against him that may not sully the chariness of our
honesty. O that my husband saw this letter! It
100   would give eternal food to his jealousy.

MRS. PAGE Why, look where he comes, and my goodman too. He's as far from jealousy as I am from
giving him cause. And that, I hope, is an unmea-
surable distance.

105   MRS. FORD You are the happier woman.

MRS. PAGE Let's consult together against this greasy
knight. Come hither.   [They retire.]

[Enter] Master Page [with] Nym, [and] Master
Ford [with] Pistol.

FORD Well, I hope it be not so.

PISTOL Hope is a curtal dog in some affairs.
110   Sir John affects thy wife.

FORD Why, sir, my wife is not young.

---

84 honesty chastity   87 boarded made advances to   94-95 fine-baited subtly
alluring   98 chariness scrupulous integrity   101-2 goodman husband
109 curtal with a docked tail   110 affects loves

PISTOL He woos both high and low, both rich and poor,
Both young and old, one with another, Ford.
He loves the gallimaufry. Ford, perpend.

FORD Love my wife?   115

PISTOL With liver burning hot. Prevent, or go thou,
Like Sir Actaeon he, with Ringwood at thy heels.
O, odious is the name!

FORD What name, sir?

PISTOL The horn, I say. Farewell.   120
Take heed, have open eye, for thieves do foot by
    night.
Take heed, ere summer comes or cuckoo birds do
    sing.
Away, Sir Corporal Nym!
Believe it, Page; he speaks sense.   [*Exit*.]

FORD [*Aside*] I will be patient; I will find out this.   125

NYM [*To Page*] And this is true; I like not the humor
of lying. He hath wronged me in some humors. I
should have borne the humored letter to her, but I
have a sword and it shall bite upon my necessity.
He loves your wife. There's the short and the long.   130
My name is Corporal Nym; I speak, and I avouch
'tis true. My name is Nym, and Falstaff loves your
wife. Adieu. I love not the humor of bread and
cheese. And there's the humor of it. Adieu. [*Exit*.]

PAGE "The humor of it," quoth 'a? Here's a fellow   135
frights English out of his wits.

FORD I will seek out Falstaff.

114 **gallimaufry** i.e., medley   114 **perpend** consider   116 **liver** (supposed seat
of love)   117 **Sir Actaeon** (accidentally coming upon Diana bathing, Actaeon was
turned into a stag for punishment and then killed by his own hounds)
117 **Ringwood** (common Elizabethan name for a hound)   118 **odious is the
name** (allusion to Actaeon as a horned beast, i.e., a cuckold)   122 **cuckoo birds**
(allusion to cuckoldom from the cuckoo's habit of laying its eggs in the nests of
other birds)   133-34 **bread and cheese** (possible allusion to the cuckoo-bread
flower, i.e., feeding cuckoldry)

133

PAGE I never heard such a drawling, affecting rogue.

FORD If I do find it—well.

140 PAGE I will not believe such a Cataian, though the priest o' th' town commended him for a true man.

FORD 'Twas a good sensible fellow—well.

[*Mrs. Page and Mrs. Ford come forward.*]

PAGE How now, Meg.

MRS. PAGE Whither go you, George? Hark you.
[*They speak aside.*]

145 MRS. FORD How now, sweet Frank. Why art thou melancholy?

FORD I melancholy? I am not melancholy. Get you home, go.

MRS. FORD Faith, thou hast some crotchets in thy
150 head now. Will you go, Mistress Page?

MRS. PAGE Have with you.—You'll come to dinner, George?
[*Enter*] *Mistress Quickly.*

[*Aside to Mrs Ford*] Look who comes yonder. She shall be our messenger to this paltry knight.

155 MRS. FORD [*Aside to Mrs Page*] Trust me, I thought on her. She'll fit it.

MRS. PAGE You are come to see my daughter Anne?

QUICKLY Ay, forsooth; and, I pray, how does good Mistress Anne?

160 MRS. PAGE Go in with us and see. We have an hour's talk with you.
[*Exeunt Mistress Page, Mistress Ford, and Mistress Quickly.*]

138 **affecting** affected   140 **Cataian** Cathaian (i.e., Chinese; not considered trustworthy by the Elizabethans)   149 **crotchets** peculiar notions   151 **Have with you** I'll go along with you

PAGE How now, Master Ford.

FORD You heard what this knave told me, did you not?

PAGE Yes, and you heard what that other told me?   165

FORD Do you think there is truth in them?

PAGE Hang 'em, slaves! I do not think the knight would offer it. But these that accuse him in his intent towards our wives are a yoke of his discarded men—very rogues, now they be out of service.   170

FORD Were they his men?

PAGE Marry were they.

FORD I like it never the better for that. Does he lie at the Garter?

PAGE Ay, marry does he. If he should intend this voyage toward my wife, I would turn her loose to him; and what he gets more of her than sharp words, let it lie on my head.   175

FORD I do not misdoubt my wife, but I would be loath to turn them together. A man may be too confident. I would have nothing lie on my head. I cannot be thus satisfied.   180

[Enter] Host.

PAGE Look where my ranting Host of the Garter comes. There is either liquor in his pate or money in his purse when he looks so merrily.—How now, mine Host.   185

HOST How now, bully rook, thou'rt a gentleman. [*Calling behind him*] Cavaliero Justice, I say!

[Enter] Shallow.

SHALLOW I follow, mine Host, I follow. Good even

168 **offer** try   169 **yoke** pair   177-78 **let it lie on my head** (1) it's my responsibility (2) I would be cuckolded   188 **Cavaliero** (Spanish title for a gentleman trained in arms)

190   and twenty, good Master Page. Master Page, will
      you go with us? We have sport in hand.

HOST Tell him, Cavaliero Justice; tell him, bully rook.

SHALLOW Sir, there is fray to be fought between Sir
      Hugh the Welsh priest and Caius the French doctor.

195 FORD Good mine Host o' th' Garter, a word with you.
                                    [*Draws him aside.*]

HOST What sayest thou, my bully rook?

SHALLOW [*To Page*] Will you go with us to behold it?
      My merry Host hath had the measuring of their
      weapons, and, I think, hath appointed them con-
200   trary places; for, believe me, I hear the Parson is
      no jester. Hark, I will tell you what our sport shall
      be.   [*They converse apart.*]

HOST Hast thou no suit against my knight, my Guest
      Cavaliero?

205 FORD None, I protest. But I'll give you a pottle of
      burnt sack to give me recourse to him and tell him
      my name is Brooke—only for a jest.

HOST My hand, bully. Thou shalt have egress and
      regress—said I well?—and thy name shall be
210   Brooke. It is a merry knight. Will you go, myn-
      heers?

SHALLOW Have with you, mine Host.

PAGE I have heard the Frenchman hath good skill in
      his rapier.

215 SHALLOW Tut, sir, I could have told you more. In these
      times you stand on distance, your passes, stoc-
      cadoes, and I know not what. 'Tis the heart, Mas-
      ter Page; 'tis here, 'tis here. I have seen the time

189-90 **Good even and twenty** good evening twenty times over (there is an error
in time here, for it is morning.)   199-200 **contrary** different   205 **pottle** two-
quart tankard   206 **burnt** heated   210-11 **mynheers** gentlemen   216 **distance**
i.e., space between fencers   216 **passes** lunges   216-17 **stoccadoes** thrusts

with my long sword I would have made you four
tall fellows skip like rats.   220

HOST Here, boys, here, here! Shall we wag?

PAGE Have with you. I had rather hear them scold
than fight.   *Exeunt [Host, Shallow, and Page].*

FORD Though Page be a secure fool and stands so
firmly on his wife's frailty, yet I cannot put off my   225
opinion so easily. She was in his company at Page's
house, and what they made there, I know not. Well,
I will look further into't; and I have a disguise to
sound Falstaff. If I find her honest, I lose not my
labor. If she be otherwise, 'tis labor well bestowed.   230
                                                       [Exit.]

Scene II. *[Falstaff's room in the Garter Inn.]*

Enter Falstaff [and] Pistol.

FALSTAFF I will not lend thee a penny.

PISTOL Why, then the world's mine oyster.
Which I with sword will open.

FALSTAFF Not a penny. I have been content, sir, you
should lay my countenance to pawn. I have grated   5
upon my good friends for three reprieves for you
and your coach-fellow Nym; or else you had
looked through the grate, like a geminy of baboons. I am damned in hell for swearing to gentlemen my friends you were good soldiers and tall   10
fellows. And when Mistress Bridget lost the handle
of her fan, I took't upon mine honor thou hadst
it not.

221 **wag** go   II.ii.5 **countenance** reputation   5-6 **grated upon** pestered
8 **geminy** pair   11-12 **handle of her fan** (often made of gold or silver)
12 **took't** swore

PISTOL Didst not thou share? Hadst thou not fifteen
15 pence?

FALSTAFF Reason, you rogue, reason. Think'st thou I'll
endanger my soul gratis? At a word, hang no more
about me; I am no gibbet for you. Go! A short
knife and a throng! To your manor of Pickt-hatch,
20 go! You'll not bear a letter for me, you rogue? You
stand upon your honor! Why, thou unconfinable
baseness, it is as much as I can do to keep the terms
of my honor precise. I, I, I myself sometimes, leaving the fear of God on the left hand and hiding
25 mine honor in my necessity, am fain to shuffle, to
hedge, and to lurch; and yet you, rogue, will
ensconce your rags, your cat-a-mountain looks,
your red-lattice phrases, and your bold-beating
oaths, under the shelter of your honor! You will not
30 do it? You!

PISTOL I do relent. What would thou more of man?

[Enter] Robin.

ROBIN Sir, here's a woman would speak with you.

FALSTAFF Let her approach.

[Enter Mistress] Quickly.

QUICKLY Give your worship good morrow.

35 FALSTAFF Good morrow, good wife.

QUICKLY Not so, and't please your worship.

FALSTAFF Good maid then.

QUICKLY I'll be sworn, as my mother was the first hour
I was born.

40 FALSTAFF I do believe the swearer. What with me?

18-19 **short knife** (for cutting purses) 19 **throng** i.e., crowd of victims
19 **Pickt-hatch** (a notorious district of London) 25 **shuffle** act underhandedly
26 **hedge** cheat 26 **lurch** pilfer 27 **cat-a-mountain** wildcat 28 **red-lattice**
i.e., alehouse 28 **bold-beating** blustering

QUICKLY Shall I vouchsafe your worship a word or
two?

FALSTAFF Two thousand, fair woman, and I'll vouchsafe
thee the hearing.

QUICKLY There is one Mistress Ford—[*glancing at*   45
Pistol and Robin] sir, I pray, come a little nearer
this ways. I myself dwell with Master Doctor Caius.

FALSTAFF Well, on; Mistress Ford, you say—

QUICKLY Your worship says very true. I pray your
worship, come a little nearer this ways.   50

FALSTAFF I warrant thee, nobody hears. Mine own
people, mine own people.

QUICKLY Are they so? God bless them and make them
his servants!

FALSTAFF Well, Mistress Ford, what of her?   55

QUICKLY Why, sir, she's a good creature. Lord, Lord,
your worship's a wanton! Well, heaven forgive you,
and all of us, I pray—

FALSTAFF Mistress Ford—come, Mistress Ford.

QUICKLY Marry, this is the short and the long of it.   60
You have brought her into such a canaries as 'tis
wonderful. The best courtier of them all, when the
court lay at Windsor, could never have brought her
to such a canary. Yet there has been knights, and
lords, and gentlemen, with their coaches. I warrant   65
you, coach after coach, letter after letter, gift after
gift; smelling so sweetly—all musk—and so rushling, I warrant you, in silk and gold; and in such
alligant terms, and in such wine and sugar of the
best and the fairest that would have won any   70
woman's heart; and I warrant you, they could never

61 canaries i.e., quandaries (?) mentally intoxicated, as with canary wine (?)
67-68 rushling i.e., rustling   69 alligant elegant (?) eloquent (?)

get an eye-wink of her. I had myself twenty angels
given me this morning; but I defy all angels—in any
such sort, as they say—but in the way of honesty;
75 and I warrant you, they could never get her so much
as sip on a cup with the proudest of them all; and
yet there has been earls—nay, which is more, pensioners; but, I warrant you, all is one with her.

FALSTAFF But what says she to me? Be brief, my good
80 she-Mercury.

QUICKLY Marry, she hath received your letter; for the
which she thanks you a thousand times; and she
gives you to notify that her husband will be absence
from his house between ten and eleven.

85 FALSTAFF Ten and eleven.

QUICKLY Ay, forsooth; and then you may come and
see the Picture, she says, that you wot of. Master
Ford, her husband, will be from home. Alas, the
sweet woman leads an ill life with him; he's a very
90 jealousy man; she leads a very frampold life with
him, good heart.

FALSTAFF Ten and eleven.—Woman, commend me to
her; I will not fail her.

QUICKLY Why, you say well. But I have another mes-
95 senger to your worship. Mistress Page hath her
hearty commendations to you too; and let me tell
you in your ear, she's as fartuous a civil modest
wife, and one, I tell you, that will not miss you
morning nor evening prayer, as any is in Windsor,
100 whoe'er be the other. And she bade me tell your
worship that her husband is seldom from home, but
she hopes there will come a time. I never knew a
woman so dote upon a man. Surely I think you
have charms, la; yes, in truth.

77-78 **pensioners** members of the royal bodyguard   80 **she-Mercury** i.e.,
messenger   87 **wot** know   90 **frampold** disagreeable   97 **fartuous** i.e., virtuous

FALSTAFF Not I, I assure thee. Setting the attraction of   105
my good parts aside, I have no other charms.

QUICKLY Blessing on your heart for't!

FALSTAFF But, I pray thee, tell me this: has Ford's wife
and Page's wife acquainted each other how they
love me?   110

QUICKLY That were a jest indeed! They have not so
little grace, I hope; that were a trick indeed! But
Mistress Page would desire you to send her your
little page, of all loves; her husband had a marvelous infection to the little page; and truly, Master   115
Page is an honest man. Never a wife in Windsor
leads a better life than she does. Do what she will,
say what she will, take all, pay all, go to bed when
she list, rise when she list, all is as she will. And,
truly, she deserves it; for if there be a kind woman   120
in Windsor, she is one. You must send her your
page; no remedy.

FALSTAFF Why, I will.

QUICKLY Nay, but do so then; and look you, he may
come and go between you both; and in any case   125
have a nay-word, that you may know one another's
mind, and the boy never need to understand anything; for 'tis not good that children should know
any wickedness. Old folks, you know, have discretion, as they say, and know the world.   130

FALSTAFF Fare thee well, commend me to them both.
There's my purse; I am yet thy debtor.—Boy, go
along with this woman. [Exeunt Mistress Quickly
and Robin.] This news distracts me.

PISTOL [Aside] This punk is one of Cupid's carriers.   135
Clap on more sails; pursue; up with your fights;

---

106 **parts** talents   114 **of all loves** for love's sake   115 **infection** i.e., affection
119 **list** pleases   126 **nay-word** password   135 **punk** strumpet   135 **carriers**
messengers   136 **fights** (screens to conceal and protect crews in naval engagements)

Give fire! she is my prize, or ocean whelm them
all!   *[Exit.]*

FALSTAFF Sayest thou so, old Jack? Go thy ways; I'll
make more of thy old body than I have done. Will
140   they yet look after thee? Wilt thou, after the expense of so much money, be now a gainer? Good
body, I thank thee, Let them say 'tis grossly done;
so it be fairly done, no matter.

[Enter] Bardolph.

BARDOLPH Sir John, there's one Master Brooke below
145   would fain speak with you, and be acquainted with
you; and hath sent your worship a morning's
draught of sack.

FALSTAFF Brooke is his name?

BARDOLPH Ay, sir.

150   FALSTAFF Call him in. *[Exit Bardolph.]* Such Brookes
are welcome to me, that o'erflows such liquor. Aha!
Mistress Ford and Mistress Page, have I encompassed you? Go to; *via!*

[Enter Bardolph, with] Ford [disguised].

FORD Bless you, sir.

155   FALSTAFF And you, sir; would you speak with me?

FORD I make bold to press with so little preparation
upon you.

FALSTAFF You're welcome. What's your will?—Give us
leave, drawer.   *[Exit Bardolph.]*

160   FORD Sir, I am a gentleman that have spent much. My
name is Brooke.

FALSTAFF Good Master Brooke, I desire more acquaintance of you.

FORD Good Sir John, I sue for yours, not to charge

152-53 encompassed outwitted   153 via go on   164 charge cause expense to

you; for I must let you understand I think myself in   165
better plight for a lender than you are, the which
hath something embold'ned me to this unseasoned
intrusion; for they say if money go before, all ways
do lie open.

FALSTAFF Money is a good soldier, sir, and will on.   170

FORD Troth, and I have a bag of money here troubles
me. If you will help to bear it, Sir John, take all, or
half, for easing me of the carriage.

FALSTAFF Sir, I know not how I may deserve to be your
porter.   175

FORD I will tell you, sir, if you will give me the hearing.

FALSTAFF Speak, good Master Brooke. I shall be glad
to be your servant.

FORD Sir, I hear you are a scholar—I will be brief   180
with you—and you have been a man long known
to me, though I had never so good means as desire
to make myself acquainted with you. I shall discover a thing to you wherein I must very much lay
open mine own imperfection; but, good Sir John,   185
as you have one eye upon my follies, as you hear
them unfolded, turn another into the register of
your own, that I may pass with a reproof the easier,
sith you yourself know how easy it is to be such
an offender.   190

FALSTAFF Very well, sir. Proceed.

FORD There is a gentlewoman in this town, her husband's name is Ford.

FALSTAFF Well, sir.

FORD I have long loved her, and, I protest to you, be-   195
stowed much on her, followed her with a doting

---

167 unseasoned unseasonable   183-84 discover reveal   189 sith since

observance, engrossed opportunities to meet her,
fee'd every slight occasion that could but niggardly
give me sight of her, not only bought many presents
200 to give her but have given largely to many to know
what she would have given. Briefly, I have pursued
her as love hath pursued me, which hath been on
the wing of all occasions. But whatsoever I have
merited—either in my mind or in my means—
205 meed, I am sure, I have received none, unless experience be a jewel. That I have purchased at an
infinite rate, and that hath taught me to say this,
"Love like a shadow flies when substance Love
    pursues;
Pursuing that that flies, and flying what pursues."

210 FALSTAFF Have you received no promise of satisfaction
at her hands?

FORD Never.

FALSTAFF Have you importuned her to such a purpose?

FORD Never.

215 FALSTAFF Of what quality was your love then?

FORD Like a fair house built on another man's ground,
so that I have lost my edifice by mistaking the place
where I erected it.

FALSTAFF To what purpose have you unfolded this to
220 me?

FORD When I have told you that, I have told you all.
Some say that though she appear honest to me, yet
in other places she enlargeth her mirth so far that
there is shrewd construction made of her. Now,
225 Sir John, here is the heart of my purpose: you are
a gentleman of excellent breeding, admirable discourse, of great admittance, authentic in your

197 **engrossed opportunities** i.e., manufactured as many opportunities as
possible   198 **fee'd** employed   205 **meed** reward   223-24 **she enlargeth ...of
her** i.e., she is so free in her merriment that she has a bad reputation   227 **great
admittance** high social prestige   227 **authentic** duly qualified

place and person, generally allowed for your many
warlike, courtlike, and learned preparations.

FALSTAFF O sir!   230

FORD Believe it, for you know it. There is money.
Spend it, spend it; spend more; spend all I have.
Only give me so much of your time in exchange
of it as to lay an amiable siege to the honesty of
this Ford's wife. Use your art of wooing; win her   235
to consent to you. If any man may, you may as
soon as any.

FALSTAFF Would it apply well to the vehemency of your
affection that I should win what you would enjoy?
Methinks you prescribe to yourself very preposter-   240
ously.

FORD O, understand my drift. She dwells so securely
on the excellency of her honor that the folly of my
soul dares not present itself. She is too bright to be
looked against. Now, could I come to her with any   245
detection in my hand, my desires had instance and
argument to commend themselves. I could drive her
then from the ward of her purity, her reputation,
her marriage vow, and a thousand other her de-
fenses, which now are too too strongly embattled   250
against me. What say you to't, Sir John?

FALSTAFF Master Brooke, I will first make bold with
your money; next, give me your hand; and last, as
I am a gentleman, you shall, if you will, enjoy
Ford's wife.   255

FORD O good sir!

FALSTAFF I say you shall.

FORD Want no money, Sir John; you shall want none.

FALSTAFF Want no Mistress Ford, Master Brooke; you
shall want none. I shall be with her, I may tell you, 260
by her own appointment. Even as you came in to

228 **allowed** approved 229 **preparations** accomplishments 246 **instance**
evidence 248 **ward** defense

me, her assistant, or go-between, parted from me.
I say I shall be with her between ten and eleven,
for at that time the jealous rascally knave her hus-
265   band will be forth. Come you to me at night; you
shall know how I speed.

FORD   I am blest in your acquaintance. Do you know
Ford, sir?

FALSTAFF   Hang him, poor cuckoldly knave! I know him
270   not. Yet I wrong him to call him poor. They say
the jealous wittolly knave hath masses of money,
for the which his wife seems to me well-favored.
I will use her as the key of the cuckoldly rogue's
coffer, and there's my harvest-home.

275   FORD   I would you knew Ford, sir, that you might
avoid him if you saw him.

FALSTAFF   Hang him, mechanical salt-butter rogue! I
will stare him out of his wits. I will awe him with
my cudgel; it shall hang like a meteor o'er the
280   cuckold's horns. Master Brooke, thou shalt know
I will predominate over the peasant, and thou shalt
lie with his wife. Come to me soon at night. Ford's
a knave, and I will aggravate his style. Thou, Master Brooke, shalt know him for knave and cuckold.
285   Come to me soon at night.   [Exit.]

FORD   What a damned Epicurean rascal is this! My
heart is ready to crack with impatience. Who says
this is improvident jealousy? My wife hath sent to
him, the hour is fixed, the match is made. Would
290   any man have thought this? See the hell of having
a false woman! My bed shall be abused, my coffers
ransacked, my reputation gnawn at; and I shall not
only receive this villainous wrong, but stand under
the adoption of abominable terms, and by him

266 **speed** succeed   271 **wittolly** cuckoldly   272 **well-favored** (1) well chosen
(2) good-looking   274 **harvest-home** i.e., reaped profits   277 **mechanical** low,
vulgar   277 **salt-butter** (1) possible derogatory allusion to Ford as a merchant (2)
ill-smelling   283 **aggravate his style** i.e., add to his title   286 **Epicurean** i.e.,
sensual   293-94 **stand under the adoption of abominable terms** submit to
being called horrible names

that does me this wrong. Terms! Names! Amaimon   295
sounds well; Lucifer, well; Barbason, well; yet
they are devils' additions, the names of fiends. But
Cuckold! Wittol!—Cuckold! The devil himself
hath not such a name. Page is an ass, a secure ass.
He will trust his wife; he will not be jealous. I will   300
rather trust a Fleming with my butter, Parson Hugh
the Welshman with my cheese, an Irishman with
my aqua vitae bottle, or a thief to walk my am-
bling gelding, than my wife with herself. Then she
plots, then she ruminates, then she devises. And   305
what they think in their hearts they may effect:
they will break their hearts but they will effect.
God be praised for my jealousy. Eleven o'clock the
hour. I will prevent this, detect my wife, be revenged on Falstaff, and laugh at Page. I will about   310
it; better three hours too soon than a minute too
late. Fie, fie, fie! Cuckold! Cuckold! Cuckold! *Exit*.

Scene III. [*A field near Windsor.*]

Enter [Doctor] Caius [and] Rugby.

CAIUS Jack Rugby!

RUGBY Sir?

CAIUS Vat is de clock, Jack?

RUGBY 'Tis past the hour, sir, that Sir Hugh promised
to meet.   5

CAIUS By gar, he has save his soul dat he is no come.
He has pray his Pible vell dat he is no come. By
gar, Jack Rugby, he is dead already if he be come.

295-96 **Amaimon ... Lucifer ... Barbason** (names of devils)   297 **additions**
titles   298 **Wittol** contented cuckold   299 **secure** confident   303 **aqua vitae**
i.e., spirits (brandy, whiskey, etc.)

RUGBY He is wise, sir. He knew your worship would
10   kill him if he came.

CAIUS By gar, de herring is no dead so as I vill kill
    him. Take your rapier, Jack. I vill tell you how I
    vill kill him.

RUGBY Alas, sir, I cannot fence.

15 CAIUS Villany, take your rapier.

RUGBY Forbear; here's company.

    [*Enter*] *Page, Shallow, Slender,* [*and*] *Host.*

HOST Bless thee, bully doctor.

SHALLOW Save you, Master Doctor Caius.

PAGE Now, good Master Doctor.

20 SLENDER Give you good morrow, sir.

CAIUS Vat be all you, one, two, tree, four, come for?

HOST To see thee fight, to see thee foin, to see thee
    traverse; to see thee here, to see thee there; to
    see thee pass thy punto, thy stock, thy reverse, thy
25   distance, thy montant. Is he dead, my Ethiopian?
    Is he dead, my Francisco? Ha, bully? What says
    my Aesculapius? My Galen? My heart of elder?
    Ha, is he dead, bully stale? Is he dead?

CAIUS By gar, he is de coward Jack-priest of de vorld.
30   He is not show his face.

HOST Thou art a Castilian King-Urinal! Hector of
    Greece, my boy!

II.iii.22 **foin** thrust   23 **traverse** move back and forth   24-25 **pass thy punto
... thy montant** (in fencing: *punto*, strike a blow with the point of the sword;
stock thrust; *reverse* backhand stroke; *distance* keeping the proper space between
combatants; *montant* upward thrust)   25 **Ethiopian** i.e., dark-bearded or dark
complexioned person   26 **Francisco** i.e., Frenchman   27 **Aesculapius** god of
medicine   27 **Galen** Greek physician   27 **heart of elder** i.e., having a soft pith,
coward   28 **stale** (slang term for a physician, from diagnosing through urine
analysis)   31 **Castilian King-Urinal** i.e., King of doctors (derogatory allusion to
Philip II of Spain)   31-32 **Hector of Greece** i.e., brave warrior

CAIUS I pray you bear vitness dat me have stay six or seven, two, tree hours for him, and he is no come.

SHALLOW He is the wiser man, Master Doctor. He is a 35 curer of souls, and you a curer of bodies. If you should fight, you go against the hair of your professions. Is it not true, Master Page?

PAGE Master Shallow, you have yourself been a great fighter, though a man of peace. 40

SHALLOW Bodykins, Master Page, though I now be old and of the peace, if I see a sword out, my finger itches to make one. Though we are justices and doctors and churchmen, Master Page, we have some salt of our youth in us. We are the sons of 45 women, Master Page.

PAGE 'Tis true, Master Shallow.

SHALLOW It will be found so, Master Page. Master Doctor Caius, I am come to fetch you home. I am sworn of the peace. You have showed yourself a 50 wise physician, and Sir Hugh hath shown himself a wise and patient churchman. You must go with me, Master Doctor.

HOST Pardon, Guest-Justice.—A word, Monsieur Mock-water. 55

CAIUS Mock-vater? Vat is dat?

HOST Mock-water, in our English tongue, is valor, bully.

CAIUS By gar, den, I have as much mock-vater as de Englishman.—Scurvy jack-dog priest! By gar, me 60 vill cut his ears.

HOST He will clapperclaw thee tightly, bully.

CAIUS Clapper-de-claw? Vat is dat?

41 **Bodykins** God's little body (an oath) 43 **make one** join in 45 **salt** liveliness 55 **Mock-water** i.e., physician (precise meaning unclear; possible corruption of muck-water or make-water, with an allusion to urine analysis) 62 **clapperclaw** thrash

HOST That is, he will make thee amends.

65 CAIUS By gar, me do look he shall clapper-de-claw me; for, by gar, me vill have it.

HOST And I will provoke him to't, or let him wag.

CAIUS Me tank you for dat.

HOST And moreover, bully—But first, Master Guest, and Master Page, and eke Cavaliero Slender [*aside to them*] go you through the town to Frogmore.

PAGE Sir Hugh is there, is he?

HOST He is there. See what humor he is in. And I will bring the doctor about by the fields. Will it do well?

75 SHALLOW We will do it.

PAGE, SHALLOW, AND SLENDER Adieu, good Master Doctor. [*Exeunt Page, Shallow, and Slender.*]

CAIUS By gar, me vill kill de priest, for he speak for a jackanape to Anne Page.

80 HOST Let him die. Sheathe thy impatience; throw cold water on thy choler. Go about the fields with me through Frogmore. I will bring thee where Mistress Anne Page is, at a farmhouse a-feasting; and thou shalt woo her. Cried game; said I well?

85 CAIUS By gar, me dank you vor dat. By gar, I love you; and I shall procure-a you de good guest: de earl, de knight, de lords, de gentlemen, my patients.

HOST For the which I will be thy adversary toward Anne Page. Said I well?

90 CAIUS By gar, 'tis good; vell said.

HOST Let us wag then.

CAIUS Come at my heels, Jack Rugby. *Exeunt.*

71 **Frogmore** (village southeast of Windsor; Caius had been waiting on the north side of the town)   84 **Cried game** (a puzzling expression, possibly from Elizabethan sporting slang, conjecturally meaning the game is under way)

ACT III

Scene I. [*A field near Frogmore.*]

Enter Evans [and] Simple. [Evans is in doublet and hose and carries a sword. Simple carries Evans' gown and a book.]

EVANS I pray you now, good Master Slender's serv-ingman, and friend Simple by your name, which way have you looked for Master Caius, that calls himself Doctor of Physic?

SIMPLE Marry, sir, the pittie-ward, the park-ward, 5 every way; Old Windsor way, and every way but the town way.

EVANS I most fehemently desire you, you will also look that way.

SIMPLE I will, sir. [*Exit.*] 10

EVANS Pless my soul, how full of cholers I am, and trempling of mind. I shall be glad if he have de-ceived me.—How melancholies I am.—I will knog his urinals about his knave's costard when I have goot opportunities for the 'ork. Pless my soul! 15

III.i.5 the pittie-ward i.e., towards Windsor Little Park   5 the park-ward i.e., towards Windsor Great Park   6 Old Windsor a village south of Frogmore   11 cholers i.e., choler, anger   13-14 knog his urinals i.e., knot his testicles   14 costard i.e., head (literally, a type of large apple)

[*Sings.*] To shallow rivers, to whose falls
    Melodious birds sings madrigals;
    There will we make our peds of roses,
    And a thousand fragrant posies.
20   To shallow—

Mercy on me, I have a great dispositions to cry.

[*Sings.*] Melodious birds sing madrigals—
    When as I sat in Pabylon—
    And a thousand vagram posies.
25   To shallow, etc.

       [*Enter Simple.*]

SIMPLE Yonder he is coming, this way, Sir Hugh.

EVANS He's welcome.

[*Sings.*] To shallow rivers, to whose falls—

Heaven prosper the right! What weapons is he?

30 SIMPLE No weapons, sir. There comes my master, Master Shallow, and another gentleman, from Frogmore, over the stile, this way.

EVANS Pray you, give me my gown—or else keep it in your arms.   [*Takes the book and reads.*]

   [*Enter*] Page, Shallow, [*and*] Slender.

35 SHALLOW How now, Master Parson. Good morrow, good Sir Hugh. Keep a gamester from the dice, and a good student from his book, and it is wonderful.

SLENDER [*Aside*] Ah, sweet Anne Page!

PAGE Save you, good Sir Hugh.

40 EVANS Pless you from His mercy sake, all of you.

SHALLOW What, the sword and the word? Do you study them both, Master Parson?

16-19 **To shallow rivers ... fragrant posies** (garbled lines from Marlowe's "The Passionate Shepherd to his Love") 23 **When as I sat in Pabylon** (from Psalm 137) 24 **vagram** i.e., fragrant 41 **word** i.e., the Bible

PAGE And youthful still—in your doublet and hose this raw rheumatic day.

EVANS There is reasons and causes for it.   45

PAGE We are come to you to do a good office, Master Parson.

EVANS Fery well; what is it?

PAGE Yonder is a most reverend gentleman who, be-like having received wrong by some person, is at   50
most odds with his own gravity and patience that ever you saw.

SHALLOW I have lived fourscore years and upward; I never heard a man of his place, gravity, and learn-ing so wide of his own respect.   55

EVANS What is he?

PAGE I think you know him: Master Doctor Caius, the renowned French physician.

EVANS Got's will, and his passion of my heart! I had as lief you would tell me of a mess of porridge.   60

PAGE Why?

EVANS He has no more knowledge in Hibocrates and Galen—and he is a knave besides, a cowardly knave as you would desires to be acquainted withal.

PAGE I warrant you, he's the man should fight with   65
him.

SLENDER [*Aside*] O sweet Anne Page!

SHALLOW It appears so by his weapons.

[*Enter*] *Host, Caius,* [*and*] *Rugby*.

Keep them asunder; here comes Doctor Caius.

PAGE Nay, good Master Parson, keep in your weapon.   70

SHALLOW So do you, good Master Doctor.

55 **wide of his own respect** indifferent to his reputation   62 **Hibocrates** i.e., Hippocrates (fifth century B.C. Greek physician)

HOST Disarm them, and let them question. Let them keep their limbs whole and hack our English.

CAIUS I pray you let-a me speak a word with your ear.
75   Verefore vill you not meet-a me?

EVANS [*Aside to Caius*] Pray you, use your patience. [*Aloud*] In good time.

CAIUS By gar, you are de coward, de Jack dog, John ape.

80 EVANS [*Aside to Caius*] Pray you, let us not be laughing-stogs to other men's humors. I desire you in friendship, and I will one way or other make you amends. [*Aloud*] I will knog your urinals about your knave's cogscomb for missing your meetings
85   and appointments.

CAIUS *Diable!* Jack Rugby, mine Host de Jarteer, have I not stay for him to kill him? Have I not, at de place I did appoint?

EVANS As I am a Christians soul, now look you, this
90   is the place appointed. I'll be judgment by mine Host of the Garter.

HOST Peace, I say, Gallia and Gaul, French and Welsh, soul-curer and body-curer.

CAIUS Ay, dat is very good, excellent.

95 HOST Peace, I say. Hear mine Host of the Garter. Am I politic? Am I subtle? Am I a Machiavel? Shall I lose my doctor? No; he gives me the potions and the motions. Shall I lose my parson, my priest, my Sir Hugh? No; he gives me the proverbs and the
100   no-verbs. Give me thy hand, terrestrial; so. Give me thy hand, celestial; so. Boys of art, I have deceived you both; I have directed you to wrong

72 **question** i.e., dispute verbally   80–81 **laughing-stogs** i.e., laughing stocks
92 **Gallia and Gaul** Wales and France   96 a **Machiavel** i.e., an intriguer (from Niccolò Machiavelli, regarded by the Elizabethans as the archintriguer)
98 **motions** bowel movements   101 **art** learning

places. Your hearts are mighty, your skins are
whole, and let burnt sack be the issue. Come, lay
their swords to pawn. Follow me, lad of peace; fol-   105
low, follow, follow.

SHALLOW Trust me, a mad Host.—Follow, gentlemen,
follow.

SLENDER [*Aside*] O sweet Anne Page!
                    [*Exeunt Shallow, Slender, Page, and Host.*]

CAIUS Ha, do I perceive dat? Have you make-a de   110
sot of us, ha, ha?

EVANS This is well! He has made us his vlouting-
stog. I desire you that we may be friends, and let
us knog our prains together to be revenge on this
same scall, scurvy, cogging companion, the Host   115
of the Garter.

CAIUS By gar, with all my heart. He promise to bring
me where is Anne Page. By gar, he deceive me too.

EVANS Well, I will smite his noddles. Pray you follow.
                                                      [*Exeunt.*]

Scene II. [*Windsor. A street.*]

[*Enter*] *Mistress Page* [*and*] *Robin.*

MRS. PAGE Nay, keep your way, little gallant. You
were wont to be a follower, but now you are a
leader. Whether had you rather lead mine eyes,
or eye your master's heels?

---

104 **Issue** conclusion   111 **sot** fool   112-13 **vlouting-stog** i.e., flouting-stock,
laughing stock   115 **scall** i.e., scald, scurvy   115 **cogging companion** cheating
rascal   III.ii.3 **Whether** i.e., I wonder whether

5   ROBIN I had rather, forsooth, go before you like a
     man than follow him like a dwarf.

     MRS. PAGE O, you are a flattering boy. Now I see
     you'll be a courtier.

                    [Enter] Ford.

     FORD Well met, Mistress Page. Whither go you?

10   MRS. PAGE Truly, sir, to see your wife. Is she at home?

     FORD Ay, and as idle as she may hang together, for
     want of company. I think if your husbands were
     dead, you two would marry.

     MRS. PAGE Be sure of that—two other husbands.

15   FORD Where had you this pretty weathercock?

     MRS. PAGE I cannot tell what the dickens his name is
     my husband had him of. What do you call your
     knight's name, sirrah?

     ROBIN Sir John Falstaff.

20   FORD Sir John Falstaff!

     MRS. PAGE He, he; I can never hit on's name. There
     is such a league between my goodman and he. Is
     your wife at home indeed?

     FORD Indeed she is.

25   MRS. PAGE By your leave, sir. I am sick till I see her.
                    [Exeunt Mistress Page and Robin.]

     FORD Has Page any brains? Hath he any eyes? Hath
     he any thinking? Sure, they sleep; he hath no use
     of them. Why, this boy will carry a letter twenty
     mile as easy as a cannon will shoot pointblank
30   twelve score. He pieces out his wife's inclination;
     he gives her folly motion and advantage. And now

11 **as idle as she may hang together** i.e., as idle as she can be without going to
pieces 15 **weathercock** (an allusion to Robin's gaudy clothes) 22 **league** friendship 30 **twelve score** i.e., at twelve score paces 30 **pieces out** i.e., assists
31 **motion** prompting

she's going to my wife, and Falstaff's boy with her.
A man may hear this shower sing in the wind. And
Falstaff's boy with her.—Good plots! They are laid,
and our revolted wives share damnation together. 35
Well, I will take him, then torture my wife, pluck
the borrowed veil of modesty from the so-seeming
Mistress Page, divulge Page himself for a secure
and willful Actaeon; and to these violent proceedings all my neighbors shall cry aim. [*Clock strikes.*] 40
The clock gives me my cue, and my assurance bids
me search. There I shall find Falstaff. I shall be
rather praised for this than mocked, for it is as
positive as the earth is firm that Falstaff is there. I
will go. 45

[*Enter*] *Page, Shallow, Slender, Host, Evans,*
Caius, [*and Rugby*].

SHALLOW, PAGE, &c. Well met, Master Ford.

FORD Trust me, a good knot. I have good cheer at
home, and I pray you all go with me.

SHALLOW I must excuse myself, Master Ford.

SLENDER And so must I, sir. We have appointed to dine 50
with Mistress Anne, and I would not break with
her for more money than I'll speak of.

SHALLOW We have lingered about a match between
Anne Page and my cousin Slender, and this day
we shall have our answer. 55

SLENDER I hope I have your good will, father Page.

PAGE You have, Master Slender. I stand wholly for
you. But my wife, Master Doctor, is for you altogether.

CAIUS Ay, be-gar, and de maid is love-a me; my 60
nursh-a Quickly tell me so mush.

HOST What say you to young Master Fenton? He

39 **Actaeon** i.e., cuckold 40 **cry aim** i.e., applaud (from archery) 47 **knot**
company

capers, he dances, he has eyes of youth, he writes
verses, he speaks holiday, he smells April and
65   May. He will carry't, he will carry't; 'tis in his buttons; he will carry't.

PAGE Not by my consent, I promise you. The gentleman is of no having. He kept company with the
wild Prince and Poins; he is of too high a region;
70   he knows too much. No, he shall not knit a knot in
his fortunes with the finger of my substance. If he
take her, let him take her simply. The wealth I
have waits on my consent, and my consent goes
not that way.

75 FORD I beseech you heartily, some of you go home
with me to dinner. Besides your cheer, you shall
have sport. I will show you a monster. Master Doctor, you shall go. So shall you, Master Page, and
you, Sir Hugh.

80 SHALLOW Well, fare you well. We shall have the freer
wooing at Master Page's.

                  [Exeunt Shallow and Slender.]

CAIUS Go home, John Rugby. I come anon.

                          [Exit Rugby.]

HOST Farewell, my hearts. I will to my honest knight
Falstaff, and drink canary with him.   *[Exit.]*

85 FORD [*Aside*] I think I shall drink in pipe-wine first
with him; I'll make him dance.—Will you go,
gentles?

ALL Have with you to see this monster.   *Exeunt.*

---

64 **speaks holiday** uses choice language   65 **carry't** win   65-66 **'tis in his
buttons** i.e., he has it in him   68 **having** property   69 **wild Prince and Poins**
(Prince Hal and Poins, characters from *1 & 2 Henry IV*)   72 **simply** by herself
without any dowry   84 **canary** a sweet wine   85 **pipe-wine** wine from the cask;
involved punning on *pipe* (1) a cask (2) a musical instrument, and on *canary* (1) a
type of wine (2) a lively dance

Scene III. [*A room in Ford's house.*]

Enter Mistress Ford [*and*] *Mistress Page.*

MRS. FORD What, John! What, Robert!

MRS. PAGE Quickly, quickly. Is the buck basket—

MRS. FORD I warrant. What, Robert, I say!

[*Enter*] *Servants* [*with a basket*].

MRS. PAGE Come, come, come!

MRS. FORD Here, set it down.   5

MRS. PAGE Give your men the charge. We must be
brief.

MRS. FORD Marry, as I told you before, John and
Robert, be ready here hard by in the brewhouse;
and when I suddenly call you, come forth, and   10
without any pause or staggering, take this basket on
your shoulders. That done, trudge with it in all
haste, and carry it among the whitsters in Datchet
Mead, and there empty it in the muddy ditch close
by the Thames side.   15

MRS. PAGE You will do it?

MRS. FORD I ha' told them over and over; they lack
no direction. Begone, and come when you are
called.   [*Exeunt Servants.*]

[*Enter*] *Robin.*

MRS. PAGE Here comes little Robin.   20

III.iii.2 **buck basket** basket for soiled linen   13 **whitsters** bleachers of linen
13-14 **Datchet Mead** (meadow between Windsor Little Park and the Thames)

MRS. FORD How now, my eyas-musket. What news
with you?

ROBIN My master, Sir John, is come in at your back
door, Mistress Ford, and requests your company.

25   MRS. PAGE You little Jack-a-Lent, have you been
true to us?

ROBIN Ay, I'll be sworn. My master knows not of
your being here, and hath threat'ned to put me into
everlasting liberty if I tell you of it; for he swears
30   he'll turn me away.

MRS. PAGE Thou'rt a good boy. This secrecy of thine
shall be a tailor to thee and shall make thee a new
doublet and hose. I'll go hide me.

MRS. FORD Do so. [*To Robin*] Go tell thy master I
35   am alone. [*Exit Robin.*] Mistress Page, remember
you your cue.

MRS. PAGE I warrant thee; if I do not act it, hiss me.
[*Exit.*]

MRS. FORD Go to, then. We'll use this unwholesome
humidity, this gross wat'ry pumpion. We'll teach
40   him to know turtles from jays.

[*Enter*] *Falstaff.*

FALSTAFF "Have I caught thee, my heavenly jewel?"
Why, now let me die, for I have lived long enough.
This is the period of my ambition. O this blessed
hour!

45   MRS. FORD O sweet Sir John!

FALSTAFF Mistress Ford, I cannot cog, I cannot prate,
Mistress Ford. Now shall I sin in my wish: I would

---

21 **eyas-musket** young male sparrow hawk; i.e., a sprightly lad   25 **Jack-a-Lent**
(an allusion to Robin's gaudy clothes, from the decorated puppet used in Lenten
games)   39 **pumpion** pumpkin   40 **turtles from jays** i.e., faithful women from
unfaithful ones   41 **"Have I ... heavenly jewel?"** (from Sir Philip Sidney's
collection of sonnets, *Astrophel and Stella*)   43 **period** end   46 **cog** fawn

thy husband were dead. I'll speak it before the best
lord; I would make thee my lady.

MRS. FORD I your lady, Sir John? Alas, I should be a   50
pitiful lady.

FALSTAFF Let the court of France show me such
another. I see how thine eye would emulate the
diamond. Thou hast the right arched beauty of the
brow that becomes the ship-tire, the tire-valiant,   55
or any tire of Venetian admittance.

MRS. FORD A plain kerchief, Sir John. My brows become nothing else, nor that well neither.

FALSTAFF Thou art a tyrant to say so. Thou wouldst
make an absolute courtier, and the firm fixture of   60
thy foot would give an excellent motion to thy gait
in a semicircled farthingale. I see what thou wert
if Fortune, thy foe, were—not Nature—thy friend.
Come, thou canst not hide it.

MRS. FORD Believe me, there's no such thing in me.   65

FALSTAFF What made me love thee? Let that persuade
thee there's something extraordinary in thee. Come,
I cannot cog and say thou art this and that, like a
many of these lisping hawthorn buds that come
like women in men's apparel and smell like Buck-   70
lersbury in simple-time. I cannot. But I love
thee, none but thee; and thou deserv'st it.

MRS. FORD Do not betray me, sir. I fear you love
Mistress Page.

FALSTAFF Thou mightst as well say I love to walk by   75

---

55 **ship-tire** headdress shaped like a ship   55 **tire-valiant** fanciful headdress
56 **tire of Venetian admittance** i.e., Venetian-style headdress   60 **absolute**
perfect   62 **semicircled farthingale** half-hooped petticoat   62-63 **I see …
friend** i.e., since you are already naturally pretty, I can imagine what you would
look like dressed for the world of high society if Fortune had not made you a
member of the bourgeois class ("Fortune thy foe" is the title of an Elizabethan
popular ballad)   69 **hawthorn buds** i.e., dandies   70-71 **Bucklersbury** (a street
in London where herbs were sold)   71 **simple-time** herb-selling season

the Counter-gate, which is as hateful to me as the reek of a limekiln.

MRS. FORD Well, heaven knows how I love you, and you shall one day find it.

80 FALSTAFF Keep in that mind; I'll deserve it.

MRS. FORD Nay, I must tell you, so you do, or else I could not be in that mind.

[Enter Robin.]

ROBIN Mistress Ford, Mistress Ford! Here's Mistress Page at the door—sweating and blowing and look-
85 ing wildly, and would needs speak with you presently.

FALSTAFF She shall not see me; I will ensconce me be-hind the arras.

MRS. FORD Pray you, do so; she's a very tattling
90 woman. *[Falstaff hides.]*

[Enter Mistress Page.]

What's the matter? How now!

MRS. PAGE O Mistress Ford, what have you done? You're shamed, y'are overthrown, y'are undone for-ever!

95 MRS. FORD What's the matter, good Mistress Page?

MRS. PAGE O well-a-day, Mistress Ford! Having an honest man to your husband, to give him such cause of suspicion!

MRS. FORD What cause of suspicion?

100 MRS. PAGE What cause of suspicion! Out upon you; how am I mistook in you!

MRS. FORD Why, alas, what's the matter?

MRS. PAGE Your husband's coming hither, woman,

---

76 **Counter-gate** (gate of the debtor's prison, known as an area of foul odors)
86 **presently** immediately   88 **arras** hanging tapestry used for wall decoration

with all the officers in Windsor, to search for a
gentleman that he says is here now in the house— 105
by your consent—to take an ill advantage of his
absence. You are undone.

MRS. FORD 'Tis not so, I hope.

MRS. PAGE Pray heaven it be not so that you have
such a man here! But 'tis most certain your hus- 110
band's coming, with half Windsor at his heels, to
search for such a one. I come before to tell you.
If you know yourself clear, why, I am glad of it;
but if you have a friend here, convey, convey him
out. Be not amazed; call all your senses to you; 115
defend your reputation, or bid farewell to your
good life forever.

MRS. FORD What shall I do? There is a gentleman, my
dear friend; and I fear not mine own shame so
much as his peril. I had rather than a thousand 120
pound he were out of the house.

MRS. PAGE For shame! Never stand "you had rather"
and "you had rather." Your husband's here at
hand; bethink you of some conveyance. In the
house you cannot hide him.—O, how have you de- 125
ceived me!—Look, here is a basket. If he be of
any reasonable stature, he may creep in here; and
throw foul linen upon him, as if it were going to
bucking. Or—it is whiting time—send him by
your two men to Datchet Mead. 130

MRS. FORD He's too big to go in there. What shall I
do?

FALSTAFF [*Rushing forward*] Let me see't, let me see't.
O let me see't! I'll in, Follow your friend's
counsel. I'll in! 135

MRS. PAGE What, Sir John Falstaff! [*Aside to Falstaff*]
Are these your letters, knight?

113 **clear** innocent 114 **friend** paramour 122 **stand** lose time over
129 **bucking** washing 129 **whiting time** bleaching time

FALSTAFF [*Aside to Mistress Page*] I love thee. Help me away.—Let me creep in here. I'll never—
[*Climbs into the basket; they cover him with foul linen.*]

140 MRS. PAGE [*To Robin*] Help to cover your master, boy. Call your men, Mistress Ford.   [*Aside to Falstaff*] You dissembling knight!

MRS. FORD What, John! Robert! John!   [*Exit Robin.*]

[*Enter Servants.*]

Go, take up these clothes here quickly. Where's
145 the cowlstaff? Look how you drumble! Carry them to the laundress in Datchet Mead. Quickly, come!

[*Enter*] Ford, Page, Caius, [*and*] Evans.

FORD [*To his companions*] Pray you, come near. If I suspect without cause, why then make sport at me;
150 then let me be your jest; I deserve it. How now, who goes here? Whither bear you this?

SERVANTS To the laundress, forsooth.

MRS. FORD Why, what have you to do whither they bear it? You were best meddle with buck-washing!

155 FORD Buck? I would I could wash myself of the buck! Buck, buck, buck! Ay, buck; I warrant you, buck—and of the season too, it shall appear. [*Exeunt Servants with the basket.*] Gentlemen, I have dreamed tonight. I'll tell you my dream.
160 Here, here, here be my keys. Ascend my chambers; search, seek, find out. I'll warrant we'll unkennel the fox. Let me stop this way first. [*Locks the door.*] So, now uncope.

PAGE Good Master Ford, be contented. You wrong
165 yourself too much.

---

145 **cowlstaff** pole for carrying a basket between two persons   145 **drumble** dawdle   156 **buck** i.e., horned beast, cuckold   157 **of the season** in season   159 **tonight** last night   161 **unkennel** dislodge   163 **uncope** i.e., flush him out (hunting)

FORD True, Master Page. Up, gentlemen; you shall see sport anon. Follow me, gentlemen. [*Exit.*]

EVANS This is fery fantastical humors and jealousies.

CAIUS By gar, 'tis no de fashion of France; it is not jealous in France.   170

PAGE Nay, follow him, gentlemen. See the issue of his search.   [*Exeunt Page, Caius, and Evans.*]

MRS. PAGE Is there not a double excellency in this?

MRS. FORD I know not which pleases me better—that my husband is deceived, or Sir John.   175

MRS. PAGE What a taking was he in when your husband asked who was in the basket!

MRS. FORD I am half afraid he will have need of washing; so throwing him into the water will do him a benefit.   180

MRS. PAGE Hang him, dishonest rascal! I would all of the same strain were in the same distress.

MRS. FORD I think my husband hath some special suspicion of Falstaff's being here, for I never saw him so gross in his jealousy till now.   185

MRS. PAGE I will lay a plot to try that, and we will yet have more tricks with Falstaff. His dissolute disease will scarce obey this medicine.

MRS. FORD Shall we send that foolish carrion Mistress Quickly to him, and excuse his throwing into   190
the water, and give him another hope to betray him to another punishment?

MRS. PAGE We will do it. Let him be sent for tomorrow, eight o'clock, to have amends.

[*Enter Ford, Page, Caius, and Evans.*]

FORD I cannot find him. May be the knave bragged   195
of that he could not compass.

176 taking fright   189 carrion i.e., body of corrupting flesh

MRS. PAGE [*Aside to Mrs. Ford*] Heard you that?

MRS. FORD You use me well, Master Ford, do you?

FORD Ay. I do so.

200 MRS. FORD Heaven make you better than your thoughts!

FORD Amen.

MRS. PAGE You do yourself mighty wrong, Master Ford.

205 FORD Ay, ay, I must bear it.

EVANS If there be any pody in the house, and in the chambers, and in the coffers, and in the presses, heaven forgive my sins at the day of judgment!

CAIUS Be-gar, nor I too; dere is nobodies.

210 PAGE Fie, fie, Master Ford, are you not ashamed? What spirit, what devil suggests this imagination? I would not ha' your distemper in this kind for the wealth of Windsor Castle.

FORD 'Tis my fault, Master Page. I suffer for it.

215 EVANS You suffer for a pad conscience. Your wife is as honest a 'omans as I will desires among five thousand, and five hundred too.

CAIUS By gar, I see 'tis an honest woman.

FORD Well, I promised you a dinner. Come, come, 220 walk in the Park. I pray you pardon me. I will hereafter make known to you why I have done this— Come, wife; come, Mistress Page—I pray you pardon me. Pray heartily, pardon me.

PAGE Let's go in, gentlemen; but, trust me, we'll mock 225 him. I do invite you tomorrow morning to my house to breakfast. After, we'll a-birding together. I have a fine hawk for the bush. Shall it be so?

207 **presses** cupboards   214 **fault** i.e., weakness   226 **a-birding** hawking
227 **fine hawk for the bush** (a hawk especially trained to fly at small birds sheltered in bushes)

FORD Anything.

EVANS If there is one, I shall make two in the com-
pany.   230

CAIUS If dere be one, or two, I shall make-a de turd.

FORD Pray you, go, Master Page.

EVANS [*Aside to Caius*] I pray you now, remembrance
tomorrow on the lousy knave, mine Host.

CAIUS [*Aside to Evans*] Dat is good, by gar; with all   235
my heart.

EVANS [*Aside to Caius*] A lousy knave, to have his
gibes and his mockeries!   *Exeunt.*

Scene IV. [*Before Page's house.*]

Enter Fenton [and] Anne Page.

FENTON I see I cannot get thy father's love;
Therefore no more turn me to him, sweet Nan.

ANNE Alas, how then?

FENTON   Why, thou must be thyself.
He doth object I am too great of birth,
And that my state being galled with my expense,   5
I seek to heal it only by his wealth.
Besides these, other bars he lays before me:
My riots past, my wild societies;
And tells me 'tis a thing impossible
I should love thee but as a property.   10

ANNE May be he tells you true.

FENTON No, heaven so speed me in my time to come!

III.iv.5 **state** estate   5 **galled with my expense** i.e., squandered away
12 **speed** prosper

167

Albeit I will confess thy father's wealth
Was the first motive that I wooed thee, Anne,
15 Yet, wooing thee, I found thee of more value
Than stamps in gold or sums in sealèd bags;
And 'tis the very riches of thyself
That now I aim at.

ANNE   Gentle Master Fenton,
Yet seek my father's love; still seek it, sir.
20 If opportunity and humblest suit
Cannot attain it, why, then—

[*Enter*] *Shallow, Slender,* [*and Mistress*] *Quickly.*

Hark you hither.
[*Takes Fenton aside.*]

SHALLOW Break their talk, Mistress Quickly. My kinsman shall speak for himself.

SLENDER I'll make a shaft or a bolt on't. 'Slid, 'tis
25 but venturing.

SHALLOW Be not dismayed.

SLENDER No, she shall not dismay me. I care not for
that, but that I am afeard.

QUICKLY [*To Anne*] Hark ye, Master Slender would
30 speak a word with you.

ANNE I come to him. [*Aside*] This is my father's
choice.
O, what a world of vile ill-favored faults
Looks handsome in three hundred pounds a year.

QUICKLY And how does good Master Fenton? Pray
35 you, a word with you.   [*They converse together.*]

SHALLOW She's coming; to her, coz. O boy, thou hadst
a father!

SLENDER I had a father, Mistress Anne; my uncle can
tell you good jests of him. Pray you, uncle, tell Mis-

16 **stamps** coins   24 **make a shaft or a bolt on't** i.e., do it one way or another
(literally, use a slender arrow or a thick one)   24 **'Slid** God's eyelid (mild oath)

tress Anne the jest how my father stole two geese 40
out of a pen, good uncle.

SHALLOW Mistress Anne, my cousin loves you.

SLENDER Ay, that I do, as well as I love any woman in
Gloucestershire.

SHALLOW He will maintain you like a gentlewoman. 45

SLENDER Ay, that I will, come cut and long-tail, under
the degree of a squire.

SHALLOW He will make you a hundred and fifty pounds
jointure.

ANNE Good Master Shallow, let him woo for himself. 50

SHALLOW Marry, I thank you for it; I thank you for
that good comfort. She calls you, coz. I'll leave you.

ANNE Now, Master Slender—

SLENDER Now, good Mistress Anne—

ANNE What is your will? 55

SLENDER My will? 'Od's heartlings, that's a pretty jest
indeed! I ne'er made my will yet, I thank God. I am
not such a sickly creature, I give heaven praise.

ANNE I mean, Master Slender, what would you with
me? 60

SLENDER Truly, for mine own part, I would little or
nothing with you. Your father and my uncle have
made motions. If it be my luck, so; if not, happy
man be his dole. They can tell you how things go
better than I can. You may ask your father; here 65
he comes.

---

42 **cousin** kinsman   46-47 **cut ... a squire** i.e., all kinds so long as they are not
too high-ranking   56 **'Od's heartlings** God's little heart (an oath)   63 **motions**
suggestions   63-64 **happy man be his dole** happiness be his portion

[Enter] Page [and] Mistress Page.

PAGE Now, Master Slender. Love him, daughter
    Anne.—
  Why, how now! What does Master Fenton here?
  You wrong me, sir, thus still to haunt my house.
70 I told you, sir, my daughter is disposed of.

FENTON Nay, Master Page, be not impatient.

MRS. PAGE Good Master Fenton, come not to my
    child.

PAGE She is no match for you.

FENTON Sir, will you hear me?

PAGE   No, good Master Fenton.
75 Come, Master Shallow; come, son Slender, in.
  Knowing my mind, you wrong me, Master Fenton.
    [Page, Shallow, and Slender enter the house.]

QUICKLY Speak to Mistress Page.

FENTON Good Mistress Page, for that I love your
    daughter
  In such a righteous fashion as I do,
80 Perforce, against all checks, rebukes, and manners,
  I must advance the colors of my love
  And not retire. Let me have your good will.

ANNE Good mother, do not marry me to yond fool.

MRS. PAGE I mean it not. I seek you a better husband.

85 QUICKLY *[To Anne]* That's my master, Master Doctor.

ANNE Alas, I had rather be set quick i' th' earth,
  And bowled to death with turnips.

MRS. PAGE Come, trouble not yourself. Good Master
    Fenton,
  I will not be your friend, nor enemy.
90 My daughter will I question how she loves you,
  And as I find her, so am I affected.

80 **checks** reproofs   81 **colors** banners   86 **quick** living

Till then, farewell, sir. She must needs go in.
Her father will be angry.
                    [*Mistress Page and Anne enter the house.*]

FENTON Farewell, gentle mistress. Farewell, Nan.

QUICKLY This is my doing now. "Nay," said I, "will   95
you cast away your child on a fool, and a physician?
Look on Master Fenton." This is my doing.

FENTON I thank thee, and I pray thee, once tonight
Give my sweet Nan this ring. There's for thy pains.
                    [*Gives the ring and some money to Quickly*
                    and then departs.]

QUICKLY Now heaven send thee good fortune! A kind   100
heart he hath. A woman would run through fire
and water for such a kind heart. But yet, I would
my master had Mistress Anne; or I would Master
Slender had her; or, in sooth, I would Master Fenton had her. I will do what I can for them all three,   105
for so I have promised, and I'll be as good as my
word—but speciously for Master Fenton. Well, I
must of another errand to Sir John Falstaff from
my two mistresses. What a beast am I to slack it!
                                    Exit.

98 once sometime 107 speciously i.e., especially 109 slack it be remiss
about it

Scene V. [*Falstaff's room in the Garter Inn.*]

Enter Falstaff.

FALSTAFF Bardolph, I say!

[*Enter*] *Bardolph.*

BARDOLPH Here, sir.

FALSTAFF Go fetch me a quart of sack—put a toast
in't. [*Exit Bardolph.*] Have I lived to be carried in
5   a basket like a barrow of butcher's offal, and to be
thrown in the Thames? Well, if I be served such
another trick, I'll have my brains ta'en out and
buttered and give them to a dog for a New-Year's
gift. The rogues slighted me into the river with as
10   little remorse as they would have drowned a blind
bitch's puppies, fifteen i' th' litter. And you may
know by my size that I have a kind of alacrity in
sinking; if the bottom were as deep as hell, I should
down. I had been drowned but that the shore was
15   shelvy and shallow—a death that I abhor, for the
water swells a man; and what a thing should I have
been when I had been swelled. I should have been
a mountain of mummy.

[*Enter Bardolph with two cups of wine.*]

BARDOLPH Here's Mistress Quickly, sir, to speak with
20   you.

FALSTAFF Come, let me pour in some sack to the
Thames water, for my belly's as cold as if I had
swallowed snowballs for pills to cool the reins. Call
her in.

III.v.3 **a toast** a piece of toast   9 **slighted** tossed contemptuously   18 **mummy**
dead flesh   23 **reins** kidneys

BARDOLPH Come in, woman.   25

[Enter Mistress] Quickly.

QUICKLY By your leave; I cry you mercy. Give your
worship good morrow.

FALSTAFF Take away these chalices. Go brew me a
pottle of sack finely.

BARDOLPH With eggs, sir?   30

FALSTAFF Simple of itself; I'll no pullet-sperm in my
brewage. *[Exit Bardolph.]* How now.

QUICKLY Marry, sir, I come to your worship from
Mistress Ford.

FALSTAFF Mistress Ford? I have had ford enough; I   35
was thrown into the ford; I have my belly full of
ford.

QUICKLY Alas the day, good heart, that was not her
fault. She does so take on with her men; they mis-
took their erection.   40

FALSTAFF So did I mine, to build upon a foolish
woman's promise.

QUICKLY Well, she laments, sir, for it that it would
yearn your heart to see it. Her husband goes this
morning a-birding. She desires you once more to   45
come to her between eight and nine. I must carry
her word quickly. She'll make you amends, I warrant you.

FALSTAFF Well, I will visit her. Tell her so, and bid
her think what a man is. Let her consider his frailty,   50
and then judge of my merit.

QUICKLY I will tell her.

FALSTAFF Do so.—Between nine and ten, sayest thou?

QUICKLY Eight and nine, sir.

26 **cry you mercy** beg your pardon   28 **chalices** drinking cups   40 **erection**
i.e., direction   44 **yearn** grieve

55 FALSTAFF Well, begone, I will not miss her.

QUICKLY Peace be with you, sir.

[Exit, leaving the door open.]

FALSTAFF I marvel I hear not of Master Brooke. He sent me word to stay within. I like his money well. —O, here he comes.

[Enter] Ford.

60 FORD Bless you, sir.

FALSTAFF Now, Master Brooke, you come to know what hath passed between me and Ford's wife?

FORD That, indeed, Sir John, is my business.

FALSTAFF Master Brooke, I will not lie to you. I was at
65 her house the hour she appointed me.

FORD And sped you, sir?

FALSTAFF Very ill-favoredly, Master Brooke.

FORD How so, sir? Did she change her determination?

FALSTAFF No, Master Brooke, but the peaking cornuto
70 her husband, Master Brooke, dwelling in a continual 'larum of jealousy, comes me in the instant
of our encounter, after we had embraced, kissed,
protested, and, as it were, spoke the prologue of
our comedy: and at his heels a rabble of his com-
75 panions, thither provoked and instigated by his distemper, and, forsooth, to search his house for his
wife's love.

FORD What, while you were there?

FALSTAFF While I was there.

80 FORD And did he search for you, and could not find you?

---

66 **sped you** did you succeed   69 **peaking cornuto** prying cuckold (with a pun on "peak" as the tip of the horn)   74 **rabble** pack   75-76 **distemper** ill temper

FALSTAFF You shall hear. As good luck would have it, comes in one Mistress Page, gives intelligence of Ford's approach; and in her invention and Ford's wife's distraction, they conveyed me into a buck 85 basket.

FORD A buck basket?

FALSTAFF By the Lord, a buck basket! Rammed me in with foul shirts and smocks, socks, foul stockings, greasy napkins, that, Master Brooke, there was 90 the rankest compound of villainous smell that ever offended nostril.

FORD And how long lay you there?

FALSTAFF Nay, you shall hear, Master Brooke, what I have suffered to bring this woman to evil for your 95 good. Being thus crammed in the basket, a couple of Ford's knaves, his hinds, were called forth by their mistress to carry me in the name of foul clothes to Datchet Lane. They took me on their shoulders; met the jealous knave their master in 100 the door, who asked them once or twice what they had in their basket. I quaked for fear lest the lunatic knave would have searched it; but Fate, ordaining he should be a cuckold, held his hand. Well, on went he for a search, and away went I for foul 105 clothes. But mark the sequel, Master Brooke. I suffered the pangs of three several deaths: first, an intolerable fright to be detected with a jealous rotten bellwether; next, to be compassed like a good bilbo in the circumference of a peck, hilt to 110 point, heel to head; and then, to be stopped in, like a strong distillation, with stinking clothes that fretted in their own grease. Think of that, a man of my kidney—think of that—that am as subject

90 that so that   97 hinds servants   108 with by   109 bellwether ram with a bell around his neck who led the flock (with an implied reference to a horned beast or cuckold)   109-10 compassed like a good bilbo bent around like a well-tempered sword blade (a test for ascertaining the quality of a good blade)   113 fretted decayed   114 kidney temperament

115 to heat as butter; a man of continual dissolution
and thaw. It was a miracle to 'scape suffocation.
And in the height of this bath, when I was more
than half stewed in grease, like a Dutch dish, to be
thrown into the Thames, and cooled, glowing hot,
120 in that surge, like a horseshoe. Think of that—hissing hot—think of that, Master Brooke!

FORD In good sadness, sir, I am sorry that for my
sake you have suffered all this. My suit then is desperate. You'll undertake her no more?

125 FALSTAFF Master Brooke, I will be thrown into Etna, as
I have been into Thames, ere I will leave her thus.
Her husband is this morning gone a-birding. I have
received from her another embassy of meeting.
'Twixt eight and nine is the hour, Master Brooke.

130 FORD 'Tis past eight already, sir.

FALSTAFF Is it? I will then address me to my appointment. Come to me at your convenient leisure, and
you shall know how I speed; and the conclusion
shall be crowned with your enjoying her. Adieu.
135 You shall have her, Master Brooke; Master Brooke,
you shall cuckold Ford.   [Exit.]

FORD Hum! Ha! Is this a vision? Is this a dream? Do
I sleep? Master Ford, awake; awake, Master Ford!
There's a hole made in your best coat, Master
140 Ford. This 'tis to be married; this 'tis to have linen
and buck baskets! Well, I will proclaim myself
what I am. I will now take the lecher; he is at my
house; he cannot 'scape me; 'tis impossible he
should. He cannot creep into a halfpenny purse,
145 nor into a pepperbox. But, lest the devil that guides
him should aid him, I will search impossible places.
Though what I am I cannot avoid, yet to be what
I would not shall not make me tame. If I have
horns to make one mad, let the proverb go with
150 me—I'll be horn-mad.   Exit.

115 dissolution liquefaction   122 sadness seriousness   128 embassy message
131 address me i.e., go

ACT IV

Scene I. [*A street.*]

Enter Mistress Page, [Mistress] Quickly,
[and] William.

MRS. PAGE Is he at Master Ford's already, think'st
thou?

QUICKLY Sure he is by this, or will be presently. But,
truly, he is very courageous mad about his throwing into the water. Mistress Ford desires you to   5
come suddenly.

MRS. PAGE I'll be with her by and by. I'll but bring
my young man here to school. Look where his master comes; 'tis a playing-day, I see.

[Enter] Evans.

How now, Sir Hugh! No school today?   10

EVANS No. Master Slender is let the boys leave to play.

QUICKLY Blessing of his heart.

MRS. PAGE Sir Hugh, my husband says my son profits
nothing in the world at his book. I pray you, ask
him some questions in his accidence.   15

EVANS Come hither, William. Hold up your head;
come.

IV.i.4 **courageous** i.e., outrageous   6 **suddenly** immediately   7 **by and by**
quickly   15 **accidence** i.e., knowledge of grammatical inflections

MRS. PAGE Come on, sirrah; hold up your head; answer your master; be not afraid.

20 EVANS William, how many numbers is in nouns?

WILLIAM Two.

QUICKLY Truly, I thought there had been one number more, because they say, "Od's nouns."

EVANS Peace your tattlings. What is "fair," William?

25 WILLIAM "*Pulcher*."

QUICKLY Polecats! There are fairer things than polecats, sure.

EVANS You are a very simplicity 'oman. I pray you peace. What is "*lapis*," William?

30 WILLIAM A stone.

EVANS And what is "a stone," William?

WILLIAM A pebble.

EVANS No, it is "*lapis*." I pray you remember in your prain.

35 WILLIAM "*Lapis*."

EVANS That is a good William. What is he, William, that does lend articles?

WILLIAM Articles are borrowed of the pronoun, and be thus declined: *Singulariter, nominativo, hic, haec,*
40 *hoc.*

EVANS *Nominativo, hig, hag, hog,* Pray you, mark: *genitivo, hujus.* Well, what is your accusative case?

WILLIAM *Accusativo, hinc.*

EVANS I pray you, have your remembrance, child:
45 *accusativo, hung, hang, hog.*

---

23 **Od's nouns** i.e., God's wounds (an oath) 26 **Polecats** (1) wildcats (2) prostitutes

QUICKLY "Hang-hog" is Latin for bacon, I warrant you.

EVANS Leave your prabbles, 'oman. What is the focative case, William?

WILLIAM O—*vocativo*, O.   50

EVANS Remember, William; focative is *caret*.

QUICKLY And that's a good root.

EVANS 'Oman, forbear.

MRS. PAGE Peace.

EVANS What is your genitive case plural, William?   55

WILLIAM Genitive case?

EVANS Ay.

WILLIAM Genitive—*horum, harum, horum*.

QUICKLY Vengeance of Jenny's case! Fie on her! Never name her, child, if she be a whore.   60

EVANS For shame, 'oman.

QUICKLY You do ill to teach the child such words. He teaches him to hick and to hack, which they'll do fast enough of themselves, and to call "horum." Fie upon you!   65

EVANS 'Oman, art thou lunatics? Hast thou no understandings for thy cases and the numbers of the genders? Thou art as foolish Christian creatures as I would desires.

MRS. PAGE Prithee, hold thy peace.   70

EVANS Show me now, William, some declensions of your pronouns.

46 **Hang-hog** (an allusion to a famous story of the jurist Sir Nicholas Bacon who told a prisoner named Hog who tried to have his death sentence commuted on grounds of kindred that "you and I cannot be of kindred unless you are hanged; for Hog is not Bacon till it be well hanged") 51 **caret** is lacking (Latin) 59 **case** pudendum (Mistress Quickly associates Latin *horum* with whore, and *harum* with hare, a slang term for a prostitute) 63 **to hick and to hack** hiccup (?) and go wenching (?; precise meaning unknown, but dissoluteness is implied)

WILLIAM Forsooth, I have forgot.

EVANS It is *qui*, *quae*, *quod*. If you forget your *qui's*,
75   your   *quae's*, and your *quod's*, you must be
preeches. Go your ways and play; go.

MRS. PAGE He is a better scholar than I thought he
was.

EVANS He is a good sprag memory. Farewell, Mis-
80   tress Page.

MRS. PAGE Adieu, good Sir Hugh. [*Exit Evans.*] Get
you home, boy. Come, we stay too long.   *Exeunt.*

Scene II. [*A room in Ford's house.*]

Enter Falstaff [*and*] *Mistress Ford.*

FALSTAFF Mistress Ford, your sorrow hath eaten up my
sufferance. I see you are obsequious in your love,
and I profess requital to a hair's breadth, not only,
Mistress Ford, in the simple office of love, but in
5   all the accoutrement, complement, and ceremony
of it. But are you sure of your husband now?

MRS. FORD He's a-birding, sweet Sir John.

MRS. PAGE [*Within*] What ho, gossip Ford. What ho!

MRS. FORD Step into th' chamber, Sir John.
                                    [*Exit Falstaff.*]

                    [*Enter*] *Mistress Page.*
10   MRS. PAGE How now, sweetheart! Who's at home besides yourself?

74-75 **qui's, quae's, quod's** (Latin *qu* was pronounced k, giving rise to bawdy
puns on *keys* = penises, *case* = pudendum, *cods* = testicles) 76 **preeches** i.e.,
breeched, flogged   79 **sprag** sprack, alert   IV.ii.2 **sufferance** suffering   2 **obsequious** devoted   8 **gossip** friend

MRS. FORD Why, none but mine own people.

MRS. PAGE Indeed?

MRS. FORD No, certainly. [*Aside to her*] Speak louder.

MRS. PAGE Truly, I am so glad you have nobody here. 15

MRS. FORD Why?

MRS. PAGE Why, woman, your husband is in his old
lunes again. He so takes on yonder with my husband, so rails against all married mankind, so curses
all Eve's daughters—of what complexion soever, 20
and so buffets himself on the forehead, crying,
"Peer out, peer out!" that any madness I ever yet
beheld seemed but tameness, civility, and patience
to this his distemper he is in now. I am glad the
fat knight is not here. 25

MRS. FORD Why, does he talk of him?

MRS. PAGE Of none but him; and swears he was carried out, the last time he searched for him, in a
basket; protests to my husband he is now here, and
hath drawn him and the rest of their company from 30
their sport to make another experiment of his suspicion. But I am glad the knight is not here. Now
he shall see his own foolery.

MRS. FORD How near is he, Mistress Page?

MRS. PAGE Hard by, at street end; he will be here 35
anon.

MRS. FORD I am undone! The knight is here.

MRS. PAGE Why then you are utterly shamed, and
he's but a dead man. What a woman are you! Away
with him, away with him. Better shame than 40
murder.

MRS. FORD Which way should he go? How should I
bestow him? Shall I put him into the basket again?

18 **lunes** lunacies   22 **Peer out** (alluding to the cuckold's horns)

[Enter Falstaff.]

FALSTAFF No, I'll come no more i' th' basket. May I
45   not go out ere he come?

MRS. PAGE Alas, three of Master Ford's brothers
watch the door with pistols that none shall issue
out; otherwise you might slip away ere he came.
But what make you here?

50   FALSTAFF What shall I do? I'll creep up into the chimney.

MRS. FORD There they always use to discharge their
birding pieces.

MRS. PAGE Creep into the kilnhole.

55   FALSTAFF Where is it?

MRS. FORD He will seek there, on my word. Neither
press, coffer, chest, trunk, well, vault, but he hath
an abstract for the remembrance of such places,
and goes to them by his note. There is no hiding
60   you in the house.

FALSTAFF I'll go out then.

MRS. PAGE If you go out in your own semblance, you
die, Sir John. Unless you go out disguised—

MRS. FORD How might we disguise him?

65   MRS. PAGE Alas the day, I know not. There is no
woman's gown big enough for him; otherwise, he
might put on a hat, a muffler, and a kerchief, and
so escape.

FALSTAFF Good hearts, devise something. Any extrem-
70   ity rather than a mischief.

MRS FORD My maid's aunt, the fat woman of Brainford, has a gown above.

54 **kilnhole** oven   58 **abstract** list   71-72 **fat woman of Brainford** (an actual
personage who kept a tavern in Brentford, a town on the Thames twelve miles east
of Windsor)

MRS. PAGE On my word, it will serve him; she's as big
as he is. And there's her thrummed hat and her
muffler too. Run up, Sir John.   75

MRS. FORD Go, go, sweet Sir John. Mistress Page and
I will look some linen for your head.

MRS. PAGE Quick, quick! We'll come dress you
straight; put on the gown the while.   [*Exit Falstaff.*]

MRS. FORD I would my husband would meet him in   80
this shape. He cannot abide the old woman of
Brainford; he swears she's a witch, forbade her my
house, and hath threat'ned to beat her.

MRS. PAGE Heaven guide him to thy husband's cudgel,
and the devil guide his cudgel afterwards!   85

MRS. FORD But is my husband coming?

MRS. PAGE Ay, in good sadness, is he; and talks of
the basket too, howsoever he hath had intelligence.

MRS. FORD We'll try that; for I'll appoint my men to
carry the basket again, to meet him at the door with   90
it, as they did last time.

MRS. PAGE Nay, but he'll be here presently. Let's go
dress him like the witch of Brainford.

MRS. FORD I'll fast direct my men what they shall do
with the basket. Go up; I'll bring linen for him   95
straight.   [*Exit.*]

MRS. PAGE Hang him, dishonest varlet, we cannot
misuse him enough.
We'll leave a proof by that which we will do,
Wives may be merry, and yet honest too.   100
We do not act that often jest and laugh;
'Tis old but true, "Still swine eats all the draff."
                                             [*Exit.*]

[*Enter Mistress Ford with two*] *Servants.*

MRS. FORD Go, sirs, take the basket again on your

74 thrummed fringed   97 dishonest unchaste   102 draff swill

shoulders. Your master is hard at door; if he bid
105   you set it down, obey him. Quickly, dispatch. [*Exit.*]

FIRST SERVANT Come, come, take it up.

SECOND SERVANT Pray heaven, it be not full of knight
again.

FIRST SERVANT I hope not; I had lief as bear so much
110   lead.   [*They lift the basket.*]

[*Enter*] *Ford, Page, Caius, Evans,* [*and*] *Shallow.*

FORD Ay, but if it prove true, Master Page, have you
any way then to unfool me again? Set down the
basket, villain. Somebody call my wife. Youth in
a basket! O you panderly rascals! There's a knot,
115   a ging, a pack, a conspiracy against me. Now shall
the devil be shamed. What, wife, I say! Come,
come forth! Behold what honest clothes you send
forth to bleaching!

PAGE Why, this passes, Master Ford! You are not
120   to go loose any longer; you must be pinioned.

EVANS Why, this is lunatics, this is mad as a mad
dog.

SHALLOW Indeed, Master Ford, this is not well, indeed.

125 FORD So say I too, sir.

[*Enter Mistress Ford.*]

Come hither, Mistress Ford; Mistress Ford, the honest woman, the modest wife, the virtuous creature
that hath the jealous fool to her husband! I suspect
without cause, mistress, do I?

130 MRS. FORD Heaven be my witness you do, if you suspect me in any dishonesty.

113-14 **Youth in a basket** (a contemporary phrase apparently connoting a
"fortunate lover") 114 **knot** band 115 **ging** gang 115-16 **Now shall the
devil be shamed** ("Speak the truth and shame the devil"—proverbial)
119 **passes** exceeds everything

FORD Well said, brazen-face; hold it out.—Come
forth, sirrah! *[Pulling clothes out of the basket.]*

PAGE This passes!

MRS. FORD Are you not ashamed? Let the clothes   135
alone.

FORD I shall find you anon.

EVANS 'Tis unreasonable. Will you take up your wife's
clothes? Come away.

FORD Empty the basket, I say!   140

MRS. FORD Why, man, why?

FORD Master Page, as I am a man, there was one
conveyed out of my house yesterday in this basket.
Why may not he be there again? In my house I
am sure he is. My intelligence is true; my jealousy   145
is reasonable. Pluck me out all the linen.
[Ford and Page pull out more clothes.]

MRS. FORD If you find a man there, he shall die a
flea's death.

PAGE Here's no man.

SHALLOW By my fidelity, this is not well, Master Ford;   150
this wrongs you.

EVANS Master Ford, you must pray, and not follow
the imaginations of your own heart. This is jealousies.

FORD Well, he's not here I seek for.   155

PAGE No, nor nowhere else but in your brain.

FORD Help to search my house this one time. If I find
not what I seek, show no color for my extremity.
Let me forever be your table-sport. Let them say
of me, "As jealous as Ford that searched a hollow   160

145 **intelligence** information   158 **show no color for my extremity** suggest no
excuse for my extravagance   159 **table-sport** i.e., laughingstock

walnut for his wife's leman." Satisfy me once
more; once more search with me.

MRS. FORD What ho, Mistress Page, come you and
the old woman down. My husband will come into
165 the chamber.

FORD Old woman? What old woman's that?

MRS. FORD Why, it is my maid's aunt of Brainford.

FORD A witch, a quean, an old cozening quean!
Have I not forbid her my house? She comes of er-
170 rands, does she? We are simple men; we do not
know what's brought to pass under the profession
of fortune-telling. She works by charms, by spells,
by th' figure, and such daubery as this is, beyond
our element; we know nothing. Come down, you
175 witch, you hag, you; come down, I say!

MRS. FORD Nay, good, sweet husband! Good gentlemen, let him not strike the old woman.

[*Enter Falstaff in woman's clothes, and Mistress Page.*]

MRS. PAGE Come, Mother Prat, come, give me your
hand.

180 FORD I'll "prat" her. [*Beats him.*] Out of my door,
you witch, you rag, you baggage, you polecat, you
runnion! Out, out! I'll conjure you, I'll fortune-
tell you! [*Exit Falstaff, running.*]

MRS. PAGE Are you not ashamed? I think you have
185 killed the poor woman.

MRS. FORD Nay, he will do it. 'Tis a goodly credit for
you.

FORD Hang her, witch!

EVANS By Jeshu, I think the 'oman is a witch indeed.

161 **leman** lover 168 **quean** hussy 168 **cozening** cheating, deceiving 173 **by
th' figure** by making wax effigies for enchantments 173 **daubery** false show
180 **prat** beat on the buttocks 182 **runnion** (abusive term for a woman)

I like not when a 'oman has a great peard; I spy   190
a great peard under his muffler.

FORD Will you follow, gentlemen? I beseech you, follow. See but the issue of my jealousy. If I cry out
thus upon no trail, never trust me when I open
again.   195

PAGE Let's obey his humor a little further. Come,
gentlemen.
[*Exeunt Ford, Page, Shallow, Caius, and Evans.*]

MRS. PAGE Trust me, he beat him most pitifully.

MRS. FORD Nay, by th' mass, that he did not; he beat
him most unpitifully, methought.   200

MRS. PAGE I'll have the cudgel hallowed and hung o'er
the altar; it hath done meritorious service.

MRS. FORD What think you? May we, with the warrant of womanhood and the witness of a good conscience, pursue him with any further revenge?   205

MRS. PAGE The spirit of wantonness is, sure, scared
out of him. If the devil have him not in fee-simple,
with fine and recovery, he will never, I think, in
the way of waste, attempt us again.

MRS. FORD Shall we tell our husbands how we have   210
served him?

MRS. PAGE Yes, by all means, if it be but to scrape
the figures out of your husband's brains. If they
can find in their hearts the poor unvirtuous fat
knight shall be any further afflicted, we two will   215
still be the ministers.

MRS. FORD I'll warrant they'll have him publicly
shamed, and methinks there would be no period to
the jest, should he not be publicly shamed.

194 **upon no trail** i.e., where there is no scent   194 **open** cry out from picking
up a scent (used of hounds)   207 **fee-simple** absolute possession   208 **fine and
recovery** (legal procedure for transferring an entailed estate into a fee-simple)
209 **waste** spoliation   213 **figures** phantasms   216 **ministers** agents

220 MRS. PAGE Come, to the forge with it; then shape it.
     I would not have things cool.   *Exeunt.*

Scene III. [*A room in the Garter Inn.*]

Enter Host and Bardolph.

BARDOLPH Sir, the Germans desire to have three of
your horses. The Duke himself will be tomorrow
at court, and they are going to meet him.

HOST What duke should that be comes so secretly?
5   I hear not of him in the court. Let me speak with
the gentlemen. They speak English?

BARDOLPH Ay, sir; I'll call them to you.

HOST They shall have my horses, but I'll make them
pay; I'll sauce them. They have had my house a
10 week at command. I have turned away my other
guests. They must come off. I'll sauce them. Come.
                                             Exeunt.

Scene IV. [*A room in Ford's house.*]

*Enter Page, Ford, Mistress Page, Mistress Ford,
and Evans.*

EVANS 'Tis one of the best discretions of a 'oman as
ever I did look upon.

IV.iii.9 **sauce them** make them pay dearly 10 **at command** reserved
11 **come off** pay IV.iv.1 **best discretions of a 'oman** most discreet woman

PAGE And did he send you both these letters at an instant?

MRS. PAGE Within a quarter of an hour.   5

FORD Pardon me, wife. Henceforth do what thou wilt.
   I rather will suspect the sun with cold
   Than thee with wantonness. Now doth thy honor
      stand,
   In him that was of late an heretic,
   As firm as faith.

PAGE   'Tis well, 'tis well; no more.   10
   Be not as extreme in submission as in offense.
   But let our plot go forward. Let our wives
   Yet once again, to make us public sport,
   Appoint a meeting with this old fat fellow,
   Where we may take him and disgrace him for it.   15

FORD There is no better way than that they spoke of.

PAGE How? To send him word they'll meet him in the
   Park at midnight? Fie, fie, he'll never come.

EVANS You say he has been thrown in the rivers, and
   has been grievously peaten as an old 'oman. Me-   20
   thinks there should be terrors in him that he should
   not come. Methinks his flesh is punished; he shall
   have no desires.

PAGE So think I too.

MRS. FORD Devise but how you'll use him when he
      comes,   25
   And let us two devise to bring him thither.

MRS. PAGE There is an old tale goes that Herne the
      Hunter,
   Sometime a keeper here in Windsor Forest,
   Doth all the wintertime, at still midnight,
   Walk round about an oak, with great ragg'd horns;   30
   And there he blasts the tree, and takes the cattle,

28 Sometime formerly   31 blasts blights   31 takes bewitches

And makes milch-kine yield blood, and shakes a
    chain
In a most hideous and dreadful manner.
You have heard of such a spirit, and well you know
35   The superstitious idle-headed eld
Received, and did deliver to our age,
This tale of Herne the Hunter for a truth.

PAGE Why, yet there want not many that do fear
In deep of night to walk by this Herne's Oak.
But what of this?

40 MRS. FORD   Marry, this is our device:
That Falstaff at that oak shall meet with us,
Disguised like Herne, with huge horns on his head.

PAGE Well, let it not be doubted but he'll come,
And in this shape. When you have brought him
    thither,
45 What shall be done with him? What is your plot?

MRS. PAGE That likewise have we thought upon, and
    thus:
Nan Page my daughter, and my little son,
And three or four more of their growth, we'll dress
Like urchins, ouphs, and fairies, green and white,
50 With rounds of waxen tapers on their heads,
And rattles in their hands. Upon a sudden,
As Falstaff, she, and I are newly met,
Let them from forth a sawpit rush at once
With some diffusèd song. Upon their sight,
55 We two in great amazedness will fly.
Then let them all encircle him about,
And, fairy-like, to pinch the unclean knight,
And ask him why, that hour of fairy revel,
In their so sacred paths he dares to tread
In shape profane.

60 MRS. FORD   And till he tell the truth,

---

35 **eld** elders 40 **device** plan 49 **urchins** goblins 49 **ouphs** elves
54 **diffusèd** i.e., cacophonous

Let the supposèd fairies pinch him sound
And burn him with their tapers.

MRS. PAGE   The truth being known,
We'll all present ourselves, dis-horn the spirit,
And mock him home to Windsor.

FORD   The children must
Be practiced well to this, or they'll ne'er do't.   65

EVANS I will teach the children their behaviors; and I
will be like a jackanapes also, to burn the knight
with my taber.

FORD That will be excellent. I'll go buy them vizards.

MRS. PAGE My Nan shall be the Queen of all the
Fairies,   70
Finely attirèd in a robe of white.

PAGE That silk will I go buy. [*Aside*] And in that tire
Shall Master Slender steal my Nan away,
And marry her at Eton. —Go, send to Falstaff
straight.

FORD Nay, I'll to him again in name of Brooke.   75
He'll tell me all his purpose. Sure, he'll come.

MRS. PAGE Fear not you that. Go, get us properties
And tricking for our fairies.

EVANS Let us about it. It is admirable pleasures and
fery honest knaveries.   80
                              [*Exeunt Page, Ford, and Evans.*]

MRS. PAGE Go, Mistress Ford,
Send Quickly to Sir John, to know his mind.
                              [*Exit Mistress Ford.*]
I'll to the Doctor. He hath my good will,
And none but he, to marry with Nan Page.
That Slender, though well landed, is an idiot;   85
And he my husband best of all affects.

61 **sound** soundly   67 **jackanapes** monkey   69 **vizards** masks   72 **tire** attire
74 **Eton** (across the river from Windsor)   77 **properties** stage properties
78 **tricking** adornment, costumes

The Doctor is well moneyed, and his friends
Potent at court. He, none but he, shall have her,
Though twenty thousand worthier come to crave
    her.
                                        [*Exit.*]

Scene V. [*The room in the Garter Inn.*]

Enter Host [*and*] *Simple.*

HOST What wouldst thou have, boor? What, thick-
skin? Speak, breathe, discuss; brief, short, quick,
snap.

SIMPLE Marry, sir, I come to speak with Sir John Fal-
5   staff from Master Slender.

HOST There's his chamber, his house, his castle, his
standing-bed and truckle bed. 'Tis painted about
with the story of the Prodigal, fresh and new. Go,
knock and call. He'll speak like an Anthropophagi-
10   nian unto thee. Knock, I say.

SIMPLE There's an old woman, a fat woman, gone up
into his chamber. I'll be so bold as stay, sir, till
she come down. I come to speak with her, indeed.

HOST Ha, a fat woman? The knight may be robbed.
15   I'll call. Bully knight, bully Sir John! Speak from
thy lungs military. Art thou there? It is thine Host,
thine Ephesian, calls.

FALSTAFF [*Above*] How now, mine Host?

HOST Here's a Bohemian-Tartar tarries the coming
20   down of thy fat woman. Let her descend, bully, let

IV.v.7 **truckle bed** trundle bed 8 **Prodigal** i.e., the Prodigal Son 9-10 **Anthro-
pophaginian** cannibal 17 **Ephesian** boon companion 19 **Bohemian-Tartar**
i.e., wild man

her descend. My chambers are honorable. Fie, privacy, fie!

[Enter] Falstaff.

FALSTAFF There was, mine Host, an old fat woman even now with me, but she's gone.

SIMPLE Pray you, sir, was't not the wise woman of Brainford? 25

FALSTAFF Ay, marry, was it, mussel-shell. What would you with her?

SIMPLE My master, sir, my Master Slender, sent to her, seeing her go thorough the streets, to know, sir, whether one Nym, sir, that beguiled him of a chain, had the chain or no. 30

FALSTAFF I spake with the old woman about it.

SIMPLE And what says she, I pray, sir?

FALSTAFF Marry, she says that the very same man that beguiled Master Slender of his chain cozened him of it. 35

SIMPLE I would I could have spoken with the woman herself. I had other things to have spoken with her too from him. 40

FALSTAFF What are they? Let us know.

HOST Ay, come; quick!

SIMPLE I may not conceal them, sir.

HOST Conceal them, or thou diest.

SIMPLE Why, sir, they were nothing but about Mistress Anne Page; to know if it were my master's fortune to have her, or no. 45

FALSTAFF 'Tis, 'tis his fortune.

SIMPLE What sir?

27 **mussel-shell** i.e., one who gapes   43 **conceal** i.e., reveal

50 FALSTAFF To have her, or no. Go; say the woman told me so.

SIMPLE May I be bold to say so, sir?

FALSTAFF Ay, Sir Tyke; who more bold?

SIMPLE I thank your worship: I shall make my master
55   glad with these tidings.   [*Exit.*]

HOST Thou art clerkly, thou art clerkly, Sir John.
Was there a wise woman with thee?

FALSTAFF Ay, that there was, mine Host; one that hath
taught me more wit than ever I learned before in
60   my life; and I paid nothing for it neither, but was
paid for my learning.

[Enter] Bardolph.

BARDOLPH Out, alas, sir, cozenage, mere cozenage!

HOST Where be my horses? Speak well them, varletto.

65 BARDOLPH Run away with the cozeners; for so soon
as I came beyond Eton, they threw me off from
behind one of them, in a slough of mire; and set
spurs and away, like three German devils, three
Doctor Faustuses.

70 HOST They are gone but to meet the Duke, villain.
Do not say they be fled: Germans are honest men.

[Enter] Evans.

EVANS Where is mine Host?

HOST What is the matter, sir?

---

53 **Sir Tyke** i.e., Master Cur   56 **clerkly** scholarly   62 **mere** pure   63-64 **varletto**
rascal   69 **Doctor Faustuses** (Faustus was a German scholar who allegedly
obtained magical powers by making a compact with Lucifer; known to the
Elizabethans primarily through Marlowe's play)   70 **villain** base fellow

EVANS Have a care of your entertainments. There is
a friend of mine come to town tells me there is three   75
cozen-germans that has cozened all the hosts of
Readins, of Maidenhead, of Colebrook, of horses
and money. I tell you for good will, look you. You
are wise and full of gibes and vlouting-stogs, and
'tis not convenient you should be cozened. Fare   80
you well.   [Exit.]

[Enter] Caius.

CAIUS Vere is mine Host de Jarteer?

HOST Here, Master Doctor, in perplexity and doubtful dilemma.

CAIUS I cannot tell vat is dat; but it is tell-a me dat   85
you make grand preparation for a Duke de Jamany.
By my trot, dere is no duke dat de court is know
to come. I tell you for good vill. Adieu.   [Exit.]

HOST Hue and cry, villain, go! [To Falstaff] Assist me,
knight. I am undone. [To Bardolph] Fly, run, hue   90
and cry, villain! I am undone!
                                    [Exeunt Host and Bardolph.]

FALSTAFF I would all the world might be cozened, for
I have been cozened and beaten too. If it should
come to the ear of the court how I have been transformed, and how my transformation hath been   95
washed and cudgeled, they would melt me out of
my fat drop by drop, and liquor fishermen's boots
with me. I warrant they would whip me with their
fine wits till I were as crestfall'n as a dried pear.
I never prospered since I forswore myself at pri-   100
mero. Well, if my wind were but long enough to
say my prayers, I would repent.

---

74 entertainments i.e., total supplies for running an inn   76 cozen-germans
(1) cousin-germans, relatives (2) cheating Germans   77 Readins Reading
83-84 doubtful fearful   97 liquor grease   99 crestfall'n i.e., undistinguished
100-1 primero (a card game)

[Enter Mistress] Quickly.

Now, whence come you?

QUICKLY From the two parties, forsooth.

105 FALSTAFF The devil take one party and his dam the other! And so they shall be both bestowed. I have suffered more for their sakes, more than the villainous inconstancy of man's disposition is able to bear.

QUICKLY And have not they suffered? Yes, I warrant
110 —speciously one of them. Mistress Ford, good heart, is beaten black and blue that you cannot see a white spot about her.

FALSTAFF What tell'st thou me of black and blue? I was beaten myself into all the colors of the rainbow;
115 and I was like to be apprehended for the Witch of Brainford. But that my admirable dexterity of wit, my counterfeiting the action of an old woman, delivered me, the knave constable had set me i' th' stocks, i' th' common stocks, for a witch.

120 QUICKLY Sir, let me speak with you in your chamber. You shall hear how things go, and, I warrant, to your content. Here is a letter will say somewhat. Good hearts, what ado here is to bring you together. Sure, one of you does not serve heaven well
125 that you are so crossed.

FALSTAFF Come up into my chamber.   *Exeunt.*

---

110 **speciously** i.e., especially   125 **crossed** thwarted

Scene VI. [*The Garter Inn.*]

Enter Fenton [and] Host.

HOST Master Fenton, talk not to me. My mind is
heavy; I will give over all.

FENTON Yet hear me speak. Assist me in my purpose,
And, as I am a gentleman, I'll give thee
A hundred pound in gold more than your loss.   5

HOST I will hear you, Master Fenton, and I will, at
the least, keep your counsel.

FENTON From time to time I have acquainted you
With the dear love I bear to fair Anne Page,
Who mutually hath answered my affection,   10
(So far forth as herself might be her chooser)
Even to my wish. I have a letter from her
Of such contents as you will wonder at,
The mirth whereof so larded with my matter
That neither singly can be manifested   15
Without the show of both. Fat Falstaff
Hath a great scene. The image of the jest
I'll show you here at large.   [*Takes out a letter.*]
                        Hark, good mine Host:
Tonight at Herne's Oak, just 'twixt twelve and one,
Must my sweet Nan present the Fairy Queen—   20
The purpose why, is here—in which disguise,
While other jests are something rank on foot,
Her father hath commanded her to slip
Away with Slender, and with him at Eton
Immediately to marry. She hath consented.   25
Now, sir,

IV.vi.14 **larded** intermixed   14 **matter** i.e., courtship problems   17 **image** form
20 **present** represent   22 **something rank** rather abundantly

Her mother (ever strong against that match
And firm for Doctor Caius) hath appointed
That he shall likewise shuffle her away,
30   While other sports are tasking of their minds,
And at the dean'ry, where a priest attends,
Straight marry her. To this her mother's plot
She, seemingly obedient, likewise hath
Made promise to the Doctor. Now, thus it rests:
35   Her father means she shall be all in white,
And in that habit, when Slender sees his time
To take her by the hand and bid her go,
She shall go with him. Her mother hath intended—
The better to denote her to the Doctor,
40   For they must all be masked and vizarded—
That quaint in green she shall be loose enrobed,
With ribands pendent, flaring 'bout her head;
And when the Doctor spies his vantage ripe,
To pinch her by the hand, and on that token
45   The maid hath given consent to go with him.

HOST Which means she to deceive, father or mother?

FENTON Both, my good Host, to go along with me.
And here it rests, that you'll procure the Vicar
To stay for me at church 'twixt twelve and one,
50   And, in the lawful name of marrying,
To give our hearts united ceremony.

HOST Well, husband your device; I'll to the Vicar.
Bring you the maid, you shall not lack a priest.

FENTON So shall I evermore be bound to thee;
55   Besides, I'll make a present recompense.   *Exeunt*

---

29 **shuffle** spirit   41 **quaint** elegantly   44 **token** signal   51 **united ceremon**
union through the marriage rite   52 **husband your device** i.e., manage your pla
prudently

ACT V

Scene I. [*The Garter Inn*.]

Enter Falstaff [*and Mistress*] *Quickly*.

FALSTAFF Prithee, no more prattling. Go. I'll hold. This is the third time; I hope good luck lies in odd numbers. Away; go. They say there is divinity in odd numbers, either in nativity, chance, or death. Away! 5

QUICKLY I'll provide you a chain, and I'll do what I can to get you a pair of horns.

FALSTAFF Away, I say; time wears. Hold up your head, and mince. [*Exit Mistress Quickly*.]

[*Enter*] *Ford*.

How now, Master Brooke. Master Brooke, the mat- 10 ter will be known tonight or never. Be you in the Park about midnight, at Herne's Oak and you shall see wonders.

FORD Went you not to her yesterday, sir, as you told me you had appointed? 15

FALSTAFF I went to her, Master Brooke, as you see, like

V.i.1 **hold** keep the engagement 3 **divinity** divination 9 **mince** trip off 14 **yesterday** (a slip; should be "this morning")

199

a poor old man; but I came from her, Master
Brooke, like a poor old woman. The same knave
Ford, her husband, hath the finest mad devil of
20   jealousy in him, Master Brooke, that ever governed
frenzy. I will tell you: he beat me grievously, in
the shape of a woman; for in the shape of man,
Master Brooke, I fear not Goliath with a weaver's
beam, because I know also life is a shuttle. I am
25   in haste. Go along with me; I'll tell you all, Master
Brooke. Since I plucked geese, played truant, and
whipped top, I knew not what 'twas to be beaten
till lately. Follow me. I'll tell you strange things of
this knave Ford, on whom tonight I will be re-
30   venged, and I will deliver his wife into your hand.
Follow. Strange things in hand, Master Brooke!
Follow.   *Exeunt.*

Scene II. [*Windsor Little Park.*]

Enter Page, Shallow, [and] Slender.

PAGE Come, come; we'll couch i' th' Castle ditch
till we see the light of our fairies. Remember, son
Slender, my daughter.

SLENDER Ay, forsooth; I have spoke with her and we
5   have a nay-word how to know one another. I come
to her in white, and cry, "mum"; she cries,
"budget"; and by that we know one another.

23-24 **Goliath with a weaver's beam** (an allusion to Goliath's staff from 1
Samuel 17:7 and 2 Samuel 21:19)   24 **life is a shuttle** (paraphrased from Job 7:6
"My days are swifter than a weaver's shuttle")   V.ii.1 **couch** hide   1 **Castle
ditch** (a ditch running along the east side of Windsor Castle)   5 **nay-word**
password   6-7 **mum ... budget** (mum ... budget, a game in which the player
pretended to be tongue-tied)

SHALLOW That's good too. But what needs either your "mum," or her "budget"? The white will decipher her well enough.—It hath struck ten o'clock.   10

PAGE The night is dark; light and spirits will become it well. Heaven prosper our sport. No man means evil but the devil, and we shall know him by his horns. Let's away; follow me.   *Exeunt*.

Scene III. [*Outside the Park*.]

Enter Mistress Page, Mistress Ford,
[and Doctor] Caius.

MRS. PAGE Master Doctor, my daughter is in green. When you see your time, take her by the hand, away with her to the deanery, and dispatch it quickly. Go before into the Park. We two must go together.   5

CAIUS I know vat I have to do. Adieu.

MRS. PAGE Fare you well, sir [*Exit Caius*.] My husband will not rejoice so much at the abuse of Falstaff as he will chafe at the Doctor's marrying my daughter. But 'tis no matter; better a little chiding   10 than a great deal of heartbreak.

MRS. FORD Where is Nan now and her troop of fairies, and the Welsh devil, Hugh?

MRS. PAGE They are all couched in a pit hard by Herne's Oak, with obscured lights which at the   15 very instant of Falstaff's and our meeting they will at once display to the night.

MRS. FORD That cannot choose but amaze him.

V.iii.18 **amaze** frighten

MRS. PAGE If he be not amazed, he will be mocked;
20 if he be amazed, he will every way be mocked.

MRS. FORD We'll betray him finely.

MRS. PAGE Against such lewdsters and their lechery,
Those that betray them do no treachery.

MRS. FORD The hour draws on. To the Oak, to the
25 Oak!   *Exeunt.*

Scene IV. [*Outside the Park.*]

Enter Evans [disguised as a Satyr] and [others as]
Fairies.

EVANS Trib, trib, fairies. Come, and remember your
parts. Be pold, I pray you. Follow me into the pit,
and when I give the watch-'ords, do as I pid you.
Come, come; trib, trib.   *Exeunt.*

Scene V. [*Herne's Oak in Windsor Little Park.*]

Enter Falstaff [disguised as Herne,] with a buck's head
upon him.

FALSTAFF The Windsor bell hath struck twelve; the
minute draws on. Now, the hot-blooded gods assist
me! Remember, Jove, thou wast a bull for thy
Europa; love set on thy horns. O powerful love,
5 that in some respects makes a beast a man; in some

22 **lewdsters** lechers V.iv.1 **Trib** i.e., trip V.v.3-4 **bull for thy Europa**
(disguise adopted by Jove for his abduction of Europa)

other, a man a beast. You were also, Jupiter, a
swan for the love of Leda. O omnipotent love, how
near the god drew to the complexion of a goose!
A fault done first in the form of a beast. O Jove, a
beastly fault! And then another fault in the sem-   10
blance of a fowl; think on't, Jove; a foul fault!
When gods have hot backs, what shall poor men
do? For me, I am here a Windsor stag; and the fattest, I think, i' th' forest. Send me a cool rut-time,
Jove, or who can blame me to piss my tallow?   15
Who comes here? My doe?

[*Enter*] *Mistress Page* [*and*] *Mistress Ford.*

MRS. FORD Sir John? Art thou there, my deer, my
male deer?

FALSTAFF My doe with the black scut! Let the sky rain
potatoes; let it thunder to the tune of "Green-   20
sleeves," hail kissing-comfits, and snow eringoes.
Let there come a tempest of provocation, I will
shelter me here.   [*Hugs her.*]

MRS. FORD Mistress Page is come with me, sweetheart.   25

FALSTAFF Divide me like a bribed buck, each a
haunch. I will keep my sides to myself, my shoulders for the fellow of this walk, and my horns I
bequeath your husbands. Am I a woodman, ha?
Speak I like Herne the Hunter? Why, now is Cupid   30
a child of conscience; he makes restitution. As I
am a true spirit, welcome!   [*Noise within.*]

6-7 **a swan for the love of Leda** (another animal disguise adopted by Jove in an
amorous adventure)   8 **complexion** temperament   14 **rut-time** (annual period
of sexual excitement for the male deer)   15 **piss my tallow** (during rut-time the
main food for the hart was the red mushroom which supposedly brought on
urination)   19 **scut** (1) tail (2) pudendum   20 **potatoes** i.e., sweet potatoes,
formerly considered aphrodisiacs   21 **kissing-comfits** perfumed sweetmeats
21 **eringoes** candied seaholly (considered an aphrodisiac)   22 **provocation**
lustful stimulation   26 **bribed** stolen   28 **fellow of this walk** forester on this
beat   29 **woodman** hunter (here, of women)   31 **of conscience** conscientious

MRS. PAGE Alas, what noise?

MRS. FORD Heaven forgive our sins!

35 FALSTAFF What should this be?

MRS. FORD } Away, away!   [*They run off.*]
MRS. PAGE

FALSTAFF I think the devil will not have me damned,
    lest the oil that's in me should set hell on fire. He
    would never else cross me thus.

*Enter Sir Hugh [Evans] like a satyr, [Anne Page] and boys
dressed like fairies, Mistress Quickly like the Queen of Fairies,
    [Pistol as Hobgoblin. They carry tapers.]*

40 QUICKLY Fairies, black, gray, green, and white,
    You moonshine revelers, and shades of night,
    You orphan heirs of fixèd destiny,
    Attend your office and your quality.
    Crier Hobgoblin, make the fairy oyes.

45 PISTOL Elves, list your names; silence, you airy toys!
    Cricket, to Windsor chimneys shalt thou leap.
    Where fires thou find'st unraked and hearths
        unswept;
    There pinch the maids as blue as bilberry.
    Our radiant Queen hates sluts and sluttery.

    FALSTAFF They are fairies; he that speaks to them shall
50   die.
    I'll wink and couch; no man their works must eye.
                                    [*Lies down upon his face.*]

---

42 orphan (possible allusion to the folklore belief that fairies were born spontan-
eously and thus had no parents)   43 office duty   43 quality profession
44 oyes hear ye (public crier's call)   47 unraked not properly covered with
coals   48 bilberry blueberry   49 sluts untidy kitchen-maids   51 wink close my
eyes

EVANS   Where's Bead? Go you, and where you find a
    maid
    That ere she sleep has thrice her prayers said,
    Raise up the organs of her fantasy,
    Sleep she as sound as careless infancy.   55
    But those as sleep and think not on their sins,
    Pinch them, arms, legs, backs, shoulders, sides, and
    shins.

QUICKLY   About, about.
    Search Windsor Castle, elves, within and out.
    Strew good luck, ouphs, on every sacred room,   60
    That it may stand till the perpetual doom,
    In state as wholesome as in state 'tis fit,
    Worthy the owner, and the owner it.
    The several chairs of Order look you scour
    With juice of balm and every precious flow'r.   65
    Each fair instalment, coat, and several crest,
    With loyal blazon, evermore be blest.
    And nightly, meadow-fairies, look you sing,
    Like to the Garter's compass, in a ring.
    Th' expressure that it bears, green let it be,   70
    More fertile-fresh than all the field to see;
    And *Honi soit qui mal y pense* write
    In emerald tufts, flow'rs purple, blue, and white—
    Like sapphire, pearl, and rich embroidery,
    Buckled below fair knighthood's bending knee—   75
    Fairies use flow'rs for their charactery.
    Away, disperse! But till 'tis one o'clock,
    Our dance of custom round about the Oak
    Of Herne the Hunter, let us not forget.

EVANS   Pray you, lock hand in hand; yourselves in
    order set;   80

---

54 **Raise up the organs of her fantasy** i.e., cause her to have pleasant
dreams   60 **ouphs** elves   61 **perpetual doom** Day of Judgment   64 **chairs of
Order** stalls of the knights of the Order of the Garter in St George's Chapel
66 **instalment** stall   66 **coat** coat of arms   66 **crest** helmet (affixed above the
stall)   67 **blazon** armorial bearings   69 **compass** circle   70 **expressure** image,
picture   72 **Honi soit qui mal y pense** Ill be to him who evil thinks (motto of
the Order of the Garter)   76 **charactery** writing (accent on second syllable)

And twenty glowworms shall our lanterns be,
To guide our measure round about the tree.
But, stay—I smell a man of middle earth.

FALSTAFF Heavens defend me from that Welsh fairy,
85   lest he transform me to a piece of cheese!

PISTOL Vile worm, thou wast o'erlooked even in thy
birth.

QUICKLY With trial-fire touch me his finger end.
If he be chaste, the flame will back descend
And turn him to no pain; but if he start,
90   It is the flesh of a corrupted heart.

PISTOL A trial, come.

EVANS   Come, will this wood take fire?
        They put the tapers to his fingers, and he starts.

FALSTAFF O, O, O!

QUICKLY Corrupt, corrupt, and tainted in desire!
About him, fairies, sing a scornful rhyme;
95   And, as you trip, still pinch him to your time.

The Song.

Fie on sinful fantasy!
Fie on lust and luxury!
Lust is but a bloody fire,
Kindled with unchaste desire,
100   Fed in heart, whose flames aspire,
As thoughts do blow them, higher and higher.
Pinch him, fairies, mutually;
Pinch him for his villainy;
Pinch him, and burn him, and turn him about,
105   Till candles and starlight and moonshine be out.

---

83 **middle earth** i.e., that section of the universe between heaven and hell,
realm of mortals   84-85 **Heavens ... cheese** (cheese was the favorite food of
Welshmen. Since Evans smells Falstaff, the latter fears he will be turned into
cheese and then devoured)   86 **o'erlooked** bewitched   97 **luxury** lasci-
viousness   98 **bloody fire** fire in the blood   102 **mutually** jointly

*Here they pinch him, and sing about him, and [Caius] the
Doctor comes one way and steals away a boy in green. And
Slender another way; he takes a boy in white. And Fenton
steals Mistress Anne. And a noise of hunting is made within,
and all the Fairies run away. Falstaff pulls off his buck's
head and rises up.*

[*Enter*] *Page, Ford,* [*Mistress Page, Mistress Ford, and
Evans*].

PAGE Nay, do not fly. I think we have watched you
now.
Will none but Herne the Hunter serve your turn?

MRS. PAGE [*To Page*] I pray you, come, hold up the
jest no higher.
[*To Falstaff*] Now, good Sir John, how like you
Windsor wives?
See you these, husband? [*Points to Falstaff's horns.*]
Do not these fair yokes   110
Become the forest better than the town?

FORD Now sir, who's a cuckold now? Master Brooke,
Falstaff's a knave, a cuckoldly knave; here are his
horns, Master Brooke. And, Master Brooke, he
hath enjoyed nothing of Ford's but his buck basket,   115
his cudgel, and twenty pounds of money, which
must be paid to Master Brooke; his horses are
arrested for it, Master Brooke.

MRS. FORD Sir John, we have had ill luck; we could
never meet. I will never take you for my love   120
again, but I will always count you my deer.

FALSTAFF I do begin to perceive that I am made an ass.

---

105 s.d. **Evans** (Q1 brings in Evans and Shallow with the others. Evans
presumably left the stage at the previous direction, when "all the Fairies run
away." He must reenter because he speaks later. Shallow speaks no lines, but he
may well belong to this group scene)   106 **watched you** i.e., caught you in the act
108 **hold up the jest no higher** i.e., put an end to the jest   118 **arrested** seized
by warrant   120 **meet** (possible aural pun on *mate*)

FORD Ay, and an ox too: both the proofs are extant.

FALSTAFF And these are not fairies? I was three or four
125   times in the thought they were not fairies; and yet
the guiltiness of my mind, the sudden surprise of
my powers, drove the grossness of the foppery
into a received belief, in despite of the teeth of all
rhyme and reason, that they were fairies. See now
130   how wit may be made a Jack-a-Lent, when 'tis upon
ill employment.

EVANS Sir John Falstaff, serve Got and leave your
desires, and fairies will not pinse you.

FORD Well said, fairy Hugh.

135   EVANS [To Ford] And leave you your jealousies too,
I pray you.

FORD I will never mistrust my wife again, till thou art
able to woo her in good English.

FALSTAFF Have I laid my brain in the sun and dried it,
140   that it wants matter to prevent so gross o'erreach-
ing as this? Am I ridden with a Welsh goat too?
Shall I have a coxcomb of frieze? 'Tis time I were
choked with a piece of toasted cheese.

EVANS Seese is not goot to give putter; your belly is
145   all putter.

FALSTAFF "Seese" and "putter"? Have I lived to stand
at the taunt of one that makes fritters of English?
This is enough to be the decay of lust and late-walk-
ing through the realm.

150   MRS. PAGE Why, Sir John, do you think though we
would have thrust virtue out of our hearts by the
head and shoulders, and have given ourselves with-

---

123 ox i.e., fool (from the expression "to make an ox of someone")   123 proofs
i.e., the long horns   127 powers faculties   127 foppery deceit   140 wants lacks
142 coxcomb of frieze fool's cap of coarse Welsh woolen cloth   148-49 late-
walking staying out late

out scruple to hell, that ever the devil could have
made you our delight?

FORD What, a hodge-pudding? A bag of flax?   155

MRS. PAGE A puffed man?

PAGE Old, cold, withered, and of intolerable entrails?

FORD And one that is as slanderous as Satan?

PAGE And as poor as Job?

FORD And as wicked as his wife?   160

EVANS And given to fornications, and to taverns, and
sack and wine and metheglins, and to drinkings
and swearings and starings, pribbles and prabbles?

FALSTAFF Well, I am your theme. You have the start of
me; I am dejected; I am not able to answer the   165
Welsh flannel. Ignorance itself is a plummet o'er
me. Use me as you will.

FORD Marry, sir, we'll bring you to Windsor, to one
Master Brooke, that you have cozened of money, to
whom you should have been a pander. Over and   170
above that you have suffered, I think to repay that
money will be a biting affliction.

PAGE Yet be cheerful, knight. Thou shalt eat a posset
tonight at my house, where I will desire thee to
laugh at my wife that now laughs at thee. Tell her   175
Master Slender hath married her daughter.

MRS. PAGE [Aside] Doctors doubt that. If Anne Page
be my daughter, she is, by this, Doctor Caius' wife.

[Enter Slender.]

SLENDER Whoa, ho, ho, father Page!

155 hodge-pudding large sausage of many ingredients   162 metheglins spiced
Welsh mead   163 starings swaggerings   165 dejected cast down   166 Welsh
flannel (teasing name for a Welshman)   166 plummet (1) garment (from
"plumbet," a woolen fabric) (2) line for sounding   177 Doctors doubt that
(expression of disbelief)

180 PAGE Son, how now; how now, son! Have you dispatched?

SLENDER Dispatched? I'll make the best in Gloucestershire know on't; would I were hanged, la, else.

PAGE Of what, son?

185 SLENDER I came yonder at Eton to marry Mistress Anne Page, and she's a great lubberly boy. If it had not been i' th' church, I would have swinged him, or he should have swinged me. If I did not think it had been Anne Page, would I might never stir—
190 and 'tis a postmaster's boy!

PAGE Upon my life, then, you took the wrong.

SLENDER What need you tell me that? I think so, when I took a boy for a girl. If I had been married to him, for all he was in woman's apparel, I would not have
195 had him.

PAGE Why, this is your own folly. Did not I tell you how you should know my daughter by her garments?

SLENDER I went to her in white, and cried, "mum,"
200 and she cried, "budget," as Anne and I had appointed; and yet it was not Anne, but a postmaster's boy.

MRS. PAGE Good George, be not angry. I knew of your purpose; turned my daughter into green; and indeed
205 she is now with the Doctor at the dean'ry, and there married.

[Enter Doctor Caius.]

CAIUS Vere is Mistress Page? By gar, I am cozened! I ha' married *un garçon*, a boy; *un* peasant, by gar, a boy; it is not Anne Page. By gar, I am cozened!

210 MRS. PAGE Why? Did you take her in green?

180-81 dispatched settled the business   187 swinged beaten   190 postmaster
master of post horses

CAIUS Ay, be-gar, and 'tis a boy. Be-gar, I'll raise all
Windsor.   [*Exit*]

FORD This is strange. Who hath got the right Anne?

PAGE My heart misgives me. Here comes Master
Fenton.   215

[*Enter Fenton and Anne Page.*]

How now, Master Fenton!

ANNE Pardon, good father! Good my mother, pardon!

PAGE Now, mistress, how chance you went not with
Master Slender?

MRS. PAGE Why went you not with Master Doctor,
maid?   220

FENTON You do amaze her. Hear the truth of it.
You would have married her most shamefully,
Where there was no proportion held in love.
The truth is, she and I, have since contracted,
Are now so sure that nothing can dissolve us.   225
Th' offense is holy that she hath committed,
And this deceit loses the name of craft,
Of disobedience, or unduteous title,
Since therein she doth evitate and shun
A thousand irreligious cursèd hours   230
Which forcèd marriage would have brought upon
her.

FORD Stand not amazed. Here is no remedy.
In love the heavens themselves do guide the state;
Money buys lands, and wives are sold by fate.

FALSTAFF I am glad, though you have ta'en a special   235
stand to strike at me, that your arrow hath
glanced.

---

221 amaze perplex   224 contracted betrothed   225 sure firmly bound in
wedlock   229 evitate avoid   236 stand hunter's place for shooting

PAGE Well, what remedy? Fenton, heaven give thee
      joy!
      What cannot be eschewed must be embraced.

FALSTAFF When night dogs run, all sorts of deer are
240   chased.

MRS PAGE Well, I will muse no further. Master
          Fenton,
          Heaven give you many, many merry days!
          Good husband, let us every one go home,
          And laugh this sport o'er by a country fire;
          Sir John and all.

245 FORD   Let it be so. Sir John,
     To Master Brooke you yet shall hold your word;
     For he tonight shall lie with Mistress Ford. *Exeunt*.

FINIS

241 muse grumble

Textual Note

Two texts of *The Merry Wives of Windsor* exist: that of the 1602 Quarto and that of the 1623 Folio. The play had been entered in the Stationers' Register on January 18, 1602, for publication by John Busby, but Busby immediately transferred his rights to Arthur Johnson. Johnson brought out Q1 later that year with Thomas Creede as his printer. In 1619, Thomas Pavier issued a second quarto that basically reprints Q1 and is therefore without textual authority. The last early quarto of the play, that of 1630, except for some changes in spelling and punctuation, was printed from the Folio. Thus Q1 and F stand as the only texts of editorial importance.

There are significant differences between these two texts. Not only is Q1 some twelve hundred lines shorter, but it omits and transposes scenes, cuts speaking parts for William and Robin, excises all references to the court and Order of the Garter, and makes a jumble of many individual passages. In sum, although coherent, the Quarto text is inferior to the Folio version. Yet the Quarto contains certain passages and readings—notably Brooke as the alias for Ford, and *cosen garmombles* in place of *cozen-germans*—which appear to be genuinely Shakespeare's.

Various theories have been advanced over the years to account for the two versions of the play. Scholarly consensus marks the Folio text as the authentic version. However, according to a strong current theory, F rests upon a 1597 mother text that had undergone minor modifications between the original production and publication of the Folio in 1623.

The Quarto version, it is posited, represents an abridgment of that mother text, illegitimately made through memorial reconstruction for a provincial acting company around 1601. The pirate was most certainly a "hired man" who played the Host in the original Lord Chamber-

lain's Men productions of the play. While making his
memorial reconstruction, this traitor actor seems to have
restored to the text the Brooke reading that had been
altered to Broome in 1597. This was done to avoid con-
flict with the family of William Brooke, Lord Cobham,
who had taken umbrage at Shakespeare's original name
for Falstaff in *1 Henry IV*—Oldcastle, a Brooke family
ancestor. At the same time, the pirate-actor, through his
playing knowledge of the original script, corrected other
anomalies, such as the confusion over the costume colors
in the fairy scene, which hasty composition had let creep
into the mother text. Thus, while Q1 must be regarded
as a corrupt text, it has helped to get us closer to Shakespeare's original version.

Trying to recapture that original version, we are further
handicapped by certain peculiarities in the Folio text. The
only stage directions indicate entries and exits; character
names are massed at the head of each scene; the play is
fully divided into acts and scenes; and there are idio-
syncrasies in punctuation. These oddities, considered col-
lectively, are now taken as an indication that the Folio
Merry Wives is a literary transcription of either the
author's manuscript or a prompt copy—it is impossible
to tell which—made by Ralph Crane, distinguished scrivener of the King's Men. Since *The Merry Wives* shares
these scribal characteristics with the three other plays
opening the Folio, it appears as if the original plan was to
have Crane make a set of literary transcriptions for all the
plays in the Folio, but the plan never was completely
executed.

The present edition is based on the Folio text. The
massed entries have been changed from the scene heads to
the appropriate places within the scene. The Latin of the
Folio's act and scene divisions has been translated into
English. The French of Dr. Caius is modernized, and the
Welsh pronunciations of Sir Hugh Evans are indicated a
little more consistently than in the Folio. For example, at
I.i.246, where the Folio in a single speech gives both
"ord" and "ort," the Signet edition alters the first to agree

TEXTUAL NOTE

with the second. Prose passages set as verse in the Folio appear here as prose. Added stage directions and indications of locale are in brackets. The name "Broome," which appears regularly in F, is here given as "Brooke," speech prefixes and abbreviations are expanded, spelling and punctuation are modernized, and obvious typographical errors are corrected. Other departures from F are listed below, the adopted reading first, in bold type, followed by the Folio reading in roman. Adopted readings from Q1 are indicated by a bracketed Q. Readings from later quartos, folios, or those by editors appear unbracketed.

I.i.45 **George** Thomas   57,60 **Shallow** Slender   124-26 **They carried ... pocket** [Q; F omits]   243 **contempt** content

I.ii.12 **seese** cheese

I.iii.14 **lime** [Q] lieu   48 **well** [Q] will   52 **legion** [Q: legians] legend   60 **oeillades** illiads   69 **cheater** Cheaters   82 **o' th'** ith'   83 **humor** honor   94 **Page** [Q] Ford   95 **Ford** [Q] Page   99 **Page** Ford   101 **mind** mine

I.iv.22 **whey face** [Q: whay coloured] wee-face   45 **boitier vert** boyteene verd

II.i.56 **praised** praise   61 **Hundredth Psalm** hundred Psalms   134 **and there's the humor of it** [Q; F omits]   205 **Ford** Shallow   210-11 **mynheers** An-heires

II.ii.24, 53, 308 **God** [Q] heauen

II.iii.54 **word** [Q; F omits]   76 **Page, Shallow and Slender** All

III.i.83 **urinals** [Q] Vrinal   84-85 **for missing your meetings and appointments** [Q; F omits]   100 **Give me thy hand, terrestrial; so** [Q; F omits]

III.iii.3 **Robert** Robin   151 **who goes here** [Q; F omits]   163 **uncope** uncape   189 **foolish** foolishion

III.iv.12 **Fenton** [F omits]   57 **God** [Q] Heauen   62 **have** hath   109 s.d. **Exit** Exeunt

III.v.88 **By the Lord** [Q] Yes   150 s.d. **Exit** Exeunt

IV.i.45 **hung** hing   66 **lunatics** Lunaties

IV.ii.18 **lunes** lines   54 **Mrs. Page** [F gives the line as part of the previous speech]   62 **Mrs. Page** [Q] Mist. Ford   94 **direct** direct direct   98 **him** [F omits]   177 **not** [F omits]   189 **Jeshu** [Q] yea and no

IV.iii.1 **Germans desire** Germane desires   7 **them** [Q] him   9 **house** [Q] houses

IV.iv.7 **cold** gold   32 **makes** make   42 **Disguised ... head** [Q, which has "Horne" for "Herne"; F omits]   60 **Mrs. Ford** Ford   72 **tire** time

TEXTUAL NOTE

IV.v.43 **Simple** Fal.   53 **Tyke** [Q] like   56 **Thou art** [Q] thou are   101-2 **to say my prayers** [Q; F omits]

IV.v.27 **ever** euen   39 **denote** deuote

V.ii.3 **daughter** [F omits]

V.iii.13 **Hugh** Herne

V.v.s.d. **with a buck's head upon him** [Q; F omits]   2 **hot-blooded** hot-bloodied   39 s.d. **Enter ... of Fairies** [Q] Enter Fairies   71 **More** Mote   91 s.d. **They ... starts** [Q; F omits]   105 s.d. **Here ... rises up** [Q, which gives "red" where we give "green," and "greene" where we give "white," and describes Anne as "being in white"]   199 **white** greene   204,210 **green** white

WILLIAM SHAKESPEARE

MUCH ADO ABOUT NOTHING

Edited by David Stevenson

MUCH ADO ABOUT NOTHING

[ACT I

Scene I. *Before Leonato's house.*]

*Enter Leonato, Governor of Messina, Hero his
daughter, and Beatrice his niece, with a Messenger.*

LEONATO I learn in this letter that Don Pedro of Aragon comes this night to Messina.

MESSENGER He is very near by this. He was not three leagues off when I left him.

LEONATO How many gentlemen have you lost in this action?　5

MESSENGER But few of any sort, and none of name.

LEONATO A victory is twice itself when the achiever brings home full numbers. I find here that Don Pedro hath bestowed much honor on a young Florentine called Claudio.　10

MESSENGER Much deserved on his part, and equally rememb'red by Don Pedro. He hath borne himself beyond the promise of his age, doing, in the figure

---

Text references are printed in **bold** type; the annotation follows in roman type.
I.i.5 **gentlemen** men of upper class   7 **sort** rank   7 **name** distinguished family

15 of a lamb, the feats of a lion. He hath indeed better
    bett'red expectation than you must expect of me to
    tell you how.

LEONATO He hath an uncle here in Messina will be
very much glad of it.

20 MESSENGER I have already delivered him letters, and
    there appears much joy in him; even so much that
    joy could not show itself modest enough without a
    badge of bitterness.

LEONATO Did he break out into tears?

25 MESSENGER In great measure.

LEONATO A kind overflow of kindness. There are no
faces truer than those that are so washed. How much
better is it to weep at joy than to joy at weeping!

BEATRICE I pray you, is Signior Mountanto returned
30 from the wars or no?

MESSENGER I know none of that name, lady. There was
none such in the army of any sort.

LEONATO What is he that you ask for, niece?

HERO My cousin means Signior Benedick of Padua.

35 MESSENGER O, he's returned, and as pleasant as ever
    he was.

BEATRICE He set up his bills here in Messina and challenged Cupid at the flight; and my uncle's fool,
reading the challenge, subscribed for Cupid and
40 challenged him at the burbolt. I pray you, how
    many hath he killed and eaten in these wars? But
    how many hath he killed? For indeed, I promised
    to eat all of his killing.

15-16 **better bett'red expectation** greatly exceeded anticipated valor   18 **uncle**
(does not appear in the play)   23 **badge** emblem   26 **kind overflow of kindness**
natural overflow of tenderness   29 **Mountanto** a fencing thrust   35 **pleasant**
lively   37 **bills** advertising placards   38 **flight** shooting contest (i.e., he thought
himself a lady-killer)   39 **subscribed** signed up   40 **burbolt** blunt arrow

LEONATO Faith, niece, you tax Signior Benedick too
much; but he'll be meet with you, I doubt it not.   45

MESSENGER He hath done good service, lady, in these
wars.

BEATRICE You had musty victual, and he hath holp to
eat it. He is a very valiant trencherman; he hath
an excellent stomach.   50

MESSENGER And a good soldier too, lady.

BEATRICE And a good soldier to a lady. But what is he
to a lord?

MESSENGER A lord to a lord, a man to a man; stuffed
with all honorable virtues.   55

BEATRICE It is so, indeed; he is no less than a stuffed
man. But for the stuffing—well, we are all mortal.

LEONATO You must not, sir, mistake my niece. There
is a kind of merry war betwixt Signior Benedick and
her. They never meet but there's a skirmish of wit   60
between them.

BEATRICE Alas, he gets nothing by that! In our last con-
flict four of his five wits went halting off, and now
is the whole man governed with one; so that if he
have wit enough to keep himself warm, let him bear   65
it for a difference between himself and his horse. For
it is all the wealth that he hath left to be known a
reasonable creature. Who is his companion now?
He hath every month a new sworn brother.

MESSENGER Is't possible?   70

BEATRICE Very easily possible. He wears his faith but
as the fashion of his hat; it ever changes with the
next block.

---

44 tax i.e., tease too hard   45 meet even   49 trencherman eater   52 to in
comparison with   56-57 stuffed man dummy   63 five wits common sense,
imagination, fancy, estimation, memory   63 halting limping   73 next block most
recent shape

MESSENGER I see, lady, the gentleman is not in your
75 books.

BEATRICE No. And he were, I would burn my study.
But I pray you, who is his companion? Is there no
young squarer now that will make a voyage with
him to the devil?

80 MESSENGER He is most in the company of the right
noble Claudio.

BEATRICE O Lord, he will hang upon him like a disease.
He is sooner caught than the pestilence, and the
taker runs presently mad. God help the noble
85 Claudio if he have caught the Benedict; it will cost
him a thousand pound ere 'a be cured.

MESSENGER I will hold friends with you, lady.

BEATRICE Do, good friend.

LEONATO You will never run mad, niece.

90 BEATRICE No, not till a hot January.

MESSENGER Don Pedro is approached.

Enter Don Pedro, Claudio, Benedick, Balthasar, and
John the Bastard.

DON PEDRO Good Signior Leonato, are you come to
meet your trouble? The fashion of the world is to
avoid cost, and you encounter it.

95 LEONATO Never came trouble to my house in the likeness of your Grace; for trouble being gone, comfort
should remain. But when you depart from me, sorrow abides, and happiness takes his leave.

DON PEDRO You embrace your charge too willingly.
100 I think this is your daughter.

LEONATO Her mother hath many times told me so.

---

75 **books** favor   76 **And if**   78 **squarer** brawler   84 **presently** immediately (the
usual sense in Shakespeare)   85 **Benedict** (the change in spelling suggests a disease
based on Benedick's name)   86 **'a** he   89 **run mad** catch the Benedict   99 **charge**
burden (of my visit)

BENEDICK Were you in doubt, sir, that you asked her?

LEONATO Signior Benedick, no; for then were you a child.

DON PEDRO You have it full, Benedick. We may guess   105
by this what you are, being a man. Truly the lady
fathers herself. Be happy, lady, for you are like an
honorable father.

BENEDICK If Signior Leonato be her father, she would
not have his head on her shoulders for all Messina,   110
as like him as she is.

BEATRICE I wonder that you will still be talking, Signior Benedick; nobody marks you.

BENEDICK What, my dear Lady Disdain! Are you yet
living?   115

BEATRICE Is it possible Disdain should die while she
hath such meet food to feed it as Signior Benedick?
Courtesy itself must convert to Disdain if you come
in her presence.

BENEDICK Then is courtesy a turncoat. But it is certain   120
I am loved of all ladies, only you excepted; and I
would I could find in my heart that I had not a hard
heart; for truly I love none.

BEATRICE A dear happiness to women! They would else
have been troubled with a pernicious suitor. I thank   125
God and my cold blood, I am of your humor for
that. I had rather hear my dog bark at a crow than
a man swear he loves me.

BENEDICK God keep your ladyship still in that mind,
so some gentleman or other shall scape a predesti-   130
nate scratched face.

BEATRICE Scratching could not make it worse and
'twere such a face as yours were.

107 **fathers herself** shows who her father is by resembling him   110 **his head**
white-haired and bearded (?)   112 **still** always (the usual sense in Shakespeare)
121 **loved of all ladies** (he had "challenged Cupid")   126-27 **of your humor
for that** in agreement on that

BENEDICK Well, you are a rare parrot-teacher.

135 BEATRICE A bird of my tongue is better than a beast of yours.

BENEDICK I would my horse had the speed of your tongue, and so good a continuer. But keep your way, a God's name! I have done.

140 BEATRICE You always end with a jade's trick. I know you of old.

DON PEDRO That is the sum of all, Leonato. Signior Claudio and Signior Benedick, my dear friend Leonato hath invited you all. I tell him we shall stay
145 here, at the least a month, and he heartily prays some occasion may detain us longer. I dare swear he is no hypocrite, but prays from his heart.

LEONATO If you swear, my lord, you shall not be forsworn. [To Don John] Let me bid you welcome, my
150 lord; being reconciled to the Prince your brother, I owe you all duty.

DON JOHN I thank you. I am not of many words, but I thank you.

LEONATO Please it your Grace lead on?

155 DON PEDRO Your hand, Leonato. We will go together.
    Exeunt. Manent Benedick and Claudio.

CLAUDIO Benedick, didst thou note the daughter of Signior Leonato?

BENEDICK I noted her not, but I looked on her.

CLAUDIO Is she not a modest young lady?

160 BENEDICK Do you question me as an honest man should do, for my simple true judgment? Or would

---

134 **parrot-teacher** i.e., monotonous speaker of nonsense   138 **continuer** staying power   140 **jade's trick** trick of a vicious horse (i.e., a sudden stop?)   142 **the sum of all** the end of the sparring match   155 s.d. **Manent** remain (Latin)   158 **noted** (1) scrutinized (2) set to music (3) stigmatized

you have me speak after my custom, as being a professed tyrant to their sex?

CLAUDIO No, I pray thee speak in sober judgment.

BENEDICK Why, i' faith, methinks she's too low for a 165
high praise, too brown for a fair praise, and too little
for a great praise. Only this commendation I can
afford her, that were she other than she is, she were
unhandsome, and being no other but as she is, I
do not like her. 170

CLAUDIO Thou thinkest I am in sport. I pray thee tell
me truly how thou lik'st her.

BENEDICK Would you buy her, that you inquire after
her?

CLAUDIO Can the world buy such a jewel? 175

BENEDICK Yea, and a case to put it into. But speak you
this with a sad brow? Or do you play the flouting
Jack, to tell us Cupid is a good hare-finder and
Vulcan a rare carpenter? Come, in what key shall
a man take you to go in the song? 180

CLAUDIO In mine eye she is the sweetest lady that ever
I looked on.

BENEDICK I can see yet without spectacles, and I see no
such matter. There's her cousin, and she were not
possessed with a fury, exceeds her as much in beauty 185
as the first of May doth the last of December. But I
hope you have no intent to turn husband, have you?

CLAUDIO I would scarce trust myself, though I had
sworn the contrary, if Hero would be my wife.

BENEDICK Is't come to this? In faith, hath not the world 190
one man but he will wear his cap with suspicion?

---

177 with a sad brow seriously   178-79 to tell us ... carpenter i.e., to mock us
with nonsense (Cupid was blind, Vulcan was a blacksmith)   191 but he ...
suspicion who (because he is unmarried) will not fear that he has a cuckold's horns

Shall I never see a bachelor of threescore again? Go
to, i' faith! And thou wilt needs thrust thy neck into
a yoke, wear the print of it and sigh away Sundays.
195   Look! Don Pedro is returned to seek you.

Enter Don Pedro.

DON PEDRO What secret hath held you here, that you
followed not to Leonato's?

BENEDICK I would your Grace would constrain me to
tell.

200   DON PEDRO I charge thee on thy allegiance.

BENEDICK You hear, Count Claudio; I can be secret as
a dumb man. I would have you think so. But, on my
allegiance—mark you this—on my allegiance! He is
in love. With who? Now that is your Grace's part.
205   Mark how short his answer is—with Hero, Leonato's short daughter.

CLAUDIO If this were so, so were it utt'red.

BENEDICK Like the old tale, my lord: "It is not so, nor
'twas not so, but indeed, God forbid it should be so!"

210   CLAUDIO If my passion change not shortly, God forbid
it should be otherwise.

DON PEDRO Amen, if you love her, for the lady is very
well worthy.

CLAUDIO You speak this to fetch me in, my lord.

215   DON PEDRO By my troth, I speak my thought.

CLAUDIO And, in faith, my lord, I spoke mine.

BENEDICK And, by my two faiths and troths, my lord,
I spoke mine.

CLAUDIO That I love her, I feel.

220   DON PEDRO That she is worthy, I know.

193-94 **thrust thy neck ... Sundays** i.e., enjoy the tiresome bondage of marriage
200 **allegiance** solemn obligation to a prince

BENEDICK   That I neither feel how she should be loved, nor know how she should be worthy, is the opinion that fire cannot melt out of me. I will die in it at the stake.

DON PEDRO   Thou wast ever an obstinate heretic in the despite of beauty.   225

CLAUDIO   And never could maintain his part but in the force of his will.

BENEDICK   That a woman conceived me, I thank her; that she brought me up, I likewise give her most 230 humble thanks. But that I will have a rechate winded in my forehead, or hang my bugle in an invisible baldrick, all women shall pardon me. Because I will not do them the wrong to mistrust any, I will do myself the right to trust none; and the fine 235 is (for the which I may go the finer), I will live a bachelor.

DON PEDRO   I shall see thee, ere I die, look pale with love.

BENEDICK   With anger, with sickness, or with hunger, 240 my lord, not with love. Prove that ever I lose more blood with love than I will get again with drinking, pick out mine eyes with a ballad maker's pen and hang me up at the door of a brothel house for the sign of blind Cupid.   245

DON PEDRO   Well, if ever thou dost fall from this faith, thou wilt prove a notable argument.

BENEDICK   If I do, hang me in a bottle like a cat and shoot at me; and he that hits me, let him be clapped on the shoulder and called Adam.   250

DON PEDRO   Well, as time shall try:

225-26 in the despite of in contempt of   228 will sexual appetite   231 rechate recheate, notes on a hunting horn   233 baldrick belt, sling (the reference here, and in rechate, is to the horns of a cuckold)   235 fine finis, result   247 notable argument famous example   248 bottle basket   250 Adam i.e., Adam Bell, one of the three superlative archers in the ballad "Adam Bell"

"In time the savage bull doth bear the yoke."

BENEDICK The savage bull may, but if ever the sensible
      Benedick bear it, pluck off the bull's horns and set
255   them in my forehead, and let me be vilely painted,
      and in such great letters as they write "Here is good
      horse to hire," let them signify under my sign "Here
      you may see Benedick the married man."

CLAUDIO If this should ever happen, thou wouldst be
260   horn-mad.

DON PEDRO Nay, if Cupid have not spent all his quiver
      in Venice, thou wilt quake for this shortly.

BENEDICK I look for an earthquake too then.

DON PEDRO Well, you will temporize with the hours.
265   In the meantime, good Signior Benedick, repair to
      Leonato's. Commend me to him and tell him I will
      not fail him at supper; for indeed he hath made
      great preparation.

BENEDICK I have almost matter enough in me for
270   such an embassage, and so I commit you—

CLAUDIO To the tuition of God. From my house, if
      I had it—

DON PEDRO The sixth of July. Your loving friend,
      Benedick.

275 BENEDICK Nay, mock not, mock not. The body of your
      discourse is sometime guarded with fragments,
      and the guards are but slightly basted on neither.
      Ere you flout old ends any further, examine your
      conscience. And so I leave you.   *Exit*.

CLAUDIO My liege, your Highness now may do me
280   good.

---

260 **horn-mad** mad with jealousy (perhaps also "sexually insatiable")   262 **Venice**
(famous for sexual license)   264 **temporize with the hours** change temper or attitude with time   269 **matter** sense   271 **tuition** custody   276 **guarded** trimmed
(used of clothing)   278 **flout old ends** i.e., indulge in derision at my expense

DON PEDRO My love is thine to teach. Teach it but
    how,
  And thou shalt see how apt it is to learn
  Any hard lesson that may do thee good.

CLAUDIO Hath Leonato any son, my lord?

DON PEDRO No child but Hero; she's his only heir.   285
  Dost thou affect her, Claudio?

CLAUDIO   O my lord,
  When you went onward on this ended action,
  I looked upon her with a soldier's eye,
  That liked, but had a rougher task in hand
  Than to drive liking to the name of love.   290
  But now I am returned and that war-thoughts
  Have left their places vacant, in their rooms
  Come thronging soft and delicate desires,
  All prompting me how fair young Hero is,
  Saying I liked her ere I went to wars.   295

DON PEDRO Thou wilt be like a lover presently
  And tire the hearer with a book of words.
  If thou dost love fair Hero, cherish it,
  And I will break with her and with her father,
  And thou shalt have her. Was't not to this end   300
  That thou began'st to twist so fine a story?

CLAUDIO How sweetly you do minister to love,
  That know love's grief by his complexion!
  But lest my liking might too sudden seem,
  I would have salved it with a longer treatise.   305

DON PEDRO What need the bridge much broader than
    the flood?
  The fairest grant is the necessity.
  Look, what will serve is fit. 'Tis once, thou lovest,
  And I will fit thee with the remedy.
  I know we shall have reveling tonight.   310

286 **affect** love   287 **ended action** war just concluded   291 **that** because
299 **break** open negotiations   303 **complexion** appearance   307 **The fairest
grant is the necessity** the most attractive giving is when the receiver really needs
something   308 **'Tis once** in short

I will assume thy part in some disguise
And tell fair Hero I am Claudio,
And in her bosom I'll unclasp my heart
And take her hearing prisoner with the force
315   And strong encounter of my amorous tale;
Then after to her father will I break,
And the conclusion is, she shall be thine.
In practice let us put it presently.   *Exeunt.*

[Scene II. *Leonato's house.*]

Enter Leonato and an old man [Antonio], brother
to Leonato.

LEONATO How now, brother? Where is my cousin
your son? Hath he provided this music?

ANTONIO He is very busy about it. But, brother, I can
tell you strange news that you yet dreamt not of.

5   LEONATO Are they good?

ANTONIO As the events stamps them. But they have
a good cover, they show well outward. The Prince
and Count Claudio, walking in a thick-pleached
alley in mine orchard, were thus much overheard
10   by a man of mine. The Prince discovered to Claudio that he loved my niece your daughter and meant
to acknowledge it this night in a dance, and if he
found her accordant, he meant to take the present
time by the top and instantly break with you of it.

15   LEONATO Hath the fellow any wit that told you this?

I.ii.1 cousin kinsman   5 they i.e., the news (plural in the sixteenth century)
6 As the events stamps them as the outcome proves them to be (a plural noun,
especially when felt to be singular, often has a verb ending in -s)   8-9 thick-
pleached alley in mine orchard walk or arbor fenced by interwoven branches in
my garden   10 discovered disclosed   13 accordant agreeing   14 top forelock

ANTONIO A good sharp fellow. I will send for him, and question him yourself.

LEONATO No, no. We will hold it as a dream till it appear itself. But I will acquaint my daughter withal, that she may be the better prepared for an 20
answer, if peradventure this be true. Go you and tell her of it.

[*Enter Attendants.*]

Cousin, you know what you have to do. O, I cry you mercy, friend. Go you with me, and I will use your skill. Good cousin, have a care this busy time. 25
Exeunt.

[Scene III. *Leonato's house.*]

Enter Sir John the Bastard and Conrade, his companion.

CONRADE What the goodyear, my lord! Why are you thus out of measure sad?

DON JOHN There is no measure in the occasion that breeds; therefore the sadness is without limit.

CONRADE You should hear reason. 5

DON JOHN And when I have heard it, what blessing brings it?

CONRADE If not a present remedy, at least a patient sufferance.

DON JOHN I wonder that thou, being (as thou say'st 10
thou art) born under Saturn, goest about to apply

23-24 **cry you mercy** beg your pardon   I.iii.1 **What the goodyear** (an expletive)
2 **out of measure sad** unduly morose   11 **under Saturn** i.e., naturally sullen

a moral medicine to a mortifying mischief. I cannot hide what I am. I must be sad when I have
cause, and smile at no man's jests; eat when I have
15 stomach, and wait for no man's leisure; sleep when
I am drowsy, and tend on no man's business; laugh
when I am merry, and claw no man in his humor.

CONRADE Yea, but you must not make the full show
of this till you may do it without controlment. You
20 have of late stood out against your brother, and he
hath ta'en you newly into his grace, where it is impossible you should take true root but by the fair
weather that you make yourself. It is needful that
you frame the season for your own harvest.

25 DON JOHN I had rather be a canker in a hedge than
a rose in his grace, and it better fits my blood to be
disdained of all than to fashion a carriage to rob
love from any. In this, though I cannot be said to
be a flattering honest man, it must not be denied
30 but I am a plain-dealing villain. I am trusted with
a muzzle and enfranchised with a clog; therefore I
have decreed not to sing in my cage. If I had my
mouth, I would bite; if I had my liberty, I would
do my liking. In the meantime let me be that I am,
35 and seek not to alter me.

CONRADE Can you make no use of your discontent?

DON JOHN I make all use of it, for I use it only. Who
comes here?

Enter Borachio.

What news, Borachio?

40 BORACHIO I came yonder from a great supper. The
Prince your brother is royally entertained by Leonato, and I can give you intelligence of an intended
marriage.

12 **mortifying mischief** killing calamity   17 **claw no man in his humor** i.e.,
flatter no man (**claw** = pat or scratch on the back; **humor** = whim)   24 **frame**
bring about   25 **canker** wild rose   27 **fashion a carriage** contrive a behavior
42 **intelligence** information

DON JOHN Will it serve for any model to build mischief on? What is he for a fool that betroths him-   45
self to unquietness?

BORACHIO Marry, it is your brother's right hand.

DON JOHN Who? The most exquisite Claudio?

BORACHIO Even he.

DON JOHN A proper squire! And who? And who?   50
Which way looks he?

BORACHIO Marry, one Hero, the daughter and heir of
Leonato.

DON JOHN A very forward March-chick! How came
you to this?   55

BORACHIO Being entertained for a perfumer, as I was
smoking a musty room, comes me the Prince and
Claudio, hand in hand in sad conference. I whipped
me behind the arras and there heard it agreed upon
that the Prince should woo Hero for himself, and   60
having obtained her, give her to Count Claudio.

DON JOHN Come, come, let us thither. This may prove
food to my displeasure. That young start-up hath
all the glory of my overthrow. If I can cross him
any way, I bless myself every way. You are both   65
sure, and will assist me?

CONRADE To the death, my lord.

DON JOHN Let us to the great supper. Their cheer is
the greater that I am subdued. Would the cook
were o' my mind! Shall we go prove what's to be   70
done?

BORACHIO We'll wait upon your lordship.
                                        Exit [with others].

47 **Marry** (an expletive, from "by the Virgin Mary")   50 **proper squire** fine young
fellow   54 **forward March-chick** precocious fellow (i.e., born in early spring)
56 **entertained for** employed as   57 **smoking** fumigating (or possibly merely
perfuming)   58 **sad** serious   66 **sure** reliable   70 **prove** try

[ACT II

Scene I. *Leonato's house.*]

Enter Leonato, his brother [Antonio], Hero his daughter, and Beatrice his niece, [also Margaret and Ursula].

LEONATO Was not Count John here at supper?

ANTONIO I saw him not.

BEATRICE How tartly that gentleman looks! I never can see him but I am heartburned an hour after.

5 HERO He is of a very melancholy disposition.

BEATRICE He were an excellent man that were made just in the midway between him and Benedick. The one is too like an image and says nothing, and the other too like my lady's eldest son, evermore
10 tattling.

LEONATO Then half Signior Benedick's tongue in Count John's mouth, and half Count John's melancholy in Signior Benedick's face—

BEATRICE With a good leg and a good foot, uncle, and
15 money enough in his purse, such a man would win any woman in the world, if 'a could get her good will.

II.i.5 **melancholy** ill-tempered   9 **eldest son** i.e., overly confident (as heir presumptive)   14 **foot** (perhaps with a pun on French *foutre*, to copulate—i.e., a good lover)

LEONATO By my troth, niece, thou wilt never get thee
a husband if thou be so shrewd of thy tongue.

ANTONIO In faith, she's too curst.   20

BEATRICE Too curst is more than curst. I shall lessen
God's sending that way, for it is said, "God sends
a curst cow short horns"; but to a cow too curst he
sends none.

LEONATO So, by being too curst, God will send you no   25
horns.

BEATRICE Just, if he send me no husband; for the
which blessing I am at him upon my knees every
morning and evening. Lord, I could not endure a
husband with a beard on his face. I had rather lie   30
in the woolen!

LEONATO You may light on a husband that hath no
beard.

BEATRICE What should I do with him? Dress him in
my apparel and make him my waiting gentle-   35
woman? He that hath a beard is more than a youth,
and he that hath no beard is less than a man; and
he that is more than a youth is not for me; and he
that is less than a man, I am not for him. Therefore
I will even take sixpence in earnest of the berrord   40
and lead his apes into hell.

LEONATO Well then, go you into hell?

BEATRICE No; but to the gate, and there will the devil
meet me like an old cuckold with horns on his head,
and say, "Get you to heaven, Beatrice, get you to   45
heaven. Here's no place for you maids." So deliver
I up my apes, and away to Saint Peter. For the

---

19 shrewd sharp   20 curst shrewish   25-26 no horns (i.e., horn used as phallic
symbol, as Beatrice's next remark makes plain)   27 just exactly   31 in the woolen
between scratchy blankets   40 in earnest (1) advance payment (2) in all seriousness
40 berrord bearward, animal keeper   41 lead his apes into hell traditional
punishment for dying unwed

heavens, he shows me where the bachelors sit,
and there live we as merry as the day is long.

50   ANTONIO [*To Hero*] Well, niece, I trust you will be
ruled by your father.

BEATRICE Yes, faith. It is my cousin's duty to make
cursy and say, "Father, as it please you." But yet
for all that, cousin, let him be a handsome fellow,
55   or else make another cursy, and say, "Father, as
it please me."

LEONATO [*To Beatrice*] Well, niece, I hope to see you
one day fitted with a husband.

BEATRICE Not till God make men of some other metal
60   than earth. Would it not grieve a woman to be
overmastered with a piece of valiant dust? To make
an account of her life to a clod of wayward marl?
No, uncle, I'll none. Adam's sons are my brethren,
and truly I hold it a sin to match in my kindred.

65   LEONATO Daughter, remember what I told you. If the
Prince do solicit you in that kind, you know your
answer.

BEATRICE The fault will be in the music, cousin, if you
be not wooed in good time. If the Prince be too
70   important, tell him there is measure in everything, and so dance out the answer. For, hear me,
Hero: wooing, wedding, and repenting is as a
Scotch jig, a measure, and a cinquepace. The first
suit is hot and hasty like a Scotch jig (and full as
75   fantastical); the wedding, mannerly modest, as a
measure, full of state and ancientry; and then comes
Repentance and with his bad legs falls into the

---

48 **bachelors** unwed persons (female as well as male)   53 **cursy** curtsy   58 **fitted**
(continues playful sexual innuendo of the scene)   59 **metal** substance   62 **marl**
earth   70 **important** importunate   70 **measure** (1) discernible time sequence
(2) moderation (the entire speech is a light parody of Sir John Davies' *Orchestra, A
Poem of Dancing* [1596]; cf. stanza 23: "Time the measure of all moving is/And
dancing is a moving all in measure")   73 **cinquepace** lively dance

cinquepace faster and faster, till he sink into his grave.

LEONATO Cousin, you apprehend passing shrewdly.   80

BEATRICE I have a good eye, uncle; I can see a church by daylight.

LEONATO The revelers are ent'ring, brother. Make good room.

[*All put on their masks.*]

Enter Prince [Don] Pedro, Claudio, and Benedick, and Balthasar [masked; and without masks Borachio and] Don John.

DON PEDRO Lady, will you walk about with your   85 friend?

HERO So you walk softly and look sweetly and say nothing, I am yours for the walk; and especially when I walk away.

DON PEDRO With me in your company?   90

HERO I may say so when I please.

DON PEDRO And when please you to say so?

HERO When I like your favor, for God defend the lute should be like the case!

DON PEDRO My visor is Philemon's roof; within the   95 house is Jove.

HERO Why then, your visor should be thatched.

DON PEDRO Speak low if you speak love.

[*Draws her aside.*]

BENEDICK Well, I would you did like me.

---

86 friend lover   93 favor face   93 defend forbid   93-94 the lute ... case i.e., your face be as ugly as your mask   95 visor mask   95 Philemon peasant who entertained Jove in his house   99 Benedick (many editors emend the Quarto, and give this and Benedick's two subsequent speeches to Balthasar; but in V.ii Benedick and Margaret spar, and they may well do so here)

100 MARGARET So would not I for your own sake, for I
have many ill qualities.

BENEDICK Which is one?

MARGARET I say my prayers aloud.

BENEDICK I love you the better. The hearers may cry
105 amen.

MARGARET God match me with a good dancer!

BALTHASAR [*Interposing*] Amen.

MARGARET And God keep him out of my sight when
the dance is done! Answer, clerk.

110 BALTHASAR No more words. The clerk is answered.

URSULA I know you well enough. You are Signior
Antonio.

ANTONIO At a word, I am not.

URSULA I know you by the waggling of your head.

115 ANTONIO To tell you true, I counterfeit him.

URSULA You could never do him so ill-well unless you
were the very man. Here's his dry hand up and
down. You are he, you are he!

ANTONIO At a word I am not.

120 URSULA Come, come, do you think I do not know you
by your excellent wit? Can virtue hide itself? Go to,
mum, you are he. Graces will appear, and there's
an end.

BEATRICE Will you not tell me who told you so?

125 BENEDICK No, you shall pardon me.

BEATRICE Nor will you not tell me who you are?

BENEDICK Not now.

BEATRICE That I was disdainful, and that I had my

114 **waggling** i.e., palsy   117 **dry** dried-up (with age)

238

good wit out of the "Hundred Merry Tales." Well,
this was Signior Benedick that said so.   130

BENEDICK What's he?

BEATRICE I am sure you know him well enough.

BENEDICK Not I, believe me.

BEATRICE Did he never make you laugh?

BENEDICK I pray you, what is he?   135

BEATRICE Why, he is the Prince's jester, a very dull
fool. Only his gift is in devising impossible slanders. None but libertines delight in him, and the
commendation is not in his wit, but in his villainy;
for he both pleases men and angers them, and then 140
they laugh at him and beat him. I am sure he is in
the fleet; I would he had boarded me.

BENEDICK When I know the gentleman, I'll tell him
what you say.

BEATRICE Do, do. He'll but break a comparison or two 145
on me; which peradventure (not marked or not
laughed at), strikes him into melancholy, and then
there's a partridge wing saved, for the fool will eat
no supper that night. [Music.] We must follow the
leaders.   150

BENEDICK In every good thing.

BEATRICE Nay, if they lead to any ill, I will leave them
at the next turning.

                    Dance. Exeunt [all except Don John,
                              Borachio and Claudio].

DON JOHN Sure my brother is amorous on Hero and
hath withdrawn her father to break with him about 155
it. The ladies follow her and but one visor remains.

129 Hundred Merry Tales a popular collection of amusing, coarse anecdotes
137 Only his his only   142 fleet group (the related meaning, group of ships, leads
to boarded me, but perhaps too there is an allusion to Fleet Prison)

BORACHIO And that is Claudio. I know him by his bearing.

DON JOHN Are not you Signior Benedick?

160 CLAUDIO You know me well. I am he.

DON JOHN Signior, you are very near my brother in his love. He is enamored on Hero. I pray you dissuade him from her; she is no equal for his birth. You may do the part of an honest man in it.

165 CLAUDIO How know you he loves her?

DON JOHN I heard him swear his affection.

BORACHIO So did I too, and he swore he would marry her tonight.

DON JOHN Come, let us to the banquet.

Exeunt. Manet Claudio.

170 CLAUDIO Thus answer I in name of Benedick
But hear these ill news with the ears of Claudio.
'Tis certain so. The Prince woos for himself.
Friendship is constant in all other things
Save in the office and affairs of love.
175 Therefore all hearts in love use their own tongues;
Let every eye negotiate for itself
And trust no agent; for beauty is a witch
Against whose charms faith melteth into blood.
This is an accident of hourly proof,
180 Which I mistrusted not. Farewell therefore Hero!

Enter Benedick.

BENEDICK Count Claudio?

CLAUDIO Yea, the same.

BENEDICK Come, will you go with me?

---

169 **banquet** light meal, or course, of fruit, wine, and dessert   174 **office** business
178 **blood** passion, desire   179 **accident of hourly proof** common happening

CLAUDIO Whither?

BENEDICK Even to the next willow, about your own   185
business, County. What fashion will you wear the
garland of? About your neck, like an usurer's chain?
Or under your arm, like a lieutenant's scarf? You
must wear it one way, for the Prince hath got your
Hero.   190

CLAUDIO I wish him joy of her.

BENEDICK Why, that's spoken like an honest drovier.
So they sell bullocks. But did you think the Prince
would have served you thus?

CLAUDIO I pray you leave me.   195

BENEDICK Ho! Now you strike like the blind man!
'Twas the boy that stole your meat, and you'll beat
the post.

CLAUDIO If it will not be, I'll leave you.   *Exit*.

BENEDICK Alas, poor hurt fowl! Now will he creep   200
into sedges. But, that my Lady Beatrice should
know me, and not know me! The Prince's fool! Ha!
It may be I go under that title because I am merry.
Yea, but so I am apt to do myself wrong. I am not
so reputed. It is the base (though bitter) disposi-   205
tion of Beatrice that puts the world into her person
and so gives me out. Well, I'll be revenged as I
may.

Enter the Prince [Don Pedro], Hero, Leonato.

DON PEDRO Now, signior, where's the Count? Did you
see him?   210

BENEDICK Troth, my lord, I have played the part of
Lady Fame. I found him here as melancholy as a

185 next nearest   185 willow symbol of unrequited love   186 County Count
192 drovier cattle dealer   197-98 beat the post i.e., strike out blindly
205-7 It is ... gives me out it is the low and harsh disposition of Beatrice to
assume her opinion of me is the world's opinion of me   212 Lady Fame goddess
of rumor

215 lodge in a warren. I told him, and I think I told
him true, that your Grace had got the good will of
this young lady, and I off'red him my company to
a willow tree, either to make him a garland, as being
forsaken, or to bind him up a rod, as being worthy
to be whipped.

DON PEDRO To be whipped? What's his fault?

220 BENEDICK The flat transgression of a schoolboy who,
being overjoyed with finding a bird's nest, shows it
his companion, and he steals it.

DON PEDRO Wilt thou make a trust a transgression?
The transgresson is in the stealer.

225 BENEDICK Yet it had not been amiss the rod had been
made, and the garland too; for the garland he might
have worn himself, and the rod he might have bestowed on you, who (as I take it) have stol'n his
bird's nest.

230 DON PEDRO I will but teach them to sing and restore
them to the owner.

BENEDICK If their singing answer your saying, by my
faith you say honestly.

DON PEDRO The Lady Beatrice hath a quarrel to you.
235 The gentleman that danced with her told her she
is much wronged by you.

BENEDICK O, she misused me past the endurance of a
block! An oak but with one green leaf on it would
have answered her; my very visor began to assume
240 life and scold with her. She told me, not thinking I
had been myself, that I was the Prince's jester, that
I was duller than a great thaw; huddling jest upon
jest with such impossible conveyance upon me
that I stood like a man at a mark, with a whole
245 army shooting at me. She speaks poniards, and
every word stabs. If her breath were as terrible as

213 in a warren i.e., in a lonely place   243 impossible conveyance incredible
dexterity   244 mark target

her terminations, there were no living near her;
she would infect to the North Star. I would not
marry her though she were endowed with all that
Adam had left him before he transgressed. She   250
would have made Hercules have turned spit, yea,
and have cleft his club to make the fire too. Come,
talk not of her. You shall find her the infernal Ate
in good apparel. I would to God some scholar
would conjure her, for certainly, while she is here,   255
a man may live as quiet in hell as in a sanctuary;
and people sin upon purpose, because they would
go thither; so indeed all disquiet, horror, and per-
turbation follows her.

Enter Claudio and Beatrice.

DON PEDRO Look, here she comes.   260

BENEDICK Will your Grace command me any service
to the world's end? I will go on the slightest errand
now to the Antipodes that you can devise to send
me on; I will fetch you a toothpicker now from the
furthest inch of Asia; bring you the length of Prester   265
John's foot; fetch you a hair off the great Cham's
beard; do you any embassage to the Pygmies—
rather than hold three words' conference with this
harpy. You have no employment for me?

DON PEDRO None, but to desire your good company.   270

BENEDICK O God, sir, here's a dish I love not! I cannot
endure my Lady Tongue.   *Exit*.

DON PEDRO Come, lady, come; you have lost the heart
of Signior Benedick.

BEATRICE Indeed, my lord, he lent it me awhile, and I   275
gave him use for it, a double heart for his single
one. Marry, once before he won it of me with false

247 **terminations** words   253 **Ate** goddess of discord   255 **conjure her** i.e.,
exorcise the devil out of her   265-66 **Prester John** legendary Christian king in
remote Asia   266 **Cham** Khan   276 **use** interest

dice; therefore your Grace may well say I have
lost it.

280 DON PEDRO You have put him down, lady; you have
put him down.

BEATRICE So I would not he should do me, my lord,
lest I should prove the mother of fools. I have
brought Count Claudio, whom you sent me to seek.

285 DON PEDRO Why, how now, Count? Wherefore are
you sad?

CLAUDIO Not sad, my lord.

DON PEDRO How then? Sick?

CLAUDIO Neither, my lord.

290 BEATRICE The Count is neither sad, nor sick, nor
merry, nor well; but civil Count, civil as an orange,
and something of that jealous complexion.

DON PEDRO I' faith, lady, I think your blazon to be
true; though I'll be sworn, if he be so, his conceit
295 is false. Here, Claudio, I have wooed in thy name,
and fair Hero is won. I have broke with her father,
and his good will obtained. Name the day of marriage, and God give thee joy!

LEONATO Count, take of me my daughter, and with
300 her my fortunes. His Grace hath made the match,
and all grace say amen to it!

BEATRICE Speak, Count, 'tis your cue.

CLAUDIO Silence is the perfectest herald of joy. I were
but little happy if I could say how much. Lady, as
305 you are mine, I am yours. I give away myself for
you and dote upon the exchange.

BEATRICE Speak, cousin; or (if you cannot) stop his
mouth with a kiss and let not him speak neither.

283 **fools babies**   291 **civil** polite (with a pun on orange of Seville)
292 **complexion** (1) disposition (2) color (i.e., yellowish for jealousy)
293 **blazon** description   294 **conceit** idea, concept

DON PEDRO In faith, lady, you have a merry heart.

BEATRICE Yea, my lord; I thank it, poor fool, it keeps   310
on the windy side of care. My cousin tells him in
his ear that he is in her heart.

CLAUDIO And so she doth, cousin.

BEATRICE Good Lord, for alliance! Thus goes everyone to the world but I, and I am sunburnt. I may   315
sit in a corner and cry "Heigh-ho for a husband!"

DON PEDRO Lady Beatrice, I will get you one.

BEATRICE I would rather have one of your father's
getting. Hath your Grace ne'er a brother like you?
Your father got excellent husbands, if a maid could   320
come by them.

DON PEDRO Will you have me, lady?

BEATRICE No, my lord, unless I might have another for
working days; your Grace is too costly to wear
every day. But I beseech your Grace pardon me.   325
I was born to speak all mirth and no matter.

DON PEDRO Your silence most offends me, and to be
merry best becomes you, for out o' question you
were born in a merry hour.

BEATRICE No, sure, my lord, my mother cried; but   330
then there was a star danced, and under that was
I born. Cousins, God give you joy!

LEONATO Niece, will you look to those things I told
you of?

BEATRICE I cry you mercy, uncle. By your Grace's   335
pardon.

Exit Beatrice.

DON PEDRO By my troth, a pleasant-spirited lady.

311 **windy** windward, safe   314-15 **Good Lord ... sunburnt** i.e., everyone gets
a husband but me, and I am ugly (**sunburnt** = tanned, and therefore ugly in the
sixteenth century)   319 **getting** begetting   335 **cry you mercy** beg your pardon

LEONATO There's little of the melancholy element in her, my lord. She is never sad but when she sleeps,
340 and not ever sad then; for I have heard my daughter say she hath often dreamt of unhappiness and waked herself with laughing.

DON PEDRO She cannot endure to hear tell of a husband.

345 LEONATO O, by no means! She mocks all her wooers out of suit.

DON PEDRO She were an excellent wife for Benedick.

LEONATO O Lord, my lord! If they were but a week married, they would talk themselves mad.

350 DON PEDRO County Claudio, when mean you to go to church?

CLAUDIO Tomorrow, my lord. Time goes on crutches till Love have all his rites.

LEONATO Not till Monday, my dear son, which is hence
355 a just sevennight; and a time too brief too, to have all things answer my mind.

DON PEDRO Come, you shake the head at so long a breathing; but I warrant thee, Claudio, the time shall not go dully by us. I will in the interim un-
360 dertake one of Hercules' labors, which is, to bring Signior Benedick and the Lady Beatrice into a mountain of affection th' one with th' other. I would fain have it a match, and I doubt not but to fashion it if you three will but minister such assistance as
365 I shall give you direction.

LEONATO My lord, I am for you, though it cost me ten nights' watchings.

CLAUDIO And I, my lord.

DON PEDRO And you too, gentle Hero?

340 ever always   366-67 ten nights' watchings ten nights awake

HERO I will do any modest office, my lord, to help my   370
cousin to a good husband.

DON PEDRO And Benedick is not the unhopefullest
husband that I know. Thus far can I praise him: he
is of a noble strain, of approved valor and confirmed honesty. I will teach you how to humor your   375
cousin, that she shall fall in love with Benedick;
and I [*to Leonato and Claudio*], with your two
helps, will so practice on Benedick that, in despite
of his quick wit and his queasy stomach, he shall
fall in love with Beatrice. If we can do this, Cupid   380
is no longer an archer; his glory shall be ours, for
we are the only love-gods. Go in with me, and I
will tell you my drift.

Exit [*with the others*].

[Scene II. *Leonato's house.*]

Enter [*Don*] *John and Borachio.*

DON JOHN It is so. The Count Claudio shall marry the
daughter of Leonato.

BORACHIO Yea, my lord; but I can cross it.

DON JOHN Any bar, any cross, any impediment will
be medicinable to me. I am sick in displeasure to   5
him, and whatsoever comes athwart his affection
ranges evenly with mine. How canst thou cross
this marriage?

BORACHIO Not honestly, my lord; but so covertly that
no dishonesty shall appear in me.   10

DON JOHN Show me briefly how.

374 **approved** tested   378 **practice on** deceive   II.ii.7 **ranges evenly** goes in a
straight line (i.e., suits me exactly)

BORACHIO I think I told your lordship, a year since, how much I am in the favor of Margaret, the waiting gentlewoman to Hero.

15 DON JOHN I remember.

BORACHIO I can, at any unseasonable instant of the night, appoint her to look out at her lady's chamber window.

DON JOHN What life is in that to be the death of this
20 marriage?

BORACHIO The poison of that lies in you to temper. Go you to the Prince your brother; spare not to tell him that he hath wronged his honor in marrying the renowned Claudio (whose estimation do you
25 mightily hold up) to a contaminated stale, such a one as Hero.

DON JOHN What proof shall I make of that?

BORACHIO Proof enough to misuse the Prince, to vex Claudio, to undo Hero, and kill Leonato. Look you
30 for any other issue?

DON JOHN Only to despite them I will endeavor anything.

BORACHIO Go then; find me a meet hour to draw Don Pedro and the Count Claudio alone; tell them that
35 you know that Hero loves me; intend a kind of zeal both to the Prince and Claudio (as in love of your brother's honor, who hath made this match, and his friend's reputation, who is thus like to be cozened with the semblance of a maid) that you
40 have discovered thus. They will scarcely believe this without trial. Offer them instances; which shall bear no less likelihood than to see me at her chamber window, hear me call Margaret Hero, hear Margaret term me Claudio; and bring them to see
45 this the very night before the intended wedding.

25 **stale** prostitute   33 **meet hour** suitable time   35 **intend** pretend
39 **cozened** cheated   41 **instances** proofs

For in the meantime I will so fashion the matter
that Hero shall be absent; and there shall appear
such seeming truth of Hero's disloyalty that jealousy shall be called assurance and all the preparation overthrown.   50

DON JOHN Grow this to what adverse issue it can, I
will put it in practice. Be cunning in the working
this, and thy fee is a thousand ducats.

BORACHIO Be you constant in the accusation, and my
cunning shall not shame me.   55

DON JOHN I will presently go learn their day of marriage.
                                        Exit [with Borachio].

[Scene III. *Leonato's garden.*]

                    Enter Benedick alone.

BENEDICK Boy!

                    [*Enter Boy.*]

BOY Signior?

BENEDICK In my chamber window lies a book. Bring it
hither to me in the orchard.

BOY I am here already, sir.   5

BENEDICK I know that, but I would have thee hence
and here again. (*Exit [Boy].*) I do much wonder
that one man, seeing how much another man is a
fool when he dedicates his behaviors to love, will,
after he hath laughed at such shallow follies in   10
others, become the argument of his own scorn by

48-49 **jealousy** mistrust II.iii.4 **orchard** garden   11 **argument** subject matter

falling in love; and such a man is Claudio. I have
known when there was no music with him but the
drum and the fife; and now had he rather hear the
15 tabor and the pipe. I have known when he would
have walked ten mile afoot to see a good armor; and
now will he lie ten nights awake carving the fashion
of a new doublet. He was wont to speak plain and
to the purpose, like an honest man and a soldier;
20 and now is he turned orthography; his words are
a very fantastical banquet—just so many strange
dishes. May I be so converted and see with these
eyes? I cannot tell; I think not. I will not be sworn
but love may transform me to an oyster; but I'll take
25 my oath on it, till he have made an oyster of me he
shall never make me such a fool. One woman is fair,
yet I am well; another is wise, yet I am well; another
virtuous, yet I am well. But till all graces be in one
woman, one woman shall not come in my grace.
30 Rich she shall be, that's certain; wise, or I'll none;
virtuous, or I'll never cheapen her; fair, or I'll never
look on her; mild, or come not near me; noble, or
not I for an angel; of good discourse, an excellent
musician, and her hair shall be of what color it
35 please God. Ha, the Prince and Monsieur Love!
[*Retiring*] I will hide me in the arbor.

Enter Prince [Don Pedro], Leonato, Claudio,
[to the sound of] music.

DON PEDRO Come, shall we hear this music?

CLAUDIO Yea, my good lord. How still the evening is,
As hushed on purpose to grace harmony!

40 DON PEDRO See you where Benedick hath hid himself?

---

15 **tabor and the pipe** music of an unmartial sort   17 **carving the fashion**
considering the design   20 **orthography** i.e., into a pedant (?)   31 **cheapen**
bargain for   32-33 **noble ... angel** (puns: both words are Elizabethan coins)
33 **discourse** conversation

CLAUDIO O, very well, my lord. The music ended,
We'll fit the kid fox with a pennyworth.

Enter Balthasar with music.

DON PEDRO Come, Balthasar, we'll hear that song
again.

BALTHASAR O, good my lord, tax not so bad a voice
To slander music any more than once. 45

DON PEDRO It is the witness still of excellency
To put a strange face on his own perfection.
I pray thee sing, and let me woo no more.

BALTHASAR Because you talk of wooing, I will sing,
Since many a wooer doth commence his suit 50
To her he thinks not worthy, yet he woos,
Yet will he swear he loves.

DON PEDRO   Nay, pray thee come;
Or if thou wilt hold longer argument,
Do it in notes.

BALTHASAR   Note this before my notes:
There's not a note of mine that's worth the noting. 55

DON PEDRO Why, these are very crotchets that he
speaks!
Note notes, forsooth, and nothing!   [*Music.*]

BENEDICK [*Aside*] Now divine air! Now is his soul
ravished! Is it not strange that sheep's guts should
hale souls out of men's bodies? Well, a horn for my 60
money, when all's done.   [*Balthasar sings.*]

The Song
Sigh no more, ladies, sigh no more,
Men were deceivers ever,

---

42 We'll ... pennyworth i.e., we'll give Benedick a little something (perhaps **kid fox** means "young fox," perhaps "known fox") 56 **crotchets** (1) whims (2) musical notes 57 **nothing** (pronounced "noting," hence a pun)

One foot in sea, and one on shore,
To one thing constant never.
Then sigh not so,
But let them go,
And be you blithe and bonny,
Converting all your sounds of woe
Into hey nonny, nonny.

Sing no more ditties, sing no moe,
Of dumps so dull and heavy;
The fraud of men was ever so,
Since summer first was leavy.
Then sigh not so, &c.

65

70

75

DON PEDRO By my troth, a good song.

BALTHASAR And an ill singer, my lord.

DON PEDRO Ha, no, no, faith! Thou sing'st well enough for a shift.

80 BENEDICK [*Aside*] And he had been a dog that should have howled thus, they would have hanged him; and I pray God his bad voice bode no mischief. I had as live have heard the night raven, come what plague could have come after it.

85 DON PEDRO Yea, marry. Dost thou hear, Balthasar? I pray thee get us some excellent music; for tomorrow night we would have it at the Lady Hero's chamber window.

BALTHASAR The best I can, my lord.

90 DON PEDRO Do so. Farewell.
                                    Exit Balthasar [with Musicians].

Come hither, Leonato. What was it you told me of today? That your niece Beatrice was in love with Signior Benedick?

CLAUDIO O, ay! [*In a low voice to Don Pedro*] Stalk on,

72 **dumps** sad songs   79 **shift** makeshift   83 **live** lief

stalk on; the fowl sits. [*In full voice*] I did never 95
think that lady would have loved any man.

LEONATO No, nor I neither; but most wonderful that
she should so dote on Signior Benedick, whom she
hath in all outward behaviors seemed ever to abhor.

BENEDICK [*Aside*] Is't possible? Sits the wind in that 100
corner?

LEONATO By my troth, my lord, I cannot tell what to
think of it, but that she loves him with an enraged
affection, it is past the infinite of thought.

DON PEDRO May be she doth but counterfeit. 105

CLAUDIO Faith, like enough.

LEONATO O God, counterfeit? There was never counterfeit of passion came so near the life of passion as
she discovers it.

DON PEDRO Why, what effects of passion shows she? 110

CLAUDIO [*In a low voice*] Bait the hook well! This fish
will bite.

LEONATO What effects, my lord? She will sit you, you
heard my daughter tell you how.

CLAUDIO She did indeed. 115

DON PEDRO How, how, I pray you? You amaze me!
I would have thought her spirit had been invincible
against all assaults of affection.

LEONATO I would have sworn it had, my lord—especially against Benedick. 120

BENEDICK [*Aside*] I should think this a gull but that
the white-bearded fellow speaks it. Knavery cannot,
sure, hide himself in such reverence.

CLAUDIO [*In a low voice*] He hath ta'en th' infection;
hold it up. 125

109 **discovers** reveals, betrays 121 **gull** trick 125 **hold** keep

DON PEDRO Hath she made her affection known to Benedick?

LEONATO No, and swears she never will. That's her torment.

130 CLAUDIO 'Tis true indeed. So your daughter says. "Shall I," says she, "that have so oft encount'red him with scorn, write to him that I love him?"

LEONATO This says she now when she is beginning to write to him; for she'll be up twenty times a night, 135 and there will she sit in her smock till she have writ a sheet of paper. My daughter tells us all.

CLAUDIO Now you talk of a sheet of paper, I remember a pretty jest your daughter told us of.

LEONATO O, when she had writ it, and was reading it 140 over, she found "Benedick" and "Beatrice" between the sheet?

CLAUDIO That.

LEONATO O, she tore the letter into a thousand half-pence, railed at herself that she should be so im-145 modest to write to one that she knew would flout her. "I measure him," says she, "by my own spirit; for I should flout him if he writ to me. Yea, though I love him, I should."

CLAUDIO Then down upon her knees she falls, weeps, 150 sobs, beats her heart, tears her hair, prays, curses— "O sweet Benedick! God give me patience!"

LEONATO She doth indeed; my daughter says so; and the ecstasy hath so much overborne her that my daughter is sometime afeard she will do a des-155 perate outrage to herself. It is very true.

DON PEDRO It were good that Benedick knew of it by some other, if she will not discover it.

143-44 halfpence i.e., small pieces   153 ecstasy madness

CLAUDIO To what end? He would make but a sport of
it and torment the poor lady worse.

DON PEDRO And he should, it were an alms to hang   160
him! She's an excellent sweet lady, and, out of all
suspicion, she is virtuous.

CLAUDIO And she is exceeding wise.

DON PEDRO In everything but in loving Benedick.

LEONATO O, my lord, wisdom and blood combating   165
in so tender a body, we have ten proofs to one that
blood hath the victory. I am sorry for her, as I have
just cause, being her uncle and her guardian.

DON PEDRO I would she had bestowed this dotage on
me; I would have daffed all other respects and   170
made her half myself. I pray you tell Benedick of it
and hear what'a will say.

LEONATO Were it good, think you?

CLAUDIO Hero thinks surely she will die; for she says
she will die if he love her not, and she will die ere   175
she make her love known, and she will die, if he
woo her, rather than she will bate one breath of
her accustomed crossness.

DON PEDRO She doth well. If she should make tender
of her love, 'tis very possible he'll scorn it; for the   180
man, as you know all, hath a contemptible spirit.

CLAUDIO He is a very proper man.

DON PEDRO He hath indeed a good outward happiness.

CLAUDIO Before God, and in my mind, very wise.

DON PEDRO He doth indeed show some sparks that are   185
like wit.

---

160 an alms a charity   165 blood passion   170 daffed all other respects put
aside all other considerations (i.e. of disparity in rank)   177 bate abate, give up
179 tender offer   181 contemptible disdainful   182 proper handsome   186 wit
intelligence

CLAUDIO And I take him to be valiant.

DON PEDRO As Hector, I assure you. And in the managing of quarrels you may say he is wise, for either he avoids them with great discretion, or undertakes them with a most Christianlike fear.

LEONATO If he do fear God, 'a must necessarily keep peace. If he break the peace, he ought to enter into a quarrel with fear and trembling.

DON PEDRO And so will he do; for the man doth fear God, howsoever it seems not in him by some large jests he will make. Well, I am sorry for your niece. Shall we go seek Benedick and tell him of her love?

CLAUDIO Never tell him, my lord; let her wear it out with good counsel.

LEONATO Nay, that's impossible; she may wear her heart out first.

DON PEDRO Well, we will hear further of it by your daughter. Let it cool the while. I love Benedick well, and I could wish he would modestly examine himself to see how much he is unworthy so good a lady.

LEONATO My lord, will you walk? Dinner is ready.
                                        [*They walk away.*]

CLAUDIO If he do not dote on her upon this, I will never trust my expectation.

DON PEDRO Let there be the same net spread for her, and that must your daughter and her gentlewomen carry. The sport will be, when they hold one an opinion of another's dotage, and no such matter. That's the scene that I would see, which will be merely a dumb show. Let us send her to call him in to dinner.
                    [*Exeunt Don Pedro, Claudio, and Leonato.*]

196-97 **large jests** broad jokes   212 **carry** manage   215 **dumb show** pantomime (because of embarrassment)

BENEDICK [*Advancing*] This can be no trick; the conference was sadly borne. They have the truth of
this from Hero. They seem to pity the lady; it seems
her affections have their full bent. Love me? Why, 220
it must be requited. I hear how I am censured. They
say I will bear myself proudly if I perceive the love
come from her. They say too that she will rather die
than give any sign of affection. I did never think to
marry; I must not seem proud. Happy are they that 225
hear their detractions and can put them to mending.
They say the lady is fair—'tis a truth, I can bear
them witness; and virtuous—'tis so, I cannot reprove
it; and wise, but for loving me; by my troth, it is
no addition to her wit, nor no great argument of her 230
folly; for I will be horribly in love with her. I may
chance have some odd quirks and remnants of wit
broken on me because I have railed so long against
marriage; but doth not the appetite alter? A man
loves the meat in his youth that he cannot endure 235
in his age. Shall quips and sentences and these
paper bullets of the brain awe a man from the
career of his humor? No, the world must be peopled. When I said I would die a bachelor, I did not
think I should live till I were married. Here comes 240
Beatrice. By this day, she's a fair lady. I do spy
some marks of love in her.

Enter Beatrice.

BEATRICE Against my will I am sent to bid you come
in to dinner.

BENEDICK Fair Beatrice, I thank you for your pains. 245

BEATRICE   I took no more pains for those thanks than
you take pains to thank me. If it had been painful,
I would not have come.

218 **sadly** seriously   220 **affections have their full bent** emotions are tightly
stretched (like a bent bow)   236 **sentences** maxims   238 **career** course

BENEDICK You take pleasure then in the message?

250 BEATRICE Yea, just so much as you may take upon a
knife's point, and choke a daw withal. You have
no stomach, signior? Fare you well.   *Exit*.

BENEDICK Ha! "Against my will I am sent to bid you
come in to dinner." There's a double meaning in
255 that. "I took no more pains for those thanks than
you took pains to thank me." That's as much as to
say, "Any pains that I take for you is as easy as
thanks." If I do not take pity of her, I am a villain;
if I do not love her, I am a Jew. I will go get her
260 picture.   *Exit*.

251 **withal** with   252 **no stomach** no wish to argue (as well as "no appetite")

[ACT III

Scene I. *Leonato's garden.*]

*Enter Hero and two Gentlewomen, Margaret
and Ursula.*

HERO Good Margaret, run thee to the parlor.
There shalt thou find my cousin Beatrice
Proposing with the Prince and Claudio.
Whisper her ear and tell her, I and Ursley
Walk in the orchard, and our whole discourse   5
Is all of her. Say that thou overheard'st us;
And bid her steal into the pleachèd bower,
Where honeysuckles, ripened by the sun,
Forbid the sun to enter—like favorites,
Made proud by princes, that advance their pride   10
Against that power that bred it. There will she hide
    her
To listen our propose. This is thy office;
Bear thee well in it and leave us alone.

MARGARET I'll make her come, I warrant you, presently.
                                                            [*Exit.*]

HERO Now, Ursula, when Beatrice doth come,   15
As we do trace this alley up and down,

***

III.i.3 **Proposing with** talking to   10-11 **Made proud ... bred it** (an Elizabethan audience of *c.*1600 would be reminded of the Earl of Essex)   12 **office**
duty   16 **trace** walk

Our talk must only be of Benedick.
When I do name him, let it be thy part
To praise him more than ever man did merit.
20   My talk to thee must be how Benedick
Is sick in love with Beatrice. Of this matter
Is little Cupid's crafty arrow made,
That only wounds by hearsay.

Enter Beatrice.

Now begin;
For look where Beatrice like a lapwing runs
25   Close by the ground, to hear our conference.

URSULA The pleasant'st angling is to see the fish
Cut with her golden oars the silver stream
And greedily devour the treacherous bait;
So angle we for Beatrice, who even now
30   Is couchèd in the woodbine coverture.
Fear you not my part of the dialogue.

HERO Then go we near her, that her ear lose nothing
Of the false sweet bait that we lay for it.
[*They approach the bower.*]
No, truly, Ursula, she is too disdainful.
35   I know her spirits are as coy and wild
As haggards of the rock.

URSULA   But are you sure
That Benedick loves Beatrice so entirely?

HERO So says the Prince, and my new-trothèd lord.

URSULA And did they bid you tell her of it, madam?

40   HERO They did entreat me to acquaint her of it;
But I persuaded them, if they loved Benedick,
To wish him wrestle with affection
And never to let Beatrice know of it.

URSULA Why did you so? Doth not the gentleman

22 **crafty** skillfully wrought   23 **only** solely   30 **woodbine coverture** honey-suckle thicket   35 **coy** disdainful   36 **haggards** wild and intractable hawks

Deserve as full as fortunate a bed   45
As ever Beatrice shall couch upon?

HERO O god of love! I know he doth deserve
As much as may be yielded to a man;
But Nature never framed a woman's heart
Of prouder stuff than that of Beatrice.   50
Disdain and Scorn ride sparkling in her eyes,
Misprizing what they look on; and her wit
Values itself so highly that to her
All matter else seems weak. She cannot love,
Nor take no shape nor project of affection,   55
She is so self-endeared.

URSULA   Sure I think so;
And therefore certainly it were not good
She knew his love, lest she'll make sport at it.

HERO Why, you speak truth. I never yet saw man,
How wise, how noble, young, how rarely featured,   60
But she would spell him backward. If fair-faced,
She would swear the gentleman should be her sister;
If black, why, Nature, drawing of an antic,
Made a foul blot; if tall, a lance ill-headed;
If low, an agate very vilely cut;   65
If speaking, why, a vane blown with all winds;
If silent, why, a block movèd with none.
So turns she every man the wrong side out
And never gives to truth and virtue that
Which simpleness and merit purchaseth.   70

URSULA Sure, sure, such carping is not commendable.

HERO No, not to be so odd, and from all fashions,
As Beatrice is, cannot be commendable.
But who dare tell her so? If I should speak,
She would mock me into air; O, she would laugh me   75
Out of myself, press me to death with wit!
Therefore let Benedick, like covered fire,

52 **Misprizing** despising 55 **project** notion 63 **black** dark-complexioned
63 **antic** grotesque figure 65 **agate very vilely cut** poorly done miniature
72 **from all fashions** contrary

Consume away in sighs, waste inwardly.
It were a better death than die with mocks,
80   Which is as bad as die with tickling.

URSULA Yet tell her of it. Hear what she will say.

HERO No; rather I will go to Benedick
And counsel him to fight against his passion.
And truly, I'll devise some honest slanders
85   To stain my cousin with. One doth not know
How much an ill word may empoison liking.

URSULA O, do not do your cousin such a wrong!
She cannot be so much without true judgment
(Having so swift and excellent a wit
90   As she is prized to have) as to refuse
So rare a gentleman as Signior Benedick.

HERO He is the only man of Italy,
Always excepted my dear Claudio.

URSULA I pray you be not angry with me, madam,
95   Speaking my fancy. Signior Benedick,
For shape, for bearing, argument, and valor,
Goes foremost in report through Italy.

HERO Indeed he hath an excellent good name.

URSULA His excellence did earn it ere he had it.
100   When are you married, madam?

HERO Why, everyday tomorrow! Come, go in.
I'll show thee some attires, and have thy counsel
Which is the best to furnish me tomorrow.
                              [*They walk away.*]

URSULA She's limed, I warrant you! We have caught
her, madam.

105 HERO If it prove so, then loving goes by haps;
Some Cupid kills with arrows, some with traps.
                              [*Exeunt Hero and Ursula.*]

84 **honest** appropriate   101 **everyday tomorrow** i.e., tomorrow I shall be
married forever   103 **furnish** dress   104 **limed** caught (as a bird is caught in
birdlime, a sticky substance smeared on branches)   105 **haps** chance

BEATRICE *[Coming forward]* What fire is in mine ears?
    Can this be true?
    Stand I condemned for pride and scorn so much?
Contempt, farewell! And maiden pride, adieu!
    No glory lives behind the back of such.   110
And, Benedick, love on; I will requite thee,
    Taming my wild heart to thy loving hand.
If thou dost love, my kindness shall incite thee
    To bind our loves up in a holy band;
For others say thou dost deserve, and I   115
Believe it better than reportingly.   *Exit.*

[Scene II. *Leonato's house.*]

*Enter Prince [Don Pedro], Claudio, Benedick,
and Leonato.*

DON PEDRO I do but stay till your marriage be consummate, and then go I toward Aragon.

CLAUDIO I'll bring you thither, my lord, if you'll vouchsafe me.

DON PEDRO Nay, that would be as great a soil in the   5
new gloss of your marriage as to show a child his
new coat and forbid him to wear it. I will only be
bold with Benedick for his company; for, from the
crown of his head to the sole of his foot, he is all
mirth. He hath twice or thrice cut Cupid's bow-   10
string, and the little hangman dare not shoot at him.
He hath a heart as sound as a bell; and his tongue
is the clapper, for what his heart thinks, his tongue
speaks.

BENEDICK Gallants, I am not as I have been.   15

116 **reportingly** i.e., mere hearsay   III.ii.3-4 **vouchsafe** permit   10-11 **cut Cupid's bowstring** i.e., avoided falling in love

LEONATO So say I. Methinks you are sadder.

CLAUDIO I hope he be in love.

DON PEDRO Hang him truant? There's no true drop of
blood in him to be truly touched with love. If he be
20   sad, he wants money.

BENEDICK I have the toothache.

DON PEDRO Draw it.

BENEDICK Hang it!

CLAUDIO You must hang it first and draw it afterwards.

25   DON PEDRO What? Sigh for the toothache?

LEONATO Where is but a humor or a worm.

BENEDICK Well, everyone cannot master a grief but
he that has it.

CLAUDIO Yet say I he is in love.

30   DON PEDRO There is no appearance of fancy in him,
unless it be a fancy that he hath to strange disguises;
as to be a Dutchman today, a Frenchman tomorrow; or in the shape of two countries at once, as a
German from the waist downward, all slops, and
35   a Spaniard from the hip upward, no doublet. Unless he have a fancy to this foolery, as it appears he
hath, he is no fool for fancy, as you would have
it appear he is.

CLAUDIO If he be not in love with some woman, there
40   is no believing old signs; 'a brushes his hat o'
mornings. What should that bode?

---

16 **sadder** graver 18 **truant** i.e., as unfaithful to his antiromantic stance
22 **Draw it** extract it (but **draw** also means eviscerate; traitors were hanged,
drawn, and quartered. **Draw it** thus leads to the exclamation **Hang it**) 26 **a
humor or a worm** (supposed causes of tooth decay, **humor** = secretion)
27-28 **Well … has it** i.e., a man has to have a grief first before he can master it
(Benedick does not admit that he has a grief; but some editors emend **cannot** to
"can") 30 **fancy** love 34 **slops** loose breeches 35 **doublet** close-fitting jacket

DON PEDRO Hath any man seen him at the barber's?

CLAUDIO No, but the barber's man hath been seen with him, and the old ornament of his cheek hath already stuffed tennis balls. 45

LEONATO Indeed he looks younger than he did, by the loss of a beard.

DON PEDRO Nay, 'a rubs himself with civet. Can you smell him out by that?

CLAUDIO That's as much as to say, the sweet youth's in love. 50

DON PEDRO The greatest note of it is his melancholy.

CLAUDIO And when was he wont to wash his face?

DON PEDRO Yea, or to paint himself? For the which I hear what they say of him. 55

CLAUDIO Nay, but his jesting spirit, which is now crept into a lutestring, and now governed by stops.

DON PEDRO Indeed that tells a heavy tale for him. Conclude, conclude, he is in love.

CLAUDIO Nay, but I know who loves him. 60

DON PEDRO That would I know too. I warrant, one that knows him not.

CLAUDIO Yes, and his ill conditions; and in despite of all, dies for him.

DON PEDRO She shall be buried with her face upwards. 65

BENEDICK Yet is this no charm for the toothache. Old

44-45 the old ornament ... tennis balls (cf. Beatrice's remark, II.i.29-30 "I could not endure a husband with a beard on his face")   48 civet perfume   54 to paint himself to use cosmetics   57 stops frets (on the lute)   63 conditions qualities   63-64 in despite of all notwithstanding   64 dies (1) pines away (2) is willing to "die" in the act of sex   65-66 She shall ... upwards (continues sexual innuendo)

signior, walk aside with me; I have studied eight or
nine wise words to speak to you, which these hobby-
70   horses must not hear.

[Exeunt Benedick and Leonato.]

DON PEDRO For my life, to break with him about Beatrice!

CLAUDIO 'Tis even so. Hero and Margaret have by
this played their parts with Beatrice, and then the
75   two bears will not bite another when they meet.

Enter John the Bastard.

DON JOHN My lord and brother, God save you.

DON PEDRO Good den, brother.

DON JOHN If your leisure served, I would speak with
you.

80   DON PEDRO In private?

DON JOHN If it please you. Yet Count Claudio may
hear, for what I would speak of concerns him.

DON PEDRO What's the matter?

DON JOHN *[To Claudio]* Means your lordship to be
85   married tomorrow?

DON PEDRO You know he does.

DON JOHN I know not that, when he knows what I
know.

CLAUDIO If there be any impediment, I pray you dis-
90   cover it.

DON JOHN You may think I love you not; let that appear hereafter, and aim better at me by that I
now will manifest. For my brother (I think he holds
you well, and in dearness of heart) hath holp to

69-70 **hobbyhorses** jokers (originally an imitation horse fastened around the waist
of a morris dancer)   77 **Good den** good evening   92 **aim better at me** judge
better of me   92 **that** that which

effect your ensuing marriage—surely suit ill spent   95
and labor ill bestowed!

DON PEDRO Why, what's the matter?

DON JOHN I came hither to tell you, and, circumstances short'ned (for she has been too long a-talk-
ing of), the lady is disloyal.   100

CLAUDIO Who? Hero?

DON JOHN Even she—Leonato's Hero, your Hero,
every man's Hero.

CLAUDIO Disloyal?

DON JOHN The word is too good to paint out her wick-   105
edness. I could say she were worse. Think you of
a worse title, and I will fit her to it. Wonder not
till further warrant. Go but with me tonight, you
shall see her chamber window ent'red, even the
night before her wedding day. If you love her then,   110
tomorrow wed her. But it would better fit your
honor to change your mind.

CLAUDIO May this be so?

DON PEDRO I will not think it.

DON JOHN If you dare not trust that you see, confess   115
not that you know. If you will follow me, I will
show you enough; and when you have seen more
and heard more, proceed accordingly.

CLAUDIO If I see anything tonight why I should not
marry her tomorrow, in the congregation where I   120
should wed, there will I shame her.

DON PEDRO And, as I wooed for thee to obtain her, I
will join with thee to disgrace her.

DON JOHN I will disparage her no farther till you are
my witnesses. Bear it coldly but till midnight, and   125
let the issue show itself.

125 coldly calmly

DON PEDRO O day untowardly turned!

CLAUDIO O mischief strangely thwarting!

DON JOHN O plague right well prevented! So will you
130   say when you have seen the sequel.   [*Exeunt.*]

[Scene III. *A street.*]

Enter Dogberry and his compartner [Verges,]
with the Watch.

DOGBERRY Are you good men and true?

VERGES Yea, or else it were pity but they should suffer
salvation, body and soul.

DOGBERRY Nay, that were a punishment too good for
5   them if they should have any allegiance in them,
being chosen for the Prince's watch.

VERGES Well, give them their charge, neighbor Dogberry.

DOGBERRY First, who think you the most desartless
10   man to be constable?

FIRST WATCH Hugh Oatcake, sir, or George Seacole,
for they can write and read.

DOGBERRY Come hither, neighbor Seacole. God hath
blessed you with a good name. To be a well-favored
15   man is the gift of fortune, but to write and read
comes by nature.

SECOND WATCH Both which, Master Constable—

DOGBERRY You have; I knew it would be your answer.
Well, for your favor, sir, why, give God thanks and

III.iii.3 **salvation** damnation (the beginning of the malapropisms basic to the
comedy of Dogberry and Verges) 7 **charge** instructions 14 **well-favored**
handsome

make no boast of it; and for your writing and read- 20
ing, let that appear when there is no need of such
vanity. You are thought here to be the most senseless and fit man for the constable of the watch.
Therefore bear you the lanthorn. This is your
charge: you shall comprehend all vagrom men; 25
you are to bid any man stand, in the Prince's
name.

SECOND WATCH How if 'a will not stand?

DOGBERRY Why then, take no note of him, but let him
go, and presently call the rest of the watch together 30
and thank God you are rid of a knave.

VERGES If he will not stand when he is bidden, he is
none of the Prince's subjects.

DOGBERRY True, and they are to meddle with none but
the Prince's subjects. You shall also make no noise 35
in the streets; for, for the watch to babble and to
talk is most tolerable, and not to be endured.

WATCH We will rather sleep than talk; we know what
belongs to a watch.

DOGBERRY Why, you speak like an ancient and most 40
quiet watchman, for I cannot see how sleeping
should offend. Only, have a care that your bills
be not stol'n. Well, you are to call at all the ale-
houses and bid those that are drunk get them to
bed. 45

WATCH How if they will not?

DOGBERRY Why then, let them alone till they are sober.
If they make you not then the better answer, you
may say they are not the men you took them for.

WATCH Well, sir. 50

25 comprehend all vagrom i.e., apprehend all vagrant   26 stand halt, stop
38 Watch (neither the Quarto nor the Folio differentiates again between First
Watch and Second Watch until the end of this scene)   42 bills constables' pikes

DOGBERRY If you meet a thief, you may suspect him, by virtue of your office, to be no true man; and for such kind of men, the less you meddle or make with them, why, the more is for your honesty.

55 WATCH If we know him to be a thief, shall we not lay hands on him?

DOGBERRY Truly, by your office you may; but I think they that touch pitch will be defiled. The most peaceable way for you, if you do take a thief, is to 60 let him show himself what he is, and steal out of your company.

VERGES You have been always called a merciful man, partner.

DOGBERRY Truly, I would not hang a dog by my will, 65 much more a man who hath any honesty in him.

VERGES If you hear a child cry in the night, you must call to the nurse and bid her still it.

WATCH How if the nurse be asleep and will not hear us?

70 DOGBERRY Why then, depart in peace and let the child wake her with crying; for the ewe that will not hear her lamb when it baes will never answer a calf when he bleats.

VERGES 'Tis very true.

75 DOGBERRY This is the end of the charge: you, constable, are to present the Prince's own person. If you meet the Prince in the night, you may stay him.

VERGES Nay, by'r lady, that I think 'a cannot.

DOGBERRY Five shillings to one on't, with any man 80 that knows the statutes, he may stay him! Marry, not without the Prince be willing; for indeed the watch ought to offend no man, and it is an offense to stay a man against his will.

VERGES By'r lady, I think it be so.

DOGBERRY Ha, ah, ha! Well, masters, good night. And   85
there be any matter of weight chances, call up me.
Keep your fellows' counsels and your own, and
good night. Come, neighbor.

WATCH Well, masters, we hear our charge. Let us go
sit here upon the church bench till two, and then   90
all to bed.

DOGBERRY One word more, honest neighbors. I pray
you watch about Signior Leonato's door; for the
wedding being there tomorrow, there is a great coil
tonight. Adieu. Be vigitant, I beseech you.   95
                    Exeunt [Dogberry and Verges].

                Enter Borachio and Conrade.

BORACHIO What, Conrade!

WATCH [*Aside*] Peace! Stir not!

BORACHIO Conrade, I say!

CONRADE Here, man. I am at thy elbow.

BORACHIO Mass, and my elbow itched; I thought there   100
would a scab follow.

CONRADE I will owe thee an answer for that; and now
forward with thy tale.

BORACHIO Stand thee close then under this penthouse,
for it drizzles rain, and I will, like a true drunkard,   105
utter all to thee.

WATCH [*Aside*] Some treason, masters; yet stand close.

BORACHIO Therefore know I have earned of Don John
a thousand ducats.

CONRADE Is it possible that any villainy should be so   110
dear?

94 **coil** to-do, turmoil 100 **Mass** (an interjection, from "by the Mass")
101 **scab** (1) crust over a wound (2) contemptible person 104 **penthouse** shed,
lean-to 105 **drunkard** (his name is based on the Spanish *borracho,* "drunkard")

BORACHIO Thou shouldst rather ask if it were possible any villainy should be so rich; for when rich villains have need of poor ones, poor ones may
115   make what price they will.

CONRADE I wonder at it.

BORACHIO That shows thou art unconfirmed. Thou knowest that the fashion of a doublet, or a hat, or a cloak, is nothing to a man.

120   CONRADE Yes, it is apparel.

BORACHIO I mean the fashion.

CONRADE Yes, the fashion is the fashion.

BORACHIO Tush! I may as well say the fool's the fool. But seest thou not what a deformed thief this fash-
125   ion is?

WATCH [Aside] I know that Deformed; 'a has been a vile thief this seven year; 'a goes up and down like a gentleman. I remember his name.

BORACHIO Didst thou not hear somebody?

130   CONRADE No; 'twas the vane on the house.

BORACHIO Seest thou not, I say, what a deformed thief this fashion is? How giddily 'a turns about all the hotbloods between fourteen and five-and-thirty? Sometimes fashioning them like Pharaoh's soldiers
135   in the reechy painting, sometime like god Bel's priests in the old church window, sometime like the shaven Hercules in the smirched worm-eaten tapestry, where his codpiece seems as massy as his club?

140   CONRADE All this I see; and I see that the fashion wears out more apparel than the man. But art not thou thyself giddy with the fashion too, that thou

117 unconfirmed innocent   119 is nothing to a man i.e., fails to reveal his actual character   135 reechy grimy, filthy   135-36 god Bel's priests (from the Apocrypha)   138 codpiece (decorative pouch at the fly of a sixteenth-century man's breeches)

hast shifted out of thy tale into telling me of the fashion?

BORACHIO Not so neither. But know that I have tonight   145
wooed Margaret, the Lady Hero's gentlewoman, by
the name of Hero. She leans me out at her mistress'
chamber window, bids me a thousand times good
night. I tell this tale vilely—I should first tell thee
how the Prince, Claudio, and my master, planted   150
and placed and possessed by my master Don John,
saw afar off in the orchard this amiable encounter.

CONRADE And thought they Margaret was Hero?

BORACHIO Two of them did, the Prince and Claudio;
but the devil my master knew she was Margaret;   155
and partly by his oaths, which first possessed them,
partly by the dark night, which did deceive them,
but chiefly by my villainy, which did confirm any
slander that Don John had made, away went Claudio enraged; swore he would meet her, as he was   160
appointed, next morning at the temple, and there,
before the whole congregation, shame her with
what he saw o'ernight and send her home again
without a husband.

FIRST WATCH We charge you in the Prince's name   165
stand!

SECOND WATCH Call up the right Master Constable.
We have here recovered the most dangerous piece
of lechery that ever was known in the commonwealth.   170

FIRST WATCH And one Deformed is one of them; I
know him; 'a wears a lock.

CONRADE Masters, masters—

SECOND WATCH You'll be made bring Deformed forth,
I warrant you.   175

151 **possessed** informed, deluded   172 **lock** lovelock, curl of hair hanging by the
ear

CONRADE Masters, never speak; we charge you let us obey you to go with us.

BORACHIO We are like to prove a goodly commodity, being taken up of these men's bills.

180 CONRADE A commodity in question, I warrant you. Come, we'll obey you.   *Exeunt.*

[Scene IV. *Leonato's house.*]

Enter Hero, and Margaret, and Ursula.

HERO Good Ursula, wake my cousin Beatrice and desire her to rise.

URSULA I will, lady.

HERO And bid her come hither.

5 URSULA Well.   [*Exit.*]

MARGARET Troth, I think your other rabato were better.

HERO No, pray thee, good Meg, I'll wear this.

MARGARET By my troth, 's not so good, and I warrant
10   your cousin will say so.

HERO My cousin's a fool, and thou art another. I'll wear none but this.

MARGARET I like the new tire within excellently, if the hair were a thought browner; and your gown's

176-77 **Masters ... with us** (Conrade is mocking the language of the Second Watch; he means, "Say no more, we will go along with you")   178-79 **We are ... bills** (Borachio continues the mockery with a series of puns: **commodity** [1] merchandise [2] profit; **taken up** [1] arrested [2] bought on credit; **bills** [1] pikes [2] bonds or sureties)   180 **in question** (1) subject to judicial examination (2) of doubtful value   III.iv.6 **rabato** ruff   13 **tire** headdress   13 **within** in the next room

a most rare fashion, i' faith. I saw the Duchess of   15
Milan's gown that they praise so.

HERO O, that exceeds, they say.

MARGARET By my troth, 's but a nightgown in respect
of yours—cloth o' gold and cuts, and laced with
silver, set with pearls, down sleeves, side-sleeves,   20
and skirts, round underborne with a bluish tinsel.
But for a fine, quaint, graceful, and excellent fashion, yours is worth ten on't.

HERO God give me joy to wear it, for my heart is exceeding heavy.   25

MARGARET 'Twill be heavier soon by the weight of a
man.

HERO Fie upon thee! Art not ashamed?

MARGARET Of what, lady? Of speaking honorably? Is
not marriage honorable in a beggar? Is not your   30
lord honorable without marriage? I think you would
have me say, "saving your reverence, a husband."
And bad thinking do not wrest true speaking, I'll
offend nobody. Is there any harm in "the heavier
for a husband"? None, I think, and it be the right   35
husband and the right wife; otherwise 'tis light,
and not heavy. Ask my Lady Beatrice else. Here
she comes.

Enter Beatrice.

HERO Good morrow, coz.

BEATRICE Good morrow, sweet Hero.   40

HERO Why, how now? Do you speak in the sick tune?

BEATRICE I am out of all other tune, methinks.

---

18 **nightgown** dressing gown 19 **cuts** slashes to show rich fabric
underneath 20 **down sleeves, side-sleeves** long sleeves covering the arms, open
sleeves hanging from the shoulder 22 **quaint** pretty, dainty 36 **light** (pun on
"wanton")

MARGARET Clap's into "Light o' love." That goes without a burden. Do you sing it, and I'll dance it.

45 BEATRICE Ye light o' love with your heels! Then, if your husband have stables enough, you'll see he shall lack no barns.

MARGARET O illegitimate construction! I scorn that with my heels.

50 BEATRICE 'Tis almost five o'clock, cousin; 'tis time you were ready. By my troth, I am exceeding ill. Heigh-ho!

MARGARET For a hawk, a horse, or a husband?

BEATRICE For the letter that begins them all, *H*.

55 MARGARET Well, and you be not turned Turk, there's no more sailing by the star.

BEATRICE What means the fool, trow?

MARGARET Nothing I; but God send everyone their heart's desire!

60 HERO These gloves the Count sent me, they are an excellent perfume.

BEATRICE I am stuffed, cousin; I cannot smell.

MARGARET A maid, and stuffed! There's goodly catching of cold.

65 BEATRICE O, God help me! God help me! How long have you professed apprehension?

MARGARET Ever since you left it. Doth not my wit become me rarely?

BEATRICE It is not seen enough. You should wear it in
70   your cap. By my troth, I am sick.

MARGARET Get you some of this distilled *Carduus*

43 **Clap's into** let us sing   44 **burden** bass part (with pun on "the heavier for a husband")   45 **Ye ... your heels** (sexual innuendo)   47 **barns** (pun on "bairns," children)   54 **H** ("ache" was pronounced "aitch")   55 **turned Turk** completely changed   57 **trow** I wonder   62 **I am stuffed** I have a head cold   63 **stuffed** filled (as with a child)   66 **apprehension** wit

Benedictus and lay it to your heart. It is the only thing for a qualm.

HERO There thou prick'st her with a thistle.

BEATRICE *Benedictus?* Why *Benedictus?* You have some moral in this *Benedictus.*   75

MARGARET Moral? No, by my troth, I have no moral meaning. I meant plain holy thistle. You may think perchance that I think you are in love. Nay, by'r lady, I am not such a fool to think what I list; nor   80 I list not to think what I can; nor indeed I cannot think, if I would think my heart out of thinking, that you are in love, or that you will be in love, or that you can be in love. Yet Benedick was such another, and now is he become a man. He swore   85 he would never marry; and yet now in despite of his heart he eats his meat without grudging. And how you may be converted I know not; but methinks you look with your eyes as other women do.

BEATRICE What pace is this that thy tongue keeps?   90

MARGARET Not a false gallop.

Enter Ursula.

URSULA Madam, withdraw. The Prince, the Count, Signior Benedick, Don John, and all the gallants of the town are come to fetch you to church.

HERO Help to dress me, good coz, good Meg, good   95
Ursula.   [*Exeunt.*]

[Scene V. *Another room in Leonato's house.*]

*Enter Leonato and the Constable [Dogberry], and
the Headborough [Verges].*

71-72 **Carduus Benedictus** blessed thistle, a medicinal herb   73 **qualm** sensation of sickness   76 **moral** special meaning   80 **list** please   87 **he eats his meat without grudging** he finds that he can still eat

LEONATO What would you with me, honest neighbor?

DOGBERRY Marry, sir, I would have some confidence with you that decerns you nearly.

LEONATO Brief, I pray you, for you see it is a busy
5   time with me.

DOGBERRY Marry, this it is, sir.

VERGES Yes, in truth it is, sir.

LEONATO What is it, my good friends?

DOGBERRY Goodman Verges, sir, speaks a little off the
10   matter—an old man, sir, and his wits are not so
blunt as, God help, I would desire they were; but,
in faith, honest as the skin between his brows.

VERGES Yes, I thank God I am as honest as any man
living that is an old man and no honester than I.

15 DOGBERRY Comparisons   are   odorous;   Palabras,
neighbor Verges.

LEONATO Neighbors, you are tedious.

DOGBERRY It pleases your worship to say so, but we
are the poor Duke's officers; but truly, for mine
20   own part, if I were as tedious as a king, I could find
in my heart to bestow it all of your worship.

LEONATO All thy tediousness on me, ah?

DOGBERRY Yea, and 'twere a thousand pound more
than 'tis; for I hear as good exclamation on your
25   worship as of any man in the city, and though I be
but a poor man, I am glad to hear it.

VERGES And so am I.

LEONATO I would fain know what you have to say.

VERGES Marry, sir, our watch tonight, excepting your
30   worship's presence, ha' ta'en a couple of as arrant
knaves as any in Messina.

III.v.15 **Palabras** (for Spanish *pocas palabras*, few words)

DOGBERRY A good old man, sir; he will be talking. As
they say, "When the age is in, the wit is out." God
help us! It is a world to see! Well said, i' faith,
neighbor Verges. Well, God's a good man. And   35
two men ride of a horse, one must ride behind. An
honest soul, i' faith, sir, by my troth he is, as ever
broke bread; but God is to be worshiped; all men
are not alike, alas, good neighbor!

LEONATO Indeed, neighbor, he comes too short of you.   40

DOGBERRY Gifts that God gives.

LEONATO I must leave you.

DOGBERRY One word, sir. Our watch, sir, have indeed
comprehended two aspicious persons, and we would
have them this morning examined before your wor-   45
ship.

LEONATO Take their examination yourself and bring
it me; I am now in great haste, as it may appear
unto you.

DOGBERRY It shall be suffigance.   50

LEONATO Drink some wine ere you go. Fare you well.

[Enter a Messenger.]

MESSENGER My lord, they stay for you to give your
daughter to her husband.

LEONATO I'll wait upon them. I am ready.
                              Exit [Leonato, with Messenger].

DOGBERRY Go, good partner, go get you to Francis   55
Seacole; bid him bring his pen and inkhorn to the
jail. We are now to examination these men.

VERGES And we must do it wisely.

DOGBERRY We will spare for no wit, I warrant you;
here's that shall drive some of them to a non-come.   60
Only get the learned writer to set down our excommunication, and meet me at the jail.   *[Exeunt.]*

60 **non-come** non compos mentis

[ACT IV

Scene I. *A church.*]

Enter Prince [Don Pedro], [Don John the] Bastard, Leonato, Friar [Francis], Claudio, Benedick, Hero, and Beatrice [and Attendants].

LEONATO Come, Friar Francis, be brief. Only to the plain form of marriage, and you shall recount their particular duties afterwards.

5   FRIAR You come hither, my lord, to marry this lady?

CLAUDIO No.

LEONATO To be married to her; Friar, you come to marry her.

FRIAR Lady, you come hither to be married to this count?

10   HERO I do.

FRIAR If either of you know any inward impediment why you should not be conjoined, I charge you on your souls to utter it.

CLAUDIO Know you any, Hero?

15   HERO None, my lord.

IV.i.3 **particular** personal

280

FRIAR Know you any, Count?

LEONATO I dare make his answer, none.

CLAUDIO O, what men dare do! What men may do!
What men daily do, not knowing what they do!

BENEDICK How now? Interjections? Why then, some   20
be of laughing, as, ah, ha, he!

CLAUDIO Stand thee by, friar. Father, by your leave,
Will you with free and unconstrainèd soul
Give me this maid your daughter?

LEONATO As freely, son, as God did give her me.   25

CLAUDIO And what have I to give you back whose
worth
May counterpoise this rich and precious gift?

DON PEDRO Nothing, unless you render her again.

CLAUDIO Sweet Prince, you learn me noble thankful-
ness.
There, Leonato, take her back again.   30
Give not this rotten orange to your friend.
She's but the sign and semblance of her honor.
Behold how like a maid she blushes here!
O, what authority and show of truth
Can cunning sin cover itself withal!   35
Comes not that blood, as modest evidence,
To witness simple virtue? Would you not swear,
All you that see her, that she were a maid,
By these exterior shows? But she is none.
She knows the heat of a luxurious bed;   40
Her blush is guiltiness, not modesty.

LEONATO What do you mean, my lord?

CLAUDIO   Not to be married,
Not to knit my soul to an approvèd wanton.

LEONATO Dear my lord, if you, in your own proof,

20-21 **some be of** some are concerned with 21 **ah, ha, he!** (examples of interjections) 22 **Stand thee by** stand aside 40 **luxurious** lustful
43 **approvèd** tested 44 **proof** experience

45   Have vanquished the resistance of her youth
        And made defeat of her virginity—

CLAUDIO I know what you would say: if I have known
            her,
        You will say she did embrace me as a husband,
        And so extenuate the 'forehand sin.
50   No, Leonato,
        I never tempted her with word too large,
        But, as a brother to his sister, showed
        Bashful sincerity and comely love.

HERO And seemed I ever otherwise to you?

55 CLAUDIO Out on thee, seeming! I will write against it.
        You seem to me as Dian in her orb,
        As chaste as is the bud ere it be blown;
        But you are more intemperate in your blood
        Than Venus, or those pamp'red animals
60   That rage in savage sensuality.

HERO Is my lord well that he doth speak so wide?

LEONATO Sweet Prince, why speak not you?

DON PEDRO   What should I speak?
        I stand dishonored that have gone about
        To link my dear friend to a common stale.

65 LEONATO Are these things spoken, or do I but dream?

DON JOHN Sir, they are spoken, and these things are
            true.

BENEDICK This looks not like a nuptial.

HERO   "True," O God!

CLAUDIO Leonato, stand I here?
        Is this the Prince? Is this the Prince's brother?
70   Is this face Hero's? Are our eyes our own?

LEONATO All this is so. But what of this, my lord?

47 **known** had intercourse with 57 **blown** blossomed 58 **blood** sexual
desire 61 **so wide** so far from the truth 64 **stale** prostitute

282

CLAUDIO Let me but move one question to your daugh-
      ter;
   And by that fatherly and kindly power
   That you have in her, bid her answer truly.

LEONATO I charge thee do so, as thou art my child.   75

HERO O, God defend me! How am I beset!
   What kind of catechizing call you this?

CLAUDIO To make you answer truly to your name.

HERO Is it not Hero? Who can blot that name
   With any just reproach?

CLAUDIO   Marry, that can Hero!   80
   Hero itself can blot out Hero's virtue.
   What man was he talked with you yesternight,
   Out at your window betwixt twelve and one?
   Now, if you are a maid, answer to this.

HERO I talked with no man at that hour, my lord.   85

DON PEDRO Why, then are you no maiden. Leonato,
   I am sorry you must hear. Upon mine honor
   Myself, my brother, and this grievèd Count
   Did see her, hear her, at that hour last night
   Talk with a ruffian at her chamber window   90
   Who hath indeed, most like a liberal villain,
   Confessed the vile encounters they have had
   A thousand times in secret.

DON JOHN Fie, fie! They are not to be named, my
      lord—
   Not to be spoke of;   95
   There is not chastity enough in language
   Without offense to utter them. Thus, pretty lady,
   I am sorry for thy much misgovernment.

CLAUDIO O Hero! What a Hero hadst thou been
   If half thy outward graces had been placed   100
   About thy thoughts and counsels of thy heart!
   But fare thee well, most foul, most fair, farewell;

73 kindly natural   91 liberal licentious

Thou pure impiety and impious purity,
For thee I'll lock up all the gates of love,
105 And on my eyelids shall conjecture hang,
To turn all beauty into thoughts of harm,
And never shall it more be gracious.

LEONATO Hath no man's dagger here a point for me?
                                    [*Hero swoons.*]

BEATRICE Why, how now, cousin? Wherefore sink you
down?

DON JOHN Come, let us go. These things, come thus to
110 light,
Smother her spirits up.
                    [*Exeunt Don Pedro, Don John, and Claudio.*]

BENEDICK How doth the lady?

BEATRICE   Dead, I think. Help, uncle!
Hero! Why, Hero! Uncle! Signior Benedick! Friar!

LEONATO O Fate, take not away thy heavy hand!
115 Death is the fairest cover for her shame
That may be wished for.

BEATRICE   How now, cousin Hero?

FRIAR Have comfort, lady.

LEONATO Dost thou look up?

FRIAR   Yea, wherefore should she not?

LEONATO Wherefore? Why, doth not every earthly thing
120 Cry shame upon her? Could she here deny
The story that is printed in her blood?
Do not live, Hero; do not ope thine eyes;
For, did I think thou wouldst not quickly die,
Thought I thy spirits were stronger than thy shames,
125 Myself would on the rearward of reproaches
Strike at thy life. Grieved I, I had but one?
Chid I for that at frugal nature's frame?

105 **conjecture** suspicion   121 **printed in her blood** written in her blushes
127 **frame** plan

O, one too much by thee! Why had I one?
Why ever wast thou lovely in my eyes?
Why had I not with charitable hand   130
Took up a beggar's issue at my gates,
Who smirchèd thus and mired with infamy,
I might have said, "No part of it is mine;
This shame derives itself from unknown loins"?
But mine, and mine I loved, and mine I praised,   135
And mine that I was proud on, mine so much
That I myself was to myself not mine,
Valuing of her—why she, O, she is fall'n
Into a pit of ink, that the wide sea
Hath drops too few to wash her clean again,   140
And salt too little which may season give
To her foul tainted flesh!

BENEDICK   Sir, sir, be patient.
For my part, I am so attired in wonder,
I know not what to say.

BEATRICE O, on my soul, my cousin is belied!   145

BENEDICK Lady, were you her bedfellow last night?

BEATRICE No, truly, not; although, until last night,
I have this twelvemonth been her bedfellow.

LEONATO Confirmed, confirmed! O, that is stronger
made
Which was before barred up with ribs of iron!   150
Would the two princes lie, and Claudio lie,
Who loved her so that, speaking of her foulness,
Washed it with tears? Hence from her! Let her die.

FRIAR Hear me a little;
For I have only been silent so long,   155
And given way unto this course of fortune,
By noting of the lady. I have marked
A thousand blushing apparitions
To start into her face, a thousand innocent shames
In angel whiteness beat away those blushes,   160
And in her eye there hath appeared a fire

141 season give act as a preservative

285

To burn the errors that these princes hold
Against her maiden truth. Call me a fool;
Trust not my reading nor my observations,
165 Which with experimental seal doth warrant
The tenor of my book; trust not my age,
My reverence, calling, nor divinity,
If this sweet lady lie not guiltless here
Under some biting error.

LEONATO   Friar, it cannot be.
170 Thou seest that all the grace that she hath left
Is that she will not add to her damnation
A sin of perjury; she not denies it.
Why seek'st thou then to cover with excuse
That which appears in proper nakedness?

175 FRIAR Lady, what man is he you are accused of?

HERO They know that do accuse me; I know none.
If I know more of any man alive
Than that which maiden modesty doth warrant,
Let all my sins lack mercy! O my father,
180 Prove you that any man with me conversed
At hours unmeet, or that I yesternight
Maintained the change of words with any creature,
Refuse me, hate me, torture me to death!

FRIAR There is some strange misprision in the princes.

185 BENEDICK Two of them have the very bent of honor;
And if their wisdoms be misled in this,
The practice of it lives in John the bastard,
Whose spirits toil in frame of villainies.

LEONATO I know not. If they speak but truth of her,
190 These hands shall tear her. If they wrong her honor,
The proudest of them shall well hear of it.
Time hath not yet so dried this blood of mine,
Nor age so eat up my invention,

165 **experimental seal** seal of experience 166 **tenor** purport 182 **maintained the change** held exchange 184 **misprision** mistaking 185 **bent** shape (or perhaps "inclination") 187 **practice** scheming 193 **invention** inventiveness

Nor fortune made such havoc of my means,
Nor my bad life reft me so much of friends,   195
But they shall find awaked in such a kind
Both strength of limb and policy of mind,
Ability in means, and choice of friends,
To quit me of them throughly.

FRIAR   Pause awhile
And let my counsel sway you in this case.   200
Your daughter here the princes left for dead.
Let her awhile be secretly kept in,
And publish it that she is dead indeed;
Maintain a mourning ostentation,
And on your family's old monument   205
Hang mournful epitaphs, and do all rites
That appertain unto a burial.

LEONATO   What shall become of this? What will this do?

FRIAR   Marry, this well carried shall on her behalf
Change slander to remorse; that is some good.   210
But not for that dream I on this strange course,
But on this travail look for greater birth.
She dying, as it must be so maintained,
Upon the instant that she was accused,
Shall be lamented, pitied, and excused   215
Of every hearer. For it so falls out
That what we have we prize not to the worth
Whiles we enjoy it; but being lacked and lost,
Why, then we rack the value, then we find
The virtue that possession would not show us   220
Whiles it was ours. So will it fare with Claudio.
When he shall hear she died upon his words,
Th' idea of her life shall sweetly creep
Into his study of imagination,
And every lovely organ of her life   225
Shall come appareled in more precious habit,
More moving, delicate, and full of life,

199 quit revenge   204 Maintain a mourning ostentation perform the outward
show of mourning   219 rack stretch   224 study of imagination meditation,
musing   225 organ physical feature   226 habit dress

Into the eye and prospect of his soul
Than when she lived indeed. Then shall he mourn,
230   If ever love had interest in his liver,
And wish he had not so accusèd her,
No, though he thought his accusation true.
Let this be so, and doubt not but success
Will fashion the event in better shape
235   Than I can lay it down in likelihood.
But if all aim, but this, be leveled false,
The supposition of the lady's death
Will quench the wonder of her infamy;
And if it sort not well, you may conceal her,
240   As best befits her wounded reputation,
In some reclusive and religious life,
Out of all eyes, tongues, minds, and injuries.

BENEDICK Signior Leonato, let the friar advise you;
And though you know my inwardness and love
245   Is very much unto the Prince and Claudio,
Yet, by mine honor, I will deal in this
As secretly and justly as your soul
Should with your body.

LEONATO   Being that I flow in grief,
The smallest twine may lead me.

250   FRIAR 'Tis well consented. Presently away;
For to strange sores strangely they strain the cure.
Come, lady, die to live. This wedding day
Perhaps is but prolonged. Have patience and
endure.
                              Exit [with all but Beatrice and Benedick].

BENEDICK Lady Beatrice, have you wept all this while?

255   BEATRICE Yea, and I will weep a while longer.

BENEDICK I will not desire that.

230 **liver** (supposed seat of love)   233 **success** what follows   234 **event** outcome
236 **But if ... false** but if all conjecture, except this (i.e., the mere supposition
of Hero's death), be aimed (**leveled**) falsely   239 **sort** turn out   244 **inwardness**
most intimate feelings

BEATRICE You have no reason. I do it freely.

BENEDICK Surely I do believe your fair cousin is wronged.

BEATRICE Ah, how much might the man deserve of me   260
that would right her!

BENEDICK Is there any way to show such friendship?

BEATRICE A very even way, but no such friend.

BENEDICK May a man do it?

BEATRICE It is a man's office, but not yours.   265

BENEDICK I do love nothing in the world so well as you.
Is not that strange?

BEATRICE As strange as the thing I know not. It were as
possible for me to say I loved nothing so well as you.
But believe me not; and yet I lie not. I confess noth-   270
ing, nor I deny nothing. I am sorry for my cousin.

BENEDICK By my sword, Beatrice, thou lovest me.

BEATRICE Do not swear and eat it.

BENEDICK I will swear by it that you love me, and I
will make him eat it that says I love not you.   275

BEATRICE Will you not eat your word?

BENEDICK With no sauce that can be devised to it. I
protest I love thee.

BEATRICE Why then, God forgive me!

BENEDICK What offense, sweet Beatrice?   280

BEATRICE You have stayed me in a happy hour. I was
about to protest I loved you.

BENEDICK And do it with all thy heart.

BEATRICE I love you with so much of my heart that none
is left to protest.   285

263 even direct 278 protest avow 281 in a happy hour just in time

BENEDICK Come, bid me do anything for thee.

BEATRICE Kill Claudio.

BENEDICK Ha! Not for the wide world!

BEATRICE You kill me to deny it. Farewell.

290 BENEDICK Tarry, sweet Beatrice.   [*He holds her.*]

BEATRICE I am gone, though I am here; there is no love in you. Nay, I pray you let me go!

BENEDICK Beatrice—

BEATRICE In faith, I will go!

295 BENEDICK We'll be friends first.   [*He lets her go.*]

BEATRICE You dare easier be friends with me than fight with mine enemy.

BENEDICK Is Claudio thine enemy?

BEATRICE Is 'a not approved in the height a villain, that
300 hath slandered, scorned, dishonored my kinswoman?
O that I were a man! What, bear her in hand until
they come to take hands; and then, with public
accusation, uncovered slander, unmitigated rancor—
O God, that I were a man! I would eat his heart in
305 the market place!

BENEDICK Hear me, Beatrice—

BEATRICE Talk with a man out at a window! A proper saying!

BENEDICK Nay, but Beatrice—

310 BEATRICE Sweet Hero, she is wronged, she is sland'red, she is undone.

BENEDICK Beat—

BEATRICE Princes and counties! Surely, a princely testimony, a goodly count, Count Comfect; a sweet gal-
315 lant surely! O that I were a man for his sake! Or that

301 **bear her in hand** fool her   314 **Comfect** sugar candy

I had any friend would be a man for my sake! But
manhood is melted into cursies, valor into compliment, and men are only turned into tongue, and trim
ones too. He is now as valiant as Hercules that only
tells a lie, and swears it. I cannot be a man with   320
wishing; therefore I will die a woman with grieving.

BENEDICK Tarry, good Beatrice. By this hand, I love
thee.

BEATRICE Use it for my love some other way than
swearing by it.   325

BENEDICK Think you in your soul the Count Claudio
hath wronged Hero?

BEATRICE Yea, as sure as I have a thought or a soul.

BENEDICK Enough, I am engaged. I will challenge him.
I will kiss your hand, and so I leave you. By this   330
hand, Claudio shall render me a dear account. As
you hear of me, so think of me. Go comfort your
cousin. I must say she is dead. And so farewell.

[Exeunt.]

[Scene II. *A prison.*]

*Enter the Constables [Dogberry and Verges] and the Town
Clerk [Sexton] in gowns, Borachio, [Conrade, and Watch].*

DOGBERRY Is our whole dissembly appeared?

VERGES O, a stool and a cushion for the sexton.

SEXTON Which be the malefactors?

DOGBERRY Marry, that am I and my partner.

317 **cursies** curtsies

5   VERGES Nay, that's certain. We have the exhibition to
     examine.

     SEXTON But which are the offenders that are to be ex-
     amined? Let them come before Master Constable.

     DOGBERRY Yea, marry, let them come before me. What
10   is your name, friend?

     BORACHIO Borachio.

     DOGBERRY Pray write down Borachio. Yours, sirrah?

     CONRADE I am a gentleman, sir, and my name is Con-
     rade.

15   DOGBERRY Write down Master Gentleman Conrade.
     Masters, do you serve God?

     BOTH Yea, sir, we hope.

     DOGBERRY Write down that they hope they serve God;
     and write God first, for God defend but God should
20   go before such villains! Masters, it is proved already
     that you are little better than false knaves, and it
     will go near to be thought so shortly. How answer
     you for yourselves?

     CONRADE Marry, sir, we say we are none.

25   DOGBERRY A marvelous witty fellow, I assure you; but
     I will go about with him. Come you hither, sirrah;
     a word in your ear. Sir, I say to you, it is thought
     you are false knaves.

     BORACHIO Sir, I say to you we are none.

30   DOGBERRY Well, stand aside. 'Fore God, they are both
     in a tale. Have you writ down that they are none?

     SEXTON Master Constable, you go not the way to ex-
     amine. You must call forth the watch that are their
     accusers.

IV.ii.12 **sirrah** (term of address used to an inferior)   26 **go about with him** get
the better of him   29 **none** (apparently pronounced the same as "known," and so
taken by Dogberry in his next speech)   30-31 **they are both in a tale** their
stories agree

292

DOGBERRY Yea, marry, that's the eftest way. Let the   35
watch come forth. Masters, I charge you in the
Prince's name, accuse these men.

FIRST WATCH This man said, sir, that Don John the
Prince's brother was a villain.

DOGBERRY Write down Prince John a villain. Why, this   40
is flat perjury, to call a prince's brother villain.

BORACHIO Master Constable!

DOGBERRY Pray thee, fellow, peace. I do not like thy
look, I promise thee.

SEXTON What heard you him say else?   45

SECOND WATCH Marry, that he had received a thousand
ducats of Don John for accusing the Lady Hero
wrongfully.

DOGBERRY Flat burglary as ever was committed.

VERGES Yea, by mass, that it is.   50

SEXTON What else, fellow?

FIRST WATCH And that Count Claudio did mean, upon
his words, to disgrace Hero before the whole assembly, and not marry her.

DOGBERRY O villain! Thou wilt be condemned into   55
everlasting redemption for this.

SEXTON What else?

WATCH This is all.

SEXTON And this is more, masters, than you can deny.   60
Prince John is this morning secretly stol'n away.
Hero was in this manner accused, in this very manner refused, and upon the grief of this suddenly died.
Master Constable, let these men be bound and
brought to Leonato's. I will go before and show him
their examination.   [*Exit.*]   65

35 eftest quickest

DOGBERRY [*To the Watch*] Come, let them be opinioned.

VERGES Let them be in the hands of Coxcomb.

DOGBERRY God's my life, where's the sexton? Let him
70   write down the Prince's officer Coxcomb. Come,
bind them. Thou naughty varlet!

CONRADE Away! You are an ass, you are an ass.

DOGBERRY Dost thou not suspect my place? Dost thou
not suspect my years? O that he were here to write
75   me down an ass! But, masters, remember that I am
an ass. Though it be not written down, yet forget
not that I am an ass. No, thou villain, thou art full
of piety, as shall be proved upon thee by good witness. I am a wise fellow; and which is more, an offi-
80   cer; and which is more, a householder; and which is
more, as pretty a piece of flesh as any is in Messina,
and one that knows the law, go to! And a rich fellow
enough, go to! And a fellow that hath had losses; and
one that hath two gowns and everything handsome
85   about him. Bring him away. O that I had been writ
down an ass!   *Exit* [*with the others*].

66-67 **opinioned** (he means "pinioned")   68 **Coxcomb** (apparently Verges
thinks this is an elegant name for one of the Watch; editors commonly emend "of
Coxcomb" to "off, Coxcomb," and give to Conrade)   71 **naughty** wicked

[ACT V

Scene I. *Before Leonato's house.*]

Enter Leonato and his brother [Antonio].

ANTONIO If you go on thus, you will kill yourself,
And 'tis not wisdom thus to second grief
Against yourself.

LEONATO   I pray thee cease thy counsel,
Which falls into mine ears as profitless
As water in a sieve. Give not me counsel,   5
Nor let no comforter delight mine ear
But such a one whose wrongs do suit with mine.
Bring me a father that so loved his child,
Whose joy of her is overwhelmed like mine,
And bid him speak of patience.   10
Measure his woe the length and breadth of mine,
And let it answer every strain for strain,
As thus for thus, and such a grief for such,
In every lineament, branch, shape, and form.
If such a one will smile and stroke his beard,   15
And sorrow wag, cry "hem" when he should groan;
Patch grief with proverbs, make misfortune drunk
With candle-wasters; bring him yet to me,

V.i.2. **second** assist 7 **suit with** accord with 12 **strain** quality, trait 16 **wag**
wave away 18 **candle-wasters** revelers (?) philosophers (?) 18 **yet** then

And I of him will gather patience.
20 But there is no such man. For, brother, men
    Can counsel and speak comfort to that grief
    Which they themselves not feel; but, tasting it,
    Their counsel turns to passion, which before
    Would give preceptial medicine to rage,
25 Fetter strong madness in a silken thread,
    Charm ache with air and agony with words.
    No, no! 'Tis all men's office to speak patience
    To those that wring under the load of sorrow,
    But no man's virtue nor sufficiency
30 To be so moral when he shall endure
    The like himself. Therefore give me no counsel;
    My griefs cry louder than advertisement.

ANTONIO Therein do men from children nothing differ.

LEONATO I pray thee peace. I will be flesh and blood;
35 For there was never yet philosopher
    That could endure the toothache patiently,
    However they have writ the style of gods
    And made a push at chance and sufferance.

ANTONIO Yet bend not all the harm upon yourself.
40 Make those that do offend you suffer too.

LEONATO There thou speak'st reason. Nay, I will do so.
    My soul doth tell me Hero is belied;
    And that shall Claudio know; so shall the Prince,
    And all of them that thus dishonor her.

Enter Prince [Don Pedro] and Claudio.

45 ANTONIO Here comes the Prince and Claudio hastily.

DON PEDRO Good den, good den.

CLAUDIO   Good day to both of you.

LEONATO Hear you, my lords—

DON PEDRO   We have some haste, Leonato.

---

24 **preceptial medicine** medicine of precepts (cf. line 17: "Patch grief with proverbs") 30 **moral** moralizing 32 **advertisement** counsel 38 **made ... sufferance** defied mischance and suffering

LEONATO Some haste, my lord! Well, fare you well,
 my lord.
 Are you so hasty now? Well, all is one.

DON PEDRO Nay, do not quarrel with us, good old man. 50

ANTONIO If he could right himself with quarreling,
 Some of us would lie low.

CLAUDIO   Who wrongs him?

LEONATO Marry, thou dost wrong me, thou dissembler,
 thou!
 Nay, never lay thy hand upon thy sword;
 I fear thee not.

CLAUDIO   Marry, beshrew my hand 55
 If it should give your age such cause of fear.
 In faith, my hand meant nothing to my sword.

LEONATO Tush, tush, man! Never fleer and jest at me.
 I speak not like a dotard nor a fool,
 As under privilege of age to brag 60
 What I have done being young, or what would do,
 Were I not old. Know, Claudio, to thy head,
 Thou hast so wronged mine innocent child and me
 That I am forced to lay my reverence by
 And, with gray hairs and bruise of many days, 65
 Do challenge thee to trial of a man.
 I say thou hast belied mine innocent child.
 Thy slander hath gone through and through her
 heart,
 And she lies buried with her ancestors;
 O, in a tomb where never scandal slept, 70
 Save this of hers, framed by thy villainy!

CLAUDIO My villainy?

LEONATO   Thine, Claudio; thine I say.

DON PEDRO You say not right, old man.

LEONATO   My lord, my lord,

55 beshrew curse (but not a strong word) 58 fleer sneer 62 head face
66 trial of a man manly test, i.e., a duel 71 framed made

I'll prove it on his body if he dare,
75   Despite his nice fence and his active practice,
His May of youth and bloom of lustihood.

CLAUDIO Away! I will not have to do with you.

LEONATO Canst thou so daff me? Thou hast killed my
child.
If thou kill'st me, boy, thou shalt kill a man.

80   ANTONIO He shall kill two of us, and men indeed.
But that's no matter; let him kill one first.
Win me and wear me! Let him answer me.
Come, follow me, boy; come, sir boy; come, follow
me.
Sir boy, I'll whip you from your foining fence!
85   Nay, as I am a gentleman, I will.

LEONATO Brother—

ANTONIO Content yourself. God knows I loved my
niece;
And she is dead, slandered to death by villains,
That dare as well answer a man indeed
90   As I dare take a serpent by the tongue.
Boys, apes, braggarts, Jacks, milksops!

LEONATO   Brother Anthony—

ANTONIO Hold you content. What, man! I know them,
yea,
And what they weigh, even to the utmost scruple;
Scrambling, outfacing, fashionmonging boys,
95   That lie and cog and flout, deprave and slander,
Go anticly, and show outward hideousness,
And speak off half a dozen dang'rous words,
How they might hurt their enemies, if they durst;
And this is all.

LEONATO But, brother Anthony—

75 nice fence elegant fencing   78 daff put off   84 foining thrusting   91 Jacks
(a contemptuous term of no precise meaning)   93 scruple smallest unit
94 Scambling brawling   94 fashionmonging fashion following   95 cog cheat
96 anticly grotesquely dressed

ANTONIO   Come, 'tis no matter.   100
  Do not you meddle; let me deal in this.

DON PEDRO Gentlemen both, we will not wake your
    patience.
  My heart is sorry for your daughter's death.
  But, on my honor, she was charged with nothing
  But what was true, and very full of proof.   105

LEONATO My lord, my lord!

DON PEDRO I will not hear you.

LEONATO No? Come, brother, away! I will be heard!

ANTONIO And shall, or some of us will smart for it.
           Exeunt ambo [Leonato and Antonio].

          Enter Benedick.

DON PEDRO See, see! Here comes the man we went to
    seek.   110

CLAUDIO Now, signior, what news?

BENEDICK Good day, my lord.

DON PEDRO Welcome, signior. You are almost come to
    part almost a fray.

CLAUDIO We had liked to have had our two noses   115
    snapped off with two old men without teeth.

DON PEDRO Leonato and his brother. What think'st
    thou? Had we fought, I doubt we should have been
    too young for them.

BENEDICK In a false quarrel there is no true valor. I   120
    came to seek you both.

CLAUDIO We have been up and down to seek thee; for
    we are high-proof melancholy, and would fain
    have it beaten away. Wilt thou use thy wit?

102 **wake your patience** arouse your indulgence (heavily ironic)   109 s.d. **ambo**
both (Latin)   118 **doubt** suspect   123 **high-proof** in the highest degree

125 BENEDICK It is in my scabbard. Shall I draw it?

DON PEDRO Dost thou wear thy wit by thy side?

CLAUDIO Never any did so, though very many have
been beside their wit. I will bid thee draw, as we do
the minstrels: draw to pleasure us.

130 DON PEDRO As I am an honest man, he looks pale.
Art thou sick, or angry?

CLAUDIO What, courage, man! What though care killed
a cat, thou hast mettle enough in thee to kill care.

BENEDICK Sir, I shall meet your wit in the career and
135 you charge it against me. I pray you choose another subject.

CLAUDIO Nay then, give him another staff. This last
was broke cross.

DON PEDRO By this light, he changes more and more.
140 I think he be angry indeed.

CLAUDIO If he be, he knows how to turn his girdle.

BENEDICK Shall I speak a word in your ear?

CLAUDIO God bless me from a challenge!

BENEDICK [Aside to Claudio] You are a villain; I jest
145 not; I will make it good how you dare, with what
you dare, and when you dare. Do me right, or I will
protest your cowardice. You have killed a sweet
lady, and her death shall fall heavy on you. Let me
hear from you.

150 CLAUDIO Well, I will meet you, so I may have good
cheer.

DON PEDRO What, a feast, a feast?

CLAUDIO I' faith, I thank him; he hath bid me to a

---

129 **draw** i.e., draw not a sword but a fiddle bow   134 **in the career** headlong
135 **charge** i.e., as in tilting with staves or lances   138 **broke cross** ineptly broken
(by crossing the opponent's shield instead of striking it headlong)   141 **turn his
girdle** challenge me (by reaching for his dagger?)   147 **protest** proclaim

calf's head and a capon; the which if I do not carve most curiously, say my knife's naught. Shall 155 I not find a woodcock too?

BENEDICK Sir, your wit ambles well; it goes easily.

DON PEDRO I'll tell thee how Beatrice praised thy wit the other day. I said thou hadst a fine wit. "True," said she, "a fine little one." "No," said I, "a great 160 wit." "Right," says she, "a great gross one." "Nay," said I, "a good wit." "Just," said she, "it hurts nobody." "Nay," said I, "the gentleman is wise." "Certain," said she, "a wise gentleman." "Nay," said I, "he hath the tongues." "That I believe," 165 said she, "for he swore a thing to me on Monday night which he forswore on Tuesday morning; there's a double tongue; there's two tongues." Thus did she an hour together transshape thy particular virtues. Yet at last she concluded with a sigh, 170 thou wast the prop'rest man in Italy.

CLAUDIO For the which she wept heartily and said she cared not.

DON PEDRO Yea, that she did; but yet, for all that, and if she did not hate him deadly, she would love him 175 dearly. The old man's daughter told us all.

CLAUDIO All, all! And moreover, God saw him when he was hid in the garden.

DON PEDRO But when shall we set the savage bull's horns on the sensible Benedick's head? 180

CLAUDIO Yea, and text underneath, "Here dwells Benedick, the married man"?

BENEDICK Fare you well, boy; you know my mind. I will leave you now to your gossiplike humor; you break jests as braggards do their blades, which God 185

155 **curiously** skillfully   156 **woodcock** stupid bird (Claudio reduces the duel to a carving up of symbols of stupidity—a calf's head, a capon, and a woodcock) 165 **hath the tongues** knows foreign languages   169 **transshape** distort 171 **prop'rest** most handsome

be thanked hurt not. [*To Don Pedro*] My lord, for
your many courtesies I thank you. I must discon-
tinue your company. Your brother the bastard is
fled from Messina. You have among you killed a
190   sweet and innocent lady. For my Lord Lackbeard
there, he and I shall meet; and till then peace be
with him.   [*Exit.*]

DON PEDRO He is in earnest.

CLAUDIO In most profound earnest; and, I'll warrant
195   you, for the love of Beatrice.

DON PEDRO And hath challenged thee?

CLAUDIO Most sincerely.

DON PEDRO What a pretty thing man is when he goes
in his doublet and hose and leaves off his wit!

Enter Constables [*Dogberry, Verges, and the
Watch, with*] *Conrade and Borachio.*

200   CLAUDIO He is then a giant to an ape; but then is an
ape a doctor to such a man.

DON PEDRO But, soft you, let me be! Pluck up, my
heart, and be sad. Did he not say my brother was
fled?

205   DOGBERRY Come you, sir. If justice cannot tame you,
she shall ne'er weigh more reasons in her balance.
Nay, and you be a cursing hypocrite once, you must
be looked to.

DON PEDRO How now? Two of my brother's men
210   bound? Borachio one.

CLAUDIO Hearken after their offense, my lord.

DON PEDRO Officers, what offense have these men
done?

200-1 He is then ... a man i.e., an ape would consider him important, but an ape
is actually a scholar (doctor) compared to such a fool   211 Hearken after
inquire into

DOGBERRY Marry, sir, they have committed false report; moreover, they have spoken untruths; secondarily, they are slanders; sixth and lastly, they have belied a lady; thirdly, they have verified unjust things; and to conclude, they are lying knaves.

DON PEDRO First, I ask thee what they have done; thirdly, I ask thee what's their offense; sixth and lastly, why they are committed; and to conclude, what you lay to their charge.

CLAUDIO Rightly reasoned, and in his own division; and, by my troth, there's one meaning well suited.

DON PEDRO Who have you offended, masters, that you are thus bound to your answer? This learned constable is too cunning to be understood. What's your offense?

BORACHIO Sweet Prince, let me go no farther to mine answer. Do you hear me, and let this count kill me. I have deceived even your very eyes. What your wisdoms could not discover, these shallow fools have brought to light, who in the night overheard me confessing to this man, how Don John your brother incensed me to slander the Lady Hero; how you were brought into the orchard and saw me court Margaret in Hero's garments; how you disgraced her when you should marry her. My villainy they have upon record, which I had rather seal with my death than repeat over to my shame. The lady is dead upon mine and my master's false accusation; and briefly, I desire nothing but the reward of a villain.

DON PEDRO Runs not this speech like iron through your blood?

CLAUDIO I have drunk poison whiles he uttered it.

DON PEDRO But did my brother set thee on to this?

224 **well suited** well dressed out   226 **bound** arraigned   227 **cunning** intelligent

BORACHIO Yea, and paid me richly for the practice
of it.

250 DON PEDRO He is composed and framed of treachery,
And fled he is upon this villainy.

CLAUDIO Sweet Hero, now thy image doth appear
In the rare semblance that I loved it first.

DOGBERRY Come, bring away the plaintiffs. By this
255 time our sexton hath reformed Signior Leonato of
the matter. And, masters, do not forget to specify,
when time and place shall serve, that I am an ass.

VERGES Here, here comes Master Signior Leonato,
and the sexton too.

*Enter Leonato, his brother [Antonio], and the
Sexton.*

260 LEONATO Which is the villain? Let me see his eyes,
That, when I note another man like him,
I may avoid him. Which of these is he?

BORACHIO If you would know your wronger, look on
me.

LEONATO Art thou the slave that with thy breath hast
killed
Mine innocent child?

265 BORACHIO   Yea, even I alone.

LEONATO No, not so, villain! Thou beliest thyself.
Here stand a pair of honorable men;
A third is fled, that had a hand in it.
I thank you, princes, for my daughter's death.
270 Record it with your high and worthy deeds.
'Twas bravely done, if you bethink you of it.

CLAUDIO I know not how to pray your patience;
Yet I must speak. Choose your revenge yourself;
Impose me to what penance your invention

272 **pray your patience** ask your forgiveness   274 **invention** imagination

Can lay upon my sin. Yet sinned I not   275
But in mistaking.

DON PEDRO   By my soul, nor I;
And yet, to satisfy this good old man,
I would bend under any heavy weight
That he'll enjoin me to.

LEONATO I cannot bid you bid my daughter live;   280
That were impossible; but I pray you both,
Possess the people in Messina here
How innocent she died; and if your love
Can labor aught in sad invention,
Hang her an epitaph upon her tomb,   285
And sing it to her bones, sing it tonight.
Tomorrow morning come you to my house;
And since you could not be my son-in-law,
Be yet my nephew. My brother hath a daughter,
Almost the copy of my child that's dead,   290
And she alone is heir to both of us.
Give her the right you should have giv'n her
     cousin,
And so dies my revenge.

CLAUDIO   O noble sir!
Your overkindness doth wring tears from me.
I do embrace your offer; and dispose   295
For henceforth of poor Claudio.

LEONATO Tomorrow then I will expect your coming;
Tonight I take my leave. This naughty man
Shall face to face be brought to Margaret,
Who I believe was packed in all this wrong,   300
Hired to it by your brother.

BORACHIO   No, by my soul, she was not;
Nor knew not what she did when she spoke to me;
But always hath been just and virtuous
In anything that I do know by her.

282 **Possess** inform   292 **right** (Hero had a right to claim Claudio as her
husband; probably there is also a pun on "rite")   300 **packed** combined, i.e., an
accomplice

305 DOGBERRY Moreover, sir, which indeed is not under white and black, this plaintiff here, the offender, did call me ass. I beseech you let it be rememb'red in his punishment. And also the watch heard them talk of one Deformed; they say he wears a key in
310 his ear, and a lock hanging by it, and borrows money in God's name, the which he hath used so long and never paid that now men grow hard-hearted and will lend nothing for God's sake. Pray you examine him upon that point.

315 LEONATO I thank thee for thy care and honest pains.

DOGBERRY Your worship speaks like a most thankful and reverent youth, and I praise God for you.

LEONATO There's for thy pains.   [*Gives money.*]

DOGBERRY God save the foundation!

320 LEONATO Go, I discharge thee of thy prisoner, and I thank thee.

DOGBERRY I leave an arrant knave with your worship, which I beseech your worship to correct yourself, for the example of others. God keep your worship!
325 I wish your worship well. God restore you to health! I humbly give you leave to depart; and if a merry meeting may be wished, God prohibit it! Come, neighbor.   [*Exeunt Dogberry and Verges.*]

LEONATO Until tomorrow morning, lords, farewell.

ANTONIO Farewell, my lords. We look for you tomor-
330 row.

DON PEDRO We will not fail.

CLAUDIO   Tonight I'll mourn with Hero.
                        [*Exeunt Don Pedro and Claudio.*]

305-6 **not under white and black** not in the official record   309 **key** ring (but perhaps Dogberry merely assumes that if a man wears a lock in his hair he must wear a key too)   319 **the foundation** (as if Leonato were a charitable institution) 320 **discharge** relieve

LEONATO [*To the Watch*] Bring you these fellows on.
     We'll talk with Margaret,
How her acquaintance grew with this lewd fellow.
                              Exeunt [*separately*].

[Scene II. *Leonato's garden.*]

Enter Benedick and Margaret [*meeting*].

BENEDICK Pray thee, sweet Mistress Margaret, deserve
     well at my hands by helping me to the speech of
     Beatrice.

MARGARET Will you then write me a sonnet in praise
     of my beauty?   5

BENEDICK In so high a style, Margaret, that no man
     living shall come over it; for in most comely truth
     thou deservest it.

MARGARET To have no man come over me! Why, shall
     I always keep belowstairs?   10

BENEDICK Thy wit is as quick as the greyhound's
     mouth; it catches.

MARGARET And yours as blunt as the fencer's foils,
     which hit but hurt not.

BENEDICK A most manly wit, Margaret; it will not hurt 15
     a woman. And so, I pray thee call Beatrice. I give
     thee the bucklers.

MARGARET Give us the swords; we have bucklers of
     our own.

BENEDICK If you use them, Margaret, you must put   20

333 **lewd** low   V.ii.6 **style** (pun on "stile," a set of steps for passing over a fence)
9 **come over me** (the beginning of an interchange of sexual innuendoes)
10 **keep belowstairs** dwell in the servants' quarters   16-17 **I give thee the
bucklers** I yield

in the pikes with a vice; and they are dangerous
weapons for maids.

MARGARET Well, I will call Beatrice to you, who I think
hath legs.   *Exit Margaret*.

25 BENEDICK And therefore will come.
[*Sings*]   The god of love,
                    That sits above
            And knows me, and knows me,
                How pitiful I deserve—
30 I mean in singing; but in loving, Leander the good
swimmer, Troilus the first employer of panders,
and a whole book full of these quondam carpetmongers, whose names yet run smoothly in the
even road of a blank verse—why, they were never
35 so truly turned over and over as my poor self in
love. Marry, I cannot show it in rhyme. I have tried.
I can find out no rhyme to "lady" but "baby," an
innocent rhyme; for "scorn," "horn," a hard rhyme;
for "school," "fool," a babbling rhyme. Very omi-
40 nous endings. No, I was not born under a rhyming
planet, nor I cannot woo in festival terms.

Enter Beatrice.

Sweet Beatrice, wouldst thou come when I called
thee?

BEATRICE Yea, signior, and depart when you bid me.

45 BENEDICK O, stay but till then!

BEATRICE "Then" is spoken. Fare you well now. And
yet, ere I go, let me go with that I came, which is,
with knowing what hath passed between you and
Claudio.

50 BENEDICK Only foul words; and thereupon I will kiss
thee.

---

21 **pikes** spikes in the center of bucklers 21 **vice** screw 30-31 **Leander ...
Troilus** (legendary lovers; Leander nightly swam the Hellespont to visit Hero,
Troilus was aided in his love for Cressida by Pandarus) 32-33 **quondam
carpetmongers** ancient boudoir knights

BEATRICE Foul words is but foul wind, and foul wind is but foul breath, and foul breath is noisome. Therefore I will depart unkissed.

BENEDICK Thou hast frighted the word out of his right 55
sense, so forcible is thy wit. But I must tell thee plainly, Claudio undergoes my challenge; and either I must shortly hear from him or I will subscribe him a coward. And I pray thee now tell me, for which of my bad parts didst thou first fall in love 60
with me?

BEATRICE For them all together, which maintained so politic a state of evil that they will not admit any good part to intermingle with them. But for which of my good parts did you first suffer love for me? 65

BENEDICK Suffer love! A good epithet. I do suffer love indeed, for I love thee against my will.

BEATRICE In spite of your heart, I think. Alas poor heart! If you spite it for my sake, I will spite it for yours, for I will never love that which my friend 70
hates.

BENEDICK Thou and I are too wise to woo peaceably.

BEATRICE It appears not in this confession. There's not one wise man among twenty that will praise himself.

BENEDICK An old, an old instance, Beatrice, that 75
lived in the time of good neighbors. If a man do not erect in this age his own tomb ere he dies, he shall live no longer in monument than the bell rings and the widow weeps.

BEATRICE And how long is that, think you? 80

BENEDICK Question: why, an hour in clamor and a quarter in rheum; therefore is it most expedient for the wise, if Don Worm, his conscience, find no impediment to the contrary, to be the trumpet of

58-59 **subscribe him** write him down   63 **politic a state** well-ordered a community   75 **instance** example   82 **rheum** tears

85　　　　his own virtues, as I am to myself. So much for
　　　　praising myself, who, I myself will bear witness, is
　　　　praiseworthy. And now tell me, how doth your
　　　　cousin?

BEATRICE Very ill.

90　BENEDICK And how do you?

BEATRICE Very ill too.

BENEDICK Serve God, love me, and mend. There will
　　　　I leave you too, for here comes one in haste.

Enter Ursula.

URSULA Madam, you must come to your uncle. Yon-
95　　　der's old coil at home. It is proved my Lady Hero
　　　　hath been falsely accused, the Prince and Claudio
　　　　mightily abused, and Don John is the author of all,
　　　　who is fled and gone. Will you come presently?

BEATRICE Will you go hear this news, signior?

100　BENEDICK I will live in thy heart, die in thy lap, and
　　　　be buried in thy eyes; and moreover, I will go with
　　　　thee to thy uncle's.　　*Exit* [*with Beatrice and Ursula*].

[Scene III. *A church.*]

Enter Claudio, Prince [*Don Pedro, Lord,*] *and
three or four with tapers* [*followed by Musicians*].

CLAUDIO Is this the monument of Leonato?

LORD It is, my lord.

[*Claudio reads from a scroll.*]

95 **old coil** plenty of confusion

Epitaph

Done to death by slanderous tongues
   Was the Hero that here lies;
Death, in guerdon of her wrongs,   5
   Gives her fame which never dies.
So the life that died with shame
Lives in death with glorious fame.
                          [Hangs up the scroll.]
Hang thou there upon the tomb,
Praising her when I am dumb.   10

CLAUDIO Now, music, sound, and sing your solemn
    hymn.

Song

Pardon, goddess of the night,
Those that slew thy virgin knight;
For the which, with songs of woe,
Round about her tomb they go.   15
Midnight, assist our moan;
Help us to sigh and groan,
    Heavily, heavily.
Graves, yawn and yield your dead,
Till death be utterèd,   20
    Heavily, heavily.

CLAUDIO Now unto thy bones good night!
    Yearly will I do this rite.

DON PEDRO Good morrow, masters; put your torches
    out.
    The wolves have preyed, and look, the gentle
      day,   25
Before the wheels of Phoebus, round about
    Dapples the drowsy east with spots of gray.
Thanks to you all, and leave us. Fare you well.

CLAUDIO Good morrow, masters; each his several way.

V.iii.5 **guerdon** reward   12 **goddess of the night** Diana, goddess of the moon
and of chastity   26 **wheels of Phoebus** wheels of the sun god's chariot

DON PEDRO Come, let us hence and put on other
30   weeds,
And then to Leonato's we will go.

CLAUDIO And Hymen now with luckier issue speeds
Than this for whom we rend'red up this woe.
Exeunt.

[Scene IV. *Leonato's house.*]

*Enter Leonato, Benedick, [Beatrice,] Margaret, Ursula,
Old Man [Antonio], Friar [Francis], Hero.*

FRIAR Did I not tell you she was innocent?

LEONATO So are the Prince and Claudio, who accused
her
Upon the error that you heard debated.
But Margaret was in some fault for this,
5   Although against her will, as it appears
In the true course of all the question.

ANTONIO Well, I am glad that all things sorts so well.

BENEDICK And so am I, being else by faith enforced
To call young Claudio to a reckoning for it.

10 LEONATO Well, daughter, and you gentlewomen all,
Withdraw into a chamber by yourselves,
And when I send for you, come hither masked.
The Prince and Claudio promised by this hour
To visit me. You know your office, brother;
15   You must be father to your brother's daughter,
And give her to young Claudio.   *Exeunt Ladies.*

ANTONIO Which I will do with confirmed countenance.

30 **weeds** apparel   32 **Hymen** god of marriage   32 **speeds** succeeds V.iv.6
question investigation   7 **sorts** turn out   17 **confirmed** steady

312

BENEDICK Friar, I must entreat your pains, I think.

FRIAR To do what, signior?

BENEDICK To bind me, or undo me—one of them.   20
    Signior Leonato, truth it is, good signior,
    Your niece regards me with an eye of favor.

LEONATO That eye my daughter lent her; 'tis most true.

BENEDICK And I do with an eye of love requite her.

LEONATO The sight whereof I think you had from me,   25
    From Claudio, and the Prince. But what's your will?

BENEDICK Your answer, sir, is enigmatical.
    But, for my will, my will is, your good will
    May stand with ours, this day to be conjoined
    In the state of honorable marriage;   30
    In which, good friar, I shall desire your help.

LEONATO My heart is with your liking.

FRIAR   And my help.
    Here comes the Prince and Claudio.

    Enter Prince [Don Pedro] and Claudio and two
               or three other.

DON PEDRO Good morrow to this fair assembly.

LEONATO Good morrow, Prince; good morrow,
    Claudio.   35
    We here attend you. Are you yet determined
    Today to marry with my brother's daughter?

CLAUDIO I'll hold my mind, were she an Ethiope.

LEONATO Call her forth, brother. Here's the friar
    ready.   [*Exit Antonio.*]

DON PEDRO Good morrow, Benedick. Why, what's the
    matter   40
    That you have such a February face,
    So full of frost, of storm, and cloudiness?

CLAUDIO I think he thinks upon the savage bull.
    Tush, fear not, man! We'll tip thy horns with gold,
45 And all Europa shall rejoice at thee,
    As once Europa did at lusty Jove
    When he would play the noble beast in love.

BENEDICK Bull Jove, sir, had an amiable low,
    And some such strange bull leaped your father's
        cow
50 And got a calf in that same noble feat
    Much like to you, for you have just his bleat.

*Enter [Leonato's] brother [Antonio], Hero, Beatrice,
Margaret, Ursula, [the ladies wearing masks].*

CLAUDIO For this I owe you. Here comes other
        reck'nings.
    Which is the lady I must seize upon?

ANTONIO This same is she, and I do give you her.

CLAUDIO Why then, she's mine. Sweet, let me see your
55   face.

LEONATO No, that you shall not till you take her hand
    Before this friar and swear to marry her.

CLAUDIO Give me your hand; before this holy friar
    I am your husband if you like of me.

60 HERO And when I lived I was your other wife; [*un-
        masking*]
    And when you loved you were my other husband.

CLAUDIO Another Hero!

HERO   Nothing certainer.
    One Hero died defiled; but I do live,
    And surely as I live, I am a maid.

---

43 **savage bull** (refers to I.i.252)   44 **tip thy horns with gold** i.e., make your
cuckolding something to be proud of   45 **Europa** Europe (though in the next line
the word designates the girl that Jupiter wooed in the guise of a bull)   52 **I owe
you** i.e., I will pay you back (for calling me a calf and a bastard)

DON PEDRO The former Hero! Hero that is dead!   65

LEONATO She died, my lord, but whiles her slander
    lived.

FRIAR All this amazement can I qualify,
    When, after that the holy rites are ended,
    I'll tell you largely of fair Hero's death.
    Meantime let wonder seem familiar,   70
    And to the chapel let us presently.

BENEDICK Soft and fair, friar. Which is Beatrice?

BEATRICE [*Unmasking*] I answer to that name. What is
    your will?

BENEDICK Do not you love me?

BEATRICE   Why, no; no more than reason.

BENEDICK Why, then your uncle, and the Prince, and
    Claudio   75
    Have been deceived—they swore you did.

BEATRICE Do not you love me?

BENEDICK   Troth, no; no more than reason.

BEATRICE Why, then my cousin, Margaret, and Ursula
    Are much deceived; for they did swear you did.

BENEDICK They swore that you were almost sick for
    me.   80

BEATRICE They swore that you were well-nigh dead for
    me.

BENEDICK 'Tis no such matter. Then you do not love
    me?

BEATRICE No, truly, but in friendly recompense.

LEONATO Come, cousin, I am sure you love the gen-
    tleman.

CLAUDIO And I'll be sworn upon't that he loves her;   85
    For here's a paper written in his hand,

66 but whiles only while   67 **qualify** abate   69 **largely** in detail

A halting sonnet of his own pure brain,
Fashioned to Beatrice.

HERO   And here's another,
Writ in my cousin's hand, stol'n from her pocket,
90   Containing her affection unto Benedick.

BENEDICK A miracle! Here's our own hands against our
hearts. Come, I will have thee; but, by this light, I
take thee for pity.

BEATRICE I would not deny you; but, by this good day,
95   I yield upon great persuasion, and partly to save
your life, for I was told you were in a consumption.

BENEDICK Peace! I will stop your mouth. [*Kisses her.*]

DON PEDRO How dost thou, Benedick, the married
man?

100 BENEDICK I'll tell thee what, Prince: a college of wit-
crackers cannot flout me out of my humor. Dost
thou think I care for a satire or an epigram? No. If
a man will be beaten with brains, 'a shall wear nothing handsome about him. In brief, since I do pur-
105 pose to marry, I will think nothing to any purpose
that the world can say against it; and therefore never
flout at me for what I have said against it; for man
is a giddy thing, and this is my conclusion. For thy
part, Claudio, I did think to have beaten thee; but in
110 that thou art like to be my kinsman, live unbruised,
and love my cousin.

CLAUDIO I had well hoped thou wouldst have denied
Beatrice, that I might have cudgeled thee out of thy
single life, to make thee a double-dealer, which out
115 of question thou wilt be if my cousin do not look
exceeding narrowly to thee.

BENEDICK Come, come, we are friends. Let's have a

87 **halting** limping   97 **Benedick** (both Quarto and Folio assign this line to
Leonato; possibly the original reading is correct, and Leonato forces Benedick to
kiss Beatrice)   114 **double-dealer** (1) married man (2) unfaithful husband

dance ere we are married, that we may lighten our
own hearts and our wives' heels.

LEONATO We'll have dancing afterward.   120

BENEDICK First, of my word; therefore play, music.
Prince, thou art sad; get thee a wife, get thee a wife!
There is no staff more reverend than one tipped with
horn.

Enter Messenger.

MESSENGER My lord, your brother John is ta'en in
flight,   125
And brought with armèd men back to Messina.

BENEDICK Think not on him till tomorrow. I'll devise
thee brave punishments for him. Strike up, pipers!
Dance. [Exeunt.]

FINIS

123-24 with horn (final reference to the horns of a cuckold)

Textual Note

The present text of *Much Ado About Nothing* is based upon the Quarto edition of the play, published in 1600. The Folio text of 1623 is a slightly edited version of this Quarto.

In I.ii Antonio is designated "Old" in the Quarto, meaning old man. In II.i Antonio's speeches are assigned to "Brother." In IV.ii "Kemp" and "Cowley," the actors intended for the roles, are assigned the speeches for Dogberry and Verges. The present edition regularizes all speech prefixes. All act and scene divisions are bracketed, since (like indications of locale) these are not in the Quarto. Spelling and punctuation have been modernized, and obvious typographical errors have been corrected. The positions of a few stage directions have been slightly altered; necessary directions that are not given in the Quarto are added in brackets. Other substantial departures from the Quarto are listed below, the adopted reading first, in bold, and then the Quarto's reading in roman type. If the adopted reading comes from the Folio, the fact is indicated by [F] following it.

I.i.s.d. [Q has "Innogen his wife," i.e., Leonato's wife, before "Hero"; she does not appear in the play] 1 **Don Pedro** Don Peter 9-10 **Don Pedro** Don Peter 195 **Enter Don Pedro** Enter don Pedro, Iohn the bastard

II.i.s.d. **Hero** his wife, Hero **niece** neece, and a kinsman 84 s.d. **Don John** or dumb Iohn 208 s.d. [Q adds "Iohn and Borachio, and Conrade"]

II.iii.138 **us of** [F] of vs

III.ii.52 **Don Pedro** [F] Bene

IV.ii.s.d. [Q places "Borachio" immediately after "Constables"]

V.iii.10 **dumb** [F] dead 22 **Claudio** Lo[rd]

V.iv.54 **Antonio** Leo 97 **Benedick** Leon

WILLIAM SHAKESPEARE

AS YOU LIKE IT

Edited by Albert Gilman

[Dramatis Personae

DUKE SENIOR, in banishment in
  the Forest of Arden
DUKE FREDERICK, his brother,
  usurper of the Dukedom
AMIENS
JAQUES } lords attending on Duke Senior
LE BEAU, a courtier
CHARLES, a wrestler
OLIVER
JAQUES } sons of Sir Rowland de Boys
ORLANDO
ADAM
DENNIS } servants to Oliver
TOUCHSTONE, a clown
SIR OLIVER MAR-TEXT, a vicar
CORIN
SILVIUS } shepherds
WILLIAM, a country fellow
HYMEN
ROSALIND, daughter to Duke Senior
CELIA, daughter to Duke Frederick
PHEBE, a shepherdess
AUDREY, a country girl
Lords, Pages, Foresters, and Attendants

Scene: Oliver's house; the court;
the Forest of Arden]

AS YOU LIKE IT

ACT I

Scene I. [*Orchard of Oliver's house.*]

Enter Orlando and Adam.

ORLANDO As I remember, Adam, it was upon this fashion
bequeathed me by will but poor a thousand crowns,
and, as thou say'st, charged my brother on his blessing
to breed me well; and there begins my sadness. My
brother Jaques he keeps at school, and report speaks   5
goldenly of his profit. For my part, he keeps me
rustically at home or, to speak more properly, stays
me here at home unkept; for call you that keeping
for a gentleman of my birth that differs not from the
stalling of an ox? His horses are bred better, for,   10
besides that they are fair with their feeding, they are
taught their manage, and to that end riders dearly
hired; but I, his brother, gain nothing under him but
growth, for the which his animals on his dunghills
are as much bound to him as I. Besides this nothing   15
that he so plentifully gives me, the something that

Text references are printed in **bold** type; the annotation follows in roman type.
I.i.2 **poor a** a mere   6 **goldenly of his profit** glowingly of his progress
6-7 **keeps me rustically** supports me like a peasant   8 **unkept** uncared for
11 **fair** handsome   12 **manage** paces

nature gave me his countenance seems to take from
me. He lets me feed with his hinds, bars me the place
of a brother, and, as much as in him lies, mines my
20 gentility with my education. This is it, Adam, that
grieves me; and the spirit of my father, which I think
is within me, begins to mutiny against this servitude.
I will no longer endure it, though yet I know no wise
remedy how to avoid it.

Enter Oliver.

25 ADAM Yonder comes my master, your brother.

ORLANDO Go apart, Adam, and thou shalt hear how he
will shake me up.

OLIVER Now, sir, what make you here?

ORLANDO Nothing. I am not taught to make anything.

30 OLIVER What mar you then, sir?

ORLANDO Marry, sir, I am helping you to mar that
which God made, a poor unworthy brother of yours,
with idleness.

OLIVER Marry, sir, be better employed, and be naught
35 awhile.

ORLANDO Shall I keep your hogs and eat husks with
them? What prodigal portion have I spent that I
should come to such penury?

OLIVER Know you where you are, sir?

40 ORLANDO O, sir, very well. Here in your orchard.

OLIVER Know you before whom, sir?

ORLANDO Ay, better than him I am before knows me. I

17 **countenance** behavior   18 **hinds** farm hands   19–20 **mines my gentility**
undermines my good birth   27 **shake me up** berate me   28 **make** you are you
doing (in the next line Orlando pretends to take the phrase to mean "accomplish")
31 **Marry** (an expletive, from "By the Virgin Mary")   34–35 **be naught awhile**
i.e., don't bother me   36–37 **Shall I ... spent** (an allusion to the story of the
Prodigal Son. See Luke 15:11–32)   39 **where** i.e., in whose presence (Orlando
pretends to take it literally)

know your are my eldest brother, and in the gentle
condition of blood you should so know me. The
courtesy of nations allows you my better in that you   45
are the first born, but the same tradition takes not
away my blood were there twenty brothers betwixt
us. I have as much of my father in me as you, albeit
I confess your coming before me is nearer to his
reverence.   50

OLIVER What, boy!   [*Strikes him.*]

ORLANDO Come, come, elder brother, you are too young
in this.   [*Seizes him.*]

OLIVER Wilt thou lay hands on me, villain?

ORLANDO I am no villain. I am the youngest son of Sir   55
Rowland de Boys; he was my father, and he is thrice
a villain that says such a father begot villains. Wert
thou not my brother, I would not take this hand from
thy throat till this other had pulled out thy tongue
for saying so. Thou hast railed on thyself.   60

ADAM Sweet masters, be patient. For your father's
remembrance, be at accord.

OLIVER Let me go, I say.

ORLANDO I will not till I please. You shall hear me. My
father charged you in his will to give me good educa-   65
tion. You have trained me like a peasant, obscuring
and hiding from me all gentlemanlike qualities. The
spirit of my father grows strong in me, and I will no
longer endure it. Therefore allow me such exercises
as may become a gentleman, or give me the poor   70
allottery my father left me by testament; with that
I will go buy my fortunes.

43-44 **in the gentle condition of blood** i.e., of the same good blood
45 **courtesy of nations** i.e., sanctioned custom of primogeniture   49-50 **your
coming ... reverence** i.e., as the eldest son you are head of the family and
therefore entitled to respect   54 **villain** (Oliver uses it in the sense of "wicked
person," but Orlando plays on its other meaning, "low-born person")
67 **qualities** accomplishments   69 **exercises** occupations   71 **allottery** share

OLIVER And what wilt thou do? Beg when that is spent?
Well, sir, get you in. I will not long be troubled with
75   you. You shall have some part of your will. I pray
you leave me.

ORLANDO I will no further offend you than becomes me
for my good.

OLIVER Get you with him, you old dog.

80   ADAM Is "old dog" my reward? Most true, I have lost
my teeth in your service. God be with my old master;
he would not have spoke such a word.

Exeunt Orlando, Adam.

OLIVER Is it even so? Begin you to grow upon me? I
will physic your rankness and yet give no thousand
85   crowns neither. Holla, Dennis!

Enter Dennis.

DENNIS Calls your worship?

OLIVER Was not Charles, the Duke's wrestler, here to
speak with me?

DENNIS So please you, he is here at the door and impor-
90   tunes access to you.

OLIVER Call him in. [*Exit Dennis.*] 'Twill be a good way;
and tomorrow the wrestling is.

Enter Charles.

CHARLES Good morrow to your worship.

OLIVER Good Monsieur Charles, what's the new news
95   at the new court?

CHARLES There's no news at the court, sir, but the old
news. That is, the old Duke is banished by his
younger brother the new Duke, and three or four
loving lords have put themselves into voluntary exile
100   with him, whose lands and revenues enrich the new

83 **grow upon me** i.e., usurp my place   84 **physic your rankness** purge your
overgrowth   97 **old Duke** i.e., Duke Senior

Duke; therefore he gives them good leave to wander.

OLIVER Can you tell if Rosalind, the Duke's daughter, be banished with her father?

CHARLES O, no; for the Duke's daughter, her cousin, so loves her, being ever from their cradles bred together, that she would have followed her exile, or have died to stay behind her. She is at the court, and no less beloved of her uncle than his own daughter, and never two ladies loved as they do.   105

OLIVER Where will the old Duke live?   110

CHARLES They say he is already in the Forest of Arden, and a many merry men with him; and there they live like the old Robin Hood of England. They say many young gentlemen flock to him every day, and fleet the time carelessly as they did in the golden world.   115

OLIVER What, you wrestle tomorrow before the new Duke?

CHARLES Marry, do I, sir; and I came to acquaint you with a matter. I am given, sir, secretly to understand that your younger brother, Orlando, hath a disposition to come in disguised against me to try a fall. Tomorrow, sir, I wrestle for my credit, and he that escapes me without some broken limb shall acquit him well. Your brother is but young and tender, and for your love I would be loath to foil him, as I must for my own honor if he come in. Therefore, out of my love to you, I came hither to acquaint you withal, that either you might stay him from his intendment, or brook such disgrace well as he shall run into, in that it is a thing of his own search and altogether against my will.   120 125 130

---

111 **Forest of Arden** Ardennes (in France; though Shakespeare may also have had in mind the Forest of Arden near his birthplace) 114-15 **fleet the time carelessly** pass the time at ease 115 **golden world** (the Golden Age of classical mythology, when men were free of sin, want, and care) 121 **fall** bout 125 **foil** throw, defeat 129 **brook** endure

OLIVER Charles, I thank thee for thy love to me, which
thou shalt find I will most kindly requite. I had myself notice of my brother's purpose herein and have
135 by underhand means labored to dissuade him from
it; but he is resolute. I'll tell thee, Charles, it is the
stubbornest young fellow of France; full of ambition,
an envious emulator of every man's good parts, a
secret and villainous contriver against me his natural
140 brother. Therefore use thy discretion. I had as lief
thou didst break his neck as his finger. And thou
wert best look to't; for if thou dost him any slight
disgrace, or if he do not mightily grace himself on
thee, he will practice against thee by poison, entrap
145 thee by some treacherous device, and never leave thee
till he hath ta'en thy life by some indirect means or
other; for, I assure thee, and almost with tears I
speak it, there is not one so young and so villainous
this day living. I speak but brotherly of him, but
150 should I anatomize him to thee as he is, I must
blush and weep, and thou must look pale and wonder.

CHARLES I am heartily glad I came hither to you. If he
come tomorrow, I'll give him his payment. If ever he
go alone again, I'll never wrestle for prize more. And
155 so God keep your worship.   *Exit*.

OLIVER Farewell, good Charles. Now will I stir this
gamester. I hope I shall see an end of him; for my
soul, yet I know not why, hates nothing more than
he. Yet he's gentle, never schooled and yet learned,
160 full of noble device, of all sorts enchantingly beloved; and indeed so much in the heart of the world,
and especially of my own people, who best know him,
that I am altogether misprized. But it shall not be so

135 **by underhand means** indirectly   138 **envious emulator** malicious rival
138 **parts** abilities   139 **natural** blood   140 **lief** soon   143–44 **grace himself
on thee** gain credit at your expense   144 **practice** plot   150 **anatomize** fully
describe   154 **go alone** i.e., walk without crutches   157 **gamester** athlete,
sportsman   159 **gentle** endowed with the qualities of a gentleman   160 **noble
device** gentlemanlike purposes   160 **all sorts** all kinds of people   163 **misprized** scorned

long; this wrestler shall clear all. Nothing remains
but that I kindle the boy thither, which now I'll go   165
about.   *Exit*.

Scene II. [*The Duke's palace*.]

Enter Rosalind and Celia.

CELIA I pray thee, Rosalind, sweet my coz, be merry.

ROSALIND Dear Celia, I show more mirth than I am
    mistress of, and would you yet I were merrier? Unless
    you could teach me to forget a banished father, you
    must not learn me how to remember any extraordi-   5
    nary pleasure.

CELIA Herein I see thou lov'st me not with the full
    weight that I love thee. If my uncle, thy banished
    father, had banished thy uncle, the Duke my father,
    so thou hadst been still with me, I could have taught   10
    my love to take thy father for mine. So wouldst thou,
    if the truth of thy love to me were so righteously
    tempered as mine is to thee.

ROSALIND Well, I will forget the condition of my estate
    to rejoice in yours.   15

CELIA You know my father hath no child but I, nor
    none is like to have; and truly, when he dies, thou
    shalt be his heir; for what he hath taken away from
    thy father perforce, I will render thee again in affec-
    tion. By mine honor, I will, and when I break that   20
    oath, let me turn monster. Therefore, my sweet Rose,
    my dear Rose, be merry.

---

164 **clear all** settle matters   I.ii.1 **sweet my coz** my sweet cousin   5 **learn** teach
10 **so** provided that   12–13 **righteously tempered** perfectly composed
14 **estate** fortune   19 **perforce** forcibly

ROSALIND From henceforth I will, coz, and devise sports.
Let me see, what think you of falling in love?

25 CELIA Marry, I prithee, do, to make sport withal; but
love no man in good earnest, nor no further in sport
neither than with safety of a pure blush thou mayst
in honor come off again.

ROSALIND What shall be our sport then?

30 CELIA Let us sit and mock the good housewife Fortune
from her wheel, that her gifts may henceforth be
bestowed equally.

ROSALIND I would we could do so, for her benefits are
mightily misplaced, and the bountiful blind woman
35   doth most mistake in her gifts to women.

CELIA 'Tis true, for those that she makes fair, she scarce
makes honest, and those that she makes honest, she
makes very ill-favoredly.

ROSALIND Nay, now thou goest from Fortune's office
40   to Nature's. Fortune reigns in gifts of the world, not
in the lineaments of Nature.

Enter [Touchstone, the] Clown.

CELIA No; when Nature hath made a fair creature, may
she not by Fortune fall into the fire? Though Nature
hath given us wit to flout at Fortune, hath not For-
45   tune sent in this fool to cut off the argument?

ROSALIND Indeed, there is Fortune too hard for Nature
when Fortune makes Nature's natural the cutter-off
of Nature's wit.

CELIA Peradventure this is not Fortune's work neither,
50   but Nature's, who perceiveth our natural wits too

27 **pure** mere   28 **come off** get away   30 **housewife** (1) woman of the house
(with a spinning wheel) (2) inconstant hussy   31 **wheel** (the wheel turned by
Fortune, blind goddess who distributed her favors at random, elevated some men
and hurled others down)   36 **fair** beautiful   37 **honest** chaste   38 **ill-favoredly**
ugly   39 **office** function   40 **gifts of the world** e.g., wealth, power   41 **lineaments of Nature** e.g., virtue, intelligence   47 **natural** born fool, halfwit
49 **Peradventure** perhaps

dull to reason of such goddesses and hath sent this
natural for our whetstone. For always the dullness of
the fool is the whetstone of the wits. How now, wit;
whither wander you?

TOUCHSTONE Mistress, you must come away to your 55
father.

CELIA Were you made the messenger?

TOUCHSTONE No, by mine honor, but I was bid to come
for you.

ROSALIND Where learned you that oath, fool? 60

TOUCHSTONE Of a certain knight that swore by his honor
they were good pancakes, and swore by his honor the
mustard was naught. Now I'll stand to it, the pancakes were naught, and the mustard was good, and
yet was not the knight forsworn. 65

CELIA How prove you that in the great heap of your
knowledge?

ROSALIND Ay, marry, now unmuzzle your wisdom.

TOUCHSTONE Stand you both forth now. Stroke your
chins, and swear by your beards that I am a knave. 70

CELIA By our beards, if we had them, thou art.

TOUCHSTONE By my knavery, if I had it, then I were;
but if you swear by that that is not, you are not forsworn; no more was this knight, swearing by his
honor, for he never had any; or if he had, he had 75
sworn it away before ever he saw those pancakes or
that mustard.

CELIA Prithee, who is't that thou mean'st?

TOUCHSTONE One that old Frederick, your father, loves.

CELIA My father's love is enough to honor him enough. 80

---

63 **naught** worthless   63 **stand to it** swear   65 **forsworn** perjured

Speak no more of him; you'll be whipped for taxation one of these days.

TOUCHSTONE The more pity that fools may not speak
wisely what wise men do foolishly.

85 CELIA By my troth, thou sayest true, for since the little
wit that fools have was silenced, the little foolery that
wise men have makes a great show. Here comes
Monsieur Le Beau.

Enter Le Beau.

ROSALIND With his mouth full of news.

90 CELIA Which he will put on us as pigeons feed their
young.

ROSALIND Then shall we be news-crammed.

CELIA All the better; we shall be the more marketable.
Bon jour, Monsieur Le Beau, what's the news?

95 LE BEAU Fair princess, you have lost much good sport.

CELIA Sport? Of what color?

LE BEAU What color, madam? How shall I answer you?

ROSALIND As wit and fortune will.

TOUCHSTONE Or as the Destinies decrees.

100 CELIA Well said; that was laid on with a trowel.

TOUCHSTONE Nay, if I keep not my rank—

ROSALIND Thou losest thy old smell.

LE BEAU You amaze me, ladies. I would have told you
of good wrestling, which you have lost the sight of.

105 ROSALIND Yet tell us the manner of the wrestling.

LE BEAU I will tell you the beginning; and if it please
your ladyships, you may see the end, for the best is

81–82 **taxation** slander 85 **troth** faith 90 **put** force 96 **color** sort 98
fortune good luck 99 **decrees** (the ending *s* was a common variant in the third
person plural) 103 **amaze** confuse 104 **lost the sight of** missed

yet to do, and here, where you are, they are coming to perform it.

CELIA Well, the beginning that is dead and buried. 110

LE BEAU There comes an old man and his three sons—

CELIA I could match this beginning with an old tale.

LE BEAU Three proper young men, of excellent growth and presence.

ROSALIND With bills on their necks, "Be it known unto 115 all men by these presents."

LE BEAU The eldest of the three wrestled with Charles, the Duke's wrestler; which Charles in a moment threw him and broke three of his ribs, that there is little hope of life in him. So he served the second, and 120 so the third. Yonder they lie, the poor old man, their father, making such pitiful dole over them that all the beholders take his part with weeping.

ROSALIND Alas!

TOUCHSTONE But what is the sport, monsieur, that the 125 ladies have lost?

LE BEAU Why, this that I speak of.

TOUCHSTONE Thus men may grow wiser every day. It is the first time that ever I heard breaking of ribs was sport for ladies. 130

CELIA Or I, I promise thee.

ROSALIND But is there any else longs to see this broken music in his sides? Is there yet another dotes upon rib-breaking? Shall we see this wrestling, cousin?

LE BEAU You must, if you stay here, for here is the 135

108 **do** be done 112 **old tale** (Le Beau's story has a "Once upon a time" beginning) 113 **proper** fine 115 **bills** notices 116 **by these presents** (part of the opening formula of many legal documents. Rosalind puns on Le Beau's use of "presence," meaning "bearing") 122 **dole** lamentation 132 **any** anyone 132–33 **broken music** music arranged in parts for different instruments

place appointed for the wrestling, and they are ready
to perform it.

CELIA Yonder sure they are coming. Let us now stay
and see it.

*Flourish. Enter Duke [Frederick], Lords, Orlando,
Charles, and Attendants.*

140 DUKE FREDERICK Come on. Since the youth will not be
entreated, his own peril on his forwardness.

ROSALIND Is yonder the man?

LE BEAU Even he, madam.

CELIA Alas, he is too young; yet he looks successfully.

145 DUKE FREDERICK How now, daughter and cousin; are
you crept hither to see the wrestling?

ROSALIND Ay, my liege, so please you give us leave.

DUKE FREDERICK You will take little delight in it, I can
tell you, there is such odds in the man. In pity of the
150 challenger's youth I would fain dissuade him, but he
will not be entreated. Speak to him, ladies; see if you
can move him.

CELIA Call him hither, good Monsieur Le Beau.

DUKE FREDERICK Do so. I'll not be by.

155 LE BEAU Monsieur the challenger, the princess calls for
you.

ORLANDO I attend them with all respect and duty.

ROSALIND Young man, have you challenged Charles the
wrestler?

160 ORLANDO No, fair princess. He is the general challenger;
I come but in as others do, to try with him the strength
of my youth.

CELIA Young gentleman, your spirits are too bold for

139 s.d. **Flourish** trumpet fanfare   144 **successfully** able to succeed   149 **such
odds in the man** i.e., the odds are all in Charles' favor   150 **fain** like to

your years. You have seen cruel proof of this man's
strength; if you saw yourself with your eyes or knew   165
yourself with your judgment, the fear of your adventure would counsel you to a more equal enterprise.
We pray you for your own sake to embrace your own
safety and give over this attempt.

ROSALIND Do, young sir. Your reputation shall not   170
therefore be misprized; we will make it our suit to
the Duke that the wrestling might not go forward.

ORLANDO I beseech you, punish me not with your hard
thoughts, wherein I confess me much guilty to deny
so fair and excellent ladies anything. But let your fair   175
eyes and gentle wishes go with me to my trial; wherein
if I be foiled, there is but one shamed that was never
gracious; if killed, but one dead that is willing to be
so. I shall do my friends no wrong, for I have none
to lament me; the world no injury, for in it I have   180
nothing. Only in the world I fill up a place, which
may be better supplied when I have made it empty.

ROSALIND The little strength that I have, I would it were
with you.

CELIA And mine to eke out hers.   185

ROSALIND Fare you well. Pray heaven I be deceived in
you!

CELIA Your heart's desires be with you!

CHARLES Come, where is this young gallant that is so
desirous to lie with his mother earth?   190

ORLANDO Ready, sir; but his will hath in it a more
modest working.

DUKE FREDERICK You shall try but one fall.

CHARLES No, I warrant your Grace you shall not entreat

171 **misprized** despised   177 **foiled** thrown   178 **gracious** graced by Fortune
181 **Only in the world I** in the world I only   185 **eke** stretch   186–87 **deceived
in you** i.e., wrong in my estimation of your strength   192 **modest working**
humble aim

195   him to a second that have so mightily persuaded him
        from a first.

        ORLANDO You mean to mock me after. You should not
        have mocked me before. But come your ways.

        ROSALIND Now Hercules be thy speed, young man!

200   CELIA I would I were invisible, to catch the strong
        fellow by the leg.   *Wrestle.*

        ROSALIND O excellent young man!

        CELIA If I had a thunderbolt in mine eye, I can tell who
        should down.   [*Charles is thrown.*] *Shout.*

205   DUKE FREDERICK No more, no more.

        ORLANDO Yes, I beseech your Grace; I am not yet well
        breathed.

        DUKE FREDERICK How dost thou, Charles?

        LE BEAU He cannot speak, my lord.

210   DUKE FREDERICK Bear him away. What is thy name,
        young man?

        ORLANDO Orlando, my liege, the youngest son of Sir
        Rowland de Boys.

        DUKE FREDERICK I would thou hadst been son to some
        man else.
215   The world esteemed thy father honorable,
        But I did find him still mine enemy.
        Thou shouldst have better pleased me with this deed
        Hadst thou descended from another house.
        But fare thee well; thou art a gallant youth;
220   I would thou hadst told me of another father.
                                        Exit Duke, [with Train].

        CELIA Were I my father, coz, would I do this?

        ORLANDO I am more proud to be Sir Rowland's son,

---

198 **come your ways** i.e., let's get started   199 **Hercules be thy speed** may
Hercules help you   206–7 **well breathed** fully warmed up   216 **still** always

His youngest son, and would not change that calling
To be adopted heir to Frederick.

ROSALIND My father loved Sir Rowland as his soul,   225
And all the world was of my father's mind.
Had I before known this young man his son,
I should have given him tears unto entreaties
Ere he should thus have ventured.

CELIA   Gentle cousin,
Let us go thank him and encourage him.   230
My father's rough and envious disposition
Sticks me at heart. Sir, you have well deserved;
If you do keep your promises in love
But justly as you have exceeded all promise,
Your mistress shall be happy.

ROSALIND   Gentleman, [gives chain]   235
Wear this for me, one out of suits with fortune,
That could give more but that her hand lacks means.
Shall we go, coz?

CELIA   Ay. Fare you well, fair gentleman.

ORLANDO Can I not say "I thank you"? My better parts
Are all thrown down, and that which here stands up   240
Is but a quintain, a mere lifeless block.

ROSALIND He calls us back. My pride fell with my
        fortunes;
I'll ask him what he would. Did you call, sir?
Sir, you have wrestled well, and overthrown
More than your enemies.

CELIA   Will you go, coz?   245

ROSALIND Have with you. Fare you well.
                                        Exit [*with Celia*].

ORLANDO What passion hangs these weights upon my
        tongue?

223 **calling** name   228 **unto** as well as   232 **Sticks** pains   234 **justly** exactly
236 **out of suits** in disfavor   237 **could** would   239 **parts** qualities   241 **quintain**
wooden post (used for tilting practice)   246 **Have with you** I'm coming
247 **passion** strong feeling

I cannot speak to her, yet she urged conference.

Enter Le Beau.

O poor Orlando, thou art overthrown!
250   Or Charles or something weaker masters thee.

LE BEAU   Good sir, I do in friendship counsel you
To leave this place. Albeit you have deserved
High commendation, true applause, and love,
Yet such is now the Duke's condition
255   That he misconsters all that you have done.
The Duke is humorous. What he is, indeed,
More suits you to conceive than I to speak of.

ORLANDO   I thank you, sir; and pray you, tell me this:
Which of the two was daughter of the Duke,
260   That here was at the wrestling?

LE BEAU   Neither his daughter, if we judge by manners,
But yet indeed the taller is his daughter,
The other is daughter to the banished Duke,
And here detained by her usurping uncle
265   To keep his daughter company, whose loves
Are dearer than the natural bond of sisters.
But I can tell you that of late this Duke
Hath ta'en displeasure 'gainst his gentle niece,
Grounded upon no other argument
270   But that the people praise her for her virtues
And pity her for her good father's sake;
And, on my life, his malice 'gainst the lady
Will suddenly break forth. Sir, fare you well.
Hereafter, in a better world than this,
275   I shall desire more love and knowledge of you.

ORLANDO   I rest much bounden to you. Fare you well.
                                        [*Exit Le Beau.*]
Thus must I from the smoke into the smother,

248 **conference** conversation   255 **misconsters** misinterprets   256 **humorous**
moody   257 **conceive** understand   262 **taller** (unless "taller" is a printer's slip
for "smaller," Shakespeare here erred. Rosalind is later said to be taller)
269 **argument** basis   274 **a better world** better times   276 **bounden** indebted
277 **smother** smothering smoke (the idea is: "Out of the frying pan into the fire")

From tyrant Duke unto a tyrant brother.
But heavenly Rosalind!   *Exit.*

Scene III. [*The palace.*]

Enter Celia and Rosalind.

CELIA Why, cousin, why, Rosalind! Cupid have mercy,
not a word?

ROSALIND Not one to throw at a dog.

CELIA No, thy words are too precious to be cast away
upon curs; throw some of them at me; come, lame   5
me with reasons.

ROSALIND Then there were two cousins laid up, when
the one should be lamed with reasons and the other
mad without any.

CELIA But is all this for your father?   10

ROSALIND No, some of it is for my child's father. O,
how full of briers is this working-day world!

CELIA They are but burrs, cousin, thrown upon thee in
holiday foolery; if we walk not in the trodden paths,
our very petticoats will catch them.   15

ROSALIND I could shake them off my coat; these burrs
are in my heart.

CELIA Hem them away.

ROSALIND I would try, if I could cry "hem," and have
him.   20

CELIA Come, come, wrestle with thy affections.

I.iii.9 **mad** melancholy   11 **child's father** i.e., future husband, Orlando   18 **Hem**
(1) cough (2) tuck   19 **cry "Hem"** clear my throat (with a pun on "him")
21 **affections** feelings

ROSALIND O, they take the part of a better wrestler than myself!

CELIA O, a good wish upon you! You will try in time,
25   in despite of a fall. But turning these jests out of service, let us talk in good earnest. Is it possible on such a sudden you should fall into so strong a liking with old Sir Rowland's youngest son?

ROSALIND The Duke my father loved his father dearly.

30   CELIA Doth it therefore ensue that you should love his son dearly? By this kind of chase, I should hate him, for my father hated his father dearly; yet I hate not Orlando.

ROSALIND No, faith, hate him not, for my sake.

35   CELIA Why should I not? Doth he not deserve well?

Enter Duke [Frederick], with Lords.

ROSALIND Let me love him for that, and do you love him because I do. Look, here comes the Duke.

CELIA With his eyes full of anger.

DUKE FREDERICK Mistress, dispatch you with your safest haste
And get you from our court.

ROSALIND   Me, uncle?

40   DUKE FREDERICK   You, cousin.
Within these ten days if that thou beest found
So near our public court as twenty miles,
Thou diest for it.

ROSALIND   I do beseech your Grace
Let me the knowledge of my fault bear with me.
45   If with myself I hold intelligence

---

24 **try** i.e., chance a bout   25-26 **turning … service** to stop joking   31 **chase** pursuit (of the argument)   35 **deserve well** i.e., deserve to be hated (if Rosalind's reasoning is valid, it follows that Celia should hate Orlando)   36 **for that** i.e., for his virtues (Rosalind takes "deserve well" in its usual sense)   40 **cousin** kinsman
45 **hold intelligence** communicate

Or have acquaintance with mine own desires,
If that I do not dream or be not frantic,
As I do trust I am not; then, dear uncle,
Never so much as in a thought unborn
Did I offend your Highness.

DUKE FREDERICK   Thus do all traitors.   50
If their purgation did consist in words,
They are as innocent as grace itself.
Let it suffice thee that I trust thee not.

ROSALIND   Yet your mistrust cannot make me a traitor.
Tell me whereon the likelihoods depends.   55

DUKE FREDERICK   Thou art thy father's daughter, there's
    enough.

ROSALIND   So was I when your Highness took his
    dukedom;
So was I when your Highness banished him.
Treason is not inherited, my lord,
Or if we did derive it from our friends,   60
What's that to me? My father was no traitor.
Then, good my liege, mistake me not so much
To think my poverty is treacherous.

CELIA   Dear sovereign, hear me speak.

DUKE FREDERICK   Ay, Celia. We stayed her for your sake,   65
Else had she with her father ranged along.

CELIA   I did not then entreat to have her stay;
It was your pleasure and your own remorse.
I was too young that time to value her,
But now I know her. If she be a traitor,   70
Why, so am I. We still have slept together,
Rose at an instant, learned, played, eat together;
And wheresoe'er we went, like Juno's swans,
Still we went coupled and inseparable.

---

47 **frantic** insane   51 **purgation** clearance   52 **grace** virtue   55 **likelihoods** possibilities   60 **friends** relatives   65 **stayed** kept   66 **ranged** wandered 68 **remorse** pity   71 **still** always   72 **eat** eaten

DUKE FREDERICK She is too subtile for thee; and her
75   smoothness,
        Her very silence and her patience,
        Speak to the people, and they pity her.
        Thou art a fool. She robs thee of thy name,
        And thou wilt show more bright and seem more
            virtuous
80   When she is gone. Then open not thy lips.
        Firm and irrevocable is my doom
        Which I have passed upon her; she is banished.

CELIA Pronounce that sentence then on me, my liege;
        I cannot live out of her company.

DUKE FREDERICK You are a fool. You, niece, provide
85   yourself;
        If you outstay the time, upon mine honor,
        And in the greatness of my word, you die.
                                    Exit Duke, &c.

CELIA O my poor Rosalind, whither wilt thou go?
        Wilt thou change fathers? I will give thee mine.
90   I charge thee be not thou more grieved than I am.

ROSALIND I have more cause.

CELIA   Thou hast not, cousin.
        Prithee be cheerful. Know'st thou not the Duke
        Hath banished me, his daughter?

ROSALIND   That he hath not.

CELIA No? Hath not? Rosalind lacks then the love
95   Which teacheth thee that thou and I am one.
        Shall we be sund'red, shall we part, sweet girl?
        No, let my father seek another heir.
        Therefore devise with me how we may fly,
        Whither to go, and what to bear with us;
100   And do not seek to take your change upon you,
        To bear your griefs yourself and leave me out;

75 **subtile** crafty 79 **virtuous** full of good qualities 81 **doom** sentence
87 **greatness** power 100 **change** i.e., change of fortune

For, by this heaven, now at our sorrows pale,
Say what thou canst, I'll go along with thee.

ROSALIND Why, whither shall we go?

CELIA To seek my uncle in the Forest of Arden.   105

ROSALIND Alas, what danger will it be to us,
Maids as we are, to travel forth so far!
Beauty provoketh thieves sooner than gold.

CELIA I'll put myself in poor and mean attire
And with a kind of umber smirch my face;   110
The like do you; so shall we pass along
And never stir assailants.

ROSALIND   Were it not better,
Because that I am more than common tall,
That I did suit me all points like a man?
A gallant curtle-ax upon my thigh,   115
A boar-spear in my hand, and, in my heart
Lie there what hidden woman's fear there will,
We'll have a swashing and a martial outside,
As many other mannish cowards have
That do outface it with their semblances.   120

CELIA What shall I call thee when thou art a man?

ROSALIND I'll have no worse a name than Jove's own
page,
And therefore look you call me Ganymede.
But what will you be called?

CELIA Something that hath a reference to my state: 125
No longer Celia, but Aliena.

ROSALIND But, cousin, what if we assayed to steal
The clownish fool out of your father's court;
Would he not be a comfort to our travel?

102 **now at our sorrows pale** now pale at our sorrows 109 **mean** lowly
110 **umber** reddish-brown color 113 **common** usually 114 **suit me at all
points** dress myself entirely 115 **curtle-ax** cutlass 118 **swashing** blustering
120 **outface** bluff 120 **semblances** appearances (of bravery) 126 **Aliena**
(Latin: the estranged one) 127 **assayed** attempted

130   CELIA He'll go along o'er the wide world with me;
          Leave me alone to woo him. Let's away
          And get our jewels and our wealth together,
          Devise the fittest time and safest way
          To hide us from pursuit that will be made
135   After my flight. Now go in we content
          To liberty, and not to banishment.   *Exeunt.*

131 **woo** coax

ACT II

Scene I. [*The Forest of Arden.*]

*Enter Duke Senior, Amiens, and two or three
Lords, like Foresters.*

DUKE SENIOR Now, my co-mates and brothers in exile,
Hath not old custom made this life more sweet
Than that of painted pomp? Are not these woods
More free from peril than the envious court?
Here feel we not the penalty of Adam;   5
The seasons' difference, as the icy fang
And churlish chiding of the winter's wind,
Which, when it bites and blows upon my body
Even till I shrink with cold, I smile and say
"This is no flattery; these are counselors   10
That feelingly persuade me what I am."
Sweet are the uses of adversity,
Which, like the toad, ugly and venomous,
Wears yet a precious jewel in his head;
And this our life, exempt from public haunt,   15
Finds tongues in trees, books in the running brooks,
Sermons in stones, and good in everything.

II.i.1 **exile** (accent on second syllable) 5 **feel we not** we do not feel (some editors emend "not" to "but") 5 **penalty of Adam** loss of Eden 6 **as** for example 7 **churlish** harsh 11 **feelingly** (1) through the senses (2) with intensity 14 **a precious jewel** (the fabled toadstone) 15 **public haunt** society

AMIENS I would not change it; happy is your Grace
That can translate the stubbornness of fortune
20   Into so quiet and so sweet a style.

DUKE SENIOR Come, shall we go and kill us venison?
And yet it irks me the poor dappled fools,
Being native burghers of this desert city,
Should, in their own confines, with forkèd heads
Have their round haunches gored.

25   FIRST LORD   Indeed, my lord,
The melancholy Jaques grieves at that,
And in that kind swears you do more usurp
Than doth your brother that hath banished you.
Today my Lord of Amiens and myself
30   Did steal behind him as he lay along
Under an oak, whose antique root peeps out
Upon the brook that brawls along this wood;
To the which place a poor sequest'red stag
That from the hunter's aim had ta'en a hurt
35   Did come to languish; and indeed, my lord,
The wretched animal heaved forth such groans
That their discharge did stretch his leathern coat
Almost to bursting, and the big round tears
Coursed one another down his innocent nose
40   In piteous chase; and thus the hairy fool,
Much markèd of the melancholy Jaques,
Stood on th' extremest verge of the swift brook,
Augmenting it with tears.

DUKE SENIOR   But what said Jaques?
Did he not moralize this spectacle?

45   FIRST LORD O, yes, into a thousand similes.
First, for his weeping into the needless stream:
"Poor deer," quoth he, "thou mak'st a testament
As worldlings do, giving thy sum of more

19 **stubbornness** hardness 22 **fools** simple creatures 23 **burghers** citizens
23 **desert** deserted 24 **forkèd heads** arrows 26 **Jaques** (dissyllabic, pronounced "Jákis") 27 **kind** way 30 **along** stretched out 32 **brawls** makes noise
33 **sequest'red** separated 41 **markèd** of noted by 44 **moralize** sermonize
46 **needless** i.e., needing no more water

To that which had too much." Then, being there
   alone,
Left and abandoned of his velvet friend: 50
" 'Tis right," quoth he, "thus misery doth part
The flux of company." Anon a careless herd,
Full of the pasture, jumps along by him
And never stays to greet him: "Ay," quoth Jaques,
"Sweep on, you fat and greasy citizens,   55
'Tis just the fashion: wherefore do you look
Upon that poor and broken bankrupt there?"
Thus most invectively he pierceth through
The body of the country, city, court,
Yea, and of this our life, swearing that we   60
Are mere usurpers, tyrants, and what's worse,
To fright the animals and to kill them up
In their assigned and native dwelling place.

DUKE SENIOR And did you leave him in this
   contemplation?

SECOND LORD We did, my lord, weeping and
   commenting   65
Upon the sobbing deer.

DUKE SENIOR   Show me the place.
I love to cope him in these sullen fits,
For then he's full of matter.

FIRST LORD I'll bring you to him straight.   *Exeunt*.

---

50 velvet i.e., courtierlike (the furry skin on the antlers, or the sleek hide, makes
the deer resemble a velvet-clad courtier)   52 flux stream   52 Anon a careless
soon an untroubled   56 wherefore do you look why should you bother looking
63 assigned allotted (by nature)   67 cope encounter   69 straight at once

Scene II. [*The palace*.]

Enter Duke [Frederick], with Lords.

DUKE FREDERICK Can it be possible that no man saw
     them?
     It cannot be; some villains of my court
     Are of consent and sufferance in this.

FIRST LORD I cannot hear of any that did see her.
5   The ladies, her attendants of her chamber,
     Saw her abed, and in the morning early
     They found the bed untreasured of their mistress.

SECOND LORD My lord, the roynish clown at whom so
     oft
     Your Grace was wont to laugh is also missing.
10   Hisperia, the princess' gentlewoman,
     Confesses that she secretly o'erheard
     Your daughter and her cousin much commend
     The parts and graces of the wrestler
     That did but lately foil the sinewy Charles,
15   And she believes, wherever they are gone,
     That youth is surely in their company.

DUKE FREDERICK Send to his brother, fetch that gallant
     hither;
     If he be absent, bring his brother to me;
     I'll make him find him. Do this suddenly,
20   And let not search and inquisition quail
     To bring again these foolish runaways.   *Exeunt.*

II.ii.3 **Are of consent and sufferance** approved and helped   8 **roynish** scurvy
13 **parts and graces** good qualities and manner   19 **suddenly** immediately
20 **quail** fail

Scene III. [*Oliver's house.*]

Enter Orlando and Adam.

ORLANDO Who's there?

ADAM What, my young master, O my gentle master,
　　O my sweet master, O you memory
　　Of old Sir Rowland, why, what make you here?
　　Why are you virtuous? Why do people love you?   5
　　And wherefore are you gentle, strong, and valiant?
　　Why would you be so fond to overcome
　　The bonny prizer of the humorous Duke?
　　Your praise is come too swiftly home before you.
　　Know you not, master, to some kind of men   10
　　Their graces serve them but as enemies?
　　No more do yours. Your virtues, gentle master,
　　Are sanctified and holy traitors to you.
　　O, what a world is this, when what is comely
　　Envenoms him that bears it!   15

ORLANDO Why, what's the matter?

ADAM   O unhappy youth,
　　Come not within these doors; within this roof
　　The enemy of all your graces lives.
　　Your brother—no, no brother, yet the son—
　　Yet not the son, I will not call him son,   20
　　Of him I was about to call his father—
　　Hath heard your praises, and this night he means
　　To burn the lodging where you use to lie
　　And you within it. If he fail of that,

II.iii.4 **make you** are you doing   7 **fond** foolish   8 **bonny prizer** stout fighter
8 **humorous** moody, temperamental   12 **No more** no better   12-13 **Your
virtues ... traitors to you** i.e., Orlando's blessed virtues have worked against
him   23 **use** are accustomed

25   He will have other means to cut you off.
      I overheard him, and his practices;
      This is no place, this house is but a butchery;
      Abhor it, fear it, do not enter it!

      ORLANDO Why, whither, Adam, wouldst thou have me
        go?

30   ADAM No matter whither, so you come not here.

      ORLANDO What, wouldst thou have me go and beg my
        food,
      Or with a base and boist'rous sword enforce
      A thievish living on the common road?
      This I must do, or know not what to do;
35   Yet this I will not do, do how I can.
      I rather will subject me to the malice
      Of a diverted blood and bloody brother.

      ADAM But do not so. I have five hundred crowns,
      The thrifty hire I saved under your father,
40   Which I did store to be my foster nurse
      When service should in my old limbs lie lame
      And unregarded age in corners thrown.
      Take that, and he that doth the ravens feed,
      Yea, providently caters for the sparrow,
45   Be comfort to my age. Here is the gold;
      All this I give you. Let me be your servant;
      Though I look old, yet I am strong and lusty,
      For in my youth I never did apply
      Hot and rebellious liquors in my blood,
50   Nor did not with unbashful forehead woo
      The means of weakness and debility;
      Therefore my age is as a lusty winter,
      Frosty, but kindly. Let me go with you;
      I'll do the service of a younger man
55   In all your business and necessities.

26 **practices** plots   27 **butchery** slaughterhouse   32 **base and boist'rous** low
and swaggering   33 **common road** highway   37 **diverted** estranged   39 **thrifty
hire I saved** wages I carefully saved   43-44 **he that ... the sparrow** (see Psalms
147:9, Luke 12:6)   49 **rebellious** i.e., causing the flesh to rebel   50 **unbashful
forehead** bold face

ORLANDO O good old man, how well in thee appears
   The constant service of the antique world,
   When service sweat for duty, not for meed!
   Thou art not for the fashion of these times,
   Where none will sweat but for promotion,   60
   And having that, do choke their service up
   Even with the having; it is not so with thee.
   But, poor old man, thou prun'st a rotten tree
   That cannot so much as a blossom yield
   In lieu of all thy pains and husbandry.   65
   But come thy ways, we'll go along together,
   And ere we have thy youthful wages spent,
   We'll light upon some settled low content.

ADAM Master, go on, and I will follow thee
   To the last gasp with truth and loyalty.   70
   From seventeen years till now almost fourscore
   Here livèd I, but now live here no more;
   At seventeen years many their fortunes seek,
   But at fourscore it is too late a week;
   Yet fortune cannot recompense me better   75
   Than to die well and not my master's debtor. *Exeunt.*

Scene IV. [*The Forest of Arden.*]

Enter Rosalind for Ganymede, Celia for Aliena, and
Clown, alias Touchstone.

ROSALIND O Jupiter, how weary are my spirits!

TOUCHSTONE I care not for my spirits if my legs were
   not weary.

ROSALIND I could find in my heart to disgrace my man's

57 **constant** faithful   57 **the antique world** the past   58 **meed** reward   65 **In lieu of** in return for   68 **low content** humble way of life   74 **week** time

5   apparel and to cry like a woman; but I must comfort
       the weaker vessel, as doublet and hose ought to
       show itself courageous to petticoat. Therefore, cour-
       age, good Aliena!

       CELIA I pray you bear with me; I cannot go no further.

10   TOUCHSTONE For my part, I had rather bear with you
       than bear you; yet I should bear no cross if I did
       bear you, for I think you have no money in your
       purse.

       ROSALIND Well, this is the Forest of Arden.

15   TOUCHSTONE Ay, now am I in Arden, the more fool I.
       When I was at home, I was in a better place, but
       travelers must be content.

                    Enter Corin and Silvius.

       ROSALIND Ay, be so, good Touchstone. Look you, who
       comes here, a young man and an old in solemn talk.

20   CORIN That is the way to make her scorn you still.

       SILVIUS O Corin, that thou knew'st how I do love her!

       CORIN I partly guess, for I have loved ere now.

       SILVIUS No, Corin, being old, thou canst not guess,
       Though in thy youth thou wast as true a lover
25   As ever sighed upon a midnight pillow.
       But if thy love were ever like to mine,
       As sure I think did never man love so,
       How many actions most ridiculous
       Hast thou been drawn to by thy fantasy?

30   CORIN Into a thousand that I have forgotten.

       SILVIUS O, thou didst then never love so heartily!
       If thou rememb'rest not the slightest folly
       That ever love did make thee run into,
       Thou hast not loved.

II.iv.6 **doublet and hose** jacket and breeches   11 **cross** (1) trouble (2) coin
stamped with a cross   29 **fantasy** love (and all its fancies)

Or if thou hast not sat as I do now,   35
Wearing thy hearer in thy mistress' praise,
Thou hast not loved.
Or if thou hast not broke from company
Abruptly, as my passion now makes me,
Thou has not loved.   40
O Phebe, Phebe, Phebe!   *Exit*.

ROSALIND Alas, poor shepherd! Searching of thy wound,
I have by hard adventure found mine own.

TOUCHSTONE And I mine. I remember, when I was in love
I broke my sword upon a stone and bid him take that   45
for coming a-night to Jane Smile; and I remember
the kissing of her batler, and the cow's dugs that her
pretty chopt hands had milked; and I remember the
wooing of a peascod instead of her, from whom I
took two cods, and giving her them again, said with   50
weeping tears, "Wear these for my sake." We that
are true lovers run into strange capers; but as all is
mortal in nature, so is all nature in love mortal in
folly.

ROSALIND Thou speak'st wiser than thou art ware of.   55

TOUCHSTONE Nay, I shall ne'er be ware of mine own wit
till I break my shins against it.

ROSALIND Jove, Jove! This shepherd's passion
Is much upon my fashion.

TOUCHSTONE And mine, but it grows something stale   60
with me.

CELIA I pray you, one of you question yond man
If he for gold will give us any food.
I faint almost to death.

TOUCHSTONE Holla, you clown!   65

36 **Wearing** exhausting   42 **Searching of** probing   43 **hard adventure** bad
luck   47 **batler** wooden paddle (used in washing clothes)   48 **chopt** chapped
49 **peascod** peapod   52-54 **as all is mortal ... folly** just as everything that lives
must die, so all who love inevitably do foolish things   55 **art ware** know   56 **wit**
wisdom   65 **clown** (1) rustic (2) fool

ROSALIND Peace, fool! He's not thy kinsman.

CORIN Who calls?

TOUCHSTONE Your betters, sir.

CORIN   Else are they very wretched.

ROSALIND Peace, I say! Good even to you, friend.

70 CORIN And to you, gentle sir, and to you all.

ROSALIND I prithee, shepherd, if that love or gold
      Can in this desert place buy entertainment,
      Bring us where we may rest ourselves and feed.
      Here's a young maid with travel much oppressed,
      And faints for succor.

75 CORIN   Fair sir, I pity her
      And wish, for her sake more than for mine own,
      My fortunes were more able to relieve her;
      But I am shepherd to another man
      And do not shear the fleeces that I graze.
80   My master is of churlish disposition
      And little recks to find the way to heaven
      By doing deeds of hospitality.
      Besides, his cote, his flocks, and bounds of feed
      Are now on sale, and at our sheepcote now,
85   By reason of his absence, there is nothing
      That you will feed on; but what is, come see,
      And in my voice most welcome shall you be.

ROSALIND What is he that shall buy his flock and pasture?

CORIN That young swain that you saw here but ere-
      while,
90   That little cares for buying anything.

ROSALIND I pray thee, if it stand with honesty,
      Buy thou the cottage, pasture, and the flock,

72 **entertainment** food and shelter 80 **churlish** miserly 81 **recks** thinks
83 **cote** cottage 83 **bounds of feed** pastures 87 **in my voice** as far as my
position allows 89 **erewhile** a short while ago 91 **stand** be consistent

And thou shalt have to pay for it of us.

CELIA And we will mend thy wages. I like this place
        And willingly could waste my time in it.   95

CORIN Assuredly the thing is to be sold.
        Go with me; if you like upon report
        The soil, the profit, and this kind of life,
        I will your very faithful feeder be
        And buy it with your gold right suddenly.   *Exeunt.* 100

Scene V. [*The forest.*]

Enter Amiens, Jaques, and others.

Song.

AMIENS Under the greenwood tree
            Who loves to lie with me,
        And turn his merry note
            Unto the sweet bird's throat,
        Come hither, come hither, come hither.   5
            Here shall he see no enemy
        But winter and rough weather.

JAQUES More, more, I prithee more!

AMIENS It will make you melancholy, Monsieur Jaques.

JAQUES I thank it. More, I prithee more! I can suck   10
        melancholy out of a song as a weasel sucks eggs.
        More, I prithee more!

AMIENS My voice is ragged. I know I cannot please you.

JAQUES I do not desire you to please me; I do desire you
        to sing. Come, more, another stanzo! Call you 'em   15
        stanzos?

93 have i.e., have the money   94 mend improve   95 waste spend   99 feeder
servant   II.v.3 turn attune, adapt

353

AMIENS What you will, Monsieur Jaques.

JAQUES Nay, I care not for their names; they owe me
nothing. Will you sing?

20 AMIENS More at your request than to please myself.

JAQUES Well then, if ever I thank any man, I'll thank
you. But that they call compliment is like th' encounter of two dog-apes, and when a man thanks
me heartily, methinks I have given him a penny and
25 he renders me the beggarly thanks. Come, sing; and
you that will not, hold your tongues.

AMIENS Well, I'll end the song. Sirs, cover the while;
the Duke will drink under this tree. He hath been all
this day to look you.

30 JAQUES And I have been all this day to avoid him. He
is too disputable for my company. I think of as many
matters as he, but I give heaven thanks and make no
boast of them. Come, warble, come.

Song.

All together here.

Who doth ambition shun
35   And loves to live i' th' sun,
Seeking the food he eats,
              And pleased with what he gets,
Come hither, come hither, come hither.
Here shall he see no enemy
40   But winter and rough weather.

JAQUES I'll give you a verse to this note that I made
yesterday in despite of my invention.

18-19 names ... nothing (Jaques plays on the word "names," a term for the
borrower's signature on a loan) 22 compliment politeness 23 dog-apes
baboons 23-25 and when ... beggarly thanks i.e., the hearty thanks of polite
society are no more sincere than the extravagant gratitude of a beggar given a small
coin 27 cover the while lay the table in the meantime 41 note tune 42 in
despite of my invention without using my imagination

AMIENS And I'll sing it.

JAQUES Thus it goes.
        If it do come to pass   45
        That any man turn ass,
        Leaving his wealth and ease
        A stubborn will to please,
        Ducdame, ducdame, ducdame.
        Here shall he see gross fools as he,   50
        An if he will come to me.

AMIENS What's that "ducdame"?

JAQUES 'Tis a Greek invocation to call fools into a
circle. I'll go sleep, if I can; if I cannot, I'll rail against
all the first-born of Egypt.   55

AMIENS And I'll go seek the Duke. His banquet is
prepared.   *Exeunt.*

Scene VI. [*The forest.*]

Enter Orlando and Adam.

ADAM Dear master, I can go no further. O, I die for
food. Here lie I down and measure out my grave.
Farewell, kind master.

ORLANDO Why, how now, Adam? No greater heart in
thee? Live a little, comfort a little, cheer thyself a   5

---

49 **Ducdame** (various derivations have been suggested: Romany *dukrā mē* ["I tell
fortunes"]; Welsh *dewch 'da mi* ["come with me"]; Latin *duc ad me* ["bring (him) to
me"]; Italian *Duc' da mè* ["duke by myself" or "duke without a dukedom"].
Probably the word is nonsense) 51 **An if** if only 53 **Greek** unintelligible
55 **first-born of Egypt** (perhaps "persons of high rank," but perhaps an allusion
to life in the Forest of Arden. Exodus 11,12 reports that when the first-born of
Egypt died, the Israelites were sent into the wilderness) 56 **banquet** light meal
II.vi.5 **comfort** take comfort

little. If this uncouth forest yield anything savage, I
will either be food for it or bring it for food to thee.
Thy conceit is nearer death than thy powers. For my
sake be comfortable, hold death awhile at the arm's
10 end. I will here be with thee presently, and if I bring
thee not something to eat, I will give thee leave to
die; but if thou diest before I come, thou art a mocker
of my labor. Well said; thou look'st cheerly, and I'll
be with thee quickly. Yet thou liest in the bleak air.
15 Come, I will bear thee to some shelter, and thou
shalt not die for lack of a dinner if there live anything
in this desert. Cheerly, good Adam.   *Exeunt.*

Scene VII. [*The forest.*]

Enter Duke Senior, and Lords, like Outlaws.

DUKE SENIOR I think he be transformed into a beast,
For I can nowhere find him like a man.

FIRST LORD My lord, he is but even now gone hence;
Here was he merry, hearing of a song.

5   DUKE SENIOR If he, compact of jars, grow musical,
We shall have shortly discord in the spheres.
Go seek him; tell him I would speak with him.

Enter Jaques.

FIRST LORD He saves my labor by his own approach.

DUKE SENIOR Why, how now, monsieur, what a life is
this,
10   That your poor friends must woo your company?
What, you look merrily.

6 **uncouth** wild   8 **conceit** thought   10 **presently** at once   II.vii.5 **compact of
jars** made up of discord   6 **discord in the spheres** (Ptolemaic astronomy taught
that the planetary spheres produced a ravishing harmony as they revolved)

JAQUES A fool, a fool! I met a fool i' th' forest,
 A motley fool! A miserable world!
 As I do live by food, I met a fool
 Who laid him down and basked him in the sun   15
 And railed on Lady Fortune in good terms,
 In good set terms, and yet a motley fool.
 "Good morrow, fool," quoth I. "No, sir," quoth he,
 "Call me not fool till heaven hath sent me fortune."
 And then he drew a dial from his poke,   20
 And looking on it with lack-luster eye,
 Says very wisely, "It is ten o'clock.
 Thus we may see," quoth he, "how the world wags.
 'Tis but an hour ago since it was nine,
 And after one hour more 'twill be eleven;   25
 And so, from hour to hour, we ripe and ripe,
 And then, from hour to hour, we rot and rot;
 And thereby hangs a tale." When I did hear
 The motley fool thus moral on the time,
 My lungs began to crow like chanticleer   30
 That fools should be so deep contemplative;
 And I did laugh sans intermission
 An hour by his dial. O noble fool,
 A worthy fool! Motley's the only wear.

DUKE SENIOR What fool is this?   35

JAQUES O worthy fool! One that hath been a courtier,
 And says, if ladies be but young and fair,
 They have the gift to know it. And in his brain,
 Which is as dry as the remainder biscuit
 After a voyage, he hath strange places crammed   40
 With observation, the which he vents

---

13 **motley** garbed in the multicolored costume of the court fool (a motley costume is commonly thought to be checkered or patched; Leslie Hotson, in *Shakespeare's Motley*, argues it was of varicolored threads but drab, like a tweed) 17 **set terms** precise phrases 19 **Call me ... fortune** (fortune proverbially favors fools) 20 **dial from his poke** sundial from his pocket 23 **wags** goes 26 **hour to hour** (perhaps with a pun on "whore") 29 **moral** moralize 30 **chanticleer** (traditional name for a rooster) 32 **sans intermission** without stop 39 **remainder biscuit** leftover hardtack 41 **vents** gives forth

In mangled forms. O that I were a fool!
I am ambitious for a motley coat.

DUKE SENIOR Thou shalt have one.

JAQUES   It is my only suit,
45   Provided that you weed your better judgments
Of all opinion that grows rank in them
That I am wise. I must have liberty
Withal, as large a charter as the wind,
To blow on whom I please, for so fools have.
50   And they that are most gallèd with my folly,
They most must laugh. And why, sir, must they so?
The why is plain as way to parish church:
He that a fool doth very wisely hit
Doth very foolishly, although he smart,
55   Not to seem senseless of the bob. If not,
The wise man's folly is anatomized
Even by the squand'ring glances of the fool.
Invest me in my motley, give me leave
To speak my mind, and I will through and through
60   Cleanse the foul body of th' infected world,
If they will patiently receive my medicine.

DUKE SENIOR Fie on thee! I can tell what thou wouldst
do.

JAQUES What, for a counter, would I do but good?

DUKE SENIOR Most mischievous foul sin, in chiding sin.
65   For thou thyself hast been a libertine,
As sensual as the brutish sting itself;
And all th' embossèd sores and headed evils
That thou with license of free foot hast caught,
Wouldst thou disgorge into the general world.

70   JAQUES Why, who cries out on pride

---

44 **suit** (1) garment (2) petition   46 **rank** luxuriant   48 **large a charter** liberal
license   50 **gallèd** chafed   55 **senseless of the bob** unaware of the hit
56 **anatomized** revealed   57 **squand'ring glances** chance hits   58 **Invest**
clothe   63 **counter** worthless coin   66 **the brutish sting** lust   67 **embossèd**
swollen   68 **license of free foot** complete freedom

That can therein tax any private party?
Doth it not flow as hugely as the sea
Till that the weary very means do ebb?
What woman in the city do I name
When that I say the city woman bears   75
The cost of princes on unworthy shoulders?
Who can come in and say that I mean her,
When such a one as she, such is her neighbor?
Or what is he of basest function
That says his bravery is not on my cost,   80
Thinking that I mean him, but therein suits
His folly to the mettle of my speech?
There then, how then, what then? Let me see wherein
My tongue hath wronged him. If it do him right,
Then he hath wronged himself. If he be free,   85
Why, then my taxing like a wild goose flies
Unclaimed of any man. But who comes here?

Enter Orlando [with his sword drawn].

ORLANDO Forbear, and eat no more!

JAQUES   Why, I have eat none yet.

ORLANDO Nor shalt not, till necessity be served.

JAQUES Of what kind should this cock come of?   90

DUKE SENIOR Art thou thus boldened, man, by thy
    distress,
Or else a rude despiser of good manners,
That in civility thou seem'st so empty?

ORLANDO You touched my vein at first. The thorny
    point
Of bare distress hath ta'en from me the show   95

---

71 **tax any private party** criticize any particular person 73 **weary very means
do ebb** (perhaps: "ostentation eventually exhausts the wealth that makes it
possible." Some editors emend "weary" to "wearer's") 76 **cost** wealth
79 **function** position 80 **his bravery ... cost** his fine dress is not paid for by
me (and therefore is not my business) 81–82 **suits ... my speech** matches his
folly to the substance of my words 85 **free** innocent 90 **kind** breed 94 **You
touched ... first** i.e., the Duke's first supposition is correct

Of smooth civility; yet am I inland bred
And know some nurture. But forbear, I say!
He dies that touches any of this fruit
Till I and my affairs are answerèd.

100   JAQUES An you will not be answered with reason, I
       must die.

       DUKE SENIOR What would you have? Your gentleness
              shall force
       More than your force move us to gentleness.

       ORLANDO I almost die for food, and let me have it!

       DUKE SENIOR Sit down and feed, and welcome to our
105   table.

       ORLANDO Speak you so gently? Pardon me, I pray you.
       I thought that all things had been savage here,
       And therefore put I on the countenance
       Of stern commandment. But whate'er you are
110   That in this desert inaccessible,
       Under the shade of melancholy boughs,
       Lose and neglect the creeping hours of time;
       If ever you have looked on better days,
       If ever been where bells have knolled to church,
115   If ever sat at any good man's feast,
       If ever from your eyelids wiped a tear
       And know what 'tis to pity and be pitied,
       Let gentleness my strong enforcement be;
       In the which hope I blush, and hide my sword.

120   DUKE SENIOR True is it that we have seen better days,
       And have with holy bell been knolled to church,
       And sat at good men's feasts, and wiped our eyes
       Of drops that sacred pity hath engend'red;
       And therefore sit you down in gentleness,
125   And take upon command what help we have
       That to your wanting may be minist'red.

96 **inland bred** brought up in civilized society   97 **nurture** good breeding
99 **answerèd** provided for   100 **An** if   100 **reason** (perhaps Jaques puns, eating
a raisin [grape])   114 **knolled** rung   118 **enforcement** support   125 **upon
command** as you wish   126 **wanting** need

ORLANDO Then but forbear your food a little while,
  Whiles, like a doe, I go to find my fawn
  And give it food. There is an old poor man
  Who after me hath many a weary step   130
  Limped in pure love. Till he be first sufficed,
  Oppressed with two weak evils, age and hunger,
  I will not touch a bit.

DUKE SENIOR   Go find him out,
  And we will nothing waste till you return.

ORLANDO I thank ye, and be blest for your good comfort!   135
                                        [*Exit*.]

DUKE SENIOR Thou seest we are not all alone unhappy:
  This wide and universal theater
  Presents more woeful pageants than the scene
  Wherein we play in.

JAQUES   All the world's a stage,
  And all the men and women merely players;   140
  They have their exits and their entrances,
  And one man in his time plays many parts,
  His acts being seven ages. At first, the infant,
  Mewling and puking in the nurse's arms.
  Then the whining schoolboy, with his satchel   145
  And shining morning face, creeping like snail
  Unwillingly to school. And then the lover,
  Sighing like furnace, with a woeful ballad
  Made to his mistress' eyebrow. Then a soldier,
  Full of strange oaths and bearded like the pard, 150
  Jealous in honor, sudden and quick in quarrel,
  Seeking the bubble reputation
  Even in the cannon's mouth. And then the justice,
  In fair round belly with good capon lined,

132 **weak evils** causing weakness   134 **waste** consume   138 **pageants** scenes
143 **seven ages** (for a survey in art and literature of the image of man's life divided
into ages, see Samuel C. Chew, '"This Strange Eventful History,"' in *Joseph
Quincy Adams Memorial Studies*, ed. James G. McManaway *et al.*)   144 **Mewling**
bawling   150 **pard** leopard   151 **Jealous** touchy   151 **sudden** rash   154 **capon
lined** (perhaps an allusion to the practice of bribing a judge with a capon)

155 With eyes severe and beard of formal cut,
     Full of wise saws and modern instances;
     And so he plays his part. The sixth age shifts
     Into the lean and slippered pantaloon,
     With spectacles on nose and pouch on side;
160 His youthful hose, well saved, a world too wide
     For his shrunk shank, and his big manly voice,
     Turning again toward childish treble, pipes
     And whistles in his sound. Last scene of all,
     That ends this strange eventful history,
165 Is second childishness and mere oblivion,
     Sans teeth, sans eyes, sans taste, sans everything.

Enter Orlando, with Adam.

DUKE SENIOR Welcome. Set down your venerable burden
     And let him feed.

ORLANDO I thank you most for him.

ADAM   So had you need.
170 I scarce can speak to thank you for myself.

DUKE SENIOR Welcome, fall to. I will not trouble you
     As yet to question you about your fortunes.
     Give us some music; and, good cousin, sing.

Song.

AMIENS
     Blow, blow, thou winter wind,
175 Thou art not so unkind
        As man's ingratitude:
     Thy tooth is not so keen,
     Because thou art not seen,
        Although thy breath be rude.
180 Heigh-ho, sing heigh-ho, unto the green holly.
     Most friendship is faining, most loving mere folly:

156 **saws** sayings   156 **modern instances** commonplace examples   158 **panta-loon** ridiculous old man (from Pantalone, a stock figure in Italian comedy)   160 **hose** breeches   163 **his** its   165 **mere** utter   175 **unkind** unnatural   181 **faining** longing (perhaps with a pun on "feigning" [pretending])

Then, heigh-ho, the holly.
This life is most jolly.

Freeze, freeze, thou bitter sky
That dost not bite so nigh   185
    As benefits forgot:
Though thou the waters warp,
Thy sting is not so sharp
    As friend rememb'red not.
Heigh-ho, sing, &c.   190

DUKE SENIOR If that you were the good Sir Rowland's
    son,
As you have whispered faithfully you were,
And as mine eye doth his effigies witness
Most truly limned and living in your face,
Be truly welcome hither. I am the Duke   195
That loved your father. The residue of your fortune
Go to my cave and tell me. Good old man,
Thou art right welcome, as thy master is.
Support him by the arm. Give me your hand,
And let me all your fortunes understand.   *Exeunt.* 200

187 **warp** turn (into ice)   193 **effigies** likeness (accent on second syllable)
194 **limned** depicted

ACT III

Scene I. [*The palace.*]

Enter Duke [Frederick], Lords, and Oliver.

DUKE FREDERICK Not see him since? Sir, sir, that cannot
    be.
    But were I not the better part made mercy,
    I should not seek an absent argument
    Of my revenge, thou present. But look to it:
5   Find out thy brother, whereso'er he is;
    Seek him with candle; bring him dead or living
    Within this twelvemonth, or turn thou no more
    To seek a living in our territory.
    Thy lands, and all things that thou dost call thine
10   Worth seizure, do we seize into our hands
    Till thou canst quit thee by thy brother's mouth
    Of what we think against thee.

OLIVER O that your Highness knew my heart in this!
    I never loved my brother in my life.

DUKE FREDERICK More villain thou. Well, push him out
15   of doors,
    And let my officers of such a nature

III.i.2 **the better part made mercy** so merciful   3 **argument** object (i.e.,
Orlando)   7 **turn** return   11 **quit** acquit   11 **mouth** testimony   16 **of such a
nature** i.e., appropriate

Make an extent upon his house and lands.
Do this expediently and turn him going.   *Exeunt*.

Scene II. [*The forest*.]

Enter Orlando, [with a paper].

ORLANDO Hang there, my verse, in witness of my love;
    And thou, thrice-crownèd Queen of Night, survey
With thy chaste eye, from thy pale sphere above,
    Thy huntress' name that my full life doth sway.
O Rosalind! These trees shall be my books,   5
    And in their barks my thoughts I'll character,
That every eye which in this forest looks
    Shall see thy virtue witnessed everywhere.
Run, run, Orlando, carve on every tree
The fair, the chaste, and unexpressive she.   *Exit*.   10

Enter Corin and [Touchstone, the] Clown.

CORIN And how like you this shepherd's life, Master
Touchstone?

TOUCHSTONE Truly, shepherd, in respect of itself, it is a
good life; but in respect that it is a shepherd's life, it
is naught. In respect that it is solitary, I like it very   15
well; but in respect that it is private, it is a very vile
life. Now in respect it is in the fields, it pleaseth me
well; but in respect it is not in the court, it is tedious.
As it is a spare life, look you, it fits my humor well;
but as there is no more plenty in it, it goes much   20

17 **Make an extent upon** seize by writ   18 **expediently** speedily   III.ii.2 **thrice-crownèd Queen of Night** Diana (goddess of the moon, the hunt, and of chastity) 4 **Thy huntress' name** i.e., Rosalind, who, because she is chaste, serves Diana 6 **character** write   8 **virtue witnessed** power attested to   10 **unexpressive she** i.e., woman beyond description   15 **naught** worthless   16 **private** lonely   19 **spare** frugal   19 **humor** disposition

against my stomach. Hast any philosophy in thee,
shepherd?

CORIN No more, but that I know the more one sickens,
the worse at ease he is; and that he that wants
money, means, and content is without three good
friends; that the property of rain is to wet and fire
to burn; that good pasture makes fat sheep, and that
a great cause of the night is lack of the sun; that he
that hath learned no wit by nature nor art may
complain of good breeding, or comes of a very dull
kindred.

TOUCHSTONE Such a one is a natural philosopher. Wast
ever in court, shepherd?

CORIN No, truly.

TOUCHSTONE Then thou art damned.

CORIN Nay, I hope.

TOUCHSTONE Truly thou art damned, like an ill-roasted
egg, all on one side.

CORIN For not being at court? Your reason.

TOUCHSTONE Why, if thou never wast at court, thou
never saw'st good manners; if thou never saw'st
good manners, then thy manners must be wicked;
and wickedness is sin, and sin is damnation. Thou
art in a parlous state, shepherd.

CORIN Not a whit, Touchstone. Those that are good
manners at the court are as ridiculous in the country
as the behavior of the country is most mockable at
the court. You told me you salute not at the court
but you kiss your hands. That courtesy would be
uncleanly if courtiers were shepherds.

TOUCHSTONE Instance, briefly. Come, instance.

21 philosophy learning   24 wants lacks   29 by nature nor art by birth or education   30 complain cry the lack   32 a natural philosopher (1) wise by nature
(2) a wise idiot   41 manners (1) behavior (2) morals   44 parlous dangerous
49 but you kiss without kissing   51 Instance proof

CORIN Why, we are still handling our ewes, and their fells you know are greasy.

TOUCHSTONE Why, do not your courtier's hands sweat? And is not the grease of a mutton as wholesome as   55
the sweat of a man? Shallow, shallow. A better instance, I say. Come.

CORIN Besides, our hands are hard.

TOUCHSTONE Your lips will feel them the sooner. Shallow again. A more sounder instance, come.   60

CORIN And they are often tarred over with the surgery of our sheep, and would you have us kiss tar? The courtier's hands are perfumed with civet.

TOUCHSTONE Most shallow man! Thou worms' meat in respect of a good piece of flesh indeed! Learn of the   65
wise, and perpend. Civet is of a baser birth than tar, the very uncleanly flux of a cat. Mend the instance, shepherd.

CORIN You have too courtly a wit for me; I'll rest.

TOUCHSTONE Wilt thou rest damned? God help thee,   70
shallow man! God make incision in thee! Thou art raw.

CORIN Sir, I am a true laborer; I earn that I eat, get that I wear, owe no man hate, envy no man's happiness, glad of other men's good, content with my   75
harm; and the greatest of my pride is to see my ewes graze and my lambs suck.

TOUCHSTONE That is another simple sin in you: to bring the ewes and the rams together and to offer to get your living by the copulation of cattle, to be bawd to   80

52 still always   53 fells fleeces   61 tarred ... surgery (shepherds used tar as an ointment)   63 civet perfume obtained from the civet cat   64 worm's meat food for worms   65 respect of comparison with   66 perpend consider   67 flux secretion   67 Mend the instance give a better example   71 make incision in thee let your blood (a common cure, here for folly)   72 raw (1) inexperienced (2) sore   73 that what   75-76 content with my harm bear with my troubles

a bell-wether and to betray a she-lamb of a twelvemonth to a crookèd-pated old cuckoldly ram, out
of all reasonable match. If thou beest not damned for
this, the devil himself will have no shepherds; I can-
85   not see else how thou shouldst 'scape.

CORIN Here comes young Master Ganymede, my new
mistress' brother.

Enter Rosalind, [reading a paper].

ROSALIND
        "From the east to western Ind,
        No jewel is like Rosalind.
90   Her worth, being mounted on the wind,
        Through all the world bears Rosalind.
        All the pictures fairest lined
        Are but black to Rosalind.
        Let no face be kept in mind
95   But the fair of Rosalind."

TOUCHSTONE I'll rhyme you so eight years together,
dinners and suppers and sleeping hours excepted. It
is the right butterwomen's rank to market.

ROSALIND Out, fool!

100 TOUCHSTONE For a taste:
        If a hart do lack a hind,
        Let him seek out Rosalind.
        If the cat will after kind,
        So be sure will Rosalind.
105   Wintred garments must be lined,
        So must slender Rosalind.
        They that reap must sheaf and bind,
        Then to cart with Rosalind.

---

81 **bell-wether** (the leading sheep of a flock carries a bell) 82 **crookèd-pated**
i.e., with crooked horns 82 **cuckoldly** (because horned) 92 **lined** drawn
95 **fair** lovely face 98 **right butterwomen's rank to market** i.e., the verses jog
along exactly like a procession of women riding to market 103 **kind** its own
kind 105 **Wintred** i.e., prepared for winter 105 **lined** stuffed 108 **to cart**
(perhaps an allusion not only to the harvest but to the custom of transporting
prostitutes to jail in a cart)

Sweetest nut hath sourest rind,
Such a nut is Rosalind.   110
He that sweetest rose will find
Must find love's prick, and Rosalind.
This is the very false gallop of verses. Why do you
infect yourself with them?

ROSALIND Peace, you dull fool! I found them on a tree.   115

TOUCHSTONE Truly the tree yields bad fruit.

ROSALIND I'll graff it with you and then I shall graff it
with a medlar. Then it will be the earliest fruit i' th'
country; for you'll be rotten ere you be half ripe, and
that's the right virtue of the medlar.   120

TOUCHSTONE You have said; but whether wisely or no,
let the forest judge.

Enter Celia, with a writing.

ROSALIND Peace! Here comes my sister reading; stand
aside.

CELIA "Why should this a desert be?   125
          For it is unpeopled? No.
     Tongues I'll hang on every tree
          That shall civil sayings show:
     Some, how brief the life of man
          Runs his erring pilgrimage,   130
     That the stretching of a span
          Buckles in his sum of age;
     Some, of violated vows
          'Twixt the souls of friend and friend;
     But upon the fairest boughs,   135
          Or at every sentence end,
     Will I 'Rosalinda' write,
          Teaching all that read to know
     The quintessence of every sprite

117 graff graft   118 medlar (1) an applelike fruit, not ready to eat until it is
almost rotten (2) interferer   120 right virtue true quality   126 For because
128 civil sayings civilized maxims   131 stretching of a span span of an open
hand   132 Buckles in limits   139 sprite soul

140   Heaven would in little show.
                Therefore heaven Nature charged
                That one body should be filled
                With all graces wide-enlarged.
                Nature presently distilled
145   Helen's cheek, but not her heart,
                Cleopatra's majesty,
                Atalanta's better part,
                Sad Lucretia's modesty.
                Thus Rosalind of many parts
150   By heavenly synod was devised,
                Of many faces, eyes, and hearts,
                To have the touches dearest prized.
                Heaven would that she these gifts should have,
                And I to live and die her slave."

155 ROSALIND O most gentle pulpiter, what tedious homily
        of love have you wearied your parishioners withal,
        and never cried, "Have patience, good people"!

     CELIA How now? Back, friends. Shepherd, go off a
        little. Go with him, sirrah.

160 TOUCHSTONE Come, shepherd, let us make an honorable
        retreat; though not with bag and baggage, yet with
        scrip and scrippage.   *Exit [with Corin].*

     CELIA Didst thou hear these verses?

     ROSALIND O, yes, I heard them all, and more too; for
165   some of them had in them more feet than the verses
        would bear.

     CELIA That's no matter. The feet might bear the verses.

     ROSALIND Ay, but the feet were lame, and could not

---

140 **in little** in miniature (i.e., the microcosm)   144 **presently** thereupon
145 **cheek ... heart** i.e., Helen's beauty but not her false heart   147 **Atalanta's
better part** i.e., Rosalind has the gracefulness but not the cruelty of Atalanta, a
huntress famed in Greek mythology for her fleetness   148 **Sad** dignified
148 **Lucretia** (a Roman matron who killed herself rather than live dishonored)
150 **synod** council   152 **touches** features   162 **scrip and scrippage** shepherd's
pouch and its contents   165 **feet** metrical units

bear themselves without the verse, and therefore
stood lamely in the verse.   170

CELIA But didst thou hear without wondering how thy
name should be hanged and carved upon these trees?

ROSALIND I was seven of the nine days out of the
wonder before you came; for look here what I found
on a palm tree. I was never so berhymed since   175
Pythagoras' time that I was an Irish rat, which I
can hardly remember.

CELIA Trow you who hath done this?

ROSALIND Is it a man?

CELIA And a chain that you once wore, about his neck.   180
Change you color?

ROSALIND I prithee who?

CELIA O Lord, Lord, it is a hard matter for friends to
meet; but mountains may be removed with earth-
quakes, and so encounter.   185

ROSALIND Nay, but who is it?

CELIA Is it possible?

ROSALIND Nay, I prithee now with most petitionary
vehemence, tell me who it is.

CELIA O wonderful, wonderful, and most wonderful   190
wonderful, and yet again wonderful, and after that,
out of all hooping!

ROSALIND Good my complexion! Dost thou think,
though I am caparisoned like a man, I have a doublet
and hose in my disposition? One inch of delay more   195

---

173 seven of the nine days (cf. the phrase "nine days' wonder")   176 **Pythagoras** (Greek philosopher who taught the doctrine of the transmigration of souls)
176 **that** when   176 **Irish rat** (it was believed that Irish sorcerers could kill rats
with rhymed spells)   178 **Trow** know   188-89 **with most petitionary vehemence** i.e., I beg you   192 **out of all hooping** beyond all measure   193 **Good
my complexion** (a mild expletive)   194 **caparisoned** dressed

is a South Sea of discovery. I prithee tell me who is
it quickly, and speak apace. I would thou couldst
stammer, that thou mightst pour this concealed man
out of thy mouth as wine comes out of a narrow-
200 mouthed bottle; either too much at once, or none at
all. I prithee take the cork out of thy mouth, that I
may drink thy tidings.

CELIA So you may put a man in your belly.

ROSALIND Is he of God's making? What manner of man?
205 Is his head worth a hat? Or his chin worth a beard?

CELIA Nay, he hath but a little beard.

ROSALIND Why, God will send more, if the man will be
thankful. Let me stay the growth of his beard, if
thou delay me not the knowledge of his chin.

210 CELIA It is young Orlando, that tripped up the wrestler's
heels and your heart both in an instant.

ROSALIND Nay, but the devil take mocking! Speak sad
brow and true maid.

CELIA I' faith, coz, 'tis he.

215 ROSALIND Orlando?

CELIA Orlando.

ROSALIND Alas the day! What shall I do with my
doublet and hose? What did he when thou saw'st
him? What said he? How looked he? Wherein went
220 he? What makes he here? Did he ask for me? Where
remains he? How parted he with thee? And when
shalt thou see him again? Answer me in one word.

CELIA You must borrow me Gargantua's mouth first;
'tis a word too great for any mouth of this age's size.
225 To say "ay" and "no" to these particulars is more
than to answer in a catechism.

195-96 **One inch ... discovery** i.e., another minute more will seem as long as
it takes to voyage to the South Seas   197 **apace** quickly   208 **stay** wait for
212-13 **sad brow and true maid** i.e., seriously and truthfully   219-20 **Wherein
went he** how was he dressed   223 **Gargantua** (a giant in Rabelais and other
writers)

ROSALIND But doth he know that I am in this forest, and in man's apparel? Looks he as freshly as he did the day he wrestled?

CELIA It is as easy to count atomies as to resolve the 230 propositions of a lover; but take a taste of my finding him, and relish it with good observance. I found him under a tree, like a dropped acorn.

ROSALIND It may well be called Jove's tree when it drops forth fruit. 235

CELIA Give me audience, good madam.

ROSALIND Proceed.

CELIA There lay he stretched along like a wounded knight.

ROSALIND Though it be pity to see such a sight, it well 240 becomes the ground.

CELIA Cry "holla" to the tongue, I prithee; it curvets unseasonably. He was furnished like a hunter.

ROSALIND O, ominous! He comes to kill my heart.

CELIA I would sing my song without a burden. Thou 245 bring'st me out of tune.

ROSALIND Do you not know I am a woman? When I think, I must speak. Sweet, say on.

Enter Orlando and Jaques.

CELIA You bring me out. Soft. Comes he not here?

ROSALIND 'Tis he! Slink by, and note him. 250

JAQUES I thank you for your company; but, good faith, I had as lief have been myself alone.

ORLANDO And so had I; but yet for fashion sake I thank you too for your society.

---

228 **freshly** handsome 230 **atomies** motes 230–31 **resolve the propositions** answer the questions 232 **good observance** close attention 234 **Jove's tree** (the oak, sacred to Jove) 236 **Give me audience** listen 242 **holla** whoa 242 **curvets** frolics 243 **furnished** dressed 244 **heart** (pun on "hart") 245 **burden** refrain

255 JAQUES God b' wi' you; let's meet as little as we can.

ORLANDO I do desire we may be better strangers.

JAQUES I pray you mar no more trees with writing love
songs in their barks.

ORLANDO I pray you mar no moe of my verses with
260   reading them ill-favoredly.

JAQUES Rosalind is your love's name?

ORLANDO Yes, just.

JAQUES I do not like her name.

ORLANDO There was no thought of pleasing you when
265   she was christened.

JAQUES What stature is she of?

ORLANDO Just as high as my heart.

JAQUES You are full of pretty answers. Have you not
been acquainted with goldsmiths' wives, and conned
270   them out of rings?

ORLANDO Not so; but I answer you right painted cloth,
from whence you have studied your questions.

JAQUES You have a nimble wit; I think 'twas made of
Atalanta's heels. Will you sit down with me, and we
275   two will rail against our mistress the world and all
our misery.

ORLANDO I will chide no breather in the world but
myself, against whom I know most faults.

JAQUES The worst fault you have is to be in love.

280 ORLANDO 'Tis a fault I will not change for your best
virtue. I am weary of you.

---

259 **moe** more   260 **ill-favoredly** badly   269-70 **conned them out of rings**
i.e., memorized the sentimental sayings inscribed in rings   271 **painted cloth**
(cheap substitute for tapestry, on which were painted pictures with trite sayings)
274 **Atalanta's heels** (Atalanta was a symbol of speed)   277 **breather** creature

JAQUES By my troth, I was seeking for a fool when I found you.

ORLANDO He is drowned in the brook. Look but in and you shall see him. 285

JAQUES There I shall see mine own figure.

ORLANDO Which I take to be either a fool or a cipher.

JAQUES I'll tarry no longer with you. Farewell, good Signior Love.

ORLANDO I am glad of your departure. Adieu, good 290 Monsieur Melancholy. [Exit Jaques.]

ROSALIND I will speak to him like a saucy lackey, and under that habit play the knave with him. Do you hear, forester?

ORLANDO Very well. What would you? 295

ROSALIND I pray you, what is't o'clock?

ORLANDO You should ask me, what time o' day. There's no clock in the forest.

ROSALIND Then there is no true lover in the forest, else sighing every minute and groaning every hour would 300 detect the lazy foot of Time as well as a clock.

ORLANDO And why not the swift foot of Time? Had not that been as proper?

ROSALIND By no means, sir. Time travels in divers paces with divers persons. I'll tell you who Time ambles 305 withal, who Time trots withal, who Time gallops withal, and who he stands still withal.

ORLANDO I prithee, who doth he trot withal?

ROSALIND Marry, he trots hard with a young maid between the contract of her marriage and the day it 310

287 cipher zero 293 habit guise 301 detect show 310 contract of her marriage betrothal

is solemnized. If the interim be but a se'nnight, Time's pace is so hard that it seems the length of seven year.

ORLANDO　Who ambles Time withal?

315　ROSALIND　With a priest that lacks Latin and a rich man that hath not the gout; for the one sleeps easily because he cannot study, and the other lives merrily because he feels no pain; the one lacking the burden of lean and wasteful learning, the other knowing no

320　burden of heavy tedious penury. These Time ambles withal.

ORLANDO　Who doth he gallop withal?

ROSALIND　With a thief to the gallows; for though he go as softly as foot can fall, he thinks himself too soon

325　there.

ORLANDO　Who stays it still withal?

ROSALIND　With lawyers in the vacation; for they sleep between term and term, and then they perceive not how time moves.

330　ORLANDO　Where dwell you, pretty youth?

ROSALIND　With this shepherdess, my sister; here in the skirts of the forest, like fringe upon a petticoat.

ORLANDO　Are you native of this place?

ROSALIND　As the cony that you see dwell where she is

335　kindled.

ORLANDO　Your accent is something finer than you could purchase in so removed a dwelling.

ROSALIND　I have been told so of many. But indeed an old religious uncle of mine taught me to speak, who

340　was in his youth an inland man; one that knew

311 **a se'nnight** seven days, a week　319 **wasteful** i.e., causing one to waste away
324 **softly** slowly　328 **term** court session　334 **cony** rabbit　335 **kindled** born
337 **purchase** acquire　337 **removed** remote　339 **religious** i.e., a member of a
religious order　340 **inland** city

courtship too well, for there he fell in love. I have heard him read many lectures against it; and I thank God I am not a woman, to be touched with so many giddy offenses as he hath generally taxed their whole sex withal.   345

ORLANDO Can you remember any of the principal evils that he laid to the charge of women?

ROSALIND There were none principal. They were all like one another as halfpence are, every one fault seeming monstrous till his fellow fault came to match it.   350

ORLANDO I prithee recount some of them.

ROSALIND No, I will not cast away my physic but on those that are sick. There is a man haunts the forest that abuses our young plants with carving "Rosalind" on their barks, hangs odes upon hawthorns, and   355 elegies on brambles; all, forsooth, deifying the name of Rosalind. If I could meet that fancy-monger, I would give him some good counsel, for he seems to have the quotidian of love upon him.

ORLANDO I am he that is so love-shaked. I pray you tell   360 me your remedy.

ROSALIND There is none of my uncle's marks upon you. He taught me how to know a man in love; in which cage of rushes I am sure you are not prisoner.

ORLANDO What were his marks?   365

ROSALIND A lean cheek, which you have not; a blue eye and sunken, which you have not; an unquestionable spirit, which you have not; a beard neglected, which you have not—but I pardon you for that, for simply your having in beard is a younger brother's revenue.   370

341 courtship (1) court manners (2) wooing   343 touched tainted   344 giddy frivolous   357 fancy-monger dealer in love   359 quotidian daily fever   364 cage of rushes i.e., prison easy to escape from   366 a blue eye i.e., dark circles under the eyes   367 unquestionable averse to conversation   369-70 simply your having truthfully what you have   370 a younger brother's revenue i.e., a small portion

Then your hose should be ungartered, your bonnet unbanded, your sleeve unbuttoned, your shoe untied, and everything about you demonstrating a careless desolation. But you are no such man: you are rather point-device in your accouterments, as loving yourself than seeming the lover of any other.

ORLANDO Fair youth, I would I could make thee believe I love.

ROSALIND Me believe it? You may as soon make her that you love believe it, which I warrant she is apter to do than to confess she does; that is one of the points in the which women still give the lie to their consciences. But in good sooth, are you he that hangs the verses on the trees wherein Rosalind is so admired?

ORLANDO I swear to thee, youth, by the white hand of Rosalind, I am that he, that unfortunate he.

ROSALIND But are you so much in love as your rhymes speak?

ORLANDO Neither rhyme nor reason can express how much.

ROSALIND Love is merely a madness, and, I tell you, deserves as well a dark house and whip as madmen do; and the reason why they are not so punished and cured is that the lunacy is so ordinary that the whippers are in love too. Yet I profess curing it by counsel.

ORLANDO Did you ever cure any so?

ROSALIND Yes, one, and in this manner. He was to imagine me his love, his mistress; and I set him every day to woo me. At which time would I, being but a moonish youth, grieve, be effeminate, changeable, longing and liking, proud, fantastical, apish, shallow,

373-74 **a careless desolation** indifferent despondency   375 **point-device in your accouterments** precise in your dress   391 **merely** completely   392 **a dark house and a whip** (the usual treatment of the insane in Shakespeare's day)   401 **moonish** changeable   402 **fantastical** capricious

inconstant, full of tears, full of smiles; for every
passion something and for no passion truly anything,
as boys and women are for the most part cattle of   405
this color; would now like him, now loathe him;
then entertain him, then forswear him; now weep
for him, then spit at him; that I drave my suitor from
his mad humor of love to a living humor of madness, which was, to forswear the full stream of the   410
world and to live in a nook merely monastic. And
thus I cured him; and this way will I take upon me
to wash your liver as clean as a sound sheep's heart,
that there shall not be one spot of love in't.

ORLANDO I would not be cured, youth.   415

ROSALIND I would cure you, if you would but call me
Rosalind and come every day to my cote and woo me.

ORLANDO Now, by the faith of my love, I will. Tell me
where it is.

ROSALIND Go with me to it, and I'll show it you; and   420
by the way you shall tell me where in the forest you
live. Will you go?

ORLANDO With all my heart, good youth.

ROSALIND Nay, you must call me Rosalind. Come, sister,   425
will you go?   *Exeunt.*

Scene III. [*The forest.*]

*Enter [Touchstone, the] Clown, Audrey; and Jaques
[apart].*

TOUCHSTONE Come apace, good Audrey. I will fetch up
your goats, Audrey. And how, Audrey, am I the man
yet? Doth my simple feature content you?

409 **humor** condition   409 **living** real   413 **liver** (thought to be the seat of love)
421 **by** along   III.iii.1 **apace** swiftly   3 **feature** appearance

AUDREY Your features, Lord warrant us! What fea-
5   tures?

TOUCHSTONE I am here with thee and thy goats, as the
most capricious poet, honest Ovid, was among the
Goths.

JAQUES [*Aside*] O knowledge ill-inhabited, worse than
10   Jove in a thatched house!

TOUCHSTONE When a man's verses cannot be understood,
nor a man's good wit seconded with the forward
child, understanding, it strikes a man more dead than
a great reckoning in a little room. Truly, I would
15   the gods had made thee poetical.

AUDREY I do not know what poetical is. Is it honest in
deed and word? Is it a true thing?

TOUCHSTONE No, truly; for the truest poetry is the most
feigning, and lovers are given to poetry, and what
20   they swear in poetry may be said as lovers they do
feign.

AUDREY Do you wish then that the gods had made me
poetical?

TOUCHSTONE I do truly; for thou swear'st to me thou
25   art honest. Now, if thou wert a poet, I might have
some hope thou didst feign.

AUDREY Would you not have me honest?

TOUCHSTONE No, truly, unless thou wert hard-favored;
for honesty coupled to beauty is to have honey a
30   sauce to sugar.

JAQUES [*Aside*] A material fool.

4 warrant save   7-8 capricious ... Goths (the Roman poet Ovid was exiled
among the Goths—pronounced in Elizabethan England the same as "goats"—for
the immorality of his verses. Touchstone plays on the words "honest" [chaste] and
"capricious" [derived from Latin *caper*, male goat])   9 ill-inhabited ill-housed
12 with by   14 great reckoning ... room large bill for poor accommodations
21 feign (1) pretend (2) desire (a pun on "fain")   28 hard-favored ugly
31 material full of good matter

AUDREY Well, I am not fair, and therefore I pray the
gods make me honest.

TOUCHSTONE Truly, and to cast away honesty upon a
foul slut were to put good meat into an unclean dish.   35

AUDREY I am not a slut, though I thank the gods I am
foul.

TOUCHSTONE Well, praised be the gods for thy foulness!
Sluttishness may come hereafter. But be it as it may
be, I will marry thee; and to that end I have been   40
with Sir Oliver Mar-text, the vicar of the next village,
who hath promised to meet me in this place of the
forest and to couple us.

JAQUES [*Aside*] I would fain see this meeting.

AUDREY Well, the gods give us joy!   45

TOUCHSTONE Amen. A man may, if he were of a fearful
heart, stagger in this attempt; for here we have no
temple but the wood, no assembly but horn-beasts.
But what though? Courage! As horns are odious,
they are necessary. It is said, "Many a man knows   50
no end of his goods." Right! Many a man has good
horns and knows no end of them. Well, that is the
dowry of his wife; 'tis none of his own getting. Horns!
Even so, poor men alone. No, no; the noblest deer
hath them as huge as the rascal. Is the single man   55
therefore blessed? No; as a walled town is more
worthier than a village, so is the forehead of a
married man more honorable than the bare brow of
a bachelor; and by how much defense is better than
no skill, by so much is a horn more precious than to   60
want.

Enter Sir Oliver Mar-text.

Here comes Sir Oliver. Sir Oliver Mar-text, you are

41 Sir (an old form of address for a priest)   47 **stagger** tremble   48 **horn-beasts**
(1) horned animals (2) cuckolds   50 **necessary** inevitable   55 **rascal** inferior deer
59 **defense** the art of defense   61 **want** i.e., lack horns

well met. Will you dispatch us here under this tree,
or shall we go with you to your chapel?

65   OLIVER MAR-TEXT   Is there none here to give the woman?

TOUCHSTONE   I will not take her on gift of any man.

OLIVER MAR-TEXT   Truly, she must be given, or the marriage is not lawful.

JAQUES   [*Comes forward*] Proceed, proceed; I'll give her.

70   TOUCHSTONE   Good even, good Master What-ye-call't.
How do you, sir? You are very well met. God 'ield
you for your last company; I am very glad to see
you. Even a toy in hand here, sir. Nay, pray be
covered.

75   JAQUES   Will you be married, motley?

TOUCHSTONE   As the ox hath his bow, sir, the horse his
curb, and the falcon her bells, so man hath his desires; and as pigeons bill, so wedlock would be
nibbling.

80   JAQUES   And will you, being a man of your breeding, be
married under a bush like a beggar? Get you to
church, and have a good priest that can tell you what
marriage is. This fellow will but join you together as
they join wainscot; then one of you will prove a
85   shrunk panel, and like green timber warp, warp.

TOUCHSTONE   [*Aside*] I am not in the mind but I were
better to be married of him than of another; for he
is not like to marry me well; and not being well
married, it will be a good excuse for me hereafter
90   to leave my wife.

63 dispatch us finish our business   70 Master What-ye-call't (Touchstone
delicately avoids the name "Jaques," which should be pronounced "jakes," a
privy)   71-72 God 'ield ... company God reward you for the last time we met
73 toy trifle   73-74 pray be covered (Jaques has removed his hat)   76 bow
yoke   84 wainscot wood paneling   86 I am not in the mind but I am not sure
but that   88-89 well married (1) legally married (2) happily married (3) married
into wealth

JAQUES Go thou with me and let me counsel thee.

TOUCHSTONE Come, sweet Audrey.
    We must be married, or we must live in bawdry.
    Farewell, good Master Oliver: not
        O sweet Oliver,   95
        O brave Oliver,
      Leave me not behind thee;
  but
        Wind away,
        Be gone, I say;   100
    I will not to wedding with thee.

OLIVER MAR-TEXT 'Tis no matter. Ne'er a fantastical
    knave of them all shall flout me out of my calling.
                                      Exeunt.

Scene IV. [*The forest.*]

Enter Rosalind and Celia.

ROSALIND Never talk to me; I will weep.

CELIA Do, I prithee; but yet have the grace to consider
    that tears do not become a man.

ROSALIND But have I not cause to weep?

CELIA As good cause as one would desire; therefore   5
    weep.

ROSALIND His very hair is of the dissembling color.

CELIA Something browner than Judas'. Marry, his kisses
    are Judas' own children.

ROSALIND I' faith, his hair is of a good color.   10

---

99 Wind turn   102 fantastical odd   III.iv.7 dissembling color i.e., red like
the hair of Judas

CELIA An excellent color. Your chestnut was ever the only color.

ROSALIND And his kissing is as full of sanctity as the touch of holy bread.

15 CELIA He hath bought a pair of cast lips of Diana. A nun of winter's sisterhood kisses not more religiously; the very ice of chastity is in them.

ROSALIND But why did he swear he would come this morning, and comes not?

20 CELIA Nay, certainly there is no truth in him.

ROSALIND Do you think so?

CELIA Yes; I think he is not a pickpurse nor a horse-stealer, but for his verity in love, I do think him as concave as a covered goblet or a worm-eaten nut.

25 ROSALIND Not true in love?

CELIA Yes, when he is in, but I think he is not in.

ROSALIND You have heard him swear downright he was.

CELIA "Was" is not "is." Besides, the oath of a lover is no stronger than the word of a tapster; they are
30 both the confirmer of false reckonings. He attends here in the forest on the Duke your father.

ROSALIND I met the Duke yesterday and had much question with him. He asked me of what parentage I was. I told him, of as good as he; so he laughed
35 and let me go. But what talk we of fathers when there is such a man as Orlando?

CELIA O, that's a brave man; he writes brave verses, speaks brave words, swears brave oaths, and breaks them bravely, quite traverse, athwart the heart of

14 holy bread (not the sacramental wafer, but bread brought to church to be blessed and then distributed to the poor)   15 cast (1) molded (2) castoff   15 Diana goddess of chastity   16 winter's sisterhood i.e., the most rigorous chastity   24 concave hollow   29 tapster waiter in a tavern   33 question talk   37 brave fine   39 traverse at an angle (instead of head-on)

his lover, as a puisny tilter, that spurs his horse but   40
on one side, breaks his staff like a noble goose. But
all's brave that youth mounts and folly guides. Who
comes here?

Enter Corin.

CORIN Mistress and master, you have oft enquired
　After the shepherd that complained of love,   45
　Who you saw sitting by me on the turf,
　Praising the proud disdainful shepherdess
　That was his mistress.

CELIA   Well, and what of him?

CORIN If you will see a pageant truly played
　Between the pale complexion of true love   50
　And the red glow of scorn and proud disdain,
　Go hence a little, and I shall conduct you,
　If you will mark it.

ROSALIND   O, come, let us remove:
　The sight of lovers feedeth those in love.
　Bring us to this sight, and you shall say   55
　I'll prove a busy actor in their play.   *Exeunt.*

Scene V. [*The forest.*]

Enter Silvius and Phebe.

SILVIUS Sweet Phebe, do not scorn me; do not, Phebe!
　Say that you love me not, but say not so
　In bitterness. The common executioner,
　Whose heart th' accustomed sight of death makes
　　hard,
　Falls not the ax upon the humbled neck   5

40 puisny inexperienced   45 complained lamented   49 pageant scene, show
III.v.5 Falls lets fall

But first begs pardon. Will you sterner be
Than he that dies and lives by bloody drops?

Enter [apart] Rosalind, Celia, and Corin.

PHEBE I would not be thy executioner.
I fly thee, for I would not injure thee.
10 Thou tell'st me there is murder in mine eye:
'Tis pretty, sure, and very probable
That eyes, that are the frail'st and softest things,
Who shut their coward gates on atomies,
Should be called tyrants, butchers, murderers.
15 Now I do frown on thee with all my heart,
And if mine eyes can wound, now let them kill thee.
Now counterfeit to swound; why, now fall down;
Or if thou canst not, O, for shame, for shame,
Lie not, to say mine eyes are murderers.
20 Now show the wound mine eye hath made in thee;
Scratch thee but with a pin, and there remains
Some scar of it; lean upon a rush,
The cicatrice and capable impressure
Thy palm some moment keeps; but now mine eyes,
25 Which I have darted at thee, hurt thee not,
Nor I am sure there is no force in eyes
That can do hurt.

SILVIUS   O dear Phebe,
If ever, as that ever may be near,
You meet in some fresh cheek the power of fancy,
30 Then shall you know the wounds invisible
That love's keen arrows make.

PHEBE   But till that time
Come thou not near me; and when that time comes,
Afflict me with thy mocks, pity me not,
As till that time I shall not pity thee.

---

7 **dies and lives** earns his living 13 **atomies** motes 17 **counterfeit to swound** pretend to swoon 23 **cicatrice and capable impressure** mark and visible impression 28 **as that ever may be near** and may the time be soon 29 **fancy** love

ROSALIND And why, I pray you? Who might be your
      mother,   35
  That you insult, exult, and all at once,
  Over the wretched? What though you have no beauty
  (As, by my faith, I see no more in you
  Than without candle may go dark to bed)
  Must you be therefore proud and pitiless?   40
  Why, what means this? Why do you look on me?
  I see no more in you than in the ordinary
  Of nature's sale-work. 'Od's my little life,
  I think she means to tangle my eyes too!
  No, faith, proud mistress, hope not after it;   45
  'Tis not your inky brows, your black silk hair,
  Your bugle eyeballs, nor your cheek of cream
  That can entame my spirits to your worship.
  You foolish shepherd, wherefore do you follow her,
  Like foggy south, puffing with wind and rain?   50
  You are a thousand times a properer man
  Than she a woman. 'Tis such fools as you
  That makes the world full of ill-favored children.
  'Tis not her glass, but you, that flatters her,
  And out of you she sees herself more proper   55
  Than any of her lineaments can show her.
  But mistress, know yourself. Down on your knees,
  And thank heaven, fasting, for a good man's love;
  For I must tell you friendly in your ear,
  Sell when you can, you are not for all markets.   60
  Cry the man mercy, love him, take his offer;
  Foul is most foul, being foul to be a scoffer;
  So take her to thee, shepherd. Fare you well.

PHEBE Sweet youth, I pray you chide a year together;
    I had rather hear you chide than this man woo.   65

ROSALIND [*Aside*] He's fall'n in love with your foulness,
  and she'll fall in love with my anger. If it be so, as

39 **Than ... to bed** i.e., your beauty is not so dazzling as to light up the room
42-43 **ordinary / Of nature's sale-work** usual product of nature's manufacture
43 **'Od's** God save   47 **bugle** black and glassy   50 **south** south wind   51 **properer**
more handsome   54 **glass** mirror   61 **Cry the man mercy** ask the man's
forgiveness   62 **Foul** (1) ugliness (2) wickedness

387

fast as she answers thee with frowning looks, I'll
sauce her with bitter words. [*To Phebe*] Why look
70   you so upon me?

PHEBE For no ill will I bear you.

ROSALIND I pray you do not fall in love with me,
For I am falser than vows made in wine.
Besides, I like you not. If you will know my house,
75   'Tis at the tuft of olives, here hard by.
Will you go, sister? Shepherd, ply her hard.
Come, sister. Shepherdess, look on him better
And be not proud. Though all the world could see,
None could be so abused in sight as he.
80   Come, to our flock.   *Exit* [*with Celia and Corin*].

PHEBE Dead shepherd, now I find thy saw of might,
"Who ever loved that loved not at first sight?"

SILVIUS Sweet Phebe.

PHEBE   Ha! What say'st thou, Silvius?

SILVIUS Sweet Phebe, pity me.

85   PHEBE Why, I am sorry for thee, gentle Silvius.

SILVIUS Wherever sorrow is, relief would be.
If you do sorrow at my grief in love,
By giving love your sorrow and my grief
Were both extermined.

90   PHEBE Thou hast my love. Is not that neighborly?

SILVIUS I would have you.

PHEBE   Why, that were covetousness.
Silvius, the time was that I hated thee;
And yet it is not that I bear thee love,
But since that thou canst talk of love so well,
95   Thy company, which erst was irksome to me,

75 **hard** near   79 **abused** deceived   81 **saw** saying   82 **Who ever ... sight**
(a line from Christopher Marlowe's poem *Hero and Leander*, published in 1598.
The "Dead shepherd" is Marlowe, who died in 1593)   89 **extermined** ended
90 **neighborly** friendly (perhaps alluding to the commandment to love one's
neighbor)   95 **erst** formerly

I will endure; and I'll employ thee too;
But do not look for further recompense
Than thine own gladness that thou art employed.

SILVIUS So holy and so perfect is my love,
  And I in such a poverty of grace,   100
  That I shall think it a most plenteous crop
  To glean the broken ears after the man
  That the main harvest reaps. Loose now and then
  A scatt'red smile, and that I'll live upon.

PHEBE Know'st thou the youth that spoke to me ere-
     while?   105

SILVIUS Not very well, but I have met him oft,
  And he hath bought the cottage and the bounds
  That the old carlot once was master of.

PHEBE Think not I love him, though I ask for him;
  'Tis but a peevish boy; yet he talks well.   110
  But what care I for words? Yet words do well
  When he that speaks them pleases those that hear.
  It is a pretty youth. Not very pretty.
  But sure he's proud. And yet his pride becomes him.
  He'll make a proper man. The best thing in him   115
  Is his complexion. And faster than his tongue
  Did make offense, his eye did heal it up.
  He is not very tall. Yet for his years he's tall.
  His leg is but so so. And yet 'tis well.
  There was a pretty redness in his lip,   120
  A little riper and more lusty red
  Than that mixed in his cheek. 'Twas just the difference
  Betwixt the constant red and mingled damask.
  There be some women, Silvius, had they marked him
  In parcels as I did, would have gone near   125
  To fall in love with him; but, for my part,
  I love him not nor hate him not. And yet
  I have more cause to hate him than to love him;
  For what had he to do to chide at me?

100 **a poverty of grace** small favor 104 **scatt'red** stray 105-6 **erewhile a**
short time ago 108 **carlot** countryman 123 **constant** uniform 123 **mingled**
damask pink and white 125 **In parcels** piece by piece

130 He said mine eyes were black and my hair black;
     And, now I am rememb'red, scorned at me.
     I marvel why I answered not again.
     But that's all one: omittance is no quittance.
     I'll write to him a very taunting letter,
135 And thou shalt bear it. Wilt thou, Silvius?

SILVIUS Phebe, with all my heart.

PHEBE   I'll write it straight;
     The matter's in my head and in my heart;
     I will be bitter with him and passing short.
     Go with me, Silvius.   *Exeunt*.

131 **rememb'red** reminded   133 **omittance is no quittance** i.e., the fact that
I did not reply does not mean I will not do so later   136 **straight** at once
138 **passing short** very curt

ACT IV

Scene I. [*The forest.*]

Enter Rosalind and Celia and Jaques.

JAQUES I prithee, pretty youth, let me be better acquainted with thee.

ROSALIND They say you are a melancholy fellow.

JAQUES I am so; I do love it better than laughing.

ROSALIND Those that are in extremity of either are 5
abominable fellows, and betray themselves to every
modern censure worse than drunkards.

JAQUES Why, 'tis good to be sad and say nothing.

ROSALIND Why then, 'tis good to be a post.

JAQUES I have neither the scholar's melancholy, which 10
is emulation; nor the musician's, which is fantastical;
nor the courtier's, which is proud; nor the soldier's,
which is ambitious; nor the lawyer's, which is politic;
nor the lady's, which is nice; nor the lover's, which
is all these: but it is a melancholy of mine own, com- 15
pounded of many simples, extracted from many
objects, and indeed the sundry contemplation of my

IV.i.5 **are in extremity of** go to extremes in   6-7 **every modern censure** i.e.,
the average man's disapproval   11 **emulation** envy   13 **politic** i.e., put on to
seem grave   14 **nice** fastidious   16 **simples** ingredients

travels, in which my often rumination wraps me in
a most humorous sadness.

20 ROSALIND A traveler! By my faith, you have great reason
to be sad. I fear you have sold your own lands to see
other men's. Then to have seen much and to have
nothing is to have rich eyes and poor hands.

JACQUES Yes, I have gained my experience.

Enter Orlando.

25 ROSALIND And your experience makes you sad. I had
rather have a fool to make me merry than experience
to make me sad—and to travel for it too.

ORLANDO Good day and happiness, dear Rosalind.

JAQUES Nay then, God b'wi'you, an you talk in
30 blank verse.   [*Exit.*]

ROSALIND Farewell, Monsieur Traveler. Look you lisp
and wear strange suits, disable all the benefits of
your own country, be out of love with your nativity,
and almost chide God for making you that counte-
35 nance you are; or I will scarce think you have swam
in a gundello. Why, how now, Orlando, where have
you been all this while? You a lover? An you serve
me such another trick, never come in my sight more.

ORLANDO My fair Rosalind, I come within an hour of
40 my promise.

ROSALIND Break an hour's promise in love? He that
will divide a minute into a thousand parts and break
but a part of the thousand part of a minute in the
affairs of love, it may be said of him that Cupid hath
45 clapped him o' th' shoulder, but I'll warrant him
heart-whole.

ORLANDO Pardon me, dear Rosalind.

18 **often rumination** constant reflection   27 **travel** (pun on "travail")   29 **an** if
31 **lisp** speak affectedly   32 **disable** disparage   33 **nativity** birthplace   36 **gundello**
gondola   45 **clapped** touched

ROSALIND Nay, an you be so tardy, come no more in my sight. I had as lief be wooed of a snail.

ORLANDO Of a snail?   50

ROSALIND Ay, of a snail; for though he comes slowly, he carries his house on his head; a better jointure, I think, than you make a woman. Besides, he brings his destiny with him.

ORLANDO What's that?   55

ROSALIND Why, horns; which such as you are fain to be beholding to your wives for; but he comes armed in his fortune and prevents the slander of his wife.

ORLANDO Virtue is no horn-maker, and my Rosalind is virtuous.   60

ROSALIND And I am your Rosalind.

CELIA It pleases him to call you so; but he hath a Rosalind of a better leer than you.

ROSALIND Come, woo me, woo me; for now I am in a holiday humor and like enough to consent. What   65 would you say to me now, an I were your very very Rosalind?

ORLANDO I would kiss before I spoke.

ROSALIND Nay, you were better speak first, and when you were graveled for lack of matter, you might take   70 occasion to kiss. Very good orators, when they are out, they will spit; and for lovers, lacking—God warn us!—matter, the cleanliest shift is to kiss.

ORLANDO How if the kiss be denied?

ROSALIND Then she puts you to entreaty, and there   75 begins new matter.

---

52 jointure marriage settlement   57 armed i.e., with horns   58 prevents (1) forestalls (2) anticipates (?)   63 leer face   70 graveled for lack of matter hard put
for something to say   72 out i.e., out of material   73 warn protect (warrant)

ORLANDO Who could be out, being before his beloved
mistress?

ROSALIND Marry, that should you, if I were your mis-
80   tress, or I should think my honesty ranker than my
wit.

ORLANDO What, of my suit?

ROSALIND Not out of your apparel, and yet out of your
suit. Am not I your Rosalind?

85   ORLANDO I take some joy to say you are, because I
would be talking of her.

ROSALIND Well, in her person, I say I will not have you.

ORLANDO Then, in mine own person, I die.

ROSALIND No, faith, die by attorney. The poor world
90   is almost six thousand years old, and in all this time
there was not any man died in his own person,
videlicet, in a love cause. Troilus had his brains
dashed out with a Grecian club; yet he did what he
could to die before, and he is one of the patterns of
95   love. Leander, he would have lived many a fair year
though Hero had turned nun, if it had not been for
a hot midsummer night; for, good youth, he went
but forth to wash him in the Hellespont, and being
taken with the cramp, was drowned; and the foolish
100   chroniclers of that age found it was "Hero of Sestos."
But these are all lies. Men have died from time to
time, and worms have eaten them, but not for love.

ORLANDO I would not have my right Rosalind of this
mind, for I protest her frown might kill me.

---

80 **honesty ranker** virtue fouler   84 **suit** (1) apparel (2) entreaty   89 **attorney**
proxy   91 **in his own person** in real life (as opposed to fiction)   92 **videlicet**
that is to say   92 **Troilus** (Priam's son, betrayed in love by Cressida and killed
by the spear of Achilles.   "As true as Troilus" became a proverbial expression)
95 **Leander** (a prototype of dedicated love, who swam the Hellespont nightly to
see his mistress, Hero of Sestos)   100 **found** gave the verdict

ROSALIND By this hand, it will not kill a fly. But come, 105
now I will be your Rosalind in a more coming-on
disposition; and ask me what you will, I will grant it.

ORLANDO Then love me, Rosalind.

ROSALIND Yes, faith, will I, Fridays and Saturdays and
all. 110

ORLANDO And wilt thou have me?

ROSALIND Ay, and twenty such.

ORLANDO What sayest thou?

ROSALIND Are you not good?

ORLANDO I hope so. 115

ROSALIND Why then, can one desire too much of a good
thing? Come, sister, you shall be the priest and marry
us. Give me your hand, Orlando. What do you say,
sister?

ORLANDO Pray thee marry us. 120

CELIA I cannot say the words.

ROSALIND You must begin, "Will you, Orlando—"

CELIA Go to. Will you, Orlando, have to wife this
Rosalind?

ORLANDO I will. 125

ROSALIND Ay, but when?

ORLANDO Why now, as fast as she can marry us.

ROSALIND Then you must say, "I take thee, Rosalind,
for wife."

ORLANDO I take thee, Rosalind, for wife. 130

ROSALIND I might ask you for your commission; but I
do take thee, Orlando, for my husband. There's a

123 Go to that's enough   131 commission license

girl goes before the priest, and certainly a woman's
thought runs before her actions.

135 ORLANDO So do all thoughts; they are winged.

ROSALIND Now tell me how long you would have her
after you have possessed her.

ORLANDO For ever and a day.

ROSALIND Say "a day," without the "ever." No, no,
140   Orlando. Men are April when they woo, December
when they wed. Maids are May when they are maids,
but the sky changes when they are wives. I will be
more jealous of thee than a Barbary cock-pigeon
over his hen, more clamorous than a parrot against
145   rain, more newfangled than an ape, more giddy in
my desires than a monkey. I will weep for nothing,
like Diana in the fountain, and I will do that when
you are disposed to be merry; I will laugh like a hyen,
and that when thou art inclined to sleep.

150 ORLANDO But will my Rosalind do so?

ROSALIND By my life, she will do as I do.

ORLANDO O, but she is wise.

ROSALIND Or else she could not have the wit to do this;
the wiser, the waywarder. Make the doors upon a
155   woman's wit, and it will out at the casement; shut
that, and 'twill out at the keyhole; stop that, 'twill fly
with the smoke out at the chimney.

ORLANDO A man that had a wife with such a wit, he
might say, "Wit, whither wilt?"

160 ROSALIND Nay, you might keep that check for it till you
met your wife's wit going to your neighbor's bed.

133 **goes before** runs ahead (Rosalind has not waited for Celia to say, "Will you,
Rosalind, have to husband")   143 **Barbary cock-pigeon** Barb pigeon ("Barbary"
suggests jealousy)   144 **against** before   145 **newfangled** given to novelty
145 **giddy** changeable   147 **like Diana in the fountain** i.e., steadily (Diana was
a popular subject for fountain statuary)   154 **Make** shut   159 **Wit, whither wilt**
i.e., where are your senses   160 **check** rebuke

ORLANDO And what wit could wit have to excuse that?

ROSALIND Marry, to say she came to seek you there. You
shall never take her without her answer unless you
take her without her tongue. O, that woman that 165
cannot make her fault her husband's occasion, let
her never nurse her child herself, for she will breed
it like a fool.

ORLANDO For these two hours, Rosalind, I will leave thee.

ROSALIND Alas, dear love, I cannot lack thee two hours! 170

ORLANDO I must attend the Duke at dinner. By two
o'clock I will be with thee again.

ROSALIND Ay, go your ways, go your ways; I knew
what you would prove. My friends told me as much,
and I thought no less. That flattering tongue of yours 175
won me. 'Tis but one cast away, and so, come
death! Two o'clock is your hour?

ORLANDO Ay, sweet Rosalind.

ROSALIND By my troth, and in good earnest, and so
God mend me, and by all pretty oaths that are not 180
dangerous, if you break one jot of your promise or
come one minute behind your hour, I will think you
the most pathetical break-promise, and the most
hollow lover, and the most unworthy of her you call
Rosalind, that may be chosen out of the gross band 185
of the unfaithful. Therefore beware my censure and
keep your promise.

ORLANDO With no less religion than if thou wert indeed
my Rosalind. So adieu.

ROSALIND Well, Time is the old justice that examines all 190
such offenders, and let Time try. Adieu.
                                        Exit [*Orlando*].

166 make ... occasion i.e., turn defense of her own actions into an accusation of
her husband's   176 one cast away i.e., one girl deserted   183 pathetical
(1) pitiful (2) passionate (?)   185 gross large   188 religion faith

CELIA You have simply misused our sex in your love-
    prate. We must have your doublet and hose plucked
    over your head, and show the world what the bird
195   hath done to her own nest.

ROSALIND O coz, coz, coz, my pretty little coz, that thou
    didst know how many fathom deep I am in love! But
    it cannot be sounded. My affection hath an unknown
    bottom, like the Bay of Portugal.

200 CELIA Or rather, bottomless, that as fast as you pour
    affection in, it runs out.

ROSALIND No, that same wicked bastard of Venus that
    was begot of thought, conceived of spleen, and born
    of madness, that blind rascally boy that abuses every
205   one's eyes because his own are out, let him be judge
    how deep I am in love. I'll tell thee, Aliena, I cannot
    be out of the sight of Orlando. I'll go find a shadow,
    and sigh till he come.

CELIA And I'll sleep.   *Exeunt.*

Scene II. [*The forest.*]

Enter Jaques; and Lords, [like] Foresters.

JAQUES Which is he that killed the deer?

LORD Sir, it was I.

JAQUES Let's present him to the Duke like a Roman
    conqueror; and it would do well to set the deer's
5   horns upon his head for a branch of victory. Have
    you no song, forester, for this purpose?

ANOTHER LORD Yes, sir.

---

192 **simply misused** completely abused   202 **bastard of Venus** Cupid
203 **thought** despondency   203 **spleen** sheer impulse

JAQUES Sing it. 'Tis no matter how it be in tune, so it
make noise enough.   *Music*.

Song.

What shall he have that killed the deer?   10
His leather skin and horns to wear:
   Then sing him home. The rest shall bear
    This burden.

Take thou no scorn to wear the horn,
It was a crest ere thou wast born,   15
   Thy father's father wore it,
   And thy father bore it.
The horn, the horn, the lusty horn,
Is not a thing to laugh to scorn.   *Exeunt*.

Scene III. [*The forest*.]

Enter Rosalind and Celia.

ROSALIND How say you now, is it not past two o'clock?
And here much Orlando!

CELIA I warrant you, with pure love and troubled brain,
he hath ta'en his bow and arrows and is gone forth
to sleep.   5

IV.ii.12-13 **The rest shall bear This burden** i.e., not only the forester who killed
the deer but all men will wear the horns of cuckoldry (many editors read the line as
a stage direction: the other foresters ["the rest"] are to join in the refrain
["burden"] after one forester has sung the first three lines of the song. If the Folio
version—here followed—is correct, it is likely that all sing the song from the
beginning) 14 **Take thou no scorn** do not be ashamed 19 **laugh to scorn**
ridicule IV.iii.2 **much** i.e., not much

Enter Silvius.

Look who comes here.

SILVIUS My errand is to you, fair youth.
My gentle Phebe bid me give you this.
I know not the contents, but, as I guess
10 By the stern brow and waspish action
Which she did use as she was writing of it,
It bears an angry tenor. Pardon me;
I am but as a guiltless messenger.

ROSALIND Patience herself would startle at this letter
15 And play the swaggerer. Bear this, bear all!
She says I am not fair, that I lack manners;
She calls me proud, and that she could not love me,
Were man as rare as phoenix. 'Od's my will!
Her love is not the hare that I do hunt.
20 Why writes she so to me? Well, shepherd, well,
This is a letter of your own device.

SILVIUS No, I protest, I know not the contents.
Phebe did write it.

ROSALIND   Come, come, you are a fool,
And turned into the extremity of love.
25 I saw her hand. She has a leathern hand,
A freestone-colored hand. I verily did think
That her old gloves were on, but 'twas her hands.
She has a housewife's hand; but that's no matter:
I say she never did invent this letter;
30 This is a man's invention and his hand.

SILVIUS Sure it is hers.

ROSALIND Why, 'tis a boisterous and a cruel style,
A style for challengers. Why, she defies me
Like Turk to Christian. Women's gentle brain
35 Could not drop forth such giant-rude invention,

18 phoenix (a legendary bird, of which there was only one in the world at any time) 24 turned into the extremity became the very essence 26 freestone-colored i.e., yellowish-brown 29 invent compose 35 giant-rude incredibly rude

Such Ethiop words, blacker in their effect
Than in their countenance. Will you hear the letter?

SILVIUS So please you, for I never heard it yet;
Yet heard too much of Phebe's cruelty.

ROSALIND She Phebes me. Mark how the tyrant writes.   40
(*Read.*) "Art thou god, to shepherd turned,
         That a maiden's heart hath burned?"
Can a woman rail thus?

SILVIUS Call you this railing?

ROSALIND (*Read.*) "Why, thy godhead laid apart,   45
              Warr'st thou with a woman's heart?"
   Did you ever hear such railing?
              "Whiles the eye of man did woo me,
              That could do no vengeance to me."
Meaning me a beast.   50
              "If the scorn of your bright eyne
              Have power to raise such love in mine,
              Alack, in me what strange effect
              Would they work in mild aspect!
              Whiles you chid me, I did love;   55
              How then might your prayers move!
              He that brings this love to thee
              Little knows this love in me;
              And by him seal up thy mind,
              Whether that thy youth and kind   60
              Will the faithful offer take
              Of me and all that I can make,
              Or else by him my love deny,
              And then I'll study how to die."

SILVIUS Call you this chiding?   65

CELIA Alas, poor shepherd!

---

40 She Phebes me i.e., she writes with her customary disdain   45 thy godhead
laid apart i.e., having assumed human form   49 vengeance harm   51 eyne eyes
54 aspect (1) look (2) planetary influence   59 seal up thy mind i.e., tell your
feelings in a letter   60 youth and kind youthful nature   62 make give

ROSALIND Do you pity him? No, he deserves no pity.
Wilt thou love such a woman? What, to make thee
an instrument, and play false strains upon thee? Not
70   to be endured! Well, go your way to her, for I see
love hath made thee a tame snake, and say this to
her: that if she love me, I charge her to love thee; if
she will not, I will never have her unless thou entreat
for her. If you be a true lover, hence, and not a word;
75   for here comes more company.   *Exit Silvius.*

Enter Oliver.

OLIVER Good morrow, fair ones. Pray you, if you know,
Where in the purlieus of this forest stands
A sheepcote, fenced about with olive trees?

CELIA West of this place, down in the neighbor bottom.
80   The rank of osiers by the murmuring stream
Left on your right hand brings you to the place.
But at this hour the house doth keep itself;
There's none within.

OLIVER If that an eye may profit by a tongue,
85   Then should I know you by description,
Such garments and such years: "The boy is fair,
Of female favor, and bestows himself
Like a ripe sister; the woman low,
And browner than her brother." Are not you
90   The owner of the house I did enquire for?

CELIA It is no boast, being asked, to say we are.

OLIVER Orlando doth commend him to you both,
And to that youth he calls his Rosalind
He sends this bloody napkin. Are you he?

95   ROSALIND I am. What must we understand by this?

OLIVER Some of my shame, if you will know of me

68-69 **make thee an instrument** use you   71 **tame snake** poor worm   77 **purlieus** borders   79 **neighbor bottom** nearby valley   80 **rank of osiers** row of willows   87 **favor** features   87 **bestows** carries   88 **ripe sister** grown-up woman (some editors emend "sister" to "forester")   88 **low** short   94 **napkin** handkerchief

What man I am, and how and why and where
This handkercher was stained.

CELIA   I pray you tell it.

OLIVER When last the young Orlando parted from you,
    He left a promise to return again   100
    Within an hour; and pacing through the forest,
    Chewing the food of sweet and bitter fancy,
    Lo, what befell. He threw his eye aside,
    And mark what object did present itself:
    Under an old oak, whose boughs were mossed with
        age   105
    And high top bald with dry antiquity,
    A wretched ragged man, o'ergrown with hair,
    Lay sleeping on his back; about his neck
    A green and gilded snake had wreathed itself,
    Who with her head, nimble in threats, approached   110
    The opening of his mouth; but suddenly,
    Seeing Orlando, it unlinked itself
    And with indented glides did slip away
    Into a bush, under which bush's shade
    A lioness, with udders all drawn dry,   115
    Lay couching, head on ground, with catlike watch
    When that the sleeping man should stir; for 'tis
    The royal disposition of that beast
    To prey on nothing that doth seem as dead.
    This seen, Orlando did approach the man   120
    And found it was his brother, his elder brother.

CELIA O, I have heard him speak of that same brother,
    And he did render him the most unnatural
    That lived amongst men.

OLIVER   And well he might so do,
    For well I know he was unnatural.   125

ROSALIND But, to Orlando: did he leave him there,
    Food to the sucked and hungry lioness?

OLIVER Twice did he turn his back and purposed so;

102 fancy love 113 indented serpentine 116 **couching** crouching 123 **render**
describe

But kindness, nobler ever than revenge,
130   And nature, stronger than his just occasion,
Made him give battle to the lioness,
Who quickly fell before him; in which hurtling
From miserable slumber I awaked.

CELIA Are you his brother?

ROSALIND   Was't you he rescued?

135 CELIA Was't you that did so oft contrive to kill him?

OLIVER 'Twas I. But 'tis not I. I do not shame
To tell you what I was, since my conversion
So sweetly tastes, being the thing I am.

ROSALIND But, for the bloody napkin?

OLIVER   By and by.
140   When from the first to last, betwixt us two,
Tears our recounts had most kindly bathed,
As how I came into that desert place:
In brief, he led me to the gentle Duke,
Who gave me fresh array and entertainment,
145   Committing me unto my brother's love,
Who led me instantly unto his cave,
There stripped himself, and here upon his arm
The lioness had torn some flesh away,
Which all this while had bled; and now he fainted,
150   And cried, in fainting, upon Rosalind.
Brief, I recovered him, bound up his wound;
And after some small space, being strong at heart,
He sent me hither, stranger as I am,
To tell this story, that you might excuse
155   His broken promise, and to give this napkin,
Dyed in his blood, unto the shepherd youth
That he in sport doth call his Rosalind.

[*Rosalind swoons.*]

CELIA Why, how now, Ganymede, sweet Ganymede!

129 **kindness** familial affection   130 **occasion** opportunity   135 **contrive** plot
139 **By and by** soon   141 **recounts** recital (of our adventures since we last
met)   144 **entertainment** hospitality   151 **recovered** revived

OLIVER Many will swoon when they do look on blood.

CELIA There is more in it. Cousin Ganymede!   160

OLIVER Look, he recovers.

ROSALIND I would I were at home.

CELIA   We'll lead you thither.
  I pray you, will you take him by the arm?

OLIVER Be of good cheer, youth. You a man! You lack
  a man's heart.   165

ROSALIND I do so, I confess it. Ah, sirrah, a body would
  think this was well counterfeited. I pray you tell
  your brother how well I counterfeited. Heigh-ho!

OLIVER This was not counterfeit. There is too great
  testimony in your complexion that it was a passion   170
  of earnest.

ROSALIND Counterfeit, I assure you.

OLIVER Well then, take a good heart and counterfeit to
  be a man.

ROSALIND So I do; but, i' faith, I should have been a   175
  woman by right.

CELIA Come, you look paler and paler. Pray you draw
  homewards. Good sir, go with us.

OLIVER That will I, for I must bear answer back
  How you excuse my brother, Rosalind.   180

ROSALIND I shall devise something. But I pray you
  commend my counterfeiting to him. Will you go?
                                        Exeunt.

167 counterfeited pretended   170-71 passion of earnest real emotion

ACT V

Scene I. [*The forest.*]

Enter [Touchstone, the] Clown and Audrey.

TOUCHSTONE We shall find a time, Audrey. Patience, gentle Audrey.

AUDREY Faith, the priest was good enough, for all the old gentleman's saying.

5 TOUCHSTONE A most wicked Sir Oliver, Audrey, a most vile Mar-text. But, Audrey, there is a youth here in the forest lays claim to you.

AUDREY Ay, I know who 'tis. He hath no interest in me in the world. Here comes the man you mean.

Enter William.

10 TOUCHSTONE It is meat and drink to me to see a clown; by my troth, we that have good wits have much to answer for. We shall be flouting; we cannot hold.

WILLIAM Good ev'n, Audrey.

AUDREY God ye good ev'n, William.

15 WILLIAM And good ev'n to you, sir.

V.i.10 **clown** yokel 12 **flouting** mocking 12 **hold** i.e., keep from mocking
14 **God ye** God give you

TOUCHSTONE Good ev'n, gentle friend. Cover thy head, cover thy head. Nay, prithee be covered. How old are you, friend?

WILLIAM Five-and-twenty, sir.

TOUCHSTONE A ripe age. Is thy name William?   20

WILLIAM William, sir.

TOUCHSTONE A fair name. Wast born i' th' forest here?

WILLIAM Ay, sir, I thank God.

TOUCHSTONE "Thank God." A good answer. Art rich?

WILLIAM Faith, sir, so so.   25

TOUCHSTONE "So so" is good, very good, very excellent good; and yet it is not, it is but so so. Art thou wise?

WILLIAM Ay, sir, I have a pretty wit.

TOUCHSTONE Why, thou say'st well. I do now remember a saying, "The fool doth think he is wise, but the wise   30 man knows himself to be a fool." The heathen philosopher, when he had a desire to eat a grape, would open his lips when he put it into his mouth, meaning thereby that grapes were made to eat and lips to open. You do love this maid?   35

WILLIAM I do, sir.

TOUCHSTONE Give me your hand. Art thou learned?

WILLIAM No, sir.

TOUCHSTONE Then learn this of me: to have is to have; for it is a figure in rhetoric that drink, being poured   40 out of a cup into a glass, by filling the one doth empty the other; for all your writers do consent that *ipse* is he. Now, you are not *ipse*, for I am he.

WILLIAM Which he, sir?

TOUCHSTONE He, sir, that must marry this woman.   45

16 **Cover thy head** (William has removed his hat) 20 **ripe** fine 40 **figure** figure of speech 43 **ipse** he himself (Latin)

Therefore, you clown, abandon—which is in the
vulgar, leave—the society—which in the boorish is,
company —of this female—which in the common is,
woman. Which together is, abandon the society of this
50   female, or, clown, thou perishest; or, to thy better
understanding, diest; or, to wit, I kill thee, make thee
away, translate thy life into death, thy liberty into
bondage. I will deal in poison with thee, or in
bastinado, or in steel; I will bandy with thee in faction;
55   I will o'errun thee with policy; I will kill thee a hundred and fifty ways. Therefore tremble and depart.

AUDREY Do, good William.

WILLIAM God rest you merry, sir.   *Exit.*

Enter Corin.

CORIN Our master and mistress seeks you. Come away,
60   away!

TOUCHSTONE Trip, Audrey, trip, Audrey. I attend, I
attend.   *Exeunt.*

Scene II. [*The forest.*]

Enter Orlando and Oliver.

ORLANDO Is't possible that on so little acquaintance you
should like her? That but seeing, you should love
her? And loving, woo? And wooing, she should
grant? And will you persever to enjoy her?

5   OLIVER Neither call the giddiness of it in question, the
poverty of her, the small acquaintance, my sudden
wooing, nor her sudden consenting; but say with me,

---

54 **bastinado** cudgeling   54 **bandy with thee in faction** i.e., argue with you as
do politicians   55 **o'errun thee with policy** overwhelm you with craft
61 **attend** come   V.ii.5 **giddiness** suddenness

I love Aliena; say with her that she loves me; consent
with both that we may enjoy each other. It shall be
to your good; for my father's house, and all the   10
revenue that was old Sir Rowland's, will I estate
upon you, and here live and die a shepherd.

Enter Rosalind.

ORLANDO You have my consent. Let your wedding be
tomorrow: thither will I invite the Duke and all's
contented followers. Go you and prepare Aliena; for   15
look you, here comes my Rosalind.

ROSALIND God save you, brother.

OLIVER And you, fair sister.   [*Exit.*]

ROSALIND O my dear Orlando, how it grieves me to see
thee wear thy heart in a scarf!   20

ORLANDO It is my arm.

ROSALIND I thought thy heart had been wounded with
the claws of a lion.

ORLANDO Wounded it is, but with the eyes of a lady.

ROSALIND Did your brother tell you how I counterfeited 25
to sound when he showed me your handkercher?

ORLANDO Ay, and greater wonders than that.

ROSALIND O, I know where you are! Nay, 'tis true.
There was never anything so sudden but the fight of
two rams and Caesar's thrasonical brag of "I came,   30
saw, and overcame"; for your brother and my sister
no sooner met but they looked; no sooner looked
but they loved; no sooner loved but they sighed; no
sooner sighed but they asked one another the reason;
no sooner knew the reason but they sought the   35
remedy: and in these degrees have they made a pair
of stairs to marriage, which they will climb incon-

11 **estate** settle   20 **scarf** sling   26 **sound** swoon   30 **thrasonical** boastful
(after the braggart soldier Thraso in Terence's comedy *Eunuchus*)   36 **degrees**
(a pun on the literal meaning, "steps")

tinent, or else be incontinent before marriage: they
are in the very wrath of love, and they will together;
40 clubs cannot part them.

ORLANDO They shall be married tomorrow, and I will
bid the Duke to the nuptial. But, O, how bitter a
thing it is to look into happiness through another
man's eyes! By so much the more shall I tomorrow
45 be at the height of heart-heaviness, by how much I
shall think my brother happy in having what he
wishes for.

ROSALIND Why then, tomorrow I cannot serve your
turn for Rosalind?

50 ORLANDO I can live no longer by thinking.

ROSALIND I will weary you then no longer with idle
talking. Know of me then, for now I speak to some
purpose, that I know you are a gentleman of good
conceit. I speak not this that you should bear a good
55 opinion of my knowledge, insomuch I say I know
you are; neither do I labor for a greater esteem than
may in some little measure draw a belief from you,
to do yourself good, and not to grace me. Believe
then, if you please, that I can do strange things. I
60 have, since I was three year old, conversed with a
magician, most profound in his art and yet not
damnable. If you do love Rosalind so near the heart
as your gesture cries it out, when your brother
marries Aliena shall you marry her. I know into what
65 straits of fortune she is driven; and it is not impossible to me, if it appear not inconvenient to you, to
set her before your eyes tomorrow, human as she is,
and without any danger.

ORLANDO Speak'st thou in sober meanings?

37-38 incontinent ... incontinent with all haste ... unchaste 54 conceit
understanding 58 to grace me to do credit to myself 60 conversed spent
time 61-62 and yet not damnable (because he practices white, not black,
magic) 63 gesture conduct 66 inconvenient unfitting 67 human as she is
i.e., Rosalind herself, not a spirit

ROSALIND By my life, I do, which I tender dearly,   70
though I say I am a magician. Therefore put you in
your best array, bid your friends; for if you will be
married tomorrow, you shall; and to Rosalind, if
you will.

Enter Silvius and Phebe.

Look, here comes a lover of mine and a lover of hers.   75

PHEBE Youth, you have done me much ungentleness
To show the letter that I writ to you.

ROSALIND I care not if I have. It is my study
To seem despiteful and ungentle to you.
You are there followed by a faithful shepherd: 80
Look upon him, love him; he worships you.

PHEBE Good shepherd, tell this youth what 'tis to love.

SILVIUS It is to be all made of sighs and tears;
And so am I for Phebe.

PHEBE And I for Ganymede.   85

ORLANDO And I for Rosalind.

ROSALIND And I for no woman.

SILVIUS It is to be all made of faith and service;
And so am I for Phebe.

PHEBE And I for Ganymede.   90

ORLANDO And I for Rosalind.

ROSALIND And I for no woman.

SILVIUS It is to be all made of fantasy,
All made of passion, and all made of wishes,
All adoration, duty, and observance,   95
All humbleness, all patience, and impatience,

70 **tender dearly** hold precious   71 **though ... magician** (a magician could
be punished with death)   78 **study** intention   79 **despiteful** scornful
93 **fantasy** fancy   95 **observance** devoted attention

411

All purity, all trial, all observance;
And so am I for Phebe.

PHEBE And so am I for Ganymede.

100 ORLANDO And so am I for Rosalind.

ROSALIND And so am I for no woman.

PHEBE If this be so, why blame you me to love you?

SILVIUS If this be so, why blame you me to love you?

ORLANDO If this be so, why blame you me to love you?

ROSALIND Why do you speak too, "Why blame you me
105   to love you?"

ORLANDO To her that is not here, nor doth not hear.

ROSALIND Pray you, no more of this; 'tis like the howling
of Irish wolves against the moon. [*To Silvius*] I will
help you if I can. [*To Phebe*] I would love you if I
110 could. Tomorrow meet me all together. [*To Phebe*] I
will marry you if ever I marry woman, and I'll be
married tomorrow. [*To Orlando*] I will satisfy you if
ever I satisfied man, and you shall be married tomorrow. [*To Silvius*] I will content you if what pleases
115 you contents you, and you shall be married tomorrow. [*To Orlando*] As you love Rosalind, meet. [*To
Silvius*] As you love Phebe, meet. And as I love no
woman, I'll meet. So fare you well. I have left you
commands.

120 SILVIUS I'll not fail if I live.

PHEBE Nor I.

ORLANDO Nor I.   *Exeunt.*

---

97 **observance** (some editors emend to "obedience") 105 **Why do you speak
too** (some editors emend to "Who do you speak to")

Scene III. [*The forest.*]

Enter [Touchstone, the] Clown and Audrey.

TOUCHSTONE Tomorrow is the joyful day, Audrey; tomorrow will we be married.

AUDREY I do desire it with all my heart; and I hope it is no dishonest desire to desire to be a woman of the world. Here come two of the banished Duke's pages. 5

Enter two Pages.

FIRST PAGE Well met, honest gentleman.

TOUCHSTONE By my troth, well met. Come, sit, sit, and a song!

SECOND PAGE We are for you. Sit i'th'middle.

FIRST PAGE Shall we clap into't roundly, without hawk- 10
ing or spitting or saying we are hoarse, which are the only prologues to a bad voice?

SECOND PAGE I'faith, i'faith! and both in a tune, like two gypsies on a horse.

Song.

It was a lover and his lass,   15
    With a hey, and a ho, and a hey nonino,
That o'er the green cornfield did pass
    In springtime, the only pretty ringtime,

V.iii.4-5 **a woman of the world** i.e., (1) married (2) fashionable 6 **honest** honorable 10 **clap into't roundly** begin directly 11-12 **the only** merely the 13 **in a tune** in unison 17 **cornfield** wheatfield 18 **ringtime** i.e., the time for giving marriage rings

When birds do sing, hey ding a ding, ding.
20   Sweet lovers love the spring.

Between the acres of the rye,
    With a hey, and a ho, and a hey nonino,
These pretty country folks would lie
    In springtime, &c.

25   This carol they began that hour,
    With a hey, and a ho, and a hey nonino,
How that a life was but a flower
    In springtime, &c.

And therefore take the present time,
30   With a hey, and a ho, and a hey nonino,
For love is crownèd with the prime
    In springtime, &c.

TOUCHSTONE Truly, young gentlemen, though there was
no great matter in the ditty, yet the note was very
35   untuneable.

FIRST PAGE You are deceived, sir. We kept time, we lost
not our time.

TOUCHSTONE By my troth, yes; I count it but time lost
to hear such a foolish song. God b' wi' you, and God
40   mend your voices. Come, Audrey.   *Exeunt.*

Scene IV. [*The forest.*]

Enter Duke Senior, Amiens, Jaques, Orlando,
Oliver, Celia.

DUKE SENIOR Dost thou believe, Orlando, that the boy
Can do all this that he hath promisèd?

---

21 **Between the acres** i.e., in the strips of unploughed land   29 **take** seize
31 **prime** spring   34 **ditty** words of the song   34 **note** melody

ORLANDO I sometimes do believe, and sometimes do not,
  As those that fear they hope, and know they fear.

Enter Rosalind, Silvius, and Phebe.

ROSALIND Patience once more, whiles our compact is
  urged.   5
  You say, if I bring in your Rosalind,
  You will bestow her on Orlando here?

DUKE SENIOR That would I, had I kingdoms to give
  with her.

ROSALIND And you say you will have her when I bring
  her?

ORLANDO That would I, were I of all kingdoms king.   10

ROSALIND You say you'll marry me, if I be willing?

PHEBE That will I, should I die the hour after.

ROSALIND But if you do refuse to marry me,
  You'll give yourself to this most faithful shepherd?

PHEBE So is the bargain.   15

ROSALIND You say that you'll have Phebe, if she will?

SILVIUS Though to have her and death were both one
  thing.

ROSALIND I have promised to make all this matter even.
  Keep you your word, O Duke, to give your daughter;
  You yours, Orlando, to receive his daughter;   20
  Keep you your word, Phebe, that you'll marry me,
  Or else, refusing me, to wed this shepherd;
  Keep your word, Silvius, that you'll marry her
  If she refuse me; and from hence I go,
  To make these doubts all even. *Exit Rosalind and Celia.* 25

DUKE SENIOR I do remember in this shepherd boy
  Some lively touches of my daughter's favor.

V.iv.4 hope i.e., hope in vain 5 compact is urged agreement is restated 18 make
all this matter even straighten out everything 27 lively living 27 favor features

ORLANDO My lord, the first time that I ever saw him
Methought he was a brother to your daughter.
30 But, my good lord, this boy is forest-born,
And hath been tutored in the rudiments
Of many desperate studies by his uncle,
Whom he reports to be a great magician,
Obscurèd in the circle of this forest.

Enter [Touchstone, the] Clown and Audrey.

35 JAQUES There is, sure, another flood toward, and
these couples are coming to the ark. Here comes a
pair of very strange beasts, which in all tongues are
called fools.

TOUCHSTONE Salutation and greeting to you all!

40 JAQUES Good my lord, bid him welcome. This is the
motley-minded gentleman that I have so often met
in the forest. He hath been a courtier, he swears.

TOUCHSTONE If any man doubt that, let him put me to
my purgation. I have trod a measure; I have flat-
45 tered a lady; I have been politic with my friend,
smooth with mine enemy; I have undone three tailors;
I have had four quarrels, and like to have fought one.

JAQUES And how was that ta'en up?

50 TOUCHSTONE Faith, we met, and found the quarrel was
upon the seventh cause.

JAQUES How seventh cause? Good my lord, like this
fellow.

DUKE SENIOR I like him very well.

55 TOUCHSTONE God 'ield you, sir; I desire you of the like.

32 **desperate** dangerous 34 **Obscurèd** hidden 35 **toward** approaching
36 **couples are coming to the ark** (cf. Genesis 7:2, "and of beasts that are not
clean by two, the male and his female") 43-44 **put me to my purgation** test
me 44 **measure** stately dance 45 **politic** crafty 46 **undone** ruined (by not
paying his bills) 47-48 **like to have fought one** almost fought over one
49 **ta'en up** settled 55 **God 'ield** God reward 55 **I desire you of the like** may
I return the compliment

I press in here, sir, amongst the rest of the country
copulatives, to swear and to forswear, according as
marriage binds and blood breaks. A poor virgin, sir,
an ill-favored thing, sir, but mine own; a poor humor
of mine, to take that that no man else will. Rich   60
honesty dwells like a miser, sir, in a poor house, as
your pearl in your foul oyster.

DUKE SENIOR By my faith, he is very swift and sententious.

TOUCHSTONE According to the fool's bolt, sir, and such   65
dulcet diseases.

JAQUES But, for the seventh cause. How did you find
the quarrel on the seventh cause?

TOUCHSTONE Upon a lie seven times removed—bear
your body more seeming, Audrey—as thus, sir. I did   70
dislike the cut of a certain courtier's beard. He sent
me word, if I said his beard was not cut well, he was in
the mind it was: this is called the Retort Courteous.
If I sent him word again it was not well cut, he would
send me word he cut it to please himself: this is called   75
the Quip Modest. If again, it was not well cut, he
disabled my judgment: this is called the Reply Churlish. If again, it was not well cut, he would answer I
spake not true: this is called the Reproof Valiant. If
again, it was not well cut, he would say I lie: this is   80
called the Countercheck Quarrelsome: and so to the
Lie Circumstantial and the Lie Direct.

JAQUES And how oft did you say his beard was not
well cut?

TOUCHSTONE I durst go no further than the Lie Circum-   85

---

57 **copulatives** couples soon to be wed 58 **blood breaks** sexual interest
wanes 59 **humor** whim 61 **honesty** virtue 63-64 **swift and sententious**
quick-witted and pithy 65 **According to the fool's bolt** (cf. the proverb "A
fool's bolt [arrow] is soon shot") 66 **dulcet diseases** pleasing weaknesses
70 **seeming** becomingly 76 **Modest** moderate 77 **disabled** did not value
81 **Countercheck** contradiction 82 **Circumstantial** indirect

stantial, nor he durst not give me the Lie Direct; and
so we measured swords and parted.

JAQUES Can you nominate in order now the degrees
of the lie?

90 TOUCHSTONE O sir, we quarrel in print, by the book, as
you have books for good manners. I will name you
the degrees. The first, the Retort Courteous; the
second, the Quip Modest; the third, the Reply Churlish; the fourth, the Reproof Valiant; the fifth, the
95 Countercheck Quarrelsome; the sixth, the Lie with
Circumstance; the seventh, the Lie Direct. All these
you may avoid but the Lie Direct, and you may avoid
that too, with an If. I knew when seven justices could
not take up a quarrel, but when the parties were
100 met themselves, one of them thought but of an If:
as, "If you said so, then I said so"; and they shook
hands and swore brothers. Your If is the only peacemaker. Much virtue in If.

JAQUES Is not this a rare fellow, my lord? He's as good
105 at anything, and yet a fool.

DUKE SENIOR He uses his folly like a stalking horse,
and under the presentation of that he shoots his wit.

Enter Hymen, Rosalind, and Celia. Still music.

HYMEN Then is there mirth in heaven
        When earthly things made even
110   Atone together.
        Good Duke, receive thy daughter;
        Hymen from heaven brought her,
            Yea, brought her hither,
        That thou mightst join her hand with his
115   Whose heart within his bosom is.

---

87 **measured swords** (swords were measured before a duel)   88 **nominate** name
90 **by the book** according to the rules   99 **take up** settle   106 **stalking horse**
(any object under cover of which a hunter pursues his game)   107 **presentation**
protection   107 s.d. **Hymen** god of marriage   107 s.d. **Still** soft   109 **made
even** i.e., reconciled   110 **Atone together** are set at one

ROSALIND [*To Duke*] To you I give myself, for I am yours.
   [*To Orlando*] To you I give myself, for I am yours.

DUKE SENIOR If there be truth in sight, you are my
   daughter.

ORLANDO If there be truth in sight, you are my Rosalind.

PHEBE If sight and shape be true,   120
   Why then, my love adieu!

ROSALIND [*To Duke*] I'll have no father, if you be not he.
   [*To Orlando*] I'll have no husband, if you be not he.
   [*To Phebe*] Nor ne'er wed woman, if you be not she.

HYMEN Peace ho! I bar confusion: 125
   'Tis I must make conclusion
      Of these most strange events.
   Here's eight that must take hands
   To join in Hymen's bands,
      If truth holds true contents.   130
[*To Orlando and Rosalind*]
   You and you no cross shall part.
[*To Oliver and Celia*]
   You and you are heart in heart.
[*To Phebe*]
   You to his love must accord,
   Or have a woman to your lord.
[*To Touchstone and Audrey*]
   You and you are sure together   135
   As the winter to foul weather.
[*To all*]
   Whiles a wedlock hymn we sing,
   Feed yourselves with questioning,
   That reason wonder may diminish
   How thus we met, and these things finish.   140

Song.
Wedding is great Juno's crown,
   O blessed bond of board and bed!

130 **If truth ... contents** if the truth is true   131 **cross** quarrel   133 **accord** agree   135 **sure together** securely bound

'Tis Hymen peoples every town;
  High wedlock then be honorèd.
145 Honor, high honor, and renown
  To Hymen, god of every town!

DUKE SENIOR O my dear niece, welcome thou art to me,
  Even daughter, welcome, in no less degree!

PHEBE [*To Silvius*] I will not eat my word, now thou
  art mine;
150 Thy faith my fancy to thee doth combine.

    Enter Second Brother [*Jaques de Boys*].

SECOND BROTHER Let me have audience for a word or two.
  I am the second son of old Sir Rowland
  That bring these tidings to this fair assembly.
  Duke Frederick, hearing how that every day
155 Men of great worth resorted to this forest,
  Addressed a mighty power, which were on foot
  In his own conduct, purposely to take
  His brother here and put him to the sword;
  And to the skirts of this wild wood he came,
160 Where, meeting with an old religious man,
  After some question with him, was converted
  Both from his enterprise and from the world,
  His crown bequeathing to his banished brother,
  And all their lands restored to them again
165 That were with him exiled. This to be true
  I do engage my life.

DUKE SENIOR   Welcome, young man.
  Thou offer'st fairly to thy brothers' wedding:
  To one, his lands withheld; and to the other,
  A land itself at large, a potent dukedom.
170 First, in this forest let us do those ends
  That here were well begun and well begot;
  And after, every of this happy number

---

144 **High** solemn 148 **Even daughter** i.e., even as a daughter 150 **combine**
unite 156 **Addressed a mighty power** prepared a mighty army 157 **conduct**
leadership 160 **old religious man** (a hermit?) 161 **question** talk 166 **engage**
pledge 167 **offer'st fairly** bring a good gift 169 **potent** powerful 170 **do
those ends** complete those purposes 172 **every** each one

That have endured shrewd days and nights with us
Shall share the good of our returnèd fortune,
According to the measure of their states.   175
Meantime forget this new-fall'n dignity
And fall into our rustic revelry.
Play, music, and you brides and bridegrooms all,
With measure heaped in joy, to th' measures fall.

JAQUES Sir, by your patience. If I heard you rightly,   180
The Duke hath put on a religious life
And thrown into neglect the pompous court.

SECOND BROTHER He hath.

JAQUES To him will I. Out of these convertites
There is much matter to be heard and learned.   185
[To Duke] You to your former honor I bequeath;
Your patience and your virtue well deserves it.
[To Orlando] You to a love that your true faith doth
   merit;
[To Oliver] You to your land and love and great allies;
[To Silvius] You to a long and well-deservèd bed;   190
[To Touchstone] And you to wrangling, for thy loving
   voyage
Is but for two months victualled. So, to your pleas-
   ures:
I am for other than for dancing measures.

DUKE SENIOR Stay, Jaques, stay.

JAQUES To see no pastime I. What you would have   195
I'll stay to know at your abandoned cave.   *Exit.*

DUKE SENIOR Proceed, proceed. We will begin these
   rites,
As we do trust they'll end, in true delights.
                                   Exit [after the dance].

---

173 **shrewd** hard 175 **measure** rank 176 **new-fall'n** newly acquired
179 **measures** dance steps 182 **thrown into ... court** given up the ceremonious
life of the court 184 **convertites** converts

[EPILOGUE]

ROSALIND It is not the fashion to see the lady the epilogue, but it is no more unhandsome than to see the
lord the prologue. If it be true that good wine needs
no bush, 'tis true that a good play needs no epilogue;
5   yet to good wine they do use good bushes, and good
plays prove the better by the help of good epilogues.
What a case am I in then, that am neither a good
epilogue, nor cannot insinuate with you in the behalf
of a good play! I am not furnished like a beggar;
10   therefore to beg will not become me. My way is to
conjure you, and I'll begin with the women. I charge
you, O women, for the love you bear to men, to like
as much of this play as please you; and I charge you,
O men, for the love you bear to women—as I per-
15   ceive by your simpering none of you hates them—
that between you and the women the play may please.
If I were a woman, I would kiss as many of you as
had beards that pleased me, complexions that liked
me, and breaths that I defied not; and I am sure, as
20   many as have good beards, or good faces, or sweet
breaths, will, for my kind offer, when I make curtsy,
bid me farewell.   *Exit.*

FINIS

Epilogue 2 **unhandsome** unbecoming 4 **no bush** no advertisement (in
Shakespeare's time vintners used an ivy bush as a sign) 8 **insinuate with you**
slyly get your approval 9 **furnished** dressed 11 **conjure** (1) solemnly entreat
(2) charm (by magic) 17 **If I were a woman** (Rosalind, of course, was played by
a boy) 18 **liked** pleased 19 **defied** disliked 22 **bid me farewell** i.e., applaud

Textual Note

As You Like It did not appear in print until the First Folio of 1623. The text is a good one and may represent a carefully prepared promptbook. Act and scene division is intelligent; exits and entrances are for the most part correctly indicated; and the stage directions are brief but generally adequate. The present edition follows the Folio text closely, admitting only those emendations that seem clearly necessary. A few directions not in the Folio but helpful in clarifying the action are placed in square brackets. Spelling and punctuation are modernized, speech prefixes are extended from abbreviations, obvious typographical errors and mislineation are corrected, and the Latin divisions into act and scene are translated. Other significant departures from the Folio (F) are listed below, the present reading in bold followed by F's reading in roman.

I.i.106 **she** hee   156 **Oliver** [F omits]

I.ii.3 **yet I were** yet were   51 **goddesses and hath** goddesses, hath   80 **Celia** Ros   88 **Le Beau** the Beu   279 **Rosalind** Rosaline [from here on, F uses either form]

I.iii.76 **her patience** per patience

II.i.49 **much** must   59 **of the country** of Countrie

II.iii.10 **some** seeme   16 **Orlando** [F omits]   29 **Orlando** Ad[am]   71 **seventeen** seauentie

II.iv.1 **weary** merry   42 **thy wound** they would   69 **you, friend** your friend

II.v.1 **Amiens** [F omits]   39-40 **no enemy ... weather** &c   44 **Jaques** Amy [i.e., Amiens]

II.vii.55 **Not to seem** Seeme   87 **comes** come   174 **Amiens** [F omits]   182 **Then** the

III.ii.125 **this a desert** this Desert   145 **her** his   155 **pulpiter** Iupiter   255 **b' wi'** buy   356 **deifying** defying

III.iv.28 **of a lover** of Louer

III.v.127-28 **yet I have** yet Haue

423

TEXTUAL NOTE

IV.i.1 **me be better** me better 18 **my** be 29 **b'wi'** buy 201 **in, it** in, in

IV.ii.7 **Another Lord** Lord

IV.iii.5 s.d. **Enter Silvius** [F places after "brain"] 8 **Phebe bid** Phebe, did bid 143 **In** I 156 **his blood** this bloud

V.ii.7 **nor her sudden** nor sodaine

V.iii.18 **In spring time** In the spring time 15-32 [the fourth stanza here appears as the second in F] 39 **b' wi'** buy

V.iv.34 s.d. **Enter ... Audrey** [F prints after line 33] 81 **so to the** so ro 114 **her hand** his hand 164 **them** him 197 **we will** wee'l

WILLIAM
SHAKESPEARE

TWELFTH
NIGHT
OR WHAT YOU
WILL

Edited by Herschel Baker

[*Dramatis Personae*

ORSINO, Duke of Illyria
SEBASTIAN, brother of Viola
ANTONIO, a sea captain, friend to Sebastian
A SEA CAPTAIN, friend to Viola
VALENTINE ⎫
CURIO ⎭ gentlemen attending on the Duke
SIR TOBY BELCH, uncle to Olivia
SIR ANDREW AGUECHEEK
MALVOLIO, steward to Olivia
FABIAN ⎫
FESTE, a clown ⎭ servants to Olivia
OLIVIA, a countess
VIOLA, sister to Sebastian
MARIA, Olivia's woman
Lords, a Priest, Sailors, Officers, Musicians,
    and Attendants

Scene: Illyria]

TWELFTH NIGHT
or, WHAT YOU WILL

ACT I

Scene I. [*The Duke's palace.*]

Enter Orsino, Duke of Illyria, Curio, and other Lords,
[*with Musicians*].

DUKE If music be the food of love, play on,
    Give me excess of it, that, surfeiting,
    The appetite may sicken, and so die.
    That strain again! It had a dying fall;
    O, it came o'er my ear like the sweet sound   5
    That breathes upon a bank of violets,
    Stealing and giving odor. Enough, no more!
    'Tis not so sweet now as it was before.
    O spirit of love, how quick and fresh art thou,
    That, notwithstanding thy capacity,   10
    Receiveth as the sea. Nought enters there,
    Of what validity and pitch soe'er,
    But falls into abatement and low price

Text references are printed in **bold** type; the annotation follows in roman type.
I.i.3 **appetite** i.e., the lover's appetite for music   4 **fall** cadence   9 **quick and fresh** lively and eager   10 **That** in that   11 **there** i.e., in the lover's "capacity"   12 **validity and pitch** value and superiority (in falconry, pitch is the highest point of a bird's flight)   13 **price** esteem

Even in a minute. So full of shapes is fancy
15   That it alone is high fantastical.

CURIO Will you go hunt, my lord?

DUKE What, Curio?

CURIO The hart.

DUKE Why, so I do, the noblest that I have.
20   O, when mine eyes did see Olivia first,
Methought she purged the air of pestilence.
That instant was I turned into a hart,
And my desires, like fell and cruel hounds,
E'er since pursue me.

Enter Valentine.

How now? What news from her?

25 VALENTINE So please my lord, I might not be admitted;
But from her handmaid do return this answer:
The element itself, till seven years' heat,
Shall not behold her face at ample view;
But like a cloistress she will veilèd walk,
30   And water once a day her chamber round
With eye-offending brine: all this to season
A brother's dead love, which she would keep fresh
And lasting in her sad remembrance.

DUKE O, she that hath a heart of that fine frame
35   To pay this debt of love but to a brother,
How will she love when the rich golden shaft
Hath killed the flock of all affections else

---

14 shapes fantasies   14 fancy love   15 high fantastical preeminently imaginative
23 fell fierce   22-24 That instant ... pursue me (Orsino's mannered play on
"hart-heart"—which exemplifies the lover's "high fantastical" wit—derives from
the story of Actaeon, a famous hunter who, having seen Diana bathing, was
transformed into a stag and torn to pieces by his hounds)   27 element sky
27 heat course   31 season preserve (by the salt in her tears)   33 remembrance
(pronounced with four syllables, "re-mem-ber-ance")   36 golden shaft (the
shaft, borne by Cupid, that causes love, as distinguished from the leaden shaft,
which causes aversion and disdain)   37 all affections else i.e., all other emotions
but love

That live in her; when liver, brain, and heart,
These sovereign thrones, are all supplied and filled,
Her sweet perfections, with one self king.   40
Away before me to sweet beds of flow'rs;
Love-thoughts lie rich when canopied with bow'rs.

Exeunt.

Scene II. [*The seacoast.*]

Enter Viola, a Captain, and Sailors.

VIOLA What country, friends, is this?

CAPTAIN This is Illyria, lady.

VIOLA And what should I do in Illyria?
My brother he is in Elysium.
Perchance he is not drowned. What think you, sailors?   5

CAPTAIN It is perchance that you yourself were saved.

VIOLA O my poor brother, and so perchance may he be.

CAPTAIN True, madam; and, to comfort you with
chance,
Assure yourself, after our ship did split,
When you, and those poor number saved with you,   10
Hung on our driving boat, I saw your brother,
Most provident in peril, bind himself
(Courage and hope both teaching him the practice)
To a strong mast that lived upon the sea;
Where, like Arion on the dolphin's back,   15

---

38 **liver, brain, and heart** (the seats respectively of sexual desire, thought, and feeling) 40 **perfections** (pronounced with four syllables) 40 **self** sole I.ii.2 **Illyria** region bordering the east coast of the Adriatic 4 **Elysium** heaven (in classical mythology, the abode of the happy dead) 8 **chance** possibility 11 **driving** drifting 13 **practice** procedure 14 **lived** i.e., floated 15 **Arion** (in classical mythology, a bard who, having leapt into the sea to escape from murderous sailors, was borne to shore by a dolphin that he charmed by his songs)

I saw him hold acquaintance with the waves
So long as I could see.

VIOLA For saying so, there's gold.
Mine own escape unfoldeth to my hope,
20   Whereto thy speech serves for authority
The like of him. Know'st thou this country?

CAPTAIN Ay, madam, well, for I was bred and born
Not three hours' travel from this very place.

VIOLA Who governs here?

25 CAPTAIN A noble duke, in nature as in name.

VIOLA What is his name?

CAPTAIN Orsino.

VIOLA Orsino! I have heard my father name him.
He was a bachelor then.

30 CAPTAIN And so is now, or was so very late;
For but a month ago I went from hence,
And then 'twas fresh in murmur (as you know
What great ones do, the less will prattle of)
That he did seek the love of fair Olivia.

35 VIOLA What's she?

CAPTAIN A virtuous maid, the daughter of a count
That died some twelvemonth since, then leaving her
In the protection of his son, her brother,
Who shortly also died; for whose dear love,
40   They say, she hath abjured the sight
And company of men.

VIOLA   O that I served that lady,
And might not be delivered to the world,
Till I had made mine own occasion mellow,
What my estate is.

---

19 **unfoldeth to my hope** i.e., reinforces my hope for my brother's safety
20 **serves for authority** i.e., tends to justify   32 **fresh in murmur** i.e., being
rumored   42 **delivered** disclosed   43-44 **made mine ... estate is** found an
appropriate time to reveal my status

CAPTAIN   That were hard to compass,
    Because she will admit no kind of suit,   45
    No, not the Duke's.

VIOLA There is a fair behavior in thee, captain,
    And though that nature with a beauteous wall
    Doth oft close in pollution, yet of thee
    I will believe thou hast a mind that suits   50
    With this thy fair and outward character.
    I prithee (and I'll pay thee bounteously)
    Conceal me what I am, and be my aid
    For such disguise as haply shall become
    The form of my intent. I'll serve this duke.   55
    Thou shalt present me as an eunuch to him;
    It may be worth thy pains. For I can sing,
    And speak to him in many sorts of music
    That will allow me very worth his service.
    What else may hap, to time I will commit;   60
    Only shape thou thy silence to my wit.

CAPTAIN Be you his eunuch, and your mute I'll be;
    When my tongue blabs, then let mine eyes not see.

VIOLA I thank thee. Lead me on.   *Exeunt.*

Scene III. [*Olivia's house.*]

Enter Sir Toby and Maria.

TOBY What a plague means my niece to take the death
    of her brother thus? I am sure care's an enemy to
    life.

MARIA By my troth, Sir Toby, you must come in

44 **compass** effect   46 **not** not even   48 **though that** even though   49 **close in** conceal   51 **character** i.e., appearance and demeanor   54-55 **become/The form of my intent** i.e., suit my purpose   59 **allow** certify   61 **wit** i.e., skill in carrying out my plan   62 **Be you his eunuch** (this part of the plan was not carried out)

5   earlier a' nights. Your cousin, my lady, takes great
       exceptions to your ill hours.

TOBY Why, let her except before excepted.

MARIA Ay, but you must confine yourself within the
       modest limits of order.

10 TOBY Confine? I'll confine myself no finer than I am.
       These clothes are good enough to drink in, and so
       be these boots too. And they be not, let them hang
       themselves in their own straps.

MARIA That quaffing and drinking will undo you. I
15   heard my lady talk of it yesterday; and of a foolish
       knight that you brought in one night here to be her
       wooer.

TOBY Who? Sir Andrew Aguecheek?

MARIA Ay, he.

20 TOBY He's as tall a man as any's in Illyria.

MARIA What's that to th' purpose?

TOBY Why, he has three thousand ducats a year.

MARIA Ay, but he'll have but a year in all these ducats.
       He's a very fool and a prodigal.

25 TOBY Fie that you'll say so! He plays o' th' viol-de-
       gamboys, and speaks three or four languages word
       for word without book, and hath all the good gifts
       of nature.

MARIA He hath indeed all, most natural; for, besides
30   that he's a fool, he's a great quarreler; and but that
       he hath the gift of a coward to allay the gust he
       hath in quarreling, 'tis thought among the prudent
       he would quickly have the gift of a grave.

I.iii.5 **cousin** (a term indicating various degrees of kinship; here, niece)   7 **except before excepted** (Sir Toby parodies the legal jargon *exceptis exceptiendis* ["with the exceptions previously noted"] commonly used in leases and contracts)   9 **modest limits of order** reasonable limits of good behavior   10 **confine** i.e., clothe   12 **And if** (a common Elizabethan usage)   20 **tall** i.e., bold and handsome   25-26 **viol-de-gamboys** bass viol   29 **natural** i.e., like a natural fool or idiot   31 **gust** gusto

TOBY By this hand, they are scoundrels and substractors that say so of him. Who are they?   35

MARIA They that add, moreover, he's drunk nightly in
your company.

TOBY With drinking healths to my niece. I'll drink to
her as long as there is a passage in my throat and
drink in Illyria. He's a coward and a coistrel that   40
will not drink to my niece till his brains turn o' th'
toe like a parish top. What, wench? *Castiliano
vulgo*; for here comes Sir Andrew Agueface.

Enter Sir Andrew.

ANDREW Sir Toby Belch. How now, Sir Toby Belch?

TOBY Sweet Sir Andrew.   45

ANDREW Bless you, fair shrew.

MARIA And you too, sir.

TOBY Accost, Sir Andrew, accost.

ANDREW What's that?

TOBY My niece's chambermaid.   50

ANDREW Good Mistress Accost, I desire better acquaintance.

MARIA My name is Mary, sir.

ANDREW Good Mistress Mary Accost.

34-35 **substractors** slanderers   40 **coistrel** knave (literally, a groom who takes
care of a knight's horse)   42 **parish top** (according to George Stevens, a large top
"formerly kept in every village, to be whipped in frosty weather, that the peasants
might be kept warm by exercise, and out of mischief while they could not work";
however, the allusion may be to the communal top-spinning whose origins are
buried in religious ritual)   42-43 **Castiliano vulgo** (a phrase of uncertain
meaning; perhaps Sir Toby is suggesting that Maria assume a grave and ceremonial manner--like that of the notoriously formal Castilians—for Sir Andrew's
benefit)   49-50 **What's that?/My niece's chambermaid** (Sir Andrew asks the
meaning of the word "accost," but Sir Toby thinks that he is referring to Maria.
Actually, she was not Olivia's chambermaid, but rather her companion, or lady in
waiting, as is made clear at I.v.162)

55 TOBY You mistake, knight. "Accost" is front her, board her, woo her, assail her.

ANDREW By my troth, I would not undertake her in this company. Is that the meaning of "accost"?

MARIA Fare you well, gentlemen.

60 TOBY And thou let part so, Sir Andrew, would thou mightst never draw sword again.

ANDREW And you part so, mistress, I would I might never draw sword again! Fair lady, do you think you have fools in hand?

65 MARIA Sir, I have not you by th' hand.

ANDREW Marry, but you shall have, and here's my hand.

MARIA Now, sir, thought is free. I pray you, bring your hand to th' butt'ry bar and let it drink.

70 ANDREW Wherefore, sweetheart? What's your meta-phor?

MARIA It's dry, sir.

ANDREW Why, I think so. I am not such an ass but I can keep my hand dry. But what's your jest?

75 MARIA A dry jest, sir.

ANDREW Are you full of them?

MARIA Ay, sir, I have them at my finger's ends. Marry, now I let go your hand, I am barren.   *Exit Maria.*

TOBY O knight, thou lack'st a cup of canary! When
80   did I see thee so put down?

ANDREW Never in your life, I think, unless you see canary put me down. Methinks sometimes I have

60 so i.e., without ceremony   64 have fools in hand i.e., are dealing with fools
66 Marry indeed (a mild interjection, originally an oath by the Virgin Mary)
69 butt'ry buttery, a storeroom for butts or casks of liquor   72 dry (1) thirsty
(2) indicative of impotence   78 barren (1) without more jests (2) dull-witted
79 canary a sweet wine from the Canary Islands

no more wit than a Christian or an ordinary man
has. But I am a great eater of beef, and I believe
that does harm to my wit.   85

TOBY No question.

ANDREW And I thought that, I'd forswear it. I'll ride
home tomorrow, Sir Toby.

TOBY *Pourquoi*, my dear knight?

ANDREW What is "*pourquoi*"? Do, or not do? I would   90
I had bestowed that time in the tongues that I have
in fencing, dancing, and bearbaiting. O, had I but
followed the arts!

TOBY Then hadst thou had an excellent head of hair.

ANDREW Why, would that have mended my hair?   95

TOBY Past question, for thou seest it will not curl by
nature.

ANDREW But it becomes me well enough, does't not?

TOBY Excellent. It hangs like flax on a distaff; and
I hope to see a huswife take thee between her legs   100
and spin it off.

ANDREW Faith, I'll home tomorrow, Sir Toby. Your
niece will not be seen; or if she be, it's four to one
she'll none of me. The Count himself here hard by
woos her.   105

TOBY She'll none o' th' Count. She'll not match above
her degree, neither in estate, years, nor wit; I have
heard her swear't. Tut, there's life in't, man.

ANDREW I'll stay a month longer. I am a fellow o' th'
strangest mind i' th' world. I delight in masques and   110
revels sometimes altogether.

---

89 **Pourquoi** why (French)   94 **Then hadst thou had an excellent head of**
hair (perhaps Sir Toby is punning on Sir Andrew's "tongues" [line 91] as "tongs"
or curling irons)   99 **distaff** stick used in spinning   100 **huswife** housewife
107 **estate** fortune   108 **there's life in't** i.e., there's hope for you yet

TOBY Art thou good at these kickshawses, knight?

ANDREW As any man in Illyria, whatsoever he be, under the degree of my betters, and yet I will not compare with an old man.

TOBY What is thy excellence in a galliard, knight?

ANDREW Faith, I can cut a caper.

TOBY And I can cut the mutton to't.

ANDREW And I think I have the back-trick simply as strong as any man in Illyria.

TOBY Wherefore are these things hid? Wherefore have these gifts a curtain before 'em? Are they like to take dust, like Mistress Mall's picture? Why dost thou not go to church in a galliard and come home in a coranto? My very walk should be a jig. I would not so much as make water but in a sink-a-pace. What dost thou mean? Is it a world to hide virtues in? I did think, by the excellent constitution of thy leg, it was formed under the star of a galliard.

ANDREW Ay, 'tis strong, and it does indifferent well in a damned-colored stock. Shall we set about some revels?

TOBY What shall we do else? Were we not born under Taurus?

112 **kickshawses** trifles (French *quelque chose*)   114 **under the degree of my betters** i.e., so long as he is not my social superior   115 **old** i.e., experienced (?) 116 **galliard** lively dance in triple time   117 **caper** (1) frisky leap (2) spice used to season mutton (hence Sir Toby's remark in the next line)   119 **back-trick** reverse step in dancing   123 **take** gather   125 **coranto** quick running dance 126-27 **sink-a-pace** cinquepace (French *cinque pas*), a kind of galliard of five steps (but there is also a scatological pun here)   128 **virtues** talents, accomplishments   129-30 **the star of a galliard** i.e., a dancing star   132 **damned-colored stock** (of the many emendations proposed for this stocking of uncertain color—"damasked-colored," "dun-colored," "dove-colored," "damson-colored," and the like—Rowe's "flame-colored" has been most popular)   135 **Taurus** the Bull (one of the twelve signs of the zodiac, each of which was thought to influence a certain part of the human body. Most authorities assigned Taurus to neither "sides and heart" nor "legs and thighs," but to neck and throat)

ANDREW Taurus? That's sides and heart.

TOBY No, sir; it is legs and thighs. Let me see thee
caper. Ha, higher; ha, ha, excellent!   *Exeunt.*

Scene IV. [*The Duke's palace.*]

Enter Valentine, and Viola in man's attire.

VALENTINE If the Duke continue these favors towards
you, Cesario, you are like to be much advanced.
He hath known you but three days and already you
are no stranger.

VIOLA You either fear his humor or my negligence,   5
that you call in question the continuance of his
love. Is he inconstant, sir, in his favors?

VALENTINE No, believe me.

Enter Duke, Curio, and Attendants.

VIOLA I thank you. Here comes the Count.

DUKE Who saw Cesario, ho?   10

VIOLA On your attendance, my lord, here.

DUKE Stand you awhile aloof. Cesario,
Thou know'st no less but all. I have unclasped
To thee the book even of my secret soul.
Therefore, good youth, address thy gait unto her;   15
Be not denied access, stand at her doors,

I.iv.5 **humor** changeable disposition   6 **that** in that   13 **no less but all** i.e.,
everything   15 **address thy gait** direct your steps

437

And tell them there thy fixèd foot shall grow
Till thou have audience.

VIOLA   Sure, my noble lord,
        If she be so abandoned to her sorrow
20   As it is spoke, she never will admit me.

DUKE Be clamorous and leap all civil bounds
        Rather than make unprofited return.

VIOLA Say I do speak with her, my lord, what then?

DUKE O, then unfold the passion of my love;
25   Surprise her with discourse of my dear faith;
        It shall become thee well to act my woes.
        She will attend it better in thy youth
        Than in a nuncio's of more grave aspect.

VIOLA I think not so, my lord.

DUKE   Dear lad, believe it;
30   For they shall yet belie thy happy years
        That say thou art a man. Diana's lip
        Is not more smooth and rubious; thy small pipe
        Is as the maiden's organ, shrill and sound,
        And all is semblative a woman's part.
35   I know thy constellation is right apt
        For this affair. Some four or five attend him,
        All, if you will; for I myself am best
        When least in company. Prosper well in this,
        And thou shalt live as freely as thy lord
        To call his fortunes thine.

40   VIOLA   I'll do my best
        To woo your lady. [Aside] Yet a barful strife!
        Whoe'er I woo, myself would be his wife.   Exeunt.

---

22 **unprofited** unsuccessful 25 **dear** intense 28 **nuncio's** messenger's 28 **aspect**
(accent on second syllable) 32 **rubious** ruby-red 32 **pipe** voice 33 **shrill and
sound** high and clear 34 **semblative** like 35 **constellation** predetermined
qualities 35 **apt** suitable 41 **barful** full of impediments

Scene V. [*Olivia's house.*]

Enter Maria and Clown.

MARIA Nay, either tell me where thou hast been, or I
will not open my lips so wide as a bristle may enter
in way of thy excuse. My lady will hang thee for
thy absence.

CLOWN Let her hang me. He that is well hanged in   5
this world needs to fear no colors.

MARIA Make that good.

CLOWN He shall see none to fear.

MARIA A good lenten answer. I can tell thee where
that saying was born, of "I fear no colors."   10

CLOWN Where, good Mistress Mary?

MARIA In the wars; and that may you be bold to say
in your foolery.

CLOWN Well, God give them wisdom that have it, and
those that are fools, let them use their talents.   15

MARIA Yet you will be hanged for being so long absent, or to be turned away. Is not that as good as a
hanging to you?

CLOWN Many a good hanging prevents a bad marriage,
and for turning away, let summer bear it out.   20

I.v.6 **fear no colors** i.e., fear nothing (with a pun on "color" meaning "flag" and
"collar" meaning "hangman's noose")   7 **Make that good** i.e., explain it
9 **lenten** thin, meager (perhaps an allusion to the colorless, unbleached linen that
replaced the customary liturgical purple or violet during Lent)   15 **talents** native
intelligence (with perhaps a pun on "talons" meaning "claws")   20 **let summer
bear it out** i.e., let the warm weather make it endurable

MARIA You are resolute then?

CLOWN Not so, neither; but I am resolved on two
points.

MARIA That if one break, the other will hold; or if
25 both break, your gaskins fall.

CLOWN Apt, in good faith; very apt. Well, go thy way!
If Sir Toby would leave drinking, thou wert as
witty a piece of Eve's flesh as any in Illyria.

MARIA Peace, you rogue; no more o' that. Here comes
30 my lady. Make your excuse wisely, you were best.
[Exit.]

Enter Lady Olivia with Malvolio
[and other Attendants].

CLOWN Wit, and't be thy will, put me into good
fooling. Those wits that think they have thee do
very oft prove fools, and I that am sure I lack thee
may pass for a wise man. For what says Quina-
35 palus? "Better a witty fool than a foolish wit."
God bless thee, lady.

OLIVIA Take the fool away.

CLOWN Do you not hear, fellows? Take away the lady.

OLIVIA Go to, y' are a dry fool! I'll no more of you.
40 Besides, you grow dishonest.

CLOWN Two faults, madonna, that drink and good
counsel will amend. For give the dry fool drink,
then is the fool not dry. Bid the dishonest man
mend himself: if he mend, he is no longer dishonest;
45 if he cannot, let the botcher mend him. Anything

---

23 **points** counts (but Maria takes it in the sense of tagged laces serving as
suspenders)   25 **gaskins** loose breeches   27-28 **thou wert as witty a piece of
Eve's flesh** i.e., you would make as clever a wife   30 **you were best** it would be
best for you   31 **and't** if it   34-35 **Quinapalus** (a sage of the Clown's invention)
39 **Go to** enough   39 **dry** stupid   40 **dishonest** unreliable   41 **madonna** my
lady   42 **dry** thirsty   45 **botcher** mender of clothes

that's mended is but patched; virtue that transgresses is but patched with sin, and sin that amends
is but patched with virtue. If that this simple syllo-
gism will serve, so; if it will not, what remedy? As
there is no true cuckold but calamity, so beauty's   50
a flower. The lady bade take away the fool; therefore, I say again, take her away.

OLIVIA Sir, I bade them take away you.

CLOWN Misprision in the highest degree. Lady, *cucullus non facit monachum*. That's as much to say   55
as, I wear not motley in my brain. Good madonna,
give me leave to prove you a fool.

OLIVIA Can you do it?

CLOWN Dexteriously, good madonna.

OLIVIA Make your proof.   60

CLOWN I must catechize you for it, madonna. Good
my mouse of virtue, answer me.

OLIVIA Well, sir, for want of other idleness, I'll bide
your proof.

CLOWN Good madonna, why mourn'st thou?   65

OLIVIA Good fool, for my brother's death.

CLOWN I think his soul is in hell, madonna.

OLIVIA I know his soul is in heaven, fool.

CLOWN The more fool, madonna, to mourn for your
brother's soul, being in heaven. Take away the fool,   70
gentlemen.

---

50 **there is no true cuckold but calamity** (although the Clown's chatter should
not be pressed too hard for significance, Kittredge's paraphrase of this difficult
passage is perhaps the least unsatisfactory: "Every man is wedded to fortune;
hence, when one's fortune is unfaithful, one may in very truth be called a
cuckold—the husband of an unfaithful wife")   54 **Misprision in the highest
degree** i.e., an egregious error in mistaken identity   54-55 **cucullus non facit
monachum** a cowl does not make a monk   59 **Dexteriously** dexterously
61-62 **Good my mouse of virtue** my good virtuous mouse (a term of playful
affection)   63 **idleness** trifling

OLIVIA What think you of this fool, Malvolio? Doth
he not mend?

MALVOLIO Yes, and shall do till the pangs of death
75   shake him. Infirmity, that decays the wise, doth
ever make the better fool.

CLOWN God send you, sir, a speedy infirmity, for the
better increasing your folly. Sir Toby will be sworn
that I am no fox, but he will not pass his word for
80   twopence that you are no fool.

OLIVIA How say you to that, Malvolio?

MALVOLIO I marvel your ladyship takes delight in such
a barren rascal. I saw him put down the other day
with an ordinary fool that has no more brain than
85   a stone. Look you now, he's out of his guard
already. Unless you laugh and minister occasion
to him, he is gagged. I protest I take these wise men
that crow so at these set kind of fools no better
than the fools' zanies.

90   OLIVIA O, you are sick of self-love, Malvolio, and
taste with a distempered appetite. To be generous,
guiltless, and of free disposition, is to take those
things for birdbolts that you deem cannon bullets.
There is no slander in an allowed fool, though
95   he do nothing but rail; nor no railing in a known
discreet man, though he do nothing but reprove.

CLOWN Now Mercury indue thee with leasing, for
thou speak'st well of fools.

Enter Maria.

MARIA Madam, there is at the gate a young gentleman
100   much desires to speak with you.

79 **I am no fox** i.e., sly and dangerous (like you)   83 **barren** stupid   83-84 **put
down ... with** bested ... by   85 **out of his guard** defenseless   86 **minister
occasion** afford opportunity (for his fooling)   88 **crow** i.e., with laughter   88 **set**
artificial   89 **zanies** inferior buffoons   91 **generous** liberal-minded   93 **birdbolts** blunt arrows   94 **allowed** licensed, privileged   97 **Mercury indue thee
with leasing** may the god of trickery endow you with the gift of deception

442

OLIVIA From the Count Orsino, is it?

MARIA I know not, madam. 'Tis a fair young man, and well attended.

OLIVIA Who of my people hold him in delay?

MARIA Sir Toby, madam, your kinsman.   105

OLIVIA Fetch him off, I pray you. He speaks nothing but madman. Fie on him! [*Exit Maria.*] Go you, Malvolio. If it be a suit from the Count, I am sick, or not at home. What you will, to dismiss it. (*Exit Malvolio.*) Now you see, sir, how your fooling   110 grows old, and people dislike it.

CLOWN Thou hast spoke for us, madonna, as if thy eldest son should be a fool; whose skull Jove cram with brains, for—here he comes—one of thy kin has a most weak pia mater.   115

Enter Sir Toby.

OLIVIA By mine honor, half drunk. What is he at the gate, cousin?

TOBY A gentleman.

OLIVIA A gentleman? What gentleman?

TOBY 'Tis a gentleman here. A plague o' these pickle-   120 herring! How now, sot?

CLOWN Good Sir Toby.

OLIVIA Cousin, cousin, how have you come so early by this lethargy?

TOBY Lechery? I defy lechery. There's one at the gate. 125

OLIVIA Ay, marry, what is he?

---

111 **old** stale, tedious   113 **Jove** (if, as is likely, Shakespeare here and elsewhere wrote "God," the printed text reflects the statute of 1606 that prohibited profane stage allusions to the deity)   115 **pia mater** brain   120-21 **pickle-herring** (to which the drunken Sir Toby attributes his hiccoughing)   121 **sot** fool   123 **Cousin** i.e., uncle (see I.iii.5)

TOBY Let him be the devil and he will, I care not.
Give me faith, say I. Well, it's all one.   *Exit.*

OLIVIA What's a drunken man like, fool?

130 CLOWN Like a drowned man, a fool, and a madman.
One draught above heat makes him a fool, the
second mads him, and a third drowns him.

OLIVIA Go thou and seek the crowner, and let him
sit o' my coz; for he's in the third degree of drink—
135 he's drowned. Go look after him.

CLOWN He is but mad yet, madonna, and the fool
shall look to the madman.   [*Exit.*]

Enter Malvolio.

MALVOLIO Madam, yond young fellow swears he will
speak with you. I told him you were sick; he takes
140 on him to understand so much, and therefore comes
to speak with you. I told him you were asleep; he
seems to have a foreknowledge of that too, and
therefore comes to speak with you. What is to be
said to him, lady? He's fortified against any denial.

145 OLIVIA Tell him he shall not speak with me.

MALVOLIO H'as been told so; and he says he'll stand
at your door like a sheriff's post, and be the supporter to a bench, but he'll speak with you.

OLIVIA What kind o' man is he?

150 MALVOLIO Why, of mankind.

OLIVIA What manner of man?

MALVOLIO Of very ill manner. He'll speak with you,
will you or no.

---

128 **faith** (in order to resist the devil)   131 **above heat** i.e., above what is
required to make a man normally warm   133 **crowner** coroner   134 **sit o' my
coz** hold an inquest on my kinsman   146 **H'as** he has   147 **sheriff's post** post
set up before a sheriff's door for placards, notices, and such   148 **but**
except   150 **of mankind** i.e., like other men

OLIVIA Of what personage and years is he?

MALVOLIO Not yet old enough for a man nor young   155
enough for a boy; as a squash is before 'tis a
peascod, or a codling when 'tis almost an apple.
'Tis with him in standing water, between boy and
man. He is very well-favored and he speaks very
shrewishly. One would think his mother's milk   160
were scarce out of him.

OLIVIA Let him approach. Call in my gentlewoman.

MALVOLIO Gentlewoman, my lady calls.   *Exit.*

Enter Maria.

OLIVIA Give me my veil; come, throw it o'er my face.
We'll once more hear Orsino's embassy.   165

Enter Viola.

VIOLA The honorable lady of the house, which is she?

OLIVIA Speak to me; I shall answer for her. Your will?

VIOLA Most radiant, exquisite, and unmatchable beauty
—I pray you tell me if this be the lady of the house,
for I never saw her. I would be loath to cast away   170
my speech; for, besides that it is excellently well
penned, I have taken great pains to con it. Good
beauties, let me sustain no scorn. I am very comptible, even to the least sinister usage.

OLIVIA Whence came you, sir?   175

VIOLA I can say little more than I have studied, and
that question's out of my part. Good gentle one,
give me modest assurance if you be the lady of the
house, that I may proceed in my speech.

---

156 **squash** unripe **peascod** (pea pod)   157 **codling** unripe apple   158 **standing water** i.e., at the turning of the tide, between ebb and flood, when it flows neither way   160 **shrewishly** tartly   172 **con** learn   173-74 **comptible** sensitive   174 **sinister** discourteous   178 **modest** reasonable

180 OLIVIA Are you a comedian?

VIOLA No, my profound heart; and yet (by the very fangs of malice I swear) I am not that I play. Are you the lady of the house?

OLIVIA If I do not usurp myself, I am.

185 VIOLA Most certain, if you are she, you do usurp yourself; for what is yours to bestow is not yours to reserve. But this is from my commission. I will on with my speech in your praise and then show you the heart of my message.

190 OLIVIA Come to what is important in't. I forgive you the praise.

VIOLA Alas, I took great pains to study it, and 'tis poetical.

OLIVIA It is the more like to be feigned; I pray you
195 keep it in. I heard you were saucy at my gates; and allowed your approach rather to wonder at you than to hear you. If you be not mad, be gone; if you have reason, be brief. 'Tis not that time of moon with me to make one in so skipping a dia-
200 logue.

MARIA Will you hoist sail, sir? Here lies your way.

VIOLA No, good swabber; I am to hull here a little longer. Some mollification for your giant, sweet lady. Tell me your mind. I am a messenger.

205 OLIVIA Sure you have some hideous matter to deliver, when the courtesy of it is so fearful. Speak your office.

180 **comedian** actor (because he has had to "con" a "part") 181 **my profound heart** my sagacious lady (a bantering compliment) 182 **that** that which 184 **usurp** counterfeit (but Viola takes it in the sense "betray," "wrong") 186 **what** i.e., your hand in marriage 187 **from my commission** beyond my instructions 190 **forgive you** excuse you from repeating 198-200 **'Tis not ... dialogue** i.e., I am not in the mood to sustain such aimless banter 202 **hull** lie adrift 203 **giant** (an ironical reference to Maria's small size) 204 **Tell me your mind. I am a messenger.** (Many editors have divided these sentences, assigning the first to Olivia and the second to Viola) 206 **when the courtesy of it is so fearful** i.e., since your manner is so truculent 207 **office** business

446

VIOLA It alone concerns your ear. I bring no overture
of war, no taxation of homage. I hold the olive
in my hand. My words are as full of peace as 210
matter.

OLIVIA Yet you began rudely. What are you? What
would you?

VIOLA The rudeness that hath appeared in me have I
learned from my entertainment. What I am, and 215
what I would, are as secret as maidenhead: to
your ears, divinity; to any other's, profanation.

OLIVIA Give us the place alone; we will hear this
divinity. [*Exit Maria and Attendants.*] Now, sir,
what is your text? 220

VIOLA Most sweet lady—

OLIVIA A comfortable doctrine, and much may be
said of it. Where lies your text?

VIOLA In Orsino's bosom.

OLIVIA In his bosom? In what chapter of his bosom? 225

VIOLA To answer by the method, in the first of his
heart.

OLIVIA O, I have read it; it is heresy. Have you no
more to say?

VIOLA Good madam, let me see your face. 230

OLIVIA Have you any commission from your lord to
negotiate with my face? You are now out of your
text. But we will draw the curtain and show you
the picture. [*Unveils.*] Look you, sir, such a one I
was this present. Is't not well done? 235

---

209 **taxation of** demand for   209 **olive** (the symbol of peace)   211 **matter**
significant content   215 **entertainment** reception   216 **maidenhead** maidenhood   217 **divinity** i.e., a sacred message   222 **comfortable** comforting
226 **method** i.e., in the theological style suggested by "divinity," "profanation,"
"text," and "doctrine"   232-33 **You are now out of your text** i.e., you have
shifted from talking of your master's heart to asking about my face   235 **this
present** just now (like portrait painters, Olivia gives the age of the subject of the
"picture" she has just revealed by drawing the "curtain" of a veil from her face)

VIOLA Excellently done, if God did all.

OLIVIA 'Tis in grain, sir; 'twill endure wind and
weather.

VIOLA 'Tis beauty truly blent, whose red and white
240 Nature's own sweet and cunning hand laid on.
Lady, you are the cruel'st she alive
If you will lead these graces to the grave,
And leave the world no copy.

OLIVIA O, sir, I will not be so hard-hearted. I will give
245 out divers schedules of my beauty. It shall be in-
ventoried, and every particle and utensil labeled
to my will: as, item, two lips, indifferent red;
item, two gray eyes, with lids to them; item, one
neck, one chin, and so forth. Were you sent hither
250 to praise me?

VIOLA I see you what you are; you are too proud;
But if you were the devil, you are fair.
My lord and master loves you. O, such love
Could be but recompensed though you were crowned
The nonpareil of beauty.

255 OLIVIA   How does he love me?

VIOLA With adorations, with fertile tears,
With groans that thunder love, with sighs of fire.

OLIVIA Your lord does know my mind; I cannot love him.
Yet I suppose him virtuous, know him noble,
260 Of great estate, of fresh and stainless youth;
In voices well divulged, free, learned, and valiant,
And in dimension and the shape of nature
A gracious person. But yet I cannot love him.
He might have took his answer long ago.

265 VIOLA If I did love you in my master's flame,

237 in grain fast-dyed, indelible 240 cunning skillful 245 schedules statements
246 utensil article 246-47 labeled to my will i.e., added as a codicil
247 item also 250 praise appraise 252 if even if 256 fertile copious
261 well divulged i.e., of good repute 262 dimension physique

448

With such a suff'ring, such a deadly life,
In your denial I would find no sense;
I would not understand it.

OLIVIA   Why, what would you?

VIOLA Make me a willow cabin at your gate
And call upon my soul within the house;   270
Write loyal cantons of contemnèd love
And sing them loud even in the dead of night;
Hallo your name to the reverberate hills
And make the babbling gossip of the air
Cry out "Olivia!" O, you should not rest   275
Between the elements of air and earth
But you should pity me.

OLIVIA You might do much. What is your parentage?

VIOLA Above my fortunes, yet my state is well.
I am a gentleman.

OLIVIA   Get you to your lord.   280
I cannot love him. Let him send no more,
Unless, perchance, you come to me again
To tell me how he takes it. Fare you well.
I thank you for your pains. Spend this for me.

VIOLA I am no fee'd post, lady; keep your purse;   285
My master, not myself, lacks recompense.
Love make his heart of flint that you shall love;
And let your fervor, like my master's, be
Placed in contempt. Farewell, fair cruelty.   *Exit*.

OLIVIA "What is your parentage?"   290
"Above my fortunes, yet my state is well.
I am a gentleman." I'll be sworn thou art.
Thy tongue, thy face, thy limbs, actions, and spirit

---

266 **deadly** doomed to die   269 **willow** (emblem of a disconsolate lover)
270 **my soul** i.e., Olivia   271 **cantons** songs   271 **contemnèd** rejected
273 **reverberate** reverberating   274 **babbling gossip of the air** i.e., echo   277 **But**
but that   279 **state** status   285 **fee'd post** i.e., lackey to be tipped   287 **Love**
make ... love may Love make the heart of him you love like flint

Do give thee fivefold blazon. Not too fast; soft, soft,
295   Unless the master were the man. How now?
Even so quickly may one catch the plague?
Methinks I feel this youth's perfections
With an invisible and subtle stealth
To creep in at mine eyes. Well, let it be.
What ho, Malvolio!

Enter Malvolio.

300 MALVOLIO   Here, madam, at your service.

OLIVIA Run after that same peevish messenger,
The County's man. He left this ring behind him,
Would I or not. Tell him I'll none of it.
Desire him not to flatter with his lord
305   Nor hold him up with hopes. I am not for him.
If that the youth will come this way tomorrow,
I'll give him reasons for't. Hie thee, Malvolio.

MALVOLIO Madam, I will.   *Exit.*

OLIVIA I do I know not what, and fear to find
310   Mine eye too great a flatterer for my mind.
Fate, show thy force; ourselves we do not owe.
What is decreed must be—and be this so!   [*Exit.*]

294 **blazon** heraldic insignia   294 **soft** i.e., take it slowly   301 **peevish** truculent
impertinent   302 **County's** Count's   304 **flatter with** encourage   310 **Mine
eye ... mind** i.e., my eye, so susceptible to external attractions, will betray my
judgment   311 **owe** own

ACT II

Scene I. [*The seacoast.*]

Enter Antonio and Sebastian.

ANTONIO Will you stay no longer? Nor will you not
that I go with you?

SEBASTIAN By your patience, no. My stars shine darkly
over me; the malignancy of my fate might perhaps
distemper yours. Therefore I shall crave of you   5
your leave, that I may bear my evils alone. It were
a bad recompense for your love to lay any of them
on you.

ANTONIO Let me yet know of you whither you are
bound.   10

SEBASTIAN No, sooth, sir. My determinate voyage is
mere extravagancy. But I perceive in you so excellent a touch of modesty that you will not extort
from me what I am willing to keep in; therefore it
charges me in manners the rather to express myself.   15
You must know of me then, Antonio, my name is
Sebastian, which I called Roderigo. My father was
that Sebastian of Messaline whom I know you have
heard of. He left behind him myself and a sister,
both born in an hour. If the heavens had been   20

II.i.3 patience permission   5 distemper disorder   11 sooth truly   11 determinate intended   12 extravagancy wandering   14-15 it charges me ...
myself i.e., civility requires that I give some account of myself   20 in an hour in
the same hour

pleased, would we had so ended! But you, sir,
altered that, for some hour before you took me
from the breach of the sea was my sister drowned.

ANTONIO Alas the day!

25 SEBASTIAN A lady, sir, though it was said she much
resembled me, was yet of many accounted beautiful.
But though I could not with such estimable wonder
overfar believe that, yet thus far I will boldly
publish her: she bore a mind that envy could not
30 but call fair. She is drowned already, sir, with salt
water, though I seem to drown her remembrance
again with more.

ANTONIO Pardon me, sir, your bad entertainment.

SEBASTIAN O good Antonio, forgive me your trouble.

35 ANTONIO If you will not murder me for my love, let
me be your servant.

SEBASTIAN If you will not undo what you have done,
that is, kill him whom you have recovered, desire
it not. Fare ye well at once. My bosom is full of
40 kindness, and I am yet so near the manners of my
mother that, upon the least occasion more, mine
eyes will tell tales of me. I am bound to the Count
Orsino's court. Farewell.   *Exit.*

ANTONIO The gentleness of all the gods go with thee.
45 I have many enemies in Orsino's court,
Else would I very shortly see thee there.
But come what may, I do adore thee so
That danger shall seem sport, and I will go.   *Exit.*

---

23 **breach** breakers   27 **with such estimable wonder** i.e., with so much esteem
in my appraisal   29 **publish** describe   33 **bad entertainment** i.e., poor reception at my hands   34 **your trouble** the trouble I have given you   35 **murder
me** i.e., by forcing me to part from you   38 **recovered** saved   40-42 **so near** ...
tales of me i.e., so overwrought by my sorrow that, like a woman, I shall weep

Scene II. [*A street near Olivia's house.*]

Enter Viola and Malvolio at several doors.

MALVOLIO Were not you ev'n now with the Countess
Olivia?

VIOLA Even now, sir. On a moderate pace I have since
arrived but hither.

MALVOLIO She returns this ring to you, sir. You might   5
have saved me my pains, to have taken it away
yourself. She adds, moreover, that you should put
your lord into a desperate assurance she will none
of him. And one thing more, that you be never so
hardy to come again in his affairs, unless it be to   10
report your lord's taking of this. Receive it so.

VIOLA She took the ring of me. I'll none of it.

MALVOLIO Come, sir, you peevishly threw it to her,
and her will is, it should be so returned. If it be
worth stooping for, there it lies, in your eye; if   15
not, be it his that finds it.   *Exit.*

VIOLA I left no ring with her. What means this lady?
Fortune forbid my outside have not charmed her.
She made good view of me; indeed, so much
That sure methought her eyes had lost her tongue,   20
For she did speak in starts distractedly.
She loves me sure; the cunning of her passion

II.ii.s.d. **several** separate 8 **desperate assurance** hopeless certainty 12 **She took the ring of me** (of the various emendations proposed for this puzzling line, Malone's "She took no ring of me" is perhaps the most attractive) 15 **eye** sight 20 **sure methought** ("sure," which repairs the defective meter of this line, has been adopted from the Second Folio. Another common emendation is "as methought") 20 **her eyes had lost her tongue** i.e., her fixed gaze made her lose the power of speech 22 **cunning** craftiness

Invites me in this churlish messenger.
None of my lord's ring? Why, he sent her none.
25   I am the man. If it be so, as 'tis,
Poor lady, she were better love a dream.
Disguise, I see thou art a wickedness
Wherein the pregnant enemy does much.
How easy is it for the proper false
30   In women's waxen hearts to set their forms!
Alas, our frailty is the cause, not we,
For such as we are made of, such we be.
How will this fadge? My master loves her dearly;
And I (poor monster) fond as much on him;
35   And she (mistaken) seems to dote on me.
What will become of this? As I am man,
My state is desperate for my master's love.
As I am woman (now alas the day!),
What thriftless sighs shall poor Olivia breathe?
40   O Time, thou must untangle this, not I;
It is too hard a knot for me t' untie.   [*Exit.*]

Scene III. [*A room in Olivia's house.*]

Enter Sir Toby and Sir Andrew.

TOBY Approach, Sir Andrew. Not to be abed after
midnight is to be up betimes; and "*Deliculo surgere*," thou know'st.

ANDREW Nay, by my troth, I know not, but I know
5   to be up late is to be up late.

25 **I am the man** i.e., whom she loves   28 **pregnant enemy** crafty fiend (i.e.,
Satan) 29 **proper false** i.e., attractive but deceitful suitors 33 **fadge** turn
out 34 **monster** (because of her equivocal position as both man and woman)
34 **fond** dote 37 **desperate** hopeless 39 **thriftless** unavailing II.iii.2-3 **Deliculo surgere** i.e., *Diluculo surgere saluberrimum est*, "it is most healthful to rise
early" (a tag from William Lily's Latin grammar, which was widely used in
sixteenth-century schools)

TOBY A false conclusion; I hate it as an unfilled can.
To be up after midnight, and to go to bed then,
is early; so that to go to bed after midnight is to go
to bed betimes. Does not our lives consist of the
four elements?   10

ANDREW Faith, so they say; but I think it rather con-
sists of eating and drinking.

TOBY Th' art a scholar! Let us therefore eat and drink.
Marian I say, a stoup of wine!

Enter Clown.

ANDREW Here comes the fool, i' faith.   15

CLOWN How now, my hearts? Did you never see the
picture of We Three?

TOBY Welcome, ass. Now let's have a catch.

ANDREW By my troth, the fool has an excellent
breast. I had rather than forty shillings I had such   20
a leg, and so sweet a breath to sing, as the fool
has. In sooth, thou wast in very gracious fooling
last night, when thou spok'st of Pigrogromitus, of
the Vapians passing the equinoctial of Queubus.
'Twas very good, i' faith. I sent thee sixpence for   25
thy leman. Hadst it?

CLOWN I did impeticos thy gratillity, for Malvolio's
nose is no whipstock. My lady has a white hand,
and the Myrmidons are no bottle-ale houses.

---

6 can tankard 9-10 the four elements i.e., air, fire, earth, and water, which
were thought to be the basic ingredients of all things 14 stoup cup 16-17 the
picture of We Three i.e., a picture of two asses, the spectator making the third
18 catch round, a simple polyphonic song for several voices 20 breast voice
21 leg i.e., skill in bowing (?) 22 gracious delightful 23-24 Pigrogromitus,
Vapians, Queubus (presumably words invented by the Clown as specimens of his
"gracious fooling" in mock learning) 26 leman sweetheart 27 impeticos thy
gratillity (more of the Clown's fooling, which perhaps means something like
"pocket your gratuity") 27-29 Malvolio's nose ... bottle-ale houses (probably
mere nonsense)

30 ANDREW Excellent. Why, this is the best fooling, when all is done. Now a song!

TOBY Come on, there is sixpence for you. Let's have a song.

ANDREW There's a testril of me too. If one knight
35 give a—

CLOWN Would you have a love song, or a song of good life?

TOBY A love song, a love song.

ANDREW Ay, ay, I care not for good life.

Clown sings.

40   O mistress mine, where are you roaming?
    O, stay and hear, your true-love's coming,
        That can sing both high and low.
    Trip no further, pretty sweeting;
    Journeys end in lovers meeting,
45   Every wise man's son doth know.

ANDREW Excellent good, i' faith.

TOBY Good, good.

Clown [sings].

    What is love? 'Tis not hereafter;
    Present mirth hath present laughter;
50   What's to come is still unsure:
    In delay there lies no plenty;
    Then come kiss me, sweet, and twenty,
        Youth's a stuff will not endure.

---

34 **testril** tester, sixpence   34-35 **If one knight give a—** (some editors have tried to supply what seems to be a missing line here, but it is probable that the Clown breaks in without permitting Sir Andrew to finish his sentence)   36-37 **of good life** i.e., moral, edifying (?)   50 **still** always   52 **Then come kiss me, sweet, and twenty** i.e., so kiss me, my sweet, and then kiss me twenty times again (some editors, taking "twenty" as an intensive, read the line as "so kiss me then, my very sweet one")

ANDREW A mellifluous voice, as I am true knight.

TOBY A contagious breath.   55

ANDREW Very sweet and contagious, i' faith.

TOBY To hear by the nose, it is dulcet in contagion.
But shall we make the welkin dance indeed? Shall
we rouse the night owl in a catch that will draw
three souls out of one weaver? Shall we do that?   60

ANDREW And you love me, let's do't. I am dog at a
catch.

CLOWN By'r Lady, sir, and some dogs will catch well.

ANDREW Most certain. Let our catch be "Thou knave."

CLOWN "Hold thy peace, thou knave," knight? I   65
shall be constrained in't to call thee knave, knight.

ANDREW 'Tis not the first time I have constrained one
to call me knave. Begin, fool. It begins, "Hold thy
peace."

CLOWN I shall never begin if I hold my peace.   70

ANDREW Good, i' faith! Come, begin.

Catch sung. Enter Maria.

MARIA What a caterwauling do you keep here? If my
lady have not called up her steward Malvolio and
bid him turn you out of doors, never trust me.

TOBY My lady's a Cataian, we are politicians, Mal-   75

---

55 **contagious breath** catchy song   57 **To hear by the nose, it is dulcet in
contagion** i.e., if we could hear through the nose, the Clown's "breath" would be
sweet and not malodorous, as "contagious" breaths usually are   58 **welkin** sky
60 **weaver** (weavers were noted for their singing)   61 **dog** clever (but in the next
line the Clown puns on **dog** i.e., latch, gripping device)   65 **Hold thy peace,
thou knave** (a line from the round proposed by Sir Andrew)   75 **My lady's a
Cataian, we are politicians** (because Sir Toby and his companions are "politicians" [i.e., tricksters, intriguers] they recognize Maria's warning of Olivia's anger
as the ruse of a "Cataian" [i.e., native of Cathay, cheater]; hence "Tilly-vally,
lady" [line 78], which means something like "Fiddlesticks, lady")

volio's a Peg-a-Ramsey, and [*sings*] "Three merry
men be we." Am not I consanguineous? Am I
not of her blood? Tilly-vally, lady. [*Sings*] "There
dwelt a man in Babylon, lady, lady."

80 CLOWN Beshrew me, the knight's in admirable fooling.

ANDREW Ay, he does well enough if he be disposed,
and so do I too. He does it with a better grace, but
I do it more natural.

85 TOBY [*Sings*] "O the twelfth day of December."

MARIA For the love o' God, peace!

Enter Malvolio.

MALVOLIO My masters, are you mad? Or what are you?
Have you no wit, manners, nor honesty, but to
gabble like tinkers at this time of night? Do ye
90 make an alehouse of my lady's house, that ye squeak
out your coziers' catches without any mitigation
or remorse of voice? Is there no respect of place,
persons, nor time in you?

TOBY We did keep time, sir, in our catches. Sneck up.

95 MALVOLIO Sir Toby, I must be round with you. My
lady bade me tell you that, though she harbors
you as her kinsman, she's nothing allied to your
disorders. If you can separate yourself and your
misdemeanors, you are welcome to the house. If
100 not, and it would please you to take leave of her,
she is very willing to bid you farewell.

---

76 **Peg-a-Ramsey** (character in an old song whose name Sir Toby uses apparently
as a term of contempt) 76–77 **Three merry men be we** (like Sir Toby's other
snatches, a fragment of an old song) 77 **consanguineous** related, kin (to Olivia)
80 **Beshrew** curse 84 **natural** (with an unintentional pun on "natural" as a term
for fool or idiot; see I.iii.29) 88 **wit** sense 88 **honesty** decency 91 **coziers'**
cobblers' 91–92 **mitigation or remorse** i.e., lowering 94 **Sneck up** go hang
95 **round** blunt

TOBY [*Sings*] "Farewell, dear heart since I must needs be gone."

MARIA Nay, good Sir Toby.

CLOWN [*Sings*] "His eyes do show his days are almost done."

MALVOLIO Is't even so?   105

TOBY [*Sings*] "But I will never die."

CLOWN [*Sings*] Sir Toby, there you lie.

MALVOLIO This is much credit to you.

TOBY [*Sings*] "Shall I bid him go?"

CLOWN [*Sings*] "What and if you do?"   110

TOBY [*Sings*] "Shall I bid him go, and spare not?"

CLOWN [*Sings*] "O, no, no, no, no, you dare not!"

TOBY Out o' tune, sir? Ye lie. Art any more than a
steward? Dost thou think, because thou art virtuous,
there shall be no more cakes and ale?   115

CLOWN Yes, by Saint Anne, and ginger shall be hot
i' th' mouth too.

TOBY Th' art i' th' right.—Go, sir, rub your chain
with crumbs. A stoup of wine, Maria!

MALVOLIO Mistress Mary, if you prized my lady's favor   120
at anything more than contempt, you would not
give means for this uncivil rule. She shall know
of it, by this hand.   *Exit*.

MARIA Go shake your ears.

102 Farewell ... gone (what follows, in crude antiphony between Sir Toby and
the Clown, is adapted from a ballad, "Corydon's Farewell to Phyllis")   113 Out
o' tune, sir? Ye lie (Sir Toby accuses the Clown of being out of tune, it seems,
because he had added an extra "no" and thus an extra note in line 112, and of lying
because he had questioned his valor in "you dare not." Then he turns to berating
Malvolio)   116 ginger (commonly used to spice ale)   118-19 rub your chain
with crumbs i.e., polish your steward's chain, your badge of office
122 give means for this uncivil rule i.e., provide liquor for this brawl   124 Go
shake your ears i.e., like the ass you are (?)

125 ANDREW 'Twere as good a deed as to drink when a
man's ahungry, to challenge him the field, and
then to break promise with him and make a fool
of him.

TOBY Do't, knight. I'll write thee a challenge; or I'll
130 deliver thy indignation to him by word of mouth.

MARIA Sweet Sir Toby, be patient for tonight. Since
the youth of the Count's was today with my lady,
she is much out of quiet. For Monsieur Malvolio,
let me alone with him. If I do not gull him into a
135 nayword, and make him a common recreation, do
not think I have wit enough to lie straight in my
bed. I know I can do it.

TOBY Possess us, possess us. Tell us something of
him.

140 MARIA Marry, sir, sometimes he is a kind of Puritan.

ANDREW O, if I thought that, I'd beat him like a dog.

TOBY What, for being a Puritan? Thy exquisite
reason, dear knight.

ANDREW I have no exquisite reason for't, but I have
145 reason good enough.

MARIA The devil a Puritan that he is, or anything
constantly but a time-pleaser; an affectioned ass,
that cons state without book and utters it by great
swarths; the best persuaded of himself; so
150 crammed, as he thinks, with excellencies that it is
his grounds of faith that all that look on him love
him; and on that vice in him will my revenge find
notable cause to work.

126 **ahungry** (characteristically, Sir Andrew confuses hunger and thirst and thus
perverts the proverbial expression)   126 **the field** i.e., to a duel   135 **nayword**
byword   138 **Possess** inform   140 **Puritan** i.e., a straight-laced, censorious
person (in lines 146-47 Maria makes it clear that she is not using the label in a
strict ecclesiastical sense, as Sir Andrew [line 141] thinks)   147 **constantly**
consistently   147 **time-pleaser** sycophant   147 **affectioned** affected   148 **cons
state without book** i.e., memorizes stately gestures and turns of phrase
149 **swarths** swaths, quantities   149 **the best persuaded of himself** i.e., who
thinks most highly of himself

TOBY What wilt thou do?

MARIA I will drop in his way some obscure epistles of   155
love, wherein by the color of his beard, the shape of
his leg, the manner of his gait, the expressure of
his eye, forehead, and complexion, he shall find
himself most feelingly personated. I can write very
like my lady your niece; on a forgotten matter we   160
can hardly make distinction of our hands.

TOBY Excellent. I smell a device.

ANDREW I have't in my nose too.

TOBY He shall think by the letters that thou wilt drop
that they come from my niece, and that she's in love   165
with him.

MARIA My purpose is indeed a horse of that color.

ANDREW And your horse now would make him an
ass.

MARIA Ass, I doubt not.   170

ANDREW O, 'twill be admirable.

MARIA Sport royal, I warrant you. I know my physic
will work with him. I will plant you two, and let
the fool make a third, where he shall find the
letter. Observe his construction of it. For this   175
night, to bed, and dream on the event. Farewell.

                                              Exit.

TOBY Good night, Penthesilea.

ANDREW Before me, she's a good wench.

TOBY She's a beagle true-bred, and one that adores
me. What o' that?   180

157 **expressure** expression   159 **personated** represented   173-74 **let the fool
make a third** (like the plan to have Viola present herself to Duke Orsino as a
eunuch [I.ii.62], this plot device was abandoned; it is Fabian, not the Clown, who
makes the third spectator to Malvolio's exposé)   175 **construction** interpretation
176 **event** outcome   177 **Penthesilea** (in classical mythology, the queen of the
Amazons)   178 **Before me** i.e., I swear, with myself as witness   179 **beagle** (one
of several allusions to Maria's small stature)

ANDREW I was adored once too.

TOBY Let's to bed, knight. Thou hadst need send for
more money.

ANDREW If I cannot recover your niece, I am a foul
185 way out.

TOBY Send for money, knight. If thou hast her not
i' th' end, call me Cut.

ANDREW If I do not, never trust me, take it how you
will.

190 TOBY Come, come; I'll go burn some sack. 'Tis too
late to go to bed now. Come, knight; come, knight.
Exeunt.

Scene IV. [*The Duke's palace.*]

Enter Duke, Viola, Curio, and others.

DUKE Give me some music. Now good morrow, friends.
Now, good Cesario, but that piece of song,
That old and antic song we heard last night.
Methought it did relieve my passion much,
5 More than light airs and recollected terms
Of these most brisk and giddy-pacèd times.
Come, but one verse.

CURIO He is not here, so please your lordship, that
should sing it.

10 DUKE Who was it?

CURIO Feste the jester, my lord, a fool that the Lady

184 **recover** win   184-85 **a foul way out** i.e., badly out of pocket   187 **Cut** i.e.,
a dock-tailed horse   190 **burn some sack** heat and spice some Spanish wine
II.iv.3 **antic** quaint   4 **passion** suffering (from unrequited love)   5 **recollected
terms** studied phrases

Olivia's father took much delight in. He is about the
house.

DUKE Seek him out, and play the tune the while.
                              [*Exit Curio.*] *Music plays.*
Come hither, boy. If ever thou shalt love,   15
In the sweet pangs of it remember me;
For such as I am all true lovers are,
Unstaid and skittish in all motions else
Save in the constant image of the creature
That is beloved. How dost thou like this tune?   20

VIOLA It gives a very echo to the seat
Where Love is throned.

DUKE   Thou dost speak masterly.
My life upon't, young though thou art, thine eye
Hath stayed upon some favor that it loves.
Hath it not, boy?

VIOLA   A little, by your favor.   25

DUKE What kind of woman is't?

VIOLA   Of your complexion.

DUKE She is not worth thee then. What years, i' faith?

VIOLA About your years, my lord.

DUKE Too old, by heaven. Let still the woman take
An elder than herself: so wears she to him,   30
So sways she level in her husband's heart;
For, boy, however we do praise ourselves,
Our fancies are more giddy and unfirm,
More longing, wavering, sooner lost and worn,
Than women's are.

VIOLA   I think it well, my lord.   35

DUKE Then let thy love be younger than thyself,

18 **motions** emotions   21 **seat** i.e., the heart (see I.i.38-39)   24 **favor** face
26 **complexion** temperament   29 **still** always   30 **wears she** she adapts herself
31 **sways she … heart** i.e., she keeps steady in her husband's affections
33 **fancies** loves   34 **worn** (many editors have adopted the reading "won" from
the Second Folio)

Or thy affection cannot hold the bent;
For women are as roses, whose fair flow'r,
Being once displayed, doth fall that very hour.

40 VIOLA And so they are; alas, that they are so.
To die, even when they to perfection grow.

Enter Curio and Clown.

DUKE O, fellow, come, the song we had last night.
Mark it, Cesario; it is old and plain.
The spinsters and the knitters in the sun,
And the free maids that weave their thread with
45   bones,
Do use to chant it. It is silly sooth,
And dallies with the innocence of love,
Like the old age.

CLOWN Are you ready, sir?

50 DUKE I prithee sing.   *Music.*

The Song.

Come away, come away, death,
    And in sad cypress let me be laid.
Fly away, fly away, breath;
    I am slain by a fair cruel maid.
55 My shroud of white, stuck all with yew,
        O, prepare it.
My part of death, no one so true
        Did share it.

Not a flower, not a flower sweet,
60   On my black coffin let there be strown;
Not a friend, not a friend greet
        My poor corpse, where my bones shall be
        thrown.

---

37 **hold the bent** i.e., maintain its strength and tension (the image is that of a bent bow)   44 **spinsters** spinners   45 **free** carefree   45 **bones** i.e., bone bobbins
46 **silly sooth** simple truth   47 **dallies** deals movingly   48 **the old age** i.e., the good old times   52 **cypress** a coffin made of cypress wood

A thousand thousand sighs to save,
  Lay me, O, where
Sad true lover never find my grave,   65
  To weep there.

DUKE There's for thy pains.

CLOWN No pains, sir. I take pleasure in singing, sir.

DUKE I'll pay thy pleasure then.

CLOWN Truly, sir, and pleasure will be paid one time   70
or another.

DUKE Give me now leave to leave thee.

CLOWN Now the melancholy god protect thee, and the
tailor make thy doublet of changeable taffeta, for
thy mind is a very opal. I would have men of such   75
constancy put to sea, that their business might be
everything, and their intent everywhere; for that's
it that always makes a good voyage of nothing.
Farewell.   *Exit*.

DUKE Let all the rest give place.
                    [*Exeunt Curio and Attendants*.]
                            Once more, Cesario,   80
Get thee to yond same sovereign cruelty.
Tell her my love, more noble than the world,
Prizes not quantity of dirty lands;
The parts that fortune hath bestowed upon her
Tell her I hold as giddily as fortune,   85
But 'tis that miracle and queen of gems
That nature pranks her in attracts my soul.

VIOLA But if she cannot love you, sir?

DUKE I cannot be so answered.

VIOLA   Sooth, but you must.

---

74 changeable i.e., with shifting lights and colors 80 give place withdraw
81 sovereign cruelty i.e., peerless and disdainful lady 84 parts gifts (of wealth
and social status) 85 giddily indifferently 86 queen of gems i.e., Olivia's
beauty 87 pranks her in adorns her with 89 Sooth truly

90   Say that some lady, as perhaps there is,
      Hath for your love as great a pang of heart
      As you have for Olivia. You cannot love her.
      You tell her so. Must she not then be answered?

      DUKE There is no woman's sides
95   Can bide the beating of so strong a passion
      As love doth give my heart; no woman's heart
      So big to hold so much; they lack retention.
      Alas, their love may be called appetite,
      No motion of the liver but the palate,
100   That suffer surfeit, cloyment, and revolt;
      But mine is all as hungry as the sea
      And can digest as much. Make no compare
      Between that love a woman can bear me
      And that I owe Olivia.

      VIOLA   Ay, but I know—

105   DUKE What dost thou know?

      VIOLA Too well what love women to men may owe.
      In faith, they are as true of heart as we.
      My father had a daughter loved a man
      As it might be perhaps, were I a woman,
      I should your lordship.

110   DUKE   And what's her history?

      VIOLA A blank, my lord. She never told her love,
      But let concealment, like a worm i' th' bud,
      Feed on her damask cheek. She pined in thought;
      And, with a green and yellow melancholy,
115   She sat like Patience on a monument,
      Smiling at grief. Was not this love indeed?
      We men may say more, swear more; but indeed
      Our shows are more than will; for still we prove
      Much in our vows but little in our love.

120   DUKE But died thy sister of her love, my boy?

95 **bide** endure   97 **retention** i.e., the ability to retain   99 **motion** stirring,
prompting   99 **liver** (seat of passion)   100 **revolt** revulsion   113 **damask** i.e.,
like a pink and white damask rose   113 **thought** brooding   118 **Our shows are
more than will** i.e., what we show is greater than the passion that we feel

VIOLA I am all the daughters of my father's house,
And all the brothers too, and yet I know not.
Sir, shall I to this lady?

DUKE   Ay, that's the theme.
To her in haste. Give her this jewel. Say
My love can give no place, bide no denay.   125

Exeunt.

Scene V. [*Olivia's garden.*]

Enter Sir Toby, Sir Andrew, and Fabian.

TOBY Come thy ways, Signior Fabian.

FABIAN Nay, I'll come. If I lose a scruple of this
sport, let me be boiled to death with melancholy.

TOBY Wouldst thou not be glad to have the niggardly
rascally sheep-biter come by some notable shame?   5

FABIAN I would exult, man. You know he brought me
out o' favor with my lady about a bearbaiting here.

TOBY To anger him we'll have the bear again, and we
will fool him black and blue. Shall we not, Sir
Andrew?   10

ANDREW And we do not, it is pity of our lives.

Enter Maria.

TOBY Here comes the little villain. How now, my
metal of India?

122 **I know not** (because she thinks that her brother may be still alive) 125 **can give no place** cannot yield 125 **denay** denial II.v.2 **scruple** smallest part 3 **boiled** (pronounced "biled," quibbling on "bile," which was thought to be the cause of melancholy) 5 **sheep-biter** i.e., sneaky dog 13 **metal of India** i.e., golden girl

MARIA Get ye all three into the box tree. Malvolio's
15   coming down this walk. He has been yonder i' the
      sun practicing behavior to his own shadow this half
      hour. Observe him, for the love of mockery; for I
      know this letter will make a contemplative idiot
      of him. Close, in the name of jesting. [*The others*
20   *hide.*] Lie thou there [*throws down a letter*]; for
      here comes the trout that must be caught with
      tickling.   *Exit.*

Enter Malvolio.

MALVOLIO 'Tis but fortune; all is fortune. Maria once
      told me she did affect me; and I have heard herself
25   come thus near, that, should she fancy, it should
      be one of my complexion. Besides, she uses me with
      a more exalted respect than anyone else that
      follows her. What should I think on't?

TOBY Here's an overweening rogue.

30 FABIAN O, peace! Contemplation makes a rare turkey
      cock of him. How he jets under his advanced
      plumes!

ANDREW 'Slight, I could so beat the rogue.

TOBY Peace, I say.

35 MALVOLIO To be Count Malvolio.

TOBY Ah, rogue!

ANDREW Pistol him, pistol him.

TOBY Peace, peace.

MALVOLIO There is example for't. The Lady of the
40   Strachy married the yeoman of the wardrobe.

18 **contemplative** i.e., self-centered   19 **Close** hide   22 **tickling** stroking, i.e.,
flattery   24 **she did affect me** i.e., Olivia liked me   25 **fancy** love   28 **follows**
serves   31 **jets** struts   31 **advanced** uplifted   33 **'Slight** by God's light (a mild
oath)   34 **Peace, I say** (many editors assign this and line 38 to Fabian on the
ground that it is his function throughout the scene to restrain Sir Toby and Sir
Andrew)   39-40 **The Lady of the Strachy** (an unidentified allusion to a great
lady who married beneath her)

ANDREW Fie on him, Jezebel.

FABIAN O, peace! Now he's deeply in. Look how imagination blows him.

MALVOLIO Having been three months married to her, sitting in my state— 45

TOBY O for a stonebow, to hit him in the eye!

MALVOLIO Calling my officers about me, in my branched velvet gown; having come from a day-bed, where I have left Olivia sleeping—

TOBY Fire and brimstone! 50

FABIAN O, peace, peace!

MALVOLIO And then to have the humor of state; and after a demure travel of regard, telling them I know my place, as I would they should do theirs, to ask for my kinsman Toby— 55

TOBY Bolts and shackles!

FABIAN O peace, peace, peace, now, now.

MALVOLIO Seven of my people, with an obedient start, make out for him. I frown the while, and perchance wind up my watch, or play with my—some 60 rich jewel. Toby approaches; curtsies there to me—

TOBY Shall this fellow live?

FABIAN Though our silence be drawn from us with cars, yet peace.

MALVOLIO I extend my hand to him thus, quenching 65 my familiar smile with an austere regard of control—

41 Jezebel (the proud and wicked queen of Ahab, King of Israel, whom Sir Andrew, muddled as usual, regards as Malvolio's prototype in arrogance) 43 blows him puffs him up 46 stonebow crossbow that shoots stones 48 branched embroidered 48-49 daybed sofa 52 to have the humor of state i.e., to assume an imperious manner 53 after a demure travel of regard i.e., having glanced gravely over my retainers 59 make out for i.e., go to fetch 60-61 play with my—some rich jewel (Malvolio automatically reaches for his steward's chain and then catches himself) 66-67 an austere regard of control i.e., a stern look of authority

TOBY And does not Toby take you a blow o' the lips then?

70 MALVOLIO Saying, "Cousin Toby, my fortunes having cast me on your niece, give me this prerogative of speech."

TOBY What, what?

MALVOLIO "You must amend your drunkenness."

75 TOBY Out, scab!

FABIAN Nay, patience, or we break the sinews of our plot.

MALVOLIO "Besides, you waste the treasure of your time with a foolish knight"—

80 ANDREW That's me, I warrant you.

MALVOLIO "One Sir Andrew"—

ANDREW I knew 'twas I, for many do call me fool.

MALVOLIO What employment have we here?
                                        [*Takes up the letter.*]

FABIAN Now is the woodcock near the gin.

85 TOBY O, peace, and the spirit of humors intimate reading aloud to him!

MALVOLIO By my life, this is my lady's hand. These be her very C's, her U's, and her T's; and thus makes she her great P's. It is, in contempt of question,
90 her hand.

ANDREW Her C's, her U's, and her T's? Why that?

MALVOLIO [*Reads*] "To the unknown beloved, this, and my good wishes." Her very phrases! By your leave, wax. Soft, and the impressure her Lucrece,

68 take give   83 employment business   84 woodcock (a proverbially stupid bird)   84 gin snare   89 in contempt of beyond   93-94 By your leave, wax i.e., excuse me for breaking the seal   94 Soft i.e., take it slowly   94 the impressure her Lucrece i.e., the seal depicts Lucrece (noble Roman matron who stabbed herself after she was raped by Tarquin, hence a symbol of chastity)

470

with which she uses to seal. 'Tis my lady. To   95
whom should this be?

FABIAN This wins him, liver and all.

MALVOLIO [*Reads*]
        "Jove knows I love,
          But who?
        Lips, do not move;   100
          No man must know."
"No man must know." What follows? The numbers
altered! "No man must know." If this should be
thee, Malvolio?

TOBY Marry, hang thee, brock!   105

MALVOLIO [*Reads*]
    "I may command where I adore,
        But silence, like a Lucrece knife,
    With bloodless stroke my heart doth gore.
        M. O. A. I. doth sway my life."

FABIAN A fustian riddle.   110

TOBY Excellent wench, say I.

MALVOLIO "M. O. A. I. doth sway my life." Nay, but
first, let me see, let me see, let me see.

FABIAN What dish o' poison has she dressed him!

TOBY And with what wing the staniel checks at it! 115

MALVOLIO "I may command where I adore." Why, she
may command me: I serve her; she is my lady.
Why, this is evident to any formal capacity. There
is no obstruction in this. And the end; what should
that alphabetical position portend? If I could make 120
that resemble something in me! Softly, "M. O. A. I."

TOBY O, ay, make up that. He is now at a cold scent.

95 **uses to seal** customarily seals   102-3 **The numbers altered** the meter
changed (in the stanza that follows)   105 **brock** badger   110 **fustian** i.e., foolish
and pretentious   111 **wench** i.e., Maria   114 **dressed** prepared for   115 **with
what wing the staniel checks at it** i.e., with what speed the kestrel (a kind of
hawk) turns to snatch at the wrong prey   118 **formal capacity** normal intelligence   119 **obstruction** difficulty

FABIAN Sowter will cry upon't for all this, though it
be as rank as a fox.

125 MALVOLIO M.—Malvolio. M.—Why, that begins my
name.

FABIAN Did not I say he would work it out? The cur
is excellent at faults.

MALVOLIO M.—But then there is no consonancy in the
130 sequel. That suffers under probation. A should
follow, but O does.

FABIAN And O shall end, I hope.

TOBY Ay, or I'll cudgel him, and make him cry O.

MALVOLIO And then I comes behind.

135 FABIAN Ay, and you had any eye behind you, you
might see more detraction at your heels than
fortunes before you.

MALVOLIO M, O, A, I. This simulation is not as the
former; and yet, to crush this a little, it would bow
140 to me, for every one of these letters are in my name.
Soft, here follows prose.

[*Reads*] "If this fall into thy hand, revolve. In my
stars I am above thee, but be not afraid of greatness. Some are born great, some achieve greatness,
145 and some have greatness thrust upon 'em. Thy
Fates open their hands; let thy blood and spirit
embrace them; and to inure thyself to what thou
art like to be, cast thy humble slough and appear
fresh. Be opposite with a kinsman, surly with
150 servants. Let thy tongue tang arguments of state;
put thyself into the trick of singularity. She thus

123-24 Sowter will cry ... as a fox i.e., the hound will bay after the false scent
even though the deceit is gross and clear   128 faults breaks in the scent
129-30 consonancy in the sequel consistency in what follows   130 suffers
under probation does not stand up under scrutiny   132 O i.e., sound of lamentation   138 simulation hidden significance   139 crush force   142 revolve reflect
143 stars fortune   147 inure accustom   148 slough skin (of a snake)
149 opposite with hostile to   150 tang arguments of state i.e., resound with
topics of statecraft   151 trick of singularity affectation of eccentricity

advises thee that sighs for thee. Remember who
commended thy yellow stockings and wished to see
thee ever cross-gartered. I say, remember. Go to,
thou art made, if thou desir'st to be so. If not, let   155
me see thee a steward still, the fellow of servants,
and not worthy to touch Fortune's fingers. Farewell.
She that would alter services with thee,
                    THE FORTUNATE UNHAPPY."

Daylight and champian discovers not more. This   160
is open. I will be proud, I will read politic authors,
I will baffle Sir Toby, I will wash off gross acquaintance, I will be point-devise, the very man.
I do not now fool myself, to let imagination jade
me, for every reason excites to this, that my lady   165
loves me. She did commend my yellow stockings of
late, she did praise my leg being cross-gartered; and
in this she manifests herself to my love, and with
a kind of injunction drives me to these habits of her
liking. I thank my stars, I am happy. I will be   170
strange, stout, in yellow stockings, and cross-
gartered, even with the swiftness of putting on. Jove
and my stars be praised. Here is yet a postscript.
[*Reads*] "Thou canst not choose but know who I
am. If thou entertain'st my love, let it appear in   175
thy smiling. Thy smiles become thee well. Therefore in my presence still smile, dear my sweet, I
prithee."
Jove, I thank thee. I will smile; I will do everything
that thou wilt have me.   *Exit*.   180

FABIAN I will not give my part of this sport for a
pension of thousands to be paid from the Sophy.

154 **cross-gartered** i.e., with garters crossed above and below the knee
160 **champian** champaign, open country   160 **discovers** reveals   161 **politic
authors** writers on politics   162 **baffle** publicly humiliate   162 **gross** low
163 **be point-devise** i.e., follow the advice in the letter in every detail   164 **jade**
trick   165 **excites to this** i.e., enforces this conclusion   169-70 **these habits of
her liking** this clothing that she likes   171 **strange** haughty   171 **stout**
proud   175 **entertain'st** accept   182 **Sophy** Shah of Persia (perhaps with
reference to Sir Anthony Shirley's visit to the Persian court in 1599, from which he
returned laden with gifts and honors)

TOBY I could marry this wench for this device.

ANDREW So could I too.

185 TOBY And ask no other dowry with her but such another jest.

Enter Maria.

ANDREW Nor I neither.

FABIAN Here comes my noble gull-catcher.

TOBY Wilt thou set thy foot o' my neck?

190 ANDREW Or o' mine either?

TOBY Shall I play my freedom at tray-trip and become thy bondslave?

ANDREW I' faith, or I either?

TOBY Why, thou hast put him in such a dream that,
195   when the image of it leaves him, he must run mad.

MARIA Nay, but say true, does it work upon him?

TOBY Like aqua-vitae with a midwife.

MARIA If you will, then, see the fruits of the sport,
      mark his first approach before my lady. He will
200   come to her in yellow stockings, and 'tis a color she
      abhors, and cross-gartered, a fashion she detests;
      and he will smile upon her which will now be so
      unsuitable to her disposition, being addicted to a
      melancholy as she is, that it cannot but turn him
205   into a notable contempt. If you will see it, follow
      me.

TOBY To the gates of Tartar, thou most excellent devil of wit.

ANDREW I'll make one too.   *Exeunt.*

---

188 **gull-catcher** fool-catcher   191 **play** gamble   191 **tray-trip** (a dice game)
197 **aqua-vitae** distilled liquors   207 **Tartar** Tartarus (in classical mythology, the infernal regions)   209 **make one** i.e., come

ACT III

Scene I. [*Olivia's garden.*]

Enter Viola and Clown [with a tabor].

VIOLA Save thee, friend, and thy music. Dost thou live by thy tabor?

CLOWN No, sir, I live by the church.

VIOLA Art thou a churchman?

CLOWN No such matter, sir. I do live by the church; 5 for I do live at my house, and my house doth stand by the church.

VIOLA So thou mayst say, the king lies by a beggar, if a beggar dwell near him; or, the church stands by thy tabor, if thy tabor stand by the church. 10

CLOWN You have said, sir. To see this age! A sentence is but a chev'ril glove to a good wit. How quickly the wrong side may be turned outward!

VIOLA Nay, that's certain. They that dally nicely with words may quickly make them wanton. 15

CLOWN I would therefore my sister had had no name, sir.

III.i.1 **Save thee** i.e., God save you   2 **live by** gain a living from (but the Clown takes it in the sense of "reside near")   2 **tabor** (1) drum (2) taborn, tavern   8 **lies** sojourns   9-10 **stands by** (1) stands near (2) upholds   12 **chev'ril** cheveril (i.e., soft kid leather)   14 **dally nicely** play subtly   15 **wanton** i.e., equivocal in meaning (but the Clown takes it in the sense of "unchaste")

475

VIOLA Why, man?

CLOWN Why, sir, her name's a word, and to dally with
20   that word might make my sister wanton. But indeed
words are very rascals since bonds disgraced them.

VIOLA Thy reason, man?

CLOWN Troth, sir, I can yield you none without
words, and words are grown so false I am loath to
25   prove reason with them.

VIOLA I warrant thou art a merry fellow and car'st
for nothing.

CLOWN Not so, sir; I do care for something; but in my
conscience, sir, I do not care for you. If that be to
30   care for nothing, sir, I would it would make you
invisible.

VIOLA Art not thou the Lady Olivia's fool?

CLOWN No, indeed, sir. The Lady Olivia has no folly.
She will keep no fool, sir, till she be married; and
35   fools are as like husbands as pilchers are to her-
rings—the husband's the bigger. I am indeed not
her fool, but her corrupter of words.

VIOLA I saw thee late at the Count Orsino's.

CLOWN Foolery, sir, does walk about the orb like
40   the sun; it shines everywhere. I would be sorry, sir,
but the fool should be as oft with your master as
with my mistress. I think I saw your wisdom there.

VIOLA Nay, and thou pass upon me, I'll no more
with thee. Hold, there's expenses for thee.

                                    [*Gives a coin.*]

45 CLOWN Now Jove, in his next commodity of hair,
send thee a beard.

21 **since bonds disgraced them** i.e., since it was required that a man's word be
guaranteed by a bond (?)   23 **Troth** by my troth   35 **pilchers** pilchards (a kind
of small herring)   39 **orb** earth   41 **but** but that   43 **pass upon me** i.e., make
me the butt of your witticisms   45 **commodity** lot, consignment

VIOLA By my troth, I'll tell thee, I am almost sick
    for one, though I would not have it grow on my
    chin. Is thy lady within?

CLOWN Would not a pair of these have bred, sir?   50

VIOLA Yes, being kept together and put to use.

CLOWN I would play Lord Pandarus of Phrygia, sir,
    to bring a Cressida to this Troilus.

VIOLA I understand you, sir. 'Tis well begged.
                                     [Gives another coin.]

CLOWN The matter, I hope, is not great, sir, begging   55
    but a beggar: Cressida was a beggar. My lady is
    within, sir. I will conster to them whence you
    come. Who you are and what you would are out of
    my welkin; I might say "element," but the word is
    overworn.   *Exit.*   60

VIOLA This fellow is wise enough to play the fool,
    And to do that well craves a kind of wit.
    He must observe their mood on whom he jests,
    The quality of persons, and the time;
    And, like the haggard, check at every feather   65
    That comes before his eye. This is a practice
    As full of labor as a wise man's art;
    For folly that he wisely shows, is fit;
    But wise men, folly-fall'n, quite taint their wit.

---

50 **these** i.e., coins of the sort that Viola had just given him   51 **put to use** put
out at interest   52-53 **I would play ... this Troilus** (in the story of Troilus and
Cressida, which supplied both Chaucer and Shakespeare the plot for major works,
Pandarus was the go-between in the disastrous love affair)   56 **Cressida was a
beggar** (in Robert Henryson's *Testament of Cressida,* a kind of sequel to Chaucer's
poem, the faithless heroine became a harlot and a beggar)   57 **conster**
explain   59 **welkin** sky   59-60 **I might say ... overworn** (perhaps a thrust at
Ben Jonson, whose fondness for the word "element" had been ridiculed by other
writers)   62 **craves** requires   62 **wit** intelligence   65 **And** (many editors, following Johnson, have emended this to "not")   65 **haggard** untrained hawk
65 **check at** leave the true course and pursue   66 **practice** skill   69 **folly-fall'n**
having fallen into folly   69 **taint their wit** i.e., betray their common sense

Enter Sir Toby and [Sir] Andrew.

70   TOBY Save you, gentleman.

VIOLA And you, sir.

ANDREW *Dieu vous garde, monsieur.*

VIOLA *Et vous aussi; votre serviteur.*

ANDREW I hope, sir, you are, and I am yours.

75   TOBY Will you encounter the house? My niece is
desirous you should enter, if your trade be to her.

VIOLA I am bound to your niece, sir; I mean, she is
the list of my voyage.

TOBY Taste your legs, sir; put them to motion.

80   VIOLA My legs do better understand me, sir, than I
understand what you mean by bidding me taste my
legs.

TOBY I mean, to go, sir, to enter.

VIOLA I will answer you with gait and entrance. But
85   we are prevented.

Enter Olivia and Gentlewoman [Maria].

Most excellent accomplished lady, the heavens rain
odors on you.

ANDREW That youth's a rare courtier. "Rain odors"—
well!

90   VIOLA My matter hath no voice, lady, but to your
own most pregnant and vouchsafed ear.

72-73 **Dieu vous garde ... votre serviteur** God protect you, sir./And you also;
your servant   75 **encounter** approach   76 **trade be to** business be with
77 **bound to** bound for (carrying on the metaphor in "trade")   78 **list**
destination   79 **Taste** try   80 **understand** i.e., stand under, support   84 **with
gait and entrance** by going and entering (with a pun on "gate")   85 **prevented**
anticipated   89 **well** i.e., well put   90 **matter hath no voice** i.e., business must
not be revealed

ANDREW "Odors," "pregnant," and "vouchsafed"—
I'll get 'em all three all ready.

OLIVIA Let the garden door be shut, and leave me to
my hearing. [*Exeunt Sir Toby, Sir Andrew, and*   95
Maria.] Give me your hand, sir.

VIOLA My duty, madam, and most humble service.

OLIVIA What is your name?

VIOLA Cesario is your servant's name, fair princess.

OLIVIA My servant, sir? 'Twas never merry world   100
Since lowly feigning was called compliment.
Y' are servant to the Count Orsino, youth.

VIOLA And he is yours, and his must needs be yours.
Your servant's servant is your servant, madam.

OLIVIA For him, I think not on him; for his thoughts,   105
Would they were blanks, rather than filled with me.

VIOLA Madam, I come to whet your gentle thoughts
On his behalf.

OLIVIA   O, by your leave, I pray you.
I bade you never speak again of him;
But, would you undertake another suit,   110
I had rather hear you to solicit that
Than music from the spheres.

VIOLA   Dear lady—

OLIVIA Give me leave, beseech you. I did send,
After the last enchantment you did here,
A ring in chase of you. So did I abuse   115
Myself, my servant, and, I fear me, you.
Under your hard construction must I sit,
To force that on you in a shameful cunning
Which you knew none of yours. What might you
think?

101 lowly feigning affected humility 105 For as for 112 music from the
spheres i.e., the alleged celestial harmony of the revolving stars and planets
113 Give me leave i.e., do not interrupt me 115 abuse deceive 117 hard
construction harsh interpretation

120 Have you not set mine honor at the stake
And baited it with all th' unmuzzled thoughts
That tyrannous heart can think? To one of your
    receiving
Enough is shown; a cypress, not a bosom,
Hides my heart. So, let me hear you speak.

VIOLA I pity you.

125 OLIVIA   That's a degree to love.

VIOLA No, not a grize; for 'tis a vulgar proof
That very oft we pity enemies.

OLIVIA Why then, methinks 'tis time to smile again.
O world, how apt the poor are to be proud.
130 If one should be a prey, how much the better
To fall before the lion than the wolf. *Clock strikes.*
The clock upbraids me with the waste of time.
Be not afraid, good youth, I will not have you,
And yet, when wit and youth is come to harvest,
135 Your wife is like to reap a proper man.
There lies your way, due west.

VIOLA   Then westward ho!
Grace and good disposition attend your ladyship.
You'll nothing, madam, to my lord by me?

OLIVIA Stay.
140 I prithee tell me what thou think'st of me.

VIOLA That you do think you are not what you are.

OLIVIA If I think so, I think the same of you.

120-21 **set mine honor ... unmuzzled thoughts** (the metaphor is from the
Elizabethan sport of bearbaiting, in which a bear was tied to a stake and harassed
by savage dogs) 122 **receiving** i.e., perception 123 **cypress** gauzelike material
125 **degree** step 126 **grize** step 126 **vulgar proof** i.e., common knowledge
134 **when wit and youth is come to harvest** i.e., when you are mature
135 **proper** handsome 136 **due west** (Olivia is perhaps implying that the sun of
her life—Cesario's love—is about to vanish) 136 **westward ho** (cry of Thames
watermen) 137 **good disposition** i.e., tranquillity of mind 141 **That you do
think you are not what you are** i.e., that you think you are in love with a man,
and are not 142 **If I think so, I think the same of you** (Olivia misconstrues
Viola's remark to mean that she is out of her mind)

VIOLA Then think you right. I am not what I am.

OLIVIA I would you were as I would have you be.

VIOLA Would it be better, madam, than I am?   145
I wish it might, for now I am your fool.

OLIVIA O, what a deal of scorn looks beautiful
In the contempt and anger of his lip.
A murd'rous guilt shows not itself more soon
Than love that would seem hid: love's night is
noon.   150
Cesario, by the roses of the spring,
By maidhood, honor, truth, and everything,
I love thee so that, maugre all thy pride,
Nor wit nor reason can my passion hide.
Do not extort thy reasons from this clause,   155
For that I woo, thou therefore hast no cause;
But rather reason thus with reason fetter,
Love sought is good, but given unsought is better.

VIOLA By innocence I swear, and by my youth,
I have one heart, one bosom, and one truth,   160
And that no woman has; nor never none
Shall mistress be of it, save I alone.
And so adieu, good madam. Never more
Will I my master's tears to you deplore.

OLIVIA Yet come again; for thou perhaps mayst move   165
That heart which now abhors to like his love.

Exeunt.

---

146 **I am your fool** i.e., you are making a fool of me   150 **love's night is noon**
i.e., love is apparent even when it is hidden   152 **maidhood** maidenhood
153 **maugre** despite   155 **clause** premise   156 **For that** that because   156 **cause**
i.e., to accept my love

Scene II. [*Olivia's house.*]

Enter Sir Toby, Sir Andrew, and Fabian.

ANDREW No, faith, I'll not stay a jot longer.

TOBY Thy reason, dear venom; give thy reason.

FABIAN You must needs yield your reason, Sir
Andrew.

5 ANDREW Marry, I saw your niece do more favors to
the Count's servingman than ever she bestowed
upon me. I saw't i' th' orchard.

TOBY Did she see thee the while, old boy? Tell me
that.

10 ANDREW As plain as I see you now.

FABIAN This was a great argument of love in her
toward you.

ANDREW 'Slight, will you make an ass o' me?

FABIAN I will prove it legitimate, sir, upon the oaths
15 of judgment and reason.

TOBY And they have been grand-jurymen since
before Noah was a sailor.

FABIAN She did show favor to the youth in your sight
only to exasperate you, to awake your dormouse
20 valor, to put fire in your heart and brimstone in
your liver. You should then have accosted her, and
with some excellent jests, fire-new from the mint,
you should have banged the youth into dumbness.
This was looked for at your hand, and this was

III.ii.3 **yield** give   11 **great argument** strong evidence   14 **legitimate** valid
19 **dormouse** i.e., sleepy

balked. The double gilt of this opportunity you   25
let time wash off, and you are now sailed into the
North of my lady's opinion, where you will hang
like an icicle on a Dutchman's beard unless you do
redeem it by some laudable attempt either of valor
or policy.   30

ANDREW And't be any way, it must be with valor; for
policy I hate. I had as lief be a Brownist as a
politician.

TOBY Why then, build me thy fortunes upon the basis
of valor. Challenge me the Count's youth to fight   35
with him; hurt him in eleven places. My niece shall
take note of it, and assure thyself there is no love-
broker in the world can more prevail in man's
commendation with woman than report of valor.

FABIAN There is no way but this, Sir Andrew.   40

ANDREW Will either of you bear me a challenge to
him?

TOBY Go, write it in a martial hand. Be curst and
brief; it is no matter how witty, so it be eloquent
and full of invention. Taunt him with the license of   45
ink. If thou thou'st him some thrice, it shall not
be amiss; and as many lies as will lie in thy sheet
of paper, although the sheet were big enough for
the bed of Ware in England, set 'em down. Go
about it. Let there be gall enough in thy ink, though   50
thou write with a goose-pen, no matter. About it!

ANDREW Where shall I find you?

25 balked let slip   25 gilt plating   26-27 the North of my lady's opinion i.e.,
her frosty disdain   28 an icicle on a Dutchman's beard (perhaps an allusion to
the arctic voyage [1596-97] of the Dutchman Willem Barents, an account of which
was registered for publication in 1598)   30 policy intrigue, trickery
32 Brownist follower of William Browne, a reformer who advocated the separation of church and state   33 politician schemer   38 can i.e., that can
43 curst petulant   45-46 the license of ink i.e., the freedom that writing
permits   46 thou'st i.e., use the familiar "thou" instead of the more formal
"you"   49 the bed of Ware a famous bedstead, almost eleven feet square,
formerly in an inn at Ware in Hertfordshire

TOBY We'll call thee at the cubiculo. Go.

Exit Sir Andrew.

FABIAN This is a dear manikin to you, Sir Toby.

55 TOBY I have been dear to him, lad, some two thousand strong or so.

FABIAN We shall have a rare letter from him, but you'll not deliver't?

TOBY Never trust me then; and by all means stir on
60 the youth to an answer. I think oxen and wainropes cannot hale them together. For Andrew, if he were opened, and you find so much blood in his liver as will clog the foot of a flea, I'll eat the rest of th' anatomy.

65 FABIAN And his opposite, the youth, bears in his visage no great presage of cruelty.

Enter Maria.

TOBY Look where the youngest wren of mine comes.

MARIA If you desire the spleen, and will laugh yourselves into stitches, follow me. Yond gull Malvolio
70 is turned heathen, a very renegado; for there is no Christian that means to be saved by believing rightly can ever believe such impossible passages of grossness. He's in yellow stockings.

TOBY And cross-gartered?

75 MARIA Most villainously; like a pedant that keeps a school i' th' church. I have dogged him like his murderer. He does obey every point of the letter that I dropped to betray him. He does smile his face into more lines than is in the new map with

53 **cubiculo** little chamber   54 **manikin** puppet   55 **been dear to him** i.e., spent his money   60-61 **wainropes** wagon ropes   64 **anatomy** cadaver   65 **opposite** adversary   67 **youngest wren** i.e., smallest of small birds   67 **mine** (most editors adopt Theobald's emendation "nine")   68 **spleen** i.e., a fit of laughter   72-73 **impossible passages of grossness** i.e., improbabilities

the augmentation of the Indies. You have not seen 80
such a thing as 'tis. I can hardly forbear hurling
things at him. I know my lady will strike him. If
she do, he'll smile, and take't for a great favor.

TOBY Come bring us, bring us where he is.

Exeunt omnes.

Scene III. [*A street.*]

Enter Sebastian and Antonio.

SEBASTIAN I would not by my will have troubled you;
But since you make your pleasure of your pains,
I will no further chide you.

ANTONIO I could not stay behind you. My desire
(More sharp than filèd steel) did spur me forth;   5
And not all love to see you (though so much
As might have drawn one to a longer voyage)
But jealousy what might befall your travel,
Being skilless in these parts; which to a stranger,
Unguided and unfriended, often prove   10
Rough and unhospitable. My willing love,
The rather by these arguments of fear,
Set forth in your pursuit.

SEBASTIAN   My kind Antonio,
I can no other answer make but thanks,
And thanks, and ever oft good turns   15

79-80 **the new map with the augmentation of the Indies** (presumably a map,
prepared under the supervision of Richard Hakluyt and others and published
about 1600, that employed the principles of projection and showed North America
and the East Indies in fuller detail than any earlier map. It was conspicuous for the
rhumb lines marking the meridians) III.iii.8 **jealousy** anxiety 9 **skilless in**
unacquainted with 12 **The rather by these arguments of fear** i.e., reinforced
by my solicitude for your safety 15 **And thanks, and ever oft good turns** (the
fact that this line is a foot too short has prompted a wide variety of emendations,
the most popular of which has been Theobald's "And thanks, and ever thanks; and
oft good turns." Later Folios omit this and the following line altogether)

Are shuffled off with such uncurrent pay.
But, were my worth as is my conscience firm,
You should find better dealing. What's to do?
Shall we go see the relics of this town?

20 ANTONIO Tomorrow, sir; best first go see your lodging.

SEBASTIAN I am not weary, and 'tis long to night.
I pray you let us satisfy our eyes
With the memorials and the things of fame
That do renown this city.

ANTONIO   Would you'ld pardon me.
25 I do not without danger walk these streets.
Once in a sea-fight 'gainst the Count his galleys
I did some service; of such note indeed
That, were I ta'en here, it would scarce be an-
    swered.

SEBASTIAN Belike you slew great number of his people?

30 ANTONIO Th' offense is not of such a bloody nature,
Albeit the quality of the time and quarrel
Might well have given us bloody argument.
It might have since been answered in repaying
What we took from them, which for traffic's sake
35 Most of our city did. Only myself stood out;
For which, if I be lapsèd in this place,
I shall pay dear.

SEBASTIAN   Do not then walk too open.

ANTONIO It doth not fit me. Hold, sir, here's my purse.
In the south suburbs at the Elephant
40 Is best to lodge. I will bespeak our diet,
Whiles you beguile the time and feed your knowl-
    edge
With viewing of the town. There shall you have me.

16 uncurrent worthless   17 worth resources   24 pardon excuse   26 the Count
his galleys the Count's warships   28 answered defended   31 quality
circumstances   32 argument cause   33 answered compensated   34 traffic's
trade's   36 lapsèd surprised and apprehended   39 Elephant an inn   40 bespeak
our diet i.e., arrange for our meals   41 Whiles while   42 have find

SEBASTIAN Why I your purse?

ANTONIO Haply your eye shall light upon some toy
    You have desire to purchase, and your store   45
    I think is not for idle markets, sir.

SEBASTIAN I'll be your purse-bearer, and leave you for
    An hour.

ANTONIO To th' Elephant.

SEBASTIAN   I do remember.   *Exeunt.*

Scene IV. [*Olivia's garden.*]

Enter Olivia and Maria.

OLIVIA I have sent after him. He says he'll come:
    How shall I feast him? What bestow of him?
    For youth is bought more oft than begged or bor-
      rowed.
    I speak too loud. Where's Malvolio? He is sad and
      civil,
    And suits well for a servant with my fortunes.   5
    Where is Malvolio?

MARIA He's coming, madam, but in very strange man-
    ner. He is sure possessed, madam.

OLIVIA Why, what's the matter? Does he rave?

MARIA No, madam, he does nothing but smile. Your   10
    ladyship were best to have some guard about you
    if he come, for sure the man is tainted in 's wits.

OLIVIA Go call him hither. I am as mad as he,
    If sad and merry madness equal be.

44 **toy** trifle 45 **store** wealth 46 **idle markets** unnecessary purchases
III.iv.1 **He says he'll come** suppose he says he'll come 2 **of** on 4 **sad and
civil** grave and formal 8 **possessed** i.e., with a devil, mad

Enter Malvolio.

15   How now, Malvolio?

MALVOLIO Sweet lady, ho, ho!

OLIVIA Smil'st thou? I sent for thee upon a sad occasion.

MALVOLIO Sad, lady? I could be sad. This does make
20   some obstruction in the blood, this cross-gartering;
      but what of that? If it please the eye of one, it is
      with me as the very true sonnet is, "Please one,
      and please all."

OLIVIA Why, how dost thou, man? What is the matter
25   with thee?

MALVOLIO Not black in my mind, though yellow in my
      legs. It did come to his hands, and commands shall
      be executed. I think we do know the sweet Roman
      hand.

30   OLIVIA Wilt thou go to bed, Malvolio?

MALVOLIO To bed? Ay, sweetheart, and I'll come to
      thee.

OLIVIA God comfort thee. Why dost thou smile so,
      and kiss thy hand so oft?

35   MARIA How do you, Malvolio?

MALVOLIO At your request? Yes, nightingales answer
      daws!

MARIA Why appear you with this ridiculous boldness
      before my lady?

40   MALVOLIO "Be not afraid of greatness." 'Twas well writ.

17 **sad** serious   22 **sonnet** (any short lyric poem)   22-23 **Please one, and
please all** i.e., so long as I please the one I love I do not care about the rest (from
"A prettie newe Ballad, intytuled: The Crow sits vpon the wall, Please one and
please all")   28-29 **the sweet Roman hand** i.e., italic writing, an elegant cursive
script more fashionable than the crabbed "secretary hand" commonly used in
Shakespeare's time   36-37 **At ... daws** i.e., should I reply to a mere servant like
you? Yes, for sometimes nightingales answer jackdaws

OLIVIA What mean'st thou by that, Malvolio?

MALVOLIO "Some are born great."

OLIVIA Ha?

MALVOLIO "Some achieve greatness."

OLIVIA What say'st thou?   45

MALVOLIO "And some have greatness thrust upon them."

OLIVIA Heaven restore thee!

MALVOLIO "Remember who commended thy yellow stockings."   50

OLIVIA Thy yellow stockings?

MALVOLIO "And wished to see thee cross-gartered."

OLIVIA Cross-gartered?

MALVOLIO "Go to, thou art made, if thou desir'st to be so."   55

OLIVIA Am I made?

MALVOLIO "If not, let me see thee a servant still."

OLIVIA Why, this is very midsummer madness.

Enter Servant.

SERVANT Madam, the young gentleman of the Count Orsino's is returned. I could hardly entreat him   60
back. He attends your ladyship's pleasure.

OLIVIA I'll come to him. [*Exit Servant.*] Good Maria, let this fellow be looked to. Where's my cousin Toby? Let some of my people have a special care of him. I would not have him miscarry for the   65
half of my dowry.

Exit [Olivia, accompanied by Maria].

58 midsummer madness extreme folly, Midsummer Eve (June 23) being traditionally associated with irresponsible and eccentric behavior 65 miscarry come to harm

MALVOLIO O ho, do you come near me now? No
worse man than Sir Toby to look to me. This con-
curs directly with the letter. She sends him on pur-
70   pose, that I may appear stubborn to him; for she
incites me to that in the letter. "Cast thy humble
slough," says she; "be opposite with a kinsman,
surly with servants; let thy tongue tang with arguments of state; put thyself into the trick of singu-
75   larity." And consequently sets down the manner
how: as, a sad face, a reverend carriage, a slow
tongue, in the habit of some sir of note, and so
forth. I have limed her; but it is Jove's doing, and
Jove make me thankful. And when she went away
80   now, "Let this fellow be looked to." "Fellow."
Not "Malvolio," nor after my degree, but "fellow." Why, everything adheres together, that no
dram of a scruple, no scruple of a scruple, no
obstacle, no incredulous or unsafe circumstance—
85   what can be said? Nothing that can be can come
between me and the full prospect of my hopes.
Well, Jove, not I, is the doer of this, and he is to
be thanked.

Enter [Sir] Toby, Fabian, and Maria.

TOBY Which way is he, in the name of sanctity? If
90   all the devils of hell be drawn in little, and
Legion himself possessed him, yet I'll speak to
him.

FABIAN Here he is, here he is! How is't with you, sir?

---

67 **come near me** i.e., begin to understand my importance   70 **stubborn**
hostile   77 **habit** clothing   77 **sir** personage   78 **limed** caught (as birds are
caught with sticky birdlime)   80 **fellow** (1) menial (2) associate (the sense in
which Malvolio takes the word)   81 **after my degree** according to my status
83 **dram** (1) minute part (2) apothecary's measure for one-eighth of an ounce
83 **scruple** (1) doubt (2) apothecary's measure for one-third of a dram
84 **incredulous or unsafe** incredible or doubtful   90 **in little** in small compass
91 **Legion** a group of devils (see Mark 5:8-9)

TOBY How is't with you, man?

MALVOLIO Go off; I discard you. Let me enjoy my   95
private. Go off.

MARIA Lo, how hollow the fiend speaks within him!
Did not I tell you? Sir Toby, my lady prays you
to have a care of him.

MALVOLIO Aha, does she so?   100

TOBY Go to, go to; peace, peace; we must deal gently
with him. Let me alone. How do you, Malvolio?
How is't with you? What, man, defy the devil?
Consider, he's an enemy to mankind.

MALVOLIO Do you know what you say?   105

MARIA La you, and you speak ill of the devil, how he
takes it at heart. Pray God he be not bewitched.

FABIAN Carry his water to th' wise woman.

MARIA Marry, and it shall be done tomorrow morning if I live. My lady would not lose him for more   110
than I'll say.

MALVOLIO How now, mistress?

MARIA O Lord.

TOBY Prithee hold thy peace. This is not the way. Do
you not see you move him? Let me alone with him.   115

FABIAN No way but gentleness; gently, gently. The
fiend is rough and will not be roughly used.

TOBY Why, how now, my bawcock? How dost thou,
chuck?

MALVOLIO Sir.   120

TOBY Ay, biddy, come with me. What, man, 'tis not

94 How is't with you, man (the Folio implausibly assigns this speech to Fabian,
but the contemptuous "man" suggests that the speaker must be Malvolio's social
superior)   96 private privacy   108 Carry his water to th' wise woman i.e.,
for analysis   115 move agitate   117 rough violent   118 bawcock fine fellow
(French *beau coq*)   119 chuck chick

for gravity to play at cherry-pit with Satan. Hang
him, foul collier!

MARIA Get him to say his prayers; good Sir Toby, get
125   him to pray.

MALVOLIO My prayers, minx?

MARIA No, I warrant you, he will not hear of godli-
ness.

MALVOLIO Go hang yourselves all! You are idle shal-
130   low things; I am not of your element. You shall
know more hereafter.   *Exit*.

TOBY Is't possible?

FABIAN If this were played upon a stage now, I could
condemn it as an improbable fiction.

135   TOBY His very genius hath taken the infection of the
device, man.

MARIA Nay, pursue him now, lest the device take air
and taint.

FABIAN Why, we shall make him mad indeed.

140   MARIA The house will be the quieter.

TOBY Come, we'll have him in a dark room and
bound. My niece is already in the belief that he's
mad. We may carry it thus, for our pleasure and
his penance, till our very pastime, tired out of
145   breath, prompt us to have mercy on him; at which
time we will bring the device to the bar and crown
thee for a finder of madmen. But see, but see.

Enter Sir Andrew.

FABIAN More matter for a May morning.

121-22 'tis not for gravity ... Satan i.e., it is unsuitable for a man of your
dignity to play a children's game with Satan   123 collier vendor of coals   129 idle
trifling   130 element sphere   135 genius nature, personality   137-38 take air
and taint be exposed and spoiled   143 carry it i.e., go on with the joke   148 More
matter for a May morning i.e., another subject for a May-Day pageant

ANDREW Here's the challenge; read it. I warrant there's
    vinegar and pepper in't.   150

FABIAN Is't so saucy?

ANDREW Ay, is't, I warrant him. Do but read.

TOBY Give me. [*Reads*] "Youth, whatsoever thou art,
    thou art but a scurvy fellow."

FABIAN Good, and valiant.   155

TOBY [*Reads*] "Wonder not nor admire not in thy
    mind why I do call thee so, for I will show thee no
    reason for't."

FABIAN A good note that keeps you from the blow of
    the law.   160

TOBY [*Reads*] "Thou com'st to the Lady Olivia, and
    in my sight she uses thee kindly. But thou liest in
    thy throat; that is not the matter I challenge thee
    for."

FABIAN Very brief, and to exceeding good sense—   165
    less.

TOBY [*Reads*] "I will waylay thee going home; where
    if it be thy chance to kill me"—

FABIAN Good.

TOBY [*Reads*] "Thou kill'st me like a rogue and a   170
    villain."

FABIAN Still you keep o' th' windy side of the law.
    Good.

TOBY [*Reads*] "Fare thee well, and God have mercy
    upon one of our souls. He may have mercy upon   175
    mine, but my hope is better, and so look to thyself.
    Thy friend, as thou usest him, and thy sworn enemy,
              ANDREW AGUECHEEK."
    If this letter move him not, his legs cannot. I'll give't
    him.   180

151 **saucy** i.e., with "vinegar and pepper"   156 **admire** marvel   172 **o' th'
windy side of the law** i.e., safe from prosecution

MARIA You may have very fit occasion for't. He is
now in some commerce with my lady and will by
and by depart.

TOBY Go, Sir Andrew. Scout me for him at the corner
185   of the orchard like a bum-baily. So soon as ever
thou seest him, draw; and as thou draw'st, swear
horrible; for it comes to pass oft that a terrible
oath, with a swaggering accent sharply twanged
off, gives manhood more approbation than ever
190   proof itself would have earned him. Away!

ANDREW Nay, let me alone for swearing.   *Exit.*

TOBY Now will not I deliver his letter; for the behavior of the young gentleman gives him out to
be of good capacity and breeding; his employment
195   between his lord and my niece confirms no less.
Therefore this letter, being so excellently ignorant,
will breed no terror in the youth. He will find it
comes from a clodpoll. But, sir, I will deliver his
challenge by word of mouth, set upon Aguecheek
200   a notable report of valor, and drive the gentleman
(as I know his youth will aptly receive it) into a
most hideous opinion of his rage, skill, fury, and
impetuosity. This will so fright them both that they
will kill one another by the look, like cockatrices.

Enter Olivia and Viola.

205 FABIAN Here he comes with your niece. Give them
way till he take leave, and presently after him.

TOBY I will meditate the while upon some horrid
message for a challenge.
                    [*Exeunt Sir Toby, Fabian, and Maria.*]

OLIVIA I have said too much unto a heart of stone

182 **commerce** conversation 185 **bum-baily** bailiff, sheriff's officer
189 **approbation** attestation 190 **proof** actual trial 191 **let me alone for
swearing** i.e., do not worry about my ability at swearing 198 **clodpoll** dunce
204 **cockatrices** fabulous serpents that could kill with a glance 205-6 **Give
them way ... after him** i.e., do not interrupt them until he goes, and then follow
him at once

494

And laid mine honor too unchary on't.   210
There's something in me that reproves my fault;
But such a headstrong potent fault it is
That it but mocks reproof.

VIOLA With the same havior that your passion bears
Goes on my master's griefs.   215

OLIVIA Here, wear this jewel for me; 'tis my picture.
Refuse it not; it hath no tongue to vex you.
And I beseech you come again tomorrow.
What shall you ask of me that I'll deny,
That honor, saved, may upon asking give?   220

VIOLA Nothing but this: your true love for my master.

OLIVIA How with mine honor may I give him that
Which I have given to you?

VIOLA   I will acquit you.

OLIVIA Well, come again tomorrow. Fare thee well.
A fiend like thee might bear my soul to hell.   225
                                              [*Exit.*]

Enter [Sir] Toby and Fabian.

TOBY Gentleman, God save thee.

VIOLA And you, sir.

TOBY That defense thou hast, betake thee to't. Of
what nature the wrongs are thou hast done him,
I know not; but thy intercepter, full of despite,   230
bloody as the hunter, attends thee at the orchard
end. Dismount thy tuck, be yare in thy preparation, for thy assailant is quick, skillful, and deadly.

VIOLA You mistake, sir. I am sure no man hath any
quarrel to me. My remembrance is very free and   235
clear from any image of offense done to any man.

210 **unchary** carelessly   214 **havior** behavior   216 **jewel** i.e., jeweled locket (?)
225 **like thee** i.e., with your attractions   230 **despite** defiance   231 **bloody as
the hunter** i.e., bloodthirsty as a hunting dog   231 **attends** awaits   232 **Dismount thy tuck** unsheathe your rapier   232 **yare** quick, prompt

TOBY You'll find it otherwise, I assure you. Therefore, if you hold your life at any price, betake you to your guard; for your opposite hath in him what
240 youth, strength, skill, and wrath can furnish man withal.

VIOLA I pray you, sir, what is he?

TOBY He is knight, dubbed with unhatched rapier and on carpet consideration, but he is a devil in
245 private brawl. Souls and bodies hath he divorced three; and his incensement at this moment is so implacable that satisfaction can be none but by pangs of death and sepulcher. "Hob, nob" is his word; "give't or take't."

250 VIOLA I will return again into the house and desire some conduct of the lady. I am no fighter. I have heard of some kind of men that put quarrels purposely on others to taste their valor. Belike this is a man of that quirk.

255 TOBY Sir, no. His indignation derives itself out of a very competent injury; therefore get you on and give him his desire. Back you shall not to the house, unless you undertake that with me which with as much safety you might answer him. There-
260 fore on, or strip your sword stark naked; for meddle you must, that's certain, or forswear to wear iron about you.

VIOLA This is as uncivil as strange. I beseech you do me this courteous office, as to know of the knight
265 what my offense to him is. It is something of my negligence, nothing of my purpose.

TOBY I will do so. Signior Fabian, stay you by this gentleman till my return.   *Exit [Sir] Toby.*

VIOLA Pray you, sir, do you know of this matter?

239 **opposite** adversary   241 **withal** with   243 **unhatched** unhacked   244 **on carpet consideration** i.e., not because of his exploits in the field but through connections at court   248 **Hob, nob** have it, or have it not   251 **conduct** escort   253 **taste** test   256 **competent** sufficient   261 **meddle** engage him, fight   265-66 **of my negligence** unintentional

FABIAN I know the knight is incensed against you,   270
even to a mortal arbitrament; but nothing of the
circumstance more.

VIOLA I beseech you, what manner of man is he?

FABIAN Nothing of that wonderful promise, to read
him by his form, as you are like to find him in the   275
proof of his valor. He is indeed, sir, the most skillful, bloody, and fatal opposite that you could possibly have found in any part of Illyria. Will you
walk towards him? I will make your peace with
him if I can.   280

VIOLA I shall be much bound to you for't. I am one
that had rather go with sir priest than sir knight. I
care not who knows so much of my mettle.

Exeunt.

Enter [Sir] Toby and [Sir] Andrew.

TOBY Why, man, he's a very devil; I have not seen
such a firago. I had a pass with him, rapier, scab-   285
bard, and all, and he gives me the stuck-in with
such a mortal motion that it is inevitable; and on
the answer he pays you as surely as your feet hits
the ground they step on. They say he has been
fencer to the Sophy.   290

ANDREW Pox on't, I'll not meddle with him.

TOBY Ay, but he will not now be pacified. Fabian
can scarce hold him yonder.

ANDREW Plague on't, and I thought he had been
valiant, and so cunning in fence, I'd have seen   295

271 **mortal arbitrament** deadly trial   283 **mettle** character, disposition
283 s.d. **Exeunt** (this stage direction, which leaves the stage empty, properly marks
the ending of the scene, but the new scene that opens with the entrance of Sir
Toby and Sir Andrew is not indicated as such in the Folio)   285 **firago** virago
(probably a phonetic spelling)   285 **pass** bout   286 **stuck-in** stoccado, thrust
287 **mortal motion** deadly pass   288 **answer** return   290 **Sophy** Shah
295 **in fence** at fencing

him damned ere I'd have challenged him. Let him let the matter slip, and I'll give him my horse, gray Capilet.

TOBY I'll make the motion. Stand here; make a good
300 show on't. This shall end without the perdition of souls. [*Aside*] Marry, I'll ride your horse as well as I ride you.

Enter Fabian and Viola.

I have his horse to take up the quarrel. I have persuaded him the youth's a devil.

305 FABIAN He is as horribly conceited of him, and pants and looks pale, as if a bear were at his heels.

TOBY There's no remedy, sir; he will fight with you for's oath sake. Marry, he hath better bethought him of his quarrel, and he finds that now scarce
310 to be worth talking of. Therefore draw for the sup-portance of his vow. He protests he will not hurt you.

VIOLA [*Aside*] Pray God defend me! A little thing would make me tell them how much I lack of a
315 man.

FABIAN Give ground if you see him furious.

TOBY Come, Sir Andrew, there's no remedy. The gentleman will for his honor's sake have one bout with you; he cannot by the duello avoid it; but he
320 has promised me, as he is a gentleman and a soldier, he will not hurt you. Come on, to't.

ANDREW Pray God he keep his oath!   [*Draws.*]

---

299 **motion** proposal   300-1 **perdition of souls** i.e., loss of life   303 **take up** settle   305 **He is as horribly conceited of him** i.e., Cesario has just as terrifying a notion of Sir Andrew   308 **oath** oath's   309 **his quarrel** the cause of his resentment   310-11 **Therefore draw for the supportance of his vow** i.e., make a show of valor merely for the satisfaction of his oath   319 **duello** duelling code

Enter Antonio.

VIOLA I do assure you 'tis against my will.   [*Draws.*]

ANTONIO Put up your sword. If this young gentleman
    Have done offense, I take the fault on me;   325
    If you offend him, I for him defy you.

TOBY You, sir? Why, what are you?

ANTONIO [*Draws*] One, sir, that for his love dares yet
    do more
    Than you have heard him brag to you he will.

TOBY Nay, if you be an undertaker, I am for you.   330
                                [*Draws.*]
Enter Officers.

FABIAN O good Sir Toby, hold. Here come the officers.

TOBY [*To Antonio*] I'll be with you anon.

VIOLA [*To Sir Andrew*] Pray, sir, put your sword up,
    if you please.

ANDREW Marry, will I, sir; and for that I promised   335
    you, I'll be as good as my word. He will bear you
    easily, and reins well.

FIRST OFFICER This is the man; do thy office.

SECOND OFFICER Antonio, I arrest thee at the suit
    Of Count Orsino.

ANTONIO   You do mistake me, sir.   340

FIRST OFFICER No, sir, no jot. I know your favor
    well,
    Though now you have no sea-cap on your head.
    Take him away. He knows I know him well.

ANTONIO I must obey. [*To Viola*] This comes with
    seeking you.

---

330 **an undertaker** one who takes up a challenge for another (with perhaps a pun
on "undertaker" as a government agent, i.e., scoundrel)   335 **for that** as for what
(i.e., his horse, "gray Capilet")   338 **office** duty   341 **favor** face

345   But there's no remedy; I shall answer it.
What will you do, now my necessity
Makes me to ask you for my purse? It grieves me
Much more for what I cannot do for you
Than what befalls myself. You stand amazed,
350   But be of comfort.

SECOND OFFICER Come, sir, away.

ANTONIO I must entreat of you some of that money.

VIOLA What money, sir?
For the fair kindness you have showed me here,
355   And part being prompted by your present trouble,
Out of my lean and low ability
I'll lend you something. My having is not much.
I'll make division of my present with you.
Hold, there's half my coffer.

ANTONIO   Will you deny me now?
360   Is't possible that my deserts to you
Can lack persuasion? Do not tempt my misery,
Lest that it make me so unsound a man
As to upbraid you with those kindnesses
That I have done for you.

VIOLA   I know of none,
365   Nor know I you by voice or any feature.
I hate ingratitude more in a man
Than lying, vainness, babbling, drunkenness,
Or any taint of vice whose strong corruption
Inhabits our frail blood.

ANTONIO   O heavens themselves!

370 SECOND OFFICER Come, sir, I pray you go.

ANTONIO Let me speak a little. This youth that you
     see here
I snatched one half out of the jaws of death;

---

345 **answer it** i.e., try to defend myself against the accusation   355 **part** partly
358 **present** present resources   359 **coffer** chest, i.e., money   360-61 **deserts to
you/Can lack persuasion** claims on you can fail to be persuasive
362 **unsound** weak, unmanly   367 **vainness** (1) falseness (2) boasting

Relieved him with such sanctity of love,
And to his image, which methought did promise
Most venerable worth, did I devotion.   375

FIRST OFFICER What's that to us? The time goes by.
    Away.

ANTONIO But, O, how vild an idol proves this god!
    Thou hast, Sebastian, done good feature shame.
    In nature there's no blemish but the mind;
    None can be called deformed but the unkind.   380
    Virtue is beauty; but the beauteous evil
    Are empty trunks, o'erflourished by the devil.

FIRST OFFICER The man grows mad; away with him!
    Come, come, sir.

ANTONIO Lead me on.   *Exit [with Officers].*

VIOLA Methinks his words do from such passion fly   385
    That he believes himself; so do not I.
    Prove true, imagination, O, prove true,
    That I, dear brother, be now ta'en for you!

TOBY Come hither, knight; come hither, Fabian. We'll
    whisper o'er a couplet or two of most sage saws.   390

VIOLA He named Sebastian. I my brother know
    Yet living in my glass. Even such and so
    In favor was my brother, and he went
    Still in this fashion, color, ornament,
    For him I imitate. O, if it prove,   395
    Tempests are kind, and salt waves fresh in love!
                                              [Exit.]

TOBY A very dishonest paltry boy, and more a
    coward than a hare. His dishonesty appears in
    leaving his friend here in necessity and denying
    him; and for his cowardship, ask Fabian.   400

375 **venerable** worthy of veneration   377 **vild** vile   378 **feature** shape, external appearance   379 **mind** (as distinguished from body or "feature")   380 **unkind** unnatural   382 **trunks** chests   382 **o'erflourished** decorated with carving and painting   390 **sage saws** wise maxims   392 **living in my glass** i.e., staring at me from my mirror   397 **dishonest** dishonorable

FABIAN A coward, a most devout coward; religious
in it.

ANDREW 'Slid, I'll after him again and beat him.

TOBY Do; cuff him soundly, but never draw thy
405   sword.

ANDREW And I do not—   [*Exit.*]

FABIAN Come, let's see the event.

TOBY I dare lay any money 'twill be nothing yet.
                          Exit [*with Sir Andrew and Fabian*].

401-2 **religious in it** i.e., dedicated to his cowardice (following "devout")
403 **'Slid** by God's eyelid   407 **event** outcome   408 **yet** after all

ACT IV

Scene I. [*Before Olivia's house.*]

Enter Sebastian and Clown.

CLOWN Will you make me believe that I am not sent
for you?

SEBASTIAN Go to, go to, thou art a foolish fellow. Let
me be clear of thee.

CLOWN Well held out, i' faith! No, I do not know   5
you; nor I am not sent to you by my lady, to bid
you come speak with her; nor your name is not
Master Cesario; nor this is not my nose neither.
Nothing that is so is so.

SEBASTIAN I prithee vent thy folly somewhere else.   10
Thou know'st not me.

CLOWN Vent my folly! He has heard that word of
some great man, and now applies it to a fool. Vent
my folly! I am afraid this great lubber, the world,
will prove a cockney. I prithee now, ungird thy   15
strangeness, and tell me what I shall vent to my
lady. Shall I vent to her that thou art coming?

SEBASTIAN I prithee, foolish Greek, depart from me.

IV.i.5 **held out** maintained 14 **lubber** lout 15 **cockney** affected fop
15-16 **ungird thy strangeness** i.e., abandon your silly pretense (of not recognizing me) 16 **vent** say 18 **Greek** buffoon

There's money for thee. If you tarry longer, I shall
20 give worse payment.

CLOWN By my troth, thou hast an open hand. These
wise men that give fools money get themselves a
good report—after fourteen years' purchase.

Enter [Sir] Andrew, [Sir] Toby, and Fabian.

ANDREW Now, sir, have I met you again? There's for
25 you!   [*Strikes Sebastian.*]

SEBASTIAN Why, there's for thee, and there, and there!
                          [*Strikes Sir Andrew.*]
Are all the people mad?

TOBY Hold, sir, or I'll throw your dagger o'er the
house.   [*Seizes Sebastian.*]

30 CLOWN This will I tell my lady straight. I would not
be in some of your coats for twopence.   [*Exit.*]

TOBY Come on, sir; hold.

ANDREW Nay, let him alone. I'll go another way to
work with him. I'll have an action of battery against
35 him, if there be any law in Illyria. Though I
stroke him first, yet it's no matter for that.

SEBASTIAN Let go thy hand.

TOBY Come, sir, I will not let you go. Come, my
young soldier, put up your iron. You are well
40 fleshed. Come on.

SEBASTIAN I will be free from thee. [*Frees himself.*]
What wouldst thou now?
If thou dar'st tempt me further, draw thy sword.

TOBY What, what? Nay then, I must have an ounce
or two of this malapert blood from you.   [*Draws.*]

23 **after fourteen years' purchase** i.e., after a long delay, at a high price
30 **straight** straightaway, at once   34-35 **have an action of battery against
him** charge him with assaulting me   36 **stroke** struck   39-40 **well fleshed** i.e.,
made eager for fighting by having tasted blood   44 **malapert** saucy

Enter Olivia.

OLIVIA Hold, Toby! On thy life I charge thee hold!   45

TOBY Madam.

OLIVIA Will it be ever thus? Ungracious wretch,
Fit for the mountains and the barbarous caves,
Where manners ne'er were preached! Out of my
    sight!
Be not offended, dear Cesario.   50
Rudesby, begone.
    [*Exeunt Sir Toby, Sir Andrew, and Fabian.*]
                I prithee gentle friend,
Let thy fair wisdom, not thy passion, sway
In this uncivil and unjust extent
Against thy peace. Go with me to my house,
And hear thou there how many fruitless pranks   55
This ruffian hath botched up, that thou thereby
Mayst smile at this. Thou shalt not choose but go.
Do not deny. Beshrew his soul for me.
He started one poor heart of mine, in thee.

SEBASTIAN What relish is in this? How runs the
    stream?   60
Or I am mad, or else this is a dream.
Let fancy still my sense in Lethe steep;
If it be thus to dream, still let me sleep!

OLIVIA Nay, come, I prithee. Would thou'dst be ruled
    by me!

SEBASTIAN Madam, I will.

OLIVIA   O, say so, and so be.   65
                                    Exeunt.

51 **Rudesby** ruffian   52 **sway** rule   53 **uncivil** barbarous   53 **extent** display
56 **botched up** clumsily contrived   58 **Beshrew** curse   59 **started** roused
59 **heart** (with a pun on "hart")   60 **What relish is in this?** i.e., what does this
mean?   61 **Or** either   62 **Lethe** in classical mythology, the river of oblivion in
Hades

Scene II. [*Olivia's house.*]

Enter Maria and Clown.

MARIA Nay, I prithee put on this gown and this beard;
make him believe thou art Sir Topas the curate;
do it quickly. I'll call Sir Toby the whilst.   [*Exit.*]

CLOWN Well, I'll put it on, and I will dissemble my-
5   self in't, and I would I were the first that ever dissembled in such a gown. I am not tall enough to
become the function well, nor lean enough to be
thought a good student; but to be said an honest
man and a good housekeeper goes as fairly as to
10   say a careful man and a great scholar. The competitors enter.

Enter [Sir] Toby [and Maria].

TOBY Jove bless thee, Master Parson.

CLOWN *Bonos dies*, Sir Toby; for, as the old hermit
of Prague, that never saw pen and ink, very wit-
15   tily said to a niece of King Gorboduc, "That that
is is"; so, I, being Master Parson, am Master Parson; for what is "that" but that, and "is" but is?

TOBY To him, Sir Topas.

CLOWN What ho, I say. Peace in this prison!

20   TOBY The knave counterfeits well; a good knave.

IV.ii.2 **Sir Topas** (the ridiculous hero of Chaucer's *Rime of Sir Thopas*, a parody of
chivalric romances) 3 **the whilst** meanwhile 4 **dissemble** disguise 7 **function** clerical office 8 **student** student 9 **good housekeeper** solid citizen
10 **careful** painstaking 10-11 **competitors** confederates 13 **Bonos dies** good
day 13-14 **the old hermit of Prague** (apparently the Clown's nonsensical
invention) 15 **King Gorboduc** (a legendary king of Britain) 20 **knave** fellow

Malvolio within.

MALVOLIO Who calls there?

CLOWN Sir Topas the curate, who comes to visit Malvolio the lunatic.

MALVOLIO Sir Topas, Sir Topas, good Sir Topas, go to my lady.   25

CLOWN Out, hyperbolical fiend! How vexest thou this man! Talkest thou nothing but of ladies?

TOBY Well said, Master Parson.

MALVOLIO Sir Topas, never was man thus wronged. Good Sir Topas, do not think I am mad. They have   30 laid me here in hideous darkness.

CLOWN Fie, thou dishonest Satan. I call thee by the most modest terms, for I am one of those gentle ones that will use the devil himself with courtesy. Say'st thou that house is dark?   35

MALVOLIO As hell, Sir Topas.

CLOWN Why, it hath bay windows transparent as barricadoes, and the clerestories toward the south north are as lustrous as ebony; and yet complainest thou of obstruction?   40

MALVOLIO I am not mad, Sir Topas. I say to you this house is dark.

CLOWN Madman, thou errest. I say there is no darkness but ignorance, in which thou art more puzzled than the Egyptians in their fog.   45

MALVOLIO I say this house is as dark as ignorance, though ignorance were as dark as hell; and I say there was never man thus abused. I am no more

26 **hyperbolical** boisterous (a term from rhetoric meaning "exaggerated in style") 33 **most modest** mildest 35 **house** madman's cell 37-38 **barricadoes** barricades 38 **clerestories** upper windows 45 **Egyptians in their fog** (to plague the Egyptians Moses brought a "thick darkness" that lasted three days; see Exodus 10:21-23)

mad than you are. Make the trial of it in any con-
50   stant question.

CLOWN What is the opinion of Pythagoras concerning
wild fowl?

MALVOLIO That the soul of our grandam might happily inhabit a bird.

55   CLOWN What think'st thou of his opinion?

MALVOLIO I think nobly of the soul and no way approve
his opinion.

CLOWN Fare thee well. Remain thou still in darkness.
Thou shalt hold th' opinion of Pythagoras ere I
60   will allow of thy wits, and fear to kill a woodcock, lest thou dispossess the soul of thy grandam.
Fare thee well.

MALVOLIO Sir Topas, Sir Topas!

TOBY My most exquisite Sir Topas!

65   CLOWN Nay, I am for all waters.

MARIA Thou mightst have done this without thy beard
and gown. He sees thee not.

TOBY To him in thine own voice, and bring me word
how thou find'st him. [To Maria] I would we were
70   well rid of this knavery. If he may be conveniently
delivered, I would he were; for I am now so far
in offense with my niece that I cannot pursue with
any safety this sport to the upshot. [To the Clown]
Come by and by to my chamber.   Exit [with Maria].

75   CLOWN [Sings] "Hey, Robin, jolly Robin,
                       Tell me how thy lady does."

49-50 **constant question** consistent topic, normal conversation   51 **Pythagoras**
(ancient Greek philosopher who expounded the doctrine of the transmigration of
souls)   53-54 **happily** haply, perhaps   60 **allow of thy wits** acknowledge your
sanity   60-61 **woodcock** (a proverbially stupid bird)   65 **I am for all waters**
i.e., I can turn my hand to any trade   71 **delivered** released   73 **upshot** conclusion
75-76 **Hey, Robin ... lady does** (the Clown sings an old ballad)

MALVOLIO Fool.

CLOWN "My lady is unkind, perdie."

MALVOLIO Fool.

CLOWN "Alas, why is she so?"   80

MALVOLIO Fool, I say.

CLOWN "She loves another." Who calls, ha?

MALVOLIO Good fool, as ever thou wilt deserve well
at my hand, help me to a candle, and pen, ink, and
paper. As I am a gentleman, I will live to be thank-   85
ful to thee for't.

CLOWN Master Malvolio?

MALVOLIO Ay, good fool.

CLOWN Alas, sir, how fell you besides your five wits?

MALVOLIO Fool, there was never man so notoriously   90
abused. I am as well in my wits, fool, as thou art.

CLOWN But as well? Then you are mad indeed, if you
be no better in your wits than a fool.

MALVOLIO They have here propertied me; keep me in
darkness, send ministers to me, asses, and do all   95
they can to face me out of my wits.

CLOWN Advise you what you say. The minister is
here.—Malvolio, Malvolio, thy wits the heavens
restore. Endeavor thyself to sleep and leave thy
vain bibble babble.   100

MALVOLIO Sir Topas.

CLOWN Maintain no words with him, good fellow.

78 perdie certainly 89 how fell you besides your five wits? i.e., how did you
happen to become mad? 90 notoriously outrageously 94 propertied i.e., used
me as a mere object, not a human being 96 face me out of my wits i.e.,
impudently insist that I am mad 97 Advise you consider carefully 97-98 The
minister is here (for the next few lines the Clown uses two voices, his own and
that of Sir Topas)

—Who, I, sir? Not I, sir. God buy you, good Sir
Topas.—Marry, amen.—I will, sir, I will.

105 MALVOLIO Fool, fool, fool, I say!

CLOWN Alas, sir, be patient. What say you, sir? I am
shent for speaking to you.

MALVOLIO Good fool, help me to some light and some
paper. I tell thee, I am as well in my wits as any
110 man in Illyria.

CLOWN Well-a-day that you were, sir.

MALVOLIO By this hand, I am. Good fool, some ink,
paper, and light; and convey what I will set down
to my lady. It shall advantage thee more than ever
115 the bearing of letter did.

CLOWN I will help you to't. But tell me true, are you
not mad indeed, or do you but counterfeit?

MALVOLIO Believe me, I am not. I tell thee true.

CLOWN Nay, I'll ne'er believe a madman till I see his
120 brains. I will fetch you light and paper and ink.

MALVOLIO Fool, I'll requite it in the highest degree. I
prithee be gone.

CLOWN [Sings]   I am gone, sir.
                 And anon, sir,
125   I'll be with you again,
                 In a trice,
                 Like to the old Vice,
                 Your need to sustain.
                 Who with dagger of lath,
130   In his rage and his wrath,
                 Cries "Ah ha" to the devil.
                 Like a mad lad,

103 **God buy you** God be with you, i.e., good-bye 107 **shent** rebuked
111 **Well-a-day that you were** alas, if only you were 117 **counterfeit** pretend
127 **Vice** (in the morality plays, a stock mischievous character who usually carried
a wooden dagger) 128 **Your need to sustain** i.e., in order to help you resist the
Devil

"Pare thy nails, dad."
Adieu, goodman devil.   *Exit.*

Scene III. [*Olivia's garden.*]

Enter Sebastian.

SEBASTIAN This is the air; that is the glorious sun;
This pearl she gave me, I do feel't and see't;
And though 'tis wonder that enwraps me thus,
Yet 'tis not madness. Where's Antonio then?
I could not find him at the Elephant;   5
Yet there he was, and there I found this credit,
That he did range the town to seek me out.
His counsel now might do me golden service;
For though my soul disputes well with my sense
That this may be some error, but no madness,   10
Yet doth this accident and flood of fortune
So far exceed all instance, all discourse,
That I am ready to distrust mine eyes
And wrangle with my reason that persuades me
To any other trust but that I am mad,   15
Or else the lady's mad. Yet, if 'twere so,
She could not sway her house, command her
    followers,
Take and give back affairs and their dispatch
With such a smooth, discreet, and stable bearing
As I perceive she does. There's something in't   20
That is deceivable. But here the lady comes.

134 **Adieu, goodman devil** (a much emended line; "goodman" [Folio "good man"], a title for a yeoman or any man of substance not of gentle birth, roughly corresponds to our "mister") IV.iii.6 **was** had been   6 **credit** belief   9 **my soul disputes well with my sense** my reason agrees with the evidence of my senses   12 **instance** precedent   12 **discourse** reason   15 **trust** belief   17 **sway** rule   18 **Take and give ... their dispatch** i.e., assume and discharge the management of affairs   21 **deceivable** deceptive

Enter Olivia and Priest.

OLIVIA Blame not this haste of mine. If you mean well,
Now go with me and with this holy man
Into the chantry by. There, before him,
25   And underneath that consecrated roof,
Plight me the full assurance of your faith,
That my most jealous and too doubtful soul
May live at peace. He shall conceal it
Whiles you are willing it shall come to note,
30   What time we will our celebration keep
According to my birth. What do you say?

SEBASTIAN I'll follow this good man and go with you
And having sworn truth, ever will be true.

OLIVIA Then lead the way, good father, and heavens
so shine
35   That they may fairly note this act of mine.

Exeunt.

24 **chantry by** nearby chapel   27 **jealous** jealous, anxious   29 **Whiles** until
29 **come to note** be made public   30 **our celebration keep** celebrate our
marriage ceremony (as distinguished from the formal compact of betrothal)
35 **fairly note** look with favor on

ACT V

Scene I. [*Before Olivia's house.*]

Enter Clown and Fabian.

FABIAN Now as thou lov'st me, let me see his letter.

CLOWN Good Master Fabian, grant me another request.

FABIAN Anything.

CLOWN Do not desire to see this letter.   5

FABIAN This is to give a dog, and in recompense desire my dog again.

Enter Duke, Viola, Curio, and Lords.

DUKE Belong you to the Lady Olivia, friends?

CLOWN Ay, sir, we are some of her trappings.

DUKE I know thee well. How dost thou, my good   10
fellow?

CLOWN Truly, sir, the better for my foes, and the
worse for my friends.

V.i.1 *his* i.e., Malvolio's

DUKE Just the contrary: the better for thy friends.

15 CLOWN No, sir, the worse.

DUKE How can that be?

CLOWN Marry, sir, they praise me and make an ass of
me. Now my foes tell me plainly I am an ass; so
that by my foes, sir, I profit in the knowledge of
20 myself, and by my friends I am abused; so that,
conclusions to be as kisses, if your four negatives
make your two affirmatives, why then, the worse
for my friends, and the better for my foes.

DUKE Why, this is excellent.

25 CLOWN By my troth, sir, no, though it please you to
be one of my friends.

DUKE Thou shalt not be the worse for me. There's
gold.

CLOWN But that it would be double-dealing, sir, I
30 would you could make it another.

DUKE O, you give me ill counsel.

CLOWN Put your grace in your pocket, sir, for this
once, and let your flesh and blood obey it.

DUKE Well, I will be so much a sinner to be a double-
35 dealer. There's another.

CLOWN *Primo, secundo, tertio* is a good play; and
the old saying is "The third pays for all." The
triplex, sir, is a good tripping measure; or the
bells of Saint Bennet, sir, may put you in mind—
40 one, two, three.

DUKE You can fool no more money out of me at this

20 **abused** deceived   21 **conclusions to be as kisses** i.e., if conclusions may be
compared to kisses (when a coy girl's repeated denials really mean assent)
21 **negatives** i.e., lips (?)   22 **affirmatives** i.e., mouths (?)   29 **double-dealing**
(1) giving twice (2) duplicity   32 **grace** (1) title of nobility (2) generosity
35 **another** i.e., coin   36 **Primo, secundo, tertio** one, two, three   36 **play**
child's game (?)   38 **triplex** triple time in dancing   39 **Saint Bennet** St Benedict
(a church)

throw. If you will let your lady know I am here
to speak with her, and bring her along with you, it
may awake my bounty further.

CLOWN Marry, sir, lullaby to your bounty till I come   45
again. I go, sir; but I would not have you to think
that my desire of having is the sin of covetousness.
But, as you say, sir, let your bounty take a nap; I
will awake it anon.   *Exit*.

Enter Antonio and Officers.

VIOLA Here comes the man, sir, that did rescue me.   50

DUKE That face of his I do remember well;
Yet when I saw it last, it was besmeared
As black as Vulcan in the smoke of war.
A baubling vessel was he captain of,
For shallow draught and bulk unprizable,   55
With which such scathful grapple did he make
With the most noble bottom of our fleet
That very envy and the tongue of loss
Cried fame and honor on him. What's the matter?

FIRST OFFICER Orsino, this is that Antonio   60
That took the *Phoenix* and her fraught from
     Candy;
And this is he that did the *Tiger* board
When your young nephew Titus lost his leg.
Here in the streets, desperate of shame and state,
In private brabble did we apprehend him.   65

VIOLA He did me kindness, sir; drew on my side;
But in conclusion put strange speech upon me.
I know not what 'twas but distraction.

42 throw throw of the dice   53 Vulcan Roman god of fire and patron of blacksmiths
54 baubling insignificant   55 For shallow draught and bulk unprizable i.e.,
virtually worthless on account of its small size   56 scathful destructive
57 bottom ship   58 very envy and the tongue of loss even enmity and the
voice of the losers   61 fraught freight, cargo   61 Candy Candia, Crete
64 desperate of shame and state i.e., recklessly disregarding his shameful past
behavior and the requirements of public order   65 brabble brawl   66 drew on
my side i.e., drew his sword in my defense   67 put strange speech upon me
spoke to me so oddly   68 distraction madness

DUKE Notable pirate, thou salt-water thief,
70   What foolish boldness brought thee to their mercies
      Whom thou in terms so bloody and so dear
      Hast made thine enemies?

ANTONIO   Orsino, noble sir,
      Be pleased that I shake off these names you give me.
      Antonio never yet was thief or pirate,
75   Though I confess, on base and ground enough,
      Orsino's enemy. A witchcraft drew me hither.
      That most ingrateful boy there by your side
      From the rude sea's enraged and foamy mouth
      Did I redeem. A wrack past hope he was.
80   His life I gave him, and did thereto add
      My love without retention or restraint,
      All his in dedication. For his sake
      Did I expose myself (pure for his love)
      Into the danger of this adverse town;
85   Drew to defend him when he was beset;
      Where being apprehended, his false cunning
      (Not meaning to partake with me in danger)
      Taught him to face me out of his acquaintance,
      And grew a twenty years removèd thing
90   While one would wink; denied me mine own purse,
      Which I had recommended to his use
      Not half an hour before.

VIOLA   How can this be?

DUKE When came he to this town?

ANTONIO Today, my lord; and for three months before,
95   No int'rim, not a minute's vacancy,
      Both day and night did we keep company.

                Enter Olivia and Attendants.

DUKE Here comes the Countess; now heaven walks on
      earth.

69 **Notable** notorious   71 **dear** grievous   79 **wrack** wreck   83 **pure** purely
84 **adverse** unfriendly   88 **to face me out of his acquaintance** i.e., brazenly to
deny any knowledge of me   91 **recommended** given

But for thee, fellow: fellow, thy words are mad-
ness.
Three months this youth hath tended upon me;
But more of that anon. Take him aside.   100

OLIVIA What would my lord, but that he may not
have,
Wherein Olivia may seem serviceable?
Cesario, you do not keep promise with me.

VIOLA Madam?

DUKE Gracious Olivia—   105

OLIVIA What do you say, Cesario?—Good my lord—

VIOLA My lord would speak; my duty hushes me.

OLIVIA If it be aught to the old tune, my lord,
It is as fat and fulsome to mine ear
As howling after music.

DUKE   Still so cruel?   110

OLIVIA Still so constant, lord.

DUKE What, to perverseness? You uncivil lady,
To whose ingrate and unauspicious altars
My soul the faithfull'st off'rings have breathed out
That e'er devotion tendered. What shall I do?   115

OLIVIA Even what it please my lord, that shall become
him.

DUKE Why should I not, had I the heart to do it,
Like to th' Egyptian thief at point of death,
Kill what I love?—a savage jealousy
That sometime savors nobly. But hear me this: 120
Since you to non-regardance cast my faith,

98 But for as for 101 but that except that which (i.e., my love) 106 Good my
lord i.e., please be silent (so Cesario may speak) 109 fat and fulsome gross and
repulsive 113 ingrate and unauspicious ungrateful and unpropitious 118 th'
Egyptian thief (in Heliodorus' *Ethiopica*, a Greek romance translated by Thomas
Underdown about 1569, the bandit Thyamis, besieged in a cave, plans to kill the
captive princess Clariclea, the object of his hopeless love; but in the darkness he
kills another woman instead) 121 non-regardance neglect

And that I partly know the instrument
That screws me from my true place in your favor,
Live you the marble-breasted tyrant still.
125　But this your minion, whom I know you love,
And whom, by heaven I swear, I tender dearly,
Him will I tear out of that cruel eye
Where he sits crownèd in his master's spite.
Come, boy, with me. My thoughts are ripe in
　　mischief.
130　I'll sacrifice the lamb that I do love
To spite a raven's heart within a dove.　　　[Going.]

VIOLA　And I, most jocund, apt, and willingly,
To do you rest a thousand deaths would die.
　　　　　　　　　　　　　　　　　　　　[Following.]

OLIVIA　Where goes Cesario?

VIOLA　　　　　　　　　　After him I love
135　More than I love these eyes, more than my life,
More, by all mores, than e'er I shall love wife.
If I do feign, you witnesses above
Punish my life for tainting of my love!

OLIVIA　Ay me detested, how am I beguiled!

VIOLA　Who does beguile you? Who does do you
140　　wrong?

OLIVIA　Hast thou forgot thyself? Is it so long?
Call forth the holy father.　　　[Exit an Attendant.]

DUKE　　　　　　　　　[To Viola] Come, away!

OLIVIA　Whither, my lord? Cesario, husband, stay.

DUKE　Husband?

OLIVIA　　　　　Ay, husband. Can he that deny?

DUKE　Her husband, sirrah?

145　VIOLA　　　　　　　　No, my lord, not I.

122 that since　123 screws forces　126 tender hold　132 apt readily　133 do
you rest give you peace　136 mores i.e., possible comparisons　145 sirrah
(customary form of address to a menial)

OLIVIA Alas, it is the baseness of thy fear
  That makes thee strangle thy propriety.
  Fear not, Cesario; take thy fortunes up;
  Be that thou know'st thou art, and then thou art
  As great as that thou fear'st.

Enter Priest.

                 O, welcome, father!   150
  Father, I charge thee by thy reverence
  Here to unfold—though lately we intended
  To keep in darkness what occasion now
  Reveals before 'tis ripe—what thou dost know
  Hath newly passed between this youth and me.   155

PRIEST A contract of eternal bond of love,
  Confirmed by mutual joinder of your hands,
  Attested by the holy close of lips,
  Strength'ned by interchangement of your rings;
  And all the ceremony of this compact   160
  Sealed in my function, by my testimony;
  Since when, my watch hath told me, toward my
    grave
  I have traveled but two hours.

DUKE O thou dissembling cub, what wilt thou be
  When time hath sowed a grizzle on thy case?   165
  Or will not else thy craft so quickly grow
  That thine own trip shall be thine overthrow?
  Farewell, and take her; but direct thy feet
  Where thou and I, henceforth, may never meet.

VIOLA My lord, I do protest.

OLIVIA   O, do not swear.   170
  Hold little faith, though thou hast too much fear.

Enter Sir Andrew.

147 **strangle thy propriety** deny your identity   150 **that him who** (i.e., the Duke)
156 **contract** betrothal   160 **compact** (accent on second syllable)   161 **Sealed
in my function** i.e., ratified by me in my priestly office   165 **a grizzle on thy
case** gray hairs on your skin   166 **craft** duplicity   167 **trip** craftiness   171 **little**
i.e., at least a little

ANDREW For the love of God, a surgeon! Send one presently to Sir Toby.

OLIVIA What's the matter?

175 ANDREW H'as broke my head across, and has given Sir Toby a bloody coxcomb too. For the love of God, your help! I had rather than forty pound I were at home.

OLIVIA Who has done this, Sir Andrew?

180 ANDREW The Count's gentleman, one Cesario. We took him for a coward, but he's the very devil incardinate.

DUKE My gentleman Cesario?

ANDREW Od's lifelings, here he is! You broke my
185 head for nothing; and that that I did, I was set on to do't by Sir Toby.

VIOLA Why do you speak to me? I never hurt you.
You drew your sword upon me without cause,
But I bespake you fair and hurt you not.

Enter [Sir] Toby and Clown.

190 ANDREW If a bloody coxcomb be a hurt, you have hurt me. I think you set nothing by a bloody coxcomb. Here comes Sir Toby halting; you shall hear more. But if he had not been in drink, he would have tickled you othergates than he did.

195 DUKE How now, gentleman? How is't with you?

TOBY That's all one! Has hurt me, and there's th' end on't. Sot, didst see Dick Surgeon, sot?

CLOWN O, he's drunk, Sir Toby, an hour agone. His eyes were set at eight i' th' morning.

---

173 **presently** immediately   175 **H'as** he has   176 **coxcomb** pate   182 **incardinate** incarnate   184 **Od's lifelings** by God's life   189 **bespake you fair** addressed you courteously   192 **halting** limping   194 **othergates** otherwise   197 **Sot** fool   199 **set** closed

TOBY Then he's a rogue and a passy measures pavin. 200
    I hate a drunken rogue.

OLIVIA Away with him! Who hath made this havoc
    with them?

ANDREW I'll help you, Sir Toby, because we'll be
    dressed together. 205

TOBY Will you help—an ass-head and a coxcomb
    and a knave, a thin-faced knave, a gull?

OLIVIA Get him to bed, and let his hurt be looked to.
                         [*Exeunt Clown, Fabian, Sir Toby,*
                                 and Sir Andrew.]

Enter Sebastian.

SEBASTIAN I am sorry, madam, I have hurt your
    kinsman;
    But had it been the brother of my blood, 210
    I must have done no less with wit and safety.
    You throw a strange regard upon me, and by that
    I do perceive it hath offended you.
    Pardon me, sweet one, even for the vows
    We made each other but so late ago. 215

DUKE One face, one voice, one habit, and two
    persons—
    A natural perspective that is and is not.

SEBASTIAN Antonio, O my dear Antonio,
    How have the hours racked and tortured me
    Since I have lost thee! 220

ANTONIO Sebastian are you?

SEBASTIAN   Fear'st thou that, Antonio?

200-1 **passy measures pavin** i.e., *passamezzo* pavan, a slow and stately dance of
eight bars (hence its relevance to the surgeon whose eyes had "set at eight")
204-5 **be dressed** have our wounds dressed 211 **with wit and safety** i.e., with a
sensible regard for my safety 212 **strange regard** unfriendly look 216 **habit**
costume 217 **A natural perspective** i.e., a natural optical illusion (like that
produced by a stereoscope, which converts two images into one) 221 **Fear'st
thou** do you doubt

ANTONIO How have you made division of yourself?
    An apple cleft in two is not more twin
    Than these two creatures. Which is Sebastian?

225 OLIVIA Most wonderful.

SEBASTIAN Do I stand there? I never had a brother;
    Nor can there be that deity in my nature
    Of here and everywhere. I had a sister,
    Whom the blind waves and surges have devoured.
230   Of charity, what kin are you to me?
    What countryman? What name? What parentage?

VIOLA Of Messaline; Sebastian was my father;
    Such a Sebastian was my brother too;
    So went he suited to his watery tomb.
235   If spirits can assume both form and suit,
    You come to fright us.

SEBASTIAN   A spirit I am indeed,
    But am in that dimension grossly clad
    Which from the womb I did participate.
    Were you a woman, as the rest goes even,
240   I should my tears let fall upon your cheek
    And say, "Thrice welcome, drownèd Viola!"

VIOLA My father had a mole upon his brow.

SEBASTIAN And so had mine.

VIOLA And died that day when Viola from her birth
245   Had numb'red thirteen years.

SEBASTIAN O, that record is lively in my soul!
    He finishèd indeed his mortal act
    That day that made my sister thirteen years.

VIOLA If nothing lets to make us happy both
250   But this my masculine usurped attire,

227-28 **Nor can there be ... everywhere** i.e., nor can I, like God, be everywhere at once   230 **Of charity** out of simple kindness   234 **suited** clothed   235 **form and suit** body and clothing   237-38 **am in that dimension ... participate** i.e., clothed in the bodily form that, like other mortals, I acquired at birth   239 **as the rest goes even** i.e., as other circumstances seem to indicate   246 **record** history (accent on second syllable)   249 **lets** interferes

Do not embrace me till each circumstance
Of place, time, fortune do cohere and jump
That I am Viola; which to confirm,
I'll bring you to a captain in this town,
Where lie my maiden weeds; by whose gentle help   255
I was preserved to serve this noble Count.
All the occurrence of my fortune since
Hath been between this lady and this lord.

SEBASTIAN [*To Olivia*] So comes it, lady, you have
    been mistook.
But nature to her bias drew in that.   260
You would have been contracted to a maid;
Nor are you therein, by my life, deceived:
You are betrothed both to a maid and man.

DUKE Be not amazed; right noble is his blood.
If this be so, as yet the glass seems true,   265
I shall have share in this most happy wrack.
[*To Viola*] Boy, thou hast said to me a thousand
    times
Thou never shouldst love woman like to me.

VIOLA And all those sayings will I over swear,
And all those swearings keep as true in soul   270
As doth that orbèd continent the fire
That severs day from night.

DUKE   Give me thy hand,
And let me see thee in thy woman's weeds.

VIOLA The captain that did bring me first on shore
Hath my maid's garments. He upon some action   275
Is now in durance, at Malvolio's suit,
A gentleman, and follower of my lady's.

OLIVIA He shall enlarge him. Fetch Malvolio hither.

252 cohere and jump i.e., fall together and agree 255 weeds clothes
260 nature to her bias drew i.e., nature followed her normal inclination
265 glass i.e., the "natural perspective" of line 217 269 over repeatedly
271 orbèd continent in Ptolemaic astronomy, the sphere of the sun
275-76 He upon some action ... Malvolio's suit i.e., at Malvolio's instigation
he is now imprisoned upon some legal charge 278 enlarge release

And yet alas, now I remember me,
280   They say, poor gentleman, he's much distract.

Enter Clown with a letter, and Fabian.

A most extracting frenzy of mine own
From my remembrance clearly banished his.
How does he, sirrah?

CLOWN Truly, madam, he holds Belzebub at the
285   stave's end as well as a man in his case may do.
Has here writ a letter to you; I should have given't
you today morning. But as a madman's epistles are
no gospels, so it skills not much when they are
delivered.

290   OLIVIA Open't and read it.

CLOWN Look then to be well edified, when the fool
delivers the madman. [*Reads in a loud voice*] "By
the Lord, madam"—

OLIVIA How now? Art thou mad?

295   CLOWN No, madam, I do but read madness. And your
ladyship will have it as it ought to be, you must
allow *vox*.

OLIVIA Prithee read i' thy right wits.

CLOWN So I do, madonna; but to read his right wits is
300   to read thus. Therefore perpend, my princess, and
give ear.

OLIVIA [*To Fabian*] Read it you, sirrah.

FABIAN (*Reads*) "By the Lord, madam, you wrong
me, and the world shall know it. Though you have
305   put me into darkness, and given your drunken
cousin rule over me, yet have I the benefit of my
senses as well as your ladyship. I have your own
letter that induced me to the semblance I put on;

281 **extracting** i.e., obliterating (in that it draws me from all thoughts of
Malvolio's "frenzy")   284-85 **he holds Belzebub at the stave's end** i.e., he
keeps the fiend at a distance   285 **case** condition   288 **skills** matters   297 **vox**
i.e., an appropriately loud voice   300 **perpend** pay attention

with the which I doubt not but to do myself much
right, or you much shame. Think of me as you   310
please. I leave my duty a little unthought of, and
speak out of my injury.

THE MADLY USED MALVOLIO."

OLIVIA Did he write this?

CLOWN Ay, madam.   315

DUKE This savors not much of distraction.

OLIVIA See him delivered, Fabian; bring him hither.
[Exit Fabian.]
My lord, so please you, these things further thought
    on,
To think me as well a sister as a wife,
One day shall crown th' alliance on't, so please you,   320
Here at my house and at my proper cost.

DUKE Madam, I am most apt t' embrace your offer.
[To Viola] Your master quits you; and for your
    service done him,
So much against the mettle of your sex,
So far beneath your soft and tender breeding,   325
And since you called me master for so long,
Here is my hand; you shall from this time be
Your master's mistress.

OLIVIA   A sister; you are she.

Enter [Fabian, with] Malvolio.

DUKE Is this the madman?

OLIVIA   Ay, my lord, this same.
How now, Malvolio?

MALVOLIO   Madam, you have done me wrong,   330
Notorious wrong.

OLIVIA   Have I, Malvolio? No.

MALVOLIO Lady, you have. Pray you peruse that letter.
You must not now deny it is your hand.

321 **proper** own   322 **apt** ready   323 **quits** releases   331 **Notorious** notable

Write from it if you can, in hand or phrase,
335   Or say 'tis not your seal, not your invention.
You can say none of this. Well, grant it then,
And tell me, in the modesty of honor,
Why you have given me such clear lights of favor,
Bade me come smiling and cross-gartered to you,
340   To put on yellow stockings, and to frown
Upon Sir Toby and the lighter people;
And, acting this in an obedient hope,
Why have you suffered me to be imprisoned,
Kept in a dark house, visited by the priest,
345   And made the most notorious geck and gull
That e'er invention played on? Tell me why.

OLIVIA Alas, Malvolio, this is not my writing,
Though I confess much like the character;
But, out of question, 'tis Maria's hand.
350   And now I do bethink me, it was she
First told me thou wast mad; then cam'st in smiling,
And in such forms which here were presupposed
Upon thee in the letter. Prithee be content.
This practice hath most shrewdly passed upon thee;
355   But when we know the grounds and authors of it,
Thou shalt be both the plaintiff and the judge
Of thine own cause.

FABIAN   Good madam, hear me speak,
And let no quarrel, nor no brawl to come,
Taint the condition of this present hour,
360   Which I have wond'red at. In hope it shall not,
Most freely I confess myself and Toby
Set this device against Malvolio here,
Upon some stubborn and uncourteous parts
We had conceived against him. Maria writ
365   The letter, at Sir Toby's great importance,

---

334 **from it** differently   335 **invention** composition   337 **in the modesty of honor** i.e., with a proper regard to your own honor   341 **lighter** lesser   345 **geck and gull** fool and dupe   349 **out of** beyond   352 **presupposed** imposed   354 **This practice hath most shrewdly passed** i.e., this trick has most mischievously worked   363 **Upon some stubborn and uncourteous parts** i.e., because of some unyielding and discourteous traits of character   365 **importance** importunity

In recompense whereof he hath married her.
How with a sportful malice it was followed
May rather pluck on laughter than revenge,
If that the injuries be justly weighed
That have on both sides passed.   370

OLIVIA Alas, poor fool, how have they baffled thee!

CLOWN Why, "some are born great, some achieve
greatness, and some have greatness thrown upon
them." I was one, sir, in this interlude, one Sir
Topas, sir; but that's all one. "By the Lord, fool, I   375
am not mad!" But do you remember, "Madam, why
laugh you at such a barren rascal? And you smile
not, he's gagged"? And thus the whirligig of time
brings in his revenges.

MALVOLIO I'll be revenged on the whole pack of you!   380
                                                    [Exit.]

OLIVIA He hath been most notoriously abused.

DUKE Pursue him and entreat him to a peace.
He hath not told us of the captain yet.
When that is known, and golden time convents,
A solemn combination shall be made   385
Of our dear souls. Meantime, sweet sister,
We will not part from hence. Cesario, come—
For so you shall be while you are a man,
But when in other habits you are seen,
Orsino's mistress and his fancy's queen.   390
                        Exeunt [all but the Clown].

                    Clown sings.

When that I was and a little tiny boy,
    With hey, ho, the wind and the rain,

---

368 **pluck on** prompt 369 **If that** if 371 **fool** (here, a term of affection and
compassion) 371 **baffled** publicly humiliated 374 **interlude** little play 384 **convents** is suitable (?) 390 **fancy's** love's s.d. **Clown sings** (since no source has
been found for the Clown's song—which certain editors have inexplicably
denounced as doggerel—we may assume that it is Shakespeare's) 391 **and** a a

A foolish thing was but a toy,
    For the rain it raineth every day.

395   But when I came to man's estate,
        With hey, ho, the wind and the rain,
      'Gainst knaves and thieves men shut their gate,
        For the rain it raineth every day.

      But when I came, alas, to wive,
400   With hey, ho, the wind and the rain,
      By swaggering could I never thrive,
        For the rain it raineth every day.

      But when I came unto my beds,
        With hey, ho, the wind and the rain,
405   With tosspots still had drunken heads,
        For the rain it raineth every day.

      A great while ago the world begun,
        Hey, ho, the wind and the rain;
      But that's all one, our play is done,
410   And we'll strive to please you every day.
                                        [*Exit.*]
                    FINIS

393 **toy** trifle   405 **tosspots** sots

Textual Note

The text of *Twelfth Night,* for which the sole source is the Folio of 1623, is, if not immaculate, so clean and tidy that it presents almost no problems. Apparently set up from the prompt copy or a transcript of it, the Folio of course contains a few misprints (like *incardinatc* for *incardinate* at V.i.182), a few presumed or obvious errors in speech-headings (like those at II.v.34, 38, where Sir Toby is perhaps confused with Fabian, or at III.iv.24, where Malvolio is assigned a speech that clearly is not his), and a few lines (for example, II.ii.12 and III.iii.15) that seem to need some sort of emendation. Moreover, the fact that the Clown is given all the lovely songs that were perhaps originally Viola's (as suggested at I.ii.57-59 and II.iv.42-43) has been cited as a token of revision. In general, however, the text, as all its editors have gratefully conceded, is one of almost unexampled purity.

In the present edition, therefore, it is followed very closely, even in such forms as *studient, jealious, wrack* (for *wreck*) and *vild,* which preserve, we may suppose, not only Shakespeare's spelling but also his pronunciation. But *prethee, divil, murther, Sathan* (for *Satan*), *Anthonio,* and *berd* (which occurs once for *beard*) are given in modern spelling. A few emendations sanctioned by long and universal approbation—like Pope's *Arion* for *Orion* at I.ii.15, Theobald's inspired *curl by* for *coole my* at I.iii.96, and Hanmer's *staniel* for *stallion* at II.v.115— have been admitted here, as have one or two superior readings from the later Folios (for example, *tang* for *langer* at III.iv.73). However, such attractive but unnecessary emendations as Pope's *south* for *sound* at I.i.5 have been rejected, and the few real cruxes have been allowed to stand, so that each reader must struggle all alone with Sir Andrew's *damned colored stock* at I.iii.132, make what he can of the mysterious Lady of the Strachy at II.v.39-40, and unravel Viola's puzzling pronouncement

TEXTUAL NOTE

at II.ii.12 without the aid of emendation.

In this edition the spelling has been modernized (with the exceptions noted above), the Latin act and scene divisions of the Folio translated, the punctuation brought into conformity with modern usage, a few lines that through compositorial error were printed as prose restored to verse (IV.ii.75-76), and a few stage directions (like the one at III.iv.14) shifted to accommodate the text. At the conclusion of the first, second, and fourth acts, the Folio has "*Finis Actus* ...," here omitted. All editorial interpolations such as the list of characters, indications of place, and stage directions implied by the text but not indicated in the Folio are enclosed in square brackets. Other material departures from the copy text (excluding obvious typographical errors) are listed below in bold type, followed in roman by the Folio reading. It will be apparent that most of them required no agonizing reappraisal.

I.ii.15 **Arion** Orion

I.iii.29 **all most,** almost   51 **Andrew** Ma.   96 **curl by coole** my   98 **me we** 112 **kickshawses** kicke-chawses   132 **set** sit   136 **That's** That

I.iv.28 **nuncio's** Nuntio's

I.v.146 **H'as** Ha's   165 s.d. **Viola** Uiolenta   256 **with fertile tears** fertill teares   302 **County's** Countes

II.ii.20 **That sure methought** That me thought   31 **our frailty** O frailtie 32 **of** if

II.iii.26 **leman** Lemon   35 **give a—** giue a   134-35 **a nayword** an ayword

II.iv.53 **Fly ... fly** Fye ... fie   55 **yew** Ew   89 **I It**   104 **know—** know.

II.v.13 **metal** Mettle   115 **staniel** stallion   144 **born** become   144 **achieve** atcheeues   159-60 **thee, THE FORTUNATE UNHAPPY./Daylight** thee, tht fortunate vnhappy daylight   177 **dear** deero

III.i.8 **king lies** Kings lyes   69 **wise men** wisemens   84 **gait** gate   93 **all ready** already   114 **here** heare

III.ii.8 **see thee the** see the   70 **renegado** Renegatho

III.iv.24 **Olivia** Mal.   73 **tang** langer   94 **How is't with you, man** [The Folio assigns this speech to Fabian]   121 **Ay, biddy** I biddy   152 **Ay, is't,** I, ist?   181 **You ... for't** Yon ... fot't   256 **competent** computent

IV.ii.6 **in** in in   15 **Gorboduc** Gorbodacke   38 **clerestories** cleere stores   73 **sport to the** sport the

V.i.201 **pavin** panyn

WILLIAM SHAKESPEARE

ALL'S WELL THAT ENDS WELL

Edited by Sylvan Barnet

ALL'S WELL THAT
ENDS WELL

ACT I

Scene I. [*Rousillon. The Count's palace.*]

*Enter young Bertram, Count of Rousillon, his mother
[the Countess], and Helena, Lord Lafew, all in black.*

COUNTESS In delivering my son from me I bury a
second husband.

BERTRAM And I in going, madam, weep o'er my
father's death anew; but I must attend his Majesty's
command, to whom I am now in ward, evermore   5
in subjection.

LAFEW You shall find of the King a husband,
madam; you, sir, a father. He that so generally
is at all times good must of necessity hold his
virtue to you, whose worthiness would stir it up   10
where it wanted, rather than lack it where there
is such abundance.

Text references are printed in **bold** type; the annotation follows in roman type.
I.i.s.d. **Rousillon** formerly a province in southern France (usually spelled "Rossil-
lion" in the Folio; the accent is on the second syllable, and -llion was probably
pronounced -yun)   1 **delivering** sending away (with pun on giving birth)   5 **to
whom I am now in ward** whose ward I now am   7 **of** in   8 **generally** impartially   9 **hold** continue   11 **where it wanted** i.e., even if it (virtue) were lacking

COUNTESS What hope is there of his Majesty's amendment?

15 LAFEW He hath abandoned his physicians, madam, under whose practices he hath persecuted time with hope, and finds no other advantage in the process but only the losing of hope by time.

COUNTESS This young gentlewoman had a father—O, 20 that "had," how sad a passage 'tis—whose skill was almost as great as his honesty; had it stretched so far, would have made nature immortal, and death should have play for lack of work. Would for the King's sake he were living! I think it would 25 be the death of the King's disease.

LAFEW How called you the man you speak of, madam?

COUNTESS He was famous, sir, in his profession, and it was his great right to be so: Gerard de Narbon.

30 LAFEW He was excellent indeed, madam. The King very lately spoke of him admiringly and mourningly; he was skillful enough to have lived still, if knowledge could be set up against mortality.

BERTRAM What is it, my good lord, the King lan-35 guishes of?

LAFEW A fistula, my lord.

BERTRAM I heard not of it before.

LAFEW I would it were not notorious. Was this gentlewoman the daughter of Gerard de Narbon?

40 COUNTESS His sole child, my lord, and bequeathed to my overlooking. I have those hopes of her good

---

20 **passage** (1) incident (2) passing away   36 **fistula** abscess   41 **overlooking** guardianship

that her education promises; her dispositions she
inherits, which makes fair gifts fairer; for where an
unclean mind carries virtuous qualities, there commendations go with pity; they are virtues and   45
traitors too. In her they are the better for their
simpleness; she derives her honesty and achieves
her goodness.

LAFEW Your commendations, madam, get from her
tears.   50

COUNTESS 'Tis the best brine a maiden can season
her praise in. The remembrance of her father never
approaches her heart but the tyranny of her sorrows takes all livelihood from her cheek. No more
of this, Helena; go to, no more, lest it be rather   55
thought you affect a sorrow than to have—

HELENA I do affect a sorrow indeed, but I have it
too.

LAFEW Moderate lamentation is the right of the dead,
excessive grief the enemy to the living.   60

COUNTESS If the living be enemy to the grief, the excess makes it soon mortal.

BERTRAM Madam, I desire your holy wishes.

LAFEW How understand we that?

COUNTESS Be thou blessed, Bertram, and succeed
thy father   65
In manners as in shape! Thy blood and virtue
Contend for empire in thee, and thy goodness

---

44 **virtuous qualities** skills (not moral qualities)   46-47 **their simpleness** being
single, unmixed   47 **derives** inherits   51 **season** preserve   54 **livelihood**
(1) vitality (2) nourishment   55 **go to** (a remonstrance, "Stop")   56 **affect** feign
(Helena enigmatically replies that she both feigns a sorrow—for her father, we
later learn—and has one; her use of the word also includes another meaning,
"love")   64 **Lafew ... that** (perhaps this line is misplaced, and should begin
Lafew's previous speech)   66 **manners** morals   66 **Thy** may thy

Share with thy birthright! Love all, trust a few,
Do wrong to none; be able for thine enemy
70   Rather in power than use, and keep thy friend
Under thy own life's key. Be checked for silence,
But never taxed for speech. What heaven more
    will,
That thee may furnish and my prayers pluck down,
Fall on thy head! Farewell. My lord,
75   'Tis an unseasoned courtier; good my lord,
Advise him.

LAFEW   He cannot want the best
That shall attend his love.

COUNTESS Heaven bless him! Farewell, Bertram.
                                        [*Exit.*]

BERTRAM The best wishes that can be forged in your
80   thoughts be servants to you! [*To Helena*] Be comfortable to my mother, your mistress, and make
much of her.

LAFEW Farewell, pretty lady; you must hold the credit
of your father.   [*Exit with Bertram.*]

85   HELENA O, were that all! I think not on my father,
And these great tears grace his remembrance more
Than those I shed for him. What was he like?
I have forgot him; my imagination
Carries no favor in't but Bertram's.
90   I am undone; there is no living, none,
If Bertram be away; 'twere all one
That I should love a bright particular star,
And think to wed it, he is so above me.
In his bright radiance and collateral light
95   Must I be comforted, not in his sphere.

69-70 **be able ... use** let your strength equal your foe's in potentiality, but do not
use it   72 **taxed** censured   76 **want** lack   80-81 **comfortable** comforting
89 **favor** (1) face (2) love token   94-95 **In his bright ... sphere** i.e., I must
content myself with his light, parallel to ("collateral") but above me; I cannot be in
his orbit

Th' ambition in my love thus plagues itself:
The hind that would be mated by the lion
Must die for love. 'Twas pretty, though a plague,
To see him every hour, to sit and draw
His archèd brows, his hawking eye, his curls,   100
In our heart's table; heart too capable
Of every line and trick of his sweet favor.
But now he's gone, and my idolatrous fancy
Must sanctify his relics. Who comes here?

Enter Parolles.

One that goes with him. I love him for his sake,   105
And yet I know him a notorious liar,
Think him a great way fool, solely a coward;
Yet these fixed evils sit so fit in him,
That they take place when virtue's steely bones
Looks bleak i' th' cold wind; withal, full oft we see   110
Cold wisdom waiting on superfluous folly.

PAROLLES Save you, fair queen!

HELENA And you, monarch!

PAROLLES No.

HELENA And no.   115

PAROLLES Are you meditating on virginity?

HELENA Ay. You have some stain of soldier in you; let me ask you a question. Man is enemy to virginity; how may we barricado it against him?

PAROLLES Keep him out.   120

HELENA But he assails; and our virginity, though valiant, in the defense yet is weak. Unfold to us some warlike resistance.

---

100 **hawking** hawklike, keen   101 **table** flat surface on which a picture is drawn
101-2 **capable/Of** receptive to   103 **fancy** lover's fantasy   104 s.d. **Parolles** (cf.
French *paroles*, "words," i.e., Talker, Braggart)   109 **take place** find acceptance
(?)   110 **withal** besides   111 **Cold ... folly** i.e., a threadbare wise servant
attending on a rich fool   112 **Save** God save   117 **stain** tincture

PAROLLES There is none. Man, setting down before
125   you, will undermine you and blow you up.

HELENA Bless our poor virginity from underminers
and blowers-up! Is there no military policy how
virgins might blow up men?

PAROLLES Virginity being blown down, man will quick-
130   lier be blown up; marry, in blowing him down
again, with the breach yourselves made you lose
your city. It is not politic in the commonwealth of
nature to preserve virginity. Loss of virginity is
rational increase, and there was never virgin got
135   till virginity was first lost. That you were made of
is metal to make virgins. Virginity by being once
lost may be ten times found; by being ever kept
it is ever lost. 'Tis too cold a companion; away
with't!

140   HELENA I will stand for't a little, though therefore
I die a virgin.

PAROLLES There's little can be said in't; 'tis against the
rule of nature. To speak on the part of virginity, is
to accuse your mothers, which is most infallible
145   disobedience. He that hangs himself is a virgin; virginity murders itself, and should be buried in highways out of all sanctified limit, as a desperate
offendress against nature. Virginity breeds mites,
much like a cheese, consumes itself to the very
150   paring, and so dies with feeding his own stomach.
Besides, virginity is peevish, proud, idle, made of
self-love which is the most inhibited sin in the

---

124 **setting down before** laying siege to   125 **blow you up** (1) explode you
(2) make you pregnant   130 **be blown up** be swollen, i.e., reach an orgasm
130 **marry** (a mild oath, "By the Virgin Mary")   134 **got** begotten   135 **That**
that which   136 **metal** (1) substance (2) coin (3) mettle, spirit   147 **sanctified**
limit consecrated ground   150 **stomach** pride

canon. Keep it not; you cannot choose but lose by't. Out with't! Within ten year it will make itself ten, which is a goodly increase, and the principal itself not much the worse. Away with't!   155

HELENA How might one do, sir, to lose it to her own liking?

PAROLLES Let me see. Marry, ill, to like him that ne'er it likes. 'Tis a commodity will lose the gloss with lying; the longer kept, the less worth. Off with't while 'tis vendible; answer the time of request. Virginity, like an old courtier, wears her cap out of fashion, richly suited, but unsuitable, just like the brooch and the toothpick, which wear not now. Your date is better in your pie and your porridge than in your cheek; and your virginity, your old virginity, is like one of our French withered pears: it looks ill, it eats drily; marry, 'tis a withered pear; it was formerly better; marry, yet 'tis a withered pear. Will you anything with it?   160   165   170

HELENA Not my virginity yet!
There shall your master have a thousand loves,
A mother, and a mistress, and a friend,
A phoenix, captain, and an enemy,   175
A guide, a goddess, and a sovereign,
A counselor, a traitress, and a dear;
His humble ambition, proud humility;
His jarring, concord, and his discord, dulcet;
His faith, his sweet disaster; with a world   180
Of pretty, fond, adoptious christendoms
That blinking Cupid gossips. Now shall he—

152-53 inhibited sin in the canon prohibited sin in the Scripture   153 Keep hoard   164 unsuitable unfashionable   165 wear not now are not now in fashion   172 yet (possibly there are missing some ensuing lines in which Helena comments on Bertram's departure, possibly the abrupt transition reveals that Helena's thoughts have not been on Parolles' talk)   175 phoenix i.e., rarity (literally, a fabulous bird)   180 disaster unfavorable star   181-82 fond ... gossips foolish, adopted names that blind ("blinking") Cupid gives as godfather ("gossips")

I know not what he shall. God send him well!
The court's a learning place, and he is one—

185 PAROLLES What one, i' faith?

HELENA That I wish well. 'Tis pity—

PAROLLES What's pity?

HELENA That wishing well had not a body in't,
Which might be felt, that we, the poorer born,
190 Whose baser stars do shut us up in wishes,
Might with effects of them follow our friends,
And show what we alone must think, which never
Returns us thanks.

Enter Page.

PAGE Monsieur Parolles, my lord calls for you.

[*Exit.*]

195 PAROLLES Little Helen, farewell. If I can remember
thee, I will think of thee at court.

HELENA Monsieur Parolles, you were born under a
charitable star.

PAROLLES Under Mars, ay.

200 HELENA I especially think, under Mars.

PAROLLES Why under Mars?

HELENA The wars hath so kept you under, that you
must needs be born under Mars.

PAROLLES When he was predominant.

205 HELENA When he was retrograde, I think rather.

PAROLLES Why think you so?

HELENA You go so much backward when you fight.

PAROLLES That's for advantage.

---

190 **baser stars** lower destinies   202 **under** in low fortune   205 **retrograde**
moving backward (astrological term)

HELENA So is running away, when fear proposes the
safety; but the composition that your valor and fear   210
makes in you is a virtue of a good wing, and I like
the wear well.

PAROLLES I am so full of businesses, I cannot answer
thee acutely. I will return perfect courtier, in the
which my instruction shall serve to naturalize   215
thee, so thou wilt be capable of a courtier's counsel,
and understand what advice shall thrust upon thee;
else thou diest in thine unthankfulness, and thine
ignorance makes thee away. Farewell. When thou
hast leisure, say thy prayers; when thou hast none,   220
remember thy friends. Get thee a good husband,
and use him as he uses thee. So, farewell.   [*Exit.*]

HELENA Our remedies oft in ourselves do lie,
Which we ascribe to heaven; the fated sky
Gives us free scope; only doth backward pull   225
Our slow designs when we ourselves are dull.
What power is it which mounts my love so high,
That makes me see, and cannot feed mine eye?
The mightiest space in fortune nature brings
To join like likes, and kiss like native things.   230
Impossible be strange attempts to those
That weigh their pains in sense, and do suppose
What hath been cannot be. Who ever strove
To show her merit that did miss her love?
The King's disease—my project may deceive me,   235
But my intents are fixed, and will not leave me.

Exit.

---

210 **composition** (1) union, mixture (2) truce, surrender   212 **wear** fashion (if
"wing" has referred not only to Parolles' flight but to a flap on his clothing, "wear"
puns—like the modern "fashion"—on habit and clothing)   215 **naturalize**
familiarize   224 **fated sky** sky (heaven) that exerts influence   230 **native** closely
related   231-33 **Impossible ... cannot be** i.e., remarkable deeds are impossible
to persons who cautiously calculate the efforts and who believe that unusual
happenings cannot take place

[Scene II. *Paris. The King's palace.*]

Flourish cornets. Enter the King of France with
letters, and divers Attendants.

KING The Florentines and Senoys are by th' ears,
     Have fought with equal fortune, and continue
     A braving war.

FIRST LORD   So 'tis reported, sir.

KING Nay, 'tis most credible. We here receive it
5   A certainty, vouched from our cousin Austria,
     With caution, that the Florentine will move us
     For speedy aid; wherein our dearest friend
     Prejudicates the business, and would seem
     To have us make denial.

FIRST LORD   His love and wisdom,
10   Approved so to your Majesty, may plead
     For amplest credence.

KING   He hath armed our answer,
     And Florence is denied before he comes;
     Yet, for our gentlemen that mean to see
     The Tuscan service, freely have they leave
     To stand on either part.

15 SECOND LORD   It well may serve
     A nursery to our gentry, who are sick
     For breathing and exploit.

I.ii.s.d. **Flourish** musical notes heralding an important person   1 **Senoys**
Sienese   1 **by th' ears** quarreling   3 **braving war** war of challenges   5 **cousin**
fellow sovereign   6 **move** petition   10 **Approved** proven   14 **The Tuscan**
service the campaign in Tuscany (N. Italy)   15 **stand on either part** serve on
either side   16 **nursery** training school   16-17 **sick/For breathing** eager for
exercise

Enter Bertram, Lafew, and Parolles.

KING   What's he comes here?

FIRST LORD It is the Count Rousillon, my good lord,
   Young Bertram.

KING   Youth, thou bear'st thy father's face.
   Frank nature, rather curious than in haste,   20
   Hath well composed thee. Thy father's moral parts
   May'st thou inherit too! Welcome to Paris.

BERTRAM My thanks and duty are your Majesty's.

KING I would I had that corporal soundness now,
   As when thy father and myself in friendship   25
   First tried our soldiership. He did look far
   Into the service of the time, and was
   Discipled of the bravest. He lasted long,
   But on us both did haggish age steal on,
   And wore us out of act. It much repairs me   30
   To talk of your good father; in his youth
   He had the wit which I can well observe
   Today in our young lords; but they may jest
   Till their own scorn return to them unnoted
   Ere they can hide their levity in honor.   35
   So like a courtier, contempt nor bitterness
   Were in his pride or sharpness; if they were,
   His equal had awaked them, and his honor,
   Clock to itself, knew the true minute when
   Exception bid him speak, and at this time   40
   His tongue obeyed his hand. Who were below him
   He used as creatures of another place,
   And bowed his eminent top to their low ranks,
   Making them proud of his humility,
   In their poor praise he humbled. Such a man   45
   Might be a copy to these younger times;

---

20 **Frank** bounteous 20 **curious** careful 26–27 **He did ... time** he had insight
into war (?) he served long in wars (?) 30 **act** action 35 **hide ... in** i.e., join ...
with (?) 40 **Exception** disapproval 41 **Who** those who 42 **another place** i.e.,
a higher rank

Which, followed well, would demonstrate them
    now
But goers backward.

BERTRAM   His good remembrance, sir,
Lies richer in your thoughts than on his tomb;
50   So in approof lives not his epitaph
As in your royal speech.

KING Would I were with him! He would always say—
Methinks I hear him now; his plausive words
He scattered not in ears, but grafted them,
55   To grow there, and to bear—"Let me not live,"
This his good melancholy oft began,
On the catastrophe and heel of pastime,
When it was out—"Let me not live," quoth he,
"After my flame lacks oil, to be the snuff
60   Of younger spirits, whose apprehensive senses
All but new things disdain; whose judgments are
Mere fathers of their garments; whose constancies
Expire before their fashions." This he wished.
I, after him, do after him wish too,
65   Since I nor wax nor honey can bring home,
I quickly were dissolvèd from my hive
To give some laborers room.

SECOND LORD   You're loved, sir;
They that least lend it you shall lack you first.

KING   I fill a place, I know't. How long is't, Count,
70   Since the physician at your father's died?
He was much famed.

BERTRAM   Some six months since, my lord.

KING If he were living, I would try him yet.

50-51 **So ... speech** i.e., the validity of his epitaph is in no way better confirmed
than in your words   53 **plausive** laudable   57 **On ... pastime** at the end
("catastrophe," "heel") of pleasure   58 **out** ended (perhaps punning on the idea
"out at heel")   59 **snuff** burnt wick that causes the lamp to smell and smolder,
preventing the lower ("younger") wick from burning brightly   60 **apprehensive**
perceptive, apt   64 **after him ... after him** later than he ... in accordance
with him

Lend me an arm. The rest have worn me out
With several applications. Nature and sickness
Debate it at their leisure. Welcome, Count,   75
My son's no dearer.

BERTRAM   Thank your Majesty.
                    Exit [the King with the rest]. Flourish.

[Scene III. *Rousillon. The Count's palace.*]

Enter Countess, Steward, and Clown.

COUNTESS   I will now hear. What say you of this
gentlewoman?

STEWARD Madam, the care I have had to even your
content I wish might be found in the calendar of
my past endeavors, for then we wound our mod-   5
esty, and make foul the clearness of our deservings, when of ourselves we publish them.

COUNTESS What does this knave here? Get you gone,
sirrah. The complaints I have heard of you I do
not all believe; 'tis my slowness that I do not, for   10
I know you lack not folly to commit them, and
have ability enough to make such knaveries yours.

CLOWN 'Tis not unknown to you, madam, I am a
poor fellow.

COUNTESS Well, sir.   15

---

74 **several applications** various treatments   I.iii.3 **even** make even, satisfy
4 **calendar** record   9 **sirrah** (term of address used to an inferior)

CLOWN No, madam, 'tis not so well that I am poor, though many of the rich are damned; but, if I may have your ladyship's good will to go to the world, Isbel the woman and I will do as we may.

20 COUNTESS Wilt thou needs be a beggar?

CLOWN I do beg your good will in this case.

COUNTESS In what case?

CLOWN In Isbel's case and mine own. Service is no heritage, and I think I shall never have the bless-
25 ing of God till I have issue o' my body; for they say barnes are blessings.

COUNTESS Tell me thy reason why thou wilt marry.

CLOWN My poor body, madam, requires it. I am driven on by the flesh, and he must needs go that
30 the devil drives.

COUNTESS Is this all your worship's reason?

CLOWN Faith, madam, I have other holy reasons, such as they are.

COUNTESS May the world know them?

35 CLOWN I have been, madam, a wicked creature, as you and all flesh and blood are, and indeed I do marry that I may repent

COUNTESS Thy marriage, sooner than thy wickedness.

CLOWN I am out o' friends, madam, and I hope to
40 have friends for my wife's sake.

COUNTESS Such friends are thine enemies, knave.

CLOWN Y'are shallow, madam, in great friends, for the knaves come to do that for me which I am

18 **go to the world** get married   19 **do** (punning on the bawdy meaning "have intercourse")   23 **case** (another bawdy pun, "pudendum")   23-24 **Service is no heritage** i.e., servants acquire no wealth (proverbial)   26 **barnes** bairns, children   32 **holy reasons** (probably there is a bawdy pun not only on "holy" but on "reasons," pronounced much like "raisings")

aweary of. He that ears my land spares my team, and gives me leave to in the crop; if I be his cuckold, he's my drudge. He that comforts my wife is the cherisher of my flesh and blood; he that cherishes my flesh and blood loves my flesh and blood; he that loves my flesh and blood is my friend: ergo, he that kisses my wife is my friend. If men could be contented to be what they are, there were no fear in marriage; for young Charbon the puritan and old Poysam the papist, howsome'er their hearts are severed in religion, their heads are both one; they may jowl horns together like any deer i' th' herd. 45 50 55

COUNTESS Wilt thou ever be a foul-mouthed and calumnious knave?

CLOWN A prophet I, madam, and I speak the truth the next way: 60

> For I the ballad will repeat,
>   Which men full true shall find,
> Your marriage comes by destiny,
>   Your cuckoo sings by kind.

COUNTESS Get you gone, sir. I'll talk with you more anon. 65

STEWARD May it please you, madam, that he bid Helen come to you. Of her I am to speak.

COUNTESS Sirrah, tell my gentlewoman I would speak with her—Helen I mean. 70

CLOWN Was this fair face the cause, quoth she,
>   Why the Grecians sackèd Troy?
> Fond done, done fond,
>   Was this King Priam's joy?

---

44 ears plows   45 in bring in   46 cuckold deceived husband (traditionally said to wear horns)   52-53 Charbon ... Poysam Flesh-eater ... Fish-eater (from French *chair bonne* = good flesh; *poisson* = fish)   55 jowl knock   60 next nearest   64 by kind according to nature (the cuckoo allegedly sang to men that they were cuckolds)   73 Fond foolishly

75   With that she sighèd as she stood,
        With that she sighèd as she stood,
            And gave this sentence then:
        Among nine bad if one be good,
        Among nine bad if one be good,
80   There's yet one good in ten.

COUNTESS What, one good in ten? You corrupt the
    song, sirrah.

CLOWN One good woman in ten, madam, which is a
    purifying o' th' song. Would God would serve the
85 world so all the year! We'd find no fault with the
    tithe-woman, if I were the parson. One in ten,
    quoth 'a! And we might have a good woman
    born but or every blazing star, or at an earth-
    quake, 'twould mend the lottery well; a man may
90 draw his heart out, ere 'a pluck one.

COUNTESS You'll be gone, sir knave, and do as I com-
    mand you!

CLOWN That man should be at woman's command,
    and yet no hurt done! Though honesty be no puri-
95 tan, yet it will do no hurt; it will wear the surplice
    of humility over the black gown of a big heart.
    I am going, forsooth. The business is for Helen to
    come hither.   *Exit*.

COUNTESS Well, now.

100 STEWARD I know, madam, you love your gentlewoman
    entirely.

COUNTESS Faith, I do. Her father bequeathed her to
    me, and she herself, without other advantage, may
    lawfully make title to as much love as she finds.

---

77 sentence wise saying   86 tithe-woman tenth woman (sent as part of the
tithe, like a tithe-pig)   87 quoth 'a says he   87 And if   88 or ... or either ...
or   95–96 wear ... heart ie., conform outwardly, masking its pride (the Church
of England required the wearing of the surplice, but clerics inclined toward
Calvinism asserted their independence by wearing beneath the surplice the black
Geneva gown)   103 advantage interest accruing to a sum of money

There is more owing her than is paid, and more   105
shall be paid her than she'll demand.

STEWARD Madam, I was very late more near her than
I think she wished me. Alone she was, and did
communicate to herself her own words to her own
ears. She thought, I dare vow for her, they touched   110
not any stranger sense. Her matter was, she loved
your son. Fortune, she said, was no goddess, that
had put such difference betwixt their two estates;
Love no god, that would not extend his might only
where qualities were level; Diana no queen of vir-   115
gins, that would suffer her poor knight surprised
without rescue in the first assault or ransom afterward. This she delivered in the most bitter touch
of sorrow that e'er I heard virgin exclaim in, which
I held my duty speedily to acquaint you withal,   120
sithence in the loss that may happen it concerns
you something to know it.

COUNTESS You have discharged this honestly; keep it
to yourself. Many likelihoods informed me of this
before, which hung so tott'ring in the balance that   125
I could neither believe nor misdoubt. Pray you
leave me. Stall this in your bosom, and I thank
you for your honest care. I will speak with you
further anon.   *Exit Steward.*

Enter Helena.

[*Aside*] Even so it was with me, when I was young;   130
If ever we are nature's, these are ours; this thorn
Doth to our rose of youth rightly belong;
Our blood to us, this to our blood is born.
It is the show and seal of nature's truth,
Where love's strong passion is impressed in youth.   135
By our remembrances of days foregone,

107 late lately   110-11 touched not any stranger sense reached no stranger's ear
116 knight i.e., chaste follower of Diana   121 sithence since   127 Stall this
keep this enclosed   131 these sorrows (?) passions (?)   133 blood passion (?)
disposition (?)

Such were our faults, or then we thought them
    none.
Her eye is sick on't; I observe her now.

HELENA What is your pleasure, madam?

COUNTESS   You know, Helen,
140   I am a mother to you.

HELENA Mine honorable mistress.

COUNTESS   Nay, a mother.
Why not a mother? When I said "a mother"
Methought you saw a serpent. What's in "mother"
That you start at it? I say I am your mother,
145   And put you in the catalogue of those
That were enwombèd mine. 'Tis often seen
Adoption strives with nature, and choice breeds
A native slip to us from foreign seeds.
You ne'er oppressed me with a mother's groan,
150   Yet I express to you a mother's care.
God's mercy, maiden, does it curd thy blood
To say I am thy mother? What's the matter,
That this distempered messenger of wet,
The many-colored Iris, rounds thine eye?
Why, that you are my daughter?

155 HELENA   That I am not.

COUNTESS I say I am your mother.

HELENA   Pardon, madam;
The Count Rousillon cannot be my brother.
I am from humble, he from honored name;
No note upon my parents, his all noble.
160   My master, my dear lord he is, and I
His servant live, and will his vassal die.
He must not be my brother.

147–48 choice ... seeds i.e., a slip that is chosen for grafting from foreign stock
becomes native to us   153 distempered disturbed   154 many-colored Iris i.e.,
teardrop (Iris was goddess of the rainbow)   155 That I am not (Helena plays on
the sense "daughter-in-law")

COUNTESS   Nor I your mother?

HELENA You are my mother, madam; would you
      were—
    So that my lord, your son, were not my brother—
    Indeed my mother! Or were you both our mothers   165
    I care no more for than I do for heaven,
    So I were not his sister. Can't no other
    But, I your daughter, he must be my brother?

COUNTESS Yes, Helen, you might be my daughter-in-
      law.
    God shield you mean it not! "Daughter" and
      "mother"   170
    So strive upon your pulse! What, pale again?
    My fear hath catched your fondness! Now I see
    The myst'ry of your loneliness, and find
    Your salt tears' head. Now to all sense 'tis gross:
    You love my son! Invention is ashamed   175
    Against the proclamation of thy passion,
    To say thou dost not. Therefore tell me true;
    But tell me then, 'tis so; for look, thy cheeks
    Confess it, t' one to th' other, and thine eyes
    See it so grossly shown in thy behaviors,   180
    That in their kind they speak it; only sin
    And hellish obstinacy tie thy tongue,
    That truth should be suspected. Speak, is't so?
    If it be so, you have wound a goodly clew;
    If it be not, forswear't; howe'er, I charge thee,   185
    As heaven shall work in me for thine avail,
    To tell me truly.

HELENA   Good madam, pardon me!

COUNTESS Do you love my son?

HELENA   Your pardon, noble mistress!

COUNTESS Love you my son?

167 **Can't no other** can it not be otherwise   170 **shield** forbid   172 **fondness**
foolishness   174 **head** source   174 **gross** obvious   181 **in their kind** according
to their nature, i.e. with tears   184 **clew** ball of string

HELENA   Do not you love him, madam?

190 COUNTESS Go not about; my love hath in't a bond
       Whereof the world takes note. Come, come, dis-
          close
       The state of your affection, for your passions
       Have to the full appeached.

HELENA   Then I confess,
       Here on my knee, before high heaven and you,
195   That before you, and next unto high heaven,
       I love your son.
       My friends were poor but honest; so's my love.
       Be not offended, for it hurts not him
       That he is loved of me; I follow him not
200   By any token of presumptuous suit,
       Nor would I have him till I do deserve him;
       Yet never know how that desert should be.
       I know I love in vain, strive against hope;
       Yet, in this captious and inteemable sieve,
205   I still pour in the waters of my love,
       And lack not to lose still. Thus, Indian-like,
       Religious in mine error, I adore
       The sun that looks upon his worshipper
       But knows of him no more. My dearest madam,
210   Let not your hate encounter with my love
       For loving where you do; but if yourself,
       Whose agèd honor cites a virtuous youth,
       Did ever, in so true a flame of liking,
       Wish chastely, and love dearly that your Dian
215   Was both herself and Love, O, then give pity
       To her whose state is such that cannot choose
       But lend and give where she is sure to lose;
       That seeks not to find that her search implies,
       But, riddle-like, lives sweetly where she dies.

193 **appeached** accused   197 **friends** relatives   204 **captious** (1) capacious (2)
deceitful   204 **inteemable** incapable of pouring forth (the sieve is capacious
enough to accept all the love poured into it, but is deceptive because it cannot pour
forth love)   206 **lack not to lose still** (1) fail not to go on losing (2) lack not a
supply to go on losing   212 **cites** demonstrates   218 **that** what   219 **lives** i.e.
stays in one place

COUNTESS Had you not lately an intent—speak truly—   220
  To go to Paris?

HELENA   Madam, I had.

COUNTESS   Wherefore? Tell true.

HELENA I will tell truth, by grace itself, I swear.
  You know my father left me some prescriptions
  Of rare and proved effects, such as his reading
  And manifest experience had collected   225
  For general sovereignty; and that he willed me
  In heedfull'st reservation to bestow them,
  As notes whose faculties inclusive were
  More than they were in note. Amongst the rest,
  There is a remedy, approved, set down,   230
  To cure the desperate languishings whereof
  The King is rendered lost.

COUNTESS   This was your motive
  For Paris, was it? Speak.

HELENA My lord your son made me to think of this;
  Else Paris, and the medicine, and the King,   235
  Had from the conversation of my thoughts
  Haply been absent then.

COUNTESS   But think you, Helen,
  If you should tender your supposèd aid,
  He would receive it? He and his physicians
  Are of a mind; he, that they cannot help him;   240
  They, that they cannot help. How shall they credit
  A poor unlearnèd virgin, when the schools,
  Emboweled of their doctrine, have left off
  The danger to itself?

HELENA   There's something in't
  More than my father's skill, which was the great'st   245

---

226 **general sovereignty** universal excellence   227 **In heedfull'st reservation**
i.e. sparingly   228-29 **notes ... in note** i.e., prescriptions ("notes") more powerful in fact than they were reported ("in note") to be   230 **approved** tested
243 **Emboweled of their doctrine** emptied of their knowledge

Of his profession, that his good receipt
Shall for my legacy be sanctified
By th' luckiest stars in heaven; and would your
    honor
But give me leave to try success, I'd venture
250   The well-lost life of mine on his Grace's cure
By such a day, an hour.

COUNTESS   Dost thou believe't?

HELENA Ay, madam, knowingly.

COUNTESS Why, Helen, thou shalt have my leave and
    love,
Means and attendants, and my loving greetings
255   To those of mine in court. I'll stay at home
And pray God's blessing into thy attempt.
Be gone tomorrow; and be sure of this,
What I can help thee to, thou shalt not miss.

                               Exeunt.

249 **try success** test the outcome

ACT II

[Scene I. *Paris. The King's palace.*]

Enter the King with divers young Lords taking
leave for the Florentine war; Bertram and
Parolles; [Attendants]. Flourish cornets.

KING Farewell, young lords! These warlike principles
    Do not throw from you; and you, my lords, farewell!
    Share the advice betwixt you; if both gain all,
    The gift doth stretch itself as 'tis received,
    And is enough for both.

FIRST LORD   'Tis our hope, sir,   5
    After well-ent'red soldiers, to return
    And find your Grace in health.

KING No, no, it cannot be; and yet my heart
    Will not confess he owes the malady
    That doth my life besiege. Farewell, young lords!   10
    Whether I live or die, be you the sons

II.i.6 **After well-ent'red soldiers** after becoming experienced soldiers 9 **owes**
owns

555

>   Of worthy Frenchmen: let higher Italy—
>   Those bated that inherit but the fall
>   Of the last monarchy—see that you come
> 15   Not to woo honor, but to wed it, when
>   The bravest questant shrinks: find what you seek,
>   That fame may cry you loud. I say, farewell.

FIRST LORD Health, at your bidding, serve your
    Majesty!

KING Those girls of Italy, take heed of them.
20   They say our French lack language to deny
    If they demand; beware of being captives
    Before you serve.

BOTH LORDS   Our hearts receive your warnings.

KING Farewell. [*To attendants*] Come hither to me.
                        [*Exit with Attendants.*]

FIRST LORD O my sweet lord, that you will stay behind
    us!

PAROLLES 'Tis not his fault, the spark.

25 SECOND LORD   O, 'tis brave wars!

PAROLLES Most admirable! I have seen those wars.

BERTRAM I am commanded here, and kept a coil with
    "Too young," and "the next year," and "'tis too
    early."

PAROLLES And thy mind stand to't, boy, steal away
    bravely.

30 BERTRAM I shall stay here the forehorse to a smock,
    Creaking my shoes on the plain masonry,
    Till honor be bought up, and no sword worn
    But one to dance with! By heaven, I'll steal away.

13–14 **Those . . . monarchy** except for those who gain by the fall of the monarchy (?) except for those who continue in the decadent ways of the past (?)   16 **questant** seeker   27 **commanded here** ordered to stay here   27 **kept a coil** bothered   29 **And if**   30 **the forehorse to a smock** i.e., in the service of women ("forehorse" = leader in a team of horses)

FIRST LORD There's honor in the theft.

PAROLLES   Commit it, Count.

SECOND LORD I am your accessary; and so farewell.   35

BERTRAM I grow to you, and our parting is a tortured
  body.

FIRST LORD Farewell, Captain.

SECOND LORD Sweet Monsieur Parolles!

PAROLLES Noble heroes, my sword and yours are kin.   40
  Good sparks and lustrous, a word, good metals.
  You shall find in the regiment of the Spinii one
  Captain Spurio, with his cicatrice, an emblem of
  war, here on his sinister cheek; it was this very
  sword entrenched it. Say to him I live, and observe   45
  his reports for me.

FIRST LORD We shall, noble Captain.   [Exeunt Lords.]

PAROLLES Mars dote on you for his novices! [To
  Bertram] What will ye do?

BERTRAM Stay the King.   50

PAROLLES Use a more spacious ceremony to the noble
  lords; you have restrained yourself within the list
  of too cold an adieu. Be more expressive to them,
  for they wear themselves in the cap of the time;
  there do muster true gait, eat, speak, and move   55
  under the influence of the most received star; and
  though the devil lead the measure, such are to be
  followed. After them, and take a more dilated
  farewell.

BERTRAM And I will do so.   60

---

41 **metals** (with the additional sense of "mettles," spirits) 43 **Spurio** (from Italian, "false") 43 **cicatrice** scar 44 **sinister** left 48 **Mars ... novices** may the god of war watch over you as his pupils 50 **Stay** support 52 **list** boundary (literally the selvage of cloth) 56 **received** fashionable 57 **measure** dance 58 **dilated** extended

PAROLLES Worthy fellows, and like to prove most
  sinewy sword-men. *Exeunt [Bertram and Parolles].*

    Enter [the King and] Lafew.

LAFEW [*Kneeling*] Pardon, my lord, for me and for
  my tidings.

KING I'll fee thee to stand up.

LAFEW [*Rising*] Then here's a man stands that has
65 brought his pardon.
  I would you had kneeled, my lord, to ask me mercy,
  And that at my bidding you could so stand up.

KING I would I had, so I had broke thy pate
  And asked thee mercy for't.

LAFEW   Good faith, across!
70 But, my good lord, 'tis thus: will you be cured
  Of your infirmity?

KING   No.

LAFEW   O, will you eat
  No grapes, my royal fox? Yes, but you will
  My noble grapes, and if my royal fox
  Could reach them. I have seen a medicine
75 That's able to breathe life into a stone,
  Quicken a rock, and make you dance canary
  With sprightly fire and motion, whose simple touch
  Is powerful to araise King Pippen, nay,
  To give great Charlemain a pen in's hand,
  And write to her a love-line.

80 KING   What "her" is this?

---

64 **I'll fee thee to stand up** i.e., please arise ("fee" = reward) 68 **pate** head
69 **across** clumsily (an unskilled tilter might break a lance "across" instead of
head-on) 72 **royal fox** (alluding to Aesop's fox who said he did not want grapes,
when he could not reach them; Lafew suggests that the King says he does not want
to be cured because he thinks he cannot be cured) 76 **Quicken** endow with
life 76 **canary** a lively dance 78 **Pippen** Pepin (died 768)

LAFEW Why, Doctor She! My lord, there's one
   arrived,
   If you will see her. Now, by my faith and honor,
   If seriously I may convey my thoughts
   In this my light deliverance, I have spoke
   With one that, in her sex, her years, profession,   85
   Wisdom and constancy, hath amazed me more
   Than I dare blame my weakness. Will you see her,
   For that is her demand, and know her business?
   That done, laugh well at me.

KING   Now, good Lafew,
   Bring in the admiration, that we with thee   90
   May spend our wonder too, or take off thine
   By wond'ring how thou took'st it.

LAFEW   Nay, I'll fit you,
   And not be all day neither.   [*Goes to door.*]

KING Thus he his special nothing ever prologues.

LAFEW Nay, come your ways.

                    Enter Helena.

KING   This haste hath wings indeed.   95

LAFEW Nay, come your ways!
   This is his Majesty; say your mind to him.
   A traitor you do look like, but such traitors
   His Majesty seldom fears. I am Cressid's uncle,
   That dare leave two together. Fare you well.   *Exit.*   100

KING Now, fair one, does your business follow us?

HELENA Ay, my good lord.
   Gerard de Narbon was my father;
   In what he did profess, well found.

KING   I knew him.

---

84 **light deliverance** jesting utterance   85 **profession** claims   90 **admiration**
wonder   92 **fit** satisfy   99 **Cressid's uncle** Pandarus (who served as go-between
for his niece and Troilus)   104 **well found** found to be skilled

HELENA The rather will I spare my praises towards
105   him;
    Knowing him is enough. On's bed of death
    Many receipts he gave me, chiefly one,
    Which as the dearest issue of his practice
    And of his old experience th' only darling,
110   He bade me store up as a triple eye,
    Safer than mine own two; more dear I have so,
    And, hearing your high Majesty is touched
    With that malignant cause wherein the honor
    Of my dear father's gift stands chief in power,
115   I come to tender it and my appliance,
    With all bound humbleness.

KING   We thank you, maiden,
    But may not be so credulous of cure,
    When our most learnèd doctors leave us, and
    The congregated College have concluded
120   That laboring art can never ransom nature
    From her inaidable estate. I say we must not
    So stain our judgment or corrupt our hope,
    To prostitute our past-cure malady
    To empirics, or to dissever so
125   Our great self and our credit, to esteem
    A senseless help, when help past sense we deem.

HELENA My duty then shall pay me for my pains.
    I will no more enforce mine office on you,
    Humbly entreating from your royal thoughts
130   A modest one to bear me back again.

KING I cannot give thee less, to be called grateful.
    Thou thought'st to help me, and such thanks I give
    As one near death to those that wish him live.
    But what at full I know, thou know'st no part,
135   I knowing all my peril, thou no art.

---

110 **triple** third, i.e., the remedy was as valuable as her eyes   115 **tender** offer
115 **appliance** (1) service (2) application, treatment   119 **congregated College**
assembled College of Physicians   120 **art** human skill   124 **empirics** quacks
125 **credit** reputation

HELENA What I can do can do no hurt to try,
    Since you set up your rest 'gainst remedy:
    He that of greatest works is finisher,
    Oft does them by the weakest minister.
    So holy writ in babes hath judgment shown,   140
    When judges have been babes; great floods have
      flown
    From simple sources; and great seas have dried
    When miracles have by the great'st been denied.
    Oft expectation fails, and most oft there
    Where most it promises, and oft it hits   145
    Where hope is coldest and despair most sits.

KING I must not hear thee; fare thee well, kind maid.
    Thy pains not used must by thyself be paid.
    Proffers not took reap thanks for their reward.

HELENA Inspirèd merit so by breath is barred.   150
    It is not so with Him that all things knows,
    As 'tis with us that square our guess by shows;
    But most it is presumption in us when
    The help of heaven we count the act of men.
    Dear sir, to my endeavors give consent;   155
    Of heaven, not me, make an experiment.
    I am not an impostor, that proclaim
    Myself against the level of mine aim,
    But know I think, and think I know most sure,
    My art is not past power, nor you past cure.   160

KING Art thou so confident? Within what space
    Hop'st thou my cure?

HELENA   The greatest grace lending grace,
    Ere twice the horses of the sun shall bring
    Their fiery torcher his diurnal ring,

---

137 **set up your rest** stake all (gambling term)   143 **the great'st** (if Helena has been thinking of the Red Sea, "the great'st" = Pharaoh)   150 **breath** i.e., your words (contrast to God's breathing into Helen is implicit in "inspirèd")   152 **square our guess by shows** make decisions by appearances   157–58 **that proclaim . . . aim** i.e., although I announce I will hit the target even before I take aim   164 **diurnal ring** daily circuit

165   Ere twice in murk and occidental damp
           Moist Hesperus hath quenched her sleepy lamp,
           Or four and twenty times the pilot's glass
           Hath told the thievish minutes how they pass,
           What is infirm from your sound parts shall fly,
170   Health shall live free, and sickness freely die.

KING Upon thy certainty and confidence
      What dar'st thou venture?

HELENA   Tax of impudence,
        A strumpet's boldness, a divulgèd shame,
        Traduced by odious ballads; my maiden's name
175   Seared otherwise; ne worse of worst, extended
        With vilest torture, let my life be ended.

KING Methinks in thee some blessèd spirit doth speak
      His powerful sound within an organ weak;
      And what impossibility would slay
180   In common sense, sense saves another way.
      Thy life is dear, for all that life can rate
      Worth name of life in thee hath estimate:
      Youth, beauty, wisdom, courage, all
      That happiness and prime can happy call.
185   Thou this to hazard needs must intimate
      Skill infinite or monstrous desperate.
      Sweet practicer, thy physic I will try,
      That ministers thine own death if I die.

HELENA If I break time, or flinch in property
190   Of what I spoke, unpitied let me die,
        And well deserved. Not helping, death's my fee,
        But if I help what do you promise me?

KING Make thy demand.

HELENA   But will you make it even?

---

165 **occidental damp** (alluding to the sun's alleged setting in the ocean)
166 **Hesperus** the evening star   167 **glass** hourglass   172 **Tax** accusation
175 **Seared** branded   175 **ne** nor   175 **extended** stretched (on the rack)
182 **estimate** value   184 **prime** springtime (of life), i.e., youth   187 **physic** medicine   189 **flinch in property** i.e., fail in any detail   193 **make it even** fulfill it

KING Ay, by my scepter and my hopes of heaven.

HELENA Then shalt thou give me with thy kingly hand   195
    What husband in thy power I will command:
    Exempted be from me the arrogance
    To choose from forth the royal blood of France
    My low and humble name to propagate
    With any branch or image of thy state;   200
    But such a one, thy vassal, whom I know
    Is free for me to ask, thee to bestow.

KING Here is my hand; the premises observed,
    Thy will by my performance shall be served;
    So make the choice of thy own time, for I,   205
    Thy resolved patient, on thee still rely.
    More should I question thee, and more I must,
    Though more to know could not be more to trust;
    From whence thou cam'st, how tended on—but rest
    Unquestioned, welcome, and undoubted blest.   210
    Give me some help here, ho! If thou proceed
    As high as word, my deed shall match thy deed.
                Flourish. Exit [*King with Helena*].

[Scene II. *Rousillon. The Count's palace.*]

Enter Countess and Clown.

COUNTESS Come on, sir. I shall now put you to the
    height of your breeding.

CLOWN I will show myself highly fed and lowly taught.
    I know my business is but to the court

II.ii.1-2 **put you to the height of** test

5   COUNTESS To the court! Why, what place make you
special, when you put off that with such contempt?
"But to the court!"

CLOWN Truly, madam, if God have lent a man any
manners, he may easily put it off at court. He that
10   cannot make a leg, put off's cap, kiss his hand, and
say nothing, has neither leg, hands, lip, nor cap;
and indeed such a fellow, to say precisely, were not
for the court. But for me, I have an answer will
serve all men.

15   COUNTESS Marry, that's a bountiful answer that fits
all questions.

CLOWN It is like a barber's chair that fits all buttocks:
the pin-buttock, the quatch-buttock, the brawn-
buttock, or any buttock.

20   COUNTESS Will your answer serve fit to all questions?

CLOWN As fit as ten groats is for the hand of an
attorney, as your French crown for your taffety
punk, as Tib's rush for Tom's forefinger, as a
pancake for Shrove Tuesday, a morris for May-
25   day, as the nail to his hole, the cuckold to his horn,
as a scolding quean to a wrangling knave, as the
nun's lip to the friar's mouth; nay, as the pudding
to his skin.

COUNTESS Have you, I say, an answer of such fitness
30   for all questions?

CLOWN From below your duke to beneath your constable, it will fit any question.

---

10 **make a leg** make obeisance (by drawing back one leg and bending the other)
18 **quatch-buttock** fat behind   21 **ten groats** (a groat was worth fourpence; ten
groats was the usual attorney's fee)   22 **French crown** (1) coin (2) bald or scabby
head (caused by syphilis, "the French disease")   22–23 **taffety punk** finely
dressed prostitute   23 **rush** ring made of rush (used in mock weddings)   24 **Shrove
Tuesday** day preceding Ash Wednesday, hence a day of feasting immediately before
Lent   24 **morris** country dance   26 **quean** prostitute   27 **pudding** sausage

COUNTESS It must be an answer of most monstrous size
that must fit all demands.

CLOWN But a trifle neither, in good faith, if the 35
learned should speak truth of it. Here it is, and all
that belongs to't. Ask me if I am a courtier; it shall
do you no harm to learn.

COUNTESS To be young again, if we could, I will be
a fool in question, hoping to be the wiser by your 40
answer. I pray you, sir, are you a courtier?

CLOWN O Lord, sir! There's a simple putting off.
More, more, a hundred of them.

COUNTESS Sir, I am a poor friend of yours, that loves
you. 45

CLOWN O Lord, sir! Thick, thick! Spare not me.

COUNTESS I think, sir, you can eat none of this homely
meat.

CLOWN O Lord, sir! Nay, put me to't, I warrant you.

COUNTESS You were lately whipped, sir, as I think. 50

CLOWN O Lord, sir! Spare not me.

COUNTESS Do you cry, "O Lord, sir!" at your whipping, and "spare not me"? Indeed, your "O Lord,
sir!" is very sequent to your whipping; you would
answer very well to a whipping, if you were but 55
bound to't.

CLOWN I ne'er had worse luck in my life in my "O
Lord, sir!" I see things may serve long, but not
serve ever.

COUNTESS I play the noble housewife with the time, 60
To entertain it so merrily with a fool.

---

35 **neither** indeed (negating the Countess' conjecture)   42 **O Lord, sir** (a phrase associated with courtiers)   46 **Thick** quickly   54 **is very sequent to** i.e., would quickly follow   56 **bound to't** (1) bound by oath to answer (2) tied to a whipping post

CLOWN O Lord, sir! Why, there't serves well again.

COUNTESS An end, sir! To your business: give Helen this,
And urge her to a present answer back.
65 Commend me to my kinsmen and my son.
This is not much.

CLOWN Not much commendation to them?

COUNTESS Not much employment for you. You understand me?

70 CLOWN Most fruitfully. I am there before my legs.

COUNTESS Haste you again.   *Exeunt.*

[Scene III. *Paris. The King's palace.*]

Enter Bertram, Lafew, and Parolles.

LAFEW They say miracles are past, and we have our philosophical persons, to make modern and familiar, things supernatural and causeless. Hence is it that we make trifles of terrors, ensconcing our-
5 selves into seeming knowledge, when we should submit ourselves to an unknown fear.

PAROLLES Why, 'tis the rarest argument of wonder that hath shot out in our latter times.

BERTRAM And so 'tis.

10 LAFEW To be relinquished of the artists—

---

64 present immediate 70 fruitfully (perhaps a bawdy punning reply, if "understand" means "have intercourse with") II.iii.2 modern commonplace 4 ensconcing fortifying 6 unknown fear i.e., inexplicable mystery 7 argument of subject for 10 artists physicians

PAROLLES So I say—both of Galen and Paracelsus.

LAFEW Of all the learned and authentic fellows—

PAROLLES Right; so I say.

LAFEW That gave him out incurable—

PAROLLES Why, there 'tis; so say I too.   15

LAFEW Not to be helped—

PAROLLES Right, as 'twere a man assured of a—

LAFEW Uncertain life and sure death.

PAROLLES Just; you say well. So would I have said.

LAFEW I may truly say it is a novelty to the world.   20

PAROLLES It is indeed; if you will have it in showing, you shall read it in what-do-ye-call there?

LAFEW [Reading] "A showing of a heavenly effect in an earthly actor."

PAROLLES That's it, I would have said the very same.   25

LAFEW Why, your dolphin is not lustier; 'fore me, I speak in respect—

PAROLLES Nay, 'tis strange, 'tis very strange; that is the brief and the tedious of it, and he's of a most facinerious spirit that will not acknowledge it to   30 be the—

LAFEW Very hand of heaven.

PAROLLES Ay, so I say.

LAFEW In a most weak—

PAROLLES And debile minister; great power, great   35

---

11 **Galen ... Paracelsus** (renowned physicians; the former was a Greek of the second century B.C., the latter a German of the sixteenth century) 26 **lustier** more vigorous 26 **'fore me** on my soul 30 **facinerious** villainous 35 **debile** weak

transcendence, which should indeed give us a
further use to be made than alone the recov'ry of
the King, as to be—

LAFEW Generally thankful.

Enter King, Helena, and Attendants.

40 PAROLLES I would have said it. You say well. Here
comes the King.

LAFEW Lustig, as the Dutchman says. I'll like a maid
the better whilst I have a tooth in my head. Why,
he's able to lead her a coranto.

45 PAROLLES Mor du vinager! Is not this Helen?

LAFEW 'Fore God, I think so.

KING Go, call before me all the lords in court.
                              [*Exit Attendant.*]
Sit, my preserver, by thy patient's side,
And with this healthful hand, whose banished sense
50 Thou hast repealed, a second time receive
The confirmation of my promised gift,
Which but attends thy naming.

Enter three or four Lords.

Fair maid, send forth thine eye. This youthful parcel
Of noble bachelors stand at my bestowing,
55 O'er whom both sovereign power and father's voice
I have to use. Thy frank election make;
Thou hast power to choose, and they none to
        forsake.

HELENA To each of you one fair and virtuous mistress
Fall, when Love please! Marry, to each but one!

60 LAFEW I'd give bay curtal and his furniture,

---

42 **Dutchman** German   44 **coranto** lively dance   45 **Mor du vinager** death of
vinager (a meaningless pseudo-French oath)   50 **repealed** recalled from banishment   56 **frank election** free choice   60 **bay curtal and his furniture** my bay
horse with the docked tail, and his trappings

My mouth no more were broken than these boys',
And writ as little beard.

KING   Peruse them well:
Not one of those but had a noble father.

HELENA *(She addresses her to a lord.)* Gentlemen,
Heaven hath through me restored the King to
    health.   65

ALL We understand it, and thank heaven for you.

HELENA I am a simple maid, and therein wealthiest
That I protest I simply am a maid.
Please it your Majesty, I have done already.
The blushes in my cheeks thus whisper me,   70
"We blush that thou shouldst choose; but, be
    refused,
Let the white death sit on thy cheek forever,
We'll ne'er come there again"

KING   Make choice and see,
Who shuns thy love shuns all his love in me.

HELENA Now, Dian, from thy altar do I fly,   75
And to imperial Love, that god most high,
Do my sighs stream. *[To First Lord]* Sir, will you
    hear my suit?

FIRST LORD And grant it.

HELENA   Thanks, sir; all the rest is mute.

LAFEW I had rather be in this choice than throw ames-
ace for my life.   80

HELENA *[To Second Lord]* The honor, sir, that flames
    in your fair eyes,
Before I speak, too threateningly replies.
Love make your fortunes twenty times above
Her that so wishes and her humble love!

---

61 **broken** broken to the bit, i.e., tamed (?) missing some teeth (?)   62 **writ**
claimed (?)   79–80 **ames-ace** two aces, the lowest throw in dicing (the line is
ironical, as one might say I would rather be in this lottery than at death's door)

SECOND LORD No better, if you please.

85   HELENA   My wish receive,
       Which great Love grant; and so, I take my leave.

LAFEW Do all they deny her? And they were sons of
       mine, I'd have them whipped, or I would send them
       to th' Turk to make eunuchs of.

HELENA [*To Third Lord*] Be not afraid that I your
90   hand should take,
       I'll never do you wrong, for your own sake.
       Blessing upon your vows, and in your bed
       Find fairer fortune if you ever wed!

LAFEW These boys are boys of ice, they'll none have
95   her. Sure they are bastards to the English; the
       French ne'er got 'em.

HELENA [*To Fourth Lord*] You are too young, too
           happy, and too good,
       To make yourself a son out of my blood.

FOURTH LORD Fair one, I think not so.

100   LAFEW There's one grape yet. I am sure thy father
       drunk wine. But if thou be'st not an ass, I am a
       youth of fourteen; I have known thee already.

HELENA [*To Bertram*] I dare not say I take you, but
           I give
       Me and my service, ever whilst I live,
105   Into your guiding power. This is the man.

KING Why then, young Bertram, take her, she's thy
           wife.

BERTRAM My wife, my liege? I shall beseech your
           Highness,
       In such a business give me leave to use
       The help of mine own eyes.

---

87 **deny her** (Lafew, at a distance, does not understand that Helena denies the
men) 96 **got** begot 101 **drunk wine** i.e., was manly

KING   Know'st thou not, Bertram,
  What she has done for me?

BERTRAM   Yes, my good lord;   110
  But never hope to know why I should marry her.

KING Thou know'st she has raised me from my sickly
  bed.

BERTRAM But follows it, my lord, to bring me down
  Must answer for your raising? I know her well;
  She had her breeding at my father's charge: 115
  A poor physician's daughter my wife! Disdain
  Rather corrupt me ever!

KING 'Tis only title thou disdain'st in her, the which
  I can build up. Strange is it that our bloods,
  Of color, weight, and heat, poured all together,   120
  Would quite confound distinction, yet stands off
  In differences so mighty. If she be
  All that is virtuous, save what thou dislik'st—
  A poor physician's daughter—thou dislik'st
  Of virtue for the name. But do not so: 125
  From lowest place when virtuous things proceed,
  The place is dignified by th' doer's deed.
  Where great additions swell's and virtue none,
  It is a dropsied honor. Good alone
  Is good, without a name; vileness is so: 130
  The property by what it is should go,
  Not by the title. She is young, wise, fair;
  In these to nature she's immediate heir;
  And these breed honor. That is honor's scorn
  Which challenges itself as honor's born   135
  And is not like the sire. Honors thrive
  When rather from our acts we them derive
  Than our foregoers. The mere word's a slave,
  Deboshed on every tomb, on every grave

---

115 **breeding** upbringing   116–17 **Disdain ... ever** may my disdain of her ruin
me forever   128 **additions swell's** titles inflate us   131 **Property** quality (here,
"good" or "vileness")   135 **challenges ... born** claims honor by descent
139 **Deboshed** debauched, debased

140   A lying trophy, and as oft is dumb
       Where dust and damned oblivion is the tomb
       Of honored bones indeed. What should be said?
       If thou canst like this creature as a maid,
       I can create the rest. Virtue and she
145   Is her own dower; honor and wealth from me.

       BERTRAM I cannot love her, nor will strive to do't.

       KING Thou wrong'st thyself, if thou shouldst strive to
         choose.

       HELENA That you are well restored, my lord, I'm glad;
         Let the rest go.

150   KING My honor's at the stake, which to defeat,
       I must produce my power. Here, take her hand,
       Proud, scornful boy, unworthy this good gift,
       That dost in vile misprision shackle up
       My love and her desert; that canst not dream
155   We, poising us in her defective scale,
       Shall weigh thee to the beam; that wilt not know,
       It is in us to plant thine honor where
       We please to have it grow. Check thy contempt;
       Obey our will, which travails in thy good;
160   Believe not thy disdain, but presently
       Do thine own fortunes that obedient right
       Which both thy duty owes and our power claims;
       Or I will throw thee from my care forever
       Into the staggers and the careless lapse
165   Of youth and ignorance; both my revenge and hate,
       Loosing upon thee in the name of justice,
       Without all terms of pity. Speak. Thine answer.

       BERTRAM Pardon, my gracious lord; for I submit
         My fancy to your eyes. When I consider
170   What great creation and what dole of honor

150 at the stake (the figure is from bearbaiting; a bear was tied to a stake, and
dogs were set upon him)   153 misprision contempt (with pun on false imprisonment)   155–56 We ... beam i.e., my (royal "we") word added to Helena will
outweigh your objection   160 presently immediately   164 staggers giddiness
(disease of animals)   169 fancy love   170 dole portion

Flies where you bid it, I find that she, which late
Was in my nobler thoughts most base, is now
The praisèd of the King; who, so ennobled,
Is as 'twere born so.

KING   Take her by the hand,
And tell her she is thine; to whom I promise   175
A counterpoise, if not to thy estate,
A balance more replete.

BERTRAM   I take her hand.

KING Good fortune and the favor of the King
Smile upon this contract; whose ceremony
Shall seem expedient on the now-born brief,   180
And be performed tonight. The solemn feast
Shall more attend upon the coming space,
Expecting absent friends. As thou lov'st her,
Thy love's to me religious; else, does err.
                    Exeunt. Parolles and Lafew stay
                    behind, commenting of this wedding.

LAFEW Do you hear, monsieur? A word with you.   185

PAROLLES Your pleasure, sir?

LAFEW Your lord and master did well to make his recantation.

PAROLLES Recantation! My lord! My master!

LAFEW Ay; is it not a language I speak?   190

PAROLLES A most harsh one, and not to be understood
without bloody succeeding. My master!

LAFEW Are you companion to the Count Rousillon?

PAROLLES To any count, to all counts; to what is man.

176–77 **A counterpoise ... replete** i.e., a reward that, if it does not equal your
estate, will overweigh it (?) 180 **expedient** swift 180 **brief** royal edict
181–83 **The solemn ... friends** the ceremonious ("solemn") feast shall await
("attend") until absent friends arrive 192 **succeeding** consequences 194 **man**
manly (but Lafew gives it another sense, "servingman")

195   LAFEW To what is count's man; count's master is of
another style.

PAROLLES You are too old, sir; let it satisfy you, you
are too old.

LAFEW I must tell thee, sirrah, I write man; to which
200   title age cannot bring thee.

PAROLLES What I dare too well do, I dare not do.

LAFEW I did think thee, for two ordinaries, to be a
pretty wise fellow; thou didst make tolerable vent
of thy travel; it might pass. Yet the scarves and the
205   bannerets about thee did manifoldly dissuade me
from believing thee a vessel of too great a burden.
I have now found thee; when I lose thee again I
care not. Yet art thou good for nothing but taking
up, and that thou'rt scarce worth.

210   PAROLLES Hadst thou not the privilege of antiquity
upon thee—

LAFEW Do not plunge thyself too far in anger, lest
thou hasten thy trial; which if—Lord have mercy on
thee for a hen! So, my good window of lattice, fare
215   thee well; thy casement I need not open, for I look
through thee. Give me thy hand.

PAROLLES My lord, you give me most egregious indignity.

LAFEW Ay, with all my heart, and thou art worthy of
it.

220   PAROLLES I have not, my lord, deserved it.

LAFEW Yes, good faith, every dram of it, and I will
not bate thee a scruple.

PAROLLES Well, I shall be wiser.

---

202 **ordinaries** tavern meals   203 **vent** free talk   204 **scarves** (military men
wore scarves, usually over the shoulder; cp. the modern *fourragère*)   206 **burden**
capacity   207 **found thee** found you out   210 **antiquity** old age   222 **bate thee
a scruple** i.e., diminish by one drop what I have said of you

LAFEW Ev'n as soon as thou canst, for thou hast to
pull at a smack o' th' contrary. If ever thou be'st   225
bound in thy scarf and beaten, thou shall find what
it is to be proud of thy bondage. I have a desire to
hold my acquaintance with thee, or rather my
knowledge, that I may say, in the default, "He is
a man I know."   230

PAROLLES My lord, you do me most insupportable
vexation.

LAFEW I would it were hell-pains for thy sake, and
my poor doing eternal; for doing I am past, as I
will by thee, in what motion age will give me leave.   235
Exit.

PAROLLES Well, thou hast a son shall take this disgrace
off me; scurvy, old, filthy, scurvy lord! Well, I must
be patient, there is no fettering of authority. I'll
beat him, by my life, if I can meet him with any
convenience, and he were double and double a   240
lord. I'll have no more pity of his age than I would
have of—I'll beat him, and if I could but meet
him again.

Enter Lafew.

LAFEW Sirrah, your lord and master's married; there's
news for you; you have a new mistress.   245

PAROLLES I most unfeignedly beseech your lordship
to make some reservation of your wrongs. He is
my good lord; whom I serve above is my master.

LAFEW Who? God?

PAROLLES Ay, sir.   250

LAFEW The devil it is that's thy master. Why dost
thou garter up thy arms o' this fashion? Dost make
hose of thy sleeves? Do other servants so? Thou

225 **pull ... contrary** i.e., take a good taste of your folly   229 **in the default**
when you fail   234 **doing** (perhaps with the bawdy meaning, "copulating")
240 **convenience** advantage

wert best set thy lower part where thy nose stands.
By mine honor, if I were but two hours younger I'd
beat thee. Methink'st thou art a general offense,
and every man should beat thee. I think thou wast
created for men to breathe themselves upon thee.

PAROLLES This is hard and undeserved measure, my
lord.

LAFEW Go to, sir. You were beaten in Italy for picking a kernel out of a pom'granate. You are a
vagabond and no true traveler. You are more saucy
with lords and honorable personages than the commission of your birth and virtue gives you heraldry.
You are not worth another word, else I'd call you
knave. I leave you.   *Exit.*

Enter Bertram.

PAROLLES Good, very good, it is so then. Good, very
good, let it be concealed awhile.

BERTRAM Undone and forfeited to cares forever!

PAROLLES What's the matter, sweetheart?

BERTRAM Although before the solemn priest I have
sworn,
I will not bed her.

PAROLLES What, what, sweetheart?

BERTRAM O my Parolles, they have married me!
I'll to the Tuscan wars and never bed her.

PAROLLES France is a dog-hole, and it no more merits
The tread of a man's foot; to th' wars!

BERTRAM There's letters from my mother; what th'
import is,
I know not yet.

PAROLLES Ay, that would be known. To th' wars, my
boy, to th' wars!

258 breathe exercise

576

He wears his honor in a box unseen,
That hugs his kicky-wicky here at home,
Spending his manly marrow in her arms,
Which should sustain the bound and high curvet   285
Of Mars's fiery steed. To other regions!
France is a stable, we that dwell in't jades;
Therefore to th' war!

BERTRAM   It shall be so. I'll send her to my house,
Acquaint my mother with my hate to her,   290
And wherefore I am fled; write to the King
That which I durst not speak. His present gift
Shall furnish me to those Italian fields
Where noble fellows strike. Wars is no strife
To the dark house and the detested wife.   295

PAROLLES   Will this capriccio hold in thee, art sure?

BERTRAM   Go with me to my chamber and advise me.
I'll send her straight away. Tomorrow
I'll to the wars, she to her single sorrow.

PAROLLES   Why, these balls bound; there's noise in it.
'Tis hard;   300
A young man married is a man that's marred.
Therefore away, and leave her bravely; go.
The King has done you wrong; but hush 'tis so.
                              Exit [*with Bertram*].

---

283 **kicky-wicky** woman (but apparently an obscene term, perhaps from French *quelque chose*, "something," a euphemism for pudendum)   285 **curvet** prancing 287 **jades** nags   296 **capriccio** caprice (an affected Italian word)

[Scene IV. *Paris. The King's palace.*]

Enter Helena and Clown.

HELENA My mother greets me kindly. Is she well?

CLOWN She is not well, but yet she has her health; she's very merry, but yet she is not well. But thanks be given she's very well and wants nothing i' th' world; but yet she is not well.

HELENA If she be very well what does she ail that she's not very well?

CLOWN Truly, she's very well indeed, but for two things.

HELENA What two things?

CLOWN One, that she's not in heaven, whither God send her quickly; the other, that she's in earth, from whence God send her quickly.

Enter Parolles.

PAROLLES Bless you, my fortunate lady!

HELENA I hope, sir, I have your good will to have mine own good fortune.

PAROLLES You had my prayers to lead them on, and to keep them on have them still. O, my knave, how does my old lady?

CLOWN So that you had her wrinkles and I her money, I would she did as you say.

PAROLLES Why, I say nothing.

II.iv.1 **well** (in his reply, the Clown plays on the Elizabethan euphemism in which the dead are said to be well, ie., well-off, being in heaven)

CLOWN Marry, you are the wiser man; for many a
man's tongue shakes out his master's undoing. To
say nothing, to do nothing, to know nothing, and   25
to have nothing, is to be a great part of your
title—which is within a very little of nothing.

PAROLLES Away, th'art a knave.

CLOWN You should have said, sir, "Before a knave
th'art a knave"; that's "Before me, th'art a   30
knave." This had been truth, sir.

PAROLLES Go to, thou art a witty fool; I have found
thee.

CLOWN Did you find me in yourself, sir, or were you
taught to find me? The search, sir, was profitable;   35
and much fool may you find in you, even to the
world's pleasure and the increase of laughter.

PAROLLES A good knave, i' faith, and well fed.
Madam, my lord will go away tonight,
A very serious business calls on him.   40
The great prerogative and rite of love,
Which as your due time claims, he does
   acknowledge,
But puts it off to a compelled restraint;
Whose want, and whose delay, is strewed with
   sweets,
Which they distil now in the curbèd time,   45
To make the coming hour o'erflow with joy,
And pleasure drown the brim.

HELENA   What's his will else?

PAROLLES That you will take your instant leave o' th'
   King,
And make this haste as your own good proceeding,

27 title possession   30 before me (punning on the sense "on my soul")
34 in by   45 curbèd time delay (?) time spent in the confining still (?)   49 as
your own good proceeding as if it originated from you

579

50   Strength'ned with what apology you think
      May make it probable need.

HELENA   What more commands he?

PAROLLES That, having this obtained, you presently
      Attend his further pleasure.

HELENA In everything I wait upon his will.

55   PAROLLES I shall report it so.   *Exit Parolles.*

HELENA I pray you. Come, sirrah.   *Exit [with Clown].*

[Scene V. *Paris. The King's palace.*]

Enter Lafew and Bertram.

LAFEW But I hope your lordship think not him a
      soldier.

BERTRAM Yes, my lord, and of very valiant approof.

LAFEW You have it from his own deliverance.

5   BERTRAM And by other warranted testimony.

LAFEW Then my dial goes not true; I took this lark
      for a bunting.

BERTRAM I do assure you, my lord, he is very great in
      knowledge, and accordingly valiant.

II.v.3 **very valiant approof** great proven valor 4 **deliverance** speech
6-7 **took this lark for a bunting** i.e., underestimated him

LAFEW I have then sinned against his experience and   10
transgressed against his valor; and my state that
way is dangerous, since I cannot yet find in my
heart to repent. Here he comes. I pray you make
us friends; I will pursue the amity.

Enter Parolles.

PAROLLES [*To Bertram*] These things shall be done, sir.   15

LAFEW Pray you, sir, who's his tailor?

PAROLLES Sir?

LAFEW O, I know him well. Ay sir, he, sir, 's a good
workman, a very good tailor.

BERTRAM [*Aside to Parolles*] Is she gone to the King?   20

PAROLLES She is.

BERTRAM Will she away tonight?

PAROLLES As you'll have her.

BERTRAM I have writ my letters, casketed my treasure,
Given order for our horses; and tonight,   25
When I should take possession of the bride,
End ere I do begin.

LAFEW [*Aside*] A good traveler is something at the
latter end of a dinner, but one that lies three thirds
and uses a known truth to pass a thousand noth-   30
ings with, should be once heard and thrice beaten.
[*Aloud*] God save you, Captain.

BERTRAM Is there any unkindness between my lord
and you, monsieur?

PAROLLES I know not how I have deserved to run into   35
my lord's displeasure.

LAFEW You have made shift to run into't, boots and
spurs and all, like him that leaped into the custard;

37 **made shift** managed

581

40   and out of it you'll run again rather than suffer
question for your residence.

BERTRAM It may be you have mistaken him, my lord.

LAFEW And shall do so ever, though I took him at's
prayers. Fare you well, my lord, and believe this of
me, there can be no kernel in this light nut; the
45   soul of this man is his clothes. Trust him not in
matter of heavy consequence; I have kept of them
tame and know their natures. Farewell, monsieur;
I have spoken better of you than you have or will
to deserve at my hand, but we must do good against
50   evil.   [*Exit.*]

PAROLLES An idle lord, I swear.

BERTRAM I think not so.

PAROLLES Why, do you not know him?

BERTRAM Yes, I do know him well, and common
speech
55   Gives him a worthy pass. Here comes my clog.

Enter Helena.

HELENA I have, sir, as I was commanded from you,
Spoke with the King, and have procured his leave
For present parting; only he desires
Some private speech with you.

BERTRAM   I shall obey his will.
60   You must not marvel, Helen, at my course,
Which holds not color with the time, nor does
The ministration and required office
On my particular. Prepared I was not
For such a business; therefore am I found
65   So much unsettled. This drives me to entreat you

39-40 **suffer question for your residence** put up with questions on why you are
there   46-47 **kept of them tame** had some of them as pets   51 **idle** foolish
55 **pass** reputation   61 **holds not color with the time** does not match the
situation

That presently you take your way for home,
And rather muse than ask why I entreat you,
For my respects are better than they seem,
And my appointments have in them a need
Greater than shows itself at the first view   70
To you that know them not. [*Gives a letter.*] This
    to my mother.
'Twill be two days ere I shall see you, so
I leave you to your wisdom.

HELENA   Sir, I can nothing say
But that I am your most obedient servant.

BERTRAM Come, come; no more of that.

HELENA   And ever shall   75
With true observance seek to eke out that
Wherein toward me my homely stars have failed
To equal my great fortune.

BERTRAM   Let that go:
My haste is very great. Farewell; hie home.

HELENA Pray sir, your pardon.

BERTRAM   Well, what would you say?   80

HELENA I am not worthy of the wealth I owe,
    Nor dare I say 'tis mine—and yet it is;
    But like a timorous thief most fain would steal
    What law does vouch mine own.

BERTRAM   What would you have?

HELENA Something, and scarce so much: nothing, in-
    deed.   85
    I would not tell you what I would, my lord.
    Faith, yes—
    Strangers and foes do sunder and not kiss.

---

68 **respects** reasons   ⸂69 **appointments** purposes   76 **observance** dutiful service
77 **homely stars** fate of low birth   81 **owe** own

BERTRAM I pray you, stay not, but in haste to horse.

90 HELENA I shall not break your bidding, good my lord.
Where are my other men? Monsieur, farewell.

Exit.

BERTRAM Go thou toward home, where I will never come
Whilst I can shake my sword or hear the drum.
Away, and for our flight.

PAROLLES   Bravely, coragio!

[*Exeunt.*]

94 **coragio** courage (Italian)

ACT III

[Scene I. *Florence. The Duke's palace.*]

Flourish. Enter the Duke of Florence, the two Frenchmen, with a troop of Soldiers.

DUKE So that from point to point now have you heard
The fundamental reasons of this war,
Whose great decision hath much blood let forth,
And more thirsts after.

FIRST LORD   Holy seems the quarrel
Upon your Grace's part; black and fearful   5
On the opposer.

DUKE Therefore we marvel much our cousin France
Would in so just a business shut his bosom
Against our borrowing prayers.

SECOND LORD   Good my lord,
The reasons of our state I cannot yield,   10

III.i.10 **yield** produce

585

But like a common and an outward man
That the great figure of a council frames
By self-unable motion; therefore dare not
Say what I think of it, since I have found
15   Myself in my incertain grounds to fail
As often as I guessed.

DUKE   Be it his pleasure.

FIRST LORD But I am sure the younger of our nature,
That surfeit on their ease, will day by day
Come here for physic.

DUKE   Welcome shall they be;
20   And all the honors that can fly from us
Shall on them settle. You know your places well;
When better fall, for your avails they fell:
Tomorrow to the field!   *Flourish; [exeunt].*

[Scene II. *Rousillon. The Count's palace.*]

Enter Countess and Clown.

COUNTESS It hath happened all as I would have had
it, save that he comes not along with her.

CLOWN By my troth, I take my young lord to be a
very melancholy man.

5   COUNTESS By what observance, I pray you?

---

13 **self-unable** **motion** impotent guess 18 **surfeit on** grow sick from
22 **When ... fell** when better places fall vacant, for you they will have fallen
III.ii.3 **troth** truth

CLOWN Why, he will look upon his boot and sing, mend the ruff and sing, ask questions and sing, pick his teeth and sing. I know a man that had this trick of melancholy sold a goodly manor for a song.

COUNTESS Let me see what he writes, and when he 10 means to come.   [*Reads a letter.*]

CLOWN I have no mind to Isbel, since I was at court. Our old lings and our Isbels o' th' country are nothing like your old ling and your Isbels o' th' court. The brains of my Cupid's knocked out, and 15 I begin to love as an old man loves money, with no stomach.

COUNTESS What have we here?

CLOWN E'en that you have there.   *Exit.*

COUNTESS [*Reads*] *a letter.* "I have sent you a 20 daughter-in-law. She hath recovered the King, and undone me. I have wedded her, not bedded her, and sworn to make the 'not' eternal. You shall hear I am run away; know it before the report come. If there be breadth enough in the world, I 25 will hold a long distance. My duty to you.
                         Your unfortunate son,
                              Bertram."
This is not well, rash and unbridled boy,
To fly the favors of so good a king,   30
To pluck his indignation on thy head
By the misprizing of a maid too virtuous
For the contempt of empire.

                    Enter Clown.

CLOWN O madam, yonder is heavy news within, between two soldiers and my young lady.   35

COUNTESS What is the matter?

CLOWN Nay, there is some comfort in the news, some

13 **lings** salt cod (but also with the sense of "lecherous men")   17 **stomach** appetite
23 **not** (with pun on "knot," the symbol of marriage)   32 **misprizing** despising

comfort; your son will not be killed so soon as I thought he would.

40 COUNTESS Why should he be killed?

CLOWN So say I, madam, if he run away, as I hear he does. The danger is in standing to't; that's the loss of men, though it be the getting of children. Here they come will tell you more. For my part, I only hear your son was run away.

45

Enter Helena and two [French] Gentlemen.

FIRST LORD Save you, good madam.

HELENA Madam, my lord is gone, forever gone.

SECOND LORD Do not say so.

COUNTESS Think upon patience. Pray you, gentlemen,
50   I have felt so many quirks of joy and grief,
That the first face of neither, on the start,
Can woman me unto't. Where is my son, I pray
    you?

SECOND LORD Madam, he's gone to serve the Duke
    of Florence.
We met him thitherward, for thence we came,
55   And, after some dispatch in hand at court,
Thither we bend again.

HELENA Look on his letter, madam, here's my
    passport.
[*Reads*] "When thou canst get the ring upon my finger, which never shall come off, and show me a
60 child begotten of thy body that I am father to, then call me husband; but in such a 'then' I write a 'never.' " This is a dreadful sentence.

COUNTESS Brought you this letter, gentlemen?

---

42 **standing to't** (1) standing one's ground (2) having sexual intercourse
52 **woman me** make me weep   57 **passport** license to wander as a beggar

FIRST LORD Ay, madam, and for the contents' sake are
    sorry for our pains.   65

COUNTESS I prithee, lady, have a better cheer.
    If thou engrossest all the griefs are thine,
    Thou robb'st me of a moiety. He was my son,
    But I do wash his name out of my blood
    And thou art all my child. Towards Florence is he?   70

SECOND LORD Ay, madam.

COUNTESS   And to be a soldier?

SECOND LORD Such is his noble purpose, and,
    believe't,
    The Duke will lay upon him all the honor
    That good convenience claims.

COUNTESS   Return you thither?

FIRST LORD Ay, madam, with the swiftest wing of
    speed.   75

HELENA [*Reads*] "Till I have no wife, I have nothing
    in France."
    'Tis bitter.

COUNTESS   Find you that there?

HELENA   Ay, madam.

FIRST LORD 'Tis but the boldness of his hand, haply,
    which his heart was not consenting to.   80

COUNTESS Nothing in France, until he have no wife!
    There's nothing here that is too good for him
    But only she, and she deserves a lord
    That twenty such rude boys might tend upon
    And call her, hourly, mistress. Who was with him?   85

FIRST LORD A servant only, and a gentleman which
    I have sometime known.

COUNTESS Parolles, was it not?

67 **thou engrossest**, you monopolize   68 **moiety** share   74 **convenience** propriety   79 **haply** perhaps

FIRST LORD Ay, my good lady, he.

COUNTESS A very tainted fellow, and full of
90   wickedness.
    My son corrupts a well-derivèd nature
    With his inducement.

FIRST LORD   Indeed, good lady,
    The fellow has a deal of that too much,
    Which holds him much to have.

95 COUNTESS Y'are welcome, gentlemen.
    I will entreat you, when you see my son,
    To tell him that his sword can never win
    The honor that he loses; more I'll entreat you
    Written to bear along.

SECOND LORD   We serve you, madam,
100   In that and all your worthiest affairs.

COUNTESS Not so, but as we change our courtesies.
    Will you draw near?   *Exit* [*with Lords and Clown*].

HELENA "Till I have no wife, I have nothing in
        France."
105   Nothing in France until he has no wife!
    Thou shalt have none, Rousillon, none in France;
    Then hast thou all again. Poor lord! Is't I
    That chase thee from thy country and expose
    Those tender limbs of thine to the event
110   Of the none-sparing war? And is it I
    That drive thee from the sportive court, where thou
    Wast shot at with fair eyes, to be the mark
    Of smoky muskets? O you leaden messengers,
    That ride upon the violent speed of fire,
115   Fly with false aim, move the still-piecing air
    That sings with piercing; do not touch my lord!

92 **his inducement** i.e., Parolles' influence 94 **holds** profits 101 **Not ...
courtesies** no, you may serve me only if I may serve you (a courteous reply)
106 **Rousillon** Bertram, Count of Rousillon 109 **event** outcome 115 **still-
piecing** ever-repairing

Whoever shoots at him, I set him there.
Whoever charges on his forward breast,
I am the caitiff that do hold him to't.
And though I kill him not I am the cause   120
His death was so effected. Better 'twere
I met the ravin lion when he roared
With sharp constraint of hunger; better 'twere
That all the miseries which nature owes
Were mine at once. No; come thou home, Rousillon.   125
Whence honor but of danger wins a scar,
As oft it loses all. I will be gone;
My being here it is that holds thee hence.
Shall I stay here to do't? No, no, although
The air of paradise did fan the house   130
And angels officed all. I will be gone,
That pitiful rumor may report my flight
To consolate thine ear. Come night, end day;
For with the dark, poor thief, I'll steal away.   *Exit.*

[Scene III. *Florence.*]

Flourish. Enter the Duke of Florence, Bertram,
Drum and Trumpets, Soldiers, Parolles.

DUKE The general of our horse thou art, and we,
    Great in our hope, lay our best love and credence
    Upon thy promising fortune.

119 caitiff wretch 122 ravin ravenous 124 owes owns, has 126–27 Whence
... all from where honor at best gains from danger a scar, and may lose everything
131 officed served III.iii.2 lay wager

BERTRAM   Sir, it is
    A charge too heavy for my strength; but yet
5   We'll strive to bear it for your worthy sake
    To th' extreme edge of hazard.

DUKE   Then go thou forth,
    And fortune play upon thy prosperous helm,
    As thy auspicious mistress!

BERTRAM   This very day,
    Great Mars, I put myself into thy file!
10   Make me but like my thoughts and I shall prove
    A lover of thy drum, hater of love.   *Exeunt omnes.*

[Scene IV. *Rousillon. The Count's palace.*]

Enter Countess and Steward.

COUNTESS Alas! And would you take the letter of her?
    Might you not know she would do as she has done,
    By sending me a letter? Read it again.

[*Steward reads the*] *letter.* "I am Saint Jaques' pilgrim,
    thither gone.
5   Ambitious love hath so in me offended
    That barefoot plod I the cold ground upon,
    With sainted vow my faults to have amended.
    Write, write, that from the bloody course of war
    My dearest master, your dear son, may hie.
10   Bless him at home in peace, whilst I from far
    His name with zealous fervor sanctify.

7 **helm** helmet   III.iv.4 **Saint Jaques' pilgrim** making a pilgrimage to St James's shrine (at Compostela, in Spain; "Jaques" is disyllabic; Já kis)   9 **hie** hurry

His taken labors bid him me forgive;
I, his despiteful Juno, sent him forth
From courtly friends with camping foes to live,
Where death and danger dogs the heels of worth.   15
He is too good and fair for death and me,
Whom I myself embrace to set him free."

[COUNTESS] Ah, what sharp stings are in her
    mildest words!
Rinaldo, you did never lack advice so much
As letting her pass so; had I spoke with her,   20
I could have well diverted her intents,
Which thus she hath prevented.

STEWARD   Pardon me, madam.
If I had given you this at overnight,
She might have been o'erta'en; and yet she writes,
Pursuit would be but vain.

COUNTESS   What angel shall   25
Bless this unworthy husband? He cannot thrive,
Unless her prayers, whom heaven delights to hear
And loves to grant, reprieve him from the wrath
Of greatest justice. Write, write, Rinaldo,
To this unworthy husband of his wife;   30
Let every word weigh heavy of her worth
That he does weigh too light. My greatest grief,
Though little he do feel it, set down sharply.
Dispatch the most convenient messenger.
When haply he shall hear that she is gone,   35
He will return; and hope I may that she,
Hearing so much, will speed her foot again,
Led hither by pure love. Which of them both
Is dearest to me, I have no skill in sense
To make distinction. Provide this messenger.   40
My heart is heavy and mine age is weak;
Grief would have tears, and sorrow bids me speak.
                                        Exeunt.

12 **taken** undertaken   13 **despiteful Juno** (alluding to Juno's persecution of
Hercules, on whom she imposed the legendary twelve labors)   17 **Whom … him**
i.e., Death … Bertram   19 **advice** discretion   23 **at overnight** last night

[Scene V. *Outside Florence.*]

A tucket afar off. Enter old Widow of Florence, her
daughter [Diana], and Mariana, with other citizens.

WIDOW Nay come, for if they do approach the city,
we shall lose all the sight.

DIANA They say the French count has done most
honorable service.

5   WIDOW It is reported that he has taken their great'st
commander, and that with his own hand he slew
the Duke's brother. [*Tucket.*] We have lost our
labor; they are gone a contrary way. Hark! You
may know by their trumpets.

10   MARIANA Come, let's return again, and suffice ourselves with the report of it. Well, Diana, take heed
of this French earl. The honor of a maid is her
name, and no legacy is so rich as honesty.

WIDOW I have told my neighbor how you have been
15   solicited by a gentleman his companion.

MARIANA I know that knave, hang him, one Parolles;
a filthy officer he is in those suggestions for the
young earl. Beware of them, Diana: their promises,
enticements, oaths, tokens, and all these engines
20   of lust, are not the things they go under; many a
maid hath been seduced by them. And the misery
is, example, that so terrible shows in the wrack of
maidenhood, cannot for all that dissuade succes-

III.v.s.d. **tucket** trumpet call heralding the approach of an important person
13 **honesty** chastity· 19 **engines** devices 20 **go under** masquerade as 23-24 **dis-**
suade succession prevent others from following

sion, but that they are limed with the twigs that
threatens them. I hope I need not to advise you   25
further, but I hope your own grace will keep you
where you are, though there were no further danger
known but the modesty which is so lost.

DIANA You shall not need to fear me.

Enter Helena, [disguised as a pilgrim].

WIDOW I hope so. Look, here comes a pilgrim. I   30
know she will lie at my house; thither they send
one another. I'll question her. God save you, pilgrim! Whither are you bound?

HELENA To Saint Jaques le Grand.
Where do the palmers lodge, I do beseech you?   35

WIDOW At the Saint Francis here beside the port.

HELENA Is this the way?

WIDOW Ay, marry, is't. (*A march afar.*) Hark you!
    They come this way.
If you will tarry, holy pilgrim,
But till the troops come by,   40
I will conduct you where you shall be lodged;
The rather for I think I know your hostess
As ample as myself.

HELENA   Is it yourself?

WIDOW If you shall please so, pilgrim.

HELENA I thank you, and will stay upon your leisure.   45

WIDOW You came, I think, from France?

HELENA   I did so.

WIDOW Here you shall see a countryman of yours
    That has done worthy service.

---

24 **limed** caught (as by birdlime, a sticky substance smeared on twigs to trap
birds) 31 **lie** lodge 35 **palmers** pilgrims 36 **port** city gate 43 **ample**
well 45 **stay upon your leisure** wait until convenient for you

HELENA   His name, I pray you.

DIANA   The Count Rousillon. Know you such a one?

50   HELENA But by the ear, that hears most nobly of him;
      His face I know not.

DIANA   Whatsome'er he is,
      He's bravely taken here. He stole from France,
      As 'tis reported, for the King had married him
      Against his liking. Think you it is so?

55   HELENA Ay, surely, mere the truth. I know his lady.

DIANA   There is a gentleman that serves the Count
      Reports but coarsely of her.

HELENA   What's his name?

DIANA   Monsieur Parolles.

HELENA   O, I believe with him,
      In argument of praise, or to the worth
60   Of the great Count himself, she is too mean
      To have her name repeated; all her deserving
      Is a reservèd honesty, and that
      I have not heard examined.

DIANA   Alas, poor lady!
      'Tis a hard bondage to become the wife
65   Of a detesting lord.

WIDOW I warrant, good creature, wheresoe'er she is,
      Her heart weighs sadly. This young maid might do
      her
      A shrewd turn, if she pleased.

HELENA   How do you mean?
      Maybe the amorous Count solicits her
      In the unlawful purpose.

70   WIDOW   He does indeed,

52 **bravely taken** well esteemed   55 **mere** absolutely   62 **reservèd honesty**
preserved chastity   68 **shrewd turn** nasty deed (with sexual implication in
"turn")

And brokes with all that can in such a suit
Corrupt the tender honor of a maid;
But she is armed for him, and keeps her guard
In honestest defense.

MARIANA   The gods forbid else!

Drum and colors. Enter Bertram, Parolles, and
the whole army.

WIDOW So, now they come.   75
That is Antonio, the Duke's eldest son;
That, Escalus.

HELENA   Which is the Frenchman?

DIANA   He—
That with the plume; 'tis a most gallant fellow.
I would he loved his wife. If he were honester
He were much goodlier. Is't not a handsome
gentleman?   80

HELENA I like him well.

DIANA 'Tis pity he is not honest. Yond's that same
knave
That leads him to these places. Were I his lady
I would poison that vile rascal.

HELENA   Which is he?

DIANA That jackanapes with scarves. Why is he
melancholy?   85

HELENA Perchance he's hurt i' th' battle.

PAROLLES Lose our drum! Well.

MARIANA He's shrewdly vexed at something. Look,
he has spied us.

WIDOW Marry, hang you!   90

MARIANA And your curtsy, for a ring-carrier!
                Exit [Bertram, with Parolles and the army].

71 **brokes** bargains   88 **shrewdly** bitterly   91 **ring-carrier** bawd

WIDOW The troop is past. Come, pilgrim, I will bring
    you
    Where you shall host; of enjoined penitents
    There's four or five, to great Saint Jaques bound,
    Already at my house.

95 HELENA   I humbly thank you.
    Please it this matron and this gentle maid
    To eat with us tonight, the charge and thanking
    Shall be for me; and, to requite you further,
    I will bestow some precepts of this virgin
    Worthy the note.

100 BOTH   We'll take your offer kindly.

Exeunt.

[Scene VI. *The Florentine camp.*]

Enter Bertram and the [two] Frenchmen, as at
first.

FIRST LORD Nay, good my lord, put him to't; let him
    have his way.

SECOND LORD If your lordship find him not a hilding,
    hold me no more in your respect.

5 FIRST LORD On my life, my lord, a bubble.

BERTRAM Do you think I am so far deceived in him?

FIRST LORD Believe it, my lord, in mine own direct

---

93 host lodge 93 enjoined bound by oath 99 of on III.vi.1 put him to't test
him 3 hilding worthless fellow

knowledge, without any malice, but to speak of him
as my kinsman, he's a most notable coward, an
infinite and endless liar, an hourly promise-breaker,   10
the owner of no one good quality worthy your lordship's entertainment.

SECOND LORD It were fit you knew him, lest reposing
too far in his virtue which he hath not, he might at
some great and trusty business in a main danger   15
fail you.

BERTRAM I would I knew in what particular action to
try him.

SECOND LORD None better than to let him fetch off his
drum, which you hear him so confidently under-   20
take to do.

FIRST LORD I, with a troop of Florentines, will suddenly surprise him; such I will have whom I am
sure he knows not from the enemy. We will bind
and hoodwink him so, that he shall suppose no   25
other but that he is carried into the leaguer of the
adversaries when we bring him to our own tents.
Be but your lordship present at his examination;
if he do not for the promise of his life and in the
highest compulsion of base fear offer to betray you   30
and deliver all the intelligence in his power against
you, and that with the divine forfeit of his soul
upon oath, never trust my judgment in anything.

SECOND LORD O, for the love of laughter, let him fetch
his drum. He says he has a stratagem for't. When   35
your lordship sees the bottom of his success in't,
and to what metal this counterfeit lump of ore will
be melted, if you give him not John Drum's entertainment your inclining cannot be removed. Here
he comes.   40

9 as my kinsman i.e., impartially   12 entertainment maintenance   19-20 fetch
off his drum recapture his drum (the loss of the drum was a military disgrace)
25 hoodwink blindfold   26 leaguer camp   31 intelligence information
38-39 John Drum's entertainment manhandling

Enter Parolles.

FIRST LORD O, for the love of laughter, hinder not the honor of his design; let him fetch off his drum in any hand.

BERTRAM How now, monsieur! This drum sticks sorely
45 in your disposition.

SECOND LORD A pox on't, let it go, 'tis but a drum.

PAROLLES "But a drum!" Is't "but a drum"? A drum so lost! There was excellent command: to charge in with our horse upon our own wings, and to rend
50 our own soldiers!

SECOND LORD That was not to be blamed in the command of the service; it was a disaster of war that Caesar himself could not have prevented if he had been there to command.

55 BERTRAM Well, we cannot greatly condemn our success; some dishonor we had in the loss of that drum, but it is not to be recovered.

PAROLLES It might have been recovered.

BERTRAM It might, but it is not now.

60 PAROLLES It is to be recovered. But that the merit of service is seldom attributed to the true and exact performer, I would have that drum or another, or *hic jacet*.

BERTRAM Why, if you have a stomach, to't, monsieur.
65 If you think your mystery in stratagem can bring this instrument of honor again into his native quarter, be magnanimous in the enterprise, and go on; I will grace the attempt for a worthy exploit. If you speed well in it, the Duke shall both speak of it
70 and extend to you what further becomes his great-

46 pox plague (literally, syphilis) 55-56 success outcome, fortune (either good or bad) 63 hic jacet here lies (Latin, beginning an epitaph) 64 stomach appetite 65 mystery art, skill 69 speed prosper

ness, even to the utmost syllable of your worthiness.

PAROLLES By the hand of a soldier, I will undertake it.

BERTRAM But you must not now slumber in it.

PAROLLES I'll about it this evening, and I will presently 75
pen down my dilemmas, encourage myself in my
certainty, put myself into my mortal preparation;
and by midnight look to hear further from me.

BERTRAM May I be bold to acquaint his Grace you
are gone about it? 80

PAROLLES I know not what the success will be, my
lord, but the attempt I vow.

BERTRAM I know, th'art valiant; and to the possibility of thy soldiership will subscribe for thee. Farewell. 85

PAROLLES I love not many words. *Exit.*

FIRST LORD No more than a fish loves water. Is not
this a strange fellow, my lord, that so confidently
seems to undertake this business, which he knows
is not to be done, damns himself to do, and dares 90
better be damned than to do't.

SECOND LORD You do not know him, my lord, as we
do. Certain it is that he will steal himself into a
man's favor and for a week escape a great deal of
discoveries, but when you find him out you have 95
him ever after.

BERTRAM Why, do you think he will make no deed at
all of this that so seriously he does address himself
unto?

FIRST LORD None in the world, but return with an in- 100
vention, and clap upon you two or three probable
lies; but we have almost embossed him. You shall

76 dilemmas arguments 77 my mortal preparation preparation for my
death (?) my weapons for killing (?) 83–84 possibility capacity 102 embossed
him exhausted him (hunting term)

see his fall tonight, for indeed he is not for your
lordship's respect.

105 SECOND LORD We'll make you some sport with the fox
ere we case him. He was first smoked by the old
lord Lafew. When his disguise and he is parted, tell
me what a sprat you shall find him; which you
shall see this very night.

110 FIRST LORD I must go look my twigs; he shall be
caught.

BERTRAM Your brother, he shall go along with me.

FIRST LORD As't please your lordship: I'll leave you.

Exit.

BERTRAM Now will I lead you to the house and show
you
The lass I spoke of.

115 SECOND LORD   But you say she's honest.

BERTRAM That's all the fault. I spoke with her but
once,
And found her wondrous cold, but I sent to her,
By this same coxcomb that we have i' th' wind,
Tokens and letters which she did re-send,
120   And this is all I have done. She's a fair creature;
Will you go see her?

SECOND LORD   With all my heart, my lord.

Exeunt.

106 **case** skin   106 **smoked** exposed (like a fox smoked out)   108 **sprat** small
fish   118 **have i' th' wind** are hunting

[Scene VII. *Florence. The Widow's house.*]

Enter Helena and Widow.

HELENA If you misdoubt me that I am not she,
  I know not how I shall assure you further,
  But I shall lose the grounds I work upon.

WIDOW Though my estate be fall'n, I was well born,   5
  Nothing acquainted with these businesses,
  And would not put my reputation now
  In any staining act.

HELENA   Nor would I wish you.
  First give me trust the Count he is my husband,
  And what to your sworn counsel I have spoken
  Is so from word to word; and then you cannot,   10
  By the good aid that I of you shall borrow,
  Err in bestowing it.

WIDOW   I should believe you,
  For you have showed me that which well approves
   Y'are great in fortune.

HELENA   Take this purse of gold,
  And let me buy your friendly help thus far,   15
  Which I will over-pay and pay again
  When I have found it. The Count he woos your
    daughter,
  Lays down his wanton siege before her beauty,
  Resolved to carry her; let her in fine consent
  As we'll direct her how 'tis best to bear it.   20
  Now his important blood will nought deny
  That she'll demand; a ring the County wears,

III.vii.3 **But ... upon** i.e., unless ("But") I reveal myself to Bertram   9 **to ...
spoken** I have confided to you, upon your oath of secrecy   19 **carry** conquer
19 **in fine** finally   21 **important** importunate, pressing   22 **County** Count

That downward hath succeeded in his house
From son to son some four or five descents
25 Since the first father wore it. This ring he holds
In most rich choice; yet, in his idle fire,
To buy his will it would not seem too dear,
Howe'er repented after.

WIDOW   Now I see
The bottom of your purpose.

30 HELENA You see it lawful then. It is no more
But that your daughter, ere she seems as won,
Desires this ring; appoints him an encounter;
In fine, delivers me to fill the time,
Herself most chastely absent. After,
35 To marry her I'll add three thousand crowns
To what is passed already.

WIDOW   I have yielded.
Instruct my daughter how she shall persever
That time and place with this deceit so lawful
May prove coherent. Every night he comes
40 With musics of all sorts, and songs composed
To her unworthiness. It nothing steads us
To chide him from our eaves, for he persists
As if his life lay on't.

HELENA   Why then tonight
Let us assay our plot, which, if it speed,
45 Is wicked meaning in a lawful deed,
And lawful meaning in a lawful act,
Where both not sin, and yet a sinful fact.
But let's about it.   [*Exeunt.*]

---

27 **will** lust 35 **To marry her** i.e., as a dowry to help her marry 37 **persever**
(accent on second syllable) 39 **coherent** in accordance 41 **steads** helps
44 **speed** prosper 45 **meaning** intention (the point of this passage is that
Bertram's intention is wicked, though his deed—copulating with his wife—will be
lawful; Helena's intention and her act will be good, and the deed will not be a sin
though in Bertram's mind he will be sinning)

ACT IV

[Scene I. *Outside the Florentine camp.*]

*Enter one of the Frenchmen, with five or six
other Soldiers in ambush.*

FIRST LORD He can come no other way but by this
hedge-corner. When you sally upon him, speak
what terrible language you will; though you understand it not yourselves, no matter; for we must not
seem to understand him, unless someone among us   5
whom we must produce for an interpreter.

FIRST SOLDIER Good captain, let me be th' interpreter.

FIRST LORD Art not acquainted with him? Knows he
not thy voice?

FIRST SOLDIER No sir, I warrant you.   10

FIRST LORD But what linsey-woolsey hast thou to
speak to us again?

IV.i.11 **linsey-woolsey** nonsense (literally a coarse fabric of linen and wool)

FIRST SOLDIER E'en such as you speak to me.

FIRST LORD He must think us some band of strangers
15 i' th' adversary's entertainment. Now he hath a
smack of all neighboring languages; therefore we
must everyone be a man of his own fancy, not to
know what we speak one to another; so we seem
to know is to know straight our purpose; choughs'
20 language, gabble enough and good enough. As for
you, interpreter, you must seem very politic. But
couch, ho! Here he comes to beguile two hours in
a sleep, and then to return and swear the lies he
forges.

Enter Parolles.

25 PAROLLES Ten o'clock. Within these three hours 'twill
be time enough to go home. What shall I say I have
done? It must be a very plausive invention that
carries it. They begin to smoke me, and disgraces
have of late knocked too often at my door. I find
30 my tongue is too foolhardy, but my heart hath the
fear of Mars before it and of his creatures, not
daring the reports of my tongue.

FIRST LORD [*Aside*] This is the first truth that e'er
thine own tongue was guilty of.

35 PAROLLES What the devil should move me to undertake the recovery of this drum, being not ignorant
of the impossibility, and knowing I had no such
purpose? I must give myself some hurts, and say
I got them in exploit. Yet slight ones will not carry
40 it. They will say, "Came you off with so little?"
And great ones I dare not give. Wherefore, what's
the instance? Tongue, I must put you into a butter-
woman's mouth, and buy myself another of Bajazet's mule if you prattle me into these perils.

---

14 **strangers** foreigners 19 **choughs'** jackdaws' 27 **plausive** plausible
42-43 **butter-woman's** i.e., shrill-voiced woman's 43-44 **Bajazet's mule**
(mules were proverbial for muteness, but "Bajazet" is inexplicable)

FIRST LORD [*Aside*] Is it possible he should know what   45
he is, and be that he is?

PAROLLES I would the cutting of my garments would
serve the turn, or the breaking of my Spanish sword.

FIRST LORD [*Aside*] We cannot afford you so.

PAROLLES Or the baring of my beard, and to say it was   50
in stratagem.

FIRST LORD [*Aside*] 'Twould not do.

PAROLLES Or to drown my clothes, and say I was
stripped.

FIRST LORD [*Aside*] Hardly serve.   55

PAROLLES Though I swore I leaped from the window
of the citadel—

FIRST LORD [*Aside*] How deep?

PAROLLES Thirty fathom.

FIRST LORD [*Aside*] Three great oaths would scarce   60
make that be believed.

PAROLLES I would I had any drum of the enemy's; I
would swear I recovered it.

FIRST LORD [*Aside*] You shall hear one anon.

PAROLLES A drum now of the enemy's—   65
Alarum within.

FIRST LORD *Throca movousus, cargo, cargo, cargo.*

ALL *Cargo, cargo, cargo, villianda par corbo, cargo.*

PAROLLES O, ransom, ransom! Do not hide mine eyes.
[*They blindfold him.*]

INTERPRETER *Boskos thromuldo boskos.*

PAROLLES I know you are the Muskos' regiment,   70
And I shall lose my life for want of language.

49 **afford you so** let you off thus   64 **anon** soon   65 s.d. **Alarum** call to arms

If there be here German, or Dane, low Dutch,
Italian, or French, let him speak to me,
I'll discover that which shall undo the Florentine.

75   INTERPRETER *Boskos vauvado*. I understand thee, and
can speak thy tongue. *Kerelybonto*. Sir, betake thee
to thy faith, for seventeen poniards are at thy
bosom.

PAROLLES O!

80   INTERPRETER O, pray, pray, pray! *Manka revania
dulche*.

FIRST LORD *Oscorbidulchos volivorco*.

INTERPRETER The General is content to spare thee yet,
And, hoodwinked as thou art, will lead thee on
85   To gather from thee. Haply thou mayst inform
Something to save thy life.

PAROLLES   O, let me live!
And all the secrets of our camp I'll show,
Their force, their purposes; nay, I'll speak that
Which you will wonder at.

INTERPRETER   But wilt thou faithfully?

PAROLLES If I do not, damn me.

90   INTERPRETER   *Acordo linta*.
Come on, thou art granted space.
                          Exit [*with Parolles guarded*].

                    A short alarum within.

FIRST LORD Go, tell the Count Rousillon and my
      brother
We have caught the woodcock and will keep him
      muffled
Till we do hear from them.

---

74 discover reveal   91 s.d. **A short alarum within** (perhaps Parolles is taken off
to a ruffle of drums)   93 **woodcock** stupid bird

SOLDIER   Captain, I will.

FIRST LORD 'A will betray us all unto ourselves; in-   95
    form on that.

SOLDIER So I will, sir.

FIRST LORD Till then, I'll keep him dark, and safely
    locked.   *Exit [with the others].*

[Scene II. *Florence. The Widow's house.*]

Enter Bertram and the maid called Diana.

BERTRAM They told me that your name was Fontibell.

DIANA No, my good lord, Diana.

BERTRAM   Titled goddess;
    And worth it, with addition. But, fair soul,
    In your fine frame hath love no quality?
    If the quick fire of youth light not your mind   5
    You are no maiden but a monument.
    When you are dead you should be such a one
    As you are now; for you are cold and stern,
    And now you should be as your mother was
    When your sweet self was got.   10

DIANA She then was honest.

BERTRAM   So should you be.

DIANA   No.

My mother did but duty; such, my lord,
As you owe to your wife.

BERTRAM   No more o' that!
I prithee, do not strive against my vows;
15 I was compelled to her, but I love thee
By love's own sweet constraint, and will forever
Do thee all rights of service.

DIANA   Ay, so you serve us
Till we serve you; but when you have our roses,
You barely leave our thorns to prick ourselves,
And mock us with our bareness.

20 BERTRAM   How have I sworn!

DIANA 'Tis not the many oaths that makes the truth,
But the plain single vow that is vowed true.
What is not holy, that we swear not by,
But take the High'st to witness; then, pray you, tell
me:
25 If I should swear by Jove's great attributes
I loved you dearly, would you believe my oaths
When I did love you ill? This has no holding,
To swear by Him whom I protest to love
That I will work against Him. Therefore your oaths
30 Are words and poor conditions but unsealed,
At least in my opinion.

BERTRAM   Change it, change it;
Be not so holy-cruel. Love is holy,
And my integrity ne'er knew the crafts
That you do charge men with. Stand no more off,
35 But give thyself unto my sick desires,
Who then recovers. Say thou art mine, and ever
My love as it begins shall so persever.

DIANA I see that men make rope's in such a scarre,
That we'll forsake ourselves. Give me that ring.

27 ill not well, not at all   30 but unsealed merely invalid   38 I see ... scarre
(possibly "scarre" means "splice" and thus "snare," but the text is probably
corrupt)

BERTRAM I'll lend it thee, my dear, but have no power   40
To give it from me.

DIANA   Will you not, my lord?

BERTRAM It is an honor 'longing to our house,
Bequeathèd down from many ancestors,
Which were the greatest obloquy i' th' world
In me to lose.

DIANA   Mine honor's such a ring;   45
My chastity's the jewel of our house,
Bequeathèd down from many ancestors,
Which were the greatest obloquy i' th' world
In me to lose. Thus your own proper wisdom
Brings in the champion Honor on my part   50
Against your vain assault.

BERTRAM   Here, take my ring.
My house, mine honor, yea, my life be thine,
And I'll be bid by thee.

DIANA When midnight comes, knock at my chamber-
window:
I'll order take my mother shall not hear.   55
Now will I charge you in the band of truth,
When you have conquered my yet maiden bed,
Remain there but an hour, nor speak to me.
My reasons are most strong and you shall know
them
When back again this ring shall be delivered;   60
And on your finger in the night I'll put
Another ring, that what in time proceeds
May token to the future our past deeds.
Adieu till then; then fail not. You have won
A wife of me, though there my hope be done.   65

BERTRAM A heaven on earth I have won by wooing
thee.   [*Exit*.]

DIANA For which live long to thank both heaven and
me!

49 proper personal   56 band bond

You may so in the end.
My mother told me just how he would woo,
70   As if she sat in's heart. She says all men
Have the like oaths. He had sworn to marry me
When his wife's dead; therefore I'll lie with him
When I am buried. Since Frenchmen are so braid,
Marry that will, I live and die a maid.
75   Only, in this disguise, I think't no sin
To cozen him that would unjustly win.   *Exit.*

[Scene III. *The Florentine camp.*]

*Enter the two French Captains, and some
two or three Soldiers.*

FIRST LORD You have not given him his mother's
letter?

SECOND LORD I have delivered it an hour since. There
is something in't that stings his nature, for on the
5   reading it he changed almost into another man.

FIRST LORD He has much worthy blame laid upon him
for shaking off so good a wife and so sweet a lady.

SECOND LORD Especially he hath incurred the everlasting displeasure of the King, who had even
10   tuned his bounty to sing happiness to him. I will
tell you a thing, but you shall let it dwell darkly
with you.

FIRST LORD When you have spoken it, 'tis dead, and I
am the grave of it.

73 **braid** deceitful (?)   76 **cozen** deceive

SECOND LORD He hath perverted a young gentlewoman   15
here in Florence, of a most chaste renown, and this
night he fleshes his will in the spoil of her honor; he
hath given her his monumental ring, and thinks
himself made in the unchaste composition.

FIRST LORD Now, God delay our rebellion! As we are   20
ourselves, what things are we!

SECOND LORD Merely our own traitors. And as in the
common course of all treasons we still see them
reveal themselves till they attain to their abhorred
ends, so he that in this action contrives against his   25
own nobility, in his proper stream o'erflows himself.

FIRST LORD Is it not meant damnable in us to be
trumpeters of our unlawful intents? We shall not
then have his company tonight?   30

SECOND LORD Not till after midnight, for he is dieted
to his hour.

FIRST LORD That approaches apace. I would gladly
have him see his company anatomized, that he
might take a measure of his own judgments, wherein   35
so curiously he had set this counterfeit.

SECOND LORD We will not meddle with him till he
come, for his presence must be the whip of the
other.

FIRST LORD In the meantime, what hear you of these   40
wars?

SECOND LORD I hear there is an overture of peace.

FIRST LORD Nay, I assure you, a peace concluded.

IV.iii.18 **monumental** serving as a memento   19 **composition** bargain
22 **Merely** utterly   26 **proper** own   26 **o'erflows** (1) betrays in talk (2) drowns
31 **dieted** restricted   34 **company anatomized** companion (i.e., Parolles) minutely analyzed   35-36 **wherein ... counterfeit** in which he has so elaborately set
this false jewel   37 **him ... he** i.e., Parolles ... Bertram

SECOND LORD What will Count Rousillon do then?
45 Will he travel higher, or return again into France?

FIRST LORD I perceive by this demand you are not altogether of his council.

SECOND LORD Let it be forbid, sir; so should I be a great deal of his act.

50 FIRST LORD Sir, his wife some two months since fled from his house. Her pretense is a pilgrimage to Saint Jaques le Grand; which holy undertaking with most austere sanctimony she accomplished; and, there residing, the tenderness of her nature became
55 as a prey to her grief; in fine, made a groan of her last breath, and now she sings in heaven.

SECOND LORD How is this justified?

FIRST LORD The stronger part of it by her own letters, which makes her story true even to the point of her
60 death. Her death itself, which could not be her office to say is come, was faithfully confirmed by the rector of the place.

SECOND LORD Hath the Count all this intelligence?

FIRST LORD Ay, and the particular confirmations, point
65 from point, to the full arming of the verity.

SECOND LORD I am heartily sorry that he'll be glad of this.

FIRST LORD How mightily sometimes we make us comforts of our losses!

70 SECOND LORD And how mightily some other times we drown our gain in tears! The great dignity that his valor hath here acquired for him shall at home be encount'red with a shame as ample.

FIRST LORD The web of our life is of a mingled yarn,
75 good and ill together; our virtues would be proud

---

51 **pretense** intention   53 **sanctimony** holiness   57 **justified** made certain
62 **rector** ruler (?) priest (?)   63 **intelligence** news

if our faults whipped them not, and our crimes would despair if they were not cherished by our virtues.

Enter a Messenger.

How now! Where's your master?

SERVANT   He met the Duke in the street, sir, of whom 80
he hath taken a solemn leave. His lordship will next morning for France. The Duke hath offered him letters of commendations to the King.

SECOND LORD   They shall be no more than needful there, if they were more than they can commend. 85

FIRST LORD   They cannot be too sweet for the King's tartness.

Enter Bertram.

Here's his lordship now. How now, my lord? Is't not after midnight?

BERTRAM   I have tonight dispatched sixteen businesses, 90
a month's length apiece. By an abstract of success: I have congied with the Duke, done my adieu with his nearest, buried a wife, mourned for her, writ to my lady mother I am returning, entertained my convoy, and between these main parcels of dis- 95
patch effected many nicer needs; the last was the greatest, but that I have not ended yet.

SECOND LORD   If the business be of any difficulty, and this morning your departure hence, it requires haste of your lordship. 100

BERTRAM   I mean the business is not ended, as fearing to hear of it hereafter. But shall we have this dia-

84-85 **They shall ... commend** i.e., the recommendations to the King will not be more than needed, even if they commend Bertram excessively (?)   91 **abstract of success** summary of my successes (?) list, in sequence (?)   92 **congied with** taken leave of   94-95 **entertained my convoy** hired my transportation   95-96 **parcels of dispatch** things to be settled   96 **nicer** (1) more trivial (2) lascivious (alluding to his affair with Diana)

logue between the Fool and the Soldier? Come,
bring forth this counterfeit module has deceived me
105   like a double-meaning prophesier.

SECOND LORD Bring him forth. [*Exeunt Soldiers.*] Has
sat i' th' stocks all night, poor gallant knave.

BERTRAM No matter, his heels have deserved it, in
usurping his spurs so long. How does he carry him-
110   self?

SECOND LORD I have told your lordship already; the
stocks carry him. But to answer you as you would
be understood, he weeps like a wench that had shed
her milk. He hath confessed himself to Morgan,
115   whom he supposes to be a friar, from the time of
his remembrance to this very instant disaster of his
setting i' th' stocks. And what think you he hath
confessed?

BERTRAM Nothing of me, has 'a?

120   SECOND LORD His confession is taken, and it shall
be read to his face. If your lordship be in't, as
I believe you are, you must have the patience to
hear it.

Enter Parolles [guarded], with his Interpreter.

BERTRAM A plague upon him! Muffled! He can say
125   nothing of me.

FIRST LORD [*Aside to Bertram*] Hush, hush! Hoodman
comes! [*Aloud*] Portotartarossa.

INTERPRETER He calls for the tortures. What will you
say without 'em?

130   PAROLLES I will confess what I know without constraint. If ye pinch me like a pasty I can say no
more.

104 **module** image   107 **gallant** finely dressed   124 **Muffled** blindfolded
126–27 **Hoodman comes** the blind man comes (customary call in the game
blindman's buff)

INTERPRETER *Bosko chimurcho.*

LORD *Boblibindo chicurmurco.*

INTERPRETER You are a merciful general. Our General 135
bids you answer to what I shall ask you out of a
note.

PAROLLES And truly, as I hope to live.

INTERPRETER "First demand of him how many horse
the Duke is strong." What say you to that? 140

PAROLLES Five or six thousand, but very weak and
unserviceable. The troops are all scattered and the
commanders very poor rogues, upon my reputation
and credit, and as I hope to live.

INTERPRETER Shall I set down your answer so? 145

PAROLLES Do. I'll take the sacrament on't, how and
which way you will.

BERTRAM [*Aside*] All's one to him. What a past-saving
slave is this!

FIRST LORD [*Aside to Bertram*] Y'are deceived, my 150
lord; this is Monsieur Parolles, the gallant mili-
tarist—that was his own phrase—that had the
whole theoric of war in the knot of his scarf, and
the practice in the chape of his dagger.

SECOND LORD [*Aside*] I will never trust a man again 155
for keeping his sword clean, nor believe he can
have everything in him by wearing his apparel
neatly.

INTERPRETER Well, that's set down.

PAROLLES "Five or six thousand horse," I said—I will 160
say true—"or thereabouts" set down, for I'll speak
truth.

FIRST LORD [*Aside*] He's very near the truth in this.

154 chape metal plate on a scabbard covering the point

BERTRAM [*Aside*] But I con him no thanks for't, in
165 the nature he delivers it.

PAROLLES "Poor rogues," I pray you say.

INTERPRETER Well, that's set down.

PAROLLES I humbly thank you, sir; a truth's a truth;
the rogues are marvelous poor.

170 INTERPRETER "Demand of him of what strength they are
a-foot." What say you to that?

PAROLLES By my troth, sir, if I were to live this present
hour, I will tell true. Let me see: Spurio, a hundred
and fifty; Sebastian, so many; Corambus, so many;
175 Jaques, so many; Guiltian, Cosmo, Lodowick, and
Gratii, two hundred fifty each; mine own company,
Chitopher, Vaumond, Bentii, two hundred fifty
each; so that the muster-file, rotten and sound,
upon my life, amounts not to fifteen thousand poll,
180 half of the which dare not shake the snow from off
their cassocks lest they shake themselves to pieces.

BERTRAM [*Aside*] What shall be done to him?

FIRST LORD [*To Bertram*] Nothing, but let him have
thanks. [*To interpreter*] Demand of him my condi-
185 tion, and what credit I have with the Duke.

INTERPRETER Well, that's set down. "You shall demand
of him whether one Captain Dumaine be i' th'
camp, a Frenchman; what his reputation is with
the Duke, what his valor, honesty, and expertness
190 in wars; or whether he thinks it were not possible
with well-weighing sums of gold to corrupt him to
a revolt." What say you to this? What do you know
of it?

PAROLLES I beseech you, let me answer to the particular
195 of the inter'gatories. Demand them singly.

INTERPRETER Do you know this Captain Dumaine?

164 con give (literally, learn) 179 poll head 181 cassocks soldiers' cloaks

618

PAROLLES I know him; 'a was a botcher's prentice in
Paris, from whence he was whipped for getting the
shrieve's fool with child, a dumb innocent that
could not say him nay.   200

BERTRAM [*Aside to Dumaine*] Nay, by your leave, hold
your hands, though I know his brains are forfeit to
the next tile that falls.

INTERPRETER Well, is this captain in the Duke of Florence's camp?   205

PAROLLES Upon my knowledge he is, and lousy.

FIRST LORD [*Aside*] Nay, look not so upon me; we
shall hear of your lordship anon.

INTERPRETER What is his reputation with the Duke?

PAROLLES The Duke knows him for no other but a poor   210
officer of mine, and writ to me this other day to
turn him out o' th' band. I think I have his letter
in my pocket.

INTERPRETER Marry, we'll search.

PAROLLES In good sadness, I do not know; either it   215
is there or it is upon a file with the Duke's other
letters in my tent.

INTERPRETER Here 'tis; here's a paper; shall I read it
to you?

PAROLLES I do not know if it be it or no.   220

BERTRAM [*Aside*] Our interpreter does it well.

FIRST LORD [*Aside*] Excellently.

INTERPRETER "Dian, the Count's a fool, and full of
gold."

PAROLLES That is not the Duke's letter, sir; that is an

---

197 **botcher's** mender's (e.g., tailor's or cobbler's)   199 **shrieve's fool** idiot girl
placed under a sheriff's charge   203 **tile that falls** i.e., accident   215 **sadness**
seriousness

225   advertisement to a proper maid in Florence, one
         Diana, to take heed of the allurement of one Count
         Rousillon, a foolish idle boy, but for all that very
         ruttish. I pray you, sir, put it up again.

    INTERPRETER Nay, I'll read it first, by your favor.

230 PAROLLES My meaning in't, I protest, was very honest
         in the behalf of the maid; for I knew the young
         Count to be a dangerous and lascivious boy, who
         is a whale to virginity, and devours up all the fry
         it finds.

235 BERTRAM [Aside] Damnable both-sides rogue!

    INTERPRETER ([Reads a] letter.) "When he swears
         oaths, bid him drop gold, and take it;
       After he scores, he never pays the score.
       Half won is match well made; match and well make
         it;
       He ne'er pays after-debts, take it before.
240   And say a soldier, Dian, told thee this:
       Men are to mell with, boys are not to kiss:
       For count of this, the Count's a fool, I know it,
       Who pays before, but not when he does owe it.
         Thine, as he vowed to thee in thine ear,
245   Parolles."

    BERTRAM [Aside] He shall be whipped through the
         army with this rhyme in's forehead.

    SECOND LORD [Aside] This is your devoted friend, sir,
         the manifold linguist, and the armipotent soldier.

250 BERTRAM [Aside] I could endure anything before but
         a cat, and now he's a cat to me.

    INTERPRETER I perceive, sir, by your General's looks,
         we shall be fain to hang you.

225 advertisement advice   228 ruttish lustful   233 fry small fish   238 Half
... make it i.e., you are halfway to success if you bargain well; so bargain well and
you will prosper (?)   241 mell mingle   249 armipotent mighty in arms (a
huffing word, like "manifold")

PAROLLES My life, sir, in any case! Not that I am
afraid to die, but that my offenses being many   255
would repent out the remainder of nature. Let me
live, sir, in a dungeon, i' th' stocks, or anywhere, so
I may live.

INTERPRETER We'll see what may be done, so you confess freely. Therefore once more to this Captain   260
Dumaine: you have answered to his reputation with
the Duke and to his valor: what is his honesty?

PAROLLES He will steal, sir, an egg out of a cloister;
for rapes and ravishments he parallels Nessus. He
professes not keeping of oaths, in breaking 'em he   265
is stronger than Hercules. He will lie, sir, with such
volubility that you would think truth were a fool;
drunkenness is his best virtue, for he will be swine-
drunk, and in his sleep he does little harm, save to
his bedclothes about him; but they know his con-   270
ditions and lay him in straw. I have but little more
to say, sir, of his honesty—he has everything that
an honest man should not have; what an honest man
should have, he has nothing.

FIRST LORD [Aside] I begin to love him for this.   275

BERTRAM [Aside] For this description of thine honesty?
A pox upon him for me, he's more and more a cat.

INTERPRETER What say you to his expertness in war?

PAROLLES Faith, sir, has led the drum before the English tragedians—to belie him I will not—and more   280
of his soldiership I know not, except in that country he had the honor to be the officer at a place
there called Mile-end, to instruct for the doubling
of files. I would do the man what honor I can, but
of this I am not certain.   285

264 Nessus centaur who attempted to rape Deianira, Hercules' wife
270-71 conditions traits   279-80 led ... tragedians i.e., been a low drummer,
leading strolling actors rather than soldiers   283 Mile-end (because the citizen
militia drilled at Mile-end, the place was a byname for military incompetence)
283-84 doubling of files drill maneuver in which pairs of men separate

FIRST LORD [*Aside*] He hath out-villained villainy so far that the rarity redeems him.

BERTRAM [*Aside*] A pox on him! He's a cat still.

INTERPRETER His qualities being at this poor price, I
290   need not to ask you if gold will corrupt him to revolt.

PAROLLES Sir, for a cardecue he will sell the fee-simple of his salvation, the inheritance of it, and cut th' entail from all remainders, and a perpetual
295   succession for it perpetually.

INTERPRETER What's his brother, the other Captain Dumaine?

SECOND LORD   [*Aside*] Why does he ask him of me?

INTERPRETER What's he?

300 PAROLLES E'en a crow o' th' same nest; not altogether so great as the first in goodness, but greater a great deal in evil. He excels his brother for a coward, yet his brother is reputed one of the best that is. In a retreat he outruns any lackey; marry, in coming on
305   he has the cramp.

INTERPRETER If your life be saved will you undertake to betray the Florentine?

PAROLLES Ay, and the captain of his horse, Count Rousillon.

310 INTERPRETER I'll whisper with the General, and know his pleasure.

PAROLLES [*Aside*] I'll no more drumming. A plague of all drums! Only to seem to deserve well, and to beguile the supposition of that lascivious young boy,
315   the Count, have I run into this danger. Yet who would have suspected an ambush where I was taken?

292 cardecue *quart d'écu* (French coin of little value)   292-93 fee-simple absolute possession   294 entail right of succession

INTERPRETER There is no remedy, sir, but you must
die. The General says you that have so traitorously
discovered the secrets of your army and made such   320
pestiferous reports of men very nobly held, can
serve the world for no honest use; therefore you
must die. Come, headsman, off with his head.

PAROLLES O Lord, sir, let me live, or let me see my
death!   325

INTERPRETER That shall you, and take your leave of all
your friends.   [*Unmuffles Parolles.*]
So, look about you. Know you any here?

BERTRAM Good morrow, noble Captain.

SECOND LORD God bless you, Captain Parolles.   330

FIRST LORD God save you, noble Captain.

SECOND LORD Captain, what greeting will you to my
Lord Lafew? I am for France.

FIRST LORD Good Captain, will you give me a copy of
the sonnet you writ to Diana in behalf of the Count   335
Rousillon? And I were not a very coward I'd compel it of you, but fare you well.
                        Exeunt [*Bertram and Lords*].

INTERPRETER You are undone, Captain, all but your
scarf; that has a knot on't yet.

PAROLLES Who cannot be crushed with a plot?   340

INTERPRETER If you could find out a country where but
women were that had received so much shame, you
might begin an impudent nation. Fare ye well, sir.
I am for France too; we shall speak of you there.
                        Exit [*with other Soldiers*].

PAROLLES Yet am I thankful. If my heart were great   345
'Twould burst at this. Captain I'll be no more,
But I will eat and drink and sleep as soft
As captain shall. Simply the thing I am
Shall make me live. Who knows himself a braggart,

350   Let him fear this; for it will come to pass
    That every braggart shall be found an ass.
    Rust, sword; cool, blushes; and Parolles live
    Safest in shame! Being fooled, by fool'ry thrive!
    There's place and means for every man alive.
355   I'll after them.   *Exit.*

[Scene IV. *Florence. The Widow's house.*]

Enter Helena, Widow, and Diana.

HELENA That you may well perceive I have not
    wronged you,
    One of the greatest in the Christian world
    Shall be my surety; 'fore whose throne 'tis needful,
    Ere I can perfect mine intents, to kneel.
5   Time was, I did him a desirèd office,
    Dear almost as his life, which gratitude
    Through flinty Tartar's bosom would peep forth,
    And answer thanks. I duly am informed
    His Grace is at Marseilles, to which place
10   We have convenient convoy. You must know
    I am supposèd dead. The army breaking,
    My husband hies him home, where, heaven aiding,
    And by the leave of my good lord the King,
    We'll be before our welcome.

WIDOW   Gentle madam,
15   You never had a servant to whose trust
    Your business was more welcome.

IV.iv.10 **convoy** transportation   11 **breaking** disbanding

HELENA   Nor you, mistress,
　　Ever a friend whose thoughts more truly labor
　　To recompense your love. Doubt not but heaven
　　Hath brought me up to be your daughter's dower,
　　As it hath fated her to be my motive   20
　　And helper to a husband. But, O strange men,
　　That can such sweet use make of what they hate,
　　When saucy trusting of the cozened thoughts
　　Defiles the pitchy night! So lust doth play
　　With what it loathes for that which is away.   25
　　But more of this hereafter. You, Diana,
　　Under my poor instructions yet must suffer
　　Something in my behalf.

DIANA   Let death and honesty
　　Go with your impositions, I am yours
　　Upon your will to suffer.

HELENA   Yet, I pray you;   30
　　But with the word the time will bring on summer,
　　When briars shall have leaves as well as thorns,
　　And be as sweet as sharp. We must away;
　　Our wagon is prepared, and time revives us.
　　All's well that ends well; still the fine's the crown. 35
　　Whate'er the course, the end is the renown.
　　　　　　　　　　　　　　　　　　Exeunt.

---

20 motive means (?)   23 saucy lascivious   23 cozened deceived   28 death
and honesty an honest death   29 impositions tasks imposed on me   31 with
the word soon (?) as the proverb says (?)   35 the fine's the crown the end is the
crown (cf. the Latin proverb, *Finis coronat opus*, "the end crowns the work")

[Scene V. *Rousillon. The Count's palace.*]

Enter Clown, Old Lady [i.e., Countess], and Lafew.

LAFEW No, no, no, your son was misled with a snipped
taffeta fellow there, whose villainous saffron
would have made all the unbaked and doughy
youth of a nation in his color. Your daughter-in-law
5   had been alive at this hour, and your son here at
home, more advanced by the King than by that red-
tailed humble-bee I speak of.

COUNTESS I would I had not known him; it was the
death of the most virtuous gentlewoman that ever
10 nature had praise for creating. If she had partaken
of my flesh and cost me the dearest groans of a
mother, I could not have owed her a more rooted
love.

LAFEW 'Twas a good lady, 'twas a good lady. We
15 may pick a thousand sallets ere we light on such
another herb.

CLOWN Indeed, sir, she was the sweet-marjoram of
the sallet, or rather, the herb of grace.

LAFEW They are not herbs, you knave, they are nose-
20 herbs.

CLOWN I am no great Nebuchadnezzar, sir; I have
not much skill in grace.

IV.v.1-2 **snipped taffeta** cloth slashed to show the colors beneath   2 **saffron**
yellow dye (used to dye starch—for ruffs—and also dough)   15 **sallets** salads
18 **herb of grace** rue   19 **not** (pun on "knot"=flower bed, leading to the
contrasting "nose-herbs"= fragrant but not tasty herbs)   22 **grace** (pun on
"grass," following the allusion to the King of Babylon who in Daniel 4:28–37 is
said to have insanely eaten grass)

LAFEW Whether dost thou profess thyself, a knave or a fool?

CLOWN A fool, sir, at a woman's service, and a knave   25
at a man's.

LAFEW Your distinction?

CLOWN I would cozen the man of his wife and do his service.

LAFEW So you were a knave at his service indeed.   30

CLOWN And I would give his wife my bauble, sir, to do her service.

LAFEW I will subscribe for thee; thou art both knave and fool.

CLOWN At your service.   35

LAFEW No, no, no.

CLOWN Why, sir, if I cannot serve you, I can serve as great a prince as you are.

LAFEW Who's that? A Frenchman?

CLOWN Faith, sir, 'a has an English name, but his   40
fisnomy is more hotter in France than there.

LAFEW What prince is that?

CLOWN The Black Prince, sir, alias the prince of darkness, alias the devil.

LAFEW Hold thee, there's my purse. I give thee not   45
this to suggest thee from thy master thou talk'st of; serve him still.

CLOWN I am a woodland fellow, sir, that always loved a great fire, and the master I speak of ever keeps a good fire. But sure he is the prince of the world; let   50
his nobility remain in's court. I am for the house

23 **Whether** which 31 **bauble** fool's stick (bawdy innuendo) 41 **fisnomy** physiognomy 43 **Black Prince** (1) Edward III, foe of the French (2) devil 46 **suggest thee from** tempt you away from

627

with the narrow gate, which I take to be too little
for pomp to enter; some that humble themselves
may, but the many will be too chill and tender, and
55   they'll be for the flow'ry way that leads to the broad
gate and the great fire.

LAFEW Go thy ways; I begin to be aweary of thee,
and I tell thee so before, because I would not fall
out with thee. Go thy ways; let my horses be well
60   looked to, without any tricks.

CLOWN If I put any tricks upon 'em, sir, they shall
be jades' tricks, which are their own right by the
law of nature.   *Exit.*

LAFEW A shrewd knave and an unhappy.

65   COUNTESS So 'a is. My lord that's gone made himself
much sport out of him; by his authority he remains
here, which he thinks is a patent for his sauciness;
and indeed he has no pace, but runs where he will.

LAFEW I like him well, 'tis not amiss. And I was about
70   to tell you, since I heard of the good lady's death
and that my lord your son was upon his return
home, I moved the King my master to speak in the
behalf of my daughter; which, in the minority of
them both, his Majesty out of a self-gracious re-
75   membrance did first propose. His Highness hath
promised me to do it—and to stop up the displeasure he hath conceived against your son there
is no fitter matter. How does your ladyship like it?

COUNTESS With very much content, my lord, and I
80   wish it happily effected.

LAFEW His Highness comes post from Marseilles, of
as able body as when he numbered thirty. 'A will
be here tomorrow, or I am deceived by him that in
such intelligence hath seldom failed.

51–52 **house with the narrow gate** heaven (with bawdy reference to vulva?)
62 **jades' tricks** mischievous doings (like those of undesirable horses)
64 **shrewd** bitter   81 **post** by rapid relays of horses

COUNTESS It rejoices me that I hope I shall see him   85
ere I die. I have letters that my son will be here
tonight. I shall beseech your lordship to remain with
me till they meet together.

LAFEW Madam, I was thinking with what manners I
might safely be admitted.   90

COUNTESS You need but plead your honorable privilege.

LAFEW Lady, of that I have made a bold charter; but
I thank my God it holds yet.

Enter Clown.

CLOWN O madam, yonder's my lord your son with a   95
patch of velvet on's face; whether there be a scar
under't or no, the velvet knows, but 'tis a goodly
patch of velvet. His left cheek is a cheek of two
pile and a half, but his right cheek is worn bare.

LAFEW A scar nobly got, or a noble scar, is a good   100
liv'ry of honor; so belike is that.

CLOWN But it is your carbonadoed face.

LAFEW Let us go see your son, I pray you. I long to
talk with the young noble soldier.

CLOWN Faith, there's a dozen of 'em with delicate   105
fine hats and most courteous feathers which bow
the head and nod at every man.   *Exeunt.*

93 **charter** claim   98 **patch of velvet** bandage (but it might cover an honorable scar or dishonorable signs of syphilis)   101 **liv'ry** badge of noble service   102 **carbonadoed** slashed (with incisions to drain venereal ulcers)

ACT V

[Scene I. *Marseilles*.]

Enter Helena, Widow, and Diana, with two Attendants.

HELENA But this exceeding posting day and night
Must wear your spirits low; we cannot help it.
But since you have made the days and nights as one,
To wear your gentle limbs in my affairs,
5   Be bold you do so grow in my requital
As nothing can unroot you.

Enter a Gentleman, a stranger.

In happy time!
This man may help me to his Majesty's ear,
If he would spend his power. God save you, sir.

GENTLEMAN And you.

V.i.1 **exceeding posting** excessive haste 5 **bold** assured 5 **requital** debt
6 **In happy time** just at the right moment

HELENA Sir, I have seen you in the court of France.   10

GENTLEMAN I have been sometimes there.

HELENA I do presume, sir, that you are not fall'n
From the report that goes upon your goodness,
And therefore, goaded with most sharp occasions
Which lay nice manners by, I put you to   15
The use of your own virtues, for the which
I shall continue thankful.

GENTLEMAN   What's your will?

HELENA That it will please you
To give this poor petition to the King,
And aid me with that store of power you have   20
To come into his presence.

GENTLEMAN The King's not here.

HELENA   Not here, sir?

GENTLEMAN   Not indeed.
He hence removed last night, and with more haste
Than is his use.

WIDOW   Lord, how we lose our pains!

HELENA All's well that ends well yet,   25
Though time seem so adverse and means unfit.
I do beseech you, whither is he gone?

GENTLEMAN Marry, as I take it, to Rousillon,
Whither I am going.

HELENA   I do beseech you, sir,
Since you are like to see the King before me,   30
Commend the paper to his gracious hand,
Which I presume shall render you no blame
But rather make you thank your pains for it.
I will come after you with what good speed
Our means will make us means.

GENTLEMAN   This I'll do for you.   35

HELENA And you shall find yourself to be well
    thanked,
  Whate'er falls more. We must to horse again.
  Go, go, provide.   *[Exeunt.]*

[Scene II. *Rousillon. The Count's palace.*]

Enter Clown and Parolles.

PAROLLES Good Master Lavatch, give my Lord
  Lafew this letter. I have ere now, sir, been better
  known to you, when I have held familiarity with
  fresher clothes; but I am now, sir, muddied in for-
5 tune's mood, and smell somewhat strong of her
  strong displeasure.

CLOWN Truly, fortune's displeasure is but sluttish if
  it smell so strongly as thou speak'st of. I will henceforth eat no fish of fortune's butt'ring. Prithee,
10 allow the wind.

PAROLLES Nay, you need not to stop your nose, sir;
  I spake but by a metaphor.

CLOWN Indeed, sir, if your metaphor stink, I will stop
  my nose, or against any man's metaphor. Prithee,
15 get thee further.

PAROLLES Pray you, sir, deliver me this paper.

CLOWN Foh! Prithee, stand away. A paper from for-

---

37 **falls** befalls   V.ii.1 **Lavatch** (apparently from French *la vache* = the cow, or
lavage = slop) 5 **mood** displeasure (with pun on mud) 10 **allow the wind** let
me have the windward side

tune's close-stool, to give to a nobleman! Look, here he comes himself.

Enter Lafew.

Here is a pur of fortune's, sir, or of fortune's   20
cat, but not a musk-cat, that has fall'n into the
unclean fishpond of her displeasure, and, as he
says, is muddied withal. Pray you, sir, use the carp
as you may, for he looks like a poor, decayed, ingenious, foolish, rascally knave. I do pity his dis-   25
tress in my similes of comfort, and leave him to
your lordship.

[*Exit.*]

PAROLLES My lord, I am a man whom fortune hath
cruelly scratched.

LAFEW And what would you have me to do? 'Tis too   30
late to pare her nails now. Wherein have you
played the knave with fortune that she should
scratch you, who of herself is a good lady and
would not have knaves thrive long under? There's
a cardecue for you. Let the justices make you and   35
fortune friends; I am for other business.

PAROLLES I beseech your honor to hear me one single
word.

LAFEW You beg a single penny more. Come, you shall
ha't; save your word.   40

PAROLLES My name, my good lord, is Parolles.

LAFEW You beg more than "word" then. Cox my
passion! Give me your hand. How does your
drum?

---

18 **close-stool** toilet   20 **pur** (1) dung (2) cat's sound (3) knave in a card game
(Lafew picks up this last meaning when he speaks)   21 **musk-cat** musk deer
(which yields perfume)   24-25 **ingenious** stupid (as though written "un-genius")
35 **cardecue** French coin   35-36 **Let ... friends** i.e., appeal to the justices for
alms   42-43 **Cox my passion** (mild oath, from "God's my passion," i.e., by
God's suffering)

45 PAROLLES O my good lord, you were the first that
found me.

LAFEW Was I, in sooth? And I was the first that lost
thee.

PAROLLES It lies in you, my lord, to bring me in some
50 grace, for you did bring me out.

LAFEW Out upon thee, knave! Dost thou put upon
me at once both the office of God and the devil?
One brings thee in grace and the other brings thee
out. [*Trumpets sound.*] The King's coming; I know
55 by his trumpets. Sirrah, inquire further after me.
I had talk of you last night; though you are a fool
and a knave you shall eat. Go to, follow.

PAROLLES I praise God for you.   [*Exeunt.*]

[Scene III. *Rousillon. The Count's palace.*]

Flourish. Enter King, Old Lady [*i.e., Countess*],
Lafew, the two French Lords, with Attendants.

KING We lost a jewel of her, and our esteem
Was made much poorer by it; but your son,
As mad in folly, lacked the sense to know
Her estimation home.

COUNTESS   'Tis past, my liege,
5   And I beseech your Majesty to make it
Natural rebellion done i' th' blade of youth,

---

46 **found me** found me out   V.iii.1 **esteem** value, i.e., reputation   4 **home** fully
6 **blade** green shoot (editors distressed by the mixed metaphor produced by "fire"
emend to "blaze")

When oil and fire, too strong for reason's force,
O'erbears it and burns on.

KING   My honored lady,
I have forgiven and forgotten all,
Though my revenges were high bent upon him   10
And watched the time to shoot.

LAFEW   This I must say—
But first I beg my pardon—the young lord
Did to his Majesty, his mother, and his lady
Offense of mighty note, but to himself
The greatest wrong of all. He lost a wife   15
Whose beauty did astonish the survey
Of richest eyes; whose words all ears took captive;
Whose dear perfection hearts that scorned to serve
Humbly called mistress.

KING   Praising what is lost
Makes the remembrance dear. Well, call him hither;   20
We are reconciled, and the first view shall kill
All repetition. Let him not ask our pardon;
The nature of his great offense is dead,
And deeper than oblivion we do bury
Th' incensing relics of it. Let him approach,   25
A stranger, no offender; and inform him
So 'tis our will he should.

GENTLEMAN   I shall, my liege.   [*Exit.*]

KING What says he to your daughter? Have you spoke?

LAFEW All that he is hath reference to your Highness.

KING Then shall we have a match. I have letters sent
    me,   30
That sets him high in fame.

---

22 **repetition** i.e., mention of what is past   25 **incensing relics** reminders that
(would) anger   29 **hath reference** is submitted

635

Enter Bertram.

LAFEW   He looks well on't.

KING I am not a day of season,
For thou mayst see a sunshine and a hail
In me at once. But to the brightest beams
35   Distracted clouds give way; so stand thou forth;
The time is fair again.

BERTRAM   My high-repented blames,
Dear sovereign pardon to me.

KING   All is whole.
Not one word more of the consumèd time.
Let's take the instant by the forward top;
40   For we are old, and on our quick'st decrees
Th' inaudible and noiseless foot of Time
Steals ere we can effect them. You remember
The daughter of this lord?

BERTRAM Admiringly, my liege. At first
45   I stuck my choice upon her, ere my heart
Durst make too bold a herald of my tongue;
Where, the impression of mine eye infixing,
Contempt his scornful perspective did lend me,
Which warped the line of every other favor,
50   Scorned a fair color or expressed it stol'n,
Extended or contracted all proportions
To a most hideous object. Thence it came
That she whom all men praised and whom myself,
Since I have lost, have loved, was in mine eye
The dust that did offend it.

55 KING   Well excused.
That thou didst love her, strikes some scores away

---

36 **blames** blameworthy deeds   39 **take … top** seize Time by the forelock
48 **perspective** optical instrument that distorts (accented on first syllable)
49 **favor** face

From the great compt; but love that comes too late,
Like a remorseful pardon slowly carried,
To the great sender turns a sour offense,
Crying "That's good that's gone." Our rash faults   60
Make trivial price of serious things we have,
Not knowing them, until we know their grave.
Oft our displeasures, to ourselves unjust,
Destroy our friends and after weep their dust;
Our own love waking cries to see what's done,   65
While shameful hate sleeps out the afternoon.
Be this sweet Helen's knell, and now forget her.
Send forth your amorous token for fair Maudlin.
The main consents are had, and here we'll stay
To see our widower's second marriage-day,   70
Which better than the first, O dear heaven, bless!
Or, ere they meet, in me, O nature, cesse!

LAFEW Come on, my son, in whom my house's name
    Must be digested; give a favor from you
    To sparkle in the spirits of my daughter,   75
    That she may quickly come. [*Bertram gives a ring.*]
      By my old beard,
    And ev'ry hair that's on't, Helen that's dead
    Was a sweet creature; such a ring as this,
    The last that e'er I took her leave at court,
    I saw upon her finger.

BERTRAM   Hers it was not.   80

KING Now pray you let me see it; for mine eye,
    While I was speaking, oft was fastened to't.
    This ring was mine, and when I gave it Helen
    I bade her, if her fortunes ever stood
    Necessitied to help, that by this token   85
    I would relieve her. Had you that craft to reave her
    Of what should stead her most?

---

57 **compt** account   58 **remorseful** compassionate   72 **cesse** cease   74 **digested** swallowed up (?) assimilated (?)   74 **favor** token   86 **reave** deprive   87 **stead** help

BERTRAM   My gracious sovereign,
    Howe'er it pleases you to take it so,
    The ring was never hers.

COUNTESS   Son, on my life,
90   I have seen her wear it, and she reckoned it
    At her life's rate.

LAFEW   I am sure I saw her wear it.

BERTRAM You are deceived, my lord; she never saw it.
    In Florence was it from a casement thrown me,
    Wrapped in a paper which contained the name
95   Of her that threw it. Noble she was, and thought
    I stood ingaged; but when I had subscribed
    To mine own fortune and informed her fully
    I could not answer in that course of honor
    As she had made the overture, she ceased
100   In heavy satisfaction and would never
    Receive the ring again.

KING   Plutus himself,
    That knows the tinct and multiplying med'cine,
    Hath not in nature's mystery more science
    Than I have in this ring. 'Twas mine, 'twas Helen's,
105   Whoever gave it you; then if you know
    That you are well acquainted with yourself,
    Confess 'twas hers, and by what rough enforcement
    You got it from her. She called the saints to surety
    That she would never put it from her finger
110   Unless she gave it to yourself in bed,
    Where you have never come, or sent it us
    Upon her great disaster.

BERTRAM   She never saw it.

KING Thou speak'st it falsely, as I love mine honor,
    And mak'st conjectural fears to come into me

96 **ingaged** not pledged (to another woman)   96–97 **subscribed/To mine own fortune** admitted my condition, i.e., that I was married   100 **heavy satisfaction** sorrowful acceptance   101 **Plutus** god of wealth   102 **tinct and multiplying med'cine** elixir that transmutes base metals to gold and multiplies gold   103 **science** knowledge

Which I would fain shut out. If it should prove   115
That thou art so inhuman—'twill not prove so,
And yet I know not—thou didst hate her deadly,
And she is dead, which nothing but to close
Her eyes myself could win me to believe,
More than to see this ring. Take him away.   120
My fore-past proofs, howe'er the matter fall,
Shall tax my fears of little vanity,
Having vainly feared too little. Away with him,
We'll sift this matter further.

BERTRAM   If you shall prove
This ring was ever hers, you shall as easy   125
Prove that I husbanded her bed in Florence,
Where yet she never was.   [*Exit guarded*.]

KING I am wrapped in dismal thinkings.

          Enter a Gentleman, [the stranger].

GENTLEMAN   Gracious sovereign,
Whether I have been to blame or no, I know not:
Here's a petition from a Florentine   130
Who hath for four or five removes come short
To tender it herself. I undertook it,
Vanquished thereto by the fair grace and speech
Of the poor suppliant, who, by this, I know
Is here attending; her business looks in her   135
With an importing visage, and she told me,
In a sweet verbal brief, it did concern
Your Highness with herself.

[KING *reads*] *a letter*. "Upon his many protestations
to marry me when his wife was dead, I blush to   140
say it, he won me. Now is the Count Rousillon a
widower, his vows are forfeited to me, and my
honor's paid to him. He stole from Florence, taking
no leave, and I follow him to his country for justice.

121–23 My fore-past ... too little the evidence already established, however the
affair turns out, will rebuke ("tax") my lightweight ("of little vanity") fears; I have
unreasonably feared too little   131 removes stopping places (changes of residence) on the King's journey   136 importing significant

145 Grant it me, O King! In you it best lies; otherwise a
seducer flourishes and a poor maid is undone.
Diana Capilet."

LAFEW I will buy me a son-in-law in a fair, and toll
for this. I'll none of him.

150 KING The heavens have thought well on thee, Lafew,
To bring forth this discov'ry. Seek these suitors.
[*Exeunt Attendants.*]
Go, speedily and bring again the Count.
I am afeard the life of Helen, lady,
Was foully snatched.

COUNTESS   Now, justice on the doers!

Enter Bertram, [guarded].

155 KING I wonder, sir, since wives are monsters to you,
And that you fly them as you swear them lordship,
Yet you desire to marry.

Enter Widow [and] Diana.

What woman's that?

DIANA I am, my lord, a wretched Florentine,
Derivèd from the ancient Capilet.
160 My suit, as I do understand, you know,
And therefore know how far I may be pitied.

WIDOW I am her mother, sir, whose age and honor
Both suffer under this complaint we bring,
And both shall cease, without your remedy.

KING Come hither, Count—do you know these
165 women?

BERTRAM My lord, I neither can nor will deny
But that I know them. Do they charge me further?

DIANA Why do you look so strange upon your wife?

48-49 **toll for** put up for sale   164 **both ... remedy** both my life ("age") and
honor will die unless you give us relief (by having Bertram marry Diana)

BERTRAM She's none of mine, my lord.

DIANA   If you shall marry,
You give away this hand, and that is mine;   170
You give away heaven's vows, and those are mine;
You give away myself, which is known mine;
For I by vow am so embodied yours
That she which marries you must marry me,
Either both or none.   175

LAFEW Your reputation comes too short for my
daughter; you are no husband for her.

BERTRAM My lord, this is a fond and desp'rate
   creature,
Whom sometime I have laughed with. Let your
   Highness
Lay a more noble thought upon mine honor,   180
Than for to think that I would sink it here.

KING Sir, for my thoughts, you have them ill to friend
Till your deeds gain them; fairer prove your honor
Than in my thought it lies.

DIANA   Good my lord,
Ask him upon his oath if he does think   185
He had not my virginity.

KING What say'st thou to her?

BERTRAM   She's impudent, my lord,
And was a common gamester to the camp.

DIANA He does me wrong, my lord; if I were so,
He might have bought me at a common price.   190
Do not believe him. O, behold this ring,
Whose high respect and rich validity
Did lack a parallel; yet for all that
He gave it to a commoner o' th' camp,
If I be one.

COUNTESS   He blushes, and 'tis hit!   195

178 fond foolish   188 gamester prostitute

Of six preceding ancestors, that gem,
Conferred by testament to th' sequent issue,
Hath it been owed and worn. This is his wife,
That ring's a thousand proofs.

KING   Methought you said
200   You saw one here in court could witness it.

DIANA I did, my lord, but loath am to produce
So bad an instrument. His name's Parolles.

LAFEW I saw the man today, if man he be.

KING Find him and bring him hither.

[*Exit an Attendant.*]

BERTRAM   What of him?
205   He's quoted for a most perfidious slave,
With all the spots o' th' world taxed and deboshed,
Whose nature sickens but to speak a truth.
Am I or that or this for what he'll utter,
That will speak anything?

KING   She hath that ring of yours.

210   BERTRAM I think she has. Certain it is I liked her,
And boarded her i' th' wanton way of youth.
She knew her distance, and did angle for me,
Madding my eagerness with her restraint,
As all impediments in fancy's course
215   Are motives of more fancy; and in fine
Her inf'nite cunning with her modern grace
Subdued me to her rate. She got the ring,
And I had that which any inferior might
At market-price have bought.

DIANA   I must be patient:
220   You that have turned off a first so noble wife,
May justly diet me. I pray you yet—
Since you lack virtue I will lose a husband—

197 **sequent issue** next heir 198 **owed** owned 205 **quoted for** known as
206 **taxed and deboshed** censured as debauched 214 **fancy's** love's
216 **modern** commonplace 221 **diet** restrain yourself from

Send for your ring, I will return it home,
And give me mine again.

BERTRAM   I have it not.

KING What ring was yours, I pray you?

DIANA   Sir, much like   225
The same upon your finger.

KING Know you this ring? This ring was his of late.

DIANA And this was it I gave him, being abed.

KING The story then goes false you threw it him
Out of a casement?

DIANA   I have spoke the truth.   230

Enter Parolles.

BERTRAM My lord, I do confess, the ring was hers.

KING You boggle shrewdly; every feather starts you.
Is this the man you speak of?

DIANA   Ay, my lord.

KING Tell me, sirrah, but tell me true, I charge you,
Not fearing the displeasure of your master,   235
Which on your just proceeding I'll keep off—
By him and by this woman here what know you?

PAROLLES So please your Majesty, my master hath been
an honorable gentleman. Tricks he hath had in him,
which gentlemen have.   240

KING Come, come, to th' purpose: did he love this
woman?

PAROLLES Faith, sir, he did love her; but how?

KING How, I pray you?

PAROLLES He did love her, sir, as a gentleman loves a   245
woman.

232 **boggle shrewdly** startle excessively   246 **woman** (in contrast to a highborn
lady)

KING How is that?

PAROLLES He loved her, sir, and loved her not.

KING As thou are a knave and no knave. What an
250   equivocal companion is this!

PAROLLES I am a poor man, and at your Majesty's
command.

LAFEW He's a good drum, my lord, but a naughty
orator.

255 DIANA Do you know he promised me marriage?

PAROLLES Faith, I know more than I'll speak.

KING But wilt thou not speak all thou know'st?

PAROLLES Yes, so please your Majesty. I did go between them as I said; but more than that, he loved
260   her, for indeed he was mad for her and talked of
Satan and of Limbo and of Furies and I know not
what; yet I was in that credit with them at that time
that I knew of their going to bed and of other motions, as promising her marriage, and things which
265   would derive me ill will to speak of; therefore I will
not speak what I know.

KING Thou hast spoken all already, unless thou canst
say they are married. But thou art too fine in thy
evidence; therefore stand aside.
This ring, you say, was yours?

270 DIANA   Ay, my good lord.

KING Where did you buy it? Or who gave it you?

DIANA It was not given me, nor I did not buy it.

KING Who lent it you?

DIANA   It was not lent me neither.

---

248 not (perhaps punning on "knot" = maidenhead) 250 equivocal companion equivocating fellow ("companion" is contemptuous) 253 naughty
(1) worthless, worth naught (2) wicked 268 fine subtle

KING Where did you find it then?

DIANA   I found it not.

KING If it were yours by none of all these ways,   275
How could you give it him?

DIANA   I never gave it him.

LAFEW This woman's an easy glove, my lord; she goes
off and on at pleasure.

KING This ring was mine; I gave it his first wife.

DIANA It might be yours or hers for aught I know.   280

KING Take her away; I do not like her now.
To prison with her. And away with him.
Unless thou tell'st me where thou hadst this ring
Thou diest within this hour.

DIANA   I'll never tell you.

KING Take her away.

DIANA   I'll put in bail, my liege.   285

KING I think thee now some common customer.

DIANA By Jove, if ever I knew man, 'twas you.

KING Wherefore hast thou accused him all this while?

DIANA Because he's guilty and he is not guilty:
He knows I am no maid, and he'll swear to't: 290
I'll swear I am a maid and he knows not.
Great King, I am no strumpet; by my life
I am either maid or else this old man's wife.

KING She does abuse our ears. To prison with her!

DIANA Good mother, fetch my bail.   [Exit Widow.]
Stay, royal sir,   295
The jeweler that owes the ring is sent for
And he shall surety me. But for this lord
Who hath abused me as he knows himself,

286 customer prostitute

645

Though yet he never harmed me, here I quit him.
300 He knows himself my bed he hath defiled,
And at that time he got his wife with child.
Dead though she be, she feels her young one kick.
So there's my riddle: one that's dead is quick.
And now behold the meaning.

Enter Helena and Widow.

KING   Is there no exorcist
305 Beguiles the truer office of mine eyes?
Is't real that I see?

HELENA   No, my good lord,
'Tis but the shadow of a wife you see,
The name and not the thing.

BERTRAM   Both, both. O, pardon!

HELENA O, my good lord, when I was like this maid,
310 I found you wondrous kind. There is your ring,
And, look you, here's your letter. This it says:
"When from my finger you can get this ring,
And is by me with child," &c. This is done.
Will you be mine, now you are doubly won?

BERTRAM If she, my liege, can make me know this
315 clearly,
I'll love her dearly, ever, ever dearly.

HELENA If it appear not plain and prove untrue,
Deadly divorce step between me and you!
O, my dear mother, do I see you living?

320 LAFEW Mine eyes smell onions, I shall weep anon.
[*To Parolles*] Good Tom Drum, lend me a handkercher. So, I thank thee. Wait on me home, I'll make
sport with thee. Let thy curtsies alone, they are
scurvy ones.

325 KING Let us from point to point this story know,
To make the even truth in pleasure flow.

299 **quit** acquit   303 **quick** (1) alive (2) pregnant   304 **exorcist** summoner of
spirits   309 **like** i.e., substitute for

[*To Diana*] If thou be'st yet a fresh uncroppèd flower,
Choose thou thy husband, and I'll pay thy dower,
For I can guess that by thy honest aid
Thou kept'st a wife herself, thyself a maid.   330
Of that and all the progress more and less
Resolvedly more leisure shall express.
All yet seems well, and if it end so meet,
The bitter past, more welcome is the sweet.

Flourish.

[*Epilogue*]

The King's a beggar now the play is done.
All is well ended if this suit be won,
That you express content; which we will pay
With strife to please you, day exceeding day.
Ours be your patience then, and yours our parts,   5
Your gentle hands lend us, and take our hearts.

Exeunt omnes.

FINIS

332 **Resolvedly** so that doubt is removed   Epilogue   1 **beggar** i.e., for applause
4 **strife** striving   5 **Ours ... parts** i.e., we will silently listen, as you have done,
and you are now the performers

Textual Note

A bookseller's reference in 1603 to "love's labor won" suggests that there was by that date a published version of a play so entitled. No copies survive. Some scholars identify this title with *All's Well*, but whatever the validity of the identification, the only authoritative text for *All's Well* is that of the First Folio (1623). Exactly what sort of text for this play the Folio's editors worked from is not certain, but probably it was either Shakespeare's finished manuscript or a scribe's copy of the manuscript. The play seems complete; it is not, for example, notably short, like *Timon of Athens*, and although it has some loose ends, they do not bulk large, as they do in *Timon*, which must be incomplete. There are, of course, puzzling words and lines, possibly as a result of a scribe's failure to transcribe accurately, and there are signs that a little tidying up remained to be done. For example, there is some inconsistency in the assignment of speeches to the two French lords, and some of their speeches are puzzlingly designated "G" and "E"—possibly the initials of actors for whom the speeches were written. And in a stage direction at III.v there is given the name "Violenta," yet no such character speaks or is addressed. Possibly Violenta was Shakespeare's first thought of a name for the widow's daughter, who is later called Diana, or possibly Violenta is a character that Shakespeare at first believed he would use in the scene but (as he worked further into the scene) decided was of no use. In a way, these minor confusions are reassuring; they suggest we have the play as Shakespeare wrote it, rather than a neat stage version that perhaps omits some of his material.

The present text modernizes spelling and punctuation, expands abbreviations, straightens out some confusion in the assignment of lines to the First and Second Lords, regularizes speech prefixes (e.g., the Folio's "Mother," "Mo.," "Coun[tess]," "La[dy]," etc., all are given as

TEXTUAL NOTE

"Countess"), and regularly gives in the stage directions "Bertram" (for the Folio's "Count," or "Count Rosse," etc.) and "Helena" (because the Folio's first stage direction and first reference to her in dialogue call her so, though the Folio later calls her "Helen"). The act divisions are translated from Latin into English. The Folio does not divide the play into scenes, giving only "Actus Primus. Scoena Prima," but the conventional and convenient scene divisions of the Globe text have been given here. These additions, and others (locales and necessary stage directions not found in the Folio) have been placed in square brackets. The position of an authentic stage direction has occasionally been slightly altered when necessary, and some passages that are printed as prose in the Folio are printed as verse here. Other substantial departures from the Folio are listed below, the present reading given first, in bold type, followed by the original reading, in roman.

I.i.134 **got** goe   155 **ten** two   165 **wear** were

I.iii.19 **I** w   115 **Diana no queen** Queene   173 **loneliness** louelinesse
179 **t'one to th'other** 'ton tooth to th'other   204 **inteemable** intemible
237 **Haply** Happily

II.i.43 **with his cicatrice, an emblem** his sicatrice, with an Emblem   64 **fee** see   146 **sits** shifts   157 **impostor** Impostrue   194 **heaven** helpe

II.ii.63 **An** And

II.iii.95 **her** heere   126 **when** whence   131 **it is** is is   295 **detested** detected

II.v.27 **End** And   29 **one** on   52 **think not** thinke

III.i.23 **the** th the

III.ii.9 **sold** hold   19 **E'en** In   115 **still-piecing** still-peering

III.v. s.d. **her daughter Diana** her daughter, Violenta   34 **le** la
66 **warrant** write

III.vi.36 **his** this   37 **ore** ours

III.vii.19 **Resolved** Resolue

IV.i.91 **art** are

IV.iii.86–89 **They ... midnight** [Folio gives to Bertram]   126 **Hush, hush** [Folio gives to Bertram]   148 **All's ... him** [Folio gives to Parolles]
208 **lordship** Lord

TEXTUAL NOTE

IV.iv.9 **Marseilles** Marcella 16 you your

IV.v.40 **name** maine 81 **Marseilles** Marcellus

V.i.6. s.d. **Gentleman, a stranger** gentle Astringer

V.ii.26 **similes** smiles

V.iii.122 **tax** taze 155 **since** sir 157 s.d. **Widow [and] Diana** Widdow, Diana, and Parolles 216 **inf'nite cunning** insuite comming

Epilogue 4 **strife** strift

WILLIAM
SHAKESPEARE

———

MEASURE FOR
MEASURE

Edited by S. Nagarsjan

The Scene: Vienna

The names of all the actors:

VINCENTIO, the Duke
ANGELO, the Deputy
ESCALUS, an ancient Lord
CLAUDIO, a young gentleman
LUCIO, a fantastic
TWO OTHER LIKE GENTLEMEN
PROVOST
THOMAS ⎫
PETER ⎬ two friars
[A Justice]
[Varrius]
ELBOW, a simple constable
FROTH, a foolish gentleman
CLOWN [Pompey, servant to Mistress Overdone]
ABHORSON, an executioner
BARNARDINE, a dissolute prisoner
ISABELLA, sister to Claudio
MARIANA, bethrothed to Angelo
JULIET, beloved of Claudio
FRANCISCA, a nun
MISTRESS OVERDONE, a bawd
[Lords, Officers, Citizens, Boy, and Attendants]

MEASURE FOR MEASURE

ACT I

Scene I. [*The Duke's palace.*]

Enter Duke, Escalus, Lords, [and Attendants].

DUKE Escalus.

ESCALUS My lord.

DUKE Of government the properties to unfold,
Would seem in me t' affect speech and discourse,
Since I am put to know that your own science   5
Exceeds, in that, the lists of all advice
My strength can give you. Then no more remains
But that, to your sufficiency as your worth is able,
And let them work. The nature of our people,
Our city's institutions, and the terms   10
For common justice, y'are as pregnant in
As art and practice hath enrichèd any
That we remember. There is our commission,
From which we would not have you warp. Call
    hither,

Text references are printed in **bold** type; the annotation follows in roman type.
I.1.3. **properties** characteristics   5 **put to know** given to understand   5 **science** knowledge   6 **lists** limits   8 **to your sufficiency ... able** (perhaps a line is missing after this line)   11 **pregnant in** full of knowledge   14 **warp** deviate

15   I say, bid come before us Angelo.

                                    [*Exit an Attendant*.]
        What figure of us, think you, he will bear?
        For you must know, we have with special soul
        Elected him our absence to supply;
        Lent him our terror, dressed him with our love,
20   And given his deputation all the organs
        Of our own pow'r. What think you of it?

ESCALUS If any in Vienna be of worth
        To undergo such ample grace and honor,
        It is Lord Angelo.

                        Enter Angelo.

DUKE   Look where he comes.

25   ANGELO Always obedient to your Grace's will,
        I come to know your pleasure.

DUKE   Angelo,
        There is a kind of character in thy life,
        That to th' observer doth thy history
        Fully unfold. Thyself and thy belongings
30   Are not thine own so proper as to waste
        Thyself upon thy virtues, they on thee.
        Heaven doth with us as we with torches do,
        Not light them for themselves; for if our virtues
        Did not go forth of us, 'twere all alike
        As if we had them not. Spirits are not finely
35   touched
        But to fine issues, nor Nature never lends
        The smallest scruple of her excellence
        But like a thrifty goddess she determines

---

16 **figure** image 16 **bear** represent 17 **soul** thought 20 **organs** means of
action 23 **undergo** enjoy 27 **character** secret handwriting 29 **belongings**
endowments 30 **proper** exclusively 32 **Heaven … do** (see Luke 11:33: "No
man, when he hath lighted a candle, putteth it in a secret place, neither under a
bushel, but on a candlestick that they which come in may see the light." Also
Matthew 7:16: "Ye shall know them by their fruits") 35-36 **Spirits … issues**
i.e., great qualities are bestowed only so that they may lead to great
achievements 37 **scruple** 1/24 oz.

Herself the glory of a creditor,
Both thanks and use. But I do bend my speech   40
To one that can my part in him advertise.
Hold therefore, Angelo:
In our remove be thou at full ourself;
Mortality and mercy in Vienna
Live in thy tongue and heart. Old Escalus,   45
Though first in question, is thy secondary.
Take thy commission.

ANGLEO   Now, good my lord,
Let there be some more test made of my mettle
Before so noble and so great a figure
Be stamped upon it.

DUKE   No more evasion.   50
We have with a leavened and preparèd choice
Proceeded to you; therefore take your honors.
Our haste from hence is of so quick condition
That it prefers itself, and leaves unquestioned
Matters of needful value. We shall write to you,   55
As time and our concernings shall importune,
How it goes with us, and do look to know
What doth befall you here. So fare you well.
To th' hopeful execution do I leave you
Of your commissions.

ANGELO   Yet give leave, my lord,   60
That we may bring you something on the way.

DUKE My haste may not admit it;
Nor need you, on mine honor, have to do
With any scruple; your scope is as mine own,
So to enforce or qualify the laws   65
As to your soul seems good. Give me your hand.
I'll privily away; I love the people,
But do not like to stage me to their eyes.
Though it do well, I do not relish well

40 use interest 40 bend address 41 advertise display prominently 43 remove
absence 46 question consideration 46 secondary subordinate 48 mettle
(pun on "metal," i.e., material) 51 leavened i.e., long-pondered 54 prefers
itself takes precedence 54 unquestioned unexamined 61 bring escort

70   Their loud applause and aves vehement.
      Nor do I think the man of safe discretion
      That does affect it. Once more, fare you well.

ANGELO The heavens give safety to your purposes.

ESCALUS Lead forth and bring you back in happiness.

75 DUKE I thank you; fare you well.   *Exit.*

ESCALUS I shall desire you, sir, to give me leave
      To have free speech with you; and it concerns me
      To look into the bottom of my place.
      A pow'r I have, but of what strength and nature,
80   I am not yet instructed.

ANGELO 'Tis so with me. Let us withdraw together,
      And we may soon our satisfaction have
      Touching that point.

ESCALUS   I'll wait upon your honor.
                                              Exeunt.

              Scene II. [*A street.*]

          Enter Lucio and two other Gentlemen.

LUCIO If the Duke, with the other dukes, come not
    to composition with the King of Hungary, why
    then all the dukes fall upon the King.

FIRST GENTLEMAN Heaven grant us its peace, but not
5   the King of Hungary's!

SECOND GENTLEMAN Amen.

LUCIO Thou conclud'st like the sanctimonious pirate,
    that went to sea with the Ten Commandments, but
    scraped one out of the table.

70 **aves** salutations   78 **To look ... place** i.e., to examine carefully the range of
my authority   I.ii.2 **composition** agreement   2 **Hungary** (perhaps a pun on
"hungry.")

SECOND GENTLEMAN "Thou shalt not steal"?   10

LUCIO Ay, that he razed.

FIRST GENTLEMAN Why, 'twas a commandment to command the captain and all the rest from their functions: they put forth to steal. There's not a soldier of us all that, in the thanksgiving before meat, do   15
relish the petition well that prays for peace.

SECOND GENTLEMAN I never heard any soldier dislike it.

LUCIO I believe thee, for I think thou never wast where grace was said.   20

SECOND GENTLEMAN No? A dozen times at least.

FIRST GENTLEMAN What, in meter?

LUCIO In any proportion, or in any language.

FIRST GENTLEMAN I think, or in any religion.

LUCIO Ay, why not? Grace is grace, despite of all   25
controversy: as, for example, thou thyself art a wicked villain, despite of all grace.

FIRST GENTLEMAN Well, there went but a pair of shears between us.

LUCIO I grant; as there may between the lists and   30
the velvet. Thou art the list.

FIRST GENTLEMAN And thou the velvet. Thou art good velvet; thou'rt a three-piled piece, I warrant thee. I had as lief be a list of an English kersey, as be piled, as thou art piled, for a French velvet. Do   35
I speak feelingly now?

LUCIO I think thou dost; and, indeed, with most pain-

23 **proportion** length   28–29 **there ... us** i.e., we are cut from the same cloth
30 **lists** selvage or border of a cloth (usually of a different material from the body)   33 **three-piled** (1) pile of a treble thickness (2) "piled" (bald) as a result of venereal disease   34 **kersey** coarse cloth (therefore "plain and honest")
35 **French velvet** (1) excellent velvet (2) French prostitute (syphilis was also known as "the French disease")   35–36 **Do ... feelingly** i.e., do I touch you there?

ful feeling of thy speech. I will, out of thine own
confession, learn to begin thy health; but, whilst I
40 live, forget to drink after thee.

FIRST GENTLEMAN I think I have done myself wrong,
have I not?

SECOND GENTLEMAN Yes, that thou hast, whether thou
art tainted or free.

Enter Bawd [Mistress Overdone].

45 LUCIO Behold, behold, where Madam Mitigation
comes! I have purchased as many diseases under
her roof as come to—

SECOND GENTLEMAN To what, I pray?

LUCIO Judge.

50 SECOND GENTLEMAN To three thousand dolors a year.

FIRST GENTLEMAN Ay, and more.

LUCIO A French crown more.

FIRST GENTLEMAN Thou art always figuring diseases in
me, but thou art full of error. I am sound.

55 LUCIO Nay, not as one would say, healthy, but so
sound as things that are hollow. Thy bones are
hollow; impiety has made a feast of thee.

FIRST GENTLEMAN How now! Which of your hips has
the most profound sciatica?

60 MISTRESS OVERDONE Well, well; there's one yonder arrested and carried to prison was worth five thousand of you all.

SECOND GENTLEMAN Who's that, I pray thee?

MISTRESS OVERDONE Marry, sir, that's Claudio, Signior
65 Claudio.

---

38 **feeling** personal experience   39–40 **learn ... thee** drink to your health but not
after you from the same cup (to avoid the infection)   50 **dolors** (pun on "dollars")
52 **French crown** (1) *écu* (2) head that has gone bald from venereal disease
57 **impiety** immorality   64 **Marry** (a light oath, from "by the Virgin Mary")

FIRST GENTLEMAN Claudio to prison? 'Tis not so.

MISTRESS OVERDONE Nay, but I know 'tis so. I saw him arrested; saw him carried away, and which is more, within these three days his head to be chopped off.   70

LUCIO But, after all this fooling, I would not have it so. Art thou sure of this?

MISTRESS OVERDONE I am too sure of it; and it is for getting Madam Julietta with child.

LUCIO Believe me, this may be. He promised to meet   75
me two hours since, and he was ever precise in promise-keeping.

SECOND GENTLEMAN Besides, you know, it draws something near to the speech we had to such a purpose.   80

FIRST GENTLEMAN But, most of all, agreeing with the proclamation.

LUCIO Away! Let's go learn the truth of it.
                              Exit [Lucio with Gentlemen].

MISTRESS OVERDONE Thus, what with the war, what with the sweat, what with the gallows, and what   85
with poverty, I am custom-shrunk.

                    Enter Clown [Pompey].

How now? What's the news with you?

POMPEY Yonder man is carried to prison.

MISTRESS OVERDONE Well; what has he done?

POMPEY A woman.   90

MISTRESS OVERDONE But what's his offense?

POMPEY Groping for trouts in a peculiar river.

MISTRESS OVERDONE What? Is there a maid with child by him?

85 sweat sweating sickness, plague   92 peculiar private

95   POMPEY No, but there's a woman with maid by him. You have not heard of the proclamation, have you?

MISTRESS OVERDONE What proclamation, man?

POMPEY All houses in the suburbs of Vienna must be plucked down.

100   MISTRESS OVERDONE And what shall become of those in the city?

POMPEY They shall stand for seed: they had gone down too, but that a wise burgher put in for them.

MISTRESS OVERDONE But shall all our houses of resort
105   in the suburbs be pulled down?

POMPEY To the ground, mistress.

MISTRESS OVERDONE Why, here's a change indeed in the commonwealth! What shall become of me?

POMPEY Come, fear not you; good counselors lack
110   no clients. Though you change your place, you need not change your trade; I'll be your tapster still. Courage, there will be pity taken on you; you that have worn your eyes almost out in the service, you will be considered.

115   MISTRESS OVERDONE What's to do here, Thomas Tapster? Let's withdraw.

POMPEY Here comes Signior Claudio, led by the provost to prison; and there's Madam Juliet.

Exeunt.

*Enter Provost, Claudio, Juliet, Officers, Lucio,
and two Gentlemen.*

CLAUDIO Fellow, why dost thou show me thus to th' world?
120   Bear me to prison, where I am committed.

PROVOST I do it not in evil disposition,

98 **suburbs** (in Shakespeare's London, the area of the brothels)   111 **tapster** bartender, waiter (here, pimp)

But from Lord Angelo, by special charge.

CLAUDIO Thus can the demigod Authority
Make us pay down for our offense by weight.
The words of heaven: on whom it will, it will;   125
On whom it will not, so. Yet still 'tis just.

LUCIO Why, how now, Claudio! Whence comes this
restraint?

CLAUDIO From too much liberty, my Lucio, liberty.
As surfeit is the father of much fast,
So every scope by the immoderate use   130
Turns to restraint. Our natures do pursue,
Like rats that ravin down their proper bane,
A thirsty evil, and when we drink, we die.

LUCIO If I could speak so wisely under an arrest, I
would send for certain of my creditors. And yet, to   135
say the truth, I had as lief have the foppery of
freedom as the mortality of imprisonment. What's
thy offense, Claudio?

CLAUDIO What but to speak of would offend again.

LUCIO What, is't murder?   140

CLAUDIO No.

LUCIO Lechery?

CLAUDIO Call it so.

PROVOST Away, sir, you must go.

CLAUDIO One word, good friend. Lucio, a word with
you.   145

LUCIO A hundred, if they'll do you any good.
Is lechery so looked after?

CLAUDIO Thus stands it with me: upon a true contract

125–26 **The words ... just** (see Romans 9:15,18: "For he saith to Moses, I will
have mercy on whom I will have mercy, and I will have compassion on whom I
will have compassion ... Therefore hath he mercy on whom he will have mercy,
and whom he will he hardeneth")   132 **ravin ... bane** greedily devour what is
poisonous to them   136 **foppery** foolishness

I got possession of Julietta's bed.
150   You know the lady, she is fast my wife,
Save that we do the denunciation lack
Of outward order. This we came not to,
Only for propagation of a dower
Remaining in the coffer of her friends,
155   From whom we thought it meet to hide our love
Till time had made them for us. But it chances
The stealth of our most mutual entertainment
With character too gross is writ on Juliet.

LUCIO With child, perhaps?

CLAUDIO   Unhappily, even so.
160   And the new deputy now for the Duke—
Whether it be the fault and glimpse of newness,
Or whether that the body public be
A horse whereon the governor doth ride,
Who, newly in the seat, that it may know
165   He can command, lets it straight feel the spur;
Whether the tyranny be in his place,
Or in his eminence that fills it up,
I stagger in—but this new governor
Awakes me all the enrollèd penalties
170   Which have, like unscoured armor, hung by th' wall
So long, that nineteen zodiacs have gone round,
And none of them been worn; and, for a name,
Now puts the drowsy and neglected act
Freshly on me. 'Tis surely for a name.

175 LUCIO I warrant it is, and thy head stands so tickle
on thy shoulders, that a milkmaid, if she be in love,
may sigh it off. Send after the Duke, and appeal
to him.

CLAUDIO I have done so, but he's not to be found.
180   I prithee, Lucio, do me this kind service:
This day my sister should the cloister enter,

---

151 **denunciation** formal announcement 153 **propagation** increase
154 **friends** relatives 161 **fault and glimpse of newness** i.e., weakness arising
from the sudden vision of new authority 168 **stagger in** am not sure 169 **enrollèd**
inscribed in the rolls of the laws 171 **zodiacs** i.e., years 175 **tickle** insecure

And there receive her approbation.
Acquaint her with the danger of my state;
Implore her, in my voice, that she make friends
To the strict deputy; bid herself assay him.   185
I have great hope in that; for in her youth
There is a prone and speechless dialect,
Such as move men; beside, she hath prosperous art
When she will play with reason and discourse,
And well she can persuade.   190

LUCIO I pray she may; as well for the encouragement
of the like, which else would stand under grievous
imposition, as for the enjoying of thy life, who I
would be sorry should be thus foolishly lost at a
game of tick-tack. I'll to her.   195

CLAUDIO I thank you, good friend Lucio.

LUCIO Within two hours.

CLAUDIO   Come, officer, away!

Exeunt.

Scene III. [*A monastery.*]

Enter Duke and Friar Thomas.

DUKE No, holy father; throw away that thought;
Believe not that the dribbling dart of love
Can pierce a complete bosom. Why I desire thee
To give me secret harbor, hath a purpose
More grave and wrinkled than the aims and ends   5
Of burning youth.

---

182 approbation novitiate   185 assay test, i.e., attempt to persuade   187 prone
winning   195 tick-tack (literally, a game using a board into which pegs were
fitted) I.iii.2 dribbling dart arrow feebly shot   3 complete protected, independent   5 wrinkled mature, aged

FRIAR THOMAS   May your Grace speak of it?

DUKE My holy sir, none better knows than you
How I have ever loved the life removed,
And held in idle price to haunt assemblies
Where youth and cost, witless bravery keeps.
I have delivered to Lord Angelo,
A man of stricture and firm abstinence,
My absolute power and place here in Vienna,
And he supposes me traveled to Poland;
For so I have strewed it in the common ear,
And so it is received. Now, pious sir,
You will demand of me why I do this.

FRIAR THOMAS Gladly, my lord.

DUKE We have strict statutes and most biting laws,
The needful bits and curbs to headstrong weeds,
Which for this fourteen years we have let slip,
Even like an o'ergrown lion in a cave,
That goes not out to prey. Now, as fond fathers,
Having bound up the threat'ning twigs of birch,
Only to stick it in their children's sight
For terror, not to use; in time the rod
Becomes more mocked than feared; so our decrees,
Dead to infliction, to themselves are dead,
And Liberty plucks Justice by the nose;
The baby beats the nurse, and quite athwart
Goes all decorum.

FRIAR THOMAS   It rested in your Grace
To unloose this tied-up Justice when you pleased,
And it in you more dreadful would have seemed
Than in Lord Angelo.

DUKE   I do fear, too dreadful:
Sith 'twas my fault to give the people scope,
'Twould be my tyranny to strike and gall them

10 **witless bravery** senseless show   12 **stricture** strictness   15 **common ear**
the ear of the people   21 **fourteen** (in I.ii.171 the time has been "nineteen" years.
Doubtless the printer's copy in both lines had either xiv or xix and in one line was
misread)   28 **Dead to infliction** utterly unenforced   29 **Liberty** license
35 **Sith** since

664

For what I bid them do; for we bid this be done
When evil deeds have their permissive pass,
And not the punishment. Therefore, indeed, my
    father,
I have on Angelo imposed the office,   40
Who may, in th' ambush of my name, strike home,
And yet my nature never in the fight
To do it slander. And to behold his sway,
I will, as 'twere a brother of your order,
Visit both prince and people. Therefore, I prithee,   45
Supply me with the habit and instruct me
How I may formally in person bear
Like a true friar. Moe reasons for this action
At our more leisure shall I render you;
Only, this one: Lord Angelo is precise,   50
Stands at a guard with envy; scarce confesses
That his blood flows, or that his appetite
Is more to bread than stone. Hence shall we see,
If power change purpose, what our seemers be.
                                    Exit [with Friar].

Scene IV. [*A nunnery*.]

Enter Isabella and Francisca, a nun.

ISABELLA And have you nuns no farther privileges?

FRANCISCA Are not these large enough?

ISABELLA Yes, truly. I speak not as desiring more,
    But rather wishing a more strict restraint
    Upon the sisterhood, the votarists of Saint Clare.   5

LUCIO (*Within*) Ho! Peace be in this place!

---

41 in th' ambush under cover   46 habit garment   48 Moe more   50 precise
fastidiously strict   51 Stands ... envy defies all malicious criticism I.iv.5 Saint
Clare (a notably strict order)

ISABELLA   Who's that which calls?

FRANCISCA It is a man's voice. Gentle Isabella,
    Turn you the key, and know his business of him.
    You may, I may not: you are yet unsworn.
    When you have vowed, you must not speak with
10   men
    But in the presence of the prioress:
    Then, if you speak, you must not show your face,
    Or, if you show your face, you must not speak.
    He calls again; I pray you, answer him.   [*Exit.*]

15 ISABELLA Peace and prosperity! Who is't that calls?

                [*Enter Lucio.*]

LUCIO Hail, virgin—if you be, as those cheek-roses
    Proclaim you are no less! Can you so stead me
    As bring me to the sight of Isabella,
    A novice of this place and the fair sister
20   To her unhappy brother, Claudio?

ISABELLA Why "her unhappy brother"? Let me ask,
    The rather for I now must make you know
    I am that Isabella and his sister.

LUCIO Gentle and fair, your brother kindly greets you.
25   Not to be weary with you, he's in prison.

ISABELLA Woe me! For what?

LUCIO For that which, if myself might be his judge,
    He should receive his punishment in thanks:
    He hath got his friend with child.

ISABELLA Sir! Make me not your story.

30 LUCIO   'Tis true.
    I would not, though 'tis my familiar sin
    With maids to seem the lapwing, and to jest,
    Tongue far from heart, play with all virgins so.
    I hold you as a thing enskied and sainted,
35   By your renouncement, an immortal spirit;

17 **stead** help   30 **story** subject for mirth   32 **lapwing** peewit (a bird which
runs away from its nest to mislead intruders)

And to be talked with in sincerity,
As with a saint.

ISABELLA You do blaspheme the good in mocking me.

LUCIO Do not believe it. Fewness and truth, 'tis thus:
Your brother and his lover have embraced;   40
As those that feed grow full, as blossoming time
That from the seedness the bare fallow brings
To teeming foison, even so her plenteous womb
Expresseth his full tilth and husbandry.

ISABELLA Someone with child by him? My cousin
     Juliet?   45

LUCIO Is she your cousin?

ISABELLA Adoptedly, as schoolmaids change their
     names
By vain, though apt, affection.

LUCIO   She it is.

ISABELLA O, let him marry her.

LUCIO   This is the point:
The Duke is very strangely gone from hence;   50
Bore many gentlemen, myself being one,
In hand and hope of action, but we do learn
By those that know the very nerves of state,
His givings-out were of an infinite distance
From his true-meant design. Upon his place,   55
And with full line of his authority,
Governs Lord Angelo, a man whose blood
Is very snow-broth; one who never feels
The wanton stings and motions of the sense,
But doth rebate and blunt his natural edge   60
With profits of the mind, study and fast.
He—to give fear to use and liberty,
Which have for long run by the hideous law,
As mice by lions—hath picked out an act,

39 **Fewness and truth** briefly and truly   42 **seedness** sowing   43 **foison** harvest
51-52 **Bore ... action** deluded ... with the hope of military action   62 **use and liberty** habitual license

65   Under whose heavy sense your brother's life
      Falls into forfeit; he arrests him on it,
      And follows close the rigor of the statute,
      To make him an example. All hope is gone,
      Unless you have the grace by your fair prayer
70   To soften Angelo. And that's my pith of business
      'Twixt you and your poor brother.

ISABELLA Doth he so? Seek his life?

LUCIO   Has censured him
      Already, and, as I hear, the provost hath
      A warrant for's execution.

75 ISABELLA Alas, what poor ability's in me
      To do him good?

LUCIO   Assay the pow'r you have.

ISABELLA My power? Alas, I doubt—

LUCIO   Our doubts are traitors,
      And makes us lose the good we oft might win,
      By fearing to attempt. Go to Lord Angelo,
80   And let him learn to know, when maidens sue,
      Men give like gods; but when they weep and kneel,
      All their petitions are as freely theirs
      As they themselves would owe them.

ISABELLA I'll see what I can do.

LUCIO   But speedily.

85 ISABELLA I will about it straight,
      No longer staying but to give the Mother
      Notice of my affair. I humbly thank you;
      Commend me to my brother; soon at night
      I'll send him certain word of my success.

LUCIO I take my leave of you.

90 ISABELLA   Good sir, adieu.

                                        Exeunt.

65 **sense** interpretation   72 **censured** pronounced judgment on   78 **makes** (a plural subject sometimes takes a verb ending in *-s*)   83 **owe** own   89 **success** outcome

ACT II

Scene I. [*A room.*]

Enter Angelo, Escalus, and Servants, Justice.

ANGELO We must not make a scarecrow of the law,
    Setting it up to fear the birds of prey,
    And let it keep one shape, till custom make it
    Their perch and not their terror.

ESCALUS   Ay, but yet
    Let us be keen, and rather cut a little,   5
    Than fall, and bruise to death. Alas, this gentleman
    Whom I would save had a most noble father.
    Let but your honor know,
    Whom I believe to be most strait in virtue,
    That, in the working of your own affections,   10
    Had time cohered with place or place with wishing,
    Or that the resolute acting of your blood
    Could have attained th' effect of your own purpose,
    Whether you had not sometime in your life
    Erred in this point which now you censure him,   15
    And pulled the law upon you.

ANGELO 'Tis one thing to be tempted, Escalus,
    Another thing to fall. I not deny,

II.i.5 **cut** prune   6 **fall** let the ax fall   9 **strait** strict   10 **affections** passions

The jury, passing on the prisoner's life,
20   May in the sworn twelve have a thief or two
Guiltier than him they try. What's open made to
     Justice,
That Justice seizes. What knows the laws
That thieves do pass on thieves? 'Tis very
     pregnant,
The jewel that we find, we stoop and take't
25   Because we see it; but what we do not see
We tread upon, and never think of it.
You may not so extenuate his offense
For I have had such faults; but rather tell me,
When I, that censure him, do so offend,
30   Let mine own judgment pattern out my death,
And nothing come in partial. Sir, he must die.

ESCALUS   Be it as your wisdom will.

ANGELO   Where is the provost?

Enter Provost.

PROVOST   Here, if it like your honor.

ANGELO   See that Claudio
Be executed by nine tomorrow morning.
35   Bring him his confessor, let him be prepared,
For that's the utmost of his pilgrimage.
                              [*Exit Provost.*]

ESCALUS   Well, Heaven forgive him, and forgive us all.
Some rise by sin, and some by virtue fall:
Some run from breaks of ice, and answer none;
40   And some condemnèd for a fault alone.

Enter Elbow, Froth, Clown [Pompey], Officers.

ELBOW   Come, bring them away. If these be good people in a commonweal that do nothing but use their
abuses in common houses, I know no law. Bring
them away.

23 **pregnant** clear   39 **Some ... ice** some escape after gross violations of chastity
(? the passage is much disputed)   40 **fault** (1) small crack in the ice (2) act of sex

ANGELO How now, sir! What's your name? And what's   45
the matter?

ELBOW If it please your honor, I am the poor Duke's
constable, and my name is Elbow. I do lean upon
justice, sir, and do bring in here before your good
honor two notorious benefactors.   50

ANGELO Benefactors? Well, what benefactors are they?
Are they not malefactors?

ELBOW If it please your honor, I know not well what
they are, but precise villains they are, that I am
sure of, and void of all profanation in the world   55
that good Christians ought to have.
comes off well; here's a wise officer.

ANGELO Go to: what quality are they of? Elbow is
your name? Why dost thou not speak, Elbow?

POMPEY He cannot, sir; he's out at elbow.   60

ANGELO What are you, sir?

ELBOW He, sir! A tapster, sir, parcel-bawd, one that
serves a bad woman whose house, sir, was, as they
say, plucked down in the suburbs, and now she
professes a hothouse, which, I think, is a very ill   65
house too.

ESCALUS How know you that?

ELBOW My wife, sir, whom I detest before Heaven
and your honor—

ESCALUS How! Thy wife?   70

ELBOW Ay, sir—whom, I thank Heaven, is an honest
woman—

ESCALUS Dost thou detest her therefore?

ELBOW I say, sir, I will detest myself also, as well as

---

58 **quality** profession   60 **out at elbow** (1) somewhat seedy (2) speechless (out at
the sound of his name)   62 **parcel-bawd** partly a bawd   65 **hothouse** bathhouse
68 **detest**, i.e., protest   71 **honest** chaste

75   she, that this house, if it be not a bawd's house, it
      is pity of her life, for it is a naughty house.

ESCALUS How dost thou know that, constable?

ELBOW Marry, sir, by my wife, who, if she had been a
      woman cardinally given, might have been accused
80   in fornication, adultery, and all uncleanliness there.

ESCALUS By the woman's means?

ELBOW Ay, sir, by Mistress Overdone's means; but as
      she spit in his face, so she defied him.

POMPEY Sir, if it please your honor, this is not so.

85 ELBOW Prove it before these varlets here, thou honor-
      able man; prove it.

ESCALUS Do you hear how he misplaces?

POMPEY Sir, she came in great with child; and longing,
      saving your honor's reverence, for stewed prunes.
90   Sir, we had but two in the house, which at that very
      distant time stood, as it were, in a fruit dish, a dish
      of some threepence; your honors have seen such
      dishes; they are not china dishes, but very good
      dishes—

95 ESCALUS Go to, go to; no matter for the dish, sir.

POMPEY No, indeed, sir, not a pin; you are therein
      in the right; but to the point. As I say, this Mistress
      Elbow, being, as I say, with child, and being great-
      bellied, and longing, as I said, for prunes; and hav-
100   ing but two in the dish, as I said, Master Froth here,
      this very man, having eaten the rest, as I said, and,
      as I say, paying for them very honestly; for, as you
      know, Master Froth, I could not give you three-
      pence again.

105 FROTH No, indeed.

POMPEY Very well, you being then, if you be remem-

76 naughty immoral   79 cardinally i.e., carnally   89 stewed prunes (supposed
to be a favorite dish among prostitutes)

b'red, cracking the stones of the foresaid prunes—

FROTH Ay, so I did indeed.

POMPEY Why, very well; I telling you then, if you be
remated'red, that such a one and such a one were   110
past cure of the thing you wot of, unless they kept
very good diet, as I told you—

FROTH All this is true.

POMPEY Why, very well, then—

ESCALUS Come, you are a tedious fool; to the purpose.   115
What was done to Elbow's wife, that he hath cause
to complain of? Come me to what was done to her.

POMPEY Sir, your honor cannot come to that yet.

ESCALUS No, sir, nor I mean it not.

POMPEY Sir, but you shall come to it, by your honor's   120
leave. And, I beseech you, look into Master Froth
here, sir, a man of fourscore pound a year, whose
father died at Hallowmas. Was't not at Hallowmas, Master Froth?

FROTH All-hallond Eve.   125

POMPEY Why, very well; I hope here be truths. He,
sir, sitting, as I say, in a lower chair, sir, 'twas in
the Bunch of Grapes, where, indeed, you have a
delight to sit, have you not?

FROTH I have so, because it is an open room, and   130
good for winter.

POMPEY Why, very well, then; I hope here be truths.

ANGELO This will last out a night in Russia,
When nights are longest there. I'll take my leave,
And leave you to the hearing of the cause,   135
Hoping you'll find good cause to whip them all.

111 wot know 117-18 Come me ... that yet (the verbs carry a sexual
innuendo) 123-24 Hallowmas All Saints' Day, November 1st 125 All-
hallond Eve October 31st

ESCALUS I think no less. Good morrow to your lordship.   *Exit* [*Angelo*].
Now, sir, come on: what was done to Elbow's wife,
once more?

140 POMPEY Once, sir? There was nothing done to her
once.

ELBOW I beseech you, sir, ask him what this man did
to my wife.

POMPEY I beseech your honor, ask me.

145 ESCALUS Well, sir; what did this gentleman to her?

POMPEY I beseech you, sir, look in this gentleman's
face. Good Master Froth, look upon his honor;
'tis for a good purpose. Doth your honor mark his
face?

150 ESCALUS Ay, sir, very well.

POMPEY Nay, I beseech you, mark it well.

ESCALUS Well, I do so.

POMPEY Doth your honor see any harm in his face?

ESCALUS Why, no.

155 POMPEY I'll be supposed upon a book, his face is the
worst thing about him. Good, then; if his face be
the worst thing about him, how could Master Froth
do the constable's wife any harm? I would know
that of your honor.

160 ESCALUS He's in the right. Constable, what say you
to it?

ELBOW First, and it like you, the house is a respected house; next, this is a respected fellow;
and his mistress is a respected woman.

165 POMPEY By this hand, sir, his wife is a more respected
person than any of us all.

155 supposed i.e., deposed   162 and if   162-63 respected i.e., suspected

ELBOW Varlet, thou liest; thou liest, wicked varlet! The time is yet to come that she was ever respected with man, woman, or child.

POMPEY Sir, she was respected with him before he 170 married with her.

ESCALUS Which is the wiser here, Justice or Iniquity? Is this true?

ELBOW O thou caitiff! O thou varlet! O thou wicked Hannibal! I respected with her before I was mar- 175 ried to her! If ever I was respected with her, or she with me, let not your worship think me the poor Duke's officer. Prove this, thou wicked Hannibal, or I'll have mine action of batt'ry on thee.

ESCALUS If he took you a box o' th' ear, you might 180 have your action of slander too.

ELBOW Marry, I thank your good worship for it. What is't your worship's pleasure I shall do with this wicked caitiff?

ESCALUS Truly, officer, because he hath some offenses 185 in him that thou wouldst discover if thou couldst, let him continue in his courses till thou know'st what they are.

ELBOW Marry, I thank your worship for it. Thou seest, thou wicked varlet, now, what's come upon thee. 190 Thou art to continue now, thou varlet; thou art to continue.

ESCALUS Where were you born, friend?

FROTH Here in Vienna, sir.

ESCALUS Are you of fourscore pounds a year?   195

FROTH Yes, and't please you, sir.

ESCALUS So. [To Pompey] What trade are you of, sir?

POMPEY A tapster, a poor widow's tapster.

172 Justice or Iniquity (personified characters in morality plays)   175 Hannibal i.e., cannibal, fleshmonger (?)

675

ESCALUS Your mistress' name?

200 POMPEY Mistress Overdone.

ESCALUS Hath she had any more than one husband?

POMPEY Nine, sir; Overdone by the last.

ESCALUS Nine! Come hither to me, Master Froth.
Master Froth, I would not have you acquainted
205 with tapsters: they will draw you, Master Froth,
and you will hang them. Get you gone, and let me
hear no more of you.

FROTH I thank your worship. For mine own part, I
never come into any room in a taphouse, but I am
210 drawn in.

ESCALUS Well, no more of it, Master Froth; farewell.
                                         [*Exit Froth.*]
Come you hither to me, Master Tapster. What's
your name, Master Tapster?

POMPEY Pompey.

215 ESCALUS What else?

POMPEY Bum, sir.

ESCALUS Troth, and your bum is the greatest thing
about you; so that, in the beastliest sense, you are
Pompey the Great. Pompey, you are partly a bawd,
220 Pompey, howsoever you color it in being a tapster,
are you not? Come, tell me true; it shall be the
better for you.

POMPEY Truly, sir, I am a poor fellow that would live.

ESCALUS How would you live, Pompey? By being a
225 bawd? What do you think of the trade, Pompey?
Is it a lawful trade?

POMPEY If the law would allow it, sir.

205 **draw you** (1) draw drinks for you (2) empty you, disembowel you   220 **color**
camouflage

ESCALUS But the law will not allow it, Pompey; nor it shall not be allowed in Vienna.

POMPEY Does your worship mean to geld and splay 230 all the youth of the city?

ESCALUS No, Pompey.

POMPEY Truly, sir, in my poor opinion, they will to't, then. If your worship will take order for the drabs and the knaves, you need not to fear the bawds. 235

ESCALUS There is pretty orders beginning, I can tell you; it is but heading and hanging.

POMPEY If you head and hang all that offend that way but for ten year together, you'll be glad to give out a commission for more heads; if this law hold 240 in Vienna ten year, I'll rent the fairest house in it after threepence a bay; if you live to see this come to pass, say Pompey told you so.

ESCALUS Thank you, good Pompey; and, in requital of your prophecy, hark you: I advise you, let me 245 not find you before me again upon any complaint whatsoever; no, not for dwelling where you do. If I do, Pompey, I shall beat you to your tent, and prove a shrewd Caesar to you; in plain dealing, Pompey, I shall have you whipped. So, for this 250 time, Pompey, fare you well.

POMPEY I thank your worship for your good counsel; [aside] but I shall follow it as the flesh and fortune shall better determine.
Whip me? No, no; let carman whip his jade. 255
The valiant heart's not whipped out of his trade.
                                                    Exit.

ESCALUS Come hither to me, Master Elbow; come hither, Master constable. How long have you been in this place of constable?

237 heading beheading   242 bay space under a single gable   255 carman whip his jade (the cartman whipped the whore after carting her through the streets; a "jade" is literally a nag)

260 ELBOW Seven year and a half, sir.

ESCALUS I thought, by the readiness in the office, you
had continued in it some time. You say, seven years
together?

ELBOW And a half, sir.

265 ESCALUS Alas, it hath been great pains to you. They
do you wrong to put you so oft upon't. Are there
not men in your ward sufficient to serve it?

ELBOW Faith, sir, few of any wit in such matters. As
they are chosen, they are glad to choose me for
270 them; I do it for some piece of money, and go
through with all.

ESCALUS Look you bring me in the names of some
six or seven, the most sufficient of your parish.

ELBOW To your worship's house, sir?

275 ESCALUS To my house. Fare you well. [*Exit Elbow*.]
What's o'clock, think you?

JUSTICE Eleven, sir.

ESCALUS I pray you home to dinner with me.

JUSTICE I humbly thank you.

280 ESCALUS It grieves me for the death of Claudio,
But there's no remedy.

JUSTICE Lord Angelo is severe.

ESCALUS   It is but needful:
Mercy is not itself, that oft looks so;
Pardon is still the nurse of second woe.
285 But yet—poor Claudio! There is no remedy.
Come, sir.   *Exeunt*.

---

266 **put you so oft upon't** i.e., impose on you the task of being constable
284 **still** always

Scene II. [*A room.*]

Enter Provost, [and a] Servant.

SERVANT He's hearing of a cause; he will come straight:
I'll tell him of you.

PROVOST   Pray you, do. [*Exit Servant.*] I'll know
His pleasure; maybe he will relent. Alas,
He hath but as offended in a dream.
All sects, all ages smack of this vice; and he   5
To die for't!

Enter Angelo.

ANGELO   Now, what's the matter, provost?

PROVOST Is it your will Claudio shall die tomorrow?

ANGELO Did not I tell thee yea? Hadst thou not order?
Why dost thou ask again?

PROVOST   Lest I might be too rash.
Under your good correction, I have seen,   10
When, after execution, judgment hath
Repented o'er his doom.

ANGELO   Go to; let that be mine.
Do you your office, or give up your place,
And you shall well be spared.

PROVOST   I crave your honor's
     pardon.
What shall be done, sir, with the groaning Juliet?   15
She's very near her hour.

ANGELO   Dispose of her
To some more fitter place, and that with speed.

II.ii.5 **sects** classes   12 **mine** i.e., my responsibility

[Re-enter Servant.]

SERVANT Here is the sister of the man condemned
　　Desires access to you.

ANGELO　　　　　　　　Hath he a sister?

20 PROVOST Ay, my good lord, a very virtuous maid
　　And to be shortly of a sisterhood,
　　If not already.

ANGELO　　　　　Well, let her be admitted.

　　　　　　　　　　　　　　　　[Exit Servant.]
　　See you the fornicatress be removed;
　　Let her have needful, but not lavish, means;
　　There shall be order for't.

　　　　　　　Enter Lucio and Isabella.

25 PROVOST　　　　　　　　'Save your honor.

ANGELO Stay a little while. *[To Isabella]* Y'are wel-
　　come: what's your will?

ISABELLA I am a woeful suitor to your honor,
　　Please but your honor hear me.

ANGELO　　　　　　　　Well; what's your suit?

ISABELLA There is a vice that most I do abhor,
30 　　And most desire should meet the blow of justice,
　　For which I would not plead, but that I must,
　　For which I must not plead, but that I am
　　At war 'twixt will and will not.

ANGELO　　　　　　　　Well: the matter?

ISABELLA I have a brother is condemned to die.
35 　　I do beseech you, let it be his fault,
　　And not my brother.

PROVOST　　　　*[Aside]* Heaven give thee moving graces.

ANGELO Condemn the fault, and not the actor of it?
　　Why, every fault's condemned ere it be done.

35 **let it be his fault** i.e., condemn his fault, not him

Mine were the very cipher of a function,
To fine the faults whose fine stands in record,   40
And let go by the actor.

ISABELLA   O just but severe law!
I had a brother, then. Heaven keep your honor.

LUCIO [*Aside to Isabella*] Give't not o'er so. To him
    again, entreat him,
Kneel down before him, hang upon his gown;
You are too cold; if you should need a pin,   45
You could not with more tame a tongue desire it.
To him, I say!

ISABELLA Must he needs die?

ANGELO   Maiden, no remedy.

ISABELLA Yes; I do think that you might pardon him,
And neither heaven nor man grieve at the mercy.   50

ANGELO I will not do't.

ISABELLA   But can you, if you would?

ANGELO Look what I will not, that I cannot do.

ISABELLA But might you do't, and do the world no
    wrong,
If so your heart were touched with that remorse
As mine is to him?

ANGELO   He's sentenced; 'tis too late.   55

LUCIO [*Aside to Isabella*] You are too cold.

ISABELLA Too late? Why, no: I, that do speak a word,
May call it again. Well, believe this:
No ceremony that to great ones 'longs,
Not the king's crown, nor the deputed sword,   60
The marshal's truncheon, nor the judge's robe,
Become them with one half so good a grace
As mercy does.
If he had been as you, and you as he,

40 fine ... fine penalize ... penalty   52 **Look what** whatever   54 **remorse**
compassion   59 **ceremony** insignia of greatness   59 **'longs** belongs

65   You would have slipped like him; but he, like you,
        Would not have been so stern.

ANGELO   Pray you, be gone.

ISABELLA I would to heaven I had your potency,
        And you were Isabel; should it then be thus?
        No; I would tell what 'twere to be a judge,
        And what a prisoner.

70   LUCIO [*Aside to Isabella*] Ay, touch him; there's the vein.

ANGELO Your brother is a forfeit of the law,
        And you but waste your words.

ISABELLA   Alas, alas!
        Why, all the souls that were were forfeit once;
        And He that might the vantage best have took
75   Found out the remedy. How would you be,
        If He, which is the top of judgment, should
        But judge you as you are? O, think on that,
        And mercy then will breathe within your lips,
        Like man new made.

ANGELO   Be you content, fair maid;
80   It is the law, not I, condemn your brother.
        Were he my kinsman, brother, or my son,
        It should be thus with him; he must die tomorrow.

ISABELLA Tomorrow! O, that's sudden! Spare him,
            spare him!
        He's not prepared for death. Even for our kitchens
85   We kill the fowl of season: shall we serve heaven
        With less respect than we do minister
        To our gross selves? Good, good my lord, bethink
            you:
        Who is that hath died for this offense?
        There's many have committed it.

LUCIO [*Aside to Isabella*]   Ay, well said.

ANGELO The law hath not been dead, though it hath
90   slept.

85 of season in season

Those many had not dared to do that evil,
If the first that did th' edict infringe
Had answered for his deed. Now 'tis awake,
Takes note of what is done, and, like a prophet,
Looks in a glass, that shows what future evils,   95
Either new, or by remissness new conceived,
And so in progress to be hatched and born,
Are now to have no successive degrees,
But here they live, to end.

ISABELLA   Yet show some pity.

ANGELO I show it most of all when I show justice,   100
For then I pity those I do not know,
Which a dismissed offense would after gall;
And do him right that, answering one foul wrong,
Lives not to act another. Be satisfied;
Your brother dies tomorrow; be content.   105

ISABELLA So you must be the first that gives this
     sentence,
And he, that suffers. O, it is excellent
To have a giant's strength; but it is tyrannous
To use it like a giant.

LUCIO [*Aside to Isabella*] That's well said.

ISABELLA Could great men thunder   110
As Jove himself does, Jove would ne'er be quiet,
For every pelting, petty officer
Would use his heaven for thunder.
Nothing but thunder. Merciful heaven,
Thou rather with thy sharp and sulfurous bolt   115
Splits the unwedgeable and gnarlèd oak
Than the soft myrtle. But man, proud man,
Dressed in a little brief authority,
Most ignorant of what he's most assured,

95-96 future ... conceived i.e., evils that will take place in future, but that are either now planned or may be planned later ("remissness"; careless omission of duty)   102 dismissed forgiven   112 pelting paltry

120   His glassy essence, like an angry ape,
        Plays such fantastic tricks before high heaven
        As makes the angels weep; who, with our spleens,
        Would all themselves laugh mortal.

        LUCIO [*Aside to Isabella*] O, to him, to him, wench!
            He will relent;
            He's coming; I perceive't.

125   PROVOST   [*Aside*] Pray heaven she win him.

        ISABELLA We cannot weigh our brother with ourself:
            Great men may jest with saints; 'tis wit in them;
            But in the less, foul profanation.

        LUCIO Thou'rt i' th' right, girl; more o' that.

130   ISABELLA That in the captain's but a choleric word,
            Which in the soldier is flat blasphemy.

        LUCIO [*Aside to Isabella*] Art avised o' that? More on't.

        ANGELO Why do you put these sayings upon me?

        ISABELLA Because authority, though it err like others,
135   Hath yet a kind of medicine in itself,
            That skins the vice o' th' top; go to your bosom,
            Knock there, and ask your heart what it doth know
            That's like my brother's fault; if it confess
            A natural guiltiness such as is his,
140   Let it not sound a thought upon your tongue
            Against my brother's life.

        ANGELO   [*Aside*] She speaks, and 'tis
            Such sense, that my sense breeds with it. [*Aloud*]
            Fare you well.

        ISABELLA Gentle my lord, turn back.

        ANGELO I will bethink me; come again tomorrow.

---

120 **glassy essence** the rational soul which reveals to man, as in a mirror, what
constitutes him a human being (?) fragile nature (?) 122 **spleens** (the spleen was
believed the seat of mirth and anger) 132 **avised** informed 136 **skins the vice**
i.e., covers the sore of vice with a skin, but does not heal it (or perhaps "skims off
the visible layer of vice")

ISABELLA Hark how I'll bribe you; good my lord, turn
    back.   145

ANGELO How? Bribe me?

ISABELLA Ay, with such gifts that heaven shall share
    with you.

LUCIO [*Aside to Isabella*] You had marred all else.

ISABELLA Not with fond sicles of the tested gold,
    Or stones whose rate are either rich or poor   150
    As fancy values them; but with true prayers
    That shall be up at heaven, and enter there
    Ere sunrise, prayers from preservèd souls,
    From fasting maids whose minds are dedicate
    To nothing temporal.

ANGELO   Well; come to me tomorrow.   155

LUCIO [*Aside to Isabella*] Go to; 'tis well; away.

ISABELLA Heaven keep your honor safe.

ANGELO   [*Aside*] Amen:
    For I am that way going to temptation,
    Where prayers cross.

ISABELLA   At what hour tomorrow
    Shall I attend your lordship?

ANGELO   At any time 'fore noon.   160

ISABELLA 'Save your honor.
         [*Exeunt Isabella, Lucio, and Provost.*]

ANGELO   From thee, even from thy virtue!
    What's this? What's this? Is this her fault or mine?
    The tempter or the tempted, who sins most?
    Ha, not she. Nor doth she tempt; but it is I
    That, lying by the violet in the sun,   165
    Do as the carrion does, not as the flow'r,
    Corrupt with virtuous season. Can it be

---

149 **fond sicles** foolish shekels   159 **cross** are at cross purposes   167 **Corrupt with virtuous season** go bad in the season that blossoms the flower

That modesty may more betray our sense
Than woman's lightness? Having waste ground
enough,
170 Shall we desire to raze the sanctuary,
And pitch our evils there? O fie, fie, fie!
What dost thou, or what art thou, Angelo?
Dost thou desire her foully for those things
That make her good? O, let her brother live:
175 Thieves for their robbery have authority
When judges steal themselves. What, do I love her,
That I desire to hear her speak again,
And feast upon her eyes? What is't I dream on?
O cunning enemy, that, to catch a saint,
180 With saints dost bait thy hook! Most dangerous
Is that temptation that doth goad us on
To sin in loving virtue. Never could the strumpet,
With all her double vigor, art and nature,
Once stir my temper; but this virtuous maid
185 Subdues me quite. Ever till now,
When men were fond, I smiled, and wond'red how.
                                                    Exit.

Scene III. [*The prison.*]

Enter Duke [disguised as a friar] and Provost.

DUKE Hail to you, provost—so I think you are.

PROVOST I am the provost. What's your will, good
friar?

DUKE Bound by my charity and my blest order,
I come to visit the afflicted spirits
5   Here in the prison. Do me the common right
To let me see them, and to make me know

171 **evils** evil structures (e.g., perhaps whorehouses or privies) 186 **fond**
infatuated

The nature of their crimes, that I may minister
To them accordingly.

PROVOST I would do more than that, if more were
    needful.

Enter Juliet.

Look, here comes one: a gentlewoman of mine,   10
Who, falling in the flaws of her own youth,
Hath blistered her report: she is with child;
And he that got it, sentenced; a young man
More fit to do another such offense
Than die for this.   15

DUKE When must he die?

PROVOST   As I do think, tomorrow.
   [*To Juliet*] I have provided for you; stay awhile,
   And you shall be conducted.

DUKE Repent you, fair one, of the sin you carry?

JULIET I do, and bear the shame most patiently.   20

DUKE I'll teach you how you shall arraign your
    conscience,
   And try your penitence, if it be sound
   Or hollowly put on.

JULIET   I'll gladly learn.

DUKE Love you the man that wronged you?

JULIET Yes, as I love the woman that wronged him.   25

DUKE So, then, it seems your most offenseful act
   Was mutually committed?

JULIET   Mutually.

DUKE Then was your sin of heavier kind than his.

JULIET I do confess it, and repent it, father.

DUKE 'Tis meet so, daughter. But lest you do repent   30

II.iii.11 **flaws** sudden gusts of wind   12 **report** reputation   21 **arraign** interrogate

As that the sin hath brought you to this shame—
Which sorrow is always toward ourselves, not
    heaven,
Showing we would not spare heaven as we love it,
But as we stand in fear—

35   JULIET I do repent me, as it is an evil,
And take the shame with joy.

DUKE   There rest.
Your partner, as I hear, must die tomorrow,
And I am going with instruction to him.
Grace go with you, *Benedicite!*   *Exit*.

40   JULIET Must die tomorrow! O injurious love,
That respites me a life, whose very comfort
Is still a dying horror.

PROVOST   'Tis pity of him.   *Exeunt*.

Scene IV. [*A room*.]

Enter Angelo.

ANGELO When I would pray and think, I think
    and pray
To several subjects: heaven hath my empty words,
Whilst my invention, hearing not my tongue,
Anchors on Isabel: heaven in my mouth,
5   As if I did but only chew his name,
And in my heart the strong and swelling evil
Of my conception. The state, whereon I studied,
Is like a good thing, being often read,
Grown seared and tedious; yea, my gravity,
10   Wherein, let no man hear me, I take pride,

39 **Benedicite** bless you   41 **respites** saves   II.iv.2 **several** separate   3 **invention** imagination   7 **conception** thought   7 **state** attitude (?) statecraft (?)
9 **seared** worn out

Could I with boot change for an idle plume
Which the air beats for vain. O place, O form,
How often dost thou with thy case, thy habit,
Wrench awe from fools, and tie the wiser souls
To thy false seeming! Blood, thou art blood.   15
Let's write "good angel" on the devil's horn,
'Tis not the devil's crest. How now, who's there?

Enter Servant.

SERVANT One Isabel, a sister, desires access to you.

ANGELO Teach her the way. [*Exit Servant.*] O heavens,
Why does my blood thus muster to my heart,   20
Making both it unable for itself,
And dispossessing all my other parts
Of necessary fitness?
So play the foolish throngs with one that swounds,
Come all to help him, and so stop the air   25
By which he should revive; and even so
The general, subject to a well-wished king,
Quit their own part, and in obsequious fondness
Crowd to his presence, where their untaught love
Must needs appear offense.

Enter Isabella.

                                    How now, fair maid?   30

ISABELLA I am come to know your pleasure.

ANGELO That you might know it, would much better
    please me
Than to demand what 'tis. Your brother cannot
    live.

ISABELLA Even so. Heaven keep your honor.

ANGELO Yet may he live awhile, and it may be,   35
As long as you or I; yet he must die.

ISABELLA Under your sentence?

11 with boot with profit   13 case (either "chance" or "outside")   13 habit
(either "behavior" or "garment")   16 horn phallus (?)   24 swounds swoons
27 general multitude

ANGELO Yea.

ISABELLA When? I beseech you that in his reprieve,
40   Longer or shorter, he may be so fitted
      That his soul sicken not.

ANGELO Ha! Fie, these filthy vices! It were as good
      To pardon him that hath from nature stol'n
      A man already made, as to remit
45   Their saucy sweetness that do coin heaven's image
      In stamps that are forbid: 'tis all as easy
      Falsely to take away a life true made,
      As to put metal in restrainèd means
      To make a false one.

50 ISABELLA 'Tis set down so in heaven, but not in earth.

ANGELO Say you so? Then I shall pose you quickly.
      Which had you rather: that the most just law
      Now took your brother's life; or, to redeem him,
      Give up your body to such sweet uncleanness
      As she that he hath stained?

55 ISABELLA   Sir, believe this:
      I had rather give my body than my soul.

ANGELO I talk not of your soul; our compelled sins
      Stand more for number than for accompt.

ISABELLA   How say you?

ANGELO Nay, I'll not warrant that; for I can speak
60   Against the thing I say. Answer to this:
      I, now the voice of the recorded law,
      Pronounce a sentence on your brother's life;
      Might there not be a charity in sin
      To save this brother's life?

ISABELLA   Please you to do't,
65   I'll take it as a peril to my soul,
      It is no sin at all, but charity.

44–45 to remit ... sweetness to pardon their lascivious pleasures
48 restrainèd forbidden   51 pose baffle (with a difficult question)   58 Stand ...
accompt are enumerated but not counted against us

ANGELO Pleased you to do't at peril of your soul,
    Were equal poise of sin and charity.

ISABELLA That I do beg his life, if it be sin,
    Heaven let me bear it. You granting of my suit,   70
    If that be sin, I'll make it my morn prayer
    To have it added to the faults of mine,
    And nothing of your answer.

ANGELO   Nay, but hear me,
    Your sense pursues not mine; either you are
      ignorant,
    Or seem so, crafty; and that's not good.   75

ISABELLA Let me be ignorant, and in nothing good,
    But graciously to know I am no better.

ANGELO Thus wisdom wishes to appear most bright
    When it doth tax itself, as these black masks
    Proclaim an enshield beauty ten times louder   80
    Than beauty could, displayed. But mark me;
    To be received plain, I'll speak more gross:
    Your brother is to die.

ISABELLA So.

ANGELO And his offense is so, as it appears,   85
    Accountant to the law upon that pain.

ISABELLA True.

ANGELO Admit no other way to save his life—
    As I subscribe not that, nor any other,
    But in the loss of question—that you, his sister,   90
    Finding yourself desired of such a person
    Whose credit with the judge, or own great place,
    Could fetch your brother from the manacles
    Of the all-binding law; and that there were
    No earthly mean to save him, but that either   95
    You must lay down the treasures of your body
    To this supposed, or else to let him suffer:

68 **poise** balance 79 **tax** censure 80 **enshield** concealed 86 **Accountant**
accountable 86 **pain** punishment 89 **subscribe** assent to 90 **But ... question** except to keep alive the argument

What would you do?

ISABELLA As much for my poor brother as myself:
100   That is, were I under the terms of death,
         Th' impression of keen whips I'd wear as rubies,
         And strip myself to death as to a bed
         That longing have been sick for, ere I'd yield
         My body up to shame.

ANGELO   Then must your brother die.

105 ISABELLA And 'twere the cheaper way.
         Better it were a brother died at once
         Than that a sister, by redeeming him,
         Should die forever.

ANGELO Were not you, then, as cruel as the sentence
110   That you have slandered so?

ISABELLA Ignomy in ransom and free pardon
         Are of two houses; lawful mercy
         Is nothing kin to foul redemption.

ANGELO You seemed of late to make the law a tyrant,
115   And rather proved the sliding of your brother
         A merriment than a vice.

ISABELLA O, pardon me, my lord. It oft falls out,
         To have what we would have, we speak not what
             we mean.
         I something do excuse the thing I hate
120   For his advantage that I dearly love.

ANGELO We are all frail.

ISABELLA   Else let my brother die,
         If not a fedary, but only he
         Owe and succeed thy weakness.

ANGELO Nay, women are frail too.

125 ISABELLA Ay, as the glasses where they view themselves,

122–23 If ... weakness (the meaning seems to be: "Let my brother die if he is the
only inheritor of human frailty instead of being a mere vassal to it")

Which are as easy broke as they make forms.
Women! Help heaven! Men their creation mar
In profiting by them. Nay, call us ten times frail;
For we are soft as our complexions are,
And credulous to false prints.

ANGELO   I think it well,   130
And from this testimony of your own sex—
Since, I suppose, we are made to be no stronger
Than faults may shake our frames—let me be bold:
I do arrest your words. Be that you are,
That is, a woman; if you be more, you're none;   135
If you be one, as you are well expressed
By all external warrants, show it now,
By putting on the destined livery.

ISABELLA I have no tongue but one; gentle my lord,
Let me entreat you speak the former language.   140

ANGELO Plainly conceive, I love you.

ISABELLA My brother did love Juliet,
And you tell me that he shall die for't.

ANGELO He shall not, Isabel, if you give me love.

ISABELLA I know your virtue hath a license in't,   145
Which seems a little fouler than it is,
To pluck on others.

ANGELO   Believe me, on mine honor,
My words express my purpose.

ISABELLA Ha! Little honor to be much believed,
And most pernicious purpose. Seeming, seeming!   150
I will proclaim thee, Angelo; look for't:
Sign me a present pardon for my brother,
Or with an outstretched throat I'll tell the world aloud
What man thou art.

---

126 forms images, appearances   130 credulous receptive   134 I do arrest your words I take you at your word   136 expressed shown to be   138 the destined livery the dress that it is the destiny of a woman to wear   147 pluck on draw on

ANGELO   Who will believe thee, Isabel?
155   My unsoiled name, th' austereness of my life,
        My vouch against you, and my place i' th' state,
        Will so your accusation overweigh,
        That you shall stifle in your own report,
        And smell of calumny. I have begun,
160   And now I give my sensual race the rein.
        Fit thy consent to my sharp appetite,
        Lay by all nicety and prolixious blushes,
        That banish what they sue for; redeem thy brother
        By yielding up thy body to my will,
165   Or else he must not only die the death,
        But thy unkindness shall his death draw out
        To ling'ring sufferance. Answer me tomorrow,
        Or, by the affection that now guides me most,
        I'll prove a tyrant to him. As for you,
170   Say what you can, my false o'erweighs your true.

                                              Exit.

ISABELLA To whom should I complain? Did I tell this,
        Who would believe me? O perilous mouths,
        That bear in them one and the selfsame tongue,
        Either of condemnation or approof;
175   Bidding the law make curtsy to their will,
        Hooking both right and wrong to th' appetite,
        To follow as it draws. I'll to my brother.
        Though he hath fall'n by prompture of the blood,
        Yet hath he in him such a mind of honor,
180   That, had he twenty heads to tender down
        On twenty bloody blocks, he'd yield them up,
        Before his sister should her body stoop
        To such abhorred pollution.
        Then, Isabel, live chaste, and, brother, die:
185   More than our brother is our chastity.
        I'll tell him yet of Angelo's request,
        And fit his mind to death, for his soul's rest.   *Exit.*

---

156 **vouch** testimony   162 **prolixious** tediously drawn-out   164 **will** carnal
appetite   167 **sufferance** torture   168 **affection** passion   174 **approof**
approval

ACT III

Scene I. [*The prison.*]

Enter Duke [as friar], Claudio, and Provost.

DUKE So then, you hope of pardon from Lord
        Angelo?

CLAUDIO The miserable have no other medicine
        But only hope:
        I have hope to live, and am prepared to die.

DUKE Be absolute for death; either death or life   5
        Shall thereby be the sweeter. Reason thus with life:
        If I do lose thee, I do lose a thing
        That none but fools would keep; a breath thou art,
        Servile to all the skyey influences,
        That dost this habitation, where thou keep'st,   10
        Hourly afflict; merely, thou art death's fool,
        For him thou labor'st by thy flight to shun,
        And yet run'st toward him still. Thou art not noble,
        For all th' accommodations that thou bear'st
        Are nursed by baseness. Thou'rt by no means
        valiant,   15
        For thou dost fear the soft and tender fork
        Of a poor worm. Thy best of rest is sleep,

III.i.5 **absolute** unconditionally prepared   9 **skyey influences** influence of the stars   10 **keep'st** dwellest   11 **fool** (the professional jester in a nobleman's household whose job was to keep his master amused)   14 **accommodations** necessities   16 **fork** forked tongue (of a snake)

And that thou oft provok'st; yet grossly fear'st
Thy death, which is no more. Thou art not thyself;
20 For thou exists on many a thousand grains
That issue out of dust. Happy thou art not,
For what thou hast not, still thou striv'st to get,
And what thou hast, forget'st. Thou art not certain,
For thy complexion shifts to strange effects,
25 After the moon. If thou art rich, thou'rt poor.
For, like an ass whose back with ingots bows,
Thou bear'st thy heavy riches but a journey,
And death unloads thee. Friend hast thou none,
For thine own bowels, which do call thee sire,
30 The mere effusion of thy proper loins,
Do curse the gout, serpigo, and the rheum,
For ending thee no sooner. Thou hast nor youth
     nor age,
But, as it were, an after-dinner's sleep,
Dreaming on both; for all thy blessèd youth
35 Becomes as agèd, and doth beg the alms
Of palsied eld, and when thou art old and rich,
Thou has neither heat, affection, limb, nor beauty,
To make thy riches pleasant. What's yet in this
That bears the name of life? Yet in this life
40 Lie hid moe thousand deaths; yet death we fear,
That makes these odds all even.

CLAUDIO   I humbly thank you.
To sue to live, I find I seek to die,
And seeking death, find life: let it come on.

Enter Isabella.

ISABELLA What, ho! Peace here; grace and good company!

PROVOST Who's there? Come in, the wish deserves a
45   welcome.

18 **provok'st** invokest   23 **certain** invariable   24-25 **For … moon** your temperament (desire?) moves to numerous things, changeable as (or "influenced by") the moon   29 **bowels** offspring   30 **The mere … loins** the very issue of your own loins   31 **serpigo** a skin disease   31 **rheum** catarrh   36 **eld** old age   37 **affection** feeling   39 **bears** deserves

DUKE Dear sir, ere long I'll visit you again.

CLAUDIO Most holy sir, I thank you.

ISABELLA My business is a word or two with Claudio.

PROVOST And very welcome. Look, signior, here's your
sister.

DUKE Provost, a word with you.   50

PROVOST As many as you please.

DUKE Bring me to hear them speak, where I may be
concealed.   [*Duke and Provost withdraw.*]

CLAUDIO Now, sister, what's the comfort?

ISABELLA Why,   55
As all comforts are, most good, most good indeed.
Lord Angelo, having affairs to heaven,
Intends you for his swift ambassador,
Where you shall be an everlasting leiger:
Therefore your best appointment make with speed;   60
Tomorrow you set on.

CLAUDIO   Is there no remedy?

ISABELLA None, but such remedy as, to save a head,
To cleave a heart in twain.

CLAUDIO   But is there any?

ISABELLA Yes, brother, you may live;
There is a devilish mercy in the judge,   65
If you'll implore it, that will free your life,
But fetter you till death.

CLAUDIO   Perpetual durance?

ISABELLA Ay, just; perpetual durance, a restraint,
Though all the world's vastidity you had,
To a determined scope.

---

59 leiger resident ambassador 60 appointment preparation 67 durance
imprisonment 69 vastidity vast spaces 70 determined scope fixed limit (i.e.,
the reprieve may win him the world, but will cost him his soul)

70 CLAUDIO   But in what nature?

ISABELLA In such a one as, you consenting to't,
        Would bark your honor from that trunk you bear,
        And leave you naked.

    CLAUDIO   Let me know the point.

ISABELLA O, I do fear thee, Claudio, and I quake,
75   Lest thou a feverous life shouldst entertain,
        And six or seven winters more respect
        Than a perpetual honor. Dar'st thou die?
        The sense of death is most in apprehension,
        And the poor beetle that we tread upon
80   In corporal sufferance finds a pang as great
        As when a giant dies.

    CLAUDIO   Why give you me this shame?
        Think you I can a resolution fetch
        From flow'ry tenderness? If I must die,
        I will encounter darkness as a bride,
85   And hug it in mine arms.

ISABELLA There spake my brother, there my father's
            grave
        Did utter forth a voice. Yes, thou must die,
        Thou art too noble to conserve a life
        In base appliances. This outward-sainted deputy,
90   Whose settled visage and deliberate word
        Nips youth i' th' head, and follies doth enmew
        As falcon doth the fowl, is yet a devil;
        His filth within being cast, he would appear
        A pond as deep as hell.

    CLAUDIO   The prenzie Angelo!

95 ISABELLA O, 'tis the cunning livery of hell,
        The damned'st body to invest and cover
        In prenzie guards. Dost thou think, Claudio,
        If I would yield him my virginity,

78 **sense** feeling 78 **apprehension** imagination 89 **appliances** devices
91 **enmew** drive into the water (as a hawk drives a fowl) 93 **cast** vomited up
94 **prenzie** (meaning uncertain; often emended to "princely", or "precise")
97 **guards** trimmings

Thou mightst be freed?

CLAUDIO   O heavens, it cannot be.

ISABELLA Yes, he would give't thee, from this rank
    offense,   100
  So to offend him still. This night's the time
  That I should do what I abhor to name,
  Or else thou diest tomorrow.

CLAUDIO   Thou shalt not do't.

ISABELLA   O, were it but my life,
  I'd throw it down for your deliverance   105
  As frankly as a pin.

CLAUDIO   Thanks, dear Isabel.

ISABELLA Be ready, Claudio, for your death tomorrow.

CLAUDIO Yes. Has he affections in him,
  That thus can make him bite the law by th' nose,
  When he would force it? Sure, it is no sin,   110
  Or of the deadly seven it is the least.

ISABELLA Which is the least?

CLAUDIO If it were damnable, he being so wise,
  Why would he for the momentary trick
  Be perdurably fined? O Isabel!   115

ISABELLA What says my brother?

CLAUDIO   Death is a fearful thing.

ISABELLA And shamèd life a hateful.

CLAUDIO Ay, but to die, and go we know not where,
  To lie in cold obstruction and to rot,
  This sensible warm motion to become   120
  A kneaded clod; and the delighted spirit
  To bathe in fiery floods, or to reside

108 affections sensual appetites 110 force enforce 111 deadly seven (pride,
envy, wrath, sloth, avarice, gluttony, lechery) 114-15 Why ... fined i.e., why for
the momentary trifle (of sexual intercourse) would he be eternally damned
119 obstruction motionlessness 120 sensible feeling 120 motion organism
121 delighted capable of delight

In thrilling region of thick-ribbèd ice;
To be imprisoned in the viewless winds,
125   And blown with restless violence round about
The pendent world; or to be worse than worst
Of those that lawless and incertain thought
Imagine howling—'tis too horrible!
The weariest and most loathèd worldly life
130   That age, ache, penury, and imprisonment
Can lay on nature is a paradise
To what we fear of death.

ISABELLA Alas, alas.

CLAUDIO   Sweet sister, let me live:
What sin you do to save a brother's life,
135   Nature dispenses with the deed so far
That it becomes a virtue.

ISABELLA   O you beast,
O faithless coward, O dishonest wretch!
Wilt thou be made a man out of my vice?
Is't not a kind of incest, to take life
From thine own sister's shame? What should I
140   think?
Heaven shield my mother played my father fair,
For such a warpèd slip of wilderness
Ne'er issued from his blood. Take my defiance,
Die, perish! Might but my bending down
145   Reprieve thee from thy fate, it should proceed.
I'll pray a thousand prayers for thy death,
No word to save thee.

CLAUDIO Nay, hear me, Isabel.

ISABELLA   O, fie, fie, fie!
Thy sin's not accidental, but a trade.
150   Mercy to thee would prove itself a bawd,
'Tis best that thou diest quickly.

CLAUDIO   O, hear me, Isabella!

126 pendent hanging in space · 135 dispenses with grants a dispensation for
142 wilderness wild nature without nurture

[*The Duke comes forward.*]

DUKE Vouchsafe a word, young sister, but one word.

ISABELLA What is your will?

DUKE Might you dispense with your leisure, I would
by and by have some speech with you: the satis-   155
faction I would require is likewise your own benefit.

ISABELLA I have no superfluous leisure; my stay must
be stolen out of other affairs, but I will attend you
awhile.

DUKE [*Aside to Claudio*] Son, I have overheard what   160
hath passed between you and your sister. Angelo
had never the purpose to corrupt her; only he hath
made an assay of her virtue to practice his judgment with the disposition of natures. She, having
the truth of honor in her, hath made him that   165
gracious denial which he is most glad to receive. I
am confessor to Angelo, and I know this to be true;
therefore prepare yourself to death. Do not satisfy
your resolution with hopes that are fallible. Tomorrow you must die; go to your knees, and make   170
ready.

CLAUDIO Let me ask my sister pardon. I am so out
of love with life, that I will sue to be rid of it.

DUKE Hold you there; farewell. [*Exit Claudio.*] Provost, a word with you.   175

[*Enter Provost.*]

PROVOST What's your will, father?

DUKE That now you are come, you will be gone.
Leave me awhile with the maid. My mind promises
with my habit no loss shall touch her by my company.   180

PROVOST In good time.   *Exit.*

DUKE The hand that hath made you fair hath made

163 assay test   179 habit religious dress   181 In good time very well

701

185

190

you good. The goodness that is cheap in beauty makes beauty brief in goodness; but grace, being the soul of your complexion, shall keep the body of it ever fair. The assault that Angelo hath made to you, fortune hath conveyed to my understanding, and, but that frailty hath examples for his falling, I should wonder at Angelo. How will you do to content this substitute, and to save your brother?

ISABELLA I am now going to resolve him. I had rather my brother die by the law than my son should be unlawfully born. But O, how much is the good Duke deceived in Angelo! If ever he return and I can speak to him, I will open my lips in vain, or discover his government.

195

DUKE That shall not be much amiss. Yet, as the matter now stands, he will avoid your accusation: he made trial of you only. Therefore fasten your ear on my advisings; to the love I have in doing good a remedy presents itself. I do make myself believe that you may most uprighteously do a poor wronged lady a merited benefit; redeem your brother from the angry law; do no stain to your own gracious person; and much please the absent Duke, if peradventure he shall ever return to have hearing of this business.

200

205

ISABELLA Let me hear you speak farther. I have spirit to do anything that appears not foul in the truth of my spirit.

210

DUKE Virtue is bold, and goodness never fearful. Have you not heard speak of Mariana, the sister of Frederick, the great soldier who miscarried at sea?

215

ISABELLA I have heard of the lady, and good words went with her name.

185 complexion character   191 resolve answer   196 discover his government expose his rule

DUKE She should this Angelo have married; was affianced to her by oath, and the nuptial appointed:
between which time of the contract and limit of the
solemnity, her brother Frederick was wracked at   220
sea, having in that perished vessel the dowry of his
sister. But mark how heavily this befell to the poor
gentlewoman: there she lost a noble and renowned
brother, in his love toward her ever most kind and
natural; with him, the portion and sinew of her for-   225
tune, her marriage dowry; with both, her combinate husband, this well-seeming Angelo.

ISABELLA Can this be so? Did Angelo so leave her?

DUKE Left her in her tears, and dried not one of them
with his comfort; swallowed his vows whole, pre-   230
tending in her discoveries of dishonor: in few, bestowed her on her own lamentation, which she yet
wears for his sake; and he, a marble to her tears,
is washed with them, but relents not.

ISABELLA What a merit were it in death to take this   235
poor maid from the world! What corruption in this
life, that it will let this man live! But how out of
this can she avail?

DUKE It is a rupture that you may easily heal, and
the cure of it not only saves your brother, but   240
keeps you from dishonor in doing it.

ISABELLA Show me how, good father.

DUKE This forenamed maid hath yet in her the continuance of her first affection; his unjust unkindness, that in all reason should have quenched her   245
love, hath, like an impediment in the current, made
it more violent and unruly. Go you to Angelo;
answer his requiring with a plausible obedience;
agree with his demands to the point; only refer
yourself to this advantage: first, that your stay with   250
him may not be long; that the time may have all

219-20 limit of the solemnity date set for the marriage ceremony
226-27 combinate betrothed   238 avail benefit

shadow and silence in it; and the place answer to
convenience. This being granted in course—and
now follows all—we shall advise this wronged maid
255   to stead up your appointment, go in your place.
If the encounter acknowledge itself hereafter, it
may compel him to her recompense: and here, by
this, is your brother saved, your honor untainted,
the poor Mariana advantaged, and the corrupt dep-
260   uty scaled. The maid will I frame and make fit
for his attempt. If you think well to carry this, as
you may, the doubleness of the benefit defends the
deceit from reproof. What think you of it?

ISABELLA The image of it gives me content already,
265   and I trust it will grow to a most prosperous perfection.

DUKE It lies much in your holding up. Haste you
speedily to Angelo: if for this night he entreat you
to his bed, give him promise of satisfaction. I will
270   presently to Saint Luke's; there at the moated
grange resides this dejected Mariana. At that
place call upon me, and dispatch with Angelo, that
it may be quickly.

ISABELLA I thank you for this comfort. Fare you well,
275   good father.   Exit.

Scene II. [Before the prison.]

Enter, [to the Duke,] Elbow, Clown
[Pompey, and] Officers.

ELBOW Nay, if there be no remedy for it, but that
you will needs buy and sell men and women like

255 stead up keep   256 encounter i.e., sexual union   260 scaled weighed
260 frame prepare   271 grange farm

beasts, we shall have all the world drink brown and
white bastard.

DUKE O heavens! What stuff is here?   5

POMPEY 'Twas never merry world since, of two
usuries, the merriest was put down, and the worser
allowed by order of law a furred gown to keep him
warm; and furred with fox and lamb skins too, to
signify that craft, being richer than innocency,   10
stands for the facing.

ELBOW Come your way, sir. 'Bless you, good father
friar.

DUKE And you, good brother father. What offense
hath this man made you, sir?   15

ELBOW Marry, sir, he hath offended the law; and, sir,
we take him to be a thief too, sir; for we have
found upon him, sir, a strange picklock, which we
have sent to the deputy.

DUKE Fie, sirrah, a bawd, a wicked bawd!   20
The evil that thou causest to be done,
That is thy means to live. Do thou but think
What 'tis to cram a maw or clothe a back
From such a filthy vice; say to thyself,
From their abominable and beastly touches   25
I drink, I eat, array myself, and live.
Canst thou believe thy living is a life,
So stinkingly depending? Go mend, go mend.

POMPEY Indeed, it does stink in some sort, sir; but
yet, sir, I would prove—   30

DUKE Nay, if the devil have given thee proofs for sin,
Thou wilt prove his. Take him to prison, officer.
Correction and instruction must both work
Ere this rude beast will profit.

ELBOW He must before the deputy, sir; he has given   35
him warning. The deputy cannot abide a whore-

III.ii.4 **bastard** sweet Spanish wine   6-7 **two usuries** lending money at interest
(a way of breeding barren metal) and fornication   11 **stands for the facing**
represents the trimming   23 **maw** belly

master; if he be a whoremonger, and comes before
him, he were as good go a mile on his errand.

DUKE That we were all, as some would seem to be,
40   From our faults, as faults from seeming, free!

Enter Lucio.

ELBOW His neck will come to your waist—a cord, sir.

POMPEY I spy comfort; I cry bail. Here's a gentleman
and a friend of mine.

LUCIO How now, noble Pompey! What, at the wheels
45   of Caesar? Art thou led in triumph? What, is there
none of Pygmalion's images, newly made woman,
to be had now, for putting the hand in the pocket
and extracting it clutched? What reply, ha? What
say'st thou to this tune, matter and method? Is't not
50   drowned i' th' last rain, ha? What say'st thou, Trot?
Is the world as it was, man? Which is the way? Is
it sad, and few words? Or how? The trick of it?

DUKE Still thus, and thus; still worse.

LUCIO How doth my dear morsel, thy mistress? Pro-
55   cures she still, ha?

POMPEY Troth, sir, she hath eaten up all her beef,
and she is herself in the tub.

LUCIO Why, 'tis good. It is the right of it; it must be
so: ever your fresh whore and your powdered bawd,
60   an unshunned consequence; it must be so. Art going
to prison, Pompey?

POMPEY Yes, faith, sir.

LUCIO Why, 'tis not amiss, Pompey. Farewell; go, say

---

38 **he were ... errand** i.e., he has a hard (or fruitless?) journey ahead   41 **cord**
i.e., the cord around the Friar's waist   46 **Pygmalion's images** i.e., prostitutes
(Pompey is compared to Pygmalion, sculptor of a female statue that came to
life)   56 **beef** prostitutes (who serve as flesh-food)   57 **in the tub** taking the cure
for venereal disease (a tub was also used for corning beef, hence the reference to
powdering—pickling—in Lucio's next speech)

I sent thee thither. For debt, Pompey? Or how?

ELBOW For being a bawd, for being a bawd.   65

LUCIO Well, then, imprison him. If imprisonment be
the due of a bawd, why, 'tis his right. Bawd is he
doubtless, and of antiquity too, bawd-born. Farewell, good Pompey. Commend me to the prison,
Pompey, you will turn good husband now, Pom-   70
pey, you will keep the house.

POMPEY I hope, sir, your good worship will be my
bail.

LUCIO No, indeed, will I not, Pompey, it is not the
wear. I will pray, Pompey, to increase your bond-   75
age. If you take it not patiently, why, your mettle
is the more. Adieu, trusty Pompey. 'Bless you, friar.

DUKE And you.

LUCIO Does Bridget paint still, Pompey, ha?

ELBOW Come your ways, sir, come.   80

POMPEY You will not bail me then, sir?

LUCIO Then, Pompey, nor now. What news abroad,
friar, what news?

ELBOW Come your ways, sir, come.

LUCIO Go to kennel, Pompey, go. [*Exeunt Elbow,*   85
Pompey, and Officers.] What news, friar, of the
Duke?

DUKE I know none. Can you tell me of any?

LUCIO Some say he is with the Emperor of Russia;
other some, he is in Rome: but where is he, think   90
you?

DUKE I know not where; but wheresoever, I wish him
well.

LUCIO It was a mad fantastical trick of him to steal

70 husband housekeeper, manager   75 wear fashion   76 mettle spirit (pun on
metal of chains)

707

95   from the state, and usurp the beggary he was never
      born to. Lord Angelo dukes it well in his absence;
      he puts transgression to't.

DUKE He does well in't.

LUCIO A little more lenity to lechery would do no
100   harm in him; something too crabbed that way, friar.

DUKE It is too general a vice, and severity must
      cure it.

LUCIO Yes, in good sooth, the vice is of a great
      kindred, it is well allied; but it is impossible to
105   extirp it quite, friar, till eating and drinking be
      put down. They say this Angelo was not made by
      man and woman after this downright way of cre-
      ation. Is it true, think you?

DUKE How should he be made, then?

110 LUCIO Some report a sea maid spawned him; some,
      that he was begot between two stockfishes. But it
      is certain that when he makes water his urine is
      congealed ice; that I know to be true. And he is a
      motion generative; that's infallible.

115 DUKE You are pleasant, sir, and speak apace.

LUCIO Why, what a ruthless thing is this in him, for
      the rebellion of a codpiece to take away the life of
      a man! Would the Duke that is absent have done
      this? Ere he would have hanged a man for the get-
120   ting a hundred bastards, he would have paid for
      the nursing a thousand. He had some feeling of the
      sport; he knew the service, and that instructed him
      to mercy.

DUKE I never heard the absent Duke much detected
125   for women; he was not inclined that way.

LUCIO O, sir, you are deceived.

110 **sea maid** (to explain his piscatory coldness)   111 **stockfishes** dried cod
114 **motion generative** masculine puppet   124-25 **detected for** accused of

708

DUKE 'Tis not possible.

LUCIO Who, not the Duke? Yes, your beggar of fifty, and his use was to put a ducat in her clack-dish; the Duke had crotchets in him. He would be drunk 130 too; that let me inform you.

DUKE You do him wrong, surely.

LUCIO Sir, I was an inward of his. A shy fellow was the Duke, and I believe I know the cause of his withdrawing. 135

DUKE What, I prithee, might be the cause?

LUCIO No, pardon; 'tis a secret must be locked within the teeth and the lips; but this I can let you understand, the greater file of the subject held the Duke to be wise. 140

DUKE Wise! Why, no question but he was.

LUCIO A very superficial, ignorant, unweighing fellow.

DUKE Either this is envy in you, folly, or mistaking. The very stream of his life and the business he hath helmed must, upon a warranted need, give him a 145 better proclamation. Let him be but testimonied in his own bringings-forth, and he shall appear to the envious a scholar, a statesman, and a soldier. Therefore you speak unskillfully; or if your knowledge be more, it is much dark'ned in your malice. 150

LUCIO Sir, I know him, and I love him.

DUKE Love talks with better knowledge, and knowledge with dearer love.

LUCIO Come, sir, I know what I know.

DUKE I can hardly believe that, since you know not 155 what you speak. But, if ever the Duke return, as our prayers are he may, let me desire you to make

129 **clack-dish** beggar's bowl (metaphorical here) 130 **crotchets** whims 133 **inward** intimate companion 139 **greater file** majority 145 **upon a warranted need** if proof be demanded 147 **bringings-forth** actions

your answer before him. If it be honest you have
spoke, you have courage to maintain it. I am bound
160 to call upon you, and I pray you, your name?

LUCIO Sir, my name is Lucio, well known to the Duke.

DUKE He shall know you better, sir, if I may live to
report you.

LUCIO I fear you not.

165 DUKE O, you hope the Duke will return no more, or
you imagine me too unhurtful an opposite. But,
indeed, I can do you little harm; you'll forswear
this again.

LUCIO I'll be hanged first; thou art deceived in me,
170 friar. But no more of this. Canst thou tell if Claudio
die tomorrow or no?

DUKE Why should he die, sir?

LUCIO Why? For filling a bottle with a tundish. I
would the Duke we talk of were returned again;
175 this ungenitured agent will unpeople the province
with continency; sparrows must not build in his
house-eaves, because they are lecherous. The Duke
yet would have dark deeds darkly answered; he
would never bring them to light. Would he were
180 returned! Marry, this Claudio is condemned for untrussing. Farewell, good friar; I prithee, pray for
me. The Duke, I say to thee again, would eat mutton on Fridays. He's not past it, yet, and I say
to thee, he would mouth with a beggar, though she
185 smelled brown bread and garlic. Say that I said so.
Farewell.   *Exit*.

DUKE No might nor greatness in mortality
Can censure 'scape; back-wounding calumny
The whitest virtue strikes. What king so strong

173 **tundish** funnel   175 **ungenitured** sexless   180–81 **untrussing** undressing
182–83 **eat mutton on Fridays** (the Duke allegedly ate mutton on a Friday,
which was a fast day, and also practiced venery; "mutton" also means "harlot,"
and Friday is the day of the planet Venus)

Can tie the gall up in the slanderous tongue?   190
But who comes here?

Enter Escalus, Provost, and [Officers with]
Bawd [Mistress Overdone].

ESCALUS Go, away with her to prison!

MISTRESS OVERDONE Good my lord, be good to me.
Your honor is accounted a merciful man, good my
lord.   195

ESCALUS Double and treble admonition, and still forfeit in the same kind! This would make mercy
swear, and play the tyrant.

PROVOST A bawd of eleven years' continuance, may
it please your honor.   200

MISTRESS OVERDONE My lord, this is one Lucio's information against me. Mistress Kate Keepdown was
with child by him in the Duke's time; he promised
her marriage; his child is a year and a quarter old,
come Philip and Jacob; I have kept it myself, and   205
see how he goes about to abuse me.

ESCALUS That fellow is a fellow of much license; let
him be called before us. Away with her to prison.
Go to, no more words. [*Exeunt Officers with Mis-*
tress Overdone.] Provost, my brother Angelo will   210
not be altered; Claudio must die tomorrow. Let him
be furnished with divines, and have all charitable
preparation. If my brother wrought by my pity,
it should not be so with him.

PROVOST So please you, this friar hath been with him,   215
and advised him for th' entertainment of death.

ESCALUS Good even, good father.

DUKE Bliss and goodness on you!

ESCALUS Of whence are you?

205 Philip and Jacob May 1st

220 DUKE Not of this country, though my chance is now
    To use it for my time; I am a brother
    Of gracious order, late come from the See
    In special business from his Holiness.

ESCALUS What news abroad i' th' world?

225 DUKE None, but that there is so great a fever on good-
    ness, that the dissolution of it must cure it, novelty
    is only in request, and it is as dangerous to be
    aged in any kind of course as it is virtuous to be
    constant in any undertaking. There is scarce truth
230 enough alive to make societies secure, but security
    enough to make fellowships accursed. Much upon
    this riddle runs the wisdom of the world. This news
    is old enough, yet it is every day's news. I pray
    you, sir, of what disposition was the Duke?

235 ESCALUS One that, above all other strifes, contended
    especially to know himself.

DUKE What pleasure was he given to?

ESCALUS Rather rejoicing to see another merry, than
    merry at anything which professed to make him
240 rejoice: a gentleman of all temperance. But leave
    we him to his events, with a prayer they may prove
    prosperous, and let me desire to know how you
    find Claudio prepared. I am made to understand
    that you have lent him visitation.

245 DUKE He professes to have received no sinister meas-
    ure from his judge, but most willingly humbles him-
    self to the determination of justice; yet had he
    framed to himself, by the instruction of his frailty,
    many deceiving promises of life; which I, by my
250 good leisure, have discredited to him, and now is
    he resolved to die.

ESCALUS You have paid the heavens your function,

225–26 fever ... cure it i.e., the dissolution of the fever alone can now restore
goodness to its pristine health   226–27 novelty is only in request change is
urgently needed   228 aged old and worn out   230 security heedlessness
231 fellowships human societies

and the prisoner the very debt of your calling. I
have labored for the poor gentleman to the extremest shore of my modesty, but my brother   255
justice have I found so severe, that he hath forced
me to tell him he is indeed Justice.

DUKE If his own life answer the straitness of his proceeding, it shall become him well; wherein if he
chance to fail, he hath sentenced himself.   260

ESCALUS I am going to visit the prisoner. Fare you
well.

DUKE Peace be with you!
     [Exeunt Escalus and Provost.]
He who the sword of heaven will bear
Should be as holy as severe;   265
Pattern in himself to know
Grace to stand, and virtue go;
More nor less to others paying
Than by self-offenses weighing.
Shame to him whose cruel striking   270
Kills for faults of his own liking.
Twice treble shame on Angelo,
To weed my vice and let his grow,
O, what may man within him hide,
Though angel on the outward side!   275
How may likeness made in crimes,
Making practice on the times,
To draw with idle spiders' strings
Most ponderous and substantial things?
Craft against vice I must apply: 280
With Angelo tonight shall lie
His old betrothèd but despisèd;
So disguise shall, by th' disguisèd,
Pay with falsehood false exacting,
And perform an old contracting.   285
       Exit.

254–55 **extremest shore of my modesty** i.e., as far as is proper
266–27 **Pattern ... go** i.e., he should have a model in himself of grace which will
stand if virtue elsewhere ebbs   273 **my** (used impersonally)   277 **Making
practice** practicing deception

ACT IV

Scene I. [*The moated grange.*]

Enter Mariana and Boy singing.

SONG

Take, O, take those lips away,
    That so sweetly were forsworn;
And those eyes, the break of day,
    Lights that do mislead the morn;
5   But my kisses bring again, bring again;
    Seals of love, but sealed in vain, sealed in vain.

Enter Duke [disguised as before].

MARIANA Break off thy song, and haste thee quick
    away.
Here comes a man of comfort, whose advice
Hath often stilled my brawling discontent.

[Exit Boy.]

10   I cry you mercy, sir; and well could wish
You had not found me here so musical.
Let me excuse me, and believe me so,
My mirth it much displeased, but pleased my woe.

DUKE 'Tis good; though music oft hath such a charm

714

To make bad good, and good provoke to harm.   15
I pray you, tell me, hath anybody inquired for me
here today? Much upon this time have I promised here
to meet.

MARIANA You have not been inquired after; I have
sat here all day.   20

Enter Isabella.

DUKE I do constantly believe you. The time is come
even now. I shall crave your forbearance a little;
may be I will call upon you anon, for some advantage to yourself.

MARIANA I am always bound to you.   *Exit.* 25

DUKE Very well met, and well come.
What is the news from this good deputy?

ISABELLA He hath a garden circummured with brick,
Whose western side is with a vineyard backed;
And to that vineyard is a planchèd gate,   30
That makes his opening with this bigger key.
This other doth command a little door
Which from the vineyard to the garden leads.
There have I made my promise
Upon the heavy middle of the night   35
To call upon him.

DUKE But shall you on your knowledge find this way?

ISABELLA I have ta'en a due and wary note upon't.
With whispering and most guilty diligence,
In action all of precept, he did show me   40
The way twice o'er.

DUKE   Are there no other tokens
Between you 'greed concerning her observance?

ISABELLA No, none, but only a repair i' th' dark,
And that I have possessed him my most stay

IV.i.28 **circummured** walled around   30 **planchèd** planked   40 **In ... precept**
teaching by gestures   42 **her observance** what she must do   44 **possessed**
informed

45 Can be but brief; for I have made him know
I have a servant comes with me along,
That stays upon me, whose persuasion is
I come about my brother.

DUKE   'Tis well borne up.
I have not yet made known to Mariana
50 A word of this. What, ho, within! Come forth.

Enter Mariana.

I pray you, be acquainted with this maid;
She comes to do you good.

ISABELLA   I do desire the like.

DUKE Do you persuade yourself that I respect you?

MARIANA Good friar, I know you do, and have found
it.

55 DUKE Take, then, this your companion by the hand,
Who hath a story ready for your ear.
I shall attend your leisure, but make haste;
The vaporous night approaches.

MARIANA Will't please you walk aside?

Exit [with Isabella].

60 DUKE O place and greatness, millions of false eyes
Are stuck upon thee; volumes of report
Run with these false and most contrarious quests
Upon thy doings; thousand escapes of wit
Make thee the father of their idle dreams,
And rack thee in their fancies.

Enter Mariana and Isabella.

65   Welcome, how agreed?

ISABELLA She'll take the enterprise upon her, father,
If you advise it.

---

47 **stays upon** waits for   47 **persuasion** conviction   62 **quests** cry of the hound
on the scent   63 **escapes** sallies

DUKE It is not my consent
But my entreaty too.

ISABELLA Little have you to say
When you depart from him, but, soft and low,
"Remember now my brother."

MARIANA Fear me not. 70

DUKE Nor, gentle daughter, fear you not at all.
He is your husband on a precontract;
To bring you thus together, 'tis no sin,
Sith that the justice of your title to him
Doth flourish the deceit. Come, let us go: 75
Our corn's to reap, for yet our tithe's to sow.

Exeunt.

Scene II. [*The prison.*]

Enter Provost and Clown [Pompey].

PROVOST Come hither, sirrah. Can you cut off a man's
head?

POMPEY If the man be a bachelor, sir, I can; but if he
be a married man, he's his wife's head, and I can
never cut off a woman's head. 5

PROVOST Come, sir, leave me your snatches, and yield
me a direct answer. Tomorrow morning are to die
Claudio and Barnardine. Here is in our prison a
common executioner, who in his office lacks a
helper. If you will take it on you to assist him, it 10
shall redeem you from your gyves; if not, you
shall have your full time of imprisonment, and your

72 precontract legally binding betrothal agreement 76 tithe tithe corn
IV.ii.4 he's his wife's head (see Ephesians 5:23: "For the husband is the head of
the wife") 6 snatches quibbles 11 gyves shackles

717

deliverance with an unpitied whipping, for you
have been a notorious bawd.

15 POMPEY Sir, I have been an unlawful bawd time out
of mind, but yet I will be content to be a lawful
hangman. I would be glad to receive some instruction
from my fellow partner.

PROVOST What, ho, Abhorson! Where's Abhorson,
20   there?

Enter Abhorson.

ABHORSON Do you call, sir?

PROVOST Sirrah, here's a fellow will help you tomorrow in your execution. If you think it meet, compound with him by the year, and let him abide
25   here with you; if not, use him for the present, and
dismiss him. He cannot plead his estimation with
you; he hath been a bawd.

ABHORSON A bawd, sir? Fie upon him! He will discredit our mystery.

30 PROVOST Go to, sir; you weigh equally; a feather will
turn the scale.   *Exit.*

POMPEY Pray, sir, by your good favor—for surely,
sir, a good favor you have, but that you have a
hanging look—do you call, sir, your occupation
35   a mystery?

ABHORSON Ay, sir; a mystery.

POMPEY Painting, sir, I have heard say, is a mystery;
and your whores, sir, being members of my occupation, using painting, do prove my occupation a
40   mystery; but what mystery there should be in hanging, if I should be hanged, I cannot imagine.

ABHORSON Sir, it is a mystery.

---

19 **Abhorson** (pun on "ab, whore, son," son from a whore)   23-24 **compound**
settle   26 **estimation** reputation   29 **mystery** craft   33 **favor** countenance

POMPEY Proof?

ABHORSON Every true man's apparel fits your thief: if
it be too little for your thief, your true man thinks it   45
big enough; if it be too big for your thief, your thief
thinks it little enough: so every true man's apparel
fits your thief.

Enter Provost.

PROVOST Are you agreed?

POMPEY Sir, I will serve him; for I do find your hang-   50
man is a more penitent trade than your bawd; he
doth oft'ner ask forgiveness.

PROVOST You, sirrah, provide your block and your ax
tomorrow four o'clock.

ABHORSON Come on, bawd. I will instruct thee in my   55
trade; follow.

POMPEY I do desire to learn, sir; and I hope, if you
have occasion to use me for your own turn,
you shall find me yare; for, truly, sir, for your
kindness I owe you a good turn.   60

PROVOST Call hither Barnardine and Claudio.

Exit [Pompey with Abhorson].

Th' one has my pity; not a jot the other,
Being a murderer, though he were my brother.

Enter Claudio.

Look, here's the warrant, Claudio, for thy death.
'Tis now dead midnight, and by eight tomorrow   65
Thou must be made immortal. Where's Barnardine?

CLAUDIO As fast locked up in sleep as guiltless labor
When it lies starkly in the traveler's bones;
He will not wake.

44-48 every ... thief (interpretation uncertain)   52 ask forgiveness (the executioner always asked the condemned man to forgive him)   58 turn execution (pun)
59 yare ready   68 starkly stiffly

PROVOST   Who can do good on him?
      Well, go, prepare yourself. [*Knocking within.*] But,
70   hark, what noise?—
      Heaven give your spirits comfort. [*Exit Claudio.*]
        By and by.
      I hope it is some pardon or reprieve
      For the most gentle Claudio. Welcome, father.

              Enter Duke [disguised as before].

DUKE The best and wholesom'st spirits of the night
      Envelop you, good provost! Who called here of
75   late?

PROVOST None since the curfew rung.

DUKE Not Isabel?

PROVOST   No.

DUKE   They will, then, ere't be long.

PROVOST What comfort is for Claudio?

DUKE There's some in hope.

80 PROVOST It is a bitter deputy.

DUKE Not so, not so; his life is paralleled
      Even with the stroke and line of his great justice.
      He doth with holy abstinence subdue
      That in himself which he spurs on his pow'r
85   To qualify in others; were he mealed with that
      Which he corrects, then were he tyrannous;
      But this being so, he's just.   [*Knocking within.*]
                        Now are they come.
                            [*Exit Provost.*]
      This is a gentle provost—seldom when
      The steelèd jailer is the friend of men.
                        [*Knocking within.*]
      How now, what noise? That spirit's possessed with
90   haste

85 **qualify** moderate   85 **mealed** stained

720

That wounds th' unsisting postern with these
  strokes.

[Enter Provost.]

PROVOST There he must stay until the officer
Arise to let him in; he is called up.

DUKE Have you no countermand for Claudio yet,
But he must die tomorrow?

PROVOST   None, sir, none.   95

DUKE As near the dawning, provost, as it is,
You shall hear more ere morning.

PROVOST   Happily
You something know; yet I believe there comes
No countermand; no such example have we.
Besides, upon the very siege of justice   100
Lord Angelo hath to the public ear
Professed the contrary.

Enter a Messenger.

             This is his lord's man.

DUKE And here comes Claudio's pardon.

MESSENGER My lord hath sent you this note, and by
me this further charge, that you swerve not from   105
the smallest article of it, neither in time, matter,
or other circumstance. Good morrow; for, as I
take it, it is almost day.

PROVOST I shall obey him.

[Exit Messenger.]

DUKE *[Aside]* This is his pardon, purchased by such
  sin   110
For which the pardoner himself is in.
Hence hath offense his quick celerity,

91 **unsisting** (perhaps "unassisting," perhaps a printer's slip for "resisting")
91 **postern** small door   100 **siege** seat

When it is borne in high authority.
When vice makes mercy, mercy's so extended,
115 That for the fault's love is th' offender friended.
Now, sir, what news?

PROVOST I told you. Lord Angelo, belike thinking
me remiss in mine office, awakens me with this un-
wonted putting-on; methinks strangely, for he hath
120 not used it before.

DUKE Pray you, let's hear.

PROVOST [*Reads*] *the letter*. "Whatsoever you may hear
to the contrary, let Claudio be executed by four
of the clock; and in the afternoon Barnardine. For
125 my better satisfaction, let me have Claudio's head
sent me by five. Let this be duly performed with a
thought that more depends on it than we must yet
deliver. Thus fail not to do your office, as you will
answer it at your peril."
130 What say you to this, sir?

DUKE What is that Barnardine who is to be executed
in th' afternoon?

PROVOST A Bohemian born, but here nursed up and
bred; one that is a prisoner nine years old.

135 DUKE How came it that the absent Duke had not
either delivered him to his liberty or executed him?
I have heard it was ever his manner to do so.

PROVOST His friends still wrought reprieves for him;
and, indeed, his fact, till now in the government
140 of Lord Angelo, came not to an undoubtful proof.

DUKE It is now apparent?

PROVOST Most manifest, and not denied by himself.

DUKE Hath he borne himself penitently in prison?
How seems he to be touched?

145 PROVOST A man that apprehends death no more dreadfully but as a drunken sleep; careless, reckless, and

117 **belike** perhaps   119 **putting-on** urging   139 **fact** evil deed

fearless of what's past, present, or to come; insensible of mortality, and desperately mortal.

DUKE He wants advice.

PROVOST He will hear none. He hath evermore had the   150
liberty of the prison; give him leave to escape hence,
he would not: drunk many times a day, if not many
days entirely drunk. We have very oft awaked him,
as if to carry him to execution, and showed him a
seeming warrant for it; it hath not moved him at all.   155

DUKE More of him anon. There is written in your
brow, provost, honesty and constancy: if I read it
not truly, my ancient skill beguiles me; but, in the
boldness of my cunning, I will lay myself in hazard. Claudio, whom here you have warrant to exe-   160
cute, is no greater forfeit to the law than Angelo who
hath sentenced him. To make you understand this
in a manifested effect, I crave but four days' res-
pite, for the which you are to do me both a
present and a dangerous courtesy.   165

PROVOST Pray, sir, in what?

DUKE In the delaying death.

PROVOST Alack, how may I do it, having the hour limited, and an express command, under penalty, to
deliver his head in the view of Angelo? I may make   170
my case as Claudio's, to cross this in the smallest.

DUKE By the vow of mine Order I warrant you, if my
instructions may be your guide. Let this Barnardine
be this morning executed, and his head borne to
Angelo.   175

PROVOST Angelo hath seen them both, and will discover the favor.

DUKE O, death's a great disguiser; and you may add

148 desperately mortal about to die without hope of the future   149 wants
needs   159 cunning knowledge   159-60 lay myself in hazard take a risk
163 in a manifested effect by open proof   165 present immediate
168-69 limited determined   176-77 discover the favor recognize the face

180 to it. Shave the head, and tie the beard; and say it
was the desire of the penitent to be so bared before his death; you know the course is common.
If anything fall to you upon this, more than thanks
and good fortune, by the saint whom I profess, I
will plead against it with my life.

185 PROVOST Pardon me, good father; it is against my oath.

DUKE Were you sworn to the Duke, or to the deputy?

PROVOST To him, and to his substitutes.

DUKE You will think you have made no offense, if the
Duke avouch the justice of your dealing?

190 PROVOST But what likelihood is in that?

DUKE Not a resemblance, but a certainty. Yet since
I see you fearful, that neither my coat, integrity,
nor persuasion can with ease attempt you, I will
go further than I meant, to pluck all fears out of
195 you. Look you, sir, here is the hand and seal of the
Duke. You know the character, I doubt not, and
the signet is not strange to you.

PROVOST I know them both.

DUKE The contents of this is the return of the Duke.
200 You shall anon overread it at your pleasure, where
you shall find, within these two days he will be
here. This is a thing that Angelo knows not; for he
this very day receives letters of strange tenor, perchance of the Duke's death, perchance entering into
205 some monastery, but by chance nothing of what is
writ. Look, th' unfolding star calls up the shepherd. Put not yourself into amazement how these
things should be: all difficulties are but easy when
they are known. Call your executioner, and off with
210 Barnardine's head; I will give him a present shrift,

180 **bared** shaved   192 **fearful** full of fear   193 **attempt** move   196 **character**
handwriting   206 **unfolding star** morning star (signaling the shepherd to lead
the sheep from the fold)   210 **shrift** absolution

and advise him for a better place. Yet you are amazed; but this shall absolutely resolve you. Come away; it is almost clear dawn.

Exit [with Provost].

Scene III. [*The prison.*]

Enter Clown [Pompey].

POMPEY I am as well acquainted here as I was in our house of profession: one would think it were Mistress Overdone's own house, for here be many of her old customers. First, here's young Master Rash; he's in for a commodity of brown paper and old 5 ginger, ninescore and seventeen pounds, of which he made five marks, ready money; marry, then ginger was not much in request, for the old women were all dead. Then is there here one Master Caper, at the suit of Master Three-pile the mercer, for 10 some four suits of peach-colored satin, which now peaches him a beggar. Then have we here young Dizzy, and young Master Deep-vow, and Master Copper-spur, and Master Starve-lackey, the rapier and dagger man, and young Drop-heir that killed 15 lusty Pudding, and Master Forthright the tilter, and brave Master Shoe-tie the great traveler, and wild Half-can that stabbed Pots, and, I think, forty more; all great doers in our trade, and are now "for the Lord's sake." 20

---

212 **resolve** convince   IV.iii.5 **commodity** (worthless goods whose purchase at a heavy price was forced on a debtor in dire need by a usurious creditor, who thus circumvented the contemporary laws against usury)   7 **marks** (a mark was about two-thirds of a pound)   12 **peaches** betrays   14 **Copper-spur** i.e., Master Pretentious (copper was a bogus substitute for gold)   16 **tilter** fighter   17 **Shoe-tie** rosette (worn by gallants)   18 **Half-can** (a larger vessel than a pot)   20 **"for the Lord's sake"** (the cry of prisoners begging alms from passers-by)

Enter Abhorson.

ABHORSON Sirrah, bring Barnardine hither.

POMPEY Master Barnardine! You must rise and be
hanged, Master Barnardine!

ABHORSON What, ho, Barnardine!

25 BARNARDINE (*Within*) A pox o' your throats! Who
makes that noise there? What are you?

POMPEY Your friends, sir; the hangman. You must
be so good, sir, to rise and be put to death.

BARNARDINE [*Within*] Away, you rogue, away! I am
30 sleepy.

ABHORSON Tell him he must awake, and that quickly
too.

POMPEY Pray, Master Barnardine, awake till you are
executed, and sleep afterwards.

35 ABHORSON Go into him, and fetch him out.

POMPEY He is coming, sir, he is coming; I hear his
straw rustle.

Enter Barnardine.

ABHORSON Is the ax upon the block, sirrah?

POMPEY Very ready, sir.

40 BARNARDINE How now, Abhorson? What's the news
with you?

ABHORSON Truly, sir, I would desire you to clap into
your prayers; for, look you, the warrant's come.

BARNARDINE You rogue, I have been drinking all night;
45 I am not fitted for't.

POMPEY O, the better, sir: for he that drinks all
night, and is hanged betimes in the morning, may
sleep the sounder all the next day.

47 **betimes** early

Enter Duke [disguised as before].

ABHORSON Look you, sir; here comes your ghostly
father. Do we jest now, think you?   50

DUKE Sir, induced by my charity, and hearing how
hastily you are to depart, I am come to advise you,
comfort you, and pray with you.

BARNARDINE Friar, not I: I have been drinking hard
all night, and I will have more time to prepare me,   55
or they shall beat out my brains with billets. I will
not consent to die this day, that's certain.

DUKE O, sir, you must; and therefore I beseech you
Look forward on the journey you shall go.

BARNARDINE I swear I will not die today for any man's   60
persuasion.

DUKE But hear you—

BARNARDINE Not a word. If you have anything to say
to me, come to my ward, for thence will not I today.
Exit.

Enter Provost.

DUKE Unfit to live or die. O gravel heart!   65
After him, fellows; bring him to the block.
[Exeunt Abhorson and Pompey.]

PROVOST Now, sir, how do you find the prisoner?

DUKE A creature unprepared, unmeet for death;
And to transport him in the mind he is
Were damnable.

PROVOST   Here in the prison, father,   70
There died this morning of a cruel fever
One Ragozine, a most notorious pirate,
A man of Claudio's years, his beard and head
Just of his color. What if we do omit
This reprobate till he were well inclined,   75
And satisfy the deputy with the visage

49 ghostly spiritual   56 billets cudgels

Of Ragozine, more like to Claudio?

DUKE O, 'tis an accident that heaven provides.
      Dispatch it presently; the hour draws on
80   Prefixed by Angelo. See this be done,
      And sent according to command, whiles I
      Persuade this rude wretch willingly to die.

PROVOST This shall be done, good father, presently;
      But Barnardine must die this afternoon,
85   And how shall we continue Claudio,
      To save me from the danger that might come
      If he were known alive?

DUKE   Let this be done:
      Put them in secret holds, both Barnardine and
        Claudio.
      Ere twice the sun hath made his journal greeting
90   To yonder generation, you shall find
      Your safety manifested.

PROVOST I am your free dependant.

DUKE Quick, dispatch, and send the head to Angelo.
                                        Exit [Provost].

      Now will I write letters to Angelo—
95   The provost, he shall bear them—whose contents
      Shall witness to him I am near at home,
      And that by great injunctions I am bound
      To enter publicly. Him I'll desire
      To meet me at the consecrated fount,
100   A league below the city; and from thence,
      By cold gradation and well-balanced form,
      We shall proceed with Angelo.

                    Enter Provost.

PROVOST Here is the head; I'll carry it myself.

DUKE Convenient is it. Make a swift return,

79 **presently** at once 80 **Prefixed** predetermined 88 **holds** cells 89 **journal**
daily 92 **your free dependant** freely at your service 101 **cold gradation**
deliberate steps

For I would commune with you of such things   105
That want no ear but yours.

PROVOST   I'll make all speed.

Exit.

ISABELLA (*Within*) Peace, ho, be here!

DUKE The tongue of Isabel. She's come to know
If yet her brother's pardon be come hither.
But I will keep her ignorant of her good,   110
To make her heavenly comforts of despair
When it is least expected.

Enter Isabella.

ISABELLA   Ho, by your leave!

DUKE Good morning to you, fair and gracious daughter.

ISABELLA The better, given me by so holy a man.
Hath yet the deputy sent my brother's pardon?   115

DUKE He hath released him, Isabel, from the world;
His head is off, and sent to Angelo.

ISABELLA Nay, but it is not so.

DUKE It is no other. Show your wisdom, daughter,
In your close patience.   120

ISABELLA O, I will to him and pluck out his eyes!

DUKE You shall not be admitted to his sight.

ISABELLA Unhappy Claudio, wretched Isabel,
Injurious world, most damnèd Angelo!

DUKE This nor hurts him nor profits you a jot;   125
Forbear it therefore, give your cause to heaven.
Mark what I say, which you shall find
By every syllable a faithful verity.
The Duke comes home tomorrow—nay, dry your
    eyes—
One of our covent, and his confessor,   130

106 want need   120 close deep, secret   130 covent convent

Gives me this instance: already he hath carried
Notice to Escalus and Angelo,
Who do prepare to meet him at the gates,
There to give up their pow'r. If you can, pace
        your wisdom
135 In that good path that I would wish it go,
And you shall have your bosom on this wretch,
Grace of the Duke, revenges to your heart,
And general honor.

ISABELLA   I am directed by you.

DUKE This letter, then, to Friar Peter give;
140 'Tis that he sent me of the Duke's return.
Say, by this token, I desire his company
At Mariana's house tonight. Her cause and yours
I'll perfect him withal, and he shall bring you
Before the Duke; and to the head of Angelo
145 Accuse him home and home. For my poor self,
I am combinèd by a sacred vow,
And shall be absent. Wend you with this letter;
Command these fretting waters from your eyes
With a light heart; trust not my holy Order,
150 If I pervert your course. Who's here?

Enter Lucio.

LUCIO Good even. Friar, where's the provost?

DUKE Not within, sir.

LUCIO O pretty Isabella, I am pale at mine heart to
see thine eyes so red; thou must be patient. I am
155 fain to dine and sup with water and bran; I dare
not for my head fill my belly; one fruitful meal
would set me to't. But they say the Duke will be
here tomorrow. By my troth, Isabel, I loved thy
brother. If the old fantastical Duke of dark cor-
160 ners had been at home, he had lived.

                                        [*Exit Isabella.*]

131 **instance** proof 134 **pace** conduct 136 **bosom** desire 146 **combinèd**
bound

DUKE Sir, the Duke is marvelous little beholding to
your reports; but the best is, he lives not in them.

LUCIO Friar, thou knowest not the Duke so well as I
do; he's a better woodman than thou tak'st him
for.   165

DUKE Well, you'll answer this one day. Fare ye well.

LUCIO Nay, tarry, I'll go along with thee: I can tell
thee pretty tales of the Duke.

DUKE You have told me too many of him already,
sir, if they be true; if not true, none were enough.   170

LUCIO I was once before him for getting a wench
with child.

DUKE Did you such a thing?

LUCIO Yes, marry, did I; but I was fain to forswear
it: they would else have married me to the rotten   175
medlar.

DUKE Sir, your company is fairer than honest. Rest
you well.

LUCIO By my troth, I'll go with thee to the lane's end.
If bawdy talk offend you, we'll have very little of   180
it. Nay, friar, I am a kind of burr; I shall stick.

Exeunt.

Scene IV. [*A room.*]

Enter Angelo and Escalus.

ESCALUS Every letter he hath writ hath disvouched
other.

---

164 **woodman** hunter (here, of women)   176 **medlar** applelike fruit edible only
when partly decayed (here, a prostitute)

ANGELO In most uneven and distracted manner. His
actions show much like to madness; pray heaven
his wisdom be not tainted. And why meet him at
the gates, and redeliver our authorities there?

ESCALUS I guess not.

ANGELO And why should we proclaim it in an hour
before his ent'ring, that if any crave redress of injustice, they should exhibit their petitions in the
street?

ESCALUS He shows his reason for that: to have a dispatch of complaints, and to deliver us from devices
hereafter which shall then have no power to stand
against us.

ANGELO Well, I beseech you, let it be proclaimed.
Betimes i' th' morn I'll call you at your house. Give
notice to such men of sort and suit as are to meet
him.

ESCALUS I shall, sir. Fare you well.   *Exit*.

ANGELO Good night.
    This deed unshapes me quite, makes me
      unpregnant,
    And dull to all proceedings. A deflow'red maid,
    And by an eminent body that enforced
    The law against it! But that her tender shame
    Will not proclaim against her maiden loss,
    How might she tongue me! Yet reason dares her no;
    For my authority bears of a credent bulk,
    That no particular scandal once can touch
    But it confounds the breather. He should have
      lived,
    Save that his riotous youth, with dangerous sense,
    Might in the times to come have ta'en revenge,
    By so receiving a dishonored life

5 ... 10 ... 15 ... 20 ... 25 ... 30

IV.iv.13 **devices** false complaints 18 **men of sort and suit** noblemen
22 **unpregnant** unreceptive 26 **maiden loss** loss of maidenhood 28 **bears of
a credent bulk** is derived from trusted material 31 **sense** feeling

732

With ransom of such shame. Would yet he had
    lived!
Alack, when once our grace we have forgot,   35
Nothing goes right; we would, and we would not.
                                                    Exit.

Scene V. [*Outside the town.*]

        Enter Duke [*in his own habit*] *and Friar Peter.*

DUKE These letters at fit time deliver me.
    The provost knows our purpose and our plot.
    The matter being afoot, keep your instruction,
    And hold you ever to our special drift,
    Though sometimes you do blench from this to that,   5
    As cause doth minister. Go call at Flavius' house,
    And tell him where I stay; give the like notice
    To Valencius, Rowland, and to Crassus,
    And bid them bring the trumpets to the gate;
    But send me Flavius first.

FRIAR PETER   It shall be speeded well.   10
                                        [*Exit.*]

                    Enter Varrius.

DUKE I thank thee, Varrius; thou hast made good
    haste.
    Come, we will walk. There's other of our friends
    Will greet us here anon, my gentle Varrius. *Exeunt.*

IV.v.1 **me** for me   5 **blench** deviate

Scene VI. [*Near the city gate.*]

Enter Isabella and Mariana.

ISABELLA To speak so indirectly I am loath:
I would say the truth; but to accuse him so,
That is your part. Yet I am advised to do it,
He says, to veil full purpose.

MARIANA   Be ruled by him.

5   ISABELLA Besides, he tells me that, if peradventure
He speak against me on the adverse side,
I should not think it strange; for 'tis a physic
That's bitter to sweet end.

MARIANA I would Friar Peter—

Enter Friar Peter.

ISABELLA   O peace! The friar is come.

FRIAR PETER Come, I have found you out a stand most
10   fit
Where you may have such vantage on the Duke,
He shall not pass you. Twice have the trumpets
        sounded.
The generous and gravest citizens
Have hent the gates, and very near upon
15   The Duke is ent'ring: therefore, hence, away!
                                        Exeunt.

IV.vi.11 **vantage** advantageous position   13 **generous** highborn   14 **hent** gathered at

ACT V

Scene I. [*The city gate.*]

Enter Duke, Varrius, Lords, Angelo, Escalus,
Lucio, [Provost, Officers, and] Citizens, at
several doors.

DUKE My very worthy cousin, fairly met.
Our old and faithful friend, we are glad to see you.

ANGELO, ESCALUS Happy return be to your royal
Grace.

DUKE Many and hearty thankings to you both.
We have made inquiry of you, and we hear   5
Such goodness of your justice, that our soul
Cannot but yield you forth to public thanks,
Forerunning more requital.

ANGELO   You make my bonds still greater.

DUKE O, your desert speaks loud, and I should wrong
it
To lock it in the wards of covert bosom,   10

V.i.1 **cousin** (a sovereign's address to a nobleman) 8 **Forerunning more**
requital preceding additional reward 10 **To ... bosom** i.e., to keep it locked
hidden in my heart

When it deserves, with characters of brass,
A forted residence 'gainst the tooth of time
And razure of oblivion. Give me your hand,
And let the subject see, to make them know
15   That outward courtesies would fain proclaim
Favors that keep within. Come, Escalus,
You must walk by us on our other hand—
And good supporters are you.

Enter [Friar] Peter and Isabella.

FRIAR PETER Now is your time: speak loud, and kneel
before him.

20   ISABELLA Justice, O royal Duke! Vail your regard
Upon a wronged—I would fain have said, a maid.
O worthy prince, dishonor not your eye
By throwing it on any other object
Till you have heard me in my true complaint,
25   And given me justice, justice, justice, justice!

DUKE Relate your wrongs. In what? By whom? Be
brief.
Here is Lord Angelo shall give you justice;
Reveal yourself to him.

ISABELLA   O worthy Duke,
You bid me seek redemption of the devil.
30   Hear me yourself, for that which I must speak
Must either punish me, not being believed,
Or wring redress from you. Hear me, O hear me,
here!

ANGELO My lord, her wits, I fear me, are not firm.
She hath been a suitor to me for her brother
Cut off by course of justice—

35   ISABELLA   By course of justice!

ANGELO And she will speak most bitterly and strange.

ISABELLA Most strange, but yet most truly, will I speak.

13 razure erasure   16 keep dwell   20 Vail your regard cast your attention

That Angelo's forsworn, is it not strange?
That Angelo's a murderer, is't not strange?
That Angelo is an adulterous thief,   40
An hypocrite, a virgin-violator;
Is it not strange, and strange?

DUKE   Nay, it is ten times strange.

ISABELLA It is not truer he is Angelo
Than this is all as true as it is strange.
Nay, it is ten times true, for truth is truth   45
To th' end of reck'ning.

DUKE   Away with her! Poor soul,
She speaks this in th' infirmity of sense.

ISABELLA O prince, I conjure thee, as thou believ'st
There is another comfort than this world,
That thou neglect me not, with that opinion   50
That I am touched with madness. Make not
    impossible
That which but seems unlike. 'Tis not impossible
But one, the wicked'st caitiff on the ground,
May seem as shy, as grave, as just, as absolute
As Angelo; even so may Angelo,   55
In all his dressings, caracts, titles, forms,
Be an arch-villain. Believe it, royal prince;
If he be less, he's nothing; but he's more,
Had I more name for badness.

DUKE   By mine honesty,
If she be mad, as I believe no other,   60
Her madness hath the oddest frame of sense,
Such a dependency of thing on thing,
As e'er I heard in madness.

ISABELLA   O gracious Duke,
Harp not on that; nor do not banish reason
For inequality, but let your reason serve   65
To make the truth appear where it seems hid,
And hide the false seems true.

54 **absolute** perfect   56 **caracts** symbols of office   65 **inequality** injustice
67 **seems** which seems

DUKE   Many that are not mad
    Have, sure, more lack of reason. What would you say?

ISABELLA I am the sister of one Claudio,
70   Condemned upon the act of fornication
    To lose his head, condemned by Angelo.
    I, in probation of a sisterhood,
    Was sent to by my brother, one Lucio
    As then the messenger—

LUCIO   That's I, and't like your Grace.
75   I came to her from Claudio, and desired her
    To try her gracious fortune with Lord Angelo
    For her poor brother's pardon.

ISABELLA   That's he indeed.

DUKE You were not bid to speak.

LUCIO   No, my good lord,
    Nor wished to hold my peace.

DUKE   I wish you now, then;
80   Pray you, take note of it, and when you have
    A business for yourself, pray heaven you then
    Be perfect.

LUCIO   I warrant your honor.

DUKE The warrant's for yourself; take heed to't.

ISABELLA This gentleman told somewhat of my tale—

85 LUCIO Right.

DUKE It may be right; but you are i' the wrong
    To speak before your time. Proceed.

ISABELLA   I went
    To this pernicious caitiff deputy—

DUKE That's somewhat madly spoken.

72 **probation** novitiate   74 **and't like** if it please   82 **perfect** thoroughly
prepared   83 **warrant** warning

ISABELLA   Pardon it;
  The phrase is to the matter.   90

DUKE Mended again. The matter: proceed.

ISABELLA In brief, to set the needless process by,
  How I persuaded, how I prayed, and kneeled,
  How he refelled me, and how I replied—
  For this was of much length—the vild conclusion   95
  I now begin with brief and shame to utter.
  He would not, but by gift of my chaste body
  To his concupiscible intemperate lust,
  Release my brother; and after much debatement,
  My sisterly remorse confutes mine honor,   100
  And I did yield to him; but the next morn betimes,
  His purpose surfeiting, he sends a warrant
  For my poor brother's head.

DUKE   This is most likely!

ISABELLA O, that it were as like as it is true!

DUKE By heaven, fond wretch, thou know'st not what
    thou speak'st,   105
  Or else thou art suborned against his honor
  In hateful practice. First, his integrity
  Stands without blemish. Next, it imports no reason
  That with such vehemency he should pursue
  Faults proper to himself: if he had so offended,   110
  He would have weighed thy brother by himself,
  And not have cut him off. Someone hath set you on;
  Confess the truth, and say by whose advice
  Thou cam'st here to complain.

ISABELLA   And is this all?
  Then, O you blessèd ministers above,   115
  Keep me in patience, and with ripened time
  Unfold the evil which is here wrapped up
  In countenance. Heaven shield your Grace from woe,

---

90 **to the matter** appropriate   94 **refelled** repelled   95 **vild** vile   100 **remorse**
pity   102 **surfeiting** satiating   107 **practice** plot   108 **imports no reason** does
not attend to reason   110 **proper** belonging

As I, thus wronged, hence unbelievèd go!

120 DUKE I know you'd fain be gone. An officer,
To prison with her! Shall we thus permit
A blasting and a scandalous breath to fall
On him so near us? This needs must be a practice.
Who knew of your intent and coming hither?

125 ISABELLA One that I would were here, Friar Lodowick.

DUKE A ghostly father, belike. Who knows that
Lodowick?

LUCIO My lord, I know him; 'tis a meddling friar,
I do not like the man. Had he been lay, my lord,
For certain words he spake against your Grace
130 In your retirement, I had swinged him soundly.

DUKE Words against me! This's a good friar, belike!
And to set on this wretched woman here
Against our substitute! Let this friar be found.

LUCIO But yesternight, my lord, she and that friar,
135 I saw them at the prison; a saucy friar,
A very scurvy fellow.

FRIAR PETER Blessed be your royal Grace!
I have stood by, my lord, and I have heard
Your royal ear abused. First, hath this woman
140 Most wrongfully accused your substitute,
Who is as free from touch or soil with her
As she from one ungot.

DUKE   We did believe no less.
Know you that Friar Lodowick that she speaks of?

FRIAR PETER I know him for a man divine and holy;
145 Not scurvy, nor a temporary meddler,
As he's reported by this gentleman;
And, on my trust, a man that never yet
Did, as he vouches, misreport your Grace.

LUCIO My lord, most villainously; believe it.

---

128 **lay** layman   130 **swinged** thrashed   136 **scurvy** worthless   145 **temporary meddler** meddler in temporal affairs

FRIAR PETER Well, he in time may come to clear
    himself,   150
  But at this instant he is sick, my lord,
  Of a strange fever. Upon his mere request,
  Being come to knowledge that there was complaint
  Intended 'gainst Lord Angelo, came I hither,
  To speak, as from his mouth, what he doth know   155
  Is true and false; and what he with his oath
  And all probation will make up full clear,
  Whensoever he's convented. First, for this woman,
  To justify this worthy nobleman,
  So vulgarly and personally accused,   160
  Her shall you hear disprovèd to her eyes,
  Till she herself confess it.

DUKE   Good friar, let's hear it.
             [Isabella is carried off guarded.]

        Enter Mariana [veiled].

  Do you not smile at this, Lord Angelo?
  O heaven, the vanity of wretched fools!
  Give us some seats. Come, cousin Angelo,   165
  In this I'll be impartial; be you judge
  Of your own cause. Is this the witness, friar?
  First, let her show her face, and after speak.

MARIANA Pardon, my lord; I will not show my face
  Until my husband bid me.   170

DUKE What, are you married?

MARIANA No, my lord.

DUKE Are you a maid?

MARIANA No, my lord.

DUKE A widow, then?   175

MARIANA Neither, my lord.

DUKE Why, you are nothing, then: neither maid,
  widow, nor wife?

157 probation proof   158 convented sent for

LUCIO My lord, she may be a punk; for many of
180 them are neither maid, widow, nor wife.

DUKE Silence that fellow. I would he had some cause
To prattle for himself.

LUCIO Well, my lord.

MARIANA My lord, I do confess I ne'er was married,
185 And I confess, besides, I am no maid.
I have known my husband; yet my husband
Knows not that ever he knew me.

LUCIO He was drunk, then, my lord; it can be no
better.

190 DUKE For the benefit of silence, would thou wert so
too!

LUCIO Well, my lord.

DUKE This is no witness for Lord Angelo.

MARIANA Now I come to't, my lord:
195 She that accuses him of fornication,
In selfsame manner doth accuse my husband,
And charges him, my lord, with such a time
When I'll depose I had him in mine arms
With all th' effect of love.

ANGELO Charges she moe than me?

200 MARIANA   Not that I know.

DUKE No? You say your husband?

MARIANA Why, just, my lord, and that is Angelo,
Who thinks he knows that he ne'er knew my body,
But knows he thinks that he knows Isabel's.

205 ANGELO This is a strange abuse. Let's see thy face.

MARIANA My husband bids me; now I will unmask.
                                    [Unveiling.]
This is that face, thou cruel Angelo,

179 punk harlot   186 known had intercourse with

Which once thou swor'st was worth the looking on;
This is the hand which, with a vowed contract,
Was fast belocked in thine; this is the body   210
That took away the match from Isabel,
And did supply thee at thy garden house
In her imagined person.

DUKE   Know you this woman?

LUCIO Carnally, she says.

DUKE   Sirrah, no more!

LUCIO Enough, my lord.   215

ANGELO My lord, I must confess I know this woman:
And five years since there was some speech of
      marriage
Betwixt myself and her, which was broke off,
Partly for that her promisèd proportions
Came short of composition, but in chief,   220
For that her reputation was disvalued
In levity; since which time of five years
I never spake with her, saw her, nor heard from her,
Upon my faith and honor.

MARIANA   Noble prince,
As there comes light from heaven and words from
      breath,   225
As there is sense in truth and truth in virtue,
I am affianced this man's wife as strongly
As words could make up vows; and, my good lord,
But Tuesday night last gone in's garden house
He knew me as a wife. As this is true,   230
Let me in safety raise me from my knees,
Or else forever be confixèd here,
A marble monument.

ANGELO   I did but smile till now;
Now, good my lord, give me the scope of justice;
My patience here is touched. I do perceive   235

211 **match** meeting 219 **proportions** dowry 220 **composition** previous
agreement 221–22 **disvalued/In levity** discredited for lightness 232 **confixèd**
fixed firmly

These poor informal women are no more
But instruments of some more mightier member
That sets them on. Let me have way, my lord,
To find this practice out.

DUKE   Ay, with my heart,
240 And punish them to your height of pleasure.
Thou foolish friar and thou pernicious woman,
Compact with her that's gone, think'st thou thy
    oaths,
Though they would swear down each particular
    saint,
Were testimonies against his worth and credit,
245 That's sealed in approbation? You, Lord Escalus,
Sit with my cousin; lend him your kind pains
To find out this abuse, whence 'tis derived.
There is another friar that set them on;
Let him be sent for.

FRIAR PETER Would he were here, my lord, for he,
250   indeed,
Hath set the women on to this complaint:
Your provost knows the place where he abides,
And he may fetch him.

DUKE   Go, do it instantly. [*Exit Provost.*]
And you, my noble and well-warranted cousin,
255 Whom it concerns to hear this matter forth,
Do with your injuries as seems you best,
In any chastisement. I for a while
Will leave you, but stir not you till you have
Well determined upon these slanderers.

260 ESCALUS My lord, we'll do it throughly.   *Exit* [*Duke*].
Signior Lucio, did not you say you knew that Friar
Lodowick to be a dishonest person?

LUCIO *Cucullus non facit monachum*; honest in
nothing but in his clothes, and one that hath spoke
265 most villainous speeches of the Duke.

236 **informal** (1) rash (2) informing   242 **Compact** in collusion   245 **approba-tion** attested integrity   263 **Cucullus non facit monachum** the cowl does not
make the monk (Latin)

ESCALUS We shall entreat you to abide here till he come, and enforce them against him; we shall find this friar a notable fellow.

LUCIO As any in Vienna, on my word.

ESCALUS Call that same Isabel here once again; I 270 would speak with her. [*Exit an Attendant.*] Pray you, my lord, give me leave to question; you shall see how I'll handle her.

LUCIO Not better than he, by her own report.

ESCALUS Say you? 275

LUCIO Marry, sir, I think, if you handled her privately, she would sooner confess; perchance, publicly, she'll be ashamed.

Enter Duke [as friar], Provost, Isabella,
[and Officers].

ESCALUS I will go darkly to work with her.

LUCIO That's the way; for women are light at mid- 280 night.

ESCALUS Come on, mistress, here's a gentlewoman denies all that you have said.

LUCIO My lord, here comes the rascal I spoke of— here with the provost. 285

ESCALUS In very good time. Speak not you to him till we call upon you.

LUCIO Mum.

ESCALUS Come, sir, did you set these women on to slander Lord Angelo? They have confessed you did. 290

DUKE 'Tis false.

ESCALUS How! Know you where you are?

DUKE Respect to your great place; and let the devil

267 enforce urge   268 notable notorious   279 darkly subtly

745

Be sometime honored for his burning throne.
295   Where is the Duke? 'Tis he should hear me speak.

ESCALUS   The Duke's in us, and we will hear you speak.
Look you speak justly.

DUKE Boldly, at least. But, O poor souls,
Come you to seek the lamb here of the fox?
300   Good night to your redress. Is the Duke gone?
Then is your cause gone too. The Duke's unjust,
Thus to retort your manifest appeal,
And put your trial in the villain's mouth
Which here you come to accuse.

305 LUCIO This is the rascal; this is he I spoke of.

ESCALUS Why, thou unreverend and unhallowed friar,
Is't not enough thou hast suborned these women
To accuse this worthy man, but in foul mouth,
And in the witness of his proper ear,
310   To call him villain? And then to glance from him
To th' Duke himself, to tax him with injustice?
Take him hence; to th' rack with him. We'll touse you
Joint by joint, but we will know his purpose.
What, "unjust"!

DUKE   Be not so hot. The Duke
315   Dare no more stretch this finger of mine than he
Dare rack his own: his subject am I not,
Nor here provincial. My business in this state
Made me a looker-on here in Vienna,
Where I have seen corruption boil and bubble
320   Till it o'errun the stew. Laws for all faults,
But faults so countenanced, that the strong statutes
Stand like the forfeits in a barber's shop,
As much in mock as mark.

ESCALUS Slander to th' state! Away with him to prison!

302 **retort** refer back 302 **manifest** clear 309 **proper** very 312 **touse** pull
317 **provincial** belonging to the province or state 322 **forfeits** extracted teeth
(barbers acted as dentists) 323 **As much ... mark** to be mocked at as much as to
be seen

ANGELO What can you vouch against him, Signior 325
Lucio? Is this the man that you did tell us of?

LUCIO 'Tis he, my lord. Come hither, goodman bald-
pate; do you know me?

DUKE I remember you, sir, by the sound of your
voice. I met you at the prison, in the absence of 330
the Duke.

LUCIO O, did you so? And do you remember what
you said of the Duke?

DUKE Most notedly, sir.

LUCIO Do you so, sir? And was the Duke a flesh- 335
monger, a fool, and a coward, as you then reported
him to be?

DUKE You must, sir, change persons with me, ere you
make that my report. You, indeed, spoke so of
him; and much more, much worse. 340

LUCIO O thou damnable fellow! Did not I pluck thee
by the nose for thy speeches?

DUKE I protest I love the Duke as I love myself.

ANGELO Hark, how the villain would close now, after
his treasonable abuses. 345

ESCALUS Such a fellow is not to be talked withal.
Away with him to prison! Where is the provost?
Away with him to prison, lay bolts enough upon
him, let him speak no more. Away with those giglets too, and with the other confederate compan- 350
ion.

DUKE [*To the Provost*] Stay, sir; stay awhile.

ANGELO What, resists he? Help him, Lucio.

LUCIO Come, sir; come, sir; come, sir; foh, sir! Why,
you bald-pated, lying rascal, you must be hooded, 355
must you? Show your knave's visage, with a pox

344 close come to agreement   349-50 giglets wanton women

to you. Show your sheep-biting face, and be
hanged an hour. Will't not off?
[*Pulls off the friar's hood, and discovers the Duke.*]

DUKE Thou art the first knave that e'er mad'st a
      Duke.
360 First, provost, let me bail these gentle three.
      [*To Lucio*] Sneak not away, sir; for the friar and you
      Must have a word anon. Lay hold on him.

LUCIO This may prove worse than hanging.

DUKE [*To Escalus*] What you have spoke I pardon.
      Sit you down.
      We'll borrow place of him. [*To Angelo*] Sir, by
365   your leave.
      Hast thou or word, or wit, or impudence,
      That yet can do thee office? If thou hast,
      Rely upon it till my tale be heard,
      And hold no longer out.

ANGELO   O my dread lord,
370 I should be guiltier than my guiltiness,
      To think I can be undiscernible,
      When I perceive your Grace, like pow'r divine,
      Hath looked upon my passes. Then, good prince,
      No longer session hold upon my shame,
375 But let my trial be mine own confession.
      Immediate sentence then, and sequent death,
      Is all the grace I beg.

DUKE   Come hither, Mariana.
      Say, wast thou e'er contracted to this woman?

ANGELO I was, my lord.

380 DUKE Go take her hence, and marry her instantly.
      Do you the office, friar, which consummate,
      Return him here again. Go with him, provost.

      Exit [*Angelo with Mariana, Friar Peter, and Provost*].

357 **sheep-biting** currish   367 **office** service   373 **passes** trespasses   374 **session** trial

ESCALUS My lord, I am more amazed at his dishonor
      Than at the strangeness of it.

DUKE   Come hither, Isabel.
      Your friar is now your prince. As I was then   385
      Advertising and holy to your business,
      Not changing heart with habit, I am still
      Attorneyed at your service.

ISABELLA   O, give me pardon,
      That I, your vassal, have employed and pained
      Your unknown sovereignty!

DUKE   You are pardoned, Isabel: 390
      And now, dear maid, be you as free to us.
      Your brother's death, I know, sits at your heart,
      And you may marvel why I obscured myself,
      Laboring to save his life, and would not rather
      Make rash remonstrance of my hidden pow'r   395
      Than let him so be lost. O most kind maid,
      It was the swift celerity of his death,
      Which I did think with slower foot came on,
      That brained my purpose. But, peace be with him.
      That life is better life, past fearing death,   400
      Than that which lives to fear. Make it your comfort,
      So happy is your brother.

      Enter Angelo, Mariana, [Friar] Peter, Provost.

ISABELLA   I do, my lord.

DUKE For this new-married man, approaching here,
      Whose salt imagination yet hath wronged
      Your well-defended honor, you must pardon   405
      For Mariana's sake. But as he adjudged your
        brother,
      Being criminal, in double violation,
      Of sacred chastity, and of promise-breach,
      Thereon dependent, for your brother's life,
      The very mercy of the law cries out   410

386 **Advertising and holy** attentive and devoted   404 **salt** lecherous

Most audible, even from his proper tongue,
"An Angelo for Claudio, death for death!"
Haste still pays haste, and leisure answers leisure;
Like doth quit like, and Measure still for Measure.
415 Then, Angelo, thy fault's thus manifested;
Which, though thou wouldst deny, denies thee
        vantage.
We do condemn thee to the very block
Where Claudio stooped to death, and with like
        haste.
Away with him.

MARIANA   O my most gracious lord,
420 I hope you will not mock me with a husband.

DUKE It is your husband mocked you with a husband.
Consenting to the safeguard of your honor,
I thought your marriage fit; else imputation,
For that he knew you, might reproach your life,
425 And choke your good to come. For his possessions,
Although by confiscation they are ours,
We do instate and widow you withal,
To buy you a better husband.

MARIANA   O my dear lord,
I crave no other, nor no better man.

430 DUKE Never crave him; we are definitive.

MARIANA Gentle my liege—   [Kneeling.]

DUKE   You do but lose your labor.
Away with him to death! [To Lucio] Now, sir, to
        you.

MARIANA O my good lord! Sweet Isabel, take my part,
Lend me your knees, and all my life to come
435 I'll lend you all my life to do you service.

DUKE Against all sense you do importune her;

414 Measure still for Measure (see Matthew 7:1–2: "Judge not, that ye be not
judged. For with what judgment ye judge, ye shall be judged: and with what
measure ye mete, it shall be measured to you again") 423 imputation accusation 430 definitive determined

Should she kneel down in mercy of this fact,
Her brother's ghost his pavèd bed would break,
And take her hence in horror.

MARIANA   Isabel,
Sweet Isabel, do yet but kneel by me,   440
Hold up your hands, say nothing, I'll speak all.
They say, best men are molded out of faults;
And, for the most, become much more the better
For being a little bad; so may my husband.
O Isabel, will you not lend a knee?   445

DUKE He dies for Claudio's death.

ISABELLA [*Kneeling*]   Most bounteous sir,
Look, if it please you, on this man condemned,
As if my brother lived. I partly think
A due sincerity governèd his deeds,
Til he did look on me. Since it is so,   450
Let him not die. My brother had but justice,
In that he did the thing for which he died.
For Angelo,
His act did not o'ertake his bad intent,
And must be buried but as an intent   455
That perished by the way. Thoughts are no
    subjects,
Intents but merely thoughts.

MARIANA   Merely, my lord.

DUKE Your suit's unprofitable; stand up, I say.
I have bethought me of another fault.
Provost, how came it Claudio was beheaded   460
At an unusual hour?

PROVOST   It was commanded so.

DUKE Had you a special warrant for the deed?

PROVOST No, my good lord; it was by private message.

DUKE For which I do discharge you of your office;
Give up your keys.

437 fact crime   438 pavèd slab-covered   456 no subjects i.e., not subject to law

465 PROVOST   Pardon me, noble lord.
     I thought it was a fault, but knew it not;
     Yet did repent me, after more advice;
     For testimony whereof, one in the prison,
     That should by private order else have died,
     I have reserved alive.

DUKE   What's he?

470 PROVOST   His name is Barnardine.

DUKE I would thou hadst done so by Claudio.
     Go fetch him hither; let me look upon him.
                                        [*Exit Provost.*]

ESCALUS I am sorry, one so learnèd and so wise
     As you, Lord Angelo, have still appeared,
475 Should slip so grossly, both in the heat of blood,
     And lack of tempered judgment afterward.

ANGELO I am sorry that such sorrow I procure,
     And so deep sticks it in my penitent heart,
     That I crave death more willingly than mercy;
480 'Tis my deserving, and I do entreat it.

               Enter Barnardine and Provost,
                    C'   ⌊muffled ⌋, Juliet.

DUKE Which is that Barnardine?

PROVOST   This, my lord.

DUKE There was a friar told me of this man.
     Sirrah, thou art said to have a stubborn soul,
     That apprehends no further than this world,
     And squar'st thy life according. Thou'rt con-
485   demned;
     But, for those earthly faults, I quit them all,
     And pray thee take this mercy to provide
     For better times to come. Friar, advise him;
     I leave him to your hand. What muffled fellow's that?

466 **knew it not** was not sure   467 **advice** thought   474 **still** ever   485 **squar'st**
regulate   486 **quit** pardon

PROVOST This is another prisoner that I saved,   490
   Who should have died when Claudio lost his head;
   As like almost to Claudio as himself.
                                                        [*Unmuffles Claudio.*]

DUKE [*To Isabella*] If he be like your brother, for his
   sake
   Is he pardoned; and, for your lovely sake,
   Give me your hand, and say you will be mine,   495
   He is my brother too; but fitter time for that.
   By this Lord Angelo perceives he's safe;
   Methinks I see a quick'ning in his eye.
   Well, Angelo, your evil quits you well;
   Look that you love your wife; her worth, worth
      yours.   500
   I find an apt remission in myself,
   And yet here's one in place I cannot pardon.
   [*To Lucio*] You, sirrah, that knew me for a fool, a
      coward,
   One all of luxury, an ass, a madman;
   Wherein have I so deserved of you,   505
   That you extol me thus?

LUCIO 'Faith, my lord, I spoke it but according to the
   trick. If you will hang me for it, you may; but I
   had rather it would please you I might be whipped.

DUKE Whipped first, sir, and hanged after.   510
   Proclaim it, provost, round about the city,
   If any woman wronged by this lewd fellow—
   As I have heard him swear himself there's one
   Whom he begot with child—let her appear,
   And he shall marry her. The nuptial finished,   515
   Let him be whipped and hanged.

LUCIO I beseech your highness, do not marry me to a
   whore. Your highness said even now, I made you a
   duke: good my lord, do not recompense me in
   making me a cuckold.   520

498 **quick'ning** animation 501 **remission** wish to forgive 504 **luxury** lust
508 **trick** fashion

DUKE Upon mine honor, thou shalt marry her.
Thy slanders I forgive; and therewithal
Remit thy other forfeits. Take him to prison,
And see our pleasure herein executed.

525 LUCIO Marrying a punk, my lord, is pressing to death,
whipping, and hanging.

DUKE Slandering a prince deserves it.
                    [*Exeunt Officers with Lucio.*]
She, Claudio, that you wronged, look you restore.
Joy to you, Mariana. Love her, Angelo;
530 I have confessed her, and I know her virtue.
Thanks, good friend Escalus, for thy much goodness;
There's more behind that is more gratulate.
Thanks, provost, for thy care and secrecy;
We shall employ thee in a worthier place.
535 Forgive him, Angelo, that brought you home
The head of Ragozine for Claudio's;
Th' offense pardons itself. Dear Isabel,
I have a motion much imports your good,
Whereto if you'll a willing ear incline,
540 What's mine is yours, and what is yours is mine.
So, bring us to our palace, where we'll show
What's yet behind, that's meet you all should know.
                                    [*Exeunt.*]

FINIS

---

528 **restore** i.e., by marriage   532 **behind** to come   532 **gratulate** gratifying
538 **motion** proposal   542 **meet** fitting

Textual Note

Our only authority for the text of *Measure for Measure* is the First Folio, whose text is on the whole a good one, probably based on a transcript of Shakespeare's manuscripts made by Ralph Crane, the scrivener of the King's Players. It seems a little disturbed in Act IV; the Duke's speech on "place and greatness" in this act would be more appropriate preceding his lines in III.ii, after the exit of Lucio. In the present text the act and scene divisions are translated from Latin and in two places depart from the Folio in order to correspond to the Globe text (the Globe's divisions are used in most books on Shakespeare): Globe I.ii is split in the Folio into a new scene after the exit of Pompey, and Globe III.ii is not marked in the Folio. The present edition corrects obvious typographical errors, modernizes spelling and punctuation, expands and regularizes speech prefixes, adjusts the lineation of a few passages, transfers the indication of locale ("The Scene: Vienna") and the *dramatis personae* ("The names of all the actors.") from the end to the beginning, and slightly alters the position of a few stage directions. Other substantial departures from the Folio are listed below, the present reading in bold and then the Folio reading in roman.

I.iii.27 **Becomes more** More   43 **it** in

I.iv.54 **givings-out** giuing-out

II.i.12 **your** our   39 **breaks** brakes

II.ii.96 **new** now   111 **ne'er** neuer

II.iv.9 **seared** feard   53 **or, to** and to   76 **Let me be** Let be   94 **all-binding** all-building

III.i.31 **serpigo** Sapego   52 **Bring me to hear them** Bring them to heare me   69 **Though** Through   130 **penury** periury   218 **by oath** oath

III.ii.26 **eat, array** eate away   48 **extracting it** extracting   153 **dearer** deare   227 **and it** and as it   278 **strings** stings

IV.i.62 **quests** Quest   64 **dreams** dreame

TEXTUAL NOTE

IV.ii.44-48 If it be too little ... fits your thief [F gives to Pompey]

IV.iii.16 Forthright Forthlight   **90 yonder** yond

IV.iv.6 redeliver reliuer

V.i.13 me we   **168 her face** your face   **426 confiscation** confutation **542 that's** that